T0287806

The Age of Ecology

The Age of Ecology

A Global History

Joachim Radkau

Translated by
Patrick Camiller

polity

First published in German as *Die Ära der Ökologie* © Verlag C.H. Beck oHG, München, 2011

This English edition © Polity Press 2014

The translation of this work was funded by Geisteswissenschaften International – Translation Funding for Humanities and Social Sciences from Germany, a joint initiative of the Fritz Thyssen Foundation, the German Federal Foreign Office, the collecting society VG WORT and the Börsenverein des Deutschen Buchhandels (German Publishers & Booksellers Association).

Polity Press
65 Bridge Street
Cambridge CB2 1UR, UK

Polity Press
350 Main Street
Malden, MA 02148, USA

ISBN-13: 978-0-7456-6216-9

A catalogue record for this book is available from the British Library.

Typeset in 10 on 11 pt Times New Roman MT by
Servis Filmsetting Ltd, Stockport, Cheshire
Printed and bound in Great Britain by Clays Ltd, St Ives PLC

The publisher has used its best endeavours to ensure that the URLs for external websites referred to in this book are correct and active at the time of going to press. However, the publisher has no responsibility for the websites and can make no guarantee that a site will remain live or that the content is or will remain appropriate.

Every effort has been made to trace all copyright holders, but if any have been inadvertently overlooked the publisher will be pleased to include any necessary credits in any subsequent reprint or edition.

For further information on Polity, visit our website: www.politybooks.com

Contents

Preface to the English Edition

For everything that happens can become a story and fine discourse,
and it may well be that we are caught up in a story.
                                Thomas Mann, *Joseph and His Brothers*
                                (Joseph to Potiphar's wife, p. 952)

The German edition of this book came out at the end of February 2011,
a fortnight before disaster struck the nuclear reactors at Fukushima. Over
the following weeks, at the Leipzig Book Fair, the final sentence about
historical moments when something new becomes possible was repeatedly
quoted and declared prophetic: 'Who knows, perhaps we shall soon be
living at such a moment.' A turbulent year ensued, with many interviews,
debates and talk shows, and I did not always feel good in the prophet's role
expected of me. Again and again the question came up: is this the end of
the nuclear age? Is the age of renewable energies around the corner? As a
70-year-old historian, I know that predictions are usually wrong. When I
began to write this book, I had no grand theory or great message in mind.
Only gradually, during its composition and related discussions, did its
political usefulness, both practical and theoretical, become clearer to me.
The following three points seemed to stand out:

(1) The standard argument of German opponents of the environmental
movement has always been that excitement about ecological issues has
emotional, and very German, roots; it is one of those cases of angst that
make Germans seem ridiculous abroad, a hysterical concoction on the part
of sensation-seeking media. This thesis, however, does not hold water if
we take a global, long-term perspective, for then it becomes apparent that
the environmental movement has the features of a New Enlightenment (a
term I actually thought for a time of using as the title of the book) and that
its origins are at least as much American and British as they are German.

For my own part, I confess that I have never felt great emotions of fear
concerning our environment; my concerns have been rational. And since
the early 1970s the main attraction of environmentalism has been that the
insight 'everything is connected with everything else' allows an enormous

number of discoveries to be made: something new every morning. These discoveries increase as one's gaze opens out to cover the whole world. Yet I have never associated such a global vision with the aim of a globally uniform protection of the environment. Rather, I believe that an international understanding of these issues is best served if we consider the different situations of various countries and accept that their policy priorities will also be different.

(2) Many environmentalists become frustrated all too quickly, concluding that there is no point in any activity, that conservationists are fighting a losing battle, that campaigns are usually unsuccessful, that the whole history of humanity is essentially one of the destruction of nature, and that the clock now shows 'five minutes to midnight' or even five minutes after, with no hope of salvation. All this shows how little many activists know about the story in which they find themselves – perhaps even the fine story that Thomas Mann's Joseph had in mind in speaking to Potiphar's wife.

Potential history is contained in this book too. A useful lesson from recent decades might be that we should take a deep breath and think in longer time frames. We might then realize that many conservationist initiatives that initially appear farcical produce an effect in the end. Environmentalism is nearly always a patchwork affair, with no grand, definitive solutions. It is therefore always possible to criticize environmental policy. But for that very reason one does well to avoid the kind of fruitless hypercriticism that is so often found in the literature.

(3) The about-turn in German energy policy after Fukushima, which, if successful, may set a precedent internationally, represents a huge victory for environmentalists, but it may also prove to be their greatest test. For renewable energies – above all, wind farms and maize-based biogas and biofuel installations – often encounter major resistance and hatred from activists fighting to preserve nature and landscapes. There is still a general confusion about how such conflicts should be rationally discussed.

Here a historical approach may help to counter the fervour of self-destructive dogmatism; once again, thinking in long time frames has its uses. As this book will show, the environmental movement did not arise as a panicky response to the threat of catastrophe, nor is it as clear as some believe that the sound of alarm bells is necessary to get something moving in political and public life. Clarity is actually impeded by panic reactions. A search for quick fixes to energy problems leads down a blind alley.

Whenever I one-sidedly emphasize the rational basis of environmentalism, my wife Orlinde has reminded me of the spiritual undertones noticeable ever since Earth Day on 22 April 1970, more clearly in the Green milieu than among leading Green politicians. This does not contradict my thesis of a new Green Enlightenment; after all, the eighteenth-century Enlightenment had its secret spiritual side. The key point is that the plethora of individual initiatives was knitted together at a rational, not a spiritual, level. The spiritual themes remained diffuse – which is not to say that they had no significance.

My chapter on the ten heroines – a word with slightly ironical connotations for modern historians – did not meet with the approbation I expected among women of my acquaintance. Orlinde, first of all, thought the portrait gallery should have included Joanna Macy (b. 1929), the founder of 'deep ecology', who sought to heal the relationship of human beings to their inner nature as well as to external nature. In a sense my biography of Max Weber was an essay in deep ecology, and many different approaches are also concealed in the present book. Yet there is much in it about which I, as a historian, would prefer for the time being to remain silent in public.

Whereas Alice Schwarzer – the most famous and most feared German feminist, author of a twin biography of Petra Kelly and the lover who killed her, Gert Bastian – found my chapter on Petra Kelly generally perceptive, Orlinde thought I had been too disparaging of this Green heroine, since chaotic people are necessary to get things moving, at least in the early days of a movement. I countered by referring to Max Weber, for whom the born politician excels in 'strong, slow drilling through hard board'; this quality is needed all the more in environmentalist politicians, and I found it lacking in the restless figure of Petra Kelly. Orlinde responded in kind, arguing that Max Weber himself had pointed out the importance of charismatic figures in historical innovation and that they often have something mad about them. However, we saw eye to eye again about the need for a historical approach; there are new departures which require the energies of Petra Kelly to drive them, but there are other situations which call for experts to draft and impose laws on such matters as water contamination. I had a number of long walks in the woods with Gertrude Lübbe-Wolff, former head of the Bielefeld water protection agency, then chair of the German Environmental Council and today a judge in the Constitutional Court. She repeatedly brought home to me that big words about conservation are so much hot air unless one also provides for institutions and instruments to make the goals a reality. But she further pointed out that environmental legislation and authorities often achieve nothing if there is not a powerful external impetus behind them.

Other friends who read parts of the text and were more attentive to academic qualities than to its spirituality made the critical point that I do not precisely define my concept of 'ecology'. This was to be expected, since arguments over the definition of terms are especially popular in Germany. But Wolfgang Haber, the grand old man of German ecology, who read through the whole manuscript, strengthened my belief that the precise scientific concept of ecology cannot be used for the purposes of political environmentalism. What I refer to is the ecology which has made world history – and that includes toxicology, natural therapies and concern for the sustainable use of natural resources, for the human habitat, biodiversity and the beauty of nature. It was the linking up of these previously disparate endeavours that led to a never-ending flow of discoveries and made it justifiable to think in terms of a new Enlightenment. Those who trace environmentalism back to specific doctrines engage with only a very limited part of the field.

Not the least of the reasons why I immediately felt environmentalism to be *my* movement is that I had always been a keen hiker and cyclist, who never considered for a moment getting a driver's licence and felt horror at the ceaseless advance of automobile culture and the destruction of cities and landscapes by motorways. In this respect, the British 'Reclaim the Streets' movement best corresponded to my feelings about the subject. I knew from my personal experience of walking and cycling that lower energy consumption need not mean giving up pleasure – on the contrary! Distancing himself from atomic energy late in life, the nuclear physicist Carl Friedrich von Weizsäcker was right to sigh: 'We would all be happier if we used less energy.' And he added: 'But we want to be unhappy.' Is that really what we want?

For some decades now, when a European has tried to write global history without being able or willing to deny that he is a European, he has laid himself open to the charge of 'Eurocentrism'. I tried as hard as I could to avoid such a limitation of vision by presenting a first draft of this book at Beijing University in 2005. But perhaps the mark of my generation's experience of life is an even greater problem than my Eurocentricity. I was accompanied on my trip to China by Frank Uekötter, a man 28 years my younger, who for two decades had been my closest interlocutor and for many years my fellow research-worker. The Chinese were therefore more than a little surprised when he promptly presented an alternative draft, one which eventually gave rise to a rival work (*Am Ende der Gewissheiten – Die ökologische Frage im 21. Jahrhundert* – Campus Verlag) that was published in the same year as the present book.

Generational cycles are of importance in the history of environmentalism, and Frank and I are forever arguing with each other in ways that reflect this difference between us. Frank complains of the growing rigidity of German environmentalism since the 1980s; I perceive greater movement over the course of time and argue that many issues of the earlier period have still not been resolved. Frank wants the environmental movement of the future to be independent of the state apparatus; I consider the interaction between movement and administration to be an existential law for environmentalism. Frank thinks that at least the German movement is too besotted with its own angst; I maintain that despite everything the core of environmentalism is a new Enlightenment.

In a sense, this book is a sequel to *Nature and Power*, first published in German in 2000 and then in an expanded American edition in 2008. Feedback from the English-speaking world, where reviewers often touched on other aspects than in Germany, gave fresh impetus to my thinking. A generally friendly review by Edward D. Melillo in *Environment and Nature in New Zealand* (vol. 5, no. 2, December 2010) regretted the absence of three themes: (1) justice, (2) 'an avowedly anti-statist and anti-corporate eco-social movement, such as the one that emerged during the Bolivian "Water War" of 2000', and (3) women! I read this only after I had finished work on the present book, but it would still be pertinent to speak of thought transmission, since these three themes are right at its heart. On the other hand, *Nature and Power* was not primarily a history of environmentalism; it was intended to show that for thousands of years the unstable relationship between man and nature has been an element in the dynamics of history.

The year after Fukushima saw an outpouring of information, debates, ideas and perspectives; almost every day brought something new. The reactions to my book – both favourable and critical – never dried up. My own copy of the first German edition came apart long ago because of all the emails and press cuttings I pasted inside it. For the present English edition I have thoroughly revised the text, taking advantage of the opportunity to reorder the flow of my ideas that threatened to burst inside my head. Now I can see many things more clearly than before, and I hope that the book has profited as a result. Yet I cannot help wondering whether the mass of history presented here does not offer insights that I have not managed to grasp.

In the wake of Fukushima, it was a standard gag among German media pundits that the Japanese, the worst hit by the disaster, seemed to be the least affected by it. Now another paradox might be placed alongside this. The Germans, who for long have been talking about phasing out nuclear energy, continue to receive nuclear-generated electricity; whereas in Japan, where the need for alternatives is officially a taboo subject, nearly all nuclear power stations have been taken out of service 'for tests'. Miranda Schreurs, an expert in Japanese environmental policy, assures me that prefectural authorities are disappointed with the results of the nuclear industry and will block any new reliance on it – although a victory for renewable energy is not yet on the cards either! (But things are changing all the time, and meanwhile the new Japanese government is announcing further nuclear projects – only the future will decide whether they are among the many bubbles of our day.) All this makes it clearer than ever that discursive history should not be confused with real history, even more in the case of environmental policy, where there is a great deal of 'symbolic politics'. It also shows that an environmental historian needs to have a feel for the irony of history.

But often one has to discover this irony through historical research. When Angela Merkel, in the wake of Fukushima, announced her intention to withdraw from nuclear energy, there was much derision about the sudden panic of a chancellor who had seemed untroubled for so long at the thought of the risks. From a historical point of view, the situation looks different. No new nuclear power station had been commissioned in the Federal Republic since 1982, so that the withdrawal from nuclear energy had already been inconspicuously brewing for thirty years.[1] Knowledge of this may be useful in weighing the high compensation demands made by leading energy corporations after the policy turn.

In the year of Fukushima I have become more keenly aware of many problems associated with environmentalism. The obsessive preoccupation with 'Stuttgart 21' (construction of the main railway station in Stuttgart) among Greens in southwest Germany, at a time when the ecological threat posed by other projects such as new airports or runways is a thousand times greater, again brought it home to me that the setting of environmental priorities is only partly a rational process. Most of all, it made me wonder whether it is wise for ecological communication to focus on climate change to the extent that – as often happens today – it comes to replace the issue of 'environmental protection'.

The wide-ranging opinions that acquaintances of mine hold about various renewable energies (without ever openly debating their differences) reminded me that the Green Enlightenment still has a long way to go. And the endless discussion on the international financial crisis, which constantly threatens to push environmental issues to the sidelines, made it as clear as it could possibly be that the fate of conservation crucially depends on whether it can be combined with strategies to address the economic crisis. The opportunity for this is there. 'Sustainability' is both an ecological and an economic goal; economic and environmental interests are coming together in the new longing for solidity.

When I have been lecturing abroad, I have repeatedly noted the extent to which environmental policy messages are bound up with particular times and places. In the case of German intellectuals, who often have an aversion to the nation-state and think of it as a leftover from an evil past, I usually warn against overestimating the importance of supranational against national institutions; democracy, transparency and political effectiveness are still today most likely to be provided at the level of nation-states. But in other countries – whether France, the USA or Japan – that would be knocking on an open door. There it is more important to recall the significance of the global horizon for the rise of environmentalism.

Right from the beginning I saw it as one aim of this book to tell the story of the environmental movement, with reference to real persons, actions and dramatic tensions. Many modern historians consider this too banal or old-fashioned; and in the ocean of literature on environmentalism (apart from journalistic reportage) the main studies have had no ambition other than to assign concrete phenomena to abstract models, with the result that no awareness of history has arisen in the practice of the movement. Environmental activism requires not only knowledge of structures but also an eye for players, situations, opportunities and dynamic potential – for possible histories.

It was also clear to me from the beginning, however, that it would be wrong to present a single master story, that this would be an arbitrary construct resting upon much too restricted a viewpoint. Nor is this just a matter of historical correctness; most of the possible histories in which I find myself provide a stimulus to act in certain ways. I would like to find myself not in a tragedy but in a success story – or at least in a comedy. The main part of my account therefore contains several histories of equal value: latent dramas that have traversed environmentalism since its earliest days. Hayden White, in his *Metahistory*,[2] taught us that historians willy-nilly follow literary models: they should be fully aware that this is what they are doing and take conscious inspiration from modern experimental literature. It seems to me that this is how we will best do justice to the novelty of environmentalism. And precisely this might be a stimulus to think more clearly, and discuss more openly, about many aspects of environmentalism.

Frequently I was pulled this way and that by alarmist literature presenting environmental problems as virtually beyond hope and another genre offering pat answers to everything. I would prefer to say of myself what Jacob von Uexküll said in 1988 at the awarding of the Alternative Nobel Prize to the courageous Brazilian environmental activist José Lutzenberger: 'He is not an optimist, he is not a pessimist; he is a possibilist.' I believe that possibilism in this sense is the best foundation not only for the writing of environmental history but also for getting something moving.

Bielefeld, May 2013
Joachim Radkau

Acknowledgements

The author and publisher wish to acknowledge the copyright images used in this book:

p. 75:   Rachel Carson. © Pittsburgh Post-Gazette/ZUMA Press/Corbis
p. 97:   David Brower. Christopher Felber/Corbis
p. 98:   Barry Commoner. The Granger Collection/Topfoto
p. 187:   Dian Fossey. Press Association/AP
p. 188:   Jane Goodall. AFP/Getty Images
p. 192:   Rudolf Bahro. Klaus Mehner/BerlinPressServices.de
p. 195:   Chico Mendes. Reuters/Str Old
p. 196:   Ken Saro-Wiwa. Lambon/Greenpeace
p. 203:   Petra Kelly. ullstein bild/Schulze-Vorberg
p. 207:   Dominique Voynet. ullstein bild/SIPA/Rex
p. 210:   Celia Hunter. Camp Denali & North Face Lodge
p. 214:   Jane Jacobs. Bob Gomel/Time Life Pictures/Getty
p. 219:   Marina Silva. Wikimedia Commons
p. 221:   Wangari Maathai. Press Association/AP
p. 225:   Vandana Shiva. Craig Golding/Getty images
p. 226:   Medha Patkar. Picture Alliance/epa
p. 230:   Dai Qing. picture-alliance/dpa
p. 234:   Ishimure Michiko. Mario Ambrosius, Tokyo
p. 291:   Rainbow warriors. Sims/Greenpeace
p. 297:   Paul Watson. Picture Alliance/epa
p. 304:   Dave Foreman. The Daily of the University of Washington/Archives
p. 309:   Tree-hugging activists. Günter Zint, panfoto
p. 310:   Chipko movement. epd-bild/Rainer Horig

The publisher apologizes for any errors or omissions in this list and would be grateful if notified of any corrections that should be incorporated in future reprints or editions of this book.

Introduction

The Green Chameleon

An impossible history? Let me begin with a confession. When the first 'environmental' initiatives began to mushroom all over the world in the early 1970s, I soon thought to myself: 'This is *my* movement!' I had not felt the same during the student revolts of '68 and after: I had enjoyed their carnivalesque side but found their revolutionary jargon both inauthentic and anachronistic. The aim of the environmentalist movement was not to re-enact past revolutions but to meet the challenges of the present day; it thus finally gave expression to a deep discontent that I and so many others had always felt but been incapable of articulating politically.

Forty years ago that was the actuality of the day, not the subject-matter of history. Until the Fukushima disaster in March 2011, however, many people in Germany – unlike in other parts of the world – thought that the environmental movement was already more history than a part of the present. The first generation of environmental historians made one discovery after another which suggested that the protest against many kinds of environmental damage had roots stretching far back into the past. So one may well ask, for example, whether the idea that something new had begun around 1970 was an optical illusion. It is an important question, and we shall have to consider it in some detail. But in any event, it can hardly be doubted that the environmental movement has since become a historical phenomenon – indeed, the symbol of a whole era. And even if one identifies with what is genuine in the movement, it is very attractive to shed greater light on it by distancing oneself to some degree. A theorist who is too close to the movement will often focus only on particular groups, goals and situations, while leaving much else out of consideration; only distance makes it possible to appreciate the range and the unity of environmentalism. Mere snapshots are often misleading, and nowhere more so than in relation to such an iridescent phenomenon. Analysis of it within a broader spatio-temporal perspective will bring many surprises and a new quality of perception.

But the way there is not simple. For many years I made notes for a history of the environmental movement, yet the suspicion kept coming over me that it might be an impossible task. The internet flooded me with information about environmentalism everywhere in the world, but it was often not easy to make out what was substantive amid the virtual. Never before had I postponed such a book project year after year; seldom had the feeling of 'I know that I know nothing' been so overpowering, sometimes without the Socratic self-assurance that this realization was wisdom itself. Often I was left only with the Pharisaic consolation that others were even more lacking in knowledge: experienced historians could display amazing ignorance in this respect, and even longstanding environmental activists could have completely wrong notions about the history in which they found themselves. But I too felt embarrassed by all the things I had forgotten or overlooked during decades of perusing huge quantities of material. Up to now there has been something shapeless about the history of environmentalism – which is why one forgets so much so easily. On the other hand, all this stimulated me not to give up. Difficulty itself represents a challenge.

In his book on 'ecological communication',[1] Niklas Luhmann remarked that eco-declarations which refer to the whole world while adopting a reproachful attitude to 'society' fall on deaf ears, since they have no addressee in modern societies divided into (and operating only through) various subsystems. At the time this had an ironical thrust: it was directed against the intellectual pipe-dream (fuelled by Habermas's theory of 'communicative action') that communication as such is already action. But as with all literature on the essentially fluid ecological movement, we must be attentive to the year in which it was written: 1986. Today it is astounding that this high priest of sociology did not yet have any idea of the rapidly advancing professionalization of environmentalism and its perfect insertion into subsystems. But the blindness seems excusable when one recalls the scene among Bielefeld sociologists in the early 1980s.

No less amazing today is Luhmann's belief that he could simply rattle off general yet accurate statements about 'ecological communication'. Famously unsociable and remote from the ecological scene, he constructed communication without much experience of his own. Over all these decades I have picked up a huge amount of 'ecological communication', for the whole area of the environment is one in which solutions usually spawn new problems and an endless supply of material for discussion. If one is not content with fixed ideas but seeks out intellectual adventure, reflection about environmental problems generates communication that can leap across scientific disciplines and span the frontiers between theory and practice or between different nations and cultures. All in all, this provides grounds for the optimism of Luhmann's opponent, Habermas, for whom such communication brings into being a cross-border public that eventually achieves something.

This effect is by no means assured, however, and in many cases it becomes apparent only over a period of time. To perceive it requires a historical approach, not momentary snapshots, even if these pass themselves off as structural analysis. What seems at first to be merely 'symbolic politics' could thus acquire real substance over the decades, only after earlier environmental protests fell flat because they did not engage an audience capable of taking effective action. The extent to which reality accords with Habermas or Luhmann cannot be determined a priori or once and for ever.

One assumption is nevertheless common to these two groundbreaking thinkers: namely, social systems – even of this transnational kind[2] – are not apparatuses ready-made for communication but are first created *by means of* communication. Yet communication requires themes. Is environmental policy such a theme, which gives rise to a new public and new social structures? That is an open question for the time being. To be sure, environmental problems cross frontiers readily enough – but do they also form structures, or are they much too diffuse and heterogeneous? Ecological communication, precisely because of its lack of frontiers, is a paradigmatic case for the Habermasian concept of a 'new obscurity'.[3] This does not exactly make it easier to concentrate one's thoughts – or to concentrate on definite goals at the level of political practice. It was in the circling of my own ideas that I first experienced environmentalism as a movement.

What is moving in the movement?

The historical empiricist who takes the word 'movement' literally has more trouble with it than the abstract system-builder. In Germany *Bewegung* was a modish term in the 1920s and a cult word during the Third Reich; it then long retained Nazi connotations after 1945, until it finally came back into fashion against a background of Americanism. As one can verify from the internet, the relevant American literature has thousands of titles containing 'environmental movement'. In the view of sociologists who insist on terminological precision, this tendency to inflate 'movement' is nothing short of scandalous. But researchers often find that, according to the very criteria tediously listed by such theoreticians, nothing much remains of 'environmental movements' in the real world today.

So, what shall I do about 'movement'? Fortunately Christof Mauch, who, as head of the German Historical Institute in Washington, promoted German–American contacts in environmental history more than anyone before him, helped me out by suggesting that I look beyond the confines of 'social movement' and focus on the most mobile and characteristic feature of the 'environmental movement': that is, the ways in which certain themes leap across the boundaries of social groups, scenes and countries, combine with other themes and give rise to new ones. The Indian historian Ranjan Chakrabarti warned me that in his country the environmental movement is made up of countless local initiatives, whose names and addresses alone would fill a 500-page handbook,[4] and that an author can get on top of it, if at all, only in terms of its various leitmotifs.

When Luhmann presents 'ecological communication' as a satyr play friskily revolving around subsystems, we may at least grant him that the environmental movement as a whole does not have a systemic logic. It cannot be understood unless living people are kept in mind. The slippery abstractions of organization theorists leave readers longing for real human beings. It is not possible to grasp social movements if one abstracts from what keeps them going, if one simply takes them as examples of general models, which inevitably have something rigid about them. The mobility of movements must be presented in the form of stories. The fact that the account will often be able to highlight only selected aspects, leaving gaps in both space and time, will be understandable to anyone who has ever grappled with such material. In many instances, something will be achieved so long as the surprising, historically novel, dimension of the story becomes apparent, while the puzzles and open questions stand out clearly and encourage further research.

The only previous history of the environmental movement from a single pen, at once wide-ranging and readable, is *Environmentalism: A Global History*, published in 2000 by the Indian historian Ramachandra Guha. Anyone looking for an accessible work of this length (150 pages) will be full of regard for the author's skill and boldness. But his construction takes risks and tends to be arbitrary in its choices, without making it clear that this is so. The German reader will be astonished to discover that he emphasizes the role of Rainer Maria Rilke – a poet held in high esteem in India – as the originator of environmental awareness in the German-speaking countries. Guha devotes a whole chapter to Gandhi, although it should first have been explained in which sense he belongs to the history of 'environmentalism'; the Indian leader appears no fewer than eighteen times in the index, whereas there is not a single entry for Greenpeace.

Guha identifies two major waves of 'environmentalism', separated by an 'age of ecological innocence' stretching roughly from the First World War until the publication of Rachel Carson's *Silent Spring* in 1962. On closer examination, however, there are many reasons to doubt the innocence of that period. Nor do Guha's stories really fit together; the narrative flow conceals many breaks; what is described as a consecutive sequence exists in reality as a tense coexistence. It therefore seems to me more accurate to tell several different stories, and to derive their arc of tension not least from within the multiplicity of forms of environmental commitment.

When the German-American literary historian Jost Hermand published his 'history of ecological consciousness'[5] in 1991, it was still possible to believe that we were living at a high point of the unfolding (in Hegel's sense) of the ecological spirit. It is a hugely erudite work, which today brings back to mind much that has been forgotten. Yet Hermand also takes much that was disparate or contradictory in the historical reality and straightens it out into a continuous development of consciousness: from

Rousseau to the *Blut und Boden* ideology, from love of dogs to solar panels. That kind of narrative will be avoided here – as will the fantasy that we currently occupy the peak of ecological consciousness. Who knows what the future may bring: perhaps ideas that are considered passé will undergo a renaissance; perhaps it will turn out that a combination of Malthus and Marx best corresponds to reality and that a synergy of population growth and the capitalist growth dynamic remains the core of the whole problem of the environment. We might even build an alliterative triumvirate by adding the name of Machiavelli, since the fact that environmentalism often becomes an instrument of power politics is also at the heart of the problem.

A vast sea of literature has existed for some time, yet it contains major gaps that are particularly striking to a historian. There is an extensive no-man's-land between *pièces d'occasion* and general works, between theoretical models and journalistic reportage, between literature about what is and literature about what ought to be. 'Movements' are shy about themselves, and written records suitable for research tend to have been kept only at a certain level of solidification. It is therefore not surprising that theoretical studies of ecological movements are more common than empirically based investigations. To be sure, 'Think globally, act locally' has been repeated as a mantra these last forty years, but there is generally a dearth of comparative transnational literature. What we have instead are mainly bookbinders' collections of various odds and ends. Environmental movements and politics are a theme without end, and we certainly do not know the end of the (hi)story.

A single history, then, does not seem a promising idea. It would even threaten to lead environmental activists astray: they might think they are in a history that gives meaning to their action, but another possibility is that they are in a different history from the one they would like to think they inhabit, and that other people with whom they try to work things out locate themselves inwardly in a different history. Champions of the 'peaceful atom' felt proud that, in accordance with their pacifist vocation, they were turning swords into ploughshares.

Do histories produce only confusing myths? Anyone who seriously experiments with narratives and counter-narratives soon realizes that there are not an infinite number of plausible histories and that certain leitmotifs or typical arcs of tension keep recurring over the course of time. Yet one should renounce any ambition to synthesize a master story out of them. René Dubos, who did more than anyone to inspire the Conference on the Environment held in Stockholm in 1972, distanced himself from the eco-prophets of doom and subscribed to less clear-cut visions of the future that allowed some room for hope.[6] It is precisely the multiplicity of possible histories which justifies an assurance that something can be done. And such 'possibilism' – José Lutzenberger's attitude referred to in the preface – is the best foundation not only for historical research but also for political commitment.

Greens without a history

On 22 April 1986 (four days before the Chernobyl nuclear disaster), at a special meeting of Green parliamentarians called to discuss anti-Semitism, Ulrich Fischer referred to the Greens' 'lack of history' as a well-known fact – and, at the same time, as a political handicap that left them helpless in the face of attacks operating with history.[7] Also in 1986, Ulrich Linse began his 'history of ecological movements in Germany' in similar vein: 'Lack of history is a distinctive feature of the "new social movements" in Germany.'[8] One would have thought that Chernobyl offered the Greens a golden opportunity to recall their historical origins in the anti-nuclear movement, but at the time everyone had suddenly turned against atomic energy and such references were no longer enough to constitute a political identity. Besides, did not the real origins go further back? But to when exactly? The Greens' lack of a historical sense had a deeper reason than mere indolence; even scholarly historians would have given them little assistance in those days. The most diverse accounts of the history and prehistory of the environmental movement still have currency today – and it remains altogether unclear whether there are any 'lessons of history' to be learned.

Under these circumstances, it is possible for opponents to spread nonsensical stories about the genesis of the environmental movement: for example, that it arose out of a reactionary romanticism close to National Socialism, or that it was a continuation of Communist totalitarianism by other means. The latter version is found especially among rabid anti-environmentalists in the USA, where a great deal can be projected onto European movements,[9] as well as in Václav Klaus's *Blue Planet in Green Shackles*, which offers the rare spectacle of shrill polemic from someone in a high political office that is supposed to embody seriousness of mind.[10] The Czech president, who takes Michael Crichton's science fiction novel *State of Fear* at face value, conjures up the nightmarish vision of a powerful global eco-clique that has taken over from the Soviet empire as a threat to newly won freedom. No whiff there of the diversity and fissiparousness of the environmental movement, or of its strong elements of grassroots democracy, or of the fact that climate alarms caused much confusion in the eco-scene while receiving encouragement from the nuclear lobby. Such books are possible only because large sections of the public are totally ignorant of the history of the movement.

In 2005 Carl Anthony, a co-founder of the Urban Habitat Program, put forward the diagnosis that 'today's environmental justice movement' suffers from a 'lack of historical context'; it knows nothing of earlier struggles to improve the life of underdogs in American cities and has been influenced by narrow mainstream definitions of the 'environment' – as if it were a question only of the surrounding world, not of access to resources.[11] This charge of deficient historical awareness might seem surprising in relation to environmentalism in America of all places. Can it not look proudly to a whole gallery of iconic figures: from Henry Thoreau through John Muir and Aldo Leopold to Rachel Carson? Yet it is no accident that the gallery ends precisely with the 'ecological revolution' of 1970.[12] Today a Green historical consciousness useful for political orientation can no longer attach itself to icons.

A new era of world history – and a New Enlightenment

In 1970 Max Nicholson, a British ecologist of international standing, published a book with the brash title *The Environmental Revolution: A Guide for the New Masters of the World*. Three decades later, on the occasion of the Johannesburg conference on sustainable development, *Time Magazine* presented its selection of 'Heroes of the Green Century', and even Ron Arnold, one of the most aggressive opponents of the environmentalists, spoke of the 'new environmental era' since the 1960s.[13] In 1992, after the Reagan and George Bush presidencies, the historian Philip Shabecoff could triumphantly proclaim: 'virtually every aspect of our personal lives, from the food we eat to the packages we use, to the way we drive and the fears we have for our children's future, has been altered by environmentalism'.[14] Really? Or is this an optical illusion on the part of those who constantly move within eco-networks and build there a virtual (and, thanks to the internet, global) world of their own?

John R. McNeill called his global environmental history of the twentieth century *Something New under the Sun* – and he marshalled an army of facts to demonstrate that, after two and a half thousand years, King Solomon's saying 'there is nothing new under the sun' (Ecclesiastes 1:9) was no longer valid. However, it is not altogether easy to say what is and is not new. For serious historians, the somewhat hyped-up euphoria of the New Age scene is reason enough to be cautious about proclaiming a new age. As McNeill himself soberly points out, much that is conventional is being conducted under the label of 'environmental politics'. An environmental historian feels particularly hesitant, since most elements of today's 'environmentalism' have had a long history under various other names – all the longer, the more the historian investigates them. One thing can be stated at once, though: the networking, wide impact and global horizons that developed from 1970 on were more or less new. Especially if one remembers some of the grotesque phenomena associated with the technocratic planning fever of the 1960s,[15] the subsequent period appears as a real watershed.

Donald Worster's seminal *History of Ecological Ideas* (1977) ends in an 'age of ecology' that he takes to be a self-evident fact. It began on 16 July 1945, with the detonation of the first atom bomb at Alamogordo in the New Mexico desert. The question is whether it marked an epochal change in material reality or in human consciousness. The bomb was first of all a brutal reality; when its existence became known, it triggered a public sense of triumph but changed the thinking of few. As Worster himself put it: 'Not until 1958 did the economic effects of atomic fallout become of more widespread concern to American scientists.'[16] Attitudes in the general public showed signs of turning only in the course of the 1960s; the 1970s would be the 'ecological decade'.

Would it be going too far to make ecology the symbol of an incipient new era? Nothing is riskier than to define the present age; the historical epochs familiar to us today usually acquired their name only in retrospect. The historian, in particular, must not forget that appellations referring to recent times are provisional. It is not difficult to come up with alternative suggestions for the last few decades: age of globalization, age of convergence following the end of the Cold War, age of worldwide economic liberalization, age of the electronic revolution, of new information and communications technology, or of great migrations. But all these proposals have a meaningfulness deficit. According to Max Weber, the hallmarks of new epochs in world history include charisma, a mixture of fear and enthusiasm, a combination of strong spiritual and material driving forces. The brief dream that the global economy, freed of all barriers, would bring worldwide prosperity and reduce the gap between rich and poor has long been over. And the expectation that globalization would make national steering of the economy redundant fizzled out at the latest in the crash of 2007–8.

After the demise of the great ideologies, popular ecology is left as the only intellectual force giving content to the new global horizon and responding to the new challenges. The very fact that (to the disappointment of quite a few activists) environmental movements repeatedly dissolve into the mainstream bears testimony to the epochal character of environmentalism; it defines the age more powerfully than even many environmentalists would like. The chameleon-like character of ecology is proof of its vitality – as philosophy of life and source of political legitimacy, as science and as watchword of protest movements. It also points to the historical novelty of the entire phenomenon. If we think back to older movements – socialist, Communist, nationalist, fascist – we will realize how quickly the 'movement' became tied down in a set of objectives and fixed ideas, and how great is the difference in this respect from the environmental movement.

At the same time, motorized road and air transport as well as atmospheric pollution have continued to grow apace in the age of ecology, and only now have the chemicalization of agriculture and the pollution of soil and groundwater got fully under way in many parts of the world. For all the knowledge about sustainability, leading corporations are geared more than ever to short-term profit maximization, and the fact that they are less tied to a particular place means that they can afford to be all the more ruthless with regard to the environment. According to ecologists working in the field, the planet's biodiversity has been continually declining. In Africa, until the 1960s an agricultural exporting region, the Global Environmental

Outlook (GEO) Study conducted by the United Nations Environment Programme (UNEP) in 2000 showed disturbing levels of environmental degradation since the 1970s.[17] The overall picture is unambiguous: ecology stands in a relationship of dialectical tension to developments in the real world but is so far the only answer to them, or anyway the only one on a scale larger than all the promises of liberalization and globalization. In this sense, it seems justified to speak of an ecological age.

The real crux, however, is that some of the problems do not yet admit of clear solutions and that they cannot all be mastered, or even directly addressed, at once. In 1991 Jost Hermand thought 'the truth about global ecological degradation was plain to see'[18] and appeared to assume that the road to salvation was also more or less clear. But today there can no longer be any talk of that – hence the meandering path of the environmental movement and the pressure for experimental policies, however fixed many individual players may be on certain goals or methods. The Hegelian maxim 'The truth is the whole' here takes on a specific meaning: the essence of the eco-age, as well as its novelty, is most apparent on a broad spatial-temporal horizon. Despite the glut of literature on the environment, the new era is still in large part terra incognita, where traditional concepts have no purchase and prevent people from recognizing what is new or being surprised at it. The novelty is precisely what is so exciting, but one's appreciation of this is vitiated if the limits of one's ambition are to range environmentalism under more general headings.

From the point of view of past experience, the environmental movement is actually an impossible phenomenon. A 2008 work on German environmental organizations by the sociologist William T. Markham – the most extensive study of its kind up to the time of writing – culminates in a Pandora's box of seemingly insoluble problems. One dilemma follows another: dilemmas of internal structure, as centralization and professionalization come into conflict with grassroots initiative; dilemmas of resource acquisition for competing organizations dependent upon the public purse or wealthy backers; dilemmas of goals and strategy, since everything is somehow interconnected in environmental politics and it is by no means clear where to start. Markham himself, who emphasizes that each step he takes is guided by theory, points out that these dilemmas stem more from the predefined theoretical model than from what happens in history.[19]

In sum, the existence of the environmental movement is something for which theory does not allow. Right from its inception, a swift end has been predicted for it – shortly after Earth Day (22 April 1970) in the case of the United States. When disaster for the Greens loomed in the wake of German unification, two books appeared hot on each other's heels: *Can the Greens Still Be Saved?* and (by a prominent member of the 'Realo' wing of the party) *Rise and Fall of the Greens.*[20] But eight years later they were part of the central government. Their history up to now illustrates the German proverb: 'Those given up for dead live longest.' Markham sums up towards the end of his investigation: 'Perhaps the most striking feature of German environmentalism is its sheer staying power.'[21] All the more surprising is it that the environmental movement has had a marginal place in recent overviews of German politics.

Admittedly, it is to some extent a matter of definition whether the major issues of the future will be seen as 'environmental problems'. It is possible, as at the height of imperialism a century ago, to define the signs of the time as a signal for struggle over ever scarcer natural resources; that may determine the future. Perhaps the age of ecology will prove to be only a temporary phase of clear-sightedness. On balance, though, this is what it has been and still is today. Voltaire once held the position that historical research had a point only if it concentrated on the worthy achievements of humanity. One may doubt this, and he himself did not succeed in the kind of historiography he demanded.[22] But if one wishes historical research to have a point, it is worth considering whether Voltaire's requirement cannot be fulfilled, at least now and then. And in fact the eco-age may be conceived as a New Enlightenment. Herein lies one point of the historical approach: the euphoria of elucidation, of rediscovering the experiences of revelation with which so much began. To be sure, this enlightenment has its own dialectic, complete with blinkers, arrogance and the pursuit of power. But, contrary to what many opponents have claimed, it is clearly not a mass psychosis originating in irrational fears. It may appear to be that in certain situations, but such an interpretation proves over time to be definitely wrong. To show this is another aim of the present book.

Chapter One

Environmentalism before the Environmental Movement

1 Good Mother Nature and the 'Appalling Wood Shortage': The Twin Face of Nature in the Decline of the Commons

From Rousseau to Romanticism: the first great age of nature worship

Anyone who wishes to tell a story must first have a beginning. The roots of modern environmentalism stretch far back in history, but is there a point at which everything began? If this means a certain person or publication, then a connoisseur of British environmental history would cite John Evelyn – the 'good Mr Evelyn', well known from Samuel Pepys's diaries – and his *Fumifugium* (1661), the first pamphlet against the scourge of city smoke, or *Sylva* (1664), the first call for afforestation. His friendship with Pepys, a naval administrator,[1] over more than forty years fits the picture, since the fleet was then the foremost consumer of timber. But Evelyn was not the originator of an afforestation movement, or of ongoing initiatives to fight coal smoke. If, instead of individuals, one looks for movements with lasting effect, then animal lovers and vegetarians, especially the Quakers, will seem more important – or else the endless quest for the near-natural garden, also British in its origins, which suggests that from early on indus-trialization and the longing for nature were closely related to each other and that a feeling for nature became the hallmark of a new cultural elite.[2]

Cultural historians prefer to begin the prehistory of environmentalism in the late eighteenth-century age of gushing enthusiasm for nature, the age of Rousseau, *Sturm und Drang* and early Romanticism. At Whitsun 1793, the Berlin students Ludwig Tieck and Wilhelm Heinrich Wackenroder went on a hiking trip in Franconian Switzerland; it counts as the historical moment when German Romanticism was first invented. 'Forest smoke, a stream flowing down a cliff, a crag leaping up in the valley – it can send me into a rapture that almost borders on madness', Tieck rejoiced.[3] But Reimar Gilsenbach, the 'cornerstone of conservationism in East Germany', main-tains that a wider historical horizon is needed to overcome the perennial narrowness of environmentalism. True conservationism, he argues, began with the great Alexander von Humboldt, whom contemporaries revered as the modern Aristotle.[4]

In reality, never before in history had there been as much talk of nature as in the period from Rousseau to Romanticism; never before had it been so much in vogue, but also so ambiguous. Historians of philosophy, who from antiquity to the Renaissance had brought a reasonable order into the history of the concept of 'nature', now increasingly gave up the task.[5] Montesquieu, in his *Considérations sur la France*, mocked nature as a lady whom everyone prided himself on knowing, with the result that her reputation was ruined. All the more remarkable, however, that the word 'nature' did not become worn out and hackneyed: in 1800, after the experiences of the Revolution, it was actually called the 'most dangerous word in the French language'.[6] Even philosophical authors of the time evidently presupposed an intuitive understanding of 'nature' and its various faces. 'Nature' became the watchword for liberation from the constraints of the old society; people discovered in the tropics and the Americas a wild, luxuriant nature – and wild 'savages' too – that they had never known in the Old World. But at the same time, scientists made vigorous advances in discovering law and order within nature.

'We obey her laws even when we resist them; we work with her, even when we want to work against her': the young Swiss Christoph Tobler, visiting Weimar in 1781, noted down such aphorisms of the 32-year-old Goethe's.[7] '*Süße, heilige Natur / Lass mich gehen auf Deiner Spur, / Leite mich an Deiner Hand / Wie ein Kind am Gängelband*' ['Sweet, holy Nature / Let me go in your tracks, / Lead me by your hand / Like a child in leading-strings']:[8] so begins the poem An die Natur [To Nature], composed in 1775 by the young poet Friedrich Leopold Graf zu Stolberg, who shocked the conservative Swiss by bathing naked with Goethe in a lake. Later, Karl Marx ridiculed this joy at being kept in nature's leading-strings as 'patriarchal drivel';[9] but paradoxically a full awareness of freedom went into this sentimentality about nature. Two centuries on, the hidden tension repeatedly burst into the open in the environmental movement: 'nature' as watchword for spontaneous living, but also as reminder that man's urge to press forward has only limited scope. At the same time: 'nature' as a passionately emotional term – a word resonating with love and enthusiasm, but also with shudders – as well as name-giver of the new natural sciences. Both are there in Goethe: his *Erlkönig* speaks of the magic of a natural spirit, but it is the rational, enlightened father who survives.

If one places Rousseau, the *Sturm und Drang* figures and the early Romantics at the origin of the environmental movement, one is implying a philosophy of history in which ideas, visions and spiritual themes come first. The nature honoured in the eighteenth century bore the features of a secularized goddess; nature worship had a pantheistic aspect. Spinoza's *Natura sive Deus* became – to quote Wolfgang Riedel – 'the most widespread nineteenth-century axiom of the philosophy of nature'.[10] But did the path lead straight from there to the modern concern for nature?

If nature was all-powerful, did that not mean its destruction was inconceivable? Immanuel Kant, whose belief in nature escaped his critique of knowledge,[11] thought it evident in 1795 (or was he making fun of such confidence?) that nature would provide people with wood even on the edge of the Arctic: 'Nature's care arouses most admiration, however, by carrying driftwood to these treeless regions, without anyone knowing exactly where it comes from. For if they did not have this material, the natives would not be able to construct either boats or weapons, or dwellings in which to live.'[12]

The great fear of wood shortage

The strange thing is that, precisely in the 1790s, Europe-wide alarms over the destruction of forest and the 'appalling wood shortage' reached their peak![13] There is a direct analogy here with *Limits to Growth*, that Club of Rome study which became a global sensation after its publication in 1972. But we have to detach ourselves from the concept of nature of the time, with its corresponding literature, to arrive at the prehistory of modern warnings about the destruction of nature. The wood shortage alarm can be found in a wide range of literature: forest records and ordinance, the archives of city forest departments, advice on new wood-saving inventions, complaints made by small and large commercial users of wood, but also in the *Cahiers de doléances* to the French government which allow us to follow the brewing of the Great Revolution. These teem with shrill cries of warning. In 1789, at the Convocation of the Estates-General, the complaints of shortage were right at the top of the agenda. According to French historians of the forest, such fears flared up like periodic bouts of malaria.[14]

Much the same was true in Germany at the time, although Heinrich Rubner calculated that in 1800 Germans had more than three times as much wood per capita at their disposal as French people.[15] In 1795, the year when Kant's *Perpetual Peace* first appeared, a prize-winning essay published in Leipzig predicted that 'life, trade and work will be made more difficult in every way for those who come after us, and our destructive acts will make them think of us with horror'. And in 1797 the inventor of a more economical oven announced: 'If the wood shortage worsens over the next twenty years at the same rate as in the past twenty, may God have mercy on us!' 'Not enough wood! High wood prices! is the general complaint in nearly all the large and small towns of Germany'; so began one forester's 'frank thoughts on the wood shortage'.[16]

Does that make things crystal-clear? Have we been looking in the wrong place for the early origins of our environmental consciousness – among poets and philosophers, instead of practical people facing everyday shortages? Things are not quite so simple, however. The complaints of wood shortage, present or future, should not be taken indiscriminately at face value. Indeed, their reality content is the object of endless controversy, in Germany and elsewhere.[17] Shortly after 1800, leading foresters were heaping scorn on the alarmists: the Bavarian reformer Joseph Hazzi, for example, sneered in 1804 that the 'frightful ado about impending shortages' was a way for 'forest charlatans' to impress the government and public opinion; and from time to time they did indeed manage to whip up a wild hysteria. The Prussian forestry expert Wilhelm Pfeil sang the same tune, suggesting that 'the ever approaching monster of the direst wood shortage' was 'a chimera that many forest people and other writers want to frighten us with, as Africans frighten their women with mumbo jumbo'. It would be splendid if wood became more expensive and fetched a decent price, since that would be a sign that things were looking up for the economy and all proprietors would finally have an incentive to keep their forest in prime condition.[18]

Since then, the story of catastrophic shortage at the end of the 'Wood Age' has served as a prelude to two heroic tales of salvation: in one, modern forestry claims to have saved countries from disaster, while in the other, economies based on fossil fuels also claim to have saved the forest by reducing the demand for firewood. But even in a declensionist history of the environment – which detects nothing but deforestation everywhere – we come across the wood shortage story. No wonder it has been the subject of endless controversy!

At first sight, the arguments for and against a 'death of the forest' alarm in the early nineteenth century sound modern. If we read the quotations in context, however, it soon becomes clear that they are part of the great controversy of the age: the liberal attack on mercantilism, the rulers' protectionist system in the Absolutist era. The long growth cycles of trees gave statist theorists a new argument for official conservation of the forest. But liberals countered that rising wood prices were the strongest inducement to afforestation; state protection was worthless, because a policeman could not be placed beside every tree, and anyway many forestry officials were corrupt; its removal would be most beneficial to those with a vital interest in forest use. The dispute remains virulent in large parts of the world today, especially as it cannot be said once and for all who is right! When Russia, seduced by the gospel of deregulation, did away with state forestry regulation in 2007, the quest for short-term profit led to such neglect of safety rules that forest fires acquired horrific proportions. Although the forest-owners' men have often been of dubious value, competent and efficient officials have been essential in modern times for the success of environmental policy.

In 1800 this was not yet so clear. A further complication was that two other issues played a role in the wood shortage controversy, so that the front lines did not always coincide: one was the clash of interests between the local firewood economy and the timber trade; the other was the dispute over the old common lands. In all seafaring nations, the naval timber supply had the highest political priority; as soon as it was impaired, by however little, the navy's champions sounded the alarm over shortages. This explains Colbert's warning cry: '*La France périra faute du bois*' [France will perish for lack of wood]. 'The timber forest cult was the state religion of the Ancien Régime', noted Andrée Corvol. And she spoke of the 'legend of deforestation' that was used to legitimate the renewal of high forest.[19]

If the high timber forest retreated a little, it did not mean much to most forest users, since nine-tenths of wood was burned as fuel. Coppice was enough for that, and it grew by itself through stump shooting, with no need for foresters or artificial afforestation. Sustainability was not an issue in relation to coppice: it was inherent in that kind of forestry, and inherent sustainability has generally been more reliable in history than any ordered from above. The stories of forest destruction that are found again and again often rest upon the fact that people were geared to the modern timber market, attentive only to the high forest and forgetful of coppice. There was indeed a crisis of the forest economy in the late eighteenth century. But it was less an ecological than an institutional crisis: the authorities and methods governing the allocation of wood were no longer keeping up with the diversity of demand. In Frankfurt, deputies of the citizenry complained as early as the mid-eighteenth century about the 'indescribable disorder in relation to wood matters' and the 'unspeakably great confusion at the Wood Office'.[20] Of course, the real wood shortage mostly hit those who were in no position either to bombard the public and officials with complaints or to pay the rising market prices – that is, the poor whose customary forest rights were being rapidly eroded. Anyone forced to buy on the open market had no interest in making a fuss about shortages, since that would only drive prices higher.

The end of the commons as a watershed

This brings us to the socially most significant controversy in this context: the struggle over the old commons, the village forest and pastureland.[21] Reformers maintained that such land was a morass of inefficiency and mismanagement and that common forest and pasture were as putrid as common whores; everyone used them and no one felt responsible for them in their own self interest. The biologist Garrett Hardin's essay *The Tragedy of the Commons* (1968) – which, in sharp opposition to the communards of '68, launched an American environmental discourse with a global impact – revived these old arguments in relation to what he called the 'global commons', paying no heed to the social control and self-regulation in the commons of old.[22] Elinor Ostrom, for her part, has shown empirically and theoretically that it is quite possible, by sealing oneself off from the outside world, to manage natural resources sustainably on a communal basis.[23] For this, in 2009, she became the first woman to be awarded the Nobel Prize for Economics.

The extent to which Ostrom's model fits the historical commons cannot be fully clarified from the sources. But there is much evidence that the symbiosis of villages with their manifest natural resources, such that any crude overuse was soon noticed, could to some extent remain stable; the main disturbance to it was insatiable rulers, with their fortresses, mines and wars, although population pressure and the allure of trade and the money economy were additional factors. A 'tragedy of the commons' occurred mainly when participants believed in the tragedy and expected the commons to dissolve in the near future, so that everyone tried to get as much as they could out of it.

This situation came about in the second half of the eighteenth century. The commons came under fire from two sides: from the rulers' foresters and agrarian reformers, and from the liberal pioneers of privatization. There is evidence to suggest that the dissolution of the commons, with its profound and extensive effects on mentalities, was the decisive process of the epoch. For the Swiss legal historian Bernd Marquardt, it spelled nothing less than the 'end of the old European environmental regime'.[24]

In the past, the commons made a 'good impression' even on an economist such as Wilhelm Roscher; its 'generosity' meant that 'nearly everywhere without great population pressure even people who, strictly speaking, had no right to common pastureland were allowed to use it'.[25] Demographic trends shook this familiar, if somewhat peevish, benevolence; then privatization and the advance of agrarian capitalism finished it off. The British agrarian historian Joan Thirsk, one of the main experts on the subject, points out that as a result of the enclosures 'the discipline of sharing things fairly with one's neighbour was relaxed, and every household became an island to itself. This was the great revolution in men's lives, greater than all the economic changes following enclosure.'[26]

The fact that rural life became less agreeable does not necessarily mean that the land was run down ecologically. On the contrary, it may be assumed that the older-style agrarian reforms which began to be widely imposed in Europe from the late eighteenth century on promoted soil ecology in more than one respect: through improved use of animal dung and through nitrogen-rich plants. Hedges defended the soil from wind erosion and offered breeding places for birds. Once again there is not just a single history. However, the liberal reformers' hope that the timber market would automatically take care of splendid forests was often disappointed.[27] And even if the commons were not well managed in purely economic terms, that is far from the same as saying that they were ecologically ruined. Today, by virtue of their species diversity, former commons landscapes are El Dorados for conservationists.[28]

When we recall those old exchanges about wood shortage and market self-regulation, today's disputes might make us think: 'That's all been seen before.' Yet, on closer inspection, the picture was very different two hundred years ago. Since the early modern age, there had been little room for doubt that the forest was an exhaustible resource. Everyone could see for themselves how quickly a tree was felled after a century's growth, and that wood burned in a chimney incomparably faster than it could be replenished. The existential threat to the forest was absolutely palpable: a tree falls with a crash, whereas its growth is imperceptible and soundless. Not even foresters could see at a glance how much wood there was in the depths of the forest, until the age of great conifer monocultures simplified the task of calculation.[29] So, there was a common tendency to think of the wood supply situation as more dramatic than it was in reality. Only modern conservationists, who would like to keep species-rich pastoral landscapes, have learned from experience how annoyingly easy it can be for the forest to grow back by itself, and that in wet climates deforestation is far from irreversible.

If accusations of overuse and warnings of impending shortage came from diverse quarters in the eighteenth century, not infrequently being traded back and forth like a tennis ball, the reason must be that they had a degree of credibility. Pure fantasies would not have been believed: the forest was too visible and too close at hand. So long as people had real organic growth before their eyes, the 'limits to growth' were a banality. In this regard, today's threats to resources – oil and gas, oceans, the atmosphere – are fundamentally different and call for new strategies and much broader coalitions to fight them.

In many respects, the wood shortage alarms that sounded in the year 1800 have a new topicality. Like the 'death of the forest' outcry in the 1980s, they were a response not so much to an acute disaster as to a crisis that threatened to strike if things went on in the same carefree way; precautions had to be presented as current crisis management before they gained political acceptance. Faced with natural growth, people had to learn to live with the limits of growth and to use regenerative resources in a sustainable manner. Around 1800 'sustainability' (*Nachhaltigkeit*) became a magic word in German forestry; two centuries later it became popular worldwide. The period around 1800 may thus be seen as a historical moment of clear-sightedness and ecological completion of the Enlightenment, which subsequently, with the triumph of coal, went into a 'two-hundred-year slumber' (in the words of Volker Hauff, the German representative on the Brundtland Commission, which invented 'sustainable development' in 1987).[30]

The impossibility of a broad Green alliance in 1800

A broad alliance for conservation and environmental protection did not come about in 1800, however, nor could it have done. 'Ecological' themes, as they are called today, were then scattered among various intellectual-political currents in partial conflict with one another. The *Ancien Régime* cultivated timber forest, the Revolution trees of liberty (which had to be uprooted and replanted for the purpose of worship). Enthusiasm for nature, which was also an enthusiasm for the natural in man, usually went together with appeals for freedom and deregulation, whereas the wood shortage alarm typically involved state-centred paternalism, calling for 'good policing' and traditional forms of regulation by the authorities. Whether nature was venerated as love object, goddess or legislator, one factor was always the liberal push for breaking old fetters and faith in the natural self-regulation of human and economic relations. Most of the forces that upheld old restrictions and supervisory bodies, and therefore had some scope for practical action to maintain a balance between man and nature, stood on the other side of the fence.[31] In the years around 1800, the great economist who pointed to the limits of growth (mostly population growth) was Thomas Malthus, but his theory had a misanthropic air, at a time when contraception was still frowned upon. To nature worshippers, such practices seemed like an act of betrayal.[32]

In France, as Andrée Corvol has written, it was the 'Restoration ultras' who conjured up a terrible deforestation.[33] Was it not under Jacobin rule that the goat – the 'poor person's cow' and worst enemy of the forest – penetrated into woodland? The French engineer F. A. Rauch, in the new 1818 edition of his *Régénération de la nature végétale*, suggested a close affinity between the political restoration and his proposed regeneration of the forest.[34] He overlooked the beneficial (if unintended) effects of the Revolution in allowing peasants to hunt freely, thereby greatly reducing the stocks of game and promoting the natural rejuvenation of deciduous forest.

In olden times, the forest was protected not only by special ordinance but to some degree also by violations of that ordinance – for example, when peasants left deadwood lying around to fertilize the soil or drove their pigs into oak or beech forest (a practice later dignified as 'forest treatment'). All in all, one has the impression that the lack of a clearly pressing problem was the ultimate reason why no broad coalition took shape on environmental issues. Whereas nowadays the law of human inertia tends towards destruction of the environment, in premodern times it probably afforded the best protection. It was so much effort to cut down and remove trees in areas off the beaten track; and rivers were often blocked by the competing interests of boatmen and rafters, water millers and farmers dependent on irrigation. Yet zealous reformers tried precisely to overcome the laws of inertia. Under such conditions, the goal of environmental protection did not animate a large movement with broad integrative power.

Too great a fixation on the term 'nature' can distract one from the true prehistory of modern environmental awareness. As a rule, rather than serving to remind people of the 'limits to growth', the evocation of 'nature' actually involved an enthusiasm for growth – often, for politicians or economists, in the context of strategies to open up a country's 'natural treasures'. It was a time when the first exact and detailed maps of whole territories were being drawn – another key turning point in the history of environmental perceptions. At a different level, the term 'natural' was used to describe the spirit of freedom that rebelled against landlords' marriage prohibitions and guild restrictions on occupational activity, as well as all the tariff barriers and staple rights that prevented trade from following the flow of rivers. 'Unnatural' were sexual practices designed to prevent conception, and a hysterical campaign against masturbation began in the eighteenth century and reached a peak with Rousseau.[35]

Since the age of Bacon, the whole modern age has had a profoundly dialectical relationship with nature: the more systematic the attempts to exploit it, the more accurately people have learned to know it and to understand its laws. The concept of 'sustainable' forestry stems from the Alpine salt works and Saxon mining and iron and steel industry, the largest consumers of wood in the eighteenth century:[36] in seeking to make the maximum use of the forest, they were forced, in their own interests, to calculate that maximum as precisely as possible. It would be wrong to infer, however – as many historians have done – that people who had not been educated about the forest lacked any sense of sustainability. The truth is that the sustainability requirement was taken for granted in the peasant economy. Everyone knew that, when an oak tree was cut down, a new one had to be grown in good time to cater for pig feed and housebuilding – they did not need to learn about 'sustainable development' from Rio. Only among the most voracious 'wood-devouring industries' did sustainability become a non-trivial matter.

Around the turn of the nineteenth century, parts of Germany became world pioneers of reforestation, and Germany as a whole the land of forest romanticism. It seems reasonable to suppose that the two were connected, yet it is surprisingly difficult to prove this. Apparently it was a question more of a dialectic than of a directly causal link. Forest romanticism may have been a subliminal reflex from the preceding wave of warnings about destruction of the forest. But what finds clearer expression in it is the idea of infinity.

At the level of individuals, Romanticism and a commitment to protection of the forest are most closely united in the person of Ernst Moritz Arndt, the pioneer of German nationalism. In 1820 he warned that the axe laid on trees threatened to become the axe 'laid on the whole nation'. Forest people must have thought this outrageous, since woodcutting was the economic purpose of their lives. But state foresters would have liked what they heard when Arndt's political values led him to demand that forest land put up for sale should be taken 'at any price' into public ownership, or when he called for business to be driven out of the forest: 'So, away with the manufacturers who are destroying the forest! Away with them from the heights and mountain tops!'[37] The Romantic pursuit of forest solitude here coincided with the forester's ideal of making decisions alone, undisturbed by customary rights of charcoal-burners and glass or pitch makers.

Nevertheless, the gnarled old oaks so beloved of the Romantics were 'bad guys' for forest economists: they did not grow any more and their wood was full of knot-holes that lowered its commercial value. Wilhelm Heinrich Riehl – another of the great ideologues of German forest romanticism, who championed professorships in forestry – complained in 1850 that 'in recent times' Germany had 'lost at least as much of its distinctive forested character' through the 'artificial conversion of proud deciduous timber forest into short-lived coniferous forest' as through 'the complete clearance of huge areas of forest'.[38]

There is one clear connection, however, between afforestation and forest romanticism. If foresters, having been the state officials most detested among the rural population in the eighteenth century,[39] advanced in the nineteenth to become the Germans' dream profession – which was by no means the case in many other countries – this was in large part the work of Romanticism. Carl Maria von Weber's *Der Freischütz* (1821), which turned the forester into an operatic hero, and whose huge success did more than all else to create a German Romanticism of the forest, still openly assumed that prospective foresters should be skilled mainly in guarding and shooting. This was precisely the type of forester that the reformers wanted to do away with. From being 'well versed in deer' (*hirschgerecht*), he should become 'well versed in wood' (*holzgerecht*)! In the end, though, the reform did not achieve its goal. Even today many foresters remain at heart more 'versed in deer', much to the disgust of those for whom wood is more important than game and the damage done by wild animals is a disgrace.

On looking back, it is clear that the forest alarms in the eighteenth century were all centred on wood. Did people see no other value in the forest? Forest romanticism did indeed see much, but it reached its peak only at the moment when the 'spectre of wood shortage'[40] was subsiding. In the course of the nineteenth century, appeals for forest protection and afforestation – from North America to British India – operated more and more with proto-ecological arguments, such as the value of the forest for soil conservation and hydrological balance, or its ostensible significance for the climate. Here, for the first time, we encounter the 'networked thinking' that modern ecologists prize, as well as the postulate of manmade climate change.

After the wood shortage alarms with which the first generation of reformers tried to mobilize governments and public opinion, these arguments functioned rather like stopgaps. But history also sheds light on the ecology of ecology. With or without forest, German landscapes had plenty of rainfall and water; the value of forest for the hydrological balance was first discovered, or anyway claimed, in Alpine Switzerland and the south of France, following periods of drought and flooding respectively. For the American afforestation movement, the water argument became central in the second half of the nineteenth century. George Perkins Marsh – who in 1864, when he was US ambassador in Florence, published *Man and Nature*, the most famous American work against environmental destruction until Rachel Carson's *Silent Spring* (1962) – could see with his own eyes the bare mountainsides of the Mediterranean, and for him nearly everything revolved around the two closely connected themes of forest and water. Germany was his model in forestry, but France was the country where the link between the two had been most thoroughly investigated.[41]

Japan: a non-Western pioneer of sustainable forestry

Japan provides an especially interesting case, being the only non-Western country to have pursued early on a systematic policy of forest protection and afforestation. Economic and ecological energies tend to be linked with each other around the world, and countries where forest conservation was institutionalized at an early date have typically been leaders in environmental protection since 1970.

In the narrow Japanese plains, steep mountains often rise up in the line of sight: this allows one to suppose that people made the connection between forest and hydrological balance quite a long time ago – earlier than in China, where the sources of the great rivers lay unknown in faraway places. (However, Japanese texts too treated forest and rivers separately until the early modern age.) Most obviously, soil erosion resulting from the deforestation of mountain slopes obstructed the rivers that irrigated rice fields; it was the misery this caused which, from the late seventeenth century on, led the shoguns in Edo (today's Tokyo) to create an erosion control authority to look after both forest and rivers.[42]

All the same, there is strong evidence that the secret of Japan's relatively successful forest conservation should be sought not so much in central initiatives as in the action of local players and peasant communities,[43] whose effectiveness has been vouchsafed by Elinor Ostrom.[44] Conservation still works best from close up; all the more was that the case in the premodern state of communications. In this respect there is a striking analogy between Japan, divided by its mountains into many mini-landscapes, and territorially fragmented Germany with its common woodlands. Although the *bakufu* issued forest protection ordinance, this central authority of the Edo shogunate, like many top administrative offices in Europe, was linked to the largest users of wood. As Conrad Totman, the leading Western researcher on Japanese forest history, notes with biting irony: 'The heart of the deforestation problem, however, lay in authorized, not unauthorized, logging. The protective measures were being taken by the principal forest predators as means of assuring their own access to forest yield, not as ways of preserving forest per se.'[45] The deforestation bound up with the weakening of regional autonomy after 1868, in the wake of the Meiji reforms, casts a retrospective glow on the forest practices of the previous period.[46]

This is still the problem of forest histories all over the world: top-down conservation is always the best documented, but it is often doubtful whether it has been the most effective. The same goes, more or less, for environmental policy as a whole. It is also the basic dilemma of the environmental protection coupled with development aid that is carried out in cooperation with government agencies, under the aegis of 'sustainable development' à la Rio 1992. As Elinor Ostrom has shown, statification of the forests, regularly justified by reference to the threat of further destruction, has in effect brought about 'open-access resources' in place of regulated commons:[47] so the issue now is to limit access again, since the corrupt and ineffectual state forestry departments often do this least of all. Much of the old German controversy over who makes the best protector of the forest has an exemplary character and can be transposed to large parts of today's world.[48] It is an endless controversy, because the validity of all answers is dependent on time and place.

The new combination of forest and climate alarms

When the French engineer F. A. Rauch first published his plea for 'regeneration' of the forest in 1802, it bore the title 'Harmonie hydro-végétale et météorologique'.[49] In it we find the new theme, at once forward-looking and dubious, of the importance of the forest for *climate*. The older view in Europe – with Scandinavia and Russia but also Tacitus' Germany in mind – was that the climate was raw and deforestation would make it milder and friendlier to humans. Most streams and rivers originated in the forest; there were clear signs that it stored water and perhaps even retained rain clouds. But since Central and Western Europe were wetter in previous centuries than they are today, and since farmers not only cleared forest but also drained low-lying land, it was not necessarily advantageous if forests distributed rain. Around 1800 there was a type of literature called 'medical topography': that is, works on the (ostensible) effects of particular landscapes on human health. They are a treasure-trove for historians researching the environmental awareness of the time, which like today was focused not least on health issues. Wet regions were generally considered unhealthy, so that forest clearances counted as beneficial.[50]

This way of thinking was increasingly overturned in the nineteenth century. Ernst Moritz Arndt, praised by Gilsenbach as the ancestor of the ecological movement, wrote in 1820: 'When trees are covered with leaves, they exhale profusely and deposit fructifying parts which, as experience teaches us, cause people and nearby fields to thrive.' Hence his main point: 'the axe laid on trees' all too often becomes an axe 'laid on the whole nation'.[51] The Mediterranean, hitherto the North's longed-for arcadia of parks and gardens, became more and more a bare, parched landscape for critical travellers inspired by the theories of agrarian and forest reformers.[52] As George P. Marsh saw it, the rain-distributing effect was ultimately the principal argument for forest conservation. The British geographer Michael Williams noted sarcastically: 'Perversely, it was Marsh's *Man and Nature* (1864) that proved to be the real catalyst to the upsurge of writing by the rainmakers after the Civil War.'[53] Again and again the *idée fixe* that, with strips of forest to retain the rain clouds, one can transform the prairies into farmland! It took a surprisingly long time for people to recognize the absurdity of such projects, so attractive was the policy goal of 'climate management'.

In British India too, forestry officials invoked climate protection more than wood supply as the justification for their strict controls.[54] Although in reality the much-coveted wood of the teak tree was their prime concern, the climate argument was a patented formula for giving top-down forest conservation a publicly useful image. Of course, such propaganda cut no ice with the forest people: indeed, it helped to make colonial conservationism suspect in the eyes of Indians in general. Things were different with regard to the hydrological balance: this was and is a valuable function of the forest, which is apparent to farmers in drought-stricken regions of the third world and has repeatedly been used by protest movements as an argument against the activities of foreign timber companies.[55]

Ecologization of 'nature's revenge'

In this connection, it is worth following the progress of the 'nature's revenge' paradigm, which played a direct role in forming the modern environmental movement. The conceptual model, first developed mainly in relation to human nature, goes back to antiquity: '*Naturam expelles furca, tamen usque recurret*' ('Drive nature out with a pitchfork and it comes back once again') is Horace's fine formulation. In recent decades it has become something of a household quotation. The 'universal goddess Natura' of late antiquity – according to Ernst Robert Curtius – is not the 'personification of an intellectual concept. She is one of the last religious experiences of the late-pagan world.'[56] In the Middle Ages, she features repeatedly with her complaints: for example, in *De planctu Naturae* by Alan de Lille (1128–1202), where she rails against sodomy as an anti-natural obstacle to reproduction.[57] In Paulus Niavis's *Iudicium Jovi*, a late fifteenth-century fantasy in which a court of the Olympian gods deliberates on the damaging effects of human mining activity, Mother Earth appears 'spattered with blood and wounded all over her body' (in the words of the god Mercury).[58] Medieval nature can only complain, not punish, and in Niavis she does not get very far.

In the modern age, nature gains greater power and can even exact revenge. In *Nemesis Divina* by Carl Linnaeus (1707–78), the great classifier who obsessively hunted for order in nature, divine vengeance is identical with nature's revenge.[59] In 1852 the satirical magazine *Fliegende Blätter* published a cartoon in which a grimly smiling tree saws a man in half; the accompanying verse reads '*Es fällt durch der Sägen und Äxte Gewalt | Der frische, fröhliche freie Wald; | Was Wunder, wenn endlich der Baum sich rächt | Und seinen Mörder in Stücken sägt*' ('Fresh forest happy and free / Falls to the blows of saw and axe. / No wonder the tree finally takes revenge / and saws its killer into pieces'). George P. Marsh's *Man and Nature* (1864) is permeated with the idea of nature's revenge. The massive deforestations in the USA, but also the smoke and soot of the new industrial concentrations, dealt a blow to the joy in progress, including for observers with a generally progressive frame of mind. Even Friedrich Engels had a place in his thought not only for the revenge of the proletariat but also – illogically, from the point of view of Marxian hopes placed in the advance of the productive forces – for the revenge of nature. 'Let us not, however, flatter ourselves overmuch on account of our human victories over nature', he wrote in his *Dialectics of Nature*. 'For each such victory nature takes its revenge on us.'[60] An originally moral-theological way of thinking acquired ever greater ecological substance, and in this secularized form it had already become common property in the nineteenth century. But in those days it was first of all sheer observation, not an impulse for action. The same is true of the idea behind Mary Shelley's *Frankenstein, or The New Prometheus* (1819): that human beings are destroying themselves through their own inventions. A century before the age of technological world wars and atomic weapons, that was still a garish fantasy, not a reality challenging us to act.

In one respect, however, the nature worship of old was in advance of modern conservationism. At a time when the word 'nature' referred also to human nature, the idea of universally innate human rights corresponded to 'natural law' or 'natural right'. Much could be projected into natural right, but at least it grounded an elementary respect for the human body. Under the influence of natural right – according to Franz Wieacker – 'the stake slowly hissed into silence from the early eighteenth century on, just as the rattling subsided in the throats of the tortured or those executed as martyrs'.[61] In the eighteenth-century cult of nature, there was a fluid transition between love of nature and love of man; it involved a love of that which is artlessly natural in human beings. But already in Rousseau, who after much persecution took refuge in 1765 on an island on Lake Biel, there is also a longing for the solitariness of nature: 'O Nature! O my mother! Here at least I am under your guardianship alone; no cunning or treacherous man can come between us here.'[62] In Romanticism this kind of love of nature became more passionate. In landscape painting, people became ever smaller and eventually disappeared altogether. But the tension between love of nature and love of man remained in latent form.

2   Nature in Need of Protection and Nature as Healing Power: Environmental Activism in the 'Nervous Age'

First data cluster: the long *fin de siècle* of urban hygiene, natural conservation and lifestyle reform

1875   UK: Public Health Act for better organization of hygienic rubbish disposal in the towns.

1876   UK: extensive ban on vivisection under the Cruelty to Animals Act, supported by the British women's movement and Queen Victoria. The Society for the Prevention of Cruelty to Animals had been founded back in 1824, and had become the RSPCA with Queen Victoria's permission to add the royal R in 1840.

1876   Founding of the Imperial Health Department in Berlin, the future workplace of Robert Koch.

1877   Founding of the International Association against River, Soil and Air Pollution.

1877   The Prussian state prohibits the discharge of untreated waste-water into rivers (a measure later relaxed under pressure from municipalities).

1878   Founding of the German Society for the Protection of Birds.

1879   German Animal Protection Congress held in Gotha; Ernst von Weber's *Folterkammern der Wissenschaft* (Torture Chambers of Science), the standard work of German anti-vivisectionism.

1880   Ernst Rudorff, *Über das Verhältnis des modernen Lebens zur Natur*, the founding text of German conservationism.

1880   The German Agricultural Council establishes a standing committee to explore the recycling of urban biological waste as fertilizer.

1880   The polar researcher Adolf Erik Nordenskjöld calls for the protection of Swedish nature and the founding of a national park.

1880   George M. Beard, *A Practical Treatise on Nervous Exhaustion (Neurasthenia)*, the founding modern work in this field.

1881   Smoke Abatement Exhibition in London.

1882   France: Law on the Restoration and Conservation of Alpine Lands.

1884   First international congress of ornithologists held in Vienna; agreement to create an international network of observation stations as the basis for bird protection measures.

1886   USA: founding of the first Audubon Society for Bird Protection.

1888   England: founding of the Arts and Crafts Exhibition Society.

1888   Institut Pasteur opens in Paris; the model for other bacteriological research centres.

1888   Heinrich Lahmann founds the Weißer Hirsch vegetarian health centre near Dresden; Eduard Bilz publishes *Das neue Naturheilverfahren* (The New Natural Healing), the best selling title on the subject at the time.

1889   Founding of the British Society for the Protection of Birds.

1889   Founding of the German League of Societies for Healthcare and Drug-Free Treatment (from 1900 the German League of Societies for Natural Living and Healing).

1890   USA: founding of Yosemite National Park.

1890   William Morris, *News from Nowhere* (the first 'ecotopia', centred on the restoration of harmony with nature).

1890   The Swiss Society to Combat Alcohol Consumption is founded on the initiative of the psychiatrist August Forel; in 1895 it fuses with the German Prohibition League to become the International Society to Combat Alcohol Consumption.

1892   Cholera epidemic in Hamburg: final proof of the need to purify river water.

1892   USA: founding of the Sierra Club, with John Muir as chair.

1893   Frederick Jackson Turner, *The Significance of the Frontier in American History* (the 'Turner thesis' that the struggle with the wilderness has marked the American character).

1893   Vegetarian Obstbaukolonie Eden founded near Oranienburg, north of Berlin.

1894   Rudyard Kipling, *The Jungle Book*.

1895   UK: founding of the National Trust for Places of Historic Interest or Natural Beauty (still the leading British association of its kind).

1895   Germany: *Die Naturfreunde* tourist club founded in association with Social Democracy.

1895   Svante August Arrhenius, the future Nobel prizewinner for physics, formulates the hypothesis of a greenhouse effect due to carbon dioxide in the atmosphere.

1897   Japan: first forest legislation; another law is passed on the preservation of temples.

1897   M. O. Bircher-Benner, the inventor of muesli, founds his sanatorium in Zurich.

1898   March: Wilhelm Wetekamp pleads before the Chamber of Deputies in Berlin for the creation of natural parks.

1898   Germany: Bird Protection League founded, with Lina Hähnle as chair.

1898   Afrikaner president Paul Krüger founds the Sabie wild reserve (from 1926 the Krüger National Park).

1898   Ebenezer Howard, *Tomorrow: A Peaceful Path to Real Reform* (the most influential book of the garden city movement).

1898   Wilhelm Bölsche, *Das Liebesleben in der Natur* (Love Life in Nature).

1900   British–German London Convention for the Preservation of Wild Animals, Birds and Fish in Africa.

1900   Founding of the World League against Vivisection.

1900   Founding of the Natural Healing Centre on Monte Verità near Ascona, which became the gathering-place for lifestyle reformers.

1901   Founding of the Wandervogel ramblers' association at Berlin-Steglitz.

1902   International Convention on the Protection of 'Useful' Birds.

1902   International Council for the Exploration of the Sea, based in Copenhagen, is established to gather information on fish stocks.

1902   Founding of the German Garden City Society.

1902   Founding of the Isar Valley Association.

1902   Hesse passes a Preservation of Ancient Monuments Act and provides for the protection of natural landmarks.
1903   Theodore Roosevelt (US president from 1901 to 1909) and John Muir hike together in Yosemite National Park.
1904   Founding of International Women's League for Bird Protection.
1904   Founding of the German League for Protection of the Countryside, as an umbrella organization for various regional leagues.
1904   Founding of the Emschergenossenschaft: the Emscher had been turning into a 'sacrificial river' to purify the Ruhr of its wastewater.
1904   Germany: *Kosmos* magazine first appears, with the aim of 'depicting living nature in all its grandeur' (an allusion to Alexander von Humboldt); it achieves a wide circulation within a few years.
1904   Upton Sinclair, *The Jungle.* Its gruesome picture of the huge Chicago slaughterhouses, especially their scandalous lack of hygiene, influences reform policies in the Progressive Era.
1905   Founding of the US Forest Service, with Gifford Pinchot as director.
1905   Anti-Smoke League founded in Baltimore; similar initiatives follow in other American cities (in 1908 the Chicago Anti-Smoke League, a women's organization, calls for electrification of the railways).
1905   Bavaria: founding of State Committee for the Care of Nature.
1906   Prussia: founding of State Office for the Care of Natural Monuments.
1906   Founding in Berlin of the German Open-Air Bathing Society.
1906   Hellerau Garden City near Dresden becomes a centre for the reform of art and design.
1906   USA: Food and Drug Act paves the way for the FDA (Food and Drug Administration), which later becomes the model for the EPA (Environmental Protection Agency).
1907   Robert Baden-Powell founds the Boy Scouts.
1908   The philosopher Theodor Lessing founds a Noise Abatement Association in Germany, with *Der Anti-Rüpel* as its press organ.
1908   Founding of the Central Office for the Prevention of Street Dust, in Berlin-Charlottenburg.
1908   Gustav Mahler's *Das Lied von der Erde*.
1909   Sweden becomes the first country to pass a Conservation Act.
1909   Wilhelm Ostwald – who, in an allusion to Kant, makes economical energy-use a 'categorical imperative' indicating the level of culture – receives the Nobel Prize for Chemistry.
1909   International Congress for Protection of the Countryside held in Paris.
1909   International Congress for the Protection of Animals in London; campaign against vivisection.
1909   Conservation Park Society founded in Stuttgart; in 1910 it acquires the Wilseder Berg, as the core of the Lüneburg Heath Protected Area.

1910   Paul Sarasin, chair of the Swiss Conservation League founded in 1909, delivers a policy report on 'world conservation' at the Eighth International Congress of Zoologists in Geneva; it calls for the establishment of a World Conservation Commission in view of the threat to animal species.

1910   Gifford Pinchot, *The Fight for Conservation*.

1910   Meeting in Tölz marks the climax of a(n unsuccessful) protest movement against the planned power station on Lake Walchen.

1911   Founding of the French Bird Protection League and the first French Conservation Area.

1911   The German writer and conservationist Hermann Löns derides the pettiness of 'conventional' natural conservation.

1911   International hygiene exhibition in Dresden (5 million visitors!).

1912   First German youth hostel opens at Burg Altena in North Rhine-Westphalia.

1913   World Conservation Congress in Berne.

1913   Founding of the British Ecological Society.

1913   Paris: the French Touring Club organizes a major international conference to bolster calls for afforestation.

1913   Meeting of the 'Free German Youth' in the Hoher Meißner massif in Hesse; a message from Ludwig Klages is entitled *Man and Earth*.

1913   Founding in Bavaria of the Conservation League, the later BUND.

1913   USA: Migratory Birds Act.

1913   Defeat of the Sierra Club's campaign against removal of Hetch Hetchy Valley from Yosemite National Park to provide water for San Francisco.

1913   Invention of the Haber-Bosch synthesis: the synthetic production of nitrogen opens the way for the chemicalization of agriculture.

1914   March: Switzerland establishes Europe's first national park, in the Engadin valley.

The Belle Époque in the history of environmentalism

Historians are inherently curious as to whether chronological detail already tells us something: simultaneity or non-simultaneity, temporal succession or concentration of data at a particular point in time. If we look for the historical origins of the modern environmental movement, the data tend to cluster in the decades around 1900: a 'long *fin de siècle*' begins to take shape, involving a 'bridge' to ecological modernity in most industrial countries, at least as noteworthy in the USA as in Britain or Germany. Many components of modern environmental movements make their public debut in that period; one is struck by the degree of simultaneity and the rapidity with which events follow one another in different countries.

Samuel P. Hays, the first to focus on government protection of natural resources in his account of the Progressive Era in America, entitled his book *Conservation and the Gospel of Efficiency* (1959). This was a reference to the climactic finale of Theodore Roosevelt's 1908 address to state governors:

> Let us remember that the conservation of our natural resources, though the gravest problem of today, is yet but part of another and greater problem to which this Nation is not yet awake, but to which it will awake in time, and with which it must hereafter grapple if it is to live – the problem of national efficiency, the patriotic duty of insuring the safety and continuance of the Nation.[63]

This drew applause from the governors: 'efficiency' was one of the buzzwords of the age and could readily be associated with patriotic appeals. In Roosevelt's mouth, it already had a meaning which, a century later, would have been conveyed by the word 'sustainability'. 'Conservation' acquired a basically anti-conservative tone, progressive and activist, which it did not have in German, for example. There are reasons why environmentalism arose as a progressive movement in the United States; a characteristic dialectic runs all the way through its history. In the very place where forest destruction and the exploitation of natural resources were taken to extremes, environmentalists were able – on the basis of a powerful civil society – to cut an especially impressive figure as saviours of the nation.

Robert H. Wiebe, who also wrote shortly before the 'ecological revolution' about the Progressive Era, gave his account what now appears an astonishing title: *The Search for Order* (1967). It is no wonder that Gifford Pinchot (the forceful legendary founder of a sustainably organized forestry) features in the book, but not John Muir, the prophet who championed national parks as a way of protecting the wilderness. For Wiebe, the spirit of that age is best embodied in Edward Bellamy's science fiction novel *Looking Backward* (1888), the 'most popular utopia in American history',[64] which offers a terrifying retrospect from a future year 2000 when American society has adopted a model of military discipline in the interests of public welfare. William Morris's utopian romance, published two years later in 1890, is seen by Jan Holm as the 'prototype of ecotopia',[65] which, though not figuring in Wiebe's book, drew on cooperative traditions for its countervision to the centralism of *Looking Backward*. A survey of the whole panorama of that time shows Morris – the greatest mind of his age in Shaw's view[66] – at least as well attuned as Bellamy to its imagined future. Around the turn of the century, the longing for a self-organized 'natural' society with no all-controlling state bureaucracy blossomed in many different forms and became a cross-frontier leitmotif of the Belle Époque.

In Germany, the many reform movements active around 1900 that seem so pregnant today had not yet found a collective term for themselves on which historians could agree. Most were treated separately under such headings as 'lifestyle reform', 'pedagogic reform', 'youth movement', 'Jugendstil' or simply 'reform movements'. In the first few decades after the Second World War, attention was focused mainly on the paths that led to National Socialism. But the truth is that, for those movements, elements such as pacifism or the quest for international understanding and small, freedom-loving communities were far more typical than chauvinism or proto-fascism. 'International' was a positively charged term, sometimes used in the self-characterization of movements that were actually regional in scope. The Deutsche Bund der Vereine für naturgemäße Lebens- und Heilweise [German League of Societies for Natural Living and Healing], the umbrella organization for natural healing societies, advocated the 'democratization of health matters' and was free of chauvinist or racist spasms, all the more remarkably because imperial nationalism was just then coming to boiling point in the Western world.[67]

But that was not only the prehistory of the world wars; it also contained quite other histories, in which much is waiting to be rediscovered in the ecological age. The view that people who abstain from meat are generally more peaceful had an established following, strengthened by numbers of ethnologists; and vegetarianism – a term covering several lifestyle reform currents – typically went together with pacifism.[68] The legendary 'First Free German Youth Congress', held in October 1913 in the Hoher Meißner massif, was a counter to the official celebrations marking the centenary of the Battle of the Nations, near Leipzig, in the Napoleonic Wars. Gustav Wyneken – a leading educational reformer and supporter of nudism – gave a speech there that people experienced as a 'paroxysm of infinite beauty'. What they remembered most was the lines: 'Seeing the valleys of our fatherland spread glistening at our feet, I cannot but wish that the day will never come when war hordes throng them. And may the day never come when we are forced to carry war into the valleys of a foreign nation.'[69]

Love of nature had many variants: one was a natural libido involving a passion for hunting and spoiling for a fight, as in the Wild West. A high-light of Theodore Roosevelt's memoirs is precisely the 'bear-hunters' meal' in the White House, to which he invited wonderful guys he felt 'proud to think of as Americans'.[70] However, love of natural landscapes was usually combined with a longing for peace; the general tone of conservation-ism was defensive, not aggressive. In no way should it be simply lumped together with a social Darwinism for which struggle was the elixir of life. The most famous and fervent declaration of love for nature made in those days is Ludwig Klages's message to the Hoher Meißner congress: *Man and Earth*. The philosopher, who abhorred war and would emigrate in 1914 to Switzerland, rebuffs Darwinism in no uncertain terms: 'Nature knows no "struggle for existence", only one stemming from a concern for life.' His message merges into a vision of a cosmic Eros that will save the earth: the 'world-creating power of love that weaves everything together'.[71] The word 'networking' did not yet exist! For Klages, lover of the wild Franziska Gräfin zu Reventlow, love of nature was one with sensual Eros. The nexus between love of nature and love of human beings was not yet broken.

'The secret warmth of the human heart has been drunk' – drunk with the destruction of nature, complains Klages.[72]

Walt Whitman, who in his lifetime had made many enemies in the USA because of his cosmic nature euphoria and sexual imagination, was now honoured in Germany ('the American Homer'[73]) almost more than in his own country. The *fin de siècle* cult of nature went together, either overtly or covertly, with a sexualization of nature. Even the most successful popularizers of Darwinism in Germany, Ernst Haeckel and Wilhelm Bölsche, were a very long way from glorifying struggle. Bölsche saw nature as a teacher of love, and in his bestseller *Das Liebesleben in der Natur*, which had a large working-class readership,[74] he described with undisguised pleasure the polymorphous sexuality of the animal and vegetable world, though hinting that homosexual intercourse was more in keeping with the nature of lower animals.[75] Rolf Peter Sieferle points out that, at least until 1914, 'nearly all social Darwinists' rejected war – if not in principle, then because they realized that modern technological warfare by no means led to selection of the best.[76] For anyone who considered 'survival of the fittest' to be the essence of Darwinism, conservation was actually against nature. But Darwinists like Haeckel and Bölsche were glowing in their love of the beauties of nature.

The protection of migratory birds, which are oblivious of national frontiers, had an inherent momentum towards international agreement. Looking back from the ecological age, our eyes can rediscover networks in the Belle Époque that were partly torn up by the two world wars. Indeed, in many areas, one has the impression that something like the environmental movement of the 1970s would have developed after 1900 if the early beginnings had not been interrupted by war and postwar emergencies – and in the USA by the boom that reactivated the illusion of unlimited resources. To be sure, the threat to the planetary ecosystem in 1900 looks altogether trivial from today's vantage point, but Klages and nature lovers already displayed a sense of alarm similar to that of modern doomsayers. In 1913 Klages could write that the 'fauna of Germania' had been almost completely wiped out. 'And who does not perceive with secret fear the yearly quickening loss of our sweet-singing birds of passage?' 'Barely a human generation ago, even in the cities, the blue summer air' was filled with 'the whirring of swallows'; now it had become 'eerily quiet' even in the countryside.[77]

There already is Rachel Carson's vision of 'silent spring', which so alarmed the American public half a century later. On closer examination, however, both reactions may seem exaggerated. The worldwide species loss was still below a calculable level: only local estimates were possible in the case of particular species. But a hundred years ago, 'nature' still referred far more than today also to nature within man – and many people seem to have felt more acutely that it was under threat. In those days, many were less accustomed than we are today to the pace of modern life, to the city environment and its sedentary lifestyle, and people had developed far fewer leisure resources to offset the damage due to civilization than we have done in our fitness-conscious age. This also explains the broad spectrum of life-style movements at the turn of the twentieth century. In comparison with the period around 1800, the general picture is unambiguous: all-powerful nature, once so threatening, had become nature under threat.

The urban environmental crisis and the hygiene movement

A real crisis, heavily perceptible to the senses, existed only in the big cities that had outgrown their old limits and threatened to choke on their own refuse and smoke. A whole generation of environmental historians has rediscovered this crisis, along with the flood of complaints that accompanied it.[78] But to find pendants to today's environmental policy in the late nineteenth or early twentieth century, one should not get too hung up on the term 'nature': much in those days came under such rubrics as 'hygiene', 'national or public health', 'urban sanitation' or 'sanitary movement'. We are certainly talking here of one of the strongest transnational reform movements of the age, which opened a new epoch in the industrial countries.[79] With regard to public hygiene, a Europe-wide network of reform-minded politicians, medical personnel and engineers was driven by a shared ethos and energy that could escalate into fanaticism and place opponents on a par with Herod's child-murderers.[80] Cleanliness in the hygienic sense fitted perfectly with the Victorian striving for moral cleanliness. But the sanitary movement also gathered momentum from social reformers and socialists, bringing forth a flood of literature and an impressive gallery of local politicians who liked to get things done.[81]

On the other hand, the sanitary movement sharply raises the question of whether it had anything to do with the conservation, natural healing and lifestyle reform movements, or whether it pointed in a different, even opposite, direction. Is it convincing proof that what today goes by the name of environmentalism did not then belong together but had a differentiated, if not internally contradictory, history?[82] These questions have to remain partly open in the present state of research, but in general it is becoming clear that the beginnings of our present ecological age cannot be altogether dated back to the period around 1900. Environmentalists and ramblers put as much distance as possible between themselves and urban spaces, but the arena of action for the sanitation movement was precisely the big cities. Typically, those active in it were eager technocrats who, even more than private entrepreneurs, pioneered comprehensive technologies such as the cascading pipes of the water supply and drainage systems beneath the cities, or the gas and electricity networks. It was a world at the opposite pole to that of the nature enthusiasts.

Many modern environmental problems actually intensified as a result of the nineteenth-century sanitary movement. To a large extent, that kind of urban sanitation was nothing other than a grand shifting of the problem. Local environmental politics is always looking for ways to solve its problems at the expense of other nearby areas or through the building of an industry-free business district at the expense of lower-class housing. In principle, this conflict was visible early on, but there was a lack of institutions capable of pursuing all-round conservation for whole regions. 'Networked thinking', such as modern ecologists demand, did exist at a rudimentary level in the nineteenth century, but it broke down when it came to the practical consequences.

Time limits of 'networked thinking'

Nevertheless, at a time when manure was still expensive, people knew even better than in the later age of artificial fertilizer that the agricultural recycling of urban food waste was the ideal solution. In the nineteenth century, public attention still focused on actual excrement, which aroused disgust but had a fertilizing value; industrial waste was not at first the big issue. The sanitation pope of Victorian England, Edwin Chadwick (1800–90), who became a kind of 'health dictator' in the eyes of his local authority opponents and declared that the social problem was ultimately one of urban sanitation,[83] turned circulation into a full-scale philosophy. 'Circulation instead of stagnation' was the answer proposed by his 'Sanitary School' – whether in relation to air, water or foodstuffs. Wastewater was to be carried into sewage farms, where after treatment it would return to the natural process of circulation. With this system, wrote Chadwick, 'we shall complete the cycle and achieve the Egyptian form of eternity, by leading the snake's tail into the snake's mouth'.[84] The more that natural circulation was disturbed, the more ambitious became the technological circulation projects.[85] In the late nineteenth century, there was a Europe-wide discussion on valuable uses for urban waste;[86] as Tim Cooper writes, Victorian England was for a time obsessed with the idea of recycling waste,[87] whereas the otherwise Anglophile chemist Justus Liebig blamed the English water closet for 'robbing other countries of the conditions for fertility' and 'meddling disgracefully with the world order'. This could not go 'unpunished'; England was 'hanging vampire-like on Europe's neck, one might even say on the world's, and sucking the blood from its heart'.[88]

Things were to be done better in the capital of the German Reich. Berlin, surrounded by sand that absorbed large amounts of fertilizer, had the world's largest sewage farms around 1900 and provided a model for distant Cairo on the edge of the desert. But the urban waste became more and more muddled and opaque; industrial toxins increasingly impaired the fertilizing value of wastewater. The Berlin sewage farms, initially hailed as 'a cultural achievement of the first order',[89] came to be seen by nature lovers as pig sties that stank to high heaven.[90] The ecological harmony between the city and its surroundings could no longer be saved.

Also the path to the perfect purification plant and perfect sludge disposal proved to be an endless slog. Changes in the composition of waste prevented the development of a disposal model applicable at all times and places. The circulation model that had given free rein to the water closet and combined sewerage systems was now merely implemented in bits and pieces: the circulation remained open and multiplied the waste problem. The striving for unattainable circulation soon aroused another ambition: what the American environmental historian Joel A. Tarr called 'the search for the ultimate sink'. A century later, we find the same shifting objectives in the history of nuclear technology: first a quest for perfect 'fuel circulation' by means of breeder reactors and reprocessing, then – when that proved unachievable – a scarcely less dubious search for the definitive storage site.

The Ruhr's epochal feat of strength, around the year 1900, involved concentrating wastewater in the Emscher (having declared it the sacrificial stretch of river), with the idea that this might make the Ruhr at least half-clean again. The Emschergenossenschaft, founded for this purpose in 1900 and later held up as the 'mother of water management',[91] remained for decades an international prototype of large-scale translocal regulation of acute environmental problems, in cooperation with the later Ruhr Resettlement Association (Ruhrsiedlungsverband) and Ruhr Valley Barrier Association (which provided the Ruhr region with clean drinking water). Of course, the wastewater from the Ruhr region ended up in the Rhine, untreated, but by then it was not far to the Netherlands frontier. Anyway, the mythical 'German stream' was in danger of degenerating into an open sewer. Only after 1991, with the coming of the new eco-age, did the 'renaturing' of the much-abused river – that is, the creation of a natural landscape along the Emscher for the first time – become a billion-euro showpiece project for a region that was trying to shake off its 'coal black' image.[92]

As long ago as 1900, the first rubbish-burning installations began shifting the waste problem up into the air. In the coal emergency of the wartime and postwar years, however, when very little combustible material of any kind was thrown away, this exit route for domestic rubbish did not develop further.[93] All the more did factories make use of it. Higher chimneys signalled a good neighbourly strategy, since they reduced the smoke nuisance in the immediate surroundings; this reached its highest point in the 1970s. But ever since it had become possible to measure atmospheric pressure with a barometer, people had known very well in theory that the earth's atmosphere was by no means never-ending and that the smoke from very high chimneys was disappearing into space.[94] Above all, it had long been demonstrated that smoke from steelworks was harmful to vegetation over long distances. But there the mining industry, without much fuss or legal action, let itself in for various compensation awards, and not a few 'smoke farmers'[95] now preferred to draw their money effortlessly rather than insist that something be done about the harmful smoke.

The highest common denominator: health!

All in all, we know of few direct links around the turn of the twentieth century between reform efforts geared to 'sanitation' and to 'nature'. The struggle against water and air pollution was usually fought out in a big-city arena very different from the green fields where ramblers and natural healers joined conservationists determined to protect nature, birds and landscape. Yet there was one high common denominator: *health*. Schopenhauer's maxim that 'health outweighs all external goods'[96] became common wisdom in an age of growing prosperity. But we still need to pay attention to the differences and phases. The first great push in urban sanitation and the centralization of a hygienic water supply and waste removal system was driven by the fear of contagious disease; cholera and typhus were even more terrifying than tuberculosis, which, though the biggest killer of the age, was insidious in its advance. The Hamburg cholera outbreak of 1892 brought the final victory of Robert Koch's bacteriological school over the rival 'miasma' explanation in terms of swampy conditions and soil impurities (whose principal figure, Max von Pettenkofer, shot himself in 1901). Since Altona, unlike neighbouring Hamburg, already had a treatment plant in operation, the fact that the epidemic was far less virulent there proved that the purification of river water was essential.[97] This vindication of the bacteriologists, however, shifted the focus away from environmental problems. Hibbert Winslow Hill, the leading American advocate of a 'new public health' strictly based on bacteriology, declared in 1916: 'The old public health was concerned with the environment; the new is concerned with the individual.'[98] Even the much-blamed 'smoke plague' was now completely underestimated as a health risk.

In 1890 Koch's presentation of his tuberculin as a possible cure for tuberculosis converted him, to quote one admirer, 'at a stroke into the greatest, most successful and most meritorious researcher of all time'[99] – although the wonder drug would soon prove to be the greatest flop in pharmaceutical history. Mountain sanatoria, with their gospel of natural healing through light and pure air, experienced a boom without precedent; the 'tuberculin exuberance', however, was left as a bad memory of a 'mental epidemic'. Often, the very advance of medical diagnostics led initially to 'therapeutic nihilism', to the belief that doctors could not achieve much; either disease prevention was seen as a matter for local politicians and engineers, or people were once more referred to the *vis medicatrix naturae* in the form of air, light and water cures, healthy diets and a balance of *quies et motus* (rest and motion). However much doctors raged against the 'cure dabblers', the philosophy of natural healing everywhere worked its way into medical practice. In 1900 the unstoppable rise of the pharmaceutical industry was not yet a fait accompli – on the contrary, drugs-based treatment seemed to many a leftover from old-style 'quackery'.[100] This was the case, quite rightly, most of all in relation to 'nervous' afflictions – which since the 1880s had developed into a fully fledged mental epidemic. 'Neurasthenia', of which the New York physician George M. Beard gave a textbook description in 1880, spread with lightning speed to Germany,[101] at a time when most transatlantic medical transfers were in the opposite direction. Shortly before 1914, it was still the commonest of all diagnoses.[102]

Nervous love of nature

The nerve doctor Willy Hellpach, one of the busiest publicists in the field who for a time gave advice to Max Weber, associated the breakthrough of Beard's 'neurasthenia' in Germany with the hangover that followed the boom of the early 1870s and the renunciation of free trade. Liberal industrialism, he argued, had itself suffered a 'nervous breakdown' around 1880.[103] The United States had similar experiences in the stormy industrialization of the post-Civil-War Age of Reconstruction. The 'nervous age' became a stock expression, and the term 'nerve hygiene' began to appear in the literature around the turn of the century.[104]

There was a close connection between the 'nervous' experience of self and the natural healing boom – not least because 'nerves' and 'nature' could both function as code words for sexuality.[105] The water, nerve and natural cure clinics that mushroomed on all sides, together with their philosophies and therapies, formed a continuum. Beard, who had once worked with Thomas Edison, still believed that neurasthenia could be cured with electrotherapy, but Paul Julius Möbius (the first in Germany to take up the new emphasis on nervous disorders) thought it was flim-flam and that only lifestyle changes could have a lasting effect.[106] In 1908, in a report to the Berlin Medical Society, the neurologist Wilhelm His argued that 'natural healing methods would achieve their most important indication, their experience-based recognition' only 'once nervous disorders had spread among the wider population'.[107]

There is considerable evidence that an inner unity of conservationist and environmentalist tendencies is most likely to be found here, even when direct linkages are not apparent. People sought relief in nature from the nervous stresses of the city; what only Romantics and disciples of Rousseau did at first became a mass movement with the advance of transport technology. 'The tradesman, the attorney comes out of the din and craft of the street,' wrote Emerson in his essay *Nature* (1836), 'and sees the sky and the woods, and is a man again.'[108] John Muir, the American prophet of national parks and the wilderness, saw nervous spirits as his confederates. In 1898 he declared: 'Thousands of tired, nerve-shaken, over-civilized people are beginning to find out going to the mountains is going home; that wilderness is a necessity; and that mountain parks and reservations are useful not only as fountains of timber and irrigating rivers, but as fountains of life.'[109] When Theodore Roosevelt met Muir in 1903 in Yosemite National Park ('the bulliest day of my life') – the photo of the two men is among the icons of American conservationism and became the title picture of a book about *American Nervousness*[110] – it was a demonstration of the nervous force reclaimed in the wildness of nature; for this president too, who always presented himself as a bundle of energy, had once felt a neurasthenic.[111] Charlotte Perkins Gilman, whose autobiography makes her a prize literary witness for the American neurasthenia of the time,[112] is also well known as the author of the first feminist ecotopia.[113] Germany and the United States, which experienced the most intense industrialization in the late nineteenth century, were the citadels of both neurasthenia[114] and conservationism by the year 1900. According to the wife of Hermann Löns, the inventor of heath romanticism, 'states of boundless depression alternated [in him] with the greatest excitability'.[115] Octavia Hill too suffered a severe breakdown before she took the initiative in founding the National Trust.[116] (Note the difference: in 1800 people sought freedom in nature; a century later they looked for peace and quiet.)

The general view is that nervousness was most rife in Protestant countries; Paolo Mantegazza (1831–1910), professor of anthropology in Florence, who himself went through severe nervous crises, acknowledged as much in his internationally successful book *The Nervous Century* (1888). This may be the solution to the puzzle of why the origins of modern environmentalism lie mainly in the Protestant countries. It has become a commonplace that the prominence of the German cultural area in modern environmentalism derives from its tradition of forest romanticism. But only in combination with nervous worry did this become capable of having a directly political impact, since everyone agreed that the quiet of the forest regenerated the nerves. A hundred years earlier, when robbers still lurked in the forest, such an idea would not have occurred to people so readily.

National differences and convergences

Then as now, a transnational comparison offers the outlines of an ecology of ecologism: characteristic differences from country to country. 'Sanitary Science is the product of the English mind': so wrote in 1885 a Dr Ballard, one of the growing number of medical officers of health (MOHs) who sustained the British public health movement.[117] The founding period of this movement lay back in the 1820s and 1840s, with hygienic and social concerns closely intertwined; Friedrich Engels's *Condition of the Working Class in England* (1845) drew heavily on the provocative hygiene reports of the time. But for a long time the MOHs were underpaid and lacked teeth; the sanitary movement became a real force only in the 1880s, when fear of epidemics won over urban reformers and engineers in large number.[118] At the same time, it spread to other Western industrial countries and gained support from ambitious men of action. Germany had an advantage in this respect because of the relatively strong position of its communal authorities; these were required to take effective measures, even if local dignitaries often had to be spurred on from above. Campaigning against cruelty to animals also went back a long time in England, having become, especially among Puritans and Quakers, one element in an influential social movement.[119] But eminent Germans such as Arthur Schopenhauer and Richard Wagner also publicly spoke out against such practices, including medical vivisection, and by 1881 the 'Reich Association of Animal Protection Societies' had more than 150 affiliates.[120] Organized animal protection came historically prior to organized natural conservation.

The cult of wilderness and national parks originated – how could it have been otherwise? – in the United States, where a new national pride turned to the monuments of nature (massive canyons and giant sequoias) to out-trump the architectural heritage of the Old World. In Europe, Scandinavians were the most likely to match the nature nationalism of the Americans, often protesting that their waterfalls were one up on Niagara. In Prussia/Germany, although Hugo Conwentz (from 1906 director of the State Office for the Care of Natural Monuments) led the way in Europe, he originally had to be content with ad hoc operations, and nature lovers could only admire with envy the great American national parks. As early as 1898, the Breslau senior schoolmaster Wilhelm Wetekamp had held them up as a model in his impassioned appeal for conservation before the Prussian chamber of deputies.[121] In 1911 Hermann Löns, gushing over the expansive heath landscape, poured scorn on the paltriness of 'conwentzional' conservation: 'The spoiling of nature, on the other hand, cannot be denied the imaginativeness of genius.'[122] In response Conwentz, more natural scientist than nature enthusiast,[123] agreed to anchor conservation more firmly in the state apparatus. He was well aware that ad hoc intervention would not be sufficient, but further state support required a clear demarcation of responsibility to avoid conflicts with the agriculture ministry. Behind Conwentz stood Friedrich Althoff, the policy strongman on scientific matters. Not only a 'movement' but also a relationship with the state and the academic world lay at the origins of conservation, in the United States as much as in Germany. Samuel P. Hays has shown that in the Theodore Roosevelt era, despite the 'grassroots' image he liked to cultivate, the protection of 'natural resources' took place in the context of central government areas of competence, as it did a generation later under Franklin D. Roosevelt. Even at that early date, a fundamental field of tension was taking shape in environmentalism.[124]

In 1909, a *Verein Naturschutzpark* founded in the Munich 'artists' den' called for the creation of American-style national parks. The meeting was attended by only 34 persons, yet by 1913 the membership had grown to 16,000 plus more than 600 corporate members – even if people in Germany could still only dream of anything on the scale of the US parks. The *Verein* made headway especially in relation to Lüneburg Heath and even won the support of Kaiser Wilhelm II. In 1912 it obtained compulsory purchase rights that enabled it to restrict hunting and to prevent construction that spoiled the landscape.[125] In those days, people liked to think of the Heath as 'primal nature'; only later, when soil and pollen experts demonstrated that it had originally been forest, did friends of the forest ridicule heath romantics for treating as wilderness a landscape that had actually been destroyed by sheep-grazing and wood consumption.[126]

Even the 'wildness' of the American West was not as untouched as its apostles claimed, since it owed its picturesque character not least to Indian burn-beating agriculture.[127] The American love of the wilderness was in reality love of a cultural landscape, only it was not aware of this. If the aesthetically motivated conservationism of the time appears naïve to us today, it is because it wanted to preserve a certain landscape as if it were a beautiful picture, without realizing – as it might have from Darwin's theory of evolution – that nature is in constant change and 'Arcadia' becomes overgrown with forest and scrub. Right up to the present day, conservationists have found it difficult to cope with the consequences of this.

Anti-alcoholism – another key component of lifestyle reform at that time – developed most strongly as a political movement in the United States, where it had behind it not only Puritan traditions but soon also modern Fordism;[128] supporters of prohibition campaigned with the same kind of moral fervour that abolitionists had displayed against slavery, although in both cases their success turned out to be something of a Pyrrhic victory. Was drunkenness against nature? That was debatable. But everyone knew that brandy did the greatest damage to *Naturvölker* or 'primitive' peoples who came into contact with modern Western civilization. In Germany, where drinking rituals were integral to the conviviality of students and soldiers, anti-alcoholism became an element in nature-oriented lifestyle reform even more than in the United States. And it began to dawn on leading psychiatrists such as Auguste Forel and Emil Kraeplin that alcohol was the worst enemy of mental health.[129] Disciples of the youth movement were afflicted with national self-loathing at the sight of beer bellies.[130] In Germany at that time, the giving up of alcohol and tobacco meant a cultural revolution. The cancer risk from smoking – unlike from factory smoke – was not yet an issue; the assertiveness of non-smokers scored successes only in the wake of the 'ecological revolution' of 1970. Vegetarianism became the new creed in the late nineteenth century, acquiring features still present today from the Zurich sanatorium founder Max Bircher-Benner, the inventor of muesli. But here there was a transatlantic affinity with the fanatical vegetarian John Harvey Kellogg, whose brother devised Kellogg's cornflakes, and who, at his sanatorium at Battle Creek, Michigan, combined a vegetarian diet with laughter exercises, Swedish gymnastics and sundry ways of stimulating bowel movements.[131]

Most of the movements discussed in this chapter were characteristic mainly of the German-speaking countries, where a Protestant-Puritan morality, reinforced by industrial performance pressure, clashed violently with excessive meat and alcohol consumption that became greater than ever with the growing prosperity. As we have seen, neurasthenia too counted as a typical disorder of Germanic-Protestant Europe. A veritable confrontation between Germanic and Roman developed especially over the issue of bird protection. In Italy, bird-catching became a mass sport in the name of the freedom to hunt. It had once been popular north of the Alps too, as Papageno's aria in *The Magic Flute* shows, and even in Prussian Westphalia everyone remained free to pursue it until 1904.[132] Around the turn of the century, however, British and German nature lovers targeted bird-catching along with deforestation as a symptom of the disturbed natural balance in Southern Europe.[133] Giovanni Salvadori – a priest who represented his native Trento province on the Austrian National Council and consistently defended the 'nutritious' bird-catching common in the South – angered the First International Congress of Ornithologists in 1884 with his polemical paper *Schützet die Insekten und gebt den Vogelfang frei*.[134] It was a sore point in those days that bird protection had a negative effect on popular nutrition. Do not birds also cause much damage? Salvadori asked. And is it really true that the insects they eat are all pests? Do these not also belong to the totality of nature? He was touching on a basic theme of species diversity that rumbles on today.

Natural conservation and habitat protection

In Wilhelmine Germany, conservationism broadened out mainly within the *Heimatschutz*, the 'homeland protection' or 'habitat protection' movement, for which the traditional farming landscape was part of nature. In some ways it was in advance of later eco-conservationism, which would focus on small natural reserves and fail to address the great bulk of the countryside; this broader horizon makes it in many respects closer to modern environmentalism.[135] *Heimat* is intimately related to 'habitat', in a sense being a transference of the concept to human beings. Since the peasant economy promoted species diversity into the nineteenth century, before the great age of land consolidation, the preservation of the traditional village unit made sense also from today's ecological viewpoint. Moreover, unlike the omnipresent goddess Natura in antiquity, the nature earmarked for conservation first had to be identified. Ernst Rudorff, the spiritual father of conservationism, also elaborated the *Heimatschutz* programme; the two went hand in hand in his view.[136] The same was true for Hugo Conwentz, who called for schools to teach *Heimat* studies and to encourage, not least through organized trips, a greater love and understanding of the local countryside. He praised a teachers' conference at the Wilseder Berg (the highest point on Lüneburg Heath) as an exemplary initiative.[137] The naturalist Emil Adolf Roßmäßler (1806–67), who as an 1848 radical lost his zoology professorship at the Forest Academy in Tharandt, had already made the link between natural conservation and habitat protection, in the journal *Aus der Heimat* that he founded in 1853.[138]

Since the Nazis' vain attempt to use *Heimatschutz* slogans to hold the front towards the end of the Second World War, many German Greens later believed that *Heimat* was a Nazi concept,[139] although a little reading would easily have told them that its roots lay more in Homer's *Odyssey* and Johanna Spyri's *Heidi* than in Adolf Hitler of all people. *Heimat* is actually a subjective concept, which, unlike 'race', cannot possibly have an onto-logical charge; it is intrinsically non-expansionist and relates to a visible, narrowly defined space. The basic feature of Germany's *Heimatschutz* was its anti-centralism and inner detachment from the post-1871 unification euphoria.[140] Nationalist tones were very seldom present, and by no means central, in its publicity; international contacts were cultivated and other countries mentioned as models.[141] Indeed, despite ever-growing hostil-ity at a political level, close cooperation developed until 1914 between the German Reich and France in the field of 'habitat protection'.[142] In October 1909 an International Homeland Conservation Congress was held in Paris, with Conwentz in the chair for the opening session;[143] a midget in the Prussian bureaucracy was a great man on the international stage. 'He caused a furore in Europe with his conception of efficient, tightly organized, conservation.'[144] He had an impact as far away as Scandinavia and Russia, and even supported the efforts of Russian conservationists to develop ideas for their own very different country.[145] The other pioneer of the internationalization of conservationism was the Swiss Paul Sarasin, who, unlike Conwentz, was a powerful orator. In him one already finds the emotive rhetoric of world salvation that brought environmentalism to the fore in the production of a meaning of life and a good conscience.

The National Trust for Places of Historic Interest or Natural Beauty – founded in 1895 and still the leading organization of its kind in Britain – also took for granted the connection between natural conservation and homeland protection, the conspicuous traditional model being not half-timbered houses and communal forests but the typically British stately homes with their 'Arcadian' landscapes. Later, jokes were told of debt-ridden noble homes being sold off to the National Trust. It was the same in Germany with the old common lands, which became idyllic places for nature lovers.[146]

A quite different, but no less significant, link between love of nature and love of homeland developed in the romanticism of the American Wild West. There too government action was ultimately required if one wished to preserve a particular area of a national park. But whereas the *Heimatschutz* appealed with some success to regional patriotism, the wil-derness cult, clashing as it did with the interests of ranchers and loggers, was not such an appropriate focus for local grassroots movements. On the other hand, anti-smoke initiatives for a long time bore the stamp of civil society much more in the United States than in Germany. As Frank Uekötter laconically remarked of the early twentieth century: 'American citizens could not confine themselves to petitioning the authorities, simply because there were no such authorities.'[147]

Conservation and urban sanitation were outwardly two different worlds, but they were both typical movements of the high industrial age that sought to grapple with its dark sides. Furthermore, although mass tourism appeared to many early conservationists as the main enemy, it was the strongest driving force behind the new longing for nature that gave conservationism its political potential. This inner tension runs all the way through the worldwide history of conservationism, right up to the present day. Never before has there been so much talk of 'enjoying nature', yet people let off steam by travelling, wrote Rudorff in his essay *Über das Verhältnis des modernen Lebens zur Natur* (1880), the programmatic text of conservationism. 'They celebrate nature, but do so by prostituting it. . . . A real mania to destroy nature in its very essence has taken hold of the world, on the pretext of making it accessible for people to enjoy.'[148] This was the complaint of those who sought solitude in nature. In reality, the effects of tourism upon conservation and the environment were by no means only negative. Spa resorts were right up front environmentally, being the first to ban smoky, foul-smelling industrial plants and to provide for clean water and air. Generally in those days, conservationists were less prejudiced towards tourism in England and France than in Germany,[149] where a typical elitism blinded them to the tourist composition of their mass base. On the other hand, health spas spread nowhere as fast as they did in Central Europe; a guide in 1971 noted that 96 per cent of the world total were still concentrated there.[150]

'Repentant butchers': hunting and conservation

Another area of tension, which has grown fiercer from its beginnings up to the present day, is that between conservationism and hunting. Love of the wild was originally geared to the pursuit of game; no other influential group had as close a relationship with untamed nature as hunters did, with the top social layers in the forefront. It was an active, not only contemplative, relationship. Many hunters believed, and still believe today, that they are the greatest lovers of nature and the ones who know it best; Theodore Roosevelt and Hermann Löns were two passionate cases in point. In 1900, on the initiative of British and German hunters, the first international conference on the conservation of African big game took place in London, and despite Anglo-German animosity due to the Boer War it resulted in a convention. Big game hunters even founded a society to combat poaching, with the resounding title Society for the Preservation of the Fauna of the Empire. The British press was quick to dub it the Penitent Butchers Club.[151] Here lies the historical origin of the African national parks – as well as the source of their problems![152]

So, there were covert as well as overt links between environmentalist organizations and other major currents of the time. 'Nature' was the magic word which, at least verbally, united many reformers: 'Return to nature and a natural lifestyle: these were the catchphrases that gave all reform efforts their bearings.'[153] A direct nexus joined animal protection, anti-vivisection and vegetarianism, not uncommonly extended also to the naturopathic and natural conservationist movements, although most bird protectionists still focused exclusively on their feathered friends and only much later, in the ecological age, became interested in the natural habitat too. But even if the word 'habitat' had not yet gained currency, there was already a realization in 1900 that farmland consolidation threatened bird species.[154] And the conviction that closeness to nature involved lifestyle issues as well as conservation was at least as spirited then as it is today.

Lifestyle and environmental awareness

Noting how his disciples blew up vegetarianism 'into an idea that could liberate humanity', the anarcho-socialist Erich Mühsam poked fun at spinach and lettuce fanatics who, for all their nature enthusiasm, were riddled with sexual inhibitions. In his 'Vegetarierlied', he had them sing:

> *Wir hassen das Fleisch, ja wir hassen Fleisch*
> *Und die Milch und die Eier und lieben keusch.*
> *Die Leichenfresser sind dumm und roh,*
> *Das Schweinevieh – das ist ebenso.*[155]

The dietary gospel of lifestyle reformers seemed especially ridiculous to workers, for whom a good chunk of sausage was very heaven. Vegetarianism, whose spiritual roots went back to the ancient Pythagoreans and early Buddhists,[156] received an essentially ethical foundation. The time was still far off when, in the name of the planetary ecosystem, people would complain of a 'cattle empire'. If the aim was to preserve the 'Arcadian' pastoral landscape, it really did not make sense to campaign against meat consumption! The ecological stability of European farming rested precisely upon the combination of agriculture and animal husbandry.

All the same, vegetarianism was by no means as banal as Mühsam believed. Far more than today, it involved a sharp break with the prevailing lifestyle; it was the 'core of the life reform movement'.[157] In 1909 an animal welfarist even claimed that 'nearly all progressive thinkers – which all free thinkers are in the end' – belong 'to the naturopathic movement, and a large percentage also subscribe to vegetarianism'.[158] This was an exaggeration, of course. But, at the same time, late modernizers had too sweeping a view of conservationism as a reactionary force hostile to progress.[159] The magic word 'reform' associated it with the intellectual world of progressivism, so that it could easily acquire even an anti-capitalist edge: Karl Liebknecht, for example, emphatically argued for the defence of nature.[160] A historical review leaves no doubt that conservationism was a typical phenomenon of modernity rather than a relic of the premodern age. Not for nothing were the first resource-protection initiatives in the USA a characteristic element of the Progressive Era.

'Monte Verità', near Ascona – where Mühsam composed his 'Vegetarierlied', and Herman Hesse and Max Weber occasionally whiled away some time – hosted a colourful spectrum of alternative movements (natural clothing, nudism, free love and free dance, anarchism and occultism) after the founding of a naturopathy centre there in 1900.[161] Unsurprisingly, it was not free of tensions. The internal cohesion of all these currents, as well as their relationship with the mainstreams of the age, remain in large part to be studied. Monographs have tended to be narrow in focus, not least because the groups in question liked to stress their heterodoxy and had none of the modern ambition to appear 'linked up'. But when one reads that the naturopathy centre was founded by Wagnerians on 'Mount Truth', that 'children of nature' danced naked there on 'Parsifal meadow' and gazed into the distance from the 'Valkyrie cliffs', one detects a half-concealed proximity to Wilhelmine culture, which also had an anti-traditional potential.[162]

Although a list of the more bizarre reform movements may come to seem like a cabinet of curiosities, a general view shows that this is a misleading impression. The sanitation movement, for example, clearly grew into an institutionalized force throughout the Western world – and in some degree the same is true of conservationism. It liked to cultivate the memory of its defeats. 'Remember Hetch Hetchy' referred to the episode when (not implausibly, on closer examination) a valley was removed from Yosemite National Park to provide water for San Francisco,[163] while on the Upper Rhine people commemorated the vain resistance to the flooding of the Laufenburg Rapids by the largest German hydroelectric power station of the age.[164] On the other hand, Friedemann Scholl summed up: 'Contrary to the often cultivated self-image, it was an extremely successful social movement. Not long after, its concerns were even recognized by the state as matters of public interest. . . . It spawned private and public institutions that would have a surprisingly long life.'[165]

The conservationist stand on Lüneburg Heath had the patronage of Wilhelm II. When one Baron von Wolff-Metternich, speaking in the Reichstag, defended the catching of birds with slings, an opponent won 'lively applause' with his sharp declaration: 'Gentlemen who defend bird-trapping should be hanged by one foot for a quarter of an hour, so that they can feel for themselves what it is like.'[166] The whole issue acquired radical tones even in the Reichstag of Imperial Germany. In Britain, both animal welfarists and supporters of the sanitary movement enjoyed the sympathy of Queen Victoria – indeed, it has been argued that the Cruelty to Animals Act of 1876 would not have been passed if she had not leaned on the medical profession.[167] These German and British inputs from above were enthusiastically replicated by Theodore Roosevelt on the other side of the Atlantic.

One link between urban sanitation and nature enthusiasm was the garden city, which, originating in England, became another nucleus of life-style reform and social-cultural utopias. It was mainly embraced by people who had given up any hope of humanizing or 'naturalizing' the big cities. But it is an irony of history that the municipal co-opting of the garden city led a rather anti-social suburbanization of lifestyles, which went together with mass motoring and carved up the landscape far more than the great conurbations had ever done.

The forest too brought together nervous individuals and other friends of nature, but it was not only a place of harmony. In the United States, the latent tension between lovers of the wild and pioneers of sustainable forestry, between preservation and conservation, became more tangible: sometimes virulent, between John Muir and Gifford Pinchot, as in the case of the Hetch Hetchy Project.[168] The conflict was all the fiercer because each in his way felt himself to be fighting for good over evil. In the south of Germany, in the dispute over the Lake Walchen power station project, conservationists clashed with campaigners for clean energy without smokestacks.[169] It seems obvious today that 'Green' movements in the year 1900 let slip many opportunities for united action – but the same holds for the Green movements of recent years. Ludwig Klages's *Man and Earth* message on the Hoher Meißner massif, to which reference has been made above, was permeated with a rapturous love of nature. But what did he want exactly? What kind of actions was he calling for? In its networking and its practical élan, the modern environmental movement is massively ahead of its predecessors at the turn of the twentieth century. Ahead too in its fundamental insights. In 1900, for example, people could still imagine that the whole problem of waste would be settled through advances in chemistry and agricultural recycling.

In other respects, however, the progress made in the last hundred years is not so clear. A recapitulation of the past is useful not least because it affords a sharper view of the present. Here too the all-pervasive 'environmental movement' exists more in the media than in reality, and big words not infrequently distract attention from the paucity of practical results. Many of the reform movements in 1900 were ultimately not about the environment but about human health – an issue which nowadays also lurks within the keyword 'environment'. Reform initiatives in 1900 had a copiously aesthetic side – *Jugendstil* in Germany and the Arts and Crafts Movement in Britain being two cases in point. But often the modern environmental movement also gained its popularity and political cutting edge especially where it rediscovered long-denied beauty and campaigned for the preservation of old city structures. With the turn to ecology, the environmental movement has forgotten a part of its own history. So, a look back can teach us that our present-day environmental awareness does not mean we stand at the end of history.

3 'The Desert Threatens': Environmental Fears in the Age of Crisis – the New Deal and Nazi Germany

The epochal significance of the Dust Bowl

One often hears it said that environmental fears are a fair-weather phenomenon; people have different worries in a time of severe crisis. If this is so, then it is significant that the Belle Époque and the long boom after the Second World War (when many middle-class people could indulge in a partly 'postmaterialist' thinking) were major periods of conservationist and environmentalist initiative. But for a long time environmental concerns have been raging in the third world; there is also an environmental awareness typical of crisis periods and crisis regions. A threat to the environment is felt especially strongly when it is associated with a threat to people's existence.

The 1930s is not yet generally thought of as an age of 'environmental movements before the environmental movement'. Yet there is much to suggest that it should be seen in this way, with the impetus coming from the United States rather than Europe. The Dust Bowl – which spread in 1934 in the Midwest as a result of devastating dust storms, seen as 'nature's revenge' for the ruthless forcing of fragile soil – led to fears that stretched far beyond the United States. This focus already put environmental awareness a little in advance of what we had at the end of the twentieth century, or even have today. For, both now and in the past, environmentalism and environmental policy have concentrated on the three great common goods: water, forest and pasture.[170] These created a need for regulation beyond the household economy, and therefore abundant material for historians and interventionist politicians. Today, global environmental initiatives concentrate on the atmosphere and the oceans; the soil, whose cultivation is a private or anyway local matter, usually remains on the margins, especially as its erosion is not spectacular in large parts of Europe. The complexity of the soil seemed to grow ad infinitum as it became increasingly subject to microscopic investigation, and its variation from place to place resulted in as many different histories. Hence the soil does not generally offer material for overarching theses and academic communities to mobilize global public opinion: no wonder that the issue does not feature prominently in most environmental debates, even though it is actually the most important. Our lives depend on the state of this final drainage basin, where toxicity is the least reversible, and statistics on worldwide soil degradation are more shocking than many other tidings of doom.[171]

In the 1930s the Dust Bowl made soil preservation a front-ranking political issue, despite the fact that government intervention traditionally encountered fierce resistance from private interests. For Donald Worster, the doyen of American environmental history and scion of a family affected by the Dust Bowl, the history of 'ecological ideas' stretches right back to the late eighteenth century, but it was only in the 1930s, 'largely as a direct consequence of the Dust Bowl experience', that soil preservation moved 'toward a more inclusive, coordinated, ecological perspective'. There had been huge dust storms in the past; but it was against the background of the world economic crisis and loss of faith in industrial capitalist progress that the Dust Bowl produced its dramatic effect. Many of the poverty-stricken farmers flooded from the Midwest to California, victims more of economic than ecological crisis. But it was the natural disaster that created material for a great saga.[172]

Almost immediately, other parts of the world woke up to the threat of soil erosion. *Deserts on the March*, Paul Sears's rousing book published in 1935 by the University of Oklahoma, at the centre of the Dust Bowl region, became 'the most important popular ecological work of the decade'. Already with a global horizon, it situated the disaster with the fundamental crisis affecting a civilization based on ruthless exploitation of the earth.[173] Twenty years later, the University of Oklahoma Press published another alarming book, *Topsoil and Civilization*, inspired by Hugh Bennett, the former head of the Soil Conservation Service, which reinterpreted American, indeed global, history as a creeping ecological suicide through plunder of the earth.[174]

Resource conservation as power politics

Richard Andrews, the historian of the American environmental movement, emphasizes the importance of the reform period under Franklin D. Roosevelt: 'The New Deal era left an unprecedented legacy of conservation achievements to American environmental policy. No other era in American history produced such an extraordinary record both of restoring and enhancing the environment, and of creating an improved sense of harmony between human communities and their environmental surroundings.'[175] Much reminds one of the older Progressive Era under Theodore Roosevelt, although this time explosive environmental problems were addressed by a government which, with greater energy than any before it, set out to intervene on a grand scale. Interior Secretary Harold L. Ickes, a 'strongman' of the new president, saw resource conservation as a recipe for hugely expanding the responsibilities of his department.[176] Since a whole generation of intellectuals lined up behind the New Deal, it acquired a dynamic of its own that justifies us in speaking not only of a new policy but of a 'movement'. Pools of politically active experts brought method, organization and management into politics on a scale never seen before.

A faith in technology that now strikes us as naïve was another hallmark of these experts. In 1934 Lewis Mumford, who would later warn of the homicidal 'mega-machine', hailed the brave new world of 'neotechnics' pioneered by Germany that would reproduce the premodern 'eotechnic' symbiosis of economy and nature in a fascinatingly new way. In keeping with the New Deal spirit, he found hydroelectric power especially fascinating: 'The smoke pall of paleotechnic industry begins to lift: with electricity the clear sky and the clean waters of the eotechnic phase come back again: the water that runs through the immaculate discs of the turbine . . . is just as pure when it emerges.'[177] The mystery of immaculate conception – now coming true in the hydroelectric power station!

In a period of mass unemployment, state intervention had greater legitimacy the more jobs it could create. Soil conservation measures seemed made for this, as the Civilian Conservation Corps (CCC) put young men to work on conservation projects, dam construction and the planting of trees.[178] In 1935, with the Dust Bowl fresh in its mind, Congress approved the establishment of the Soil Conservation Service (SCS) under Hugh Hammond Bennett; it was the first agency of its kind anywhere in the world. Like David Lilienthal, the head of the Tennessee Valley Authority (which cooperated with the SCS), 'Big Hugh' was a strong man with missionary traits well suited to the role of saviour.[179] Boiling with rage, he pointed out that an equivalent of 200 farms, each of 40 acres, was lost daily through erosion, and that water or wind carried away three billion tons of soil a year – enough to fill a freight train stretching eighteen times round the Equator.[180] In the years beginning with 1935, nearly all the states of the USA passed soil conservation laws. *Fortune* wrote in 1935: 'It is conceivable that when the history of our generation comes to be written in the perspective of a hundred years the saving of the broken lands will stand out as the great and most enduring achievement of the time.'[181]

All these activities involved an emotional appeal to the 'grassroots democracy' typical of the New Deal and soil conservationism, especially as it was clear in principle that farmers would be decisive for any extensive practical application.[182] The SCS operated across regions controlled by the farmers themselves: 1,670 regions had been established by 1947.[183] The objectives were as well intentioned as those of later third world development aid, which was strongly influenced by the New Deal. But it is in the nature of a large organization armed with experts that it favours a bureaucratic, 'top-down' political style. All in all, the New Deal represented the greatest push towards administrative centralism in American history, so that by 1940, the American farmer worked in a system that was dominated by the interplay among large public and private organizations.[184]

With such an approach, it is easier to build dams and power stations than the kind of terraced fields and windbreak forest planned by the Soil Protection strategists. 'Only scattered patches of the New Deal Shelter Belt project were ever actually planted, and even fewer have survived.' Where such tree hedges exist, in keeping with local conditions and requirements, the initiative for them was generally taken by farmers themselves.[185] The Tennessee Valley Authority (TVA), the flagship of the New Deal, concentrated its energies on high-profile dam and power station projects, while soil conservation (totally reliant on unspectacular local efforts) and forest programmes lagged behind.[186] The irrigated soil, so long as it remained wet, was not blown away by the wind: this seemed to be the answer to the Dust Bowl horror. Only later was it realized that the Midwest projects – or, to be more specific, those drawing on the Ogallala aquifer – had placed excessive strain on the groundwater.[187] In 1951, in the spirit of 'local democracy', a corporation was founded for this to be controlled by farmers: the High Plains Underground Water Conservation District; it worked better in Nebraska than Texas, but the basic problem remained that the use of this non-renewable resource condemned agriculture to long-term decline.[188]

In general, the progress in the soil sciences was far greater than the practical improvements brought by the New Deal.[189] It did open the 'great era of dam building',[190] first in the USA, then in many other parts of the world – a classic example of how the attempt to solve environmental problems through radical measures on a grand scale can create new and often more intractable problems. In the last few decades, the campaign against dams has become a central issue for third world environmental movements. David Lilienthal, famous as the head of the TVA, became the first chair of the Atomic Energy Commission after the war, and later the TVA planned one nuclear power station after another.[191] The 'peaceful atom' became associated with perspectives similar to those which shaped the later environmental movement: that is, an emission-free energy source accessible to every region in the world and, thanks to fast breeders, capable of providing an inexhaustible supply. The same Lilienthal, we should note, went on to become one of the first prominent nuclear sceptics.[192]

The 'history of ecological ideas' recalled by Donald Worster runs partly crossways to the history of what was done. It was precisely in the 1920s and 1930s that Frederic Clements, brought up in the Nebraska prairie, developed his theory of the natural 'climax state' of a landscape and of a 'climax community' in ecology. This implied that, for all nature's dynamism, there was an equilibrium that man could not change with impunity, and that the 'back to nature' idea had a sound ecological basis.[193] Even Hugh Bennett argued that in principle it was better to give up agriculture in parts of the Great Plains and to return the former prairies to grass; but he was first of all an activist and project-maker, who had no idea what to do with these pearls of wisdom.[194] Not only nostalgia for the Wild West but also sober calculation pointed to such conclusions in arid regions, since the costs of irrigating them far outweighed the agricultural yield, and the most enthusiastic partisans of 'free enterprise' could survive there on farming only with massive government subsidies.[195] Later, in the eco-age, scientific and popular ecology changed positions: academics soon moved away from climax theory and no longer recognized any stable equilibrium; while conservationists and environmentalists needed at least the fiction of such states to have criteria for what needed protection. Today they still find it difficult to do without the fiction.

*Making environmental policy scientific: the 'ploughman's folly'
and 'game management'*

The soil conservation of the New Deal era made history mainly by attack-
ing the plough, the traditional embodiment of agriculture. 'Plough,
plough, plough', Cato the Elder hammered into the heads of Roman
farmers, and Pliny the Elder added: 'Plough with all your might!'[196] But
that was a time when ploughs were still wooden and, by modern standards,
did no more than scratch the soil. In the age of steel and motorized trac-
tors, it was necessary to relearn how to farm on fragile soil. In 1937 the
US Department of Agriculture (USDA) produced an educational film:
The Plow that Broke the Plains, whose very title blamed the plough for
the Dust Bowl, and which had to be withdrawn after vigorous protests
from the farming lobby.[197] In 1943 Edward H. Faulkner, an agronomist
from erosion-threatened Ohio, published a bestseller, *The Plowman's Folly*,
which identified not only deep ploughing of fragile soil but tillage itself
as 'sabotage' of nature.[198] In the Midwest, the plough was increasingly
replaced by the harrow. Agrarian chemistry supported this quiet revolution in soil processing, since weeds were no longer ploughed in and a
dramatically increased demand for herbicides could be catered for. In this
respect too, the soil conservation of the New Deal era ran counter to the
preoccupations of the eco-age, initiated by Rachel Carson's sounding of
the alarm against pesticides.

The new attention to natural resources, together with the activism and
'scientific management' typical of the New Deal era, was also palpable in
other areas of environmental policy. In 1933 the forestry scientist Aldo
Leopold brought out his *Game Management*, which became the 'Bible of
the wildlife profession'[199] and posthumously established his publisher in
the gallery of the great American pioneers of environmentalism; 'thinking
like a mountain', though somewhat obscure, would be his most commonly
quoted phrase.[200] In 1935 he helped to found the Wilderness Society,
which, alongside the Sierra Club going back to 1892, was the most important organizational link between the old and the new ecologism. According
to Leopold's biographer, Susan Flader, the year 1935 'marked a reorientation in his thinking from a historical and recreational to a predominantly
ecological and ethical justification for wilderness'.[201] The areas to be
protected were no longer only canyons and waterfalls.

Leopold's formative experience had been in 1906, when the Kaibab
forest in the Grand Canyon had been declared a game reserve. Wolves,
coyotes and cougars were shot to protect the deer, with the result that the
number of these grew over eighteen years from 4,000 to nearly 100,000.
But this increase – apparently a record in game management – caused
severe damage to the forest, and the deer population eventually fell back
sharply as a result of starvation.[202] The lesson for Leopold was that predatory game were also part of the ecological balance.[203] From then on, for
emotional as well as ecological reasons, he missed the sight of them when-

ever he travelled in Germany's forests. 'Just knowing a bear was nearby gave a special spice to a whole region. That scent has disappeared from the German mountains; it has fallen victim to the misguided zeal of game-keepers and livestock owners.'[204]

In densely populated Central Europe, where predatory wild animals were virtually wiped out centuries ago, the damage caused by game is an old theme, not a recent discovery. Yet the reintroduction of wolves and bears was not a subject of debate there, and for hunters the lure of the forest lay in its roe deer and stags. At the time when Aldo Leopold wrote his *Game Management*, Goering was pushing through his *Reichsjagdgesetz* (1934) in Nazi Germany – a law which limited the number of people entitled to hunt and increased the stock of game to levels damaging to the forest.[205] Goering's own hunting fever undermined Nazi autarky policy (which aimed at maximum reliance on national resources), while Aldo Leopold showed how forest and game conservation could be made compatible with each other. This is not to say that Leopold was in every respect a New Dealer: he watched with sadness how CCC people beat 'protected routes' through the wilderness as a way of controlling fire risks and predatory game.[206] Did he believe that wildfires were also part of the wilderness? On 21 April 1948, he lost his life battling a prairie fire – a hero's end quite in keeping with the fire-fighting traditions of American forestry.

From toxicology to ecology: origins of environmentalism in occupational medicine

For Robert Gottlieb, the historian of American environmentalism, the gallery of eco-heroines began long before Rachel Carson with Alice Hamilton (1869–1970), who owed her fame to pioneering studies of toxins and occupational diseases (above all, lead poisoning).[207] Indeed, the origins of the modern environmental movement lie at least as much in toxicology as in ecology, and occupational medicine was the first to demonstrate the pathogenic effect of many environmental toxins. This research gained fresh momentum in the 1930s, when the mood was critical of industry and capitalism, and expanded its horizon beyond the factory floor. In retrospect, it can be seen that the 'turn' in occupational medicine[208] led to a focus not only on workplace toxins but also on the human environment. Only then did toxicology become politics and bring occupational medicine out of the shadows.

Later, Rachel Carson obtained key information on DDT-related cancer risks from Wilhelm Hueper, the director of the Environmental Cancer Section of the National Cancer Institute.[209] Yet there has been very little systematic study of the relationship between occupational medicine and the environmental movement. It has not been without its tensions. As far as occupational medicine was concerned, a problem ceased to be posed if the toxin in question was ventilated away from the factory floor into the environment; the once so combative Alice Hamilton, for example, looked back contentedly in 1948 from retirement and concluded that American industry had been aware of the health issues.[210] For environmental researchers, however, the problem was only just beginning – and this could not fail to disturb the arrangement between occupational medicine and industrial corporations.[211] Medical minds that looked only for individual causes and culpable lawbreakers tended to view research findings as counterproductive if they identified multiple toxic influences on the environment. Nevertheless, when all is said and done, occupational medicine and environmental research had a mutually reinforcing effect.

The campaign against smoke also intensified in the New Deal years, acquiring a sheriff-like hero in the shape of Raymond Tucker. Appointed St Louis Commissioner of Smoke Regulation in 1937, he reacted with great energy to the unprecedented smog that hit the city in autumn 1939. The next year, the city council passed a law to regulate all sources of smoke in its jurisdiction. 'Never before', writes Frank Uekötter, 'had a single engineer possessed such power in the American movement against air pollution – and, as time would show, never thereafter.'[212]

Until the Tucker era, smoke control in St Louis had been a history of frustration; now the turnaround was visible from one year to the next.[213] In 1940, Pittsburgh, the archetypal Smoke City, followed suit, mutating into the trailblazer with its punctilious 'smoke control movement'.[214] It might seem strange today that for half a century none of these anti-smoke campaigns targeted tobacco smoke, although it was far more damaging to the health than chimney emissions. Was the cigarette in those days too inseparably bound up with the lifestyle of progressive intellectuals? Only the Nazi regime, which would have gradually eradicated such people altogether, waged a campaign against tobacco.[215] Germany was also the leader in research into the link between asbestos and lung cancer, which was first recognized there in 1943 as an occupational disease.[216] And the health risk from radioactivity was more warily investigated than in other Western countries: on this point, Nazi concerns for genetic make-up proved productive. In the 1950s a German book *Das lustige Atom* [The Merry Atom], which described the history of atomic research in rhyme and was often given as a gift in the nuclear community, contained the verse:

Schon jetzt erscheint uns manchmal hart
Was sich an Chromosomen paart;
Was durch Bestrahlung werden kann,
Da denkt man lieber gar nicht dran.[217]

The Dust Bowl alarm goes around the world

It is worth considering the New Deal era in such detail, for, whereas the 1920s saw the beginnings of US industrial hegemony, the 1930s were the decade of incipient US hegemony in the domains later grouped under environmental policy. Alerted by the Dust Bowl expert community, other regions of the world discovered soil erosion as a major problem. The impact in Australia was especially rapid, with disputes, as in the American Midwest, over whether the desert had to be accepted as a fact of nature or whether irrigation could transform it into farmland. The latter vision was presented in 1918 in a work by Edwin J. Brady of more than a thousand pages: *Australia Unlimited*, but it rested on the false assumption that the groundwater beneath Australia's deserts was inexhaustible. Without a constant and plentiful supply, the agricultural destruction of grass cover threatened to turn even steppe into desert, while sand storms laid even Australia's farming districts to waste. Expert knowledge derived from the Dust Bowl greatly sharpened such fears.[218] And unlike in the Tennessee Valley, dams were not an option to provide irrigation on a grand scale.

In the United States, the Dust Bowl did not remain as a permanent issue but gave way to a new optimism in the 1940s with the wartime boom, the return of wetter weather, irrigation projects and advances in agrochemicals. It was a different story in Australia, however, where the ecologist Francis Ratcliffe – a man with a background in British India – produced a report on erosion (*Flying Fox and Drifting Sand: The Adventures of a Biologist in Australia*, 1938) which contributed to the creation of soil conservation authorities in New South Wales (1938) and Victoria (1940).[219] Referring not only to soil ecology but also to climate experiences over the previous half-century, Ratcliffe warned that the expansion of agriculture, and especially the introduction of European-style permanent grazing, would in the long run inevitably destroy the very foundations on which it rested.[220] In its concern for the soil, Australia in the 1930s and 1940s was ahead of postwar environmentalism. This later activism would be spellbound by the wilderness, but the most 'endangered species' in the fifth continent is agricultural land, which faces the threat of salinization and groundwater depletion.

The Dust Bowl experience could be read in very different ways. One invoked the 'limits to growth' as fundamental, while the other took the soil crisis as a challenge requiring large-scale irrigation projects. It was this second approach which made the real impact on development policy in the postwar decades, so much so that 'development' became synonymous all over the world with the construction of giant dams. This optimistic-activist version of New Dealism was present in unadulterated form in Walter Clay Lowdermilk, the dynamic assistant chief of the SCS and president of the American Geophysical Union, a man much admired by Roosevelt's famous secretary of agriculture Henry A. Wallace. The reports of Lowdermilk's trips as a soil conservation adviser, from North Africa to China,[221] are a fascinating source even today.[222] Although not himself of Jewish origin, he became (in Wallace's words) the most perfect Zionist convert one could imagine. In 1939, on a trip to Palestine, he spoke by radio from Jerusalem of his 'Eleventh Commandment': 'Thou shalt inherit the holy earth as a faithful steward conserving its resources and productivity from generation to generation. Thou shalt safeguard thy fields from soil erosion, thy living waters from drying up, thy forests from desolation, and protect thy hills from overgrazing by the herds, that thy descendants may have abundance forever.' He proposed setting up a 'Jordan Valley Authority', by analogy with the TVA, although by no stretch of the imagination could the Jordan compare with the Tennessee in water volume.

Admiring the settlers who created oases in the parched land, but troubling himself little over the limited supply of irrigation water, he offered a powerful ideology for the Zionists to use. Arab invaders, Bedouin and fellahin had turned the Promised Land of milk and honey into a desert, and now the Zionists would turn it back into a Garden of Eden by means of irrigation, tree-planting and contour farming.[223] The same held even for the Negev Desert, which had never been green. So long as the Bedouin held sway there, all effort was in vain; they would drive their camels onto the fields and allow the irrigation systems to go to rack and ruin. 'Only an energetic people, using methods of dry farming and constructing dams to conserve flood and rain waters, can make the Negeb fertile.'[224] Lowdermilk's vision of history built on the one propagated by French colonizers in North Africa, in which Rome's 'former granary' that nomads had turned into desert would again become a green El Dorado thanks to modern irrigation systems.[225] Bedouin cast in the role of the short-sighted Yankee farmers responsible for the Dust Bowl! That extensive grazing is good for the soil, whereas irrigation systems exacerbate the fragility of eco-systems, is something that would only be discovered later in the eco-age.[226]

In principle, the Soviet Union should have been the main focus of soil discourse, for the black earth of the Ukraine was famous for its fertility, though also long threatened by wind erosion in particular. A disastrous dust storm occurred there in 1928, and others soon followed.[227] Russian scientists were then far ahead of their American counterparts in soil research, including the study of ecology and erosion;[228] not for nothing did many soil types bear Russian names. In Russia, at least as much as in the German *Blut und Boden* literature, a patriotic rhetoric was combined with awareness of the danger to the steppe soil.[229] Although the theory that woodland debased soil quality was sometimes aired, advocates of afforestation belts made the breakthrough to soil conservation in the 1930s. In 1936, water-retaining forest in river catchment areas in the European USSR was even placed under legal protection.[230] In the same year, an all-Soviet conference on the struggle against soil erosion was held at the Soil Science Institute in Moscow.[231]

On the other hand, the lack of a self-aware civil society in Stalinist Russia stood in the way of lively public debate. If forest conservationists are to serve their purpose, they must be attuned to local conditions: this theoretical insight was not lost on people in the Soviet Union, but the central planning system complied with it even less than the New Deal style of planning. There too, giant dams were held up alongside steel plants as epitomes of development, and scarcely anywhere in the West were the incentives for extensive irrigation as attractive as they were in large areas of the southern USSR.[232] It was only under Khrushchev, however, that ecologically ruthless projects to irrigate large arid regions reached their climax; he came from Ukraine and, unfortunately for Soviet agriculture, had trained as an agrarian expert.[233] In parts of the former German Democratic Republic, the soil still suffers today from the fact that large-scale units after the collectivization of agriculture threw the lessons of the Dust Bowl to the wind.

Soil awareness and Blut und Boden*: the Alwin Seifert phenomenon*

Nazi Germany is a curious and contradictory case with regard to soil conservation and environmental policy. The alliterative formula *Blut und Boden* (blood and soil) has often been quoted to describe Nazi ideology, although it is an open question whether *Boden* was here a metaphor or a more definite image. In any event, one would look in vain for the word in the index of Hitler's *Mein Kampf*. With its high levels of rainfall and silt, Germany faced different soil problems from those in the American Midwest. During the war a shortage of fertilizer was the main problem. Afterwards, amid the general enthusiasm for agrochemicals, negative experiences began to appear from the excessive use of chemical fertilizer[234] – sometimes also, in a similarity with the American situation, as a result of taking drainage too far. 'Until now we have lived in a state of unconscious economic hydrophobia', claimed an official economic adviser in Hesse in 1926, although his criticism applied less to farmers (who had learned in modern times the usefulness of irrigated meadows) than to politicians in charge of agriculture.[235] In his view, their sole ambition for water not immediately needed for agriculture was to conduct it to the sea as quickly and completely as possible, by means of straightened streams and rivers. If Germans continued to do this, they would face 'a dangerous drying out of the top layers of earth' and a threat to their whole culture.[236]

Ten years later, the Dust Bowl fresh in his mind, Alwin Seifert (1890–1972) issued precisely such a warning, with the rhetorical force of a prophet. He was the most striking figure in environmental politics during the Nazi period – in many respects a charismatic phenomenon, in others a 'cross between court jester and Cassandra'.[237] An excellent self promoter, his real importance has sometimes been exaggerated beyond the sphere of ecological discourse; he became known as a lecturer on garden and cemetery construction at the Munich Institute of Technology, and after 1933 as 'Reich Landscape Lawyer' employed on motorway construction. As a colleague of Fritz Todt, the general highways inspector, he advocated that the autobahns should have sweeping lines corresponding to the landscape and, instead of roadside ditches, embankments planted with indigenous species. One admirer of his passion for natural landscaping drooled that 'the whole of Germany is his garden', but a more sober way of putting it would be that his autobahn consultancy was the icing on the cake. After all, Todt was a powerful man, and the gruff male friendship that developed between him and Seifert was along the proverbial lines of '*Pack schlägt sich, Pack verträgt sich*' ['riffraff come to blows one minute and make it up the next'].[238] The *mésalliance* of autobahn construction and landscape planning is somewhat reminiscent of Robert Moses, who planned huge green spaces around New York in the decades after 1926 and, with a brutality unmatched by anyone before or since, carved motorways through the city so that people could access them as quickly as possible.[239] After 1945, Seifert remained in people's memory as the man who championed natural gardens and the use of skilfully made, non-chemical compost.[240]

Seifert's main interest for us, however, lies in the offensive he waged in 1935 against the penchant of German hydraulic engineering for straight lines, which he tried to banish from the autobahn builders. In mystical tones, he wrote of how nature was 'everywhere a closed living organism', and of how rivers too were living beings that should not be wantonly crushed with concrete.[241] His argument was essentially rational, however, like that of the Hesse politician who complained of German 'hydrophobia'. The traditional drive to get water on its way as fast as possible had its origins in an age when the climate in Europe was wetter, but since the 1880s the German climate had been growing warmer and drier. The new times were actually good times, but the opportunity they offered would be wasted if the attitude to water typical of the earlier age was continued.[242] The Dust Bowl was already a warning sign that, if things went on as before, German soil would 'flow away towards Russia' and Germans would become, like the Slavs, a 'steppe people' in their landscape and their souls.[243] Water was therefore a 'to be or not to be' question for the German nation.[244]

Seifert's self-ingratiation with nationalist ideology may be understood as a tactic, since at the same time he repeatedly referred to other nations as models that put Germans to shame with the sensitivity to nature they showed in hydraulic engineering and road-building. He also looked to the Soil Conservation Service as a model, when experts across the Atlantic were praising German soil conservation as an example to be followed.[245] In the United States, soil conservation and hydraulic engineering went hand in hand; in the controversy aroused by Seifert this was not the case. He could demonstrate his 'steppification' thesis only on an ad hoc basis.[246] To what extent was his alarm well founded? With hindsight, it looks rather similar to the 'dying forest' alarm after 1980: an insidious danger was blown up into an imminent catastrophe. Two decades later, as agriculture minister, the future president of the Federal Republic, Heinrich Lübke, was still recognizing the reality of the danger.[247]

Did Seifert's attacks during the Nazi period have an effect? Of course he provoked an uproar among hydraulic engineers, but Todt stuck with him in the controversy, especially as he had a lot of support in academic circles and autobahn construction came off better in any comparison with the straightening of rivers: 'Whereas road-building has learned to work

in association with nature,' Todt wrote, 'hydraulic engineering is dominated by the use of concrete, straight lines and precise shapes.'[248] Seifert's
polemic did not take aim at any core Nazi policies. David Blackbourn's
The Conquest of Nature – which refers to the conquest of German nature
by hydraulic engineering – reaches its climax in the Third Reich, giving
a superficial reader the impression that hydraulic engineering was at the
centre of Nazi policy, and that National Socialism signified a peak of
hydraulic supremacy. The reality is otherwise. In 1935, when the Reich
Labour Office cut through a meander of the River Ems near Warendorf,
the local Nazi press boasted that the combined 'popular strength of the
Third Reich' had achieved victory in the 'thousand-year battle' with the
violence of water.[249] (In 1946, after regulation of the Ems, the largest floods
in living memory occurred.) But straightening operations there or on the
Luppe in Leipzig – which met with protests among conservationists[250] –
were 'small beer' (*Pritzelkram*, as Löns might have said) in comparison
with the huge New Deal projects in the Tennessee Valley. Anyway, the
great age of German dam construction under Otto Intze was over by then.
Blackbourn himself remarks that the Hoover Dam, completed in 1936,
accumulated nearly two hundred times as much water as Germany's then-
largest dam, the one on Lake Eder built in 1914.[251]

To be sure, drainage and river regulation were among the tasks of the
Reich Labour Office. But already in *Mein Kampf* Hitler had made no
secret of his mistrust of 'internal colonization', since it distracted people's minds from external expansion.[252] Walther Schoenichen, director
of the Prussian State Agency for the Care of Natural Monuments and
from 1933 the most voluble propagandist for Nazi-style conservation,
was able to publish a critical 'appeal from the German landscape to the
Labour Office'.[253] In 1936 Hans Klose – who, without being a Nazi Party
member, succeeded Schoenichen in his post[254] – attended the first Reich
Conservation Congress in Berlin and, with the 1935 Conservation Law
behind him, openly polemicized: 'No one in this hall will fail to be horrified by the thought that, if the often excessive removal of water for agriculture and labour service continues unabated, it will in a few years almost
totally distort these natural resources and leave our fatherland deprived of
them.'[255]

Conservation and National Socialism

Hitler was personally so little interested in conservation that he did not
mention it in *Mein Kampf* even when he could have used it to counter
the idea that 'internal colonization' offered a solution to the limits of
Germany's food supply.[256] He called nature 'the cruel queen of all wisdom',
and that kind of nature needed no protection. By contrast, Seifert referred
back to the Darwinian view that a 'ruthless struggle of all against all'
prevails in nature; this 'received opinion' corresponded to 'yesterday's

constant emphasis on that which divides and separates, on individual being'.[257] It was also Hitler's opinion, though!

The relationship between conservation and National Socialism was the object of repeated controversy.[258] In fact, this way of posing the question is too general: it assumes that the ideas of conservation and landscape protection were one and the same, and that National Socialism was a consistent system of thought with a single position on nature. Nazi ideology was in large part a conglomerate, however: the 'typical Nazi' existed only in propaganda and in caricatures of the movement. In reality it contained a wide variety of human types: not only romantic nature worshippers but also, in at least the same degree, enthusiastic technocrats. In any event, the hunter in close contact with nature (who did not embody the whole of conservationism) was one of the Nazi prototypes. One can recognize him in the person of Goering decked out in his glorious green huntmaster's costume, who would have liked to make the Schorfheide reserve comparable in size to an American national park, but was unable to get his way against other departments of the state.[259]

'Public welfare before private benefit' (*Gemeinnutz geht vor Eigennutz*) was the Nazi slogan. Sometimes conservationists managed to enforce their definition of public advantage,[260] but military and economic elites also demanded that it serve their interests. There was no fixed party line on nature; public discussion was possible up to a point, and initiatives with the character of a movement could develop without an initial impetus from Nazi leadership circles. For example, a Committee to Save Deciduous Forest formed within the Deutscher Heimatbund, even strengthening its activity after the beginning of the war and issuing a public memorandum in 1941. One poetaster lamented there:

O deutscher Wald, o Büchengrün
Und Kraft der starken Eichen
O deutscher Wald, du sinkst dahin
Von deines Würgers Streichen![261]

Note that the 'slayer' was he who followed the high felling levels ordered under the war economy. The memorandum had wide reverberations, and one thing that stands out among the host of different positions is that in 1941, in the middle of the war, nationalist tones were secondary to ecological and hydrological voices.[262]

It would not be right to view the conservationism of that period simply as an instrument of the Nazi regime. It also happened that conservationists had some success in instrumentalizing the Nazi apparatus for their own ends. The poet Ludwig Finckh campaigned for more than twenty-five years against the stone quarries belonging to Baron von Hornstein, which in his view were ruining the 'holy' Hohenstoffeln, a striking basalt peak in his native Hegau region near Lake Constance. And in the end he managed to win Himmler and Goering onto his side. With even fewer scruples than Schoenichen, he did not hesitate to play on *völkisch* or anti-Semitic registers;[263] yet, as a friend of Herman Hesse, he saw his mission as being 'to stand up for everything repressed, violated and unrecognized'.[264] The Finckh case gives some idea of the ambiguity of conservationism in the Nazi period. Not infrequently those who gave reason to doubt their National Socialist conviction made a special show of stalwartness,[265] while those sitting more firmly in the saddle had no need to do that. In any event, it may be said to the honour of environmentalists that they seem to have stooped only rarely to anti-Semitic attacks, although they could easily have invoked the view, common among Zionists as well as anti-Semites, that two thousand years without a homeland had left the Jews with no relationship to nature and the soil.[266]

The Nazi period is not without significance in the history of conservationism and environmentalism, but there is more than one way of interpreting it. Hans Klose, who, as director of the Reich Conservation Agency from 1938 to 1945, played a decisive role in the story, later maintained that the years between 1939 and 1945 saw 'undoubtedly the peak of German conservationism during those fifty years', and yet 'the forces destructive of nature' grew 'immeasurably' from 1933 on.[267] The Nazi government, often tireless in its display of activity, sought from the beginning to adopt a high profile on environmental matters. Between 1933 and 1935, Goering rushed through one measure after another: a ban on vivisection, an animal protection law,[268] a hunting law that prohibited the 'unprofessional' shotgun method, a law against destruction of the forest, and a new Reich Conservation Law.[269] In 1934 the East Elban landowner Walter von Keudell, an enlightened opponent of deforestation and spruce monoculture, became head of the newly created Reich Forest Agency and, with the unyielding resolve of the times, sought to impose his own model of sustainable forestry.[270]

The Reich minister of agriculture, Richard Darré, who was furiously opposed to chemical 'test-tube thinking' and the 'demonic grin of capitalism', took public positions close to the 'organic farming' of later years.[271] To save on the use of foreign currency for fertilizer imports, local authorities were required in 1935–6 to check all wastewater discharge for possible agricultural use before allowing it through to sewage treatment plants.[272] The Reich Conservation Law of 1935 – which, alone in the world and going far beyond the protection of 'natural monuments', ordered any landscape-altering projects to include a conservationist dimension and even the possibility of confiscation – ushered in years of veritable euphoria among conservationists. The simple threat of confiscation, though applied only exceptionally, made landowners willing to sell. 'Never in German history have so many nature reserves been designated within such a brief period.'[273]

Conservation, however, had neither the apparatus nor the enforcement powers to intervene decisively in area planning. In such matters, the Nazi regime was a long way from the ruthlessness and radicalism of its military or racial policy; it remained impotent when environmental considerations clashed with important economic or military interests – not, of course, a peculiarity of the Third Reich. Keudell lost his positions when his promotion of mixed forest cut across the Four Year Plan and the requirement for rapid maximum yields. A penchant for non-chemical farming stretched as far as Himmler and Bormann, the two men closest to Hitler during the war,[274] but in practice it was the IGFarben experts who called the shots. When the aim was to maximize calorie yield in the agricultural 'production battle', even forced maize-growing flew in the face of Darré's eco-philosophy[275] – much as the eucalyptus tree, the enemy of the forest par excellence, crossed the threshold of acceptability.[276] Wood research was given an unprecedented boost, and forest experts were triumphant that indigenous wood was finally valued as highly as metals. As late as July 1939, a Congress of the German Forest Union was held at the Kroll opera house in Berlin, amid 'unheard-of glitter and luxury' in Goering's bombastic style,[277] but the goal of a new 'wood age' bound up with Nazi autarkic policies ultimately called into question the autonomy of forestry. It would prove a seminal conflict of objectives.

Such clashes are also the norm today; it is in the nature of things that different policies on conservation should get in each other's way. In the totalitarian state, however, it was more difficult than in a democracy to argue out differences in public, even when conservation and environmental issues did not affect core Nazi policies and were in principle open for discussion. In any event, various rivalries meant that no broad Green alliance ever came about in Nazi Germany. At first Goering was something like a Nazi Green icon, but the whole issue was for him mainly subordinate to his hunting passion – and anyway, in so far as he escaped inertia, his main activities were development of the air force and the Four Year Plan. As for Seifert and Darré, so close to each other in their philosophy of nature, a hostile rivalry developed between the two men. Even municipal projects for the recycling of waste horrified Seifert on account of his landscape aesthetic, while many foresters 'hit the roof' when it came to Keudell's *dirigiste* vision of 'permanent forest'.[278] People rhapsodized over the 'German forest', but the forestry and timber sector was a long way from a consensus over what it should actually look like – not to speak of agreement on conservation.

The picture is not all negative, however. Although the confiscation clause in the Reich Conservation Law was the stuff of conflict, relations between conservationists and farmers were generally friendlier than they became sixty years later under the EU's fauna and flora directive. In the 1930s, when farmers did not yet have chemical pesticides, they still needed birds to multiply as a protection against insect attack. It is true that, for farmers who had reclaimed moorland at great effort, the conservationist restoration of heath landscapes was a real pain in the neck. Yet farmers and conservationists stood together in opposing military encroachment in areas such as Lüneburg Heath, and farmers, being courted by the Nazi regime, could engage in protest actions that would have landed others in a concentration camp.[279]

In the context of autarky – here too Goering's hand is visible – the Nazi government kept up a barrage of propaganda on recycling. Long after 1945, German ears echoed with a song of which no one knew for sure whether it was Nazi or satirically anti-Nazi:

Knochen, Eisen, Lumpen und Papier,
Ausgeschlagene Zähne sammeln wir.
Hermann Göring, ja, wir danken dir,
Alles sammeln wir.[280]

This revaluation of waste continued after the war, but then it was a result of necessity, not of ecological rationality. Thus, in the postwar coal shortage, not only forests but even windbreak hedges were torn up by the roots, and regions of northern Germany were afflicted with wind erosion on a scale not seen since the eighteenth century. It was an American-style Dust Bowl scenario, and Seifert's warning appeared more topical than it had ten years before: 'The conversion of Germany into dry arid steppe really is in full flow.'[281] And in 1947 *Die Wüste droht*, the book by the journalist Anton Metternich from which this quotation is taken, presented a German pendant to the American Dust Bowl literature, also with a global and world-historical horizon. Large parts of it already have the tenor of modern eco-apocalypses. Its reflections are also influenced, however, by the panaceas then on offer: towards the end, for example, we find a chapter on 'synthetic liver sausage' and artificial 'egg white', at a time when Germans had no choice but to engage in non-chemical agriculture – and still went hungry. The wings of ecological thought were clipped in a situation of shortages; only in better times was that thought able to spread them more fully again. In the harsh postwar climate, it went without saying that one did not throw away anything that could still be put to some use. But in the long period of rising prosperity that followed, the change was more drastic than at any previous time in history. This was the springboard for a new environmental awareness, which stood in a dialectical relationship with the actual course of things.

4   Think Big! A Charismatic Intermezzo on the Olympian Heights

The forgotten advances in the postwar period

Early policy initiatives of the League of Nations and UNESCO, the founding of the International Union for the Conservation of Nature (IUCN) in 1948 and of the World Wildlife Fund (WWF) that grew out of it in 1961, the manifold conservationist activities of Julian Huxley, Max Nicholson and their influential circle of choice friends: all this fell into near-oblivion in the years when the term 'environmental movement' made everyone think of mass protests. Only recently has Anna Wöbse rediscovered this prehistory of the eco-age and shown that 'nature' experienced an 'explosion of new semantic assignment' in the postwar period.[282] Was this a mere flourish in world history? With hindsight, surely something more than that. For the global horizon is constitutive of modern environmentalism. Countless activists feel euphoric about doing something to save the world, even if it is always a problem to define its practical import. As we have seen, the term 'international' already had positive connotations among environmentalists around the year 1900, but these received a durable and expanding institutional form only after 1945. A comparison with the (by no means negligible) activities of the interwar League of Nations[283] shows the quite new impetus behind the approach of the UNESCO milieu to nature.[284]

Peace opened people's eyes to common human problems: more, those who cared about a lasting peace were led to search for tasks that bonded humanity together and required international cooperation. By and large, though not always and everywhere, the cross-border character of many environmental problems has given an impetus for wider understanding and cooperation. Environmental awareness correlates not only with environmental problems but also with tides of international politics; it is no accident that its highpoints occur in periods of international détente. Of course, where the issue is access to vital resources, it provides plenty of material for conflict. But, far more than ideological confrontations and questions of national prestige, environmental problems have tended to generate an atmosphere of rational regulation – up to now, at least.

Since the world is large and complex, and global risks are not evident to the senses, global environmental issues have the twin face of a real and a constructed problem. Moreover, two or three generations ago, our perception of the earth's ecosystem was far less complex and statistical than it is today. Unlike pollution caused by industrial plants, problems of the planet do not manifest themselves per se; there have to be groups of people and institutions with an interest in tackling them.

The dilemma of internationalism in the interwar period: environmental initiatives in the League of Nations

Personnel working for the League of Nations in the interwar period already recognized cross-border spheres of activity, especially with regard to such glaring issues as oil spill in international waters or the ruthless overhunting of whales. The latter reached unprecedented dimensions in the steamship age, especially after the First World War, when whalers – which were at the same time floating factories – completed their decimation of stocks in the northern hemisphere and pushed into the waters of the Antarctic. The methods of refining whale oil for margarine production – first invented in the 1920s and unknown to many consumers – spurred on the industrialization of the whaling sector.[285] From then on, an Argentinean diplomat by the name of José León Suárez fought for decades with great passion to protect the whale. As in the case of forest and game conservation, it was possible to appeal without any sentimentality to the interest that hunters and consumers themselves had in the principle of sustainability. But how should quotas be fairly distributed among various countries, and how should respect for them be enforced?

These problems remained unsolved. It was mainly the traditional whaling nations – Britain and Norway – which pushed through the Geneva Convention of 1931; the use of the status quo as the guideline meant that they came off best from the quota allocation. But the newcomers, headed by Japan and from 1933 Nazi Germany, flouted the Geneva restrictions.[286] The atmosphere of growing international hostility made coordinated action impossible, and in the end war proved to be the only effective form of conservation. All British and Japanese factory ships, as well as a majority of Norwegian ones, were sunk by torpedoes.[287]

Peace brought the return of international whaling conferences, but also of ruthless hunting practices. Following a conference in Washington in 1946, an International Whaling Commission (IWC) was set up in 1949, but it was a prisoner to the short-term interests of whaling nations. Cocking a snook at the IWC, Aristotle Onassis – the most extravagant billionaire of the postwar decades – deployed his factory ship *Olympic Challenger* in 1949 under various flags. His cynicism was truly without equal: he had the bar stools of his private yacht *Christina* covered with the skins of whale penises, tracked whales by aircraft, and spared neither pregnant cows nor the growing young.[288] From then until the spectacular Greenpeace operations, international species conservation concentrated more on elephants than whales, more on the largest land animals than sea creatures, and more on Africa than the oceans.

The choice of animal icons was really something special. The protection of whales and elephants could only be organized from a distance, since it lacked the underpinning of regional grassroots movements. Moreover, the conservation of African big game had a smack of colonialism: it created a front against the indigenous population, unless they happened to profit from safari tourism. By contrast, in the case of migratory birds – which gave momentum per se to transnational conservation – there was a far better chance of peppering the global horizon with local initiatives

An instructive example is the campaign in the 1950s over the Knechtsand, off the coast of northern Germany. It centred on an uninhabited island in the Weser estuary, which the British occupation forces were given for bombing practice in return for handing back Heligoland to the German state. Local fishermen protested against this at first, but without success. Then a wider movement began to take shape in 1954, in the name of bird conservation, since an estimated 75,000 shelducks gathered there in late summer during the moulting season. On 8 September 1957, 300 demonstrators organized a happening before the Knechtsand on twenty picturesquely decorated cutters – a show for the media, which could easily have been staged in the later Greenpeace era. On closer examination, it was clear that only a section of the protesters were interested in bird conservation, yet the action found an echo among British bird conservationists (who had some influence in the armed forces) and had a successful result. The schoolteacher who initiated the protest movement, Bernhard Freemann, became popular in the British media, and, although the West German government refrained from intervening, the British unilaterally suspended bombing practice there in 1958. 'Not for nothing did Britain see itself as a "nation of animal lovers" and count as the enlightened core country of the traditional animal and bird conservation movement', writes Anna Wöbse.[289] In the end, nature played a trick on nature conservation, as the rescued Knechtsand gradually turned into mere sandbank. However, the novel operation of September 1957 opened the way for a series of further initiatives, which after the 1970s – in cooperation with the Netherlands and Denmark, though sharply at odds with local people concerned about their dykes and crab fishing[290] – led to the creation of the Wadden Sea National Park of Lower Saxony.

UNESCO and IUCN – Julian Huxley and his circle

International agreement in the realm of conservation was easiest to achieve during the first two postwar decades. The initiative came mainly from the biologist Julian Huxley (1887–1975), the first secretary-general of UNESCO, and from the Swiss Conservation League. At the UNESCO conference held in 1947 in Mexico City, Huxley managed to convince the organization (whose title refers to education, science and culture) that its remit should also include nature, since the enjoyment of nature is part of culture, and the preservation of 'rare and interesting animals and plants' is a scientific duty.[291] In the same year, an international conservation conference took place in Brunnen, Switzerland; the decisive impulse for the new organization came from the Swiss Conservation League, led by Charles Bernard, which could proudly point to the fact that the national park in the Engadine was Europe's oldest.

For a time, it was a confused scene. Petty jealousies developed between Continental Europeans and Anglo-Americans, but the latter too were disunited and, in all this, the Western countries were almost on their own. The main issue in dispute was whether the new organization should be autonomous or remain an organ of UNESCO. The Continental Europeans managed to get their way over (at least formal) autonomy, but the organization was provided with only minimal funding; it later looked like perhaps the wrong decision, in view of the key role that the UN and UNESCO would play as forums of international environmental policy.[292] In those days, it was feared that US hegemony came with UNESCO; only later did hostility to international organizations become widespread in the United States itself. The controversies of those 'rather chaotic but nevertheless euphoric founding years'[293] were anyway a sign of a dawning awareness that, beyond fine words, some important new directions might possibly be taken.

The IUCN first came into being as the International Union for the Preservation of Nature (IUPN), but the word 'preservation' sounded too backward-looking and insufficiently activist in British and American ears.[294] In the United States, 'conservation' had had a more powerful ring since the days of Theodore Roosevelt and Gifford Pinchot, denoting not only the protection of nature but also the sustainable management of important economic resources; it was a bridge to what would later be called 'environmental politics'. Resolutions along such lines existed right from the start,[295] even though in practice the organization limited itself to the conservation niche. American members, in particular, forced it to rename itself the IUCN in 1956, when half of its tiny budget was coming from the United States.[296]

In August–September 1949, Lake Success in New York State witnessed the curious spectacle of two parallel conferences: the mammoth UNSCCUR (United Nations Scientific Conference on the Conservation and Utilization of Resources), to which 4,000 experts from around the world were invited, and the IUPN–UNESCO Conference on Conservation. Participants were divided over whether this simultaneity was more indicative of cooperation or of competition. Max Nicholson (1904–2003), the influential, strong-willed founder of the British Council for Nature and the British Trust for Ornithology, considered the whole enterprise premature, on the grounds that the UN understood nothing about conservation, and that a base of strong national organizations (with Britain in the lead) should be developed before embarking on grand international ventures.[297] At the same time, however, he stressed that 'we' and the Americans were 'internationally minded'.[298] Although the Cold War was already raging and the Soviet Union kept away from the UNSCCUR – China had never been represented by forestry experts – the early postwar vision of One World still prevailed. Jimmy G. Crowther, a member of the UNESCO staff, even suggested in all seriousness a project to make the whole of the earth's surface a 'global park'. Having studied the US national park administrations, he was confident that the technical problems of supervising such a park could be solved. A leading French figure in the IUPN, Roger Heim, delighted his colleagues with a plan to turn the Camargue, the El Dorado of European migratory birds, into an international park.[299]

In its early years, the IUPN was a historically unique specimen: a 'hybrid of governmental and non-governmental bodies',[300] in a sense the first GONGO (government-organized non-governmental organization),[301] and thus a model for later combinations of state initiative and self-organization. These would have found it difficult to survive without UNESCO behind them – and without the widespread feeling in such circles that something needed to be done internationally to protect nature and natural resources. Decisive in all this was the personal commitment of Julian Huxley, who straddled the IUPN and UNESCO, offering intellectual authority as well as visionary passion and a conviction that ecology should be a practical science in the service of humanity.[302] Always on the go (unless crippled by a periodic bout of depression), with a characteristic mix of biological-zoological competence and enthusiastic dilettantism, he often appeared as a jack of all trades and looked ahead from the non-political specialist discipline to the later popular ecology.

The soul of the early UNESCO and IUPN did not lie in any apparatus, but rather – long before the internet age – in an elite group of up-and-coming academics,[303] who, despite their many differences, shared a basic feeling that the time had come (after the dreadful war and the abyss of chauvinism and racism) to lay the foundations of a better world: a peaceful, social, cultivated world intent on preserving its roots in nature. It was the job of leading scientists to point the way, since the future belonged to science, and, rightly understood, science would lead in practice to the betterment of the world. The routine of environmental politics would often make people forgetful of the moments of euphoria and sudden inspiration that had punctuated its beginnings![304] Later, the IUPN also performed important service in statistical work: it was the source of the 'Red List', first presented to the world public in 1966, which became the 'most successful and perhaps best-known instrument of species conservation'.[305]

In his speech to the UN Environment Conference held in Stockholm in 1972, Gunnar Myrdal, a prominent member of this elite known for his faith in the power of books and science, still took it for granted that concern for the earth's ecosystem should originate among scientists conscious of their responsibility, not from a broad mass movement.[306] Leading figures in this scene, such as the historians Desmond Bernal and Joseph Needham (the future author of a huge work on science and technology in Chinese history), were Communists, however independently minded, or were at least interested in reaching agreement with the Soviet Union and rejecting the global supremacy of American capitalism.

In the 1950s, the Cold War put a dampener on the vision of One World, but some of it managed to survive, especially as there were interludes of détente. Because of its greater vulnerability, people in Europe were far more aware than in the United States that it would be suicidal to take things as far as a real war, and so even at the tensest moments of the East–West conflict there were always undercurrents eager to calm things down. Broadly speaking, it would not be wrong to situate the international communication with nature within this context. The upsurges of environmentalism in the 1970s and 1990s also occurred in periods of détente, even if the German Greens first experienced the turn of 1989–90 as a huge letdown. So long as the nuclear 'chicken' game continued to be the stuff of nightmares, the main worry was survival over the next few years, not the future of generations to come.

Edward Steichen's *The Family of Man*, which opened on 24 January

1955 at the New York Museum of Modern Art and proved to be the most successful photo exhibition in history, was characteristic of the One World mentality. The 503 exhibits, comprising 273 pictures from 68 countries, were meant to show 'the essential oneness of mankind throughout the world', the elemental phenomena of fear and joy, tears and laughter, love and death being spontaneously understandable to people everywhere. The typical reviewer criticized the fact that it depicted human beings as insect-like creatures, not as bearers of culture; one even jibed that it would be better to move *The Family of Man* from the Museum of Modern Art to the Museum of Natural History.[307] In those days, human nature was often included in the international communication with nature.

The tsetse fly as super-conservationist: overpopulation as the main danger

What was the acute threat to nature? For IUCN circles, the number one danger was not industrial emissions but overpopulation.[308] This may appear surprising, because what people then dreaded most in Europe was loss of life in war, not a surplus of human beings. But postwar short-ages did make them aware of the finitude of natural resources, giving a new impetus to Malthusian concerns.[309] As for the United States, it was only now that Malthusianism made its first appearance. The spectre of overpopulation features in two basic works of American environmental-ism, both published in 1948: *Our Plundered Planet* by Fairfield Osborn, the director of the New York Zoological Society, and *Road to Survival* by the ornithologist William Vogt.[310] In the latter, however, one recognizes the special viewpoint of the champions of African national parks, who saw their wilderness dream threatened by new settlers. The otherwise humane Julian Huxley, for example, felt glad that the tsetse fly was infecting people and cattle with the often deadly sleeping sickness. Wrongly thought of as 'Africa's scourge', it only struck down livestock – wild animals were immune from the pathogen – and therefore maintained intact 'the wonderful hierarchy of the original wild creatures'. 'Thanks to the tsetse fly,' he wrote, 'large stretches of land were put "out of bounds" and devoted to preserving nature. . . . Is it therefore absurd to suggest that a monument should be erected to that insect, as the saviour of Africa and its unique fauna?'[311]

The pros and cons of the tsetse fly dated back to the turn of the century, when sleeping sickness had devastated whole regions in East Africa, yet big game hunters had noted the advance of the wilderness with grim satisfaction.[312] In the 1950s and 1960s, Huxley was not alone in praising the insect; Bernhard Grzimek likewise pointed out that it was preserving 'large parts of wet, tropical Africa'.[313] Huxley did not, however, advocate inhumane ways of preventing overpopulation, but held in high regard Margaret Sanger, the promoter of contraception and the 'anti-baby pill' developed in the 1950s.[314] By then, birth control was losing the sourly misanthropic and puritanical overtones of the old Malthusianism. The protection of wild nature was no longer associated with repression of the wild nature within human beings: an epochal change in the relationship between man and nature.

In the age of nuclear euphoria: green visions for the icy wastes

Since Julian Huxley often sounds like a founder of the later environmental movement, we find it all the more amazing today that he was such a staunch supporter of nuclear energy, and – typically of the 1950s euphoria – not only in the context of power stations. At a time when civilian atomic energy scarcely existed, all kinds of dreams could be happily invested in it. Huxley agreed with Desmond Bernal, the physicist and later author of a celebrated four-volume *Science in History*, that the 'peaceful atom' had many possible uses: 'excavation for dams; moving of earth to create new reservoirs for irrigation; melting the polar ice-caps to free new land and ameliorate the climate (though this would have the disadvantage of raising the sea-level by over a hundred feet and flooding areas like north-east India and Holland)' and above all the generation of electricity.[315] It is enough to list these to appreciate the starkness of the later change in perception.

As early as autumn 1945, with Hiroshima still fresh in people's minds, Huxley outlined this vision to a 'huge rally in Madison Square Gardens', which had expected him to explain the future of a world with atomic weapons. And in 1970, when the vision had long since evaporated, he repeated it in his memoirs without any critical distance, accepting the dark side of global warming as an embarrassing, but simply unavoidable, side effect of an (essentially beneficial) warmer climate in the North. One has a presentiment of 'Think Big!' and everything associated with it. But the Swede Georg Borgstrom began his book *The Hungry Planet* (1965) – which brings us closer to the 'ecological revolution' of 1970 – with the laconic remark that, if 'the Arctic and Antarctic' were converted 'into giant food-producing hothouses heated by atomic power', the meltwater would drown 'a major part' of mankind.[316]

'In the visions of the fifties, the atom was like the Rhine gold in Wagner's opera: it brings happiness to the good and peaceful, but ruin to the bad and power-hungry.'[317] The 'peaceful atom', which seemed to fit in with the 'swords into ploughshares' slogan, did help to drive out fears of the atom bomb; the common emphasis on peace, typical of the early postwar decades, may be found both in the 'Göttingen Manifesto'[318] of 1957 (composed by West German nuclear physicists) and in the French 'atomic pope' Frédéric Joliot-Curie.[319] The most fanatical expressions figure in *Das Prinzip Hoffnung* (1959), the magnum opus of the prophet-philosopher Ernst Bloch, who sees nuclear energy (equated by ill-informed enthusiasts with the imminent achievement of nuclear fusion[320]) as right up there alongside solar energy:

> Just as the chain reactions on the sun bring us heat, light and life, so atomic energy, in a different machinery from that of the bomb, in the blue atmosphere of peace, creates fertile land out of the desert, and spring out of ice. A few hundred pounds of uranium and thorium would be enough to make the Sahara and the Gobi desert disappear, and to transform Siberia and Northern Canada, Greenland and the Antarctic into a Riviera.[321]

Visibly enamoured of his own naïvety, the philosopher, unlike Huxley, does not even find it worth mentioning the consequences of rising sea levels. One can see why Hans Jonas later entitled his contrary work of eco-philosophy *Das Prinzip Verantwortung*, the 'principle of responsibility'.[322]

Bloch thought *Brave New World*, the dystopian novel by Julian's brother Aldous Huxley, 'idiotic'.[323] But in the 1950s there were still seamless transitions between eco-visions and scientific-technological dreams of omnipotence – indeed, also sceptical side currents. Since Hiroshima, in fact, it had been suspected that even civilian nuclear technology had its quirks; many could not help associating it with the bomb. None other than Robert Oppenheimer, the legendary 'father' of the atom bomb, pointed out in November 1945 at an early 'symposium on nuclear energy' that there was a technological affinity between reactors and bombs, and that every reactor also produced bomb-grade fissile material. Yet a 'utopian hope in the unlimited availability of atomic power broke through' immediately after Hiroshima, as it seemed that the 'peaceful atom' might be the 'radiating centre of a new world',[324] and this vision was reflected in the scientific elites around Julian Huxley or Desmond Bernal and their well-meaning dreams of power.

Huxley – like Gregory Pincus, the inventor of the contraceptive pill – participated in the famous (or infamous) colloquium volume of the Ciba Foundation, *Man and His Future* (1963), which had a 'worldwide echo',[325] and in which the geneticist J. B. S. Haldane, alluding to the horrific Thalidomide scandal, speculated that it would soon be possible to breed astronauts with stunted limbs, who could make it to Alpha Centauri without carrying unnecessary weight – or else astronauts with four short legs adapted to the high gravity on Jupiter.[326] The German edition was co edited by Robert Jungk, the vociferous future campaigner against nuclear energy, who had once acclaimed German nuclear researchers in particular as the heralds of a new responsible science.[327]

In the same volume, the 76-year-old Julian Huxley published a forceful plea for the steering of human evolution. 'It is clear that the general quality of the world's population is not very high, is beginning to deteriorate, and could and should be improved', precisely for the sake of the harmonious coexistence of human beings with one another and with nature. Human evolution has so far 'lurched from one crisis to another', and now it is on the path to self-destruction; the task of science is self-evidently to ensure that it becomes 'a self-correcting cybernetic process'.[328] (Cybernetics was the modish science of the 1960s.) Ten or twenty years later, such pronouncements shocked people as scientific delusions of grandeur. But it is worth looking back not least because many things were said clearly then that would later be camouflaged. Positions taken in the eco-age should also be checked to see whether they contain an element of megalomania between the lines, or whether they aim at going beyond man's present-day capacities in a way that is conceivable only through global genetic engineering. In the 1960s as today, one finds an unclarified juxtaposition of transcendence and immanence in thinking about nature. After all, with its Enlightenment origins, naturalism was an alternative to metaphysical transcendentalism, and biologists had a deeply rooted belief in the existence of an organically determined human nature. One can see that the *Family of Man* exhibition too belonged to the One World conceptual universe of the fifties. The network of UNESCO and IUCN intellectual elites should not be thought of as having a system of thought free from contradictions!

Even the Huxley brothers, whose interests often overlapped and who kept in close touch with each other throughout their lives, had quite different ideas and styles of thought: Aldous with his famous scepticism towards technology; Julian with a periodically resurgent tendency to technocratic utopianism.[329] But Aldous Huxley too, shortly before his death, wrote a positive (eco-)utopia of his own: the novel *Island* (1962), of which Ernest Callenbach later supposedly said that, if he had not read it, he would probably never have written his *Ecotopia*.[330] *Island* appeared in the same year as *Silent Spring*, and Aldous Huxley, like Rachel Carson, was terminally ill with cancer at the time. The crux of his idyll on the fictitious island of Pala was the prevention of population growth, and even the introduction of eugenic practices by means of artificial insemination;[331] he saw this as the priority, in the same way as his brother, whereas in *Brave New World* he had still caricatured attempts to intervene in natural reproduction. Julian Huxley's memoirs, however, mention *Island* only in passing and without comment;[332] there is no indication that the ecotopia set in the South Seas meant anything to him. What the two brothers had in common was spontaneous and followed no discursive logic. Julian wrote the preface to the British edition of *Silent Spring*, yet made no mention of Rachel Carson in his memoirs. Aldous complained to him, with Rachel Carson's description of the effects of DDT in mind, that with songbirds 'we are losing half the basis for English poetry'.[333]

One lodestar of the 1950s was Albert Schweitzer; he was close to God for many who set their sights on peace, humanity, closeness to nature and third world aid. Rachel Carson dedicated *Silent Spring* to him, quoting as an epigraph his statement that a return to original forms of human existence was the only salvation. 'Man has lost the capacity to foresee and to forestall. He will end by destroying the earth.' Julian and Aldous Huxley also visited Schweitzer, but Julian confesses in his otherwise discreet memoirs that he found him disappointing: 'There was more proclamation than scientific analysis in his utterances; a hollowness in his main theme – that all life must be equally respected.'[334] Such was indeed not Julian Huxley's view, and the missionary doctors' cure for African poverty seemed to him misguided if it dramatically reduced infant mortality without doing anything to limit births. Furthermore, Huxley knew that Schweitzer's slogans could have no real teeth. A commitment to life *tout court* was not possible, only to life in a clearly defined sense: and in Africa that meant to endangered big game. Schweitzer in Lambarene, who did not look down on Africa from an aeroplane, saw things differently: he still experienced wild nature as overpowering, delighted at the clearing of primeval forest, and approved the killing of wild elephants that destroyed plantations.[335] In his situation, of course, he could not behave otherwise! As *Der Spiegel* reported on 14 September 1960, Schweitzer even turned sharply against Grzimek's pursuit of elephant conservation: 'The destruction of plantations by elephants is becoming a catastrophe.'[336]

Success through summit diplomacy and infectious enthusiasm

Huxley's memoirs give an impression of amazing success – not through organization, tenacious lobbying and political campaigning, but above all through discussions at the top and a charm offensive to arouse a dormant love of nature in elite individuals. In 1930 Huxley approached the socialist theoretician Sydney Webb, then British colonial secretary, to gain his support for wild game reserves. But Webb's spontaneous reaction was dismissive: 'Game for him, with his socialist sympathies, meant something for landowners to shoot, and Reserves meant Preserves, where mammals and birds were kept safe for rich men's sport. However, I explained the real position. . ., and within a few years national parks were established in all three East African territories.'[337]

It was that easy (assuming we can believe him), at least in colonial times – perhaps also in the African *ancien régime*. Thirty-three years later, delegates to an IUCN conference in Addis Ababa visited a fine game reserve, felt enthusiastic about it, and 'decided at once that it should be declared a national park; it had everything needed – fine hilly scenery, splendid trees and many interesting birds, some species restricted to Ethiopia'.[338] Ecology, it seems, exists only to confirm what is felt spontaneously and intuitively. When Huxley writes about nature in Central Africa, the prevailing mood is one of enthusiasm.

As Anna Wöbse writes, Africa became an 'ecological playground' and identity-forming El Dorado for the conservation elite.[339] No doubt it was a Western, not an African, way of looking at Africa, even if Huxley and his friends abhorred apartheid. The national parks had their origins in the reserves imposed on the continent by colonial big game hunters, but conservationists had meanwhile broken loose from the hunters. Grzimek, on the other hand, whose promotion of national parks was taken up by the new world power, television, and used more effectively than ever before, clashed violently with the big game hunters,[340] who claimed, not altogether wrongly,[341] that his alarming figures about wild animal decimation had been plucked out of the air.[342] All the more did Grzimek appeal to the interest of new African states in encouraging tourism as a source of foreign currency. At the IUCN conference in Arusha (Tanzania), sponsored by the Food and Agriculture Organization of the UN (FAO) and UNESCO in 1961, he explained to the head of government Julius Nyerere that Tanzania simply could not compete with the Alps or the Rocky Mountains at the level of tourist attractions. 'If tourists come here,' he said, 'it's because they can easily and safely watch elephants, lions, giraffes and rhinos – a wealth of wild animals that does not exist anywhere else.' Nyerere admitted that he did not care much for animals and could not imagine spending a free day watching crocodiles, but he knew that Europeans and Americans got pleasure out of it. Wild animals would become Tanzania's third largest source of income, after sisal and diamonds, and so he was willing to protect them.[343]

Of the new African leaders, Nyerere was thought to be the most level-headed and to have the greatest integrity. But Grzimek did not hesitate to make similar advances to Uganda's bloodthirsty dictator, Idi Amin, when he showed himself willing to use his power to protect the national parks.[344] Grzimek vehemently encouraged resettlement of the Massai outside his beloved Serengeti, with no thought for the fact that the ostensible 'wild' was marked by the humans living there. Even from an American view-point, Grzimek did more than anyone before him to make a fine art out of wilderness publicity, mobilizing unprecedented means and African person-nel for the purpose. Yet this type of conservation, widely replicated in sub-sequent years, turned out (in the view of a later WWF expert) to be a fatal dead end: not only because it was conducted against indigenous people, but also on account of its fixation on big game instead of whole ecosys-tems.[345] Even a reputed bio-ecologist like Julian Huxley got so carried away that he failed to notice the touristic, ultimately non-ecological, nature of this strategy and praised the Serengeti and the local research institute as 'the world's largest ecological laboratory'.[346]

A contempt for humanity could lie hidden in the passion for the wild. In his memoirs, Julian Huxley relates that in 1939, when he was secretary of the London Zoological Society, Churchill asked him what would happen to the zoo in the event of war, and he replied that they would shoot all the dangerous animals that might escape during an air raid. Churchill pon-dered for a while and suddenly said: 'What a pity!' Then the old warrior burst out: 'Imagine a great air-raid over this great city of ours – squadrons of enemy planes dropping their bombs on London, houses smashed into ruins, fires breaking out everywhere – corpses lying in the smoking ashes – and lions and tigers roaming the desolation in search of the corpses – and you're going to shoot them! What a pity!' Afterwards, Huxley took him to see the giant panda. And Churchill, a bosom buddy in his enthusiasm for wild animals, enthused: 'It has exceeded all my expectations . . . and they were *very* high.'[347] This might well have been how the future logo of the World Wildlife Fund was born!

From the IUCN to the World Wildlife Fund – the wilderness vision becomes a reality

The way in which Julian Huxley and his group kept abreast of the times is a million miles from the clubbishness of regional conservationism. Nevertheless, the IUCN had something oddly imaginary about it. Its annual budget in the mid-1950s was around $33,000[348] – which meant that it scarcely existed as an organization. There were no fixed contributions from member-states;[349] the IUCN lived on handouts. In essence it was a high-sounding name and a select network. It could initiate conservation projects only if they were part of the trend: it had no power to force anything through against resistance. In 1948, at the time of its founding, the IUPN drew up the first 'Red Lists' of rare and endangered species,[350] but it had nothing like a comprehensive database for the issuing of reliable statements that could hold up in the event of conflicts.[351] Alarm calls were capable of influencing only those with the right predisposition.

From the vantage of the 1950s, historians for whom only hard facts count would have thought the IUCN worthy of no more than a footnote. Only in retrospect can we see how international conservation emerged, at first imperceptibly, from its niche, and how its imaginary construction slowly but surely acquired material substance – not least through the new power of the visual media, which Grzimek used to virtuoso effect.[352] This became evident in 1961 with the founding of the WWF, which grew out of the IUCN milieu. The actual impetus was a concern that decolonization would imperil the national parks set up by the colonial powers, but also that the IUCN was facing an acute financial crisis. The WWF too, under its founding president Prince Philip, confidently presented itself as a 'high society' organization, with no ambition to become a grassroots movement. But, whereas the IUCN was always struggling to survive, the new Fund at long last had money, money, money – plus all the magic of modern colour photography to publicize itself.

From the beginning, the WWF realized that its task was not only to combat African poachers but above all to preserve wildlife habitats; and the simplest way to do this was by purchasing the lands in question, so that it was no longer necessary to deal with African district chiefs. The basic idea came from Victor Stolan, a Czech refugee who had succeeded in business in England: it was to make a turn to the super-rich. As he put it: 'There must be a way to the conscience and the heart and pride and vanity of the very rich people to persuade them to sink their hands very deeply into their pockets.' There was indeed a way, and it proved to be amazingly wide and direct, especially when Max Nicholson threw himself behind the project with the slogan 'conservation costs money';[353] in Germany, the former Volkswagen boss Kurt Lotz became the chair of WWF Deutschland. The WWF appointed 'rangers', in olive-green uniforms and jeeps, to patrol the conservation areas[354] – quite a different breed from the old-style nature lover. In this period, when Rachel Carson's *Silent Spring* was causing an outcry, international conservancy and environmentalism was acquiring unmistakably novel features – but also internal tensions on a new scale. For the first major sponsor of WWF, Royal Dutch Shell, produced pesticides as by far its most profitable chemical goods – with the result that, although WWF kept silent publicly about the DDT controversy triggered by Carson's book, a vigorous controversy erupted inside the organization.[355]

From the campaign against nuclear tests to mistrust of the 'peaceful atom'

A new dynamism also came from a very different quarter: the protest movement against atmospheric nuclear tests, represented by prominent scientists and Nobel prizewinners such as Linus Pauling, which eventually led to the US–Soviet agreement to end tests in 1963. While Donald Worster dates the beginning of the 'age of ecology' to 16 July 1945 – the first atomic bomb explosion at Alamogordo – he also points out that the dangers of radioactive fallout began to cause great disquiet among American scientists only after 1958.[356] It was also then that the early enthusiasm for the 'peaceful atom' gave way to disenchantment.[357] Now there was no longer just a consensus-oriented conservationism, but also national and international protest movements underpinned by local initiatives. One centre of the resistance to nuclear tests was St Louis, which under Raymond Tucker had already seen campaigns against industrial pollution and lay in an area with especially high fallout. The Committee for Nuclear Information (note the use of 'information' as a weapon), founded there in 1958 by academics and lay people, created quite a stir over the years with its exhibitions and publications, including an alarming report entitled *Nuclear War in St. Louis.*

In places such as St Louis, when the public discovered the dangers of low-level radiation, protests against nuclear testing passed straight on to warnings concerning civilian nuclear technology. It was there that Barry Commoner, later a leading figure of the 'ecological revolution', first acquired a high political profile.[358] In Europe, which was spared nuclear tests, the transition was not as direct as in the United States, but an Austrian–German 'World League for the Preservation of Life', founded in 1958, became the earliest cell of an anti-nuclear movement, taking inspiration from the eco-apocalyptic book *Morgen holt dich der Teufel* [The Devil will Call for You Tomorrow] (1968) by the Austrian forester Günther Schwab. This protest, however, remained mostly local until the 1970s, retaining a parochial flavour for intellectuals who lived in the imaginative world of nuclear euphoria and thought that this made them progressive. In any event, the first major scientific compendium of environmental risks in the German language – the 600-page *Im Würgegriff des Fortschritts* [In the Stranglehold of Progress] (1961), by the doctor Bodo Manstein, which was dedicated to Prime Minister Nehru of India as a neutral mediator in the Cold War and declared radioactivity (not only the bomb) to be a life-and-death question for humanity – expressed deep disquiet over the 'precipitate expansion' of civilian nuclear technology and, without reaching a definitive judgement, had a great deal to say about its potential risks.[359]

Rachel Carson

In 1960, when Rachel Carson (1907–64) was working on *Silent Spring*, her editor Paul Brooks at Houghton Mifflin was struck by her analogy between the risks of pesticides and radioactivity. It was so dramatic, he wrote to her, 'that people can't help getting the idea. In a sense, all this publicity about fallout gives you a head start in awakening people to the dangers of chemicals.'[360] It is therefore surprising that keywords such as 'fallout', 'nuclear weapons' and 'radioactivity' do not feature in the index of *Silent Spring*; it is left to the reader to make the connection. The author's warnings refer chiefly to pesticides, especially DDT, and she keeps out of the political controversy concerning nuclear weapons. Yet she thinks politically, in the sense that her focus on a single objective is designed to have the maximum impact. This tension has accompanied the environmental movement from the beginning: it must set priorities for practical reasons, but in doing so it inevitably neglects other issues that may possibly prove more serious in the course of time.

Rachel Carson (1907–64) originally worked as a biologist for the US Bureau of Fisheries.

Despite (or because of) violent attacks by the chemicals industry, *Silent Spring* was an instant success;[361] a series of excerpts in *New Yorker* led to the placing of 40,000 advance orders for the book before it finally appeared in September 1962. One senator promptly put it on a par with *Uncle Tom's Cabin*, the Bible of the anti-slavery movement, while *Time Magazine* even compared it to Darwin's *Origin of Species*. Clearly it could be read as a literary as well as a scientific work, and its impact was due not least to this synthesis of technical instruction and poetic vision that has made it outlive many another eco-bestseller. Its extraordinary success shows, however, the extent to which the terrain had been prepared for its message. The IUPN/IUCN had early on pointed to the dangers of herbicides and insecticides[362] – though more for non-human nature than for human beings. For her part, Rachel Carson argued that DDT was a threat mainly to humans, since it entered the food chain at the end of which stood man.

These soundings of the alarm received attention only around 1960, since in the fifties DDT was still hailed for its miraculous victory over the malaria that had afflicted wet tropical regions of the South for centuries. The World Health Organization made DDT the centre of one of its principal campaigns to save the world. But once they no longer had to fear malaria, nature lovers could not only experience unclouded joy at the marsh landscapes but also line up pesticides in their sights. From now on, cancer was the *grande peur* of the industrial countries – with the exception of Japan. This change was at the root of the modern environmental movement: not by chance did President Nixon call for a 'war on cancer' in parallel to a 'war on pollution'.[363] Rachel Carson's original impulse was a love of nature, but what she added to traditional conservationism was an ability to present the threat to man in a convincing fashion. This concern, and not just a selfless love of nature, allowed the environmental movement to become a major force. Rachel Carson's work on *Silent Spring* went hand in hand with a growing fear of cancer, to which she referred in the book at ever greater length.[364]

Having served during the war in the Fish and Wildlife Service, one of the New Deal authorities over which Ickes presided, Rachel Carson had published an earlier bestseller, *The Sea Around Us*, in 1951 and received acclaim as the 'literary woman of the year'. It may be thought surprising that this did not make her attentive to new dimensions of environmental damage, but in those days she was still lost in raptures over the sea and even described approvingly the efforts of engineers to exploit oil beneath its surface; only in 1960, in the preface to a new edition, did she speak of the dangers that radioactive contamination posed to the oceans.[365] Again when she wrote *Silent Spring*, her hopes of another bestseller led her to aim for a careful balance between sober analysis and nightmarish visions, between a conservationism that appealed to intellectual elites and an alarmism geared to the wider public. President Kennedy, who liked to display his openness to new science and bold reforms – including, in Vietnam, to new kinds of biological warfare – expressed an early interest in Rachel Carson's warnings and invited her onto his panel of advisers. For the time being, of course, this had little practical effect: the banning of DDT came only ten years later, when industry was anyway losing interest in the chemical, not least because of growing resistance among insects.[366] In 1968 Germany's Central Horticultural Association published a brochure, *Keine Angst vor Pflanzenschutz* [No Fear of Pesticides], which revealed that fear of plant conservation had existed, and perhaps still did.[367] At the Stockholm environmental conference in 1972 opinions were divided about DDT.[368] And even the American Environmental Protection Agency (EPA), once praised for combativeness in some areas, irritated activists with its 'bite inhibition' on the issue of pesticides.[369]

As a marine biologist, Rachel Carson felt a special empathy with salmon: it moved her that these fish swam away from the nutrient-rich ocean, progressing up rivers with great difficulty and danger to regain their place of origin. Since the nineteenth century this homeward journey had sensitized quite a few anglers, in both Europe and the United States, to the river pollution and ecological disturbances resulting from dams;[370] Rachel Carson's love of salmon was selfless. However, *Silent Spring* appealed first and foremost to people's love of birds, in an attempt to mobilize the bird protectors who had always been the core of conservationism. But Rachel Carson could also have warm feelings towards insects, the natural prey of birds; no wonder that Ernst Jünger – transformed from Germany's most famous wartime author into a keen entomologist – confessed to admiring her.[371] Her love of nature was many-sided; in this too she was ahead of many others, a born integrationist who built a solid bridge to ecology. Those obsessed with one particular species tend to protect it at the expense of others, so that their eyes are closed to the wholeness of nature.

One major reason why *Silent Spring* was an instant success in America is that the Thalidomide scandal had erupted there just two months before.[372] West Germany was even worse affected, since its health authorities reacted more sluggishly than the US Food and Drugs Administration, which, though not realizing the danger at first, listened to the courageous pharmacologist Frances Oldham Kelsey and tightened its controls.[373] The German drugs industry had a great tradition, and unlike its American counterpart was left to supervise itself. Until the 1960s there was actually a 'culture of limitless trust',[374] which went back to an earlier time when patience was seen as 'the most important quality of a good chemist'.[375] In terms of its immediately visible consequences, the Thalidomide disaster was far graver than the German scandals of the eco-age; the shockingly weak response of politicians and the public sheds a sharp light on the callousness of a period when 'the pill' epitomized the brave new world and the new boom in natural therapies lay far in the future. The American lead in this respect was connected to the fact that the new environmentalism came above all from the United States.

Rachel Carson did not yet speak on behalf of a protest movement. She was no labour leader – although, as developments in the sixties made clear, it was perfectly possible to mobilize the United Farm Workers against the explosive growth of pesticides.[376] With a strong sense of decency and public spirit, she agreed to give radio and television interviews, but it is hard to imagine her in front of a microphone issuing shrill alarms. The full-throated champions of private property could not damage her as they did later environmental bureaucrats, for her starting point was precisely that indiscriminate aerial spraying of DDT was a violation of property rights. Nor did she overindulge in doomsday scenarios or the creation of enemy images. In this respect, it is instructive to compare *Silent Spring* with the incendiary *Der Tanz mit der Teufel* (1958) [Dancing with the Devil], in which Günther Schwab, the co-founder of the 'World League for the Preservation of Life', had exposed the dangers of DDT several years earlier.[377] Environmental pollution as an attack by the devil on mankind – enlightenment in the guise of demonology! Though excellently informed for its time, it was not the kind of book that could be quoted by intellectuals. Schwab dedicated it to an elite of great minds, but he was never one of them himself.

Rachel Carson, on the other hand, was surrounded by a select group; her biographer even refers to an 'inner circle'.[378] Although she corresponded with a host of experts, she wrote her book all on her own – as a scientific private detective, so to speak. Since her younger days, she had kept in touch with the long-established Audubon Society for the protection of birds, but it was only after the publication of *Silent Spring* that she contacted David Brower, the pugnacious executive director of the Sierra Club, who had been trying since 1952 to shift that traditional organization to a more offensive policy on the environment.[379] Her book became the Bible of a movement only in the wake of the 'ecological revolution' in 1970. The spell of the Cold War had to be broken before the hour of ecology sounded.[380] Two decades later, it was the transformations in the Eastern bloc that again opened up global environmental issues.

Silent Spring came into being not in public debates but in the intimate atmosphere of Rachel Carson's passionate relationship with Dorothy Freeman, a woman five years her elder, who was married to the managing director of an agribusiness corporation. Reading the correspondence between the two women, one feels thrown back to the Romantic Age. In one of the long, tender letters that Dorothy wrote to the terminally ill Rachel, she agrees with her friend that Wagner's luxuriant Venusberg music from *Tannhäuser* is more fitting than Hindemith's modern sounds to their state of mind.[381] That too made *Silent Spring* a classic. Unlike in Schwab's story of grinning devils who hatch the ruin of mankind, the horror here has an undertone of longing for love and beauty. The old unity of eros with love of nature lives on in Rachel Carson.

Chapter Two

The Great Chain Reaction: The 'Ecological Revolution' in and around 1970

Second data cluster: the great synchronization around 1970

1965	Three books: Murray Bookchin and Louis Herber, *The Crisis of the Cities*; Alexander Mitscherlich, *Die Unwirtlichkeit unserer Städte*; Georg Borgstrom, *The Hungry Planet*.
1965–70	US Air Force sprays 41 million litres of the Agent Orange, Agent White and Agent Blue herbicides on Vietnamese forests and rice fields; the terms 'ecocide' and 'ecological Auschwitz' are coined to describe it.
Jan. 1965	On the initiative of Kenneth Hahn, the Los Angeles County Board of Supervisors asks the federal attorney general to investigate whether the car and petroleum industries are conspiring against a reduction of exhaust gases.
Feb. 1965	Oleg Volkov (1900–96), *Tuman nad Baikalom* (Fog over Baikal): first major public attack in the Soviet Union on the industrial contamination of Lake Baikal.
1965	Adlai Stevenson, US ambassador to the UN (and former presidential candidate): 'We travel together, passengers on a little spaceship, preserved from annihilation only by the care, the work, and I will say the love we give our fragile craft.'
Nov. 1965	First world congress on air purification held in Buenos Aires; the International Union of Air Pollution Prevention Associations (IUAPPA) is founded at the urging of the US Air Pollution Control Association.
1965	The Deutscher Naturschutzring, the German conservation umbrella organization, publishes *Nature in Danger*, with supportive letters from Christian Democrat leaders Konrad Adenauer and Franz Josef Strauß and the Federal president, Karl Heinrich Lübke.
1966	The biologist Barry Commoner, a leading figure in the

	protest movement against nuclear weapons testing and the Vietnam War, founds the Center for the Biology of Natural Systems and wages campaigns against industrial pollutant emissions.
1966	In Crotonville (New York), a movement led by Robert Kennedy campaigns against growing pollution of the Hudson and a planned hydroelectric power station.
1966	Aberfan disaster in Wales: a coal slagheap collapses and buries part of the village. Mounting pressure for waste disposal controls.
1966	The IUPN publishes *The Red Data Book*, the first 'Red List' of endangered species to be made public.
June 1966	Discovery of 'China syndrome' in US Advisory Committee on Reactor Safeguards: i.e., the possibility of an unstoppable reactor core meltdown (David Okrent: a 'revolution' in assessment of reactor safety).
15 July 1966	In agreement with leading conservationists, the Bavarian government plans a Bavarian Forest National Park, the first in Germany. After lively public debate, a statutory order is passed accordingly on 22 July 1969.
5 Oct. 1966	The 'Enrico Fermi' experimental breeder reactor near Detroit is destroyed by a mega-accident; it is later revealed in J. G. Fuller's *We Almost Lost Detroit*.
Xmas 1966	The medievalist Lynn White gives a lecture on the 'Historical Origins of Our Ecological Crisis' (founding text of environmental history).
Xmas 1966	Under the slogan 'Christmas in Kathmandu', hippies gather in the hashish centre and capital of Nepal.
1966/7	GROMET Project: the US tries to win India as an ally by spraying silver iodide on clouds to release rain (without much success and despite Pakistani protests).
1967	New York: founding of Environmental Defense (ED), one of the largest US environmental NGOs, which, partly in cooperation with chemical enterprises, especially targets new toxic substances.
1967	England: a 'volcano of discontent' erupts over the elitist conduct of the management board at an extraordinary congress of the National Trust for Places of Historic Interest or Natural Beauty. Conflict over the building of a motorway through 'inalienable' Trust land. Appeal director Conrad Rawnsley accuses the Trust 'of being bankrupt in ideas, bankrupt in leadership, bankrupt in the common touch'.
1967	Swedish scientist Svante Oden publishes the first widely discussed study of the impact of acid rain on forests, waters and crop yields.

1967	Sweden establishes a Conservation Agency.
18 Mar. 1967	*Torrey Canyon* supertanker disaster off the south coast of England; images of the 'oil plague' cause public outrage.
1 Nov. 1967	Arvid Parvo, Malta's delegate to the UN, calls on the General Assembly to protect the oceans as the 'common heritage of mankind'. Ongoing international negotiations begin on the regulation of sea use.
1967	Dominican Republic: President Joaquin Balaguer launches a drastic forest conservation policy, which is followed by further environmental measures.
1967	Under pressure from food crises, the Indian government embarks on the forced sterilization of couples with more than three children.
1967	Julius Nyerere, the future president of Tanganyika, issues the Arusha Manifesto, which sets a framework for conservation in postcolonial Africa.
1967	Roderick Frazier Nash, *Wilderness and the American Mind*.
1968	The Council of Europe issues a Water Charter and a 'European Clean Air Charter', with the principle that polluters, not taxpayers, should foot the bill. It declares 1970 European Conservation Year.
1968	Sweden's proposal for a UN conference on environmental issues is adopted by the 23rd General Assembly.
1968	USA: founding of the Union of Concerned Scientists, which organizes public hearings on nuclear risk studies.
1968	Paul Ehrlich, *The Population Bomb*; Garrett Hardin, *The Tragedy of the Commons*.
1968	Barry Commoner, 'The Killing of a Great Lake', an article warning of the biological death of Lake Erie.
1968	US Defense Secretary Robert McNamara, who already considers the Vietnam War unwinnable, transfers to the directorship of the World Bank.
1968	René Dubos (1901–82), *So Human an Animal* (a basic work of environmental ethics, against antibiotics). His *Only One Earth* report, jointly authored with Barbara Ward, becomes the foundation for the Stockholm Environmental Conference in 1972.
1968	French scientists and conservationists found a national Federation of Conservation Societies (FFSPN); its first major campaign is over the government's authorization of a ski centre in the Vanoise National Park (created only six years earlier, in 1963).
1968	Günther Schwab (co-founder of the 'World League for the Preservation of Life') publishes *Morgen holt dich*

	der Teufel, the first German polemical text against civilian nuclear technology.
Feb./Mar. 1968	Japan: first clashes between police and demonstrators over plans to build a large airport at Narita, near Tokyo.
1 Mar. 1968	New York: Robert Moses, in charge of city planning for forty-four years, is removed after years of campaigning by Jane Jacobs against his brutal clearances.
4 Apr. 1968	Martin Luther King is assassinated at Memphis, Tennessee.
6–7 Apr. 1968	The Club of Rome is constituted at the Accademia die Lincei in Rome, with the aim of analysing global problems in their interconnection.
10–11 May 1968	Paris: Night of the Barricades marks the peak of the student movement.
July 1968	Max-Otto Bruker, *Der Notstand der Demokratie – aufgezeigt am Kernkraftwerk Würgassen* (one of the first supraregional German polemics against civilian nuclear power).
Sep. 1968	UNESCO Man and Biosphere Conference in Paris: the main precursor of Stockholm 1972. Origin of the UN's Man and Biosphere programme (1970) and of the Biosphere Reserve alternative to the national park model.
28 Oct. 1968	Start of US hearings on Rachel Carson's claims about the effects of DDT; these reveal the lack of independent testing by the chemical industry.
1969–73	Catastrophic drought in the Sahel.
1969	Growing 'nuclear controversy' in the USA; the protests against nuclear weapons tests begin to focus also on civilian atomic installations.
1969	A heated controversy on the Trans-Alaska Pipeline, the 'most ambitious construction project in American history' to develop the 'largest oil field in American history'. It is approved only after the onset of the 1973 oil crisis.
1969	Sheldon Novick, *The Careless Atom* (pathbreaking work on the risks of civilian nuclear technology).
1969	The Japanese writer Ishimure Michiko publishes *Kugai Jodo* (*Paradise in the Sea of Sorrow*), her sensational literary account of Minamata disease caused by methyl mercury discharge.
1969	USA: the National Environmental Policy Act (NEPA) requires the Federal authorities to check any major decision for its effects on the environment; this leads in 1970 to the founding of the EPA, headed by William

Ruckelshaus, which is answerable to the president and is given policing powers by Congress in 1988: not just the launching but the increasingly effective enforcement of environmental standards.

1969	USA: Endangered Species Act.
1969	Canada: 'Pollution Probe' constituted at Toronto University; it will become the country's leading environmental organization.
1969	England: Royal Commission on Environmental Pollution is constituted.
1969	In the aftermath of Venice's disastrous high tide of November 1966, UNESCO publishes an extensive report on the threat to the city from a combination of environmental factors.
Jan. 1969	Miners and miners' widows found the West Virginia Black Lung Association, with large-scale publicity and the active support of Ralph Nader.
Mar. 1969	Copenhagen: a spectacular happening launches the NOAH environmental organization.
7 June 1969	An 'ecology action group' in Berkeley demolishes its car and makes a sculpture out of the pieces. Happenings become a form of action of the nascent environmental movement.
22 June 1969	Cleveland (Ohio): industrial oil waste sets the Cuyahoga River on fire, in a spectacle that shakes the American public.
19 July 1969	Neil Armstrong is the first man on the moon.
15–17 Aug. 1969	Woodstock: approximately 400,000 people attend 'Three Days of Peace and Music', the climax of the hippy and rock music movement.
Sep. 1969	USA: Friends of the Earth breaks away from the Sierra Club (dating back to 1892), mainly because of its refusal to oppose nuclear power projects. David Brower launches the new organization with a slogan – 'Think globally, act locally' – which has since been adopted in many places by the environmental movement.
1969	Protest movement against nuclear power stations planned at Monticello on the Mississippi.
Nov. 1969	Tenth General Assembly of the IUCN in Delhi proclaims 'quality of life', not just conservation, as its overarching objective ('The time has come for a new strategic approach').
Nov. 1969	Shocking photos of the US Army massacre at My Lai on 16 March 1968 are published all over the world.
7 Nov. 1969	In an informal meeting with Hans-Dietrich Genscher, the new West German interior minister, his think-tank

adviser Peter Menke-Glückert proposes 'environment' (*Umwelt*) as the US-style collective name for a new set of responsibilities within the ministry. The results include new laws on lead in petrol, waste management, emission control, aircraft noise, and environmental statistics, which place the Federal Republic ahead of the rest of Europe.

Dec. 1969   Willy Brandt appoints Bernhard Grzimek federal commissioner for conservation issues. Grzimek resigns in 1973, saying that he feels his work is undervalued.

1 Jan. 1970   President Nixon signs the National Environmental Policy Act, which obliges the Federal government to vouch for all its activities and their environmental implications.

1 Jan. 1970   Sweden bans most uses of DDT, initially for a two-year period.

1970   USA: Natural Resources Defense Council (NRDC) is established with the support of the Ford Foundation. It comes out of a 'Riverkeeper' initiative, which campaigned against pollution of the Hudson.

1970   USA: Occupational Safety and Health Administration Act (OSHA).

1970   Lewis Mumford, *The Pentagon of Power*; Gordon Rattray Taylor, *Doomsday Book: Can the World Survive?*; Arthur R. Tamplin and John W. Gofman, *'Population Control' through Nuclear Pollution*; Charles A. Reich, *The Greening of America*; Dee Brown, *Bury My Heart at Wounded Knee*.

7 Feb. 1970   Barry Commoner on the cover of *Time*.

12 Mar. 1970   Tokyo Resolution (symposium of the International Social Science Council on environmental issues): 'Everyone has the right to an environment that is not detrimental to their health or well-being and does not endanger nature or its aesthetic attraction.' In July 1970 there is a public outcry that children are dying in Tokyo of photochemical smog. In November the Japanese cabinet submits fourteen bills on pollution, which are all approved by Parliament. A Conservation Agency is established the following year, on 1 July 1971.

24 Mar. 1970   Representatives of the Sierra Club and Friends of the Earth, together with other environmental activists and Congressmen, found the Citizens' League against the Sonic Boom. It reaches a wide public on Earth Day (22 April) and wages a successful campaign against the Supersonic Transport project. Since this has no pros-

	pect of profitability and is a danger to the earth's ozone layer, the Senate votes it down later in the year.
1970	Major floods on the southern fringe of the Himalayas become the 'turning point in the ecological history of the region' (Ramachandra Guha); protest movement targets deforestation and contempt for traditional village rights. Out of this emerges the Chipko movement, largely kept going by women and Gandhi supporters, which for a long time will be the best-known third world environmental movement.
1970	Nobel Peace Prize for Norman Borlaug, the 'father of the Green Revolution'.
22 Apr. 1970	Earth Day celebrated on the initiative of Congressman Gaylord Nelson, with approx. 10,000 participants in Washington and more than 20 million worldwide.
1970	World Climate Conference at the Massachusetts Institute of Technology (MIT).
1970	California Environmental Quality Act. Governor Ronald Reagan, though inwardly an opponent of environmentalism, tries to present California as the policy frontrunner.
1970	An environment ministry is established in France.
May 1970	East Germany passes a Landeskulturgesetz (on landscape, nature and environment conservation, recycling and soil improvement); a Ministry for Environmental Protection and Water Management comes into being on 1 January 1972.
1970	European Conservation Year, already declared as such in 1963 by the Council of Europe.
1970	The OECD, noted since 1968 for studies and recommendations on environmental issues (with the EEC playing a leading role), establishes an Environment Committee.
1970	Founding of the Bavarian Forest National Park, the first in Germany on the American model.
1970	Conservation groups, mainly formed out of bird protection, fishing and rambling societies, wage 'aggressive' public campaigns against the discharge of untreated wastewater into Lake Constance and overdevelopment of its shores.
Sep. 1970	France: Jacques Cousteau, world famous for his underwater films, begins to warn in public about marine pollution.
19 Sep. 1970	First squats in Frankfurt-am-Main; 'urban warfare' begins there in autumn 1971.
5 Oct. 1970	*Der Spiegel* features the environment on its front cover

	for the first time ('Poisoned Environment'), considering this to be a completely new issue in Germany.
2 Nov. 1970	Headline in the *Süddeutsche Zeitung*: 'Nuclear Battle over Würgassen [power station]'.
1970	USA: the Resource Conservation and Recovery Act (RCRA) empowers the EPA to monitor the handling and recycling of waste, especially toxic waste.
late 1970	US Congress passes a new and tougher Clean Air Act, which for the first time sets binding national targets for air quality. (The UK's Clean Air Act dates back to 1956.)
7 Dec. 1970	Willy Brandt's genuflection at the monument to the Warsaw Ghetto uprising: the most striking moment of the 'new Ostpolitik'.
24 Dec. 1970	Horst Stern's TV programme 'Observations on the Red Deer' sharply attacks the hunting lobby and its overcultivation of game that is damaging the forest.
1971	The Bonn government sets up an advisory council on environmental issues.
1971	West Germany: the 'Aircraft Noise Act' requires appropriate commissions to be created for all commercial airports.
Mar. 1971	Beginning of 'Cod War' between Iceland and Britain, when Reykjavik extends its territorial waters to 50 miles in response to the decline of fish stocks.
12 Apr. 1971	Some 1,500 protesters march to the Fessenheim nuclear power station in Alsace: the first major European demonstration of its kind. In July, 15,000 turn out to protest against the building of Bugey nuclear power station on the Rhone.
1971	Greenpeace is founded in Vancouver. It first attracts attention with an operation against French nuclear testing on the Mururoa atoll in the South Seas; the battle cry 'Better active than radioactive!' is subsequently used also against 'peaceful' nuclear technology.
1971	At the request of Governor Tom McCall, Oregon initiates exemplary legislation on environmental protection.
1971	First spectacular action by Friends of the Earth, whose supporters dump 1,500 disposable bottles outside the Schweppes company gates in Britain.
1971	The Japanese Mitsui corporation loses a legal action that victims of itai-itai disease (cadmium poisoning, first recognized in 1955) had brought against it.
1971	A ministry for the environment is created in France.
1971	First 'environmental adviser' at the World Bank.
1971	The EPA declares asbestos to be an atmospheric health

	hazard; its removal becomes one of the early focuses of environmental policy.
1971	USA: all cigarette advertising on the radio is banned.
1971	Niigata scandal in Japan: effective protests against a chemical plant that had been discharging mercury-laden wastewater into a river with toxic effects.
1971	Barbara Ward founds the International Institute for Environment and Development (IIED).
1971	Barbara Ward and René Dubos, *Only One Earth*, a fundamental text for the 1972 Environment Conference in Stockholm.
1971	Ramsar conference in Iran leads to the Convention on Wetlands of International Importance.
1971	Barry Commoner, *The Closing Circle*.
1971	Bo Gunnarsson, *Japan's Ecological Harakiri*, published in Stockholm.
1971	Konrad Lorenz, *Civilized Man's Eight Deadly Sins*, with 'overpopulation' and 'habitat destruction' as numbers one and two.
27 Dec. 1971	Alvin M. Weinberg, the longstanding director of the Oak Ridge nuclear research centre, states in a public lecture: 'We nuclear people have made a Faustian bargain with society.'
Feb. 1972	Nixon in China; an acupuncture boom gets under way in the West, associated with the growing popularity of natural healing.
1972	Dennis L. Meadows et al., *The Limits to Growth: Report of the Club of Rome.*
1972	France: Les Amis de la Terre, under Brice Lalonde's leadership, organize their first major demonstration: La Vélorution attracts some 20,000 cyclists in Paris.
1972	Hans Dollinger, *Die totale Autogesellschaft* (a detailed account of direct and indirect damage caused by the spread of motoring).
June 1972	UN Environment Conference in Stockholm; only Romania takes part from the Eastern bloc, but China, only recently admitted to the UN, is also there. Deforestation in Amazonia is described as an 'ecological Hiroshima'. More than 400 NGOs are represented; the UN contributes to their being publicly recognized institutions. Founding of the United Nations Environmental Programme (UNEP), with Maurice Strong as director.
1972	India: the Pani-Panchayat movement begins to emerge in response to the severe drought in Maharashtra State, made worse by the high water use of sugar cane

	plantations; the movement calls for everyone living in the area to have the right to water.
1972	Founding of the first Green parties, in Australia and New Zealand.
1972	UNESCO World Heritage Convention.
1972	The film *Home* features a fictitious speech by the Indian chief Seattle, which will often be cited in the ecological literature as an authentic confirmation of Indian harmony with nature.
1972	Founding of the BBU environmental umbrella organization in Germany: Bundesverband Bürgerinitiativen Umweltschutz.
2 July 1972	The 'Ecology Group' around Hubert Weinzierl and Konrad Lorenz presents an 'Ecological Manifesto'.
Oct. 1972	First Conference of EC environmental ministers in Bonn. They agree to include environmental protection among the tasks of the Community, although in practice this has few real consequences until the late 1980s.
1972	On the initiative of the USA, the London Dumping Convention agrees on a black list of substances whose dumping at sea is strictly forbidden, and a grey list allowed on certain conditions. Monitoring is left to the signatory states; there is no provision for sanctions.
1972	USA: Clean Water Act (pendant to the Clean Air Act!): first set of binding national standards for the chemical, and later biological, purity of water.
1972	USA: Federal Environmental Pesticides Control Act (FEPCA); banning of DDT (Rachel Carson, *Silent Spring*, 1962!); mandate to check all other (50,000) pesticides. Also in 1972, DDT is banned in Switzerland. (In 1968 the USA had prohibited the import of Swiss cheese because of its DDT content.)
1972	USA: Office of Technology Assessment (OTA) established by Congress as a neutral advisory body (abolished in 1995).
1972	USA: Toxic Substances Control Act (TSCA) empowers the EPA to check whether chemicals are injurious to health.
1972	West Germany: so-called Würgassen judgement of the Federal Administrative Court gives priority to safety over the promotion of nuclear energy in the interpretation of the Atomic Act.
1972	The British anti-vivisectionist Olive Parry sets fire to herself.
1972	The Mexican psychologist and environmental activist Fernando Césarman transfers the concept of 'ecocide',

originally used by the movement against the Vietnam War, to civil spheres of the relationship with nature (*Ecocido: Estudio psicoanalítico de la destrucción del medio ambiente*).

1972   Gregory Bateson, *Steps to an Ecology of Mind.*
1972   Turning point in worldwide population trends ('demographic transition'), as growth begins to slow.

The year of triumph

When Max Nicholson, an early pioneer of conservation, published his book *The Environmental Revolution* in 1970, it had a subtitle that testified to the global intoxication with power: *A Guide for the New Masters of the World*. Martin Holdgate, director-general of the IUCN from 1988 to 1994 and perhaps the man most familiar with the past history of conservation and environmentalism, still spoke thirty years later of the 'environmental explosion' during the years from 1966 to 1975.[1] Back in 1970, a few months after the moon landing of 19 July 1969, Nicholson boasted:

> The pride of having reached the moon is cancelled out by the humiliation of having gone so far to making a slum of our own native planet. Quite suddenly the long struggle of a small minority to secure conservation of nature has been overtaken by a broad wave of awakening mass opinion. . . . Old values, habits of thought and established practices are being challenged all over the world.[2]

All this, he claimed, added, up to nothing less than a revolution, an 'environmental revolution'.

It is a grand irony of history that the very triumph of space travel made us aware how empty the cosmos is, and that the images of 'our blue planet', with its vulnerable, wafer-thin atmosphere, aroused a new and tender concern. 'Spaceship Earth' became the stock phrase of environmentalism. But a spaceship needs a captain to stop it crashing; again we see the dream of power ensconced in the global gaze.

Curiously, however, Nicholson – who knows the *longue durée* better than anyone – offers no explanation for this turn with which he is abruptly confronted. He even concedes that 'revolutions, unfortunately, have a way of surprising revolutionaries', of causing them to lose foresight and control.[3] He avoids the Girondiste Vergniaud's famous verdict that revolution, like Saturn, devours its own children, yet that too would be appropriate in his case; his name fell into oblivion even in ecological circles, and four decades after it was published in a number of languages *Environmental Revolution* can be picked up on the internet for the token price of a penny. Did the 'environmental revolution' never take place, or is the very oblivion a sign of a dramatic shift of horizon? In 1986 Edward Goldsmith and Nicholas

Hildyard (the editors of *The Ecologist*) published a collection entitled *Green Britain or Industrial Wasteland?*, which sharply criticized the idea that Britain was a green pioneer. But today that too can be bought for a penny on the internet; the deindustrialization that has taken place in Britain since the 1980s makes many traditional complaints about industrial poisoning of the environment appear exaggerated. In 1987 Nicholson published another book: *The New Environmental Age*. The Duke of Edinburgh wrote the foreword, showing that the author, like the WWF, moved in the best circles. Now the talk is no longer of a revolution but of decentred 'interactions'.[4] And in his gallery of honour devoted to the 'Pioneers of Conservation', Nicholson speaks of mere names from long ago that virtually no one has heard of.

To the irritation of veteran environmentalists, the tens of thousands of young enthusiasts who observed Earth Day on 22 April 1970 in Washington and many other cities believed that they were the first to have discovered the acute threat to nature; most of them had no idea at all of the long list of their predecessors.[5] This is why many environmental historians have sought to demonstrate the historical falsity of this conception of a 'ground zero'. In reality, the roots go so far back that a historian is often exhausted by the time he or she makes it to the year 1970. Nevertheless, more than forty years on, it seems thoroughly wrong to downplay the importance of that watershed.

Frank Uekötter, who has given us the most detailed account of anti-smoke campaigns in German and American cities from the nineteenth century on, speaks of a 'quiet revolution' and the inconspicuous yet irresistible rise of a 'precautionary principle' in the period around 1960.[6] On the other hand, in the early years after 1970, nothing new happened in terms of effective measures: rather, legislative activism meant that 'chaos ruled supreme' in day-to-day administrative practice.[7] Yet Uekötter also speaks of an 'ecological revolution' or even an 'ecological big bang', albeit more for the United States than Germany.[8] Many conservationists began to feel overrun by the new 'environmentalists', complaining that they had been doing the same for ages without making such a fuss about it. Still, Hubert Weinzierl, the grand old man of Bavarian conservation, admitted with more than thirty years' hindsight: 'Only the changing mood in social policy around the end of the sixties created the soil for new social movements, and hence for a durable ecological movement. European Conservation Year, 1970, saw the breakthrough of an overall vision in which the earth was recognized as the common home of all living creatures.'[9]

All in all, there is much evidence that the 'ecological revolution' in and around 1970 marked a real turning point, not a pseudo-event. The term 'revolution' may tempt us into a misleading history centred on dramatic events, but let us not lapse too quickly into story-telling! Even if one generally shies away from long lists of historical data, it will be useful in the present case to allow the mass of pure facts and data, previously missing in most history books, to work on us first for a while. The scale of the concurrence alone has its fascination. Were we to begin with a particular history, only a small section of these facts would come into our purview. Sometimes it is useful to know the precise data and their temporal sequence; that anyway provides initial clues as to causes and effects. But perhaps what is decisive is not causal relations but reciprocation and synergy effects. Let us allow all these data to remain at first alongside and after one another, without defining in advance the main actions or key actors, what is central or marginal, what does and does not belong.

A pure list of data leaves many questions open, yet it contains reasonably clear answers (typically of a 'yes, but' or 'no, but' kind) to certain basic questions. At first sight, it seems trivial to mention that the strongest impulse for the new environmentalism came from the United States. But this was later often forgotten in wide circles of the European environmental movement, especially when America under Reagan and Bush Jr became the bastion of a policy rollback. The precedence of the United States stems not only from the combativeness of civil society but also from the fact that the exploitation of resources had long been particularly ruthless there. In Germany, the spraying of DDT from aircraft happened only in the GDR. In 1970 it became known that much higher amounts of DDT were stored in American than West German corpses.[10]

Yet, somehow or other, common ground soon developed in environmental matters between the United States and its European allies. American environmentalists, who called for government intervention and were denounced for this as crypto-Communists,[11] could cite evidence from across the Atlantic that welfare provision was a good old Western tradition. Seldom have Europeans received such charming compliments from an American for their environmental awareness as they did from Jeremy Rifkin, a pioneering thinker on issues to do with the environment and technology.[12] Within Europe, as we have seen, a leading role soon fell to the Federal Republic of Germany, where environmental activism took on an American tempo. Until then, Britain had been in the lead on 'Green' issues such as landscape, nature and bird protection – a source of pride for conservationists – and these sectors continued to be strong and well-organized there.[13] The British lagged behind, however, in new areas such as the fight against nuclear energy, emissions and acid rain, being seen on the Continent as a brake until the new Green dynamism had an impact on the British Isles.[14]

The ecological turn in East Asia

The simple facts appear to show that the 'ecological revolution' of 1970 was overwhelmingly Western. It did, however, immediately leap over to the non-Western country that had had the greatest success in keeping up with the West industrially: Japan. Until then, the Japanese 'culture of silence' had applied also to environmental scandals (it lasted until Fukushima in relation to nuclear technology), but now local protests started to have a real public resonance; sections of the Japanese media and administrative elites executed a dramatic about-face (at least on some egregious instances of environmental pollution) and sought to present Japan internationally as a frontrunner. As early as 1956, 'Minamata disease' (caused by mercury emissions from the Chisso chemical corporation) had shocked local public opinion but been covered up elsewhere. In 1969, Ishimure Michiko's *Paradise in the Sea of Sorrow* became a bestseller and, like *Silent Spring*, was compared to *Uncle Tom's Cabin*.[15]

Note the difference: Rachel Carson's spring of the dead birds was a fantasy; the human torments described by the Japanese writer were real. The later outcry in Germany – 'First the forest dies, then man' – was the expression of an apocalyptic fiction; in Minamata first cats, then human beings, really had been dying. But Japanese environmentalists were not alone in raising the alarm about mercury; the biologist Barry Commoner – featured on the front cover of *Time* (7 February 1970), in another sign of the ecological turn – also focused his campaigns on mercury, whose dangers, known since antiquity, had acquired new dimensions through the rapid growth of synthetic chemistry.[16]

While the Soviet Union and its satellites boycotted the 1972 Environment Conference in Stockholm because of the exclusion of the GDR – which did not prevent Moscow and Washington from signing an agreement on protection of the environment[17] – the People's Republic of China decided to take part. Outwardly it presented itself as a very critical voice, branding 'neocolonialism' as the main danger to the environment and wanting nothing to do with birth control or a ban on nuclear weapons testing, but in reality the flood of information in Stockholm concerning environmental risks had a lasting impact on Chinese participants. Ten years later Qu Geping, one of the Chinese delegates and from 1973 deputy director of a newly created state conservation agency, stated in no uncertain terms that the Stockholm summit had been a 'turning point' in world history, since when 'Chinese environmentalism had entered a new phase of development'. China, he said, had actively supported the conference and learned a great deal from it; it had inspired the holding of the first national environmental conference in 1973.[18] Whereas the Maoist government had still denounced birth control as reactionary Malthusianism, China began in 1980 to horrify Western human rights activists with the rigour of its curbs on demographic growth. In 1994 Qu Geping published an environmental history of China, in which its population increase over thousands of years was presented as an eternal curse that had ruined its soil.[19]

UNESCO and space travel: the global as reality and fiction

Stockholm 1972 brings us to the crucial significance of international conferences and transnational communication in general. For those who value only palpable realities and concrete effects – as do many environmental activists who not only give grand speeches but want to achieve something visible – the international level has something imaginary and disembodied, and there will always be a suspicion that international lobbying amounts to a variety of tourism. In most of the literature on American environmentalism, Stockholm either does not feature at all or has only a marginal position; the wish to appear as a genuinely American movement is much stronger. For European environmental initiatives, however, the summit had been a source of encouragement and enhanced status ever since the UN General Assembly voted it through back in 1968. Several countries – from France to the GDR – had tried to raise their profile on environmental policy in the run-up to Stockholm 1972. At the beginning of that year, East Berlin actually created a new environment ministry – fourteen years before the Federal Republic did so – but there is still little information available about its activity. In fact, from the late sixties on the GDR discharged all the saline from its potash industry into the River Werra, yet maintained (until 1968) an agreement negotiated in 1913 between the adjacent owners of the time. Symbolic politics by no means always coincided with real politics.

Emotional talk of One World was essential for the new environmental movement as it found expression from the second half of the sixties on. Photos from space gave tangible reality to the 'blue planet' and its atmosphere, so that, although the small-scale ecology of the time was still far from giving scientific substance to 'the earth's ecosystem', it looked quite different from the old papier-mâché globes that used to lie on people's desks. Ironically, the very success of space flights in the 1960s destroyed their magic: small wonder, then, that NASA only reluctantly came to the view that life on Mars was impossible.[20] If imaginative people in the fifties believed we could always emigrate to other heavenly bodies if conditions on earth became too difficult, space travel made us aware how empty and lifeless space is, and that this planet of ours is all we have.

In a sense, it was a 'Copernican turn' in reverse: whereas the earth since Copernicus had been just one planet among others, it was now again something unique in the cosmos: something at once beautiful and vulnerable.[21] In 1966 Barbara Ward (later Baroness Jackson of Lodsworth) published *Spaceship Earth*, and her subsequent *Only One Earth: The Care and Maintenance of a Small Planet* (1971), co-authored with the microbiologist René Dubos and written under great time pressure with the help of advisers from fifty-eight countries, became the key book for the Stockholm conference. To appreciate the change in the global horizon, one need only recall how Hermann Löns had scorned conservationism in 1911 as 'small beer' (*Pritzelkram*). Now those who campaigned against the pollution of a little stream did so in the proud belief that they were doing their bit to save the world.

If one focuses only on grassroots movements, belittling the 'top-down' impulses and elitist features of the new environmentalism, one takes in only half the history – often not even that. The simple facts speak for themselves. In the German media in the seventies and eighties, the eco-scene retained (especially for opponents) an image of long-haired hippies and outsiders that was relevant only to a particular time and place. What was often seen as a subculture was in reality a segment of the new high culture. On the whole, an environmental commitment put one in good, indeed the best, society – not usually in society whose idealism was beyond doubt. Its leading figures were more likely to have a glamorous background: the Canadian businessman Maurice Strong, first executive director of UNEP, general secretary of the Stockholm conference and two decades later of the Rio summit, came from the petroleum and energy sector; and Aurelio Peccei, the 'strongman' of the Club of Rome and the driving force behind *Limits to Growth*, was director of the Latin American section of Fiat and boss of Olivetti. For a neo-Marxist from the '68 student movement, quite a few protagonists of environmentalism seemed at first – to put it mildly – strange and disconcerting.

Politics to the fore

From the mid-1970s, when opinions diverged over the nuclear question, the environmental protest movement mobilized large numbers of people, including many '68ers. The sequence of events shows, however, that politics was the priority in the Federal Republic. As early as 1969, 'the environment' had not been without significance in the general elections, and on 7 November a policy meeting with Genscher, the new interior minister, came up with the idea of American-style 'conservationism': that is, a packaging of various administrative initiatives that had previously been handled separately.[22] Later, it was often heard from the opposing side that sensationalist media people unleashed an environmental hysteria – but the evidence does not support this.

Even *Der Spiegel*, which has often been ascribed a pioneering role, published its first environmental front cover only on 5 October 1970, calling for a 'profound rethink' but noting that, whereas 'the first signs of this [were] visible in USA, Japan and Sweden', there was as yet 'not the slightest inkling in the Federal Republic'.[23] Today, whole batches of historical studies show that many components of the new 'environmental awareness' already stretched back more than a century; the *Spiegel* quotation thus says a great deal about how that prehistory unfolded outside the very layer of critical/reform-minded intellectuals from which it recruited its editors and readers.

Subsequent events bore out the confident assertion at the interior ministry in 1969 that 'we have invented the environmental movement'.[24] Not altogether, though. The ministry initiative actually originated with Peter Menke-Glückert, a thoroughly anti-bureaucratic bureaucrat (more think-tanker than civil servant), who was capable of deriding his colleagues as 'bureaufascists', and who used the cross-border environmental dynamism to confound administrative routines. When he showed up somewhere, no one knew whether he was there as a civil servant or as a stand-alone figure. In his way – and this too was typical of the new-style environmentalists – he combined criticism of blind growth mania with the planning optimism of the sixties, a voguish futurology and an insistence on science and 'system' in politics. This was part of the background to his enthusiasm for 'environmental politics'.[25] He had brought this new trend straight from the USA, knew more in general about the world than most officials at the interior ministry in Bonn, and was director of the Science Resource Division of the OECD (unlike the EEC, a pioneer on environmental issues). In this latter capacity, he attended the UNESCO Biosphere Conference in Paris in 1968. He once said that he got his 'sense for firm logistical mastery' from America and his 'high awareness of liberty' from the OECD.[26]

Menke-Glückert thus embodied the new style of the early Brandt era. In his own speeches, Brandt happily took over the new key phrase 'quality of life', but in general one has the impression that, though at least outwardly open to new trends, he was more or less unaffected by the environmental movement.[27] He still lived immersed in the ideas of modernity: the revolutionary romanticism of '68 was more understandable to him than the new emphasis on nature. As mayor of West Berlin, he would have liked to build a nuclear power station on a Wannsee island so that his part of the city could have its own source of electricity – a project which, never discussed in public, was vetoed by Bonn when it became clear that West Berliners should have been evacuated during a major incident in the GDR (a few years after the building of the Wall!). Again in the early seventies, Brandt supported the BASF project for a nuclear power station close to the city, which even members of the nuclear 'community' thought questionable, and which eventually ran into the sand.[28] Olof Palme (Sweden) and Bruno Kreisky (Austria), two charismatic Social Democrat leaders of the 1970s, championed nuclear energy in accordance with the traditional belief in progress; and the redefinition of 'left' and 'progressive' by opponents of nuclear power faced them with the gravest dilemmas of their time in office.

All the same, Brandt's new Ostpolitik probably contributed to the milder climate in which environmental politics flourished – a kind of '*Sturm und Drang* period',[29] experienced much as in Washington. A key impetus came from below, however. Action groups mushroomed in the period around 1970, so prolifically that by 1972 it was possible to establish an umbrella organization: the Bundesverband Bürgerinitiativen Umweltschutz (BBU). In many cases, Niklas Luhmann's scenario of 'ecological communication' was not at all applicable: many initiatives were not aimed in the void at 'society'– which, as Luhmann jibed, has neither an address nor a telephone – but at the competent authorities; this was indeed one of the merits of the new environmental politics, even when it did not bring about anything directly. Without the movement in civil society, environmental politics would have been no more than a passing fashion and gone by the board under Brandt's successor, Helmut Schmidt. The Bonn environmental policy-makers, at least as much as their American counterparts, were aware that without the *Bürgerinitiativen* they would be fighting a losing battle.[30]

In the United States, the birthplace of environmental politics, the 'movement' was more to the fore than in Germany. Admittedly it was a question more of initiatives by social elites in contact with government than of revolts from below. However, new and combative forces asserted themselves in the late sixties alongside the older, more consensus-oriented Sierra Club, Audubon Society and Wilderness Society. This fitted the age of the civil rights movement and the protests against the Vietnam War, but it also reflected a situation where the old procedures of community regulation, established in campaigns against smoke and neighbourhood water pollution, no longer had much purchase.[31] Neither car exhaust gases, radioactive fallout or air-sprayed DDT, nor the growing flood of industrial emissions that people could not see or smell, were amenable to the old consensus approach. The new environmentalism had to grapple not only with material waste but also with phenomena such as the rubbish dumps that had sprung up everywhere around the world, and which the existing institutions had conspicuously failed to control.

Leaders pointing in different directions: David Brower and Barry Commoner

It was a sign of the times when David Brower (1912–2000), a charismatic bundle of energy – one historian called him the 'Bismarck', another the 'arch-druid' of wilderness lovers[32] – attacked the Sierra Club (of which he had been executive director since 1953) for its pusillanimous style of work and excessive willingness to compromise, and broke away to found Friends of the Earth, soon to grow into an international organization. In the eyes of his admirers, Brower was no less than the 'inventor of modern American environmentalism' – though, of course, he was not the only candidate for that title. In his heart, he was above all a passionate lover of the wild,[33] and as a token of this he was willing, if push came to shove, to wage open war on the Forest Service and the dam projects of the Bureau of Reclamation. In the late sixties he also joined the campaign against nuclear energy, and in that too he felt let down by the Sierra Club;[34] those whose sole obsession was to keep the canyons of the West free of hydroelectric power stations saw nuclear energy as a welcome relief. (Most of the older generation of conservationists in Switzerland and Upper Bavaria were similarly pro-nuclear.) Friends of the Earth founded the first transnational anti-nuclear information network. American information experts were decisive in giving intellectual support to opponents of the atomic lobby in other countries, which tried to present anyone who contradicted it as incompetent.

David Brower (1912–2000; here shown in 1995) founded several organizations, including Friends of the Earth in 1969.

In 1970, according to *Time Magazine*, many Americans saw Barry Commoner as the leader of the new combative 'environmentalism'. A microbiologist by training, but increasingly dissatisfied with the discipline, he embodied more wholeheartedly than many colleagues the new type of critical 'politico-scientist'.[35] Already active in the late fifties campaign against nuclear weapons testing, and then in the movement against the Vietnam War, he differed from Brower in being a spokesperson of the New Left. He did not come out of the old wilderness romanticism, but represented a new style of conservationist protest that had expanded its focus from nuclear weapons to civilian nuclear technology.[36] 'Everything is connected to everything else' was his 'first law of ecology': he thus avoided a fixation on just one risk, going on to track down industrial mercury emissions and issuing warnings to the public about the impact of phosphate-based detergents on rivers. According to the historian of science Donald Fleming, who was suspicious of the new environmentalism among his colleagues, Barry Commoner's exaggerated account in 1968 of the 'alleged "killing" of Lake Erie' by phosphates was 'probably the most famous horror story of the New Conservation movement'.[37]

Oddly enough, although Brower and Commoner were both active in the anti-nuclear campaign around 1970, they appear not really to have known each other. Commoner receives no mention in Brower's 550-page memoirs, and in Egan's biography they meet only once, after Brower has encouraged Paul Ehrlich to write his *Population Bomb*, triggering a major dispute with Commoner. Similarly, in England, Max Nicholson and Ernst F. Schumacher – the author of the cult book *Small Is Beautiful* (1973), who was then the most important economic theorist on the eco-scene – seem to have ignored each other.

The biologist Barry Commoner (1917–2012; here shown in 1974) founded the
Center for the Biology of Natural Systems in 1996 and led campaigns against
industrial pollution. In 1970 he was featured on the cover of *Time Magazine*.

This raises an important point that has received little attention until
now. The various American environmental organizations did not merge
into a single large movement, but all too often, whether openly or in less
visible ways, developed an especially intense rivalry in fundraising and the
soliciting of publicity. Positive stimuli or challenges were always needed to
bring about the networking of initiatives; politicians created the common
target groups and arenas, and repeatedly also the common adversary who
brought the centrifugal Green movements back together.

Earth Day

Earth Day, first celebrated on 22 April 1970 and since then every year
in many American cities, was perceived by the public as a spectacular
overture to the new eco-age and, in the words of its national coordinator
Denis Hayes, 'the largest organized demonstration in human history'.[38]
As we have seen, its origins lay in an initiative of a Democatic senator
from Wisconsin, Gaylord Nelson. One of the greatest ironies in the
history of environmentalism is that it received its main impetus under
President Nixon of all people – the poison dwarf par excellence in the eyes
of reform-minded intellectuals. The EPA was created during his term of
office, and fundamental pieces of legislation followed one after the other.
By himself Nixon would never have come up with such an idea, nor was
he exactly proud of this achievement of his administration; he sometimes
spoke of it with downright cynicism. But, in view of the fiasco in Vietnam,

he needed something with a progressive tinge to take the wind out of his opponents' sails, and environmentalism came along just in the nick of time. Behind Nixon stood an experienced environmental activist known to him since 1955, Russell E. Train, who had founded the African Wildlife Leadership Foundation and was now chair of the President's Council of Environmental Quality. The importance of individual actors should not be underestimated.[39]

Bearing in mind the later controversies, it is surprising that the National Environmental Policy Act (NEPA) – which created the EPA and required the Federal authorities to check all major measures for their environmental impact – passed through Congress without lengthy debate or lobbying: 'the environment' seemed to command a consensus in those early days.[40] The paperback edition of *Silent Spring* even appeared with a quotation from Nixon on its cover![41] But in 1972 he drew back from environmentalism when he realized that his toying with it did not please most of the Republican business world.[42] Without a broad movement, but also without the institutions founded at that time, environmentalism would soon have been history, in both Washington and Bonn.

Later it was often argued that the new thing about the environmental movement was its selfless 'postmaterialism'.[43] If this were the case, its current prospects would be bleak – for material security has again become the prime concern in the wake of the economic crisis. The truth is, rather, that in 1970 the (seemingly) selfless love of nature and enthusiasm for the wild was anything but new; it was the leitmotif of a long-institutionalized conservationism, which now found itself being overshadowed by new struggles. The decision to convene the Stockholm Conference was taken in 1968, at the UNESCO Biosphere Conference in Paris, and the new keyword 'biosphere' evoked not only the old wilderness ideal but a human-friendly nature in which life was worth living. Any other model would have been out of the question in UN circles, at a time when parts of Africa and Asia were threatened with famine. Only because the issue at stake was not a law of nature but human well-being or even survival did environmentalism acquire a political potential, especially in the international arena. 'Quality of life' was a characteristic ideal in the early ecological era. Much that had once been included under 'sanitation' or 'public health' flowed into the new environmentalism and gave it political impetus. It was another sign of the times when cigarette advertising was banned on the radio in 1971 in the United States.[44] The old anti-smoke campaigns had never got round to the idea of targeting tobacco smoke as well. From now on, the most effective environmental alarms typically concerned pollutants that were a danger to health.

At the same time, however, environmental initiatives directed their fire against the kind of urban redevelopment that was a legacy of the old hygiene movement. Such initiatives find no place in a purely ecological view of the environmental movement, but in reality protests against the destruction of established urban structures were often central to it. There is no counterpart in the German literature to Rachel Carson's *Silent Spring*; if one were to look for a comparable turning point, it would probably have to be a polemical work such as Alexander Mitscherlich's *Unwirtlichkeit unserer Städte* (1965) [The Inhospitableness of Our Cities]. Horror at the unbearable situation brought about by the motor car is one of the key environmental themes in the media in the 1960s, and not only in West Germany. Yet it was still possible then to think of a solution in terms of more express routes. The title story of *Der Spiegel* 35 (1969), 'Wucher mit dem Quadratmeter' (that is, 'profiteering from the square metre'), suggested that the legal scope for compulsory purchase orders should be increased to allow for an expansion of the autobahn system. Two years later, the title of issue 27 (1971), 'Massentod auf Deutschlands Straßen' [Mass Death on Germany's Roads], with a coffin blazoned across the cover, gave a clear new message: an end to the speed madness!

Origins in fear and disasters?

In later years, one often heard it said that the new environmental awareness originated in fear, traumas or – as critics put it – hysteria. Today we have grown used to news items about damage to the environment, but when such reports were still new the horror of them caused many a shudder. Perhaps the most striking chronological aspect, however, is that no disaster can be identified in any way as the chief impetus for the new 'environmental boom'. Concentration on one disaster had fixed people's minds on a single threat, but the ecological revolution arose out of a conceptual association of various risks. Senator Gaylord Nelson supposedly got the idea for Earth Day after an oil slick appeared off Santa Barbara, Los Angeles,[45] but that disaster, caused by Union Oil Company drilling operations, was soon forgotten and did not enter into the collective memory of the eco-scene.[46] In England, pictures of dying birds off the coast of Cornwall following the *Torrey Canyon* shipwreck produced public outrage for a while, but it too did not stay in the memory elsewhere, despite the fact that oil supertankers owned by dubious companies and flying dubious flags were a perfect target for attack. The fact is that London's 'killer smog' of December 1952, which caused thousands of deaths, far exceeded all the environmental scandals that were fresh in people's minds in 1970. The 'ecological revolution' of that year rested upon at least a half-dozen concerns: the nuclear risk, the rubbish crisis, water and air pollution, overpopulation and species loss. To combine these into one was mainly the work of the intellect.

The initial impetus for Sweden to call the first international conference on the environment was a number of signs that British industrial emissions were causing the acid rain that damaged its forests.[47] However, there was no full-scale alarm at the time:[48] one erupted in Germany only ten years later, amid fears about 'dying forests'. At the Stockholm Conference, Sweden did not manage to foreground the 'acid rain' issue; the scientific evidence was incidental and made no impact.[49] In general, it may be seen as a paradox that the environmental *prise de conscience* occurred at the very time when smoky factory chimneys were disappearing from the advanced industrial countries and environmental damage was less glaring than ten or twenty years earlier. As for radioactivity, which aroused the strongest protests in Germany and other countries, it was not perceptible to any sense organ. There is much to be said for Jeremy Rifkin's view that the environmental breakthrough should be included among the great enlightenments of world history, rather than the great fears. But this does not mean that environmental awareness did not unleash a 'dialectic of enlightenment' as soon as it was combined with political power.[50]

Gordon Rattray Taylor's *Doomsday Book: Can the World Survive?*, which hit the bookshops at just the right time, soon became an international bestseller, but the author, best known for his previous *Sex in History*, was not to be taken all that seriously as a prophet of doom. Jost Hermand prefers to think of the Club of Rome's 'doomsday shock of 1972' as the real big bang.[51] But this is refuted by the sequence of events, since the environmental boom began considerably earlier and provided the background for the huge success of *Limits to Growth*. Two decades before, most of the world's inhabitants would have thought it a banal truth that there were limits to growth. Menke-Glückert – who, like Günter Hartkopf, the state secretary responsible in Bonn since 1969 for environmental issues, banked more on optimism than pessimism – considered *Limits to Growth* to be poorly founded and to some extent even counterproductive and debilitating; the Club of Rome was an 'elite club of would-be statesmen', which wanted to impose its pessimistic view of things on humanity.[52] Barry Commoner, for his part, described *Limits to Growth* as 'a step back', drawing fire from Paul R. Ehrlich for his alleged lack of ecological competence.[53] The Club of Rome study immediately unleashed a boisterous debate among elite intellectuals:[54] it was highly stimulating, but most unlikely to traumatize whole masses of people. Besides, in the new environmental awareness, the concern over limits to growth overlapped with an opposite fear that unchecked growth would produce unintended negative consequences for the quality of life. Had the prediction of impending limits to growth been reliable, there would have been far fewer fears for the environment.

Significantly, and in contradiction to the magazine's usual emphasis on pictorial clarity, the cover of *Der Spiegel*'s first lead issue on the environment – 5 October 1970 – was divided into four images: clouds of red smoke, mountains of rubbish, a dried lake with driftwood, and a child's doll together with exhaust gases in a traffic jam. Nor was there agreement on which was the current priority. The headline of the title story, 'Man Is Destroying the Earth', referred to chemical wastewater, but then followed such a jumble of facts that one wonders how it did not strike the editors long before publication. Again, no particular disaster had triggered a chain reaction of fears. At most in Japan – where industrial policy had previously shown exemplary disregard for local populations – four major pollution scandals ushered in the eco-age.[55] Margaret A. McKean, who had first-hand experience of the country and wrote the most detailed Western study of that early period, began with the terse observation: 'Japan was literally the most polluted nation on earth', but after the first decade of the eco-age it 'now has the strictest pollution standards in the world'.[56] There too, however, a simple stimulus-reaction schema has only limited explanatory power; for the mercury poisoning at Minamata Bay had been known to people in the region since 1956. Only in the eco-age did environmental disasters become public scandals instead of being hushed up – and force politicians to do something about them.[57]

Buried in the regional press in West Germany and regarded by most intellectuals there as rather parochial,[58] nuclear dangers were already an issue in the American 'ecological revolution' of 1970. The leading critics in the USA were experts with inside knowledge, who had broken away from the nuclear establishment: a type then very thin on the ground in Germany. Since the second half of the 1960s, even the inner circle of the Advisory Committee on Reactor Safeguards (ACRS) had been leaking more and more information about the possibility of reactor accidents that could not be controlled with the procedures then in place and would require the evacuation of whole regions.[59] This led to the unofficial rule that nuclear power stations should be built only in lightly populated areas,[60] whereas in West Germany new ones were still being planned for the Frankfurt[61] and Mannheim-Ludwigshafen regions.[62]

Alvin M. Weinberg, a demigod of US nuclear research and long-time director of the Oak Ridge research centre, said at Christmas 1971 in a talk in Philadelphia to the American Association for the Advancement of Science: 'We nuclear people have made a Faustian bargain with society.'[63] For those who know Goethe's play, this sounds eerily cryptic. Spontaneously one identifies the nuclear researcher with Faust, but is he not here really the devil? Anyway, it is clear that criticisms have to base themselves mainly on hypothetical risks, not on real accidents. The late consequences of Britain's Windscale reactor accident of 8 October 1957 were unknown at the time to the public, as were the most unsettling aspects of the accident of 5 October 1966 in the 'Enrico Fermi' breeder reactor, thirty miles from Detroit (which were finally revealed in 1975 in the exposé *We Almost Lost Detroit*, based on ostensible statements by one of the engineers involved).[64] Compared with the battle scenes that later accompanied German nuclear policy, the 'controversy' in the United States took fairly 'civil' forms.

In sum, the formative period of the eco-age was defined much more by the intellect than by pure emotion;[65] the leading role of scientists was enough to guarantee this. Or were they too driven by hidden fears? On the day before Earth Day, Barry Commoner declared to students at Harvard: 'You are the first generation in the history of man to carry strontium-90 in your bones and DDT in your fat; your bodies will record in time the full effects of environmental destruction on mankind.'[66] At a DDT hearing in

Washington, it was claimed that a cannibal chief had forbidden his fellow-tribesmen to eat Americans because they contained too much DDT.[67] There is some evidence that fear of cancer – which took over from the old fear of infectious diseases – was a subterranean impulse behind the new environmental awareness and the common denominator in a variety of phobias, especially of radiation.[68] Cancer became a metaphor for environmental dangers: 'growth as an end in itself is the ideology of the cancer cell'. 'Was it fear of cancer, that great standby of all environmental demagogues, that stirred our worries about the Earth?', asked James Lovelock – with noticeable irony, because he considered nuclear energy unavoidable.[69] Since cancer breeds such panic that many prefer not to speak of it – Rachel Carson too was publicly silent about her own affliction with the disease – we often need to read between the lines; that makes any definite proof difficult. Cancer had not been an issue in the old smoke debate, but from the 1950s the evidence began to pile up that air pollution increased the risk of cancer.[70] Industrial emissions progressed from a municipal to a national theme. In the 1960s, suspicions grew about the carcinogenic effects of car exhaust gases. Kenneth Hahn, a member of the Los Angeles Board of Supervisors, wrote on 16 February 1970 to the attorney general that there was reason to believe in a conspiracy by the car and petroleum industries to block the production of cars and fuels without harmful exhaust gases.[71] The EPA tried to make its mark in the war on cancer, though with little success; it lacked the necessary competence.[72]

Was the ecocide in Vietnam the origin?

It has been argued that a major anthropogenic environmental disaster did after all trigger the 'ecological revolution' in 1970: namely, the biological warfare conducted by the US Air Force in Vietnam, when more than forty million litres of aircraft-sprayed Agent Orange (plus other herbicides) defoliated large areas of forest.[73] Arthur Galston, professor of plant biology at Yale, coined the term 'ecocide' for this (by analogy with 'genocide') and called for a tribunal similar to that which tried the Nazi war criminals.[74] In Vietnam, the nightmare conjured up a few years before in *Silent Spring* became reality: Vietnamese estimates suggest that as many as a million people suffered its consequences over three generations, and it has since been shown that thousands of American soldiers were also affected. In 1970, no other acute eco-disaster anywhere in the world remotely compared in scale or obscenity to the ecocide in Vietnam.

Carl Amery thinks it obvious that the American student revolt got from Agent Orange the 'decisive adrenalin surge' that made it the engine of the new environmentalism.[75] Yet it is rather surprising that, after all that has since come to light, Vietnam played quite a marginal role in the ecological upsurge of the time. It does not feature at all in David Brower's extensive memoirs, which instead celebrate President Johnson's signing of the

Wilderness Act on 3 September 1964 as one of the greatest successes of his life.[76] The environmental movement was *not* a direct continuation of the movement against the Vietnam War, but rather corresponded to the wide-spread search for consensus: a major new purpose across a divided society. The ecocide theme would have thrown it back to the old scenario of strug-gle, while the theme of war would have distracted it from the newly recog-nized primary issue of the time, the *unintended* consequences of peaceful progress. Anyway, in 1970 President Nixon undertook to respect the Geneva Protocol of 1925 on biological weapons, which the United States had not signed at the time. When dioxin – the toxin contained in Agent Orange – was discovered ten years later in waste on Love Canal, Niagara Falls, it became a cause célèbre for the environmental movement, although that scandal was minute in comparison with the ecocide in Vietnam. Only afterwards did Ralph Nader sound the alarm: 'Three ounces of dioxin could kill more than a million people.'[77]

Vietnam activists headed by Barry Commoner were among the initiators of Earth Day on 22 April 1970,[78] but slogans denouncing ecocide did not dominate the scene, and many supporters of the New Left took part with mixed feelings.[79] Commoner himself complained about the 'confusion of Earth Week' (note how the Day has become a Week!): 'Earth Week mir-rored personal convictions more than objective knowledge.'[80] In the US media, however, Earth Day was celebrated as a world-historic event. In the words of one contemporary observer: 'Not since the Japanese attack on Pearl Harbor has any public issue received such massive support in all the news media, local as well as national.'[81] A conservative anti-ecological Fronde had not yet taken shape; Earth Day was mainly a pageant dis-playing what the nation held in common, not an arena for big battles. According to a journalist, the day went off in a 'surprisingly lighthearted' manner, even if demonstrators carried dead fish across Fifth Avenue to highlight the pollution of the Hudson. The next day, the *New York Times* wrote of the campaign: 'Conservatives were for it. Liberals were for it. Democrats, Republicans and Independents were for it. So were the ins, the outs, the executive and legislative branches of Government.'[82]

In its euphoria of unity through enlightenment, which for a bliss-ful moment covered over differences,[83] Earth Day reminds one of the Woodstock Festival and its 'flower children' eight months earlier. In his lecture of 1966 on the 'historical roots of our ecological crisis' (which became the founding text of environmental history[84]), the medievalist Lynn White had placed the Beatnik precursors of the hippies on a par with Francis of Assisi, as pioneers of the reconciliation between man and nature; the hippy scene returned this historian's compliment.[85] The 700-page encyclopaedia of hippy culture, which teems with keywords on the 'environmental movement', describes it as 'evolved from the hippie *back-to-the-earth* movement'.[86] There would seem to be a link between the atmospheres in the two. It has scarcely ever been investigated and is not easy to demonstrate empirically,[87] yet it is plausible both logically and psychologically. For the natural environment can best be preserved if human beings rediscover that love and the enjoyment of nature afford greater joy than the endless pursuit of money and consumer goods. In 1970, when Elisabeth Mann-Borgese (1918–2002), the youngest daughter of Thomas Mann and a famed 'sea woman', presented proposals for marine protection laws at a Pacem in Maribus conference in Malta, she first asked the participants to sing together 'We all live on a yellow submarine': a Woodstock atmosphere among the elite of sea law experts!

Notwithstanding hippy touches, one often found oneself in remarkably serious company at the Earth Day festivities. The Natural Resources Defense Council (NRDC) – one of the new environmental NGOs that did effective lobbying in Washington – was founded in 1970, with financial support from the Ford Foundation, by students at Yale Law School and campaigners against the planned hydroelectric power station on the Hudson;[88] in general, graduates from Yale Law School, one of the finest in the country, were to be found with striking frequency in the new ecological upsurge.[89] Denis Hayes, the organizer of Earth Day, came from there; and Charles A. Reich, whose bestseller *The Greening of America* appeared in 1970, taught there. More than in other countries, professionalism was an early characteristic of the environmental movement; a historical narrative moving 'from spontaneous initiative to professional organization', perhaps suggested by the German experience, would not fit what happened in the United States. The two were colourfully intertwined from the start. Reich thought he could glimpse at Woodstock the first light of the coming 'revolution', the rebellion of a newly conscious youth against the sclerotic corporate state; and he took as his motto for *The Greening of America* Woody Guthrie's 'This Land Is Your Land' and The Youngbloods' 'Get Together' (which, according to *Rolling Stone* magazine, was the 'informal anthem of the late sixties').[90] German protesters at the Gorleben nuclear waste storage facility still kept themselves warm in the spring air of 1979 by dancing to 'This Land Is Your Land'.[91] In the United States, however, environmentalism also had a decidedly conservative element from very early on. One of its most influential programmatic texts was *The Tragedy of the Commons*, Garrett Hardin's essay of 1968.

In the United States a new elite formed around environmental issues, self-assertive and well informed, with a broad horizon even at regional level. To be sure, its position within the scientific establishment was often still insecure; the 'ecology' it invoked was not necessarily the same as the hitherto non-political, parochial discipline that went by the same name,[92] just as many of its warnings about dangers to the earth's ecosystem lacked an exact scientific basis. But if we compare it with earlier large movements, it immediately becomes clear that *information* – whether obtained through science or from travel – had never before been so central to a movement. For the historian Samuel Hays, 'the politics of science' sums up the new environmental politics that began in 1970.[93] To the drumbeat of *Limits to Growth*, whose data had the technological support of MIT behind them, a belief in the computer – if not the computer itself – made history for the time, although the simplest mathematical logic could have made it clear that permanent growth was an absurdity.[94] A close link between conservation and popular science had existed ever since the natural history associations of the nineteenth century,[95] and the more specialized and incomprehensible science was to lay people, the more did popularization (once the province of distinguished experts) become a special kind of conventional media form. It is not least at this level that the environmental movement has its place in the sociology of science.

Woodstock was an end, Earth Day a beginning. The latter was not a sub-cultural happening but an event that united subculture and high culture as well as people on both sides of the bitter argument over the Vietnam War. But this festival of unity was not the end of history – more like a beginning, although once again a first disillusionment would soon follow. A protest potential and countercultural element remained inside the environmental movement, in the United States as elsewhere, and it found a new lease of life as soon as a front formed against it. One of its quickest and most spectacular successes, however, came in 1970 when it converged with those arguing in terms of economic rationality to oppose the Supersonic Transport (SST) Project jointly promoted by the government and industry; it had anyway been clear for a long time to many economic analysts that, apart from infuriating people in their flight path, the planned aircraft had no prospect of making a profit. Eventually even Boeing, the main contractor, lost interest. What sounded to the public like a victory for ecology – since activists had been targeting the sonic boom as an eco-scandal – was really at least as much a victory for economics. Given the crisis of space travel, even NASA distanced itself from the SST Project (which it had previously gone along with) and tried to prove its own ecological credentials by disclosing the dangers of supersonic flight to the ozone layer.[96] Convergences with economic and research apparatuses, whether open or hidden, have remained to this day a precondition for the success of the environmental movement, not least with the advent of the electronic revolution.

1968 and 1970

There has been surprisingly little study of environmental initiatives in their ambiguous and multifaceted relationship with the student revolt and sixties subculture. Especially in its style of action, though not consistently or everywhere, the environmental movement succeeded to the legacy of '68, with its sit-ins, teach-ins, happenings, demonstrations, occupations of squares and clashes with the police. Earth Day was itself a teach-in: one of unprecedented dimensions. There were numerous personal continuities between the movements of the sixties and seventies: Daniel Cohn-Bendit and Rudi Dutschke, the French and German student leaders, found their way to the Greens.

This does not necessarily mean that there was an ideological continuity. True, a rejection of the technological form of progress and consumer society was already one of the leitmotifs of 1968,[97] while in many cases the environmental movement had anti-capitalist features precisely in its founding period; not infrequently one has the impression that its rhetoric replaced the exploited proletariat with exploited nature. In those days, little was known about the horrific damage to the environment in the Communist countries. Nor was there much concern about it: the subject would only have been a distraction. Even such a comparatively independent thinker as Hans-Magnus Enzensberger, whose radical socialism got its first cold shower in Cuba, wrote in 1973 in his *Kursbuch*, the seismograph of the New Left: 'Chinese society certainly offers the best chances for the ecological survival of human beings. A thrifty handling of natural resources is an essential component of Chinese culture.' The Chinese government, he argued, was 'the only one in the world' to have developed 'consistent strategies to ward off catastrophe'.[98] And yet nature was something very different from the proletariat; that was impossible to overlook as one went deeper into environmental questions. One of Dutschke's mentors had been Ernst Bloch, whose enthusiasm for the 'peaceful atom' went even further than that of the Western nuclear lobby. As late as 1977, Dutschke sighed in a notebook entry that the 'mass mobilization' against nuclear power stations was causing him 'theoretical and political difficulties', so that he preferred to read the adventure novels of Karl May to his children.[99] He and many other '68ers arrived at the new consciousness of nature only after a series of political disappointments and existential crises; nature had not been the issue in '68. Environmental activists would have happily poured water into the petrol tank of Willibald – the traditional working-class excavator operator celebrated in a famous children's song by Dieter Süverkrup (1970).

Fusion with parts of the '68 scene was a secondary issue precisely for the West German environmental movement, where it was posed mainly by the anti-nuclear movement and the targets it offered for '68-style action and anti-capitalist positions. In Denmark – where things were otherwise less turbulent – the environmentalist protests began as early as March 1969 with a happening that carried drama to a sickening extreme, putting most German happenings in the shade. At a conference in Copenhagen University, which included prominent figures from the respectable natural history society NOA, a student group entered the auditorium and locked the doors. One of them reported:

> We locked them all in. We were about twenty people. After we had locked the doors, we cut off the ventilation and started to poison them. It was pretty violent. We got up on the stage and talked about air pollution. We burnt garbage and tobacco in large quantities. We poured waste water from a nearby factory in an aquarium with goldfish who slowly died. On the side walls we showed films about cancer

and pollution and we had a loudspeaker with a traffic alarm blasting. We sprayed water in the audience from Endrup lake. And we had taken along a wild duck which we covered with oil. 'Come and save it', we screamed. 'You talk about pollution. Why don't you do anything about it?' Finally we cut off its head to end its suffering, and we walked down along the first row of chairs so that all who were sitting there got blood on their clothes. After one hour we opened the doors and said that we wanted to start an environmental movement, and that the founding meeting was being held in the next room.

Such was the launch of NOAH.[100]

This happening – which enraged animal lovers – was a one-off in the 'ecological revolution' that took place in and around 1970. Anyway, it did not unleash chaos but was the prelude to the creation of a new organization. That was the difference from German happenings in the same period. NOAH presented itself as a movement that finally took the goals of the old NOA seriously, and it joined forces with Friends of the Earth, which was founded in the same year.

The 'population bomb'

A common denominator in the emergent environmental movement, both in the United States and elsewhere, was horror at the unchecked growth of the world population. Even more than the atom bomb, it was this analogously named 'population bomb' – the title of Paul R. Ehrlich's best-seller of 1968 – which unsettled many environmentalists. While Alvin M. Weinberg, the intellectual supremo of the nuclear community, tried to use population growth as an argument for breeder reactors that would provide endless energy,[101] the nuclear dissidents John W. Gofman and Arthur R. Tamplin, who worked at the renowned Lawrence Laboratory, alluded in the sarcastic title of their book to the population bomb rather than the atom bomb: *'Population Control' through Nuclear Pollution* (1970). Even before the uproar surrounding *Limits to Growth*, the demographic limits imposed by natural resources but scorned by human blindness provided the foundation for modern environmental consciousness. The logic of Garrett Hardin's *The Tragedy of the Commons*, first published in 1968, also implied that population growth was the core of all environmental problems.[102] As we have seen, it was already an old theme for defenders of the (mainly African) wilderness, and in the 1960s the 'population explosion' in India and resulting famines were hitting the headlines.[103] Ehrlich referred not only to statistics but also to his own experience: in 1966, riding a taxi on a 'stinking hot night in Delhi', he was suddenly overcome by the 'hellish' sense that he was drowning in a human tide;[104] in the 1970s, he predicted, 'hundreds of millions' would be starving.[105] As for Barry Commoner, he never received as many critical missives at any other time as he did when, though not contesting that demographic pressure would exacerbate the critical situation in parts of the third world, he doubted the idea that population growth was currently a primary ecological problem.[106]

Yet another event that fell in the watershed year of 1970 was the awarding of the Nobel Peace Prize to Norman E. Borlaug for his work in cultivating types of grains. He was hailed as the 'father of the Green Revolution' – when 'Green' was more ambiguous than it would be a decade later. Claiming that without DDT his successes 'would have been impossible', Borlaug fulminated that the world was condemned to starve to death if a 'powerful and hysterical interest group' managed to obtain the banning of chemical fertilizer by means of 'senseless laws';[107] the volume was just as loud as in the attacks of the chemical industry on Rachel Carson. New grain types had apparently improved India's food situation in the 1970s, to a degree that no one could have foreseen in the previous decade. Paul Ehrlich, in particular, came in for a lot of jibes. Yet in 1996, in an angry riposte to his critics, he could point with some justice to what was already known in principle at the Stockholm conference in 1972:[108] that the 'Green Revolution', with its high use of water and herbicides in a situation of continued population growth, would exacerbate the long-term environmental crisis. And in arguing this, Ehrlich could appeal to Borlaug himself.[109]

Ehrlich's main point was that, in large parts of the world, the Green Revolution promoted the decline of traditional small farmers and the loss of agricultural knowledge based on long experience – a process which probably has its greatest reach amid all the transformations of recent times. So, population increase has led to the explosive growth of slums. Whereas in 1968 it had still been possible to dismiss criticism of India's unrestricted population growth as Western arrogance, by the 1990s strict birth control had long been official government policy.

A standard reproach against the 'population bomb' rhetoric is that it distracts attention from the guilt of the first world[110] and suggests that development aid is pointless and harmful. But none other than Nehru was a declared supporter of 'family planning' from the early fifties on,[111] while even Gunnar Myrdal, an advocate of development aid and pioneer of the Scandinavian welfare state, could say in 1972 at the Stockholm Conference that 'in a sense' population growth was 'the key factor in the environmental problem'.[112] Barbara Ward and René Dubos speak in *Only One Earth* of the population explosion, without inverted commas.[113] In the Bundesrepublik, Georg Picht, then a pioneering reformer, took a firm position in *Mut zur Utopie* [Courage for Utopia] (1970) in favour of immediate and 'systematic birth control';[114] only much later did the Greens denounce the 'falsehood' of a causal connection between environmental destruction and overpopulation.[115]

In and of itself, the 'population bomb' did not offer a suitable target for a movement to attack, yet in 1970 a women's action group called Zero Population Growth began to operate in the United States, not without some tension with feminists.[116] Even parts of the Peace and Love scene, enjoying new freedoms thanks to the pill, could see some attraction in propaganda for contraception, since it involved a counterpower to the conservative establishment.[117] At the time, American Indians had considerable kudos in the eco-scene, and there were precedents (albeit not exactly attractive ones) for the deliberate lowering of birth-rates. Among the Cheyenne, famous from John Ford's last Westerns, a man of character would swear at the birth of his first son not to have any more children for seven or even fourteen years.[118] It is true that massive coercion was legitimate in Ehrlich's 'population bomb' model. But it was just then that a sudden drop in birth-rates due to the pill began to manifest itself in the West, so that it was possible to imagine that love, nothing but love, would replace coercion in the not too distant future.

Konrad Lorenz, the best-known behavioural scientist of his time – whose *Civilized Man's Eight Deadly Sins* (1971) became a key environmental text in the German-speaking world, and who passionately supported the Austrian protest movement[119] – called overpopulation the first deadly sin. Nor were his reasons only ecological: 'warm, heartfelt human love' would die out if people lived too closely packed alongside one another and everyone did not have some space of their own.[120] In 1973 Lorenz received the Nobel Prize for Medicine and Physiology.

But what could environmentalists do to affect trends in the third world? Crucially, there seemed to be no practical tasks in relation to the 'population explosion' of which they complained; it was therefore not much good as the common denominator for a movement. In the Western world, there was more reason to worry about declining birth-rates than about population growth. To be sure, the new environmental awareness did not correspond in general to any demographic discourse. This is indeed the point: the 'ecological revolution' of 1970 cannot be explained by one particular causality – the result of a recent environmental disaster, specific discourses or the interests of distinct social groups. Definite causes may be apparent in relation to temporally and spatially limited histories, but they begin to fray as soon as the horizon widens a little. Even Edda Müller, who emphasizes the priority of politics in West Germany, cannot help thinking that the Bonn inventors of environmental politics were not yet aware of 'the scope, and later explosiveness, of the issue'; she even suspects that it 'always remained unclear' what was likely to provide the decisive impetus.[121] A study of the parallel emergence of environmental activism in France finds itself with nothing but 'unanswered questions' about its origins.[122] Even Commoner asserted in 1971: 'Despite the constant reference to palpable, everyday life experiences – foul air, polluted water and rubbish heaps – there is an air of unreality about the environmental crisis.'[123]

What does the vain search for a sufficient cause demonstrate?

In his famous study *Suicide* (1897), a founding work of sociology, Émile Durkheim operated *per exclusionem*: that is, he successively ruled out one cause after another for the frequency of suicide in certain countries and places, before arriving at the real point: the cause is 'society', or, more precisely, social anomie. Similarly, one might be tempted to seek the ultimate reason for the puzzling genesis of modern environmental consciousness in the emergence of *global society*. Does today's talk of globalization not have its main root in sixties rhetoric about 'Spaceship Earth' and our threatened 'blue planet'? We need to be careful, though. Up to now 'global society' has been an airy structure whose real existence is uncertain. The same is true of 'postmaterialist society' – a concept that used to be thought of as having explanatory value. Since 1970 the greed for resource-guzzling consumption has by no means died away; pessimists even think that it has never been greater. We should not forget that, even in criminal cases, the search for a culprit *per exclusionem* can be deceptive. One never knows whether every possibility has been eliminated.

Durkheim wanted to say that conventional historical-causal explanations are naïve, and that one must think rather in terms of social systems and their interrelations. The ecological revolution of 1970 offers a prime example of this. Yet precisely here we should not dismiss as naïve the possibility that the ultimate cause lies in environmental problems themselves, and that there is after all something like a logic of history (not in particular problems, though, but in their connection by the intellect). The environmental movement is a diffuse phenomenon, but the problems also present themselves diffusely, and over forty years ago they were still far harder to grasp than they are today. It could be that this very fact was mirrored in the environmental movement.

For it became blatantly obvious that a massive new problem-complex had opened up behind all individual problems. It had already appeared in the wake of the first great industrialization boom in the late nineteenth century, but then the war came along and distorted our view of it. The end of the era of world wars, then the crumbling of the Cold War fronts, freed our view of common problems facing humanity, after decades of historically unprecedented growth both demographic and economic, as well as growth of atmospheric emissions and fossil fuel burning. Christian Pfister's 'fifties syndrome' has much to be said for it: that is, the thesis that the 1950s brought novel dimensions of anthropogenic environmental change, beside which everything before it seems ancient.[124]

Another point is also important here. Environmental protection became a task *sui generis* at a time when the secure elements in man's relationship with the environment were fast disappearing. For most of human history, the law of inertia had been a guarantee against truly insatiable using up of the environment; without modern technology it had been such an exhausting effort to cut down whole forests, to extract coal from deep underground and fish from the oceans. Even in the railway age, large parts of the world remained undeveloped and immeasurable natural resources went untouched. But all this has changed dramatically since the middle of the twentieth century. The law of inertia keeled over, as it were, so that the pillage of nature would have had no bounds if things had simply been allowed to go on.

Or think of the technological revolution that since the 1950s has dwarfed all previous changes in agriculture! Previously it had been in the farmers' own interest, at least in the Old World, to keep their ecosystem intact – which meant a degree of diversification, a correct combination of land cultivation and livestock farming, and careful attention to the recycling of animal waste, humus levels and the hedges that protect the soil and provide nests for birds that eat harmful insects. A large part of this ecological stability built into agriculture was lost as a result of chemical fertilizer, pesticides and animal factories. And whereas techno-optimists a generation earlier had still expected that sewage farms, recycling and sundry chemical inventions would more or less automatically solve the waste problem, this whole range of hopes proved to be a complete illusion. Indeed, after the end of the immediate postwar period, the refuse problem increased exponentially and took on a new dimension with the spread of non-recyclable plastic waste. However meticulous the search for causal links in the 'ecological revolution', one always comes to the heart of the matter itself – to the huge knot of problems it addressed.

As soon as the environmental movement crossed a threshold of political power and got down to action, it had to set priorities amid the confusion and to aim for certain solutions. Since, in 'networked thinking', everything is linked to everything else, far-sighted ecologists saw that there was always something unsatisfactory and provisional in such decisions; this inner tension continues to define environmental protection today, consciously or unconsciously. And with the decisions began the conflicts. The rash of American laws enacted from 1970 on not only set upper limits to the acceptable pressure on the environment, but also prescribed certain technical approaches: car exhaust systems with catalytic converters, filters for wastewater pipes, cleaning devices for power station emissions. The Americans were often superior to Europeans in this practical sense for the concrete and technical, but the harmony of Earth Day soon vanished and the clashes began between industry and environmental agencies.[125] On the other hand, American activists – unlike their counterparts in Europe – were well provided with legal experts, who found an inexhaustible field for activity in the new legislation. Once this was up and running, the work of perfecting it could scarcely be halted – even under the Reagan administration.[126]

Beginning in 1970, the new 'environmental politics' took a previously heterogeneous batch of efforts, each with its own history, and made of them one large entity with a tendency to become global. But this unification was inevitably won at the price of inner tensions that still give the eco-age its inherent drama: partly open, partly latent. René Dubos, the main inspiration behind the Stockholm Conference of 1972, took up David Brower's watchword: 'Think globally, act locally!'[127] It was an obvious paradox, which sounded good when the thinking and the acting first began – but, as in the Progressive Era and the age of the New Deal, there was no question of a pre-established harmony between the grass-roots movements and top-level conceptions of planning. The most tangible result of Stockholm was the establishment of the UNEP in Nairobi, the first major UN agency to be located in a third world country, but it became an apparatus without teeth that wags later derided as a 'junk store',[128] and which clashed with the decision-making and responsibilities of more established UN organizations, the FAO and the World Health Organization (WHO).[129] A tension between the impetus towards central planning and local autonomy still runs through environmental protection in many parts of the world. The term 'environmental protection' itself has the old dualism of 'conservation' and 'public health', often only externally joined to each other; the two lived off different passions and operated with different human types, and this contrast keeps showing through. For centuries, to be drawn to nature partly reflected a love of humanity, but partly also a horror of human beings en masse; it is an ambiguity that still clings to the love of nature. Tensions that were still latent until 1970 have burst into the open and contributed to a situation where there is no longer only mainstream environmentalism but a multiplicity of different histories. Once empowered, the ecological enlightenment is subject to the dialectic of enlightenment.

Chapter Three

Networked Thinking and Practical Priorities: An Endless Interplay

In 1970, accustomed by his research at NASA to a global view, James Lovelock suddenly had the thought that the whole earth, including its inorganic part, should be conceived as a great creature in which everything was vitally linked to everything else. This 'Gaia' theory was a hypothesis – or better: a vision, which remains difficult to test empirically. It did not give humans much opportunity for action; they would have needed the Good Lord for that. For if everything is linked to everything else, moreover in a global dimension, where can man begin if there are disturbing signs that Gaia is ill? Lovelock disapproves of the way in which many environmental activists have targeted nuclear technology – as if the risks it presents were germane to the life of Gaia. Yet he too has his hobby horse, his clearly defined priority, and that is the English hedge landscape of his childhood. Hedges protect the soil; birds nest in them. So he finds it unforgivable that anti-nuclear demonstrators have forgotten the struggle against land consolidation and agricultural mechanization.

Is that applied Gaia theory? Of course, the protection of hedges can be justified ecologically – but its prioritization, as Lovelock candidly admits, owes more to his youthful love and sense of beauty than to ecology.[1] The way in which priorities come about is one of the most exciting questions in the history of environmentalism. Spontaneously, human beings do not react to all risks but only to some; and their selection is not always a matter of rational choice. It ought to become rational in the environmental movement. But what is rational is not so clear-cut. It might be asked why there were not many more passionate debates about these questions – to which one answer is that it is often very difficult to discuss priorities rationally. Environmentalism has had to live with this dilemma up to the present day. It is astonishing that it has been able to do so.

Towards the end of his *Collapse*, Jared Diamond writes: 'People often ask, "What is the single most important environmental population problem in the world today?" A flip answer would be: "the single most important problem is our misguided focus on identifying the single most important problem".'[2] But this way of dressing down the questioner is not fair. Someone lost in contemplating the interconnectedness of nature or overawed by the coming apocalypse can speak like that, but someone who wants to get something moving – in the belief that it may be possible at least to postpone the apocalypse – is right to pose the question. Everyone knows from their daily experience that if you try to do everything at once you don't get anything done. This simple fact creates a permanent tension, which has kept environmentalism moving from its beginnings up to today and is unlikely ever to find a definitive resolution. Ecology as such does not give rise to a clear concrete imperative, although one repeatedly has the impression that it does.

Daniel J. Fiorino, who, more than many other authors, has written on American environmental policy from the actors' viewpoint and on the basis of insider knowledge, is emphatic: 'The challenge in environmental policy is the classic political and administrative need to set priorities. . . . Environmental policy is replete with choices. How do we compare an ecological risk like the loss of a wetland with a health risk like the increased incidence of lung cancer near a chemical plant?'[3] The founders of West German environmental policy confirmed that the point was 'to set priorities', 'to differentiate the important from the unimportant'.[4] An activist might counter: why is it necessary to prioritize these risks? Why is there a contradiction between preserving the wetland and forcing the chemical plant to cease harmful emissions? Fiorino would reply that this was not thinking strategically, since in both cases (assuming the wetland is attractive for economic use) one would be dealing with powerful economic interests, and it would be unwise to fight on two fronts at the same time. All historical experience speaks in favour of concentrating one's forces at a single point; the more contentious the objective, the greater the validity of this principle. In 1989 Ernst Ulrich von Weizsäcker had the following requirement of 'ecological Realpolitik': 'We must abandon exaggerated and hysterical demands that blur our vision of priorities and make it more difficult to reach the broad basis of agreement on the drastic steps needed for the turn to earth politics.'[5] Those who want to discuss ad infinitum love the endless interactions opened up by ecology; those who prefer action, with a view to achieving something, may in some situations actually experience 'networked thinking' as a diversionary tactic! We are talking about a tension in environmentalism for which there can be no definitive solution.

Olson's paradox and environmental protection

It might be objected that environmental protection is more or less in the interests of all human beings. Even in the earliest days of the movement, there was talk of overcoming the traditional narrow focus on such goals as protecting particular birds in a particular marshland;[6] this became the butt of jokes in which some wanted to protect storks, while others wanted to protect frogs from storks. But love for particular plants or animals often expresses a special kind of militancy, whereas a non-specific love of nature has something diffuse. This brings us to Olson's paradox that resolute small groups, held together by a special common interest and continual face-to-face contact, are more able to assert themselves than a large anonymous collective with a very general interest. This is the great opportunity for lobbies and local single-issue campaigns – as well as the most delicate problem for environmental politics in the broadest sense of the term. Frank Uekötter expresses this in a paradoxical formula: 'The larger the group, the less the individual incentive to represent the interests of the group.'[7]

The aim of the environmental movements is to use Olson's paradox at first but to cheat it a little in the longer term. Were it a natural law with unlimited validity, any environmental politics worthy of the name would be doomed to failure. During the modern age, however, albeit to an extent that varies greatly from country to country, loyalties have developed beyond archaic clans. The opportunity for environmental politics depends essentially on this process – but also on people's readiness to fight to preserve their own immediate lifeworld. One-sided advocates of 'Think globally' have coined the deprecatory term NIMBY, 'Not in My Backyard', for local initiatives. But the environmental movement is unlikely to make progress towards really universalist thinking if it casts off any NIMBY themes. For reasons that have to do with human nature, a basic tension will remain. And contrary to what was long thought, especially in Germany, there is no collective instinct to preserve the species, only an individual urge to survive and reproduce, a selfish instinct towards 'sustainability'.[8] Robert Kennedy Jr, who headed the 'Riverkeeper' campaign against pollution of the Hudson, once even reported approvingly that his fellow-campaigners were changing the derogatory label 'NIMBY' into a term of honour![9]

'Everything Is Connected to Everything Else', but often in a very special way

In 1970 the tension between networked thinking and a practical need to set priorities was impressively embodied in the person of Barry Commoner. 'Everything Is Connected to Everything Else', like that with capital letters,[10] was his 'first law of ecology', all the more remarkable because he was really a born campaigner, who needed to have a clear objective. But, as a scientific ecologist, he was also aware that all priorities for environmental protection are specific in time and place. He was not happy with the course of Earth Day on 22 April 1970: he admitted to being surprised, and not pleasantly so, at the sudden public 'turbulence' over themes with which he and others like him had been grappling for years. 'What surprised me most', he wrote, 'were the numerous, confident explanations of the cause and cure of the crisis', which always expressed a presumptuous belief that one had discovered the single cause and cure.[11] He spent five pages sardonically reviewing the motley attributions of blame, including the overpopulation thesis of Paul Ehrlich and Garrett Hardin, which together reflected the many sides of modern environmental politics. But this diversity was not known to the individuals in question, and the obsession with holding the ultimate truth produced an involuntary splitting of the whole eco-scene. This too makes understandable Commoner's anger over Ehrlich's 'population bomb'. Commoner had no wish to deny that population growth may contribute to a growing burden on the environment, but he thought it misleading and practically unhelpful to regard it as the one big bomb. Realistically, he saw that people can effectively cripple environmental movements if, for all their verbal zeal, they remain focused on problems that divert attention from what needs to be done here and now.

Although Commoner rejected an exclusive concentration on one cause and cure, he did think that a limited number of risks should be given priority: (1) radioactive fallout from nuclear weapons tests; (2) car exhaust gases, reaching a scandalous level in the Los Angeles smog; (3) damage to the soil and groundwater from chemical fertilizers, especially nitrates; (4) the destruction of water ecosystems, with Lake Erie as the most glaring example; (5) harmful emissions from new industrial sectors; and (6) dangers to the earth's atmosphere, already mentioned occasionally in relation to the contentious issue of supersonic aircraft.[12] The 'wilderness' theme is not mentioned! Subsequently, he also concentrated – as did the German environmental movement – on problems of energy production;[13] he was discovering solar power as an alternative to nuclear energy.[14] This whole issue provided not only targets for attack but also a positive project, although the sun's potential and the optimum technological path to its use were as yet unclear.

The birth of priorities: a mysterious process

In what ways do priorities take shape? This is the big question, to which there is no general answer. Often clarification is possible only through the analysis of historical sources, since protest movements prefer to present their object as one whose importance goes without saying. As we have seen, the 'ecological revolution' of 1970 was not preceded by a major environmental disaster that automatically defined priorities. It may be suggested that the rational choice model helps to explain the decision-making process that leads to priorities. But what does 'rational' mean in this case? There is rationality at an abstract level – to make economic activity and lifestyles environmentally tolerable again – but not once this goal is translated into concrete tasks.

An institutional problem would seem to lie behind this deficiency. In the view of some ministry officials, a priority is 'essential' above all when the environmental problem at issue comes under their own competence or is suited to expand its responsibilities and raise its political profile. Thus, the nuclear power conflict was an irritant for environmental politicians in the Bonn interior ministry of the 1970s, because it gave them nothing to do: energy policy came under economics and technology, until 1986, after Chernobyl, when the newly founded environment ministry also acquired responsibility for reactor safety. Interior ministry officials, with Günter Hartkopf at their head, had wanted to create a policy lobby together with the civil movements,[15] but now what happened to them was like the experience of Goethe's 'Sorcerer's Apprentice': 'No longer can I rid myself / Of the spirits that I've summoned.' From the viewpoint of action groups, it is rational to concentrate on goals that offer the largest mobilization of support and funding. For scientists, it is rational to define the environmental priorities in such a way that they can utilize their own special skills. For media people, what counts most is the alarming and tangible aspect of the problems. Ideally, all these four players will work together, but such cooperation is usually not a smooth process resulting from the logic of the matter.

The problem of priorities is especially striking in German conservancy circles, where, as we have seen, it is said mockingly that NABU and BUND – the largest environmental NGOs – could not agree because the one had the protection of storks at heart, while the other wanted to protect frogs from storks. Since one species eats others in the animal world, there could easily be similar jokes about protectors of cormorants and fish, or raptors and songbirds. The *Spiegel* editor Jochen Bölsche, who is committed to conservationism, complained: 'Bird protectors and cat lovers are evidently incapable of grasping what their activities have in common.'[16] Well, ecology offers the common denominator. But the various activists could be grouped into one front only through the intellect, not through the emotions; mere love of a particular species made them blind.

The tenfold origin of the environmental movement

In the 'ecological revolution' of 1970, the new 'networked thinking' went together with the networking of several policy-making and administrative departments that already had histories of their own, and in many European countries a long statist tradition greater than in the United States.

1 The longest tradition in Germany and other Central and Western European countries is *forest conservation*: not in the American sense of preserving the wild, but in the sense of sustainable forestry and, in mountain regions, the designation of protected forest areas.

2 A sometimes longer, though far from always effective, tradition is *water conservation*: active maintenance of the domestic and industrial water supply and the purity of wells and open waters. In former times, the sheer availability and (since the nineteenth-century epidemics) cleanness of water were the main concern, together with the hygienic disposal of wastewater.

3 *Air pollution control* – or, more specifically, smoke abatement. This too began in the late nineteenth century, but for a long time it came far behind water hygiene, because fear of epidemics was not a factor – cancer worries came later – and the concept of air purity was both legally and technically harder to grasp than that of a clean water supply.

4 The *protection of animals*, especially birds, spread from England (also in the late nineteenth century) and became a popular and passionately committed movement mainly in Northwest Europe.

5 The *protection of nature*, in the sense of landscape conservation, which was first institutionalized in Prussia in 1906 and often (not only in Germany) associated with cultural heritage and bird protection, was a relative latecomer in comparison with most of the other fields of activity mentioned here.

6 *Labour protection*, provided with medical backup, also has a tradition going back to the nineteenth century: many environmental hazards were first demonstrated in the sphere of occupational medicine. The scientific basis of Rachel Carson's *Silent Spring* lay more in toxicology than in ecology.

7 *Consumer protection*, strongly allied with environmentalism (especially in the USA) since the 1970s, has also kept up with the times since the hygiene movement of the nineteenth century; concern over unclean or adulterated foodstuffs actually goes back to the pre-industrial age. Ralph Nader, who built up a whole staff around him and won great respect in the sixties for his attacks on poor car safety, later focused more on atmospheric pollutants, including radioactivity, and by 1970 was seen by many as one of the leaders (along with Brower and Commoner) of the environmental movement.[17]

8 *Natural healing*, involving faith in the curative powers of light, air, water and a 'natural' lifestyle, was probably one of the strongest forces driving the environmental movement. It first took off around 1900, from Germany to the United States. In the decades after 1970, 'alternative' therapies experienced a new boom, although, as Robert Jütte noted in 1996, 'so far the ecological movement has not found its way to a convincing position on matters of health'.[18]

9 Protests against *noise* reached a first peak in the 'nervous age' around 1900[19] and – as the campaign against aircraft noise shows – also lay at the origin of the 'ecological revolution' of 1970.[20] Later, though, the opposition to a new runway (Startbahn West) at Frankfurt airport followed the ecologically correct course of directing its main actions against large-scale deforestation.

10 Last but not least is *Heimatschutz* – the German term for the protection of village, urban and landscape heritage making up the *human habitat*. In parts of the third world, this may be said to include the struggle for traditional village rights to nearby woodland.

'Networked thinking' did not automatically integrate these older fields with one another; if they had developed an institutional life of their own, they usually preserved it after 1970. In fact, the major push to bring them together under the rubric of 'environmental protection' allowed rivalries to burst forth, as in the United States between wilderness supporters and advocates of sustainable forestry or in Germany between conservationists and environmentalists. As Anna Wöbse has noted, the focus on separate protection interests led to a 'division of the world' into one part to be saved and another (much larger) part that there was no hope of saving;[21] the new environmentalism thus involved an attempt to reunify the world – although it was still a long way from achieving it. In the eyes of many environmental politicians, conservation lawyers are still apolitical 'dicky-bird lovers', for whom environmental politicians are cold technocrats prepared to wave any wind park through for the sake of renewable energy. After 1970, many conservationists felt overwhelmed by the new environmentalists[22] – nor were they so wrong, from their own point of view. Often they could not keep up with the new style of politics and remained outside the newly emerging networks. Yet, in the Old World and the New, conservation was still the sunny side of environmentalism: reduced emission targets do not warm the cockles of the heart.

So long as these various bodies worked for themselves, there was no problem of priorities. Nor did one appear after 1970 if the previous routines were simply continued. It might even be argued in principle that the most sensible course was to deal with environmental issues within existing departments such as energy, transport or farming, instead of carving a special composite out of them.[23] What large-scale networking actually achieved should be critically assessed on a case-by-case basis. The sudden spread of the concept of the environment occurred at a time of major terminological expansion in political discourses, when it was eloquently claimed that fashionable disciplines such as cybernetics, systems theory and futurology were putting politics on a 'scientific' footing. 'Environment' too was in constant danger of becoming a mere part of this bubble.

Specification and potential enlargement of the concept

Like Hegel's world spirit,[24] the general term 'environment' needs to be repeatedly made more specific if it is to remain alive. One comparative study of the British and Indian news media concludes that 'global environmental issues' as such mean nothing to most Indians or even have overtones of mental colonialism; specific local issues to do with hygiene, health hazards, waste disposal and water management are what really arouse people.[25] Continual harping on a global, all-inclusive concept of the environment may actually be a barrier to global understanding. In parts of the third world it smacks so much of the first world that it would probably be better to speak of particular problems of the soil, so that people realize their own vital issues are at stake. In this respect, there is a significant analogy between problems of understanding between cultures and between generations. At a time when the early eco-scene was becoming the older generation, children at schools were heard saying that 'the environment' was a 'mega-out' – yet, despite predictions that they were becoming resigned, new generations have grown into environmentalism. It has always been possible to mobilize young people, especially on issues involving specific damage to the environment. The above-mentioned study, based on findings in the 1990s, even speaks of something common to Britain and India: 'It is not that people are not concerned with environmental issues at all; it is just that they do not have a high profile unless they have a detectable local impact.'[26]

Thus, the term 'environment' contains not only an expansive programme but also a permanent tension – and for that very reason an element of dynamism that keeps the environmental movement in motion. Alois Glück, a Bavarian environmental politician from the early years, recalls that 'from roughly 1976–77' environmental politics became 'a pretty exhausting business', once attempts were made to develop it 'in a holistic and ecological direction', instead of restricting it to the protection of certain animal species in danger of losing their habitat. In the end, however,, this networking effort was productive, so that environmental politics gained 'a new and quite distinctive political dynamism'.[27]

Robert Poujade, the first French environment minister, pointed out that the simple term 'environment', as it is now understood, has an 'imperialist' quality in that it legitimates ever more extensive intervention.[28] But he proved completely unable to exploit this imperial potential with his still tiny 'ministry of the impossible'; the lack of a clearly defined sphere of competence was a severe handicap at first. The multifaceted character of environmentalism still favours the natural inclination of state bureaucracies to spread responsibility. There is always a danger that many things will remain unconnected or even at odds with one another, especially if no think-tanks are there to integrate them.

1 On the Ecology of Ecologism

The picture becomes much more complicated in an international perspective, making it trickier to arrive at a common scale of priorities where this is necessary (as in the global commons). When Barbara Ward and René Dubos, in the run-up to the Stockholm Conference of 1972, consulted experts from around the world for their *Only One Earth*, they heard advice in Asia that each country should first learn 'to manage its own ecosystem'. There are 'many different worlds in our one world', and they differ 'not only in physical characterization and economic structures but also – more important – in their cultural traditions'.[29]

Is this diversity only a transitional state that further understanding will

take us beyond? The Australian zoologist Tim Flannery argues the opposite in his bestseller on the climate problem (*The Weathermakers*, 2005);
he even maintains that both the economic and ecological dynamics are
increasing regional differentiation in the United States and elsewhere. 'The
People of the Midwest have probably never felt so distant from those living
in New York, while the Californians feel more than ever that they are a law
unto themselves. This diversity threatens to tear modern America apart,
and communication technologies (themselves a result of the "American
revolution") are involved in a race against time to prevent this.'[30] Similarly,
a number of broad-based empirical studies have concluded that, despite
the spread of transnational networks, the general picture of European
environmental movements – from England to Greece, and from Sweden to
Spain – has not become more homogeneous. This is a surprising finding, in
view of the current assumption that the environmental movement is being
'Europeanized'.[31]

In principle, national differences are a universally known fact, yet their
special prominence in the sphere of environmental protection has been
the object of surprisingly little research. In 1990, in what is still a unique
quantitative study, Wolfgang Rüdig did publish a global survey of the
resistance to nuclear energy and append percentage figures for the extent
to which various countries had completed or exceeded the nuclear plans
they had in 1974 (when the resistance first got off the ground): the lack of
correlation between the two sets of data is baffling.[32] Again and again, the
simple figures for environmental initiatives in this or that country, and for
the people participating in them, come as a surprise and present us with
questions. Qualitative aspects, such as the frequency of violent actions, are
probably connected to the stance of those on the opposing side; environmental movements cannot be understood if they are seen in isolation.

Social scientists like to explain the differences by the specific institutional
and social-cultural setting. But, precisely where nature is the issue, one
should not disregard natural factors – considered not as determinants, but
as a challenge to human creativity. It would be illogical if there were no
ecology of the eco-movement! And it would also be illogical to use a single
pre-existing yardstick to assess the various environmental priorities in different parts of the world, or to write off some countries as actors in world
politics because they do not fulfil certain criteria of one's own country.

Environmental problems – it seems a trivial point – are posed differently in advanced and backward industrial countries, in densely and
lightly populated lands, at temperate and tropical latitudes, in arid and wet
regions. The more populous a country, the more critical is the state of its
rubbish dumps, and the greater the threat that its roads will seize up. In
arid regions, the competition for water dominates everything else; not for
nothing is the original meaning of rivals 'riparian neighbours'. Nor is it
any wonder that *las guerras del agua* (water wars) feature so prominently
among Spanish environmental conflicts, especially in times of growing
drought.[33] On the other hand, a relatively lightly populated country such

as Spain can boast of Europe's greatest species diversity without having done much to achieve it,[34] whereas densely populated countries with saturation levels of intensive farming find it much more difficult to set aside protected wildlife areas. In Italy, for example, almost all the conservation areas are old cultivated landscapes; wilderness is not an issue in the ecological scene there. In Germany too, as researchers delved deeper into the country's history, the primal forest became an imagined Romantic object that was thought to exist as a reality only in the colonial world.[35] A wilderness movement, as in the United States or Australia, could not develop in Germany: what was the Dragon's Rock, the birthplace of German conservationism in 1836, in comparison with the grandiose canyons and giant redwoods of the American West, or the natural wonders of Australia? The loving preservation of nature also varies in its methods – partly, it is true, for natural reasons. In Australia and New Zealand, whose ecosystems have been isolated for millions of years, the main war is against non-native species that multiply there with less restraint than anywhere else in the world. 'In New Zealand conservation is primarily about killing', as Doug Mende, of the Mount Bruce National Wildlife Centre, brutally puts it.[36]

Of course, the cultural backgrounds should not be overlooked. The United States and Australia lacked ancient temples and Gothic cathedrals; that left only natural landmarks as national monuments. Russia's history has been marked by its overabundance of forest, yet this has given so much trouble that the romanticism often associated with this has not become really popular there; Leonid Leonov's *The Russian Forest* (1953), for example, reads like a kind of *Bildungsroman*, meant to popularize official afforestation policies. The great historian Vasily Klyuchevsky (1841–1911) referred to the 'Russian's unfriendly or deprecatory attitude to the forest': 'He has never loved his forest. If he entered the shadowy semi-darkness, he was seized with an apprehension that he could not account for to himself.' The river had quite a different effect: 'It made him feel alive, so that he became bosom friends with it. He loved his river, and for nothing else in the country did he have such tender words in his songs.'[37] Not surprisingly, the Russian environmental movement developed mainly to protest against the pollution of Lake Baikal and the planned diversion of great Siberian rivers into non-Russian regions of Central Asia.[38]

The lure of ecological determinism: the case of Japan

A Western nature lover visiting Japan for the first time feels disappointed that its national parks do not seem to mean much to a people so noted for its love of nature: there is no comparison with the significance they have in the United States ('the best idea America ever had'!). People familiar with Japan say this is easy to explain: what people mainly love there is 'not wild nature but nature as the bearer of a function for culture and society'.[39] Western literature on the country is fond of contrasting it with the West, as if the tea ceremony were the quintessence of Japan. But American society too has its conformist side; and not only Westerners but also Japanese are fond of niches where they can live life to the full. In Japan, it is not only the trim garden-nature that is cultivated but – as many temple groves show – also opulent, seemingly wild nature.

National parks of American dimensions, however, are unthinkable in the narrow, densely populated lowlands of Japan; and on the steep mountain slopes, where it has become too expensive to use the wood, forests have been growing wild for decades, much to the annoyance of foresters[40] – no wonder the country has no Wilderness Society that enjoys popular support! Indeed, the depopulation of forest areas and the decay of mountain villages are the environmental problem that conservationists try to address.[41] That too is not altogether peculiar to Japan: many French friends of the environment are also fond of traditional farm landscapes and complain of the *exode rural* that has grown dramatically since 1945, giving rise to new wildernesses that have less wildlife and are aesthetically less appealing.[42]

To be sure, there is reason to be cautious with ecological determinism, especially in countries where one does not really understand the cultural background. If two-thirds of Japan is covered with forest, this is spontaneously attributed to the fact that those two-thirds are hard-to-farm mountainous terrain. But in North China, for example, many mountains lack forest cover and the slopes are terraced for agriculture. In former times that also used to be the case in Japan. Conrad Totman even ventures the thesis: 'Judging by its specific interaction of geography and history, Japan ought to be an (ecologically) ruined country.'[43] A glance at the map may not be not enough to explain its relatively sustainable forest management since the eighteenth century. But it would be perverse to explain Japan's handling of the environment without any reference to that environment.

After the reactor disaster at Fukushima on 12 March 2011, people around the world were puzzled that this hi-tech country par excellence, where severe earthquakes are part of the tectonic structure, should have designed nuclear power plants with so little heed to the danger. One obvious reason for this is that the Japanese thought for a long time that they could rely on their position as the world leader in anti-earthquake architecture.[44] But there are time limits to man's overcoming of natural challenges; it can lead to a false sense of security – not only in Japan.

Small differences: the case of Europe

Much the same is true of many other countries. In the Alpine lands, both nature and politicians favour organic farming, since a high degree of mechanization does not suit the terrain, and the Alps would lose their attraction to tourists (a key element in the economy) if local farmers were to disappear and the wide open pastures became covered with forest. In

England and France too, many conservationists perceive the traditional rural landscape as something worth preserving. The Council for the Protection of Rural England is a characteristic component of the British environmental movement,[45] and the old farming world belongs to the *patrimoine* defended by like-minded people in France. Germans are struck that this aspect is missing from their otherwise diverse movement; 'nature' is seen there mainly as a world requiring protection from farmers, set apart from agricultural landscapes where species diversity has been in decline. In this respect, modern German perceptions of the environment are more American than European. Things used to be different, when there was an alliance between conservationism and countryside protection, but a reaction against the ideology of *Blut und Boden* inoculated German intellectuals against agrarian nostalgia.

In view of its geography, one might think that the Netherlands would have the most to fear from a rise in sea levels due to global warming. But dyke construction has been a routine matter there for five centuries, and the population is relaxed about its partly submarine location. It is easy to understand that cycling is so common there, but not that this traditional land of windmills, unlike Denmark, is not pioneering modern wind rotors. Not wind but a political tailwind has been in short supply there. Yet per capita spending on conservation and environmental protection is greater than in any other country!

David Elliott, a technologist who switched from nuclear to renewable energy, remarked in 2007 that no Continental country is as endowed as Britain is with wind, wave and tidal energy sources, yet it continues to rely on coal and nuclear power and lags behind in the use of renewable energy.[46] The German Democratic Republic, a small, fairly flat country short of foreign currency, was predestined to be a land of bicycles: the much-derided motto of Communist leader Walter Ulbricht, 'Overtake, without catching up!', could actually have had a future there. However, it soon changed course, so that the slogan 'Cycle lanes for East Berlin!' caught on only when the days of the GDR were numbered. More than in the West, bicycles were a *sine qua non* for environmental protesters. On the other hand, given the all-pervasive smell of coal smoke, it is hardly surprising that nuclear energy remained attractive to many citizens of the GDR longer than it did in West Germany.

Germany's current leading position in solar technology is, of course, not due to special favours from the sun; it makes about as much sense as 'growing bananas in Alaska', joked Jürgen Grossmann, the boss of the RWE electricity giant,[47] However, Bavaria's leading role in the German sector is the result of natural endowments: not only is it sunnier than the North; it also suffered for a long time under the dominance of coal from the Ruhr. Though the bastion of political conservatism, Bavaria also claims to be in the vanguard of conservationism – a combination that surprises people in North Germany, where 'eco' is most often associated with the left. This can be explained partly by Bavaria's tourism industry, but partly also by its unbroken link between natural conservation and cultural heritage. The BUND (Bund für Umwelt und Naturschutz Deutschland, the long-established environmental protection society) had Bavarian roots going back to the days of Imperial Germany, and in the 1990s more than half its membership still came from Bavaria. Many right–left polarizations in the North were avoided here in the South.[48]

Different paths in transport policy

A 2006 questionnaire of experts in twenty countries about the sectors that pose the greatest obstacles to environmental protection listed the following: (1) energy, (2) road transport, (3) agriculture and (4) construction.[49] Clearly these are all sectors with a strongly national and regional complexion, and, needless to say, the options for transport policy – a sinew of environmental policy – are strongly determined by geographical factors. The best European example of this is Switzerland, which is the 'number one railway country' and has energetically used high toll charges to curb truck haulage.[50] The narrowness of Alpine valleys makes it easier to present this concentration on rail as a patriotic duty, further promoted by the fact that much of road transport involves foreign transit vehicles. The canton of Uri, which for centuries had occupied a key position commanding the Gothard Pass, was at first naïvely jubilant over a massive railway and motorway upgrade of the old pass route; it realized too late that the explosion of through traffic had simply turned it into a noisy backwater.[51]

Of course, the geography of transport policy provides no more than the framework: it is not the determining factor, and besides, the framework can be interpreted in more ways than one. From the early 1970s on, German policy-makers gambled on the Transrapid – the magnetic levitation train, such as the one in which the contented inhabitants of Ernst Callenbach's *Ecotopia* (1975) escape all clatter as they glide through the countryside at 360 km an hour. But it was a fantasy at the time. As with so many 'new technologies', the devil lay in the detail: the first trial runs soon showed that the 'whispering arrow' caused as much noise as a low-flying aircraft when it was travelling at full speed. In any event, it could seldom reach full speed in the cramped Federal Republic; the whole project ended in failure, especially as it would have required new infrastructure to be built.[52] Environmentally friendly only on certain clearly defined conditions, it was ill suited to a thickly populated country with a dense pre-existing rail network.

Similarly out of place in the Bundesrepublik is the idea, dominant since the 1970s, that superfast cars are key to the country's success, and that the kind of speed limit normal in other countries would be a stab in the back for the leading sector of the German economy. At a time when Germany still enjoys world respect as a leader in environmental policy, its environmentalists feel ashamed at the repeated postponement of speed curbs on its roads. Even after the catalytic converter came on line, German carmakers lagged at least a decade behind the Americans and Japanese, until they discovered the competitive advantage it would give them in comparison with European rivals.[53] The German environmental movement, otherwise so pugnacious, displayed inhibitions all through the seventies when it came to the damage caused by motor vehicles.[54] Whereas Americans traditionally become more agitated than Germans over any restriction on individual freedom, the roles were reversed in this case. Defying all arguments, the car lobby and its clientele adopted a stance on speed limits that was more in the style of American anti-environmentalists.

A comparison with militant protest movements in Britain against the expansion of road traffic and motorway construction – the Carmageddon campaign and the Reclaim the Streets, Roadblock and Road Alert revolts that peaked in the 1990s[55] – makes it even clearer how much the power of the car lobby hems in the German environmental movement. The integrity of typical English parkland, with its Arcadian aura, is a central value for British environmentalists,[56] whereas policy-makers have often argued that England, unlike Central European countries, is not overburdened with transit traffic and that it has no interest in slapping high charges on goods vehicles.[57] English politicians also tend to drag their feet within the EU on the matter of emission standards – which is to be explained by their island position in Northwest Europe, where west winds usually whisk emissions off to other countries.

As early as the nineteenth century, a distinctively Scottish environmentalism was observable within the British Isles, and in recent years this has gained a new lease of life amid the rise of a new Scottish nationalism. While Scots were making their mark on British economic thought, Scottish botanists and medical men were helping to shape environmental awareness within the British Empire.[58] At home they had bare mountains before their eyes, so that in the colonies – from South Africa to New Zealand – many of them developed a real tree-planting mania, in sharp conflict with the general British indifference to the forest.[59] For the Scottish doctor Hugh Cleghorn, 'conservator of the forests' in Madras from 1858 on, the value of the forest lay not only in its wood but above all in its beneficial influence on the climate and human health. He complained that, of all European nations, the British had the least appreciation of the forest, and that this had carried over to the ruthless destructiveness of settlers in the United States.[60] Today, the Scots have an ambivalent attitude to environmental history: the traumatic memory of the eighteenth-century Highland Clearances is still alive,[61] yet many learned to love the beauty of the broad, bare peaks, with their special fauna and flora, and protested along with the WWF against state-subsidized conifer afforestation – at the very time when alarms were sounding in Germany over the 'death of the forest': 'Who still wants to holiday in Scotland', asked one German journalist, 'when every road passes through a dark tunnel made of spruce wood?'[62] Still, there is more to Scotland than the Highlands. Since the 1990s, the special Scottish potential for protest has also been vented in one of Europe's environmental justice movements, which has targeted the high levels of pollution on the Dirty Scotland Trail from Edinburgh to Glasgow.[63]

From the Hudson to the Colorado: American contrasts

In the United States too there are marked regional differences in environmental awareness, and they are certainly not attributable to natural variations alone. One of the 'incubators' of the American environmental movement was the valley of the River Hudson, whose eponymous school of painting is somewhat reminiscent of German Romanticism centred on the Rhine.[64] The Hudson Valley 'Riverkeeper' organization – which had Robert Kennedy Jr among its members and soon grasped how to play on the political, journalistic and legal registers – became a model for the development of environmentalism.[65] However, the beauty and endangered status of the river were probably less significant than the proximity of New York City. The Northeast was the core region of the movement, being the one with the earliest settlements, the densest population and the highest concentration of intellectuals.

In terms of political climate and environmental awareness, the contrast with the Southern states is so striking that one is tempted – by analogy with Weber's famous theory of capitalism and the Puritan-Protestant ethic – to postulate a link between environmentalism and the same ethic, especially as a comparable North–South contrast is observable within European environmental movements. 'Evidently a liberal electorate combined with an ethically inclined political culture is the best guarantee of an innovative environmental politics',[66] commented Kristine Kern, also with regard to the weakness of environmentalism in the South and Midwest, despite the fact that they were the most affected by soil exhaustion and erosion.[67] The pressure of objective ecological problems cannot by itself explain the genesis of the environmental movement.

It is striking that the other two regional bastions of American environmentalism, though very different from each other, are on the West Coast: Oregon and California. According to Kristine Kern, Oregon is even 'the most innovative state of the USA in environmental policy', having made itself the 'environmental model for the nation' as early as the 1970s.[68] California, for its part, strove to move beyond Hetch Hetchy (1906–13), the first ecological controversy centred on a dam, which had sullied the state's reputation in the eyes of friends of the wilderness ('Remember Hetch Hetchy!'). Catching up and eventually overtaking its neighbouring state to the north, it became the centre of hippy and student countercultures, so that by 1975 it seemed natural for Ernest Callenbach to situate his Ecotopia there.[69]

Oregon, the first hippy paradise in the 1960s,[70] saw a coming together of environmental initiatives at the top and the grassroots: Governor Tom

McCall became a linchpin of the new environmentalism, while the student-based Nature's Conspiracy mobilized people against the deforestation of virgin forest, its 'Make Love, Not Lumber' being a variation on the anti-Vietnam War slogan 'Make Love, Not War'.[71] Here ecological awareness combined with pride in a still relatively intact environment; the state is almost half-covered with forest, of which 60 per cent is publicly owned, and government foresters do not immediately provoke agitation in support of private property. The endangered northern spotted owl, an iconic figure of nature under threat and the object of a decades-long controversy between friends of the wilderness and timber companies,[72] is native to the forests of Oregon, where the first habitat-protection initiatives developed. No other animal has caused as much fuss in the American eco-age as this species of owl, virtually unknown outside the United States. But Oregon's environmental image of itself, unlike that of gold-grabbing California, can also draw on a solid and upright tradition.[73] A version of the Weber thesis that replaced the spirit of capitalism with the spirit of ecologism would be quite appropriate here.

California too has its state pride: for example, it is host to no fewer than 99 per cent of giant redwoods – icons of the wild ever since the days of John Muir.[74] But here environmentalism also contains a hefty portion of what Mike Davis calls 'ecology of fear':[75] fear, that is, of forest fires and earthquakes,[76] plus (in the case of Los Angeles, the smog and automobile capital) a horror of exhaust gases. In the early 1960s, the world's first successful anti-nuclear campaign developed north of San Francisco against the planned nuclear power plant on Bodega Bay, which became famous around the same time from Hitchcock's *The Birds* (1963). But if the original impetus was landscape protection, the decisive argument was eventually the risk of earthquakes; the trauma of the destruction of San Francisco in 1906 was still present in the collective memory.[77] Yet as late as 1976 President Carter announced plans for thirty-six new nuclear power plants in California, whose coastline is at risk from earthquakes, and a Green California movement sprang up in protest.[78] But there was an older tradition of environmentalism in the state: the campaign against smog – with car exhaust gases suspected as the cause – actually began in 1943 and peaked in the 1960s; no other pollution battle attracted greater publicity at the time, with the result that the United States took the lead internationally in catalytic converters.[79] North California also became the American pioneer in solar energy, although it soon learned that silicon processing was by no means an ecologically innocent craft. A newly founded Silicon Valley Toxics Coalition went on to launch a nationwide Campaign for Responsible Technology.[80]

Arnold Schwarzenegger, who in 2003 took over as film star governor of California, was following in the footsteps of Ronald Reagan in 1966, but unlike his predecessor he championed the struggle for, not against, environmental protection. This was not only a niche for ageing hippies, but had for a long time been an arena for men of action to prove themselves.

In comparison with the more homogeneous Oregon, California is a state marked by unusual, and still increasing, social-cultural contrasts: between a conservative middle class and countercultural strata, or between millionaire paradises and slum districts with burgeoning ethnic subcultures. Around the end of the millennium, the proportion of whites had fallen below 50 per cent.[81] The Californian environmental movement began in 1965 with a 'slow-growth rebellion' – or, to be more specific, with squatting initiatives in rich neighbourhoods concerned about air quality and open views over the surrounding nature.[82] In 1999, however, California's Environmental Justice Act put it ahead of the rest of the United States.[83] Whether environmentalism is socially divisive or exercises an integrative potential is a particularly fascinating question in California.

A new ecological contrast between America and Europe

Significant differences in environmental policy exist not only between regions but also more widely. A fundamental division between the USA and the EU has begun to taken shape only in the last few decades; the environmental movement originally presented itself as an American achievement, but this has been increasingly forgotten since the Reagan era. Today US anti-environmentalists construct the enemy image of un-American Eurocrats legislating on ecological matters, blind to the sanctity of private property and the freedom to dispose of it as one wishes.[84] Meanwhile, a pioneering environmentalist like Jeremy Rifkin can idealize Europe as a region of ancient wisdom, which, after many crises, has learned the art of precautionary planning and is aware that individual freedom of action is not the highest good.[85] For many Americans, the experience of their own vulnerability on 11 September 2001 came as a profound shock – or even the beginning of a new epoch (*not* the ecological age). For Europeans, their vulnerability had been self-evident at least since the two world wars: it was a basic feeling that also extended to the environment. The United States had long thought of itself as the land of unlimited opportunity, whereas in Europe the 'limits to growth' were only temporarily forgotten during the postwar boom years. Across the Atlantic, the idea of freedom was inseparably bound up with relentless advance into open spaces;[86] in the Old World, it became obvious long ago that society could not continue indefinitely without careful thought for the future.

Yet by 1970 the United States was displaying greater vigour in environmental policy than most other countries. Washington buried in good time its supersonic flight ambitions, whereas Paris and London pressed on for decades with their economically and ecologically senseless Concorde project. 'The very fact that the Americans did not wish to see a supersonic transport develop in Europe only hardened French resolve to see the project through.'[87] Sometimes it was advantageous that economic rationality ranked higher in the USA than in many parts of Europe; indeed, the fact that it was more difficult to hide behind government supervisory responsibilities (as in the European *étatiste* tradition) meant that the 'polluter pays' principle could be legally enforced with greater strictness. The antagonistic American justice system, in which the plaintiff has the burden of proving damage and his or her lawyers show a detective-like zeal motivated by profit, was more likely to favour thorough investigations than one in which these were left up to an overworked public prosecutor able to draw on less specialist knowledge. Cases relating to the environment have repeatedly offered thrilling courtroom battles to the American public.

The American system did not work, however, when it was a question of hypothetical dangers rather than demonstratable injuries; the obligation to take precautions has still not been enforced in the United States, whereas in the EU it has for many years been asserted at least in principle, though by no means everywhere in practice.[88] The contrasting attitudes in Europe and America have been especially apparent since the 1990s in relation to the dangers of genetic engineering and climate change. It is remarkable how a broad consensus on gene technology restrictions developed in the EU, without anything like a Chernobyl effect to drive it on.

The key question is the burden of proof: whether it has to be demonstrated that a technology is harmful or that it is not harmful. In the case of new technologies with a high hypothetical risk, the tendency in Europe has been to insist on the latter. This does not mean that the consequences have always been consistently drawn; detailed administrative work is worlds apart from the affirmation of basic principles.[89] But for environmental lawyers, who developed into a special professional group, the fleshing out of the precautionary principle became a productive challenge. Restrictions on gene technology partly corresponded to the interests of European farmers, who were anyway afflicted with overproduction and could use the restrictions to keep food imports out of the EU, without violating the World Trade Organization's free trade provisions. In any event, since harvests are less threatened by pests in temperate climates than in hot regions, the EU had less need of genetic modifications to increase crop resistance.

Differences between the Old and the New World are not unbridgeable. The idea of tackling the dangers to the earth's atmosphere with 'market-based instruments' (i.e., trade in emission rights) first appeared in the early 1970s in the EPA's Clean Air Act Program; it was very American in conception and initially encountered defensive reflexes in Europe,[90] where it seemed to express a demoralizing retreat or even the prostitution of 'Mother Nature'.[91] Instead of leading by example, the world's financially strongest corporations could cover any amount of pollution by purchasing emission rights from poorer countries, and these countries had an incentive to produce the greatest possible emission levels so that they could later sell off emission rights at the highest price. The success of this strategy requires the price of the emission bond to be so high that it strongly encourages reductions, and the emissions to be no higher than the level defined by the purchased rights. So far neither of these conditions is on the agenda; the EU's longstanding reservations about such trading appear as justified as ever. Yet, in the context of deregulation, it has more supporters than ever in Europe and actually became official EU policy post-Kyoto, whereas the United States of all countries has begun to backtrack.[92] It also fits into the picture that, when the US Congress ran into protests against supersonic aircraft in 1972,[93] it took the lead internationally by setting up the Office of Technological Assessment (OTA). However, it abolished it in 1995[94] – when none other than Al Gore was vice-president, and just when technological assessment was coming into fashion in Europe.

The gap between the first and third worlds

Up to now we have mainly been considering the Western world, leaving Japan to one side. There is no doubt that the modern environmental movement originated in the West – or, to be more precise, the Northwest – and that Western influences have played a role in many non-Western initiatives. But as early as the Stockholm Conference of 1972, the most delicate issue in international environmental policy was whether the first and third worlds could find common ground, or whether the gulf between them was unbridgeable. From the beginning, objections were heard that environmental awareness was a luxury for rich countries, which, after a long period of rampant economic growth, were suddenly discovering 'limits' in order to prevent the poorer countries from catching up, and which, having used their own natural resources to the limit, now expected the third world to leave its remaining undeveloped areas intact for wilderness lovers in the first world. The contradiction certainly provided plenty of material for fiery rhetoric!

On the other hand, it soon became clear that environmental problems greatly impaired life chances in the third world, more so than in the leading industrial countries. In many countries of Africa and Asia, a newly sharpened awareness of the issues gave the impetus for endless discoveries. Yet is it true that this had nothing in common with, or even pointed in an opposite direction from, environmental awareness in the first world: did it concern the survival crisis facing humanity, rather than the protection of nature from human beings?

The Australian activist Timothy Doyle, whose sketch of the differences in environmental initiatives around the world is the most impressive so far (2005), identifies six leitmotifs and movement types that are mainly distributed among six different countries: forest movements in the USA, anti-mining movements in the Philippines, wilderness movements in Australia, anti-roads movements in England, river movements in India, and – last but not least – anti-nuclear movements in Germany. Anyone who has grappled with the thorny problem of grouping the world's environmental movements into some reasonable structure will not lack respect for Doyle's tour de force. As he puts it, the inspiration for his book came in a church pew on the Philippines island of Mindanao, when he realized that a 'huge gulf' was opening between the movements of rich and poor countries, and that it was thoroughly wrong to cover this over with environmental rhetoric. His aim was to home in on the fundamental split at the level of political experiences:

> This book is more of a celebration of differences than similarities: more evidence of the fact that there are many environmental movements across the earth, rather than one. Environmental movements across the globe must persist in this salutation of diversity and resist the all-powerful but understandable urges to overly homogenize opposition, using the justification of global resistance and, in doing so, creating one environmental movement.[95]

In this way of seeing things, it would be altogether aberrant to seek to hammer out global environmental priorities at summit conferences, and we should be extremely glad that such approaches keep grinding to a halt. Doyle also speaks disparagingly of the 'concept of sustainable development', which the Rio summit of 1992 made into a magical incantation, but which is in reality a monstrosity dreamed up by 'the public relations industry working for big business interests'. Agreed upon as a compromise formula by the first and the third world, it is still unclear whether it has any real substance and integrative potential.[96] For Doyle, the practical import of 'sustainable development' is simply to give legitimacy to the exploitation of natural resources by those who can afford a PR department to cultivate their eco-image. Rather, the only possible common denominator of environmental movements around the world would be an awareness and affirmation of their diversity; that alone makes it meaningful to group them all under the term 'environmental movements'.

There too lies the practical value of this global history of the eco-age. Yet that is not all. Doyle would personally accept that the wilderness movement in his native Australia has effected a reconciliation between the first and third worlds, by regarding the Aborigines as 'natural allies'.[97] More generally, however, the wilderness cult tends to divide the two worlds from each other, since most inhabitants of the third world are not 'people of the wild' (if there are such people at all). Nevertheless, there are three objections to a one-sided emphasis on the gulf between the first and the third world:

(1) Although it has been common for more than half a century to speak of the 'third world' as a fact associated with certain images of poverty and hope, one easily forgets that it is really a highly imaginary entity: a Western construct that public figures (including in the third world itself) use to attract development aid, but one that contains a misleading suggestion of homogeneity and forthcoming 'development'.[98] The truth is that countries like Brazil and Bangladesh are worlds apart; Africa has become a third

world within the third world. From the beginning, 'third world' was a blanket term that produced questionable blanket judgements; today it has become an outright anachronism.[99]

Third world spokespersons are not among those who go hungry and often do not represent their interests. True, the group dynamic at summit conferences has repeatedly led to an opposition between the first and third worlds, but the real 'ecology of the ecological movement' is more varied and does not lend itself to such dualism. If many self-styled spokespersons of the third world claim that its values are quite different from those of the first world, especially in environmental matters, such assurances should be treated with caution; particular interests may well lie behind them. The very dangers of pesticides with which Rachel Carson first aroused America's environmental awareness have become more glaring, also in leading third world countries, as a result of the Green Revolution that was still in its infancy at the time she was writing.

(2) Doyle's identification of certain countries with particular types of environmental movement has an essentially ideal-typical character. In reality, each country takes up a much wider range of theses, and to some extent the central ones have changed over time. The American environmental movement, as it spread in a chain reaction around 1970, was something different from the redwoods cult previously carried on by the Sierra Club and the Wilderness Society. The mobility of the environmental movement is apparent not least in its leitmotifs. Over the decades, the German movement too has been characterized by a broad spectrum of objectives; it would never have made history if it had been no more than a single-issue campaign against nuclear energy.

(3) For a long time now, none of Doyle's six leitmotifs has been characteristic of just one country; they have all leaped across international frontiers. Although Doyle uses them for the purposes of differentiation, they are at least equally suited for the definition of transnational links. Environmentalism, as a global phenomenon, may manifest itself very diversely in individual countries, and it may not be associated everywhere with the same social milieu, yet many links are apparent in a whole network of common themes. Exaggerating a little, within a long-term global perspective, one might say that it is not group interests but particular issues that have been the main players in the eco-age.

Issue leaps

Not only Britain but also Germany abounded in campaigns against motorways, although they often lacked transregional dimensions or an integrative philosophy. The anti-nuclear movement, though stronger in the Federal Republic than elsewhere and subject to hysterical attacks from the nuclear lobby, is by no means a uniquely German phenomenon. Forest protection movements are not peculiar to the United States but are probably the most common type of environmentalist movement across the globe. The struggle to preserve rivers can also be found in many parts of the world, from the Danube to the Colorado; the movement against the damming of the Nagara ('Japan's last free-flowing river'), which began in 1988, derived fresh stimulation from Indian activists locked in battle against the Narmada high dam.[100] Complaints about mining pollution are not confined to the modern Philippines but – as Paulus Niavis's *Klage der Natur* testifies – have been heard in Germany since the fifteenth century.

A collective volume on environmental politics and protests in Southeast Asia (1998)[101] is organized not by country but by issue: conflicts over high dams, forest use, mining, harmful pollution, and tourism projects in Thailand and Bali. The absence of wilderness protection movements is no surprise; protests against extensive logging by foreign companies involve forest rights. Again the whole spectrum seems very exotic in comparison with the eco-scene in Western countries, yet there are several areas of overlap. Although the actual issues differ, forest and water – the two great commons in history – feature repeatedly in dam conflicts, from the Danube to the Mekong, as do problems relating to mining and the effects of water and air pollution on human health; the contributors cover protests in the more industrial countries against landscape destruction by motorways and the risks associated with particular technologies (especially nuclear energy and chemistry), and there are also accounts of animal and wilderness protection movements. These problem areas appear interlinked, partly if not on all points, and there is an inner logic that takes us from one issue to another. The knowledge that the forest and watercourse conditions are bound up with each other is here generally at the root of 'networked thinking'. The struggle against water and air pollution, a classical arena of environmental protection, leads on to discussion of various harmful emissions and the risks of modern technologies.

With Pirandello into the global history of the environmental movement

In a global perspective, the problems are not as varied as the players. They can perhaps be considered within discrete episodes, though not assigned as such to particular group interests and discourses; rather, they are taken up by different players in various countries and at various times. In the 1920s Luigi Pirandello created an uproar with his *Six Characters in Search of an Author*. Similarly, if we were to make a play out of the history of the environmental movement, we might allude to Commoner's six chief dangers by calling it *Six Issues in Search of Players*; further subdivision might then yield nine or even a full dozen issues. It would be a modern play, without the classical unity of time and place, without actors fixed once and for all, and without a definitive ending.

The very first issue common to environmental movements around the world is one omitted by Timothy Doyle but referring back to industrial medicine: namely, *poison*. Were we to leaf through decades of environmental headlines in a magazine like *Der Spiegel*, we would find this running through them like a red thread and symbolized by a skull and cross-bones.[102] Günter Hartkopf, state secretary at the German interior ministry from 1969 to 1983 and, as such, the leading force in Bonn's environmental policy, used to bring up the issue of 'sacrifices' in discussions – and by that he meant human sacrifices. For example, 'when a discussion on local air purification measures considered whether (particularly delicate) gladioli had to be able to grow in the affected areas, he would ask whether there were damaging effects on human health'.[103] If there were, environmental protection was most likely to become part of the policy-making process, in the first as well as the third world.

To repeat: what was new in and after 1970 was a concern not for nature as such but for human beings! Harmful emissions not only justified inter-vention by the authorities, but were often targeted by protest movements, especially in countries that had previously had no effective system of supervision. This defined a clear goal, a clear legitimacy, and often also feasible solutions as well as a group of vitally affected persons whom the campaign could mobilize. It was mainly poisoning scandals that unleashed the Japanese environmental movement and got politicians moving. A special Japanese path? But even Carolyn Merchant's *Columbia Guide to American Environmental History* (2002) features the Antitoxics Movement as the only concrete example of a modern environmental movement.[104]

Since socially disadvantaged groups were usually the most exposed to dangerous emissions, the Environmental Justice movement reactivated this original focus of the eco-age and established a link with local environmental protests in the third world. As a rule, campaigns against toxic waste were local. But since poor third world countries increasingly offer themselves as dumping grounds for the first world, many such movements jumped across national frontiers – especially as they provided an ideal focus for Greenpeace's spectacular sea-based operations.[105] Environmentalists were able to demonstrate solidarity in action with the third world.

To return to Pirandello: the toxicity issue, which typically moves between the political heights and the grassroots, sought out changing players.[106] Criticism of nuclear power – originally a theme of conservative anti-modernists – was taken up by neo-Marxists in the 1970s. Ecofeminists joined with traditionalist mountain farmers in rejecting gene technology. Passionate hunters got enthusiastic about the wilderness, but so too did passionate opponents of hunting. Conservation exerted an attraction for misanthropes as well as for lovers of the whole of creation.

The issues did not always find the right players for them. Someone full of rage at existing conditions often seeks to join the protest movement around at the time – which since 1970 has often meant an environmental movement – and in some situations will even vent their rage against fellow-campaigners. Ideally, environmentalism needed people with ties in their family and locality, and with a keen sense of responsibility for future generations, who felt bound by certain rules and values and, when appropriate, viewed the state as a positive force for order. But such people are often not prepared for confrontation with the state, or have no time for a new commitment. After 1970, then, it was typically '68ers who, having failed in their previous objectives, could be mobilized to campaign against environmental scandals: single people without children, for whom homeland, family, standards and laws were deeply suspect. What counted for them above everything was their spontaneous impulses, and they liked nothing more than travelling around the world. This did not necessarily mean that they ended up doing nothing for environmentalism. The history of the eco-age provides material for success stories as well as tragedies, but also quite a lot of material for comedies.

2 Water and the Atom

The oldest arena of environmental politics

Water, more than forest or soil, is an element of mobility and interconnectedness, but also one that displays the 'ecology of the eco-movement', the power of geographical and cultural differences. To the best of my knowledge, what we today call 'environmental awareness' first arose in connection with water – not with the sea (that came later) but with inland waters.[107] Regulatory traditions here go back to the early river civilizations with which recorded history begins: thousands of years before the modern age intensified the regulation of forest use. Historically, as well as ecologically, the priority of water issues in many parts of the world is not difficult to understand: whether one dammed up a river or extracted water from it, quarrels constantly arose with others living beside it and called for regulation and a degree of forward planning. Moreover, to be viable, environmental policies in relation to water soon developed into a balancing strategy that taught networked thinking. Venice was an early pioneer of this art: it had to protect itself against high tides, but also to prevent the silting up of its lagoon. In the long run, single-minded *de*-watering would lead to crisis just as surely as the endless watering of arid regions.

The Spanish Conquistadors were less circumspect than the Venetians. In conquering Mexico, Cortés's men experienced Tenochtitlán, the lakeside capital of the Aztecs that they called the 'Venice of the West', as a dangerous trap, and afterwards, instead of agreeing to maintain the Aztec ecosystem, they turned the lake into a clogged-up sewer by discharging waste and faeces into it. This raised not only the incidence of disease but also the danger of flooding, since the capacity of the lake to retain water was severely reduced. For centuries Mexican environmental policy was therefore dominated by the practice of *desagüe* or drainage, until a salt steppe spread into the valley of Mexico and dust storms ravaged the city.[108]

Alexander von Humboldt already described the obsession with *desagüe* (which continued down to the 1950s!) as a 'stupidity': 'But the Spanish have looked on the water as an enemy. Apparently they want this New Spain to be just as dry as the interior of their old Spain. They want nature to be like their morality, and they are not making a bad job of it.'[109] That is not the full story, however. In comparison with the Yankees' later ambition to irrigate areas captured from Mexico and turn them into farmland, historians have seen the relative rationality of the Spanish settlers; they came from arid regions themselves and accepted what they found in Mexico, engaging in extensive forms of agriculture.[110]

Water has been a continual focus of environmental conflicts and politics. Municipal sanitation in late nineteenth-century Europe gave the highest priority to hygiene in the supply and drainage of water. Subsequently, administrations in Central and Western Europe targeted at least the worst cases of pollution, so that water-related issues were not at first a central concern for the new environmental movement. But the age of reforms around the year 1900 largely passed by the more backward local government systems of Southern Europe, where the supply of water was anyway more problematic and basic demands for municipal sanitation had still to be addressed.[111] As for water-deprived parts of the third world, the European-style hygienic 'hydropolis' has been achievable only in wealthy districts of the big cities; a fixation on this sanitation model is almost automatically associated with socially discriminatory environmental policies.[112]

The new explosiveness of water policy

There is much evidence that water problems are becoming a greater priority worldwide. If global warming continues, its effects will be especially apparent in the water supply of many parts of the world. Modern technology makes it possible to carry water over ever greater distances and to extract it, like other natural resources, from politically less powerful areas. In this way, the core countries are able to cover up the overuse of their own water resources. In the 1990s the US Sun Belt Water Corporation attempted to import Canadian water on a large scale into parched areas of California, but the Canadian government eventually vetoed the project and sued for billions of dollars in compensation.[113] The water supply in the increasingly parched region around Beijing was one of the factors behind the construction of the giant Three Gorges dam on the Yangtze,[114] which led to the most voluble environmental controversy in China's modern history. We are likely to hear of more conflicts of this kind in the future. For although North China is in danger of drying up, the means exist to pump water into it from the South. In 2006 a book entitled *How Tibet's Water Will*

Save China caused a stir in the Chinese public and considerable disquiet in India. The author, Li Ling, a retired army officer and nationalist, proposed diverting several rivers from the Tibetan high plateau to North China: a gigantic project, with no historical precedent, but in the realm of the possible thanks to modern technology.[115]

It might be logical (eco-logical) to demand that every region should keep its natural water resources, and that water should be priced at a level that induces consumers to think and to use it more economically. This was the philosophy behind the global water conference in Dublin in 1992, where, unlike at the Rio summit in the same year, the experts met by themselves and paid less attention to social policy aspects.[116] The situation was amazingly reminiscent of the conflict in Germany two centuries ago, when many people were still used to receiving the 'bare household necessity' of wood free of charge but were told by reformers that wood had to fetch a proper price in the interests of good forest management. Often, however, it is precisely in areas with little water of their own (where water would fetch the highest price) that the mass of the population are the poorest. In scarcely any other sphere is it so important, and so tricky, to synthesize social and environmental policy! And scarcely anywhere is there such a bad synergy of profit and environmental damage; the more that the water is polluted, the more people are told to buy it in bottles from supermarkets, at a price that can be driven higher and higher. History shows that a concern for clean drinking water is one of the strongest impulses behind environmentalism. But its efficacy turns into its opposite as soon as the profit motive holds sway, and profits grow as clean water becomes scarcer and more expensive.

Water projects could rely on preferential support from the World Bank. But for them to be creditworthy, the water had to be sold at a price that more or less covered repayment of the loan. The best-known prototype of the resulting conflicts was the 'Cochabamba water war' in Bolivia in 1999–2000, when privatization of the water supply on World Bank advice pushed the price up to a level that forced poor people to spend a large part of their income on water. This soon led to a veritable uprising and general strike, in which large numbers of Bolivians – many speak of millions – poured towards Cochabamba. After some bloody clashes, the resistance won through and the privatization was reversed. The privatization was intended to set an example, as we can see from the fact there are similar projects today in all parts of the world, from Bolivia to Berlin. For their part, leaders of the protest movement issued the Cochabamba Declaration, which numbered the right to water among the human rights that had to be defended. No other disputed resource raises the question of survival so sharply, and in no other case was it so easy to define and justify a natural right. 'Water Is Life': the now world-famous Coordinadora de Defensa del Agua y de la Vida grew out of the Cochabamba movement.[117]

People in the North still take it for granted that drinking water flows out of municipal pipes, yet this boon is highly unusual in today's world. Water and air are basic elements in the world and for all forms of life; the term 'natural right' has an evident meaning in relation to them. But who decides how much water each person is entitled to, and what quality it should have? Should drinking water be kept separate from other kinds? Or is that a fundamental misconception, since it allows the low-grade pollution of most water when many have no option other than to drink it? Here too there seems no point in trying to come up with a general answer; it is a classic example of the ecology of environmental protection. The same is true of hydraulic engineering.

Large dams as targets of protest movements

In 1999 the writer Arundhati Roy, the best-known spokesperson of radical Indian eco-activism, who has contemptuously distanced herself from the hygiene-oriented environmentalism of the new middle classes, put large dams in the same league as atom bombs in terms of their destructive impact.[118] Dams and nuclear power plants are the technological mega-projects which have aroused the strongest protests around the world and are the ones most likely to jump across the frontiers of nations and cultures. This is an irony of history, if we recall Mumford's gushing enthusiasm for environmentally friendly 'new technology' and its incarnation in hydroelectric power stations. Water power, like nuclear power, drew to itself hopes that would later become a driving force of the environmental movement: hopes in an inexhaustible, eco-friendly energy source not dependent on smokestacks or the using up of fossil fuels.

Opinions about hydropower are still divided in the international eco-scene. The reasons for this are obvious: it makes a difference whether you create an artificial lake in the central German uplands or in the tropics. In the Sauerland even conservationists have sooner or later come to accept them, especially considering that, once nature has reconquered their shores, they have an attraction of their own and offer a breeding ground for birds. By the time you reach the Alps, however, this has changed to support for nuclear energy as an alternative. Further south, where evaporation is enormous, or in river cultures, where expensive farmland can be lost and the stagnant water become a hotbed for pathogens and eventually threaten to silt up, the building of large dams is often economically irrational, explicable only because the Tennessee Valley Authority model defined it for decades as the paragon of progress and 'development'. Nehru's description of large dams as the 'temples of modern India' became a catchphrase to be found in every school textbook.[119] Sunderlal Bahugana, on the other hand, the spokesperson of India's Chipko movement, cursed large dams as 'monuments of twentieth-century stupidity',[120] while Vandana Shiva complained that dam-building became a veritable 'epidemic' after Independence.[121] In sharp contrast, anyone who did not live near a river could hope to be one of the winners; campaigners against the Narmada dam, for example, feared they would be lynched if they ventured into the powerful neighbouring state of Gujarat.[122]

A trailblazer in international eco-communication was *The Social and Environmental Effects of Large Dams*, a 400-page work written by Edward Goldsmith and Nicholas Hildyard (from the British magazine *The Ecologist*) and published in 1984 by the Sierra Club. It is remarkable in more ways than one. Whereas – as we have seen – it is not easy to reconcile ecology with social justice in commercialization of the water supply, these two authors thought the situation was clear-cut in the case of large dams: they were ecologically disastrous, economically absurd (because they led in the long run to silting and soil salination) and above all anti-social. Typically commissioned by a local ruler as a prestige project, they served the interests of the core countries at the expense of the poor peasantry. Protest movements against them might also work in campaigns for the environment and for social justice – although regions far away from the hydropower stations that hoped to benefit from the electricity they generated often had very different notions of 'justice'. Besides, 'large' dams were not the only targets for the protest movements. But what did 'large' mean exactly? According to Goldsmith and Hildyard, it was to be defined qualitatively rather than quantitatively – by the scale of the environmental impact. Their 'small' alternative consisted not of a general model but of specific historical examples, most notably the *qanat* irrigation networks of ancient Iran, whose underground course prevented evaporation and other problems.[123] The authors wrote in detail about small-scale models from the past that had been adapted to local needs; few other early works of the environmental movement testify to such a deep and knowledgeable awareness of history.

Environmentally aware sections of the American public did not have to look to the third world for evidence of the irrationality of large dams and irrigation systems: they could see it in the West of their own country, the model of free enterprise![124] The old hatred felt by friends of the wilderness for Hetch Hetchy and other dams on the Colorado came alive again with new arguments: 'The finest fantasy of eco-warriors is the destruction of the [Glen Canyon] dam and the liberation of the Colorado', admitted Dave Foreman with brutal frankness.[125] By the 1990s, although 'Earth First!' leaders usually contained themselves and most protests against existing dams were unsuccessful, the time was over when they were held up across the globe as monuments to the future.[126]

Flood defence and opportunities for irrigation were the arguments most widely used to justify dam-building in the eyes of the peasantry 'Anyone opposed to irrigation is an enemy of the nation', thundered even Tirunellai N. Seshan, at the time India's state secretary for environmental issues, who had the image of an honest, independent-minded man familiar with the ecological evils of large dams and otherwise given to sarcasm about the politicians' penchant for mega-projects.[127] In India, as elsewhere, the interests of the electricity companies tended to outweigh others. And the energy potential of large dams fascinated engineers and politicians alike.[128]

The Aswan high dam, the first project of its kind in the third world and for decades the most spectacular, notoriously failed to serve the fellahin but *destroyed* the natural flooding of the Nile that had fertilized the fields for millennia with particles of mud. The original dam at Aswan, built in 1900 according to the plans of the historically aware Sir William Willcocks,[129] had been provided with sluices so that much of the mud would continue to pass through.[130] But, as John McNeill sums it up, a form of economy by far the longest-lasting and most sustainable in world history came to an end when the new dam was completed under the direction of Soviet engineers.[131] That was in 1971 – in the age of the 'ecological revolution'. How extraordinary, one might think, that there were no cries of outrage at the time! But that too would appear to be significant: the problems of agrarian sustainability were rediscovered only later over a period of time; the Aswan dam was charged with the symbolism of 'development'; and most of the Islamic world is still today a blank on the world map of the environmental movement, even though green is the colour of Islam, and traditional sharia law provides for exact regulation of water use and communal upkeep of the irrigation systems put in place by fellahin at the bottom end of the social hierarchy.[132] It is true that since 1988 Egypt has had the first Green party in the Arab world, but it too did not dare to broach the 'Aswan dam' issue, concentrating instead – in keeping with its urban intellectual roots – on problems of municipal sanitation.[133] At the time when the Aswan dam was being built, the main complaint of an international public focused on conservation was that it would involve the flooding of ancient temples; that was one of the origins of UNESCO's Heritage of Mankind programme.[134]

Revolt against the 'temples of modern India'

Hydraulic specialists traditionally viewed India as the 'fairy-tale land of irrigation', which exceeded 'even China in the diversity of its methods' that mirrored the variety of local conditions.[135] In the nineteenth century, British engineers still learned to respect the achievements of the Mogul period, which ranged from small artificial lakes to vast installations. This historical background makes it understandable that the post-Independence government had special ambitions in this sphere; one estimate is that, between 1947 and 1982, 15 per cent of all government expenditure went on the construction of dams, so that India was the world leader in hydroelectric power. Yet, given the importance of irrigation in the country's history, most of the wide valleys suitable for artificial lakes were densely populated; it is thought that between 1947 and 1992 such projects drove as many as 20 million people from their home region.[136] In 2001 Arundhati Roy even suggested the incredible figure of 56 million![137] In the third world, where the cultural divide between central bureaucracies and the village world is often even sharper than in old industrial countries, it is quite common for planners to show a provocative disregard for local people. Indeed, it sometimes happened in the 1960s that villagers first realized the size of the artificial lake from rising water levels.[138]

We can see why in the 1980s the 'fairy-tale land of irrigation' became the centre of struggles against dam projects, and why its broad protest movements, especially against the Sardar Sarovar dam on the Narmada river north of Mumbai (then the 'largest dam project in the world'), set an example that was followed in other countries.[139] It was meant to be the final construction in the Narmada Valley Development Project, which altogether provided for no fewer than 30 large, 135 medium-sized and 3,000 small dams along the hitherto untouched river.[140] Spiritually inspired publications on the Sardar Sarovar conflict emphasize that the Narmada – whose pebbles 'look like little *lingas*, the phallic symbols of the god Shiva'[141] – is holier even than the Ganges. But this quality has not kept local people from using and polluting the water of either river; everyone takes its use for irrigation for granted, and religious traditions offer no satisfactory explanation for the resistance. In the case of the Narmada, it was the decades-long dispute among riparian states over control of the water which repeatedly delayed dam projects.[142] Other factors seem more important than spiritual links to the river, and the protest movement itself drew upon India's rich hydraulic traditions. Many villages had some competence in the field and centuries of experience of supplying themselves with water. They did not need the grand project, which actually threatened their own irrigation systems. Indira Gandhi herself, and Rajiv Gandhi after her, were frightened of the human costs of large dams;[143] but even as government leaders they found themselves incapable of stopping the project machinery once it was up and running.

A social or ecological conflict?

To be sure, most campaigners were concerned not with ecology as such but with the threat to the rights of indigenous people. Vandana Shiva refers to a key aspect of all large dam projects: even if they may potentially be useful to many people, they generally go together with the cancellation of traditional village use-rights and the disempowerment of village communities.[144] In large parts of the world, this is the downside of all environmental policy; its ultimate effect, albeit under the slogan of 'sustainable development', is to strengthen the power of the central authorities. It might therefore be asked whether we are really talking about an environmental conflict. Is ecology not merely the outward appearance of what is essentially a social conflict of world-historic dimensions, over the assertion of modern power apparatuses against the old peasant worlds?

In any event, ecology has placed a major new weapon in the hands of those old worlds. The shaking of fixed ideas of technological progress, the sharper awareness of unintended consequences, the Small Is Beautiful idea, the demand for 'networked thinking': all this has contributed to the exemplary character and growth of the opposition to large dams. A simple chronology indicates that this first acquired chances of success only in the ecological era, when it did not remain stuck in desperate rearguard actions but grew more self-confident, found new allies and became capable of dealing with political conflict.

In the years between Chernobyl and Rio, from 1986 to 1992, environmental concerns reached a new international peak. The resistance to large dam projects, from Austria to Indonesia, was at its height in the 1980s, and 28 September 1989 saw the first great rally against the Narmada dam: the Narmada Bachao Andolan or 'Save the Narmada Movement'.[145] In view of the World Bank's involvement in the Narmada project, US Congressmen staged a hearing in 1989 and invited Indian representatives of the resistance to attend it. Since Japan too had a stake in funding the project, Japanese NGOs organized an international Narmada symposium the following year, after which Tokyo pulled out of the project. In late 1990 large numbers of people flocked to a sit-in at the main construction site,[146] in a spectacular demonstration that recalled the famous salt march led by Mahatma Gandhi.

NGOs pressured the World Bank for years to end its support for the project, causing it to commission a special report in 1992. This drew the devastating conclusion that the whole design stage had been sloppy and unprofessional. It had not even been thought worth calculating with reasonable accuracy the number of people who would be displaced; it now turned out that the final total would be 240,000, rather than the 90,000 originally envisaged.[147] Nothing played a greater role than the Narmada scandal in bringing about the subsequent 'social-ecological turn'; indeed, it had such an impact on the image of the Bank that demands were voiced for its dissolution.[148] In the end, the World Bank decided to withdraw from the project.[149] It was no longer possible to stop completion of the Sardar Sarovar dam, however, and a series of further dams is planned for the Narmada valley. Some of these are already under construction, providing ample material for future controversy. But 'even if we lose this struggle, we shall win the battle', predicted Medha Patkar, the internationally famous spokesperson of the resistance movement.[150]

The Three Gorges dam on the Yangtze

The resistance to large dams is a striking example of how, in the eco-age, new thinking carries certain issues around the world, attracting very different players with different cultural backgrounds. It seems natural to compare the Narmada campaign in India with Chinese criticism of the Three Gorges dam project in the densely populated Yangtze valley; it

came to the attention of the world, also in 1989, through the documentation supplied by the courageous engineer Dai Qing, who was sentenced
to ten months in prison for her pains.[151] This gigantic project, completely
overshadowing the one on the Narmada, stretches for more than 600 kilometres, and the power station is supposed to generate as much electricity
as sixteen large nuclear facilities. It was thought at first that two million
people would need to be resettled, but the figure crept up by several million
more.[152]

The conflict scenario in China was completely different from the one
in India, a country with a lively civil society teeming with local initiatives.
Villagers had lost most of their autonomy under the Communist dictatorship and were in no position to sustain the resistance. Dai Qing described
the objective style of a debate among experts, which, for all its restraint,
makes us aware of millennia of hydraulic experience and respect for the
river's might based on numerous flood disasters. The Three Gorges project
had been discussed internally for three decades, but its scale had cooled
even Mao Zedong's ardour, especially as it would make the country more
vulnerable militarily and local peasant communes were meant to form the
basis of Communist rule. Dai Qing was supported by Li Rui, Mao's former
secretary for industrial affairs and vice-minister for water resources and
electricity, who appealed to 'the laws of nature' and, using party jargon,
accused enthusiasts for the project of leftist emotionalism and arbitrary
subjectivism.[153]

In 1957 the feisty hydraulics expert Huang Wanli, who had once worked
for the Tennessee Valley Authority, also invoked the 'laws of nature' in
his critique of the Sanmenxia dam project on the River Hoangho, which
turned into a fiasco because of the sludge load that had given the Yellow
River its name. Later, in his eighties and still not opposed to large dams
in principle, he sent letters warning against the Three Gorges project to
the Chinese head of government Jiang Zemin and to President Clinton,
and played off experiences from China's past against the deficient local
knowledge of the Soviet advisers.[154] As to Dai Qing, the issue was not
only the Yangtze but also, increasingly, freedom of opinion and policy
competence.[155] The fact that the project was becoming a political trial of
strength may be one reason why the Chinese government stuck to its guns.
However, after 181 metres of the high dam were completed, the government began to distance itself from the project,[156] and disquiet over the
flooding of a historic landscape became politically acceptable. In 2007 a
huge canvas by Liu Xiaodong, *The New Migrants of the Three Gorges*, was
auctioned by the founder of a Beijing restaurant chain for something like
two million euros.[157]

Far from being isolated instances, the Narmada and Three Gorges
controversies were prototypes for environmental protest movements as far
away as South Africa and Brazil. Especially in South, East and Southeast
Asia, the opposition to large dams has developed into a full-blown
movement – whether on the Mekong (which rises in Yunnan in southern

China and flows through several Southeast Asian countries), in the Kedungombo area of central Java, or in numerous other projects.[158] In the case of rivers that cross national frontiers, the disputes have in part been conducted by the respective governments.

In densely populated river cultures, for example, it is not surprising that internal conflicts mainly revolve around the resettlement of people from flooded valleys. But there is also a markedly symbolic dimension, on both sides. For enthusiasts a dam embodies the magical concept of 'development', whereas for opponents it has become the Leviathan of state power.[159] Supporters also argue that large dams are 'symbols of justice in distributing the benefits of development among the provinces'[160] – another example of how social justice can be used to justify wholesale state incursions, as the history of Communism repeatedly shows. Ecology too is Janus-faced in terms of power politics: it functions not only as a weapon of resistance but also as a legitimation of rule. The Indonesian 'transmigration project' to move millions of poor people from Java to other islands, which is considered the 'most ambitious resettlement project in the world', was justified on something like ecological grounds – by reference to the intolerable overpopulation of Java.

A new ecological basis for the right to a homeland

But as soon as we get more specific, ecological reasoning also provides arguments in the opposite direction. Not the least promising of its aspects is the rational foundation it gives for the right to a homeland (which to champions of progress and mobility is simply an expression of the law of inertia). The Indonesian 'transmigration project' led not only to mass impoverishment but also a large-scale ecological disaster, since the settlers had no relationship to their new environment and were unfamiliar with conditions there.[161] Even parts of the Indonesian army sympathized with the anti-dam movement and failed to move against demonstrators.[162]

The writer Valentin Rasputin, one of the spiritual fathers of the Russian environmental movement, wrote in his *Farewell to Matyora* (1976) of the anti-dam thrust contained in the love of one's country: it was a new tone in the Soviet Union, where mega-dams had been hailed for generations as the cathedrals of Communism. Rasputin's heroine is an old woman – a perfect specimen of a lively Russian peasant, deeply attached to her homeland – who remains in her village even when it is flooded by a dam reservoir.[163] The author himself, in a letter to the Russian head of government, threatened to commit suicide on Red Square if the plan to divert Siberian rivers to Central Asia was implemented.[164] Medha Patkar announced in 1989, in a letter to the executive director of the World Bank, that she and her fellow-campaigners would not leave the Narmada valley even if it were flooded.[165] The product of Rasputin's literary imagination was carried over into the real world!

The ambiguity of ecology on the Danube

The movement against the planned hydropower station near Hainburg, 60 kilometres down river from Vienna, takes us into a very different atmosphere. The project, which threatened to flood the pastoral landscape dear to nature lovers, originated in the days of the Third Reich, but it did not get further than the drawing board until the early 1980s. The World Wildlife Fund launched a 'Save the Meadows!' campaign. And when the clearance of riverside forest began in December 1984, conservationists occupied the area, bringing work to a temporary halt on 2 January 1985 after a brutal police operation had aroused widespread disgust among the public. The internationally best-known Austrian of the day – the behavioural scientist Konrad Lorenz, then in his eighties, who had received a Nobel Prize in 1973 and authored the seminal *Civilized Man's Eight Deadly Sins* – placed himself at the head of the protest movement and, together with other academics and environmentalists, called for a referendum on the Hainburg project.[166] On 7 May 1984 an effective event was staged for the media: an 'animal press conference', at which spokespersons for the campaign appeared in the guise of red deer, black storks, bluethroats and fire-bellied toads. Although, unlike on the Narmada, this was not actually a human habitat but a species-rich stretch of nature, Lorenz and his colleagues were convinced that most of the Austrian population would consider the Danube meadows a part of their homeland worth preserving. The government in Vienna played for time, initially deciding to postpone the project.

Lorenz had previously put his head above the parapet in a successful campaign against the Zwentendorf nuclear power plant. But now he quarrelled with his old friend Otto Koenig (once nicknamed 'Lorenzulus', because he even copied Lorenz's beard style). Koenig too was a respected behavioural scientist and a leading light in Austrian conservationism, but he had started thinking in a different environmental framework: he believed that, since the country had to be supplied with energy somehow or other, hydropower was the only option left if coal and nuclear were excluded. As early as 1970 he had given advice on environmental sustainability to the Danube power stations that were building one dam after another upstream from Vienna, and with the support of the company in question he had founded an Institute of Eco-Ethology.[167] The Danube was not the Nile or the Hoangho, and a dam there did not spell ecological disaster. Did not rivers left to themselves also clog up and form delightful lakes, offering breeding grounds to whole flocks of birds? What it meant to think ecologically was not altogether clear in relation to hydropower situations, at least at temperate latitudes.

For Otto Koenig, the conflicts over hydropower were a sign that conservation had to be rethought from scratch in the eco-age: it had to shift its focus from the mere protection of familiar landscapes to an active and holistic strategy for the development of a nationwide environmentally sustainable economy. 'Conservationism today stands at the wrong front', he complained after the campaign against the Hainburg project. There were 'scarcely any undisturbed landscapes' left to preserve; sometimes, habitat protection could succeed 'only through targeted revitalization', through the creation of 'second-hand living space'. This was to borrow a term from Konrad Lorenz, for whom anyone with a knowledge of history must realize that, because of canal-building, the Neusiedler See paradise so dear to nature lovers is actually a 'second-hand living space'. But conservation or no, 'our main concern today is for detoxification of the environment': again the toxic leitmotif! 'In this age of madness, genuine conservationists must think holistically, plan holistically and act holistically.' They must fight 'at the right fronts', 'where the issue really is survival, not some media-driven spectacle'. Hydropower stations are therefore an 'important step' in the right direction. And, without mentioning Lorenz by name: 'I know there are zoologists and botanists for whom a particular landscape with trees or a few larvae in a familiar pool are more important than people affected by exhaust gases. They are the "conservationists" who drive by car to occupy a riverside meadow.'[168] Seldom has a leading environmental activist stated the problem of priorities in such a down-to-earth and provocative manner.

Originally cutting across conservation: the anti-nuclear movement

Whereas the anti-hydropower front was incomprehensible to Italian conservationists – hydraulic engineering is a very old tradition in Italy – old-style conservationists in the Alpine lands, like the Sierra Club in the American West, actually accepted nuclear power plants as a way of averting the disfigurement of valleys with dam walls. For Koenig, on the other hand, the fight against nuclear energy took priority, even though he was horrified by the 'grotesque game of Indians and revolution' in which many of his fellow-campaigners engaged.[169] This brings us to the heart of the conflict. In 1979 the German movement peaked with a 100,000-strong demonstration in Hanover on 31 March, not long after a majority of Austrians had opted out of nuclear power in a referendum on 5 November 1978. Robert Jungk proclaimed an 'informal International' of resistance, from Scandinavia to Australia.[170]

No other issue was so central to the new environmental movement, unaffected by conservationist traditions, which sprang up mostly in Central Europe but not only there. It originated in a civil movement, not in the activity of politicians – although information too was in there from the start.[171] It remains evident today that there were rational reasons for this concentration on the nuclear dangers. For protest movements, it was an advantage to have nuclear power plants as such massive objects of attack, whereas the ecological hazards of chemicals, motoring or agriculture were more difficult to grasp at a single point. Environmental politicians who wanted to create a lobby for themselves out of the citizens' initiatives felt at a loss in the face of this new priority, since energy policy lay outside their field of competence. Later, the struggle against nuclear technology was often motivated in ecological terms: the splitting of the atom, which interfered with the basic elements of the universe, appeared as a sin against creation. At first, however, the issue was not nature but technological safety and human health; the new protest movement fitted in with the worldwide anti-toxic campaigns.

The 'pathfinder' role of nuclear technology: facing a hypothetical risk

But the anti-nuclear movement was also a herald of things to come, since the dangers in question, unlike nearly every other environmental issue then making the headlines, did not essentially translate into damaging effects that were visible and proven: they involved a *hypothetical risk*. This was something new. And its importance for the future, for the world in which we now live, is clear if we think of the risks of genetic engineering, climate change and marine ecosystems, or even the particularly hypothetical risk of 'electrosmog'.

None other than Wolf Häfele, the powerfully eloquent originator of the fast breeder project at Karlsruhe nuclear research centre, pointed to this 'pathfinder' role way back in 1973[172] – partly, no doubt, to remind the gathering opposition that nuclear risks with their characteristic uncertainties were not alone in the landscape of the new technologies. This tension runs through the whole history of environmentalism. Acute and tangible risks are most likely to excite public protests, but it is the chronic and imperceptible ones that tend to be the most serious. However, the anti-nuclear movement, which arose long before the incidents at Three Mile Island and Chernobyl, demonstrates that these new kinds of risk are capable of mobilizing large numbers of people.

Or is Hiroshima the ultimate origin of the anti-nuclear movement: a visible, public catastrophe of the most horrific kind? Against this, it may be pointed out that in the fifties (one thinks of the 'Göttingen Manifesto' issued by German nuclear scientists in 1957) intellectuals and opinion-makers had sharply differentiated between the bomb and the 'peaceful atom'. And in the 1970s German opponents of nuclear power still regarded the issue of 'the Bomb' as a diversion; it was more likely to be brought up by the pro-nuclear lobby, which argued that nuclear weapons, not civilian uses, were the real danger. The peaceful atom thus became a kind of whipping boy, in a role that it by no means deserved.

The anti-nuclear movement was not from the outset a component, or indeed catalyst, of a broader environmentalism. In many cases, the initial fixation on this one issue was so colossal simply because the absorbing detailed study of nuclear risks left little time for anything else. Both this early prioritization, and the way in which the focus on the nuclear issue eventually extended to a wider spectrum of environmental risks, are of exemplary significance, especially in Germany.

No need to explain the German anomaly?

It is true that the anti-nuclear movement was by no means as peculiar to Germany as the atom lobby often claimed and many activists themselves believed. But even systematic global comparisons have shown that the Federal Republic was way out in front; its figure of 120,000 participants for a single demonstration has still not been matched anywhere in the world.[173] Also distinctive is the tenacity with which the movement held up over the decades, surviving a generation change and a decline in media interest. This is evidently connected to another German lead – to the unique successes of the Greens, whose main origin lay in the anti-nuclear movement. When they first emerged, at the end of the 1970s, the main dividing line between their supporters and opponents was the question of nuclear energy. This was the solid point of reference, at least in Germany, amid the confusing spectrum of environmental issues.

Things seemed very simple to activists in Germany: nuclear technology was highly dangerous, so resistance to it was natural enough; the only thing requiring explanation was why this remained weaker in other countries. From a purely German viewpoint, the controversy unfolded with an inner logic out of the development of nuclear technology itself. Three arguments may be given in support of this.

1 The German nuclear industry at first preferred to develop its own reactors, and there was an awareness that they needed to be considerably safer in the densely populated Federal Republic than in the United States. However, American light water reactors became standard at the latest by 1967, although in the view of US experts the high 'residual risk' meant that these were acceptable only in lightly populated areas, such as did not exist in the Federal Republic.[174] An 'ecology of the eco-movement' therefore logically accounts for the vigour of the resistance in Germany.
2 Until the 1960s expert circles talked with remarkable candour about the dangers of nuclear energy, but once billions had been invested in light water reactors a new code of practice put an end to discussions of the maximum risk. It was therefore logical that these should take place instead among the opposition public.[175]
3 So long as nuclear energy was a vision for the future, any number of pipe dreams could be projected onto it – and in fact the 1950s witnessed a veritable nuclear euphoria, in Germany and many other parts of the world. This stopped at the moment when nuclear power plants became a huge reality. Once a power station was planned nearby, it made sense to ask more warily than before whether one could rely on the safety procedures in the event of a major accident.[176]

In a sense, the dispute over nuclear energy has been the largest public controversy so far in the history of the Bundesrepublik: its duration, from the action at Wyhl (1975) to the present, belies all claims about short-lived fashions in today's media world; its vigour was such that the largest demonstrations outdid those of the student movement in 1968; and it has involved great numbers of people and a range of often high-level arguments. The enthusiasm of the movement did not come only from a common rejection of top-down paternalism; it also had an intrinsic intellectual attractiveness, not least because of attempts to bridge the gap between the social and natural sciences.

All this was true of other countries as well. Yet the Federal Republic did occupy a special place, and to appreciate this better a comparison with nuclear controversies, or the lack of controversies, in three other countries is especially instructive: that is, in France, the United States and Japan.

France

Few people know today that the first major European demonstration against a planned nuclear plant took place not in Germany but in France: on 12 April 1971, in the Alsatian commune of Fessenheim. Shortly afterwards, ten times as many demonstrators (roughly 15,000) poured into the reactor construction site in Bugey, on the right bank of the Rhone, ending the campaign with a great 'anti-nuclear festival' in July.[177] These actions did not lead to success, unlike the resistance that began in 1974 to the planned chemical plant near Marckolsheim in Alsace. The atmosphere was marked by French traditions of *l'action directe*, farmers' resistance and 1968-style countercultural happenings, but also by the growing assertiveness of regional movements.

Under the aegis of ecology, Alsatians were able to display a new self-awareness that would have been regarded as treasonable a few decades earlier. On 28 December 1971, representatives of some fifty anti-nuclear groups from various countries met in Strasbourg, and observers already thought they could detect that 'a phase of "spontaneous" individual actions was passing over to one of organization and concerted operations'. Models from across the Rhine were important in the occupation at Wyhl on 18 February 1975, when the West German anti-nuclear movement first hit the headlines as a large-scale militant phenomenon. In 1974 a Battelle Institute study had found that, out of some 10,000 German press articles on nuclear energy, only a small fraction took a negative attitude; contrary to what was later claimed, the primary impulse did not come from the media.[178]

Only in the subsequent period, when France had become the undisputed citadel of atomic energy, did it become popular to construct an ideal-typical contrast between France, the land of reason and faith in progress, and Germany, the land of Romanticism and dissatisfaction with modernity; the German nuclear lobby, in particular, liked to pour scorn on an alleged national tradition of hostility to technology. There may be a small kernel of truth in this opposition, but it would be easy to adduce a host of facts that contradict it. Nor does the history of technology in Germany exactly fit the picture, and – whatever many Germans believe[179] – 'Vive l'atome!' did not sum up the overwhelming mood in France. Rather, there were significant levels of protest, and opinion surveys reveal that nuclear anxiety was not much less widespread in France than in the Bundesrepublik.[180]

To some extent, the differences between the two countries are explicable in ecological terms. Three are obvious enough and may partly account for the fact that the opposition was much less effective in France. First, France is much less densely populated than West Germany and has far smaller coal reserves at its disposal. From the 1950s on, the political rhetoric in Paris assumed that France's industrial backwardness in comparison with Germany and Britain had been due to its relative shortage of coal, whereas now nuclear energy seemed to offer it a golden opportunity.[181] In any event, France closed the gap even in the absence of large coal deposits. Second, in the 1960s, solar energy installations in the Pyrenees and wave power projects on the Atlantic coast aroused considerable public attention, although in the end their significance was more symbolic than real. The great age of renewable energies had not yet arrived. Third, France had an arsenal of nuclear weapons, so that the country's organizational apparatus was in a totally different league from Germany's Atomic Commission. Besides, nationalist motives were associated with nuclear technology in De Gaulle's France; these also existed on the quiet in the Federal Republic, although no one dared to voice them in public. Many overheads of the nuclear arms race – especially the high costs of uranium enrichment – could be disguised by 'peaceful' technology.

Atom bomb production not only gave a start-up advantage for the 'peaceful atom'; it also represented a burden on reactor development that was always in tension with the needs of the energy industry. For 'national' motives, the Commissariat à l'energie atomique (CEA) under De Gaulle insisted on gas graphite reactors, which promised to make France independent of American technology, whereas Electricité de France (EDF) would have liked to use the cheaper American light water reactors, as the German energy industry did at the time. Under these conditions, no self-contained nuclear community developed in the De Gaulle era – a situation which, for French critics of nuclear technology, was advantageous for a while. But when De Gaulle's successor, Georges Pompidou, opted instead for light water reactors, the nuclear front closed. After the oil crisis of autumn 1973, the French government – unperturbed by the mounting criticism of nuclear energy – deployed all its powers to place virtually the whole of the country's electricity supply on a nuclear foundation and 'left everyone breathless with its draconian boldness'[182] in making France the world leader in nuclear technology.

In the late 1970s, the opposition to nuclear projects was even more violent in France than in the Federal Republic. If it eventually ground to a halt, the decisive reason was probably the strength of French centralism, since above all there protest movements need to be based on more than outrage to have a chance of success. In the 1960s, the German nuclear industry had a horror of French bureaucracy and *planification* and was filled with distrust of the European Atomic Community (Euratom), originally nicknamed the 'European Community for Peaceful Production of the French Atom Bomb'. Even the *Industriekurier*, then the leading mouthpiece of German industry, relayed this 'witticism'.[183] In the 1970s, however, the German nuclear industry began to feel envious of French centralism.

German licensing procedures for nuclear power plants had at least formally a decentralized element: they laid down schedules for local discussion, which gave a forum for critics who were being asked to live next door to one. It is true that such discussions often proved farcical, since the *Land* government had often made up its mind already, but this meant that critics felt furious at being slighted and faith in the approval process was destroyed. Then there were the incidents with the police! Most German students in the revolt of '68 thought the police force was particularly brutal because it had many former Nazis in its ranks. But anyone who took part in demonstrations in France against the Malville breeder project soon realized that this was a mistake. As a brochure *Against the Atomic State*, with texts by Wolf Biermann, Klaus Traube and Günter Wallraf, forcefully put it: 'In comparison with Malville, Brokdorf was like going for a stroll. The police fired smoke, gas and percussion grenades as in war.'[184] In the abstract, this may have been a chance for anti-nuclear activists to experience suffering and become heroes; demonstrators in France had an even sturdier enemy image than in the Federal Republic. But in the late seventies the age of the Che Guevara cult was over. The environmental movement was brimming with an emotive new feeling for *life*; its spirit of martyrdom was exiguous indeed.

The United States

Most German anti-nuclear activists were not aware that the earliest impetus for their campaign came from the United States. Holger Strohm, who put together the first extensive German compendium of anti-nuclear arguments (*Friedlich in die Katastrophe*, 1973), was chair of the German section of Friends of the Earth, and he had acquired his unrivalled information from transatlantic connections. Curiously, these American origins of the nuclear energy controversy have been forgotten by many US historians. In the three thick volumes of the *Encyclopedia of World Environmental History* (2004), for example, nuclear technology and the anti-nuclear movement are marginal issues; the Chernobyl reactor disaster, which defined a new era for German environmentalists, is not even awarded an independent article. An environmental historian for whom nuclear power is the number one issue cannot but find this puzzling, especially as no environmental movement has as marked a sense of history as the American.

This difference is partly due to the lack of temporal synchronization between the anti-nuclear campaigns in America and Germany. In the United States, the struggle came to a head as early as the 1960s, when there was a direct transition from the movement against atmospheric nuclear weapons testing to protests against civilian nuclear power plants. One connective link was the campaign against the Plowshare Program, whose title alluded to the pacifist 'Swords into Ploughshares' – in fact, a project for the civilian use of atom bombs to create a new lock-free Panama Canal ('Panatomic Canal') at sea level across the Isthmus.[185] The criticism of nuclear plants grew sharper in the late sixties, when tests showed that in major incidents the emergency cooling system could only be relied upon to a limited extent: or, in plain language, that a major catastrophe making the 'peaceful atom' akin to a nuclear bomb was a real possibility.[186]

By the mid-seventies, however, when the anti-nuclear campaign in West Germany was at its height, things had quietened down again in the United States. There had been no decision to wind down nuclear energy, but nor had any new plants been commissioned. The main reason for this was the high costs involved. Meanwhile, the key issue for environmental activists had become a ban on the export of weapons-grade fissile material.[187] During Jimmy Carter's presidency, mainly for anti-proliferation reasons in the interests of the existing monopoly states, the US administration turned against fast breeder reactors and reprocessing plants – the very projects which (as at Kalkar and Gorleben) were becoming the target of vigorous protests in West Germany.[188] There was thus little motivation for large protest movements in the USA, even after the major incident at Three Mile Island in March 1979. Since the international Gorleben symposium was meeting during those very days in Hanover with Carl Friedrich von Weizsäcker[189] in the chair – the Christian Democrat government in Lower Saxony pulled out of the reprocessing project at the end, signalling what an industry spokesperson called a 'Cannae-like' defeat for German nuclear policy – Three Mile Island may possibly have had a greater impact in Germany than in the United States.[190]

Until a few years previously, it would have been a demonstration of competence in the field to call for 'closing of the fuel cycle' – that is, for the building of breeder reactors and reprocessing plants to make nuclear power akin to renewable energy. 'Closing the fuel cycle', with a sideswipe at America's 'throwaway economy' and lack of interest in recycling, would even have sounded an ecological note. But when reprocessing turned out to be one of the most unpleasant risk sectors of nuclear technology, which did not even promise to be cost-effective, nuclear energy lost the last remnant of its kudos as an environmentally friendly and renewable 'new technology'.[191] In the United States, where people had always had a more sober and business-like attitude to nuclear energy, it had lost that remnant long ago.

Another difference between America and Germany deserves consideration here. In the United States, distinguished scientists were from the beginning at the forefront of campaigns against nuclear projects. Critics never found themselves left in the lurch by science. No less a figure than David Lilienthal, the first post-1945 chair of the Atomic Energy Commission (AEC) and formerly a charismatic New Deal project leader, became openly sceptical about nuclear energy in 1960.[192] Then, in the course of the sixties, the Union of Concerned Scientists – which had cut its teeth on criticisms of atomic weapons – developed into the brains trust of the movement against nuclear power plants.[193] Gofman and Tamplin, the spokespersons of the growing attack on the AEC (which was later dissolved), had once been leading experts on nuclear technology. Now they described the AEC as a pack of inveterate liars and crooks, which never learned from its mistakes and practised 'an insidious form of sadism and genocide': no streetfighter could have put it more sharply.[194] At least as prominent was Barry Commoner, whose head graced the cover of *Time Magazine*'s first issue on the environment in February 1970. In him everything was rolled into one: protest against nuclear weapons testing, against the Vietnam War and against civilian nuclear plants – all resting on a foundation of broad ecological competence.

For a long time, the German anti-nuclear movement lacked figures of comparable scientific repute. The nuclear physicists who issued the 'Göttingen Manifesto' in April 1957, speaking out against the supply of atomic weapons to the Bundeswehr, also emphatically supported the 'peaceful atom' and stuck to this position in the following period.[195] In the United States there was a much more direct historical link between criticisms of civilian atomic energy and nuclear weapons. This was perfectly in tune with the basically pacifist tendency of the environmental movement, which in 1980, against the background of rearmament and a new peace movement, also became central to the German Greens.

Japan

This of all countries had no major controversy regarding nuclear power, at least until the Fukushima disaster of 11 March 2011 (now referred to as 3/11!). It is a very curious lack. After all, Japan was the first, and so far the only, direct victim of nuclear weapons. When the twenty-three-man crew of the *Lucky Dragon*, a Japanese tuna-fishing vessel, sailed into the fallout of an American hydrogen bomb test in March 1954 and came down with radiation sickness, an international movement developed against nuclear weapons testing in the atmosphere.[196] The Japanese plains are much more densely populated than the Federal Republic of Germany, and the 'residual risk' of nuclear technology is correspondingly greater – not to speak of the fact that Japan is one of the most earthquake-prone countries in the world. (In the United States, the risk of earthquakes was the compelling argument used by the first action group against a nuclear energy project, at Bodega Bay in California.) And since the Japanese electrical industry – more far-sighted than the German in this respect – made an early decision to con-centrate on electronics rather than nuclear technology, atomic power had no 'national' argument in its favour; on the contrary, the reactors had to be imported from the USA.

So how was it that no major protest movement developed in Japan? This is one of those questions that cry out for international comparisons; one does not get far if one focuses only on Japan. A deep psychological factor may be that Japan used to have one of the lowest cancer rates in the industrialized world, and that – as one can see from the face masks often worn in big cities – the fear of bacteria and harmful dust was more powerful. Probably, however, the main reason is that people could see no alternative to nuclear power. Japan has little coal of its own, and depend-ence on Chinese imports would have been a nightmare. The world's major oil reserves lie even further from Japan than from Europe, while wind power does not inspire much confidence in a country plagued by typhoons. Fortunately, the car industry learned much earlier there than in Germany that, in the short term, energy-saving is by far the most efficient source of power. But since the 'wood age' finally ended around 1960, electric air conditioning has been the favourite way of heating interior spaces (much to the disgust of energy planners).

And Hiroshima? In Tokyo there is only a small, hidden and little-visited monument to the victims of atomic weapons. When the German Green leader Petra Kelly went to Japan in 1976, she was baffled and appalled at the widespread indifference to the nuclear risk;[197] people preferred to say nothing about the whole subject. Victims had to endure discrimination; a 'culture of remembrance' had not developed.[198] Europeans who know the country well explain that the Japanese tend to display a serene cheerful-ness and dislike speaking of misfortune and suffering.[199] One may doubt whether such a blanket judgement is sustainable, especially as dissenting voices are to be found in Japanese literature. Nor should we forget that in Germany too, under the influence of the 'Göttingen Manifesto', the public's attitude to the 'peaceful atom' was for a long time unconnected to fear of the Bomb.

Depth psychologists may speculate that fear of the Bomb, repressed in the subconscious, was the underlying cause for the rage that many envi-ronmental activists felt about nuclear power stations. But if we stick to conscious, documented history, then Japan is an argument against this.

In the case of other environmental disasters, the Japanese 'culture of silence' ended much earlier. This was apparent in the Minimata tragedy, when, as we have seen, mercury discharged by a chemical corporation severely damaged the health of people living on a bay in Kyushu island, and Ishimure Michiko's *Paradise in the Sea of Sorrow* acquired a significance comparable to that of Rachel Carson's *Silent Spring* for the American environmental movement. This raises an important point. When we ask why there was no major anti-nuclear campaign in a particular country, we must consider whether other conflicts were not uppermost at the time. Anyone who took part in the German nuclear controversy knows that it took up much time and energy, and that it is not possible to get involved simultaneously in several campaigns; the drive is not there, even if time is not wanting.

Again we find the basic dilemma of the environmental movement: the range of issues is huge, and many are connected to one another, but our forces are limited and activists must focus on a particular objective. Why was there not a major struggle over nuclear energy in England, where the first big (though long downplayed) reactor accident occurred on 8 October 1957, at Windscale? Perhaps the answer is that British conservationists and environmentalists had traditionally concentrated on quite different goals that absorbed their potential for militancy: bird protection, animal rights, anti-hunting campaigns, later opposition to motorways, Reclaim the Streets? In the GDR, following Chernobyl, even intellectuals deeply frustrated at conditions in their country sometimes expressed irritation over the fuss in the West: East Germans were nearly choking on coal smoke and would be more than happy to have nuclear power instead; the way protesters got worked up in West Germany was typical of a country living in luxury.

In short, to understand the conflict over nuclear energy, it is necessary to avoid a total fixation on power plants and to keep in mind the wider picture. Of course, this does not always remain the same: it did not in Japan, either. As in Germany, women in particular were mobilized in the wake of Chernobyl. There too, with a twenty-year delay, the once-vaunted 'closing of the fuel cycle' was identified as the sorest point: the major incidents involving the Monju fast-breeder reactor in 1995 and the Tokaimura reprocessing plant in 1997, which revealed an expected amateurism and nearly ended in catastrophe, unleashed a wave of public outrage over the nuclear industry that had never been seen before in Japan.[200] Another wave of protest, though remaining local, followed in 2004 in response to a major incident at the Mihama power plant.[201] The key factor is probably that all the protests up to Fukushima remained disparate and did not really impinge on mainstream opinion formation. The interaction of civic protests with government authorities, the media and the academic world, which was so decisive for the success of environmentalists in the West, appears to have been lacking in Japan, at least in the case of nuclear dangers.

Before Fukushima, anti-nuclear activism in Japan focused on the final storage of highly radioactive waste.[202] Much the same was true in South Korea, where revelations that a permanent disposal site was under secret preparation led to a veritable uprising on the island of Anmyeondo.[203] In this respect, there is even a parallel with anti-nuclear developments in

Germany. These have a logic of their own; for as soon as nuclear plants were in existence, the transportation of spent fuel offered campaigners a clear target, and it was no solution to leave the waste inside the plant or to dump it in some forgotten corner where no one would disturb it. A satisfactory final solution was anyway not possible, given that plutonium has a half-life of thousands of years, and this undeniable Achilles heel was only underlined by the shilly-shallying of those whom the protesters targeted. The prospect of becoming a nuclear dumping ground was especially infuriating, so it was relatively easy to organize local protest actions. And even with their limitations, these repeatedly highlighted the dilemma from which there was no escape in principle.

What explains Germany's leading role in the anti-nuclear campaign?

Champions of nuclear technology in Germany have often claimed that the vigorous resistance is due to a typically German angst and Romantic hostility to technology. Put like that, the argument is easy to refute; the German forest was threatened far more by smoky coal-fired power stations than it is by nuclear plants. But what is true is that, after two world wars, Germans had a particularly strong longing for security and an aversion to anything associated with rearmament. In any event, a German tradition of cautiousness is visible in relation to technology, at least as much among anti-technicists as among technicians.[204] Friedrich Münzinger's *Atomkraft*, the standard West German work of the fifties on reactor construction, is full of warnings about the risks of nuclear technology, such as one would find twenty years later only in the writings of anti-nuclear campaigners. In his view, the euphoria of the fifties was an 'atomic power psychosis', explicable only by the 'mental confusion that had severely affected the world for years'. Such promises as 'that atomic power will soon ease the lot of the man in the street in unheard-of ways' were 'mere blarney unruffled by any expert knowledge'. Münzinger noted with satisfaction that many Germans were 'warier than Americans, for example' of nuclear installations.[205] He was by no means hostile to technology as such, however, and had considerable experience of supervising the construction of large power stations. For this very reason, he was aware of the size of the risks that physicists never even suspected in their laboratories. As far back as 1942, in his book *Ingenieure*, he had argued that a precise knowledge of risks was part of the skill of a good engineer and differentiated him from technically minded lay people.

What of Romanticism as a prime source of the German lead in the nuclear controversy? It is an attractive idea to follow the ways in which environmental protests associated themselves over the years with the old German forest romanticism. The link did not exist at the beginning. It first appears clearly among the environmentalists in Alsace, from whose ranks the future French Green leader Antoine Waechter emerged, and who, as ecologists, no longer had to fear being suspected of German sympathies because of their love of homeland and forest.[206] In Germany the latter was the domain of foresters, who were proud of a long tradition of sustainability; there seemed to be no particular need to worry about the forest. A link between anti-nuclear protests and forest romanticism first came about during the campaign over the Gorleben radioactive waste facility in Lower Saxony, where protesters founded a 'Free Republic of Wendland', lived in the style of a rural commune, embraced trees and climbed treetops when police tried to clear the area by force. Thirty years later one of these 'tree ladies', Rebekka Harms, became a Green Euro MP.

The 'dying forest' alarm, sounded by *Der Spiegel*'s front cover of 16 November 1981, turned this alliance of environmentalism and forest romanticism into a torrent. Yet this very alarm, which seems exaggerated today, broke up the united front, contradicting the view of those who would derive the course of the movement from the logic of environmental discourse itself. For now it was coal-fired power stations that became the target of criticism – a tendency later reinforced by the climate change alarm – and many partisans of nuclear energy began inwardly to rejoice. Years later, of course, their sense of triumph would be tainted by Chernobyl.

At any public debate on nuclear energy in the seventies, it was usually easy to tell at once who belonged to which side: those in favour were correctly dressed, in a grey suit and tie, with a neat hairstyle and controlled body language, whereas those against tended to be younger, long-haired, more colourfully (or at least casually) dressed, and more relaxed in their body language. All in all, it was a perfect illustration of Pierre Bourdieu's concept of habitus. Often, this external impression prompted further conclusions, as if two fundamentally different cultures, world-views and human types were involved. Nowadays, representatives of the two camps cannot be identified straight off in this way: the opponents of nuclear energy may be more advanced in years than its supporters; the anti-nuclear campaigners of yesterday have become the older generation.

Thirty years or more ago, however, it was already possible to know that the German nuclear controversy did not express a cultural conflict with deep historical roots. Just a little earlier, in the 1960s, the fronts had been completely different: typical intellectuals regarded nuclear energy as the epitome of progress for which it was worth fighting (other social groups, as surveys showed, were more sceptical). Those who thought of themselves as 'left-wing' or 'progressive' used to criticize government ministers for not promoting this energy of the future with sufficient resolve, allegedly because of their conservatism, inertia, aloofness from science, or dogmatic economic liberalism.[207]

Admittedly there was no lack of sceptical voices. But they were to be heard where in retrospect one would have least expected to find them: among precursors of Ludwig Erhard's 'social market economy', among experienced engineers such as Friedrich Münzinger, or at the head of the RWE, by far the largest electricity producer of the time. In the fifties and sixties, the RWE had spared no expense or effort to open up brown coal fields in the Lower Rhine region; coal had been its triumph, nuclear energy a disruptive factor giving competitors a potential advantage. In 1959 its boss, Heinrich Schöller, referred to the climate of 'atomic hysteria' and warned that Germans might be 'taken in' (*böse hereinfallen*) by the forced pace of reactor construction![208] Such scepticism persisted at the top until the late sixties. And in the seventies, the RWE was not properly prepared when it had to defend the front line of nuclear power against a storm of resistance.

The '68 student movement and the birth of anti-nuclear protests

Here we come to an intriguing problem of continuity. In the United States the leading role of Barry Commoner spans the periods, and in the Bundesrepublik there were a number of similar figures. But in general '68ers began to take an interest in nuclear technology only *after* Wyhl 1975 had revealed the emergence of a broad protest movement: in fact, they had great difficulty in theoretically justifying the new position, which at first arose simply out of a spontaneous empathy with the protesters. Among neo-Marxists in the New Left, and not only them, it was a common view that the advance of the productive forces required social progress, and that this rested on the increasing scientific complexity of the productive forces, represented above all by nuclear power. This theory was popular among intellectuals, in both East and West, not least because it assigned them a flattering role as pioneers. The first long polemical tract in German against nuclear technology came from the Austrian forester Günther Schwab (1904–2006), the founder of the 'World League for the Preservation of Life', who later became discredited by right-wing extremism.[209]

But around 1970 the landscape underwent a dramatic change. With Earth Day and the invention of environmental politics in the United States, the Stockholm conference of 1972, European Conservation Year and many other things happening around the world, conservation and environmental protection were given an international 'progressive' facelift. An old concern became fresh and new. This alone made it possible for the New Left to pour into environmental activism, and for environmental protection to become a struggle-oriented movement. Nowhere else could the aggressive style of major demonstrations be acted out as it was at nuclear installations. No issue other than the risks of nuclear power came close to being the bridge between 1968 and the environmental movement. Later questions did not provide the same kind of ideal target.

The anti-nuclear campaign was hardest for Marxist-Leninist positions to justify, since the Soviet Union did not exactly provide a shining example. Maoists were the easiest to mobilize, and for years their groups dominated the action during clashes with the police. True, Mao's Little Red Book said nothing against nuclear technology, but the rhetoric of direct action and links with the peasantry was suited to agitation against nuclear plants, which were mostly located in remote farming areas. The Maoist Nina Gladitz worked with wine-growers and fisherfolk to make an enthralling documentary in the region around Wyhl – for which the pro-Moscow German Communist Party (DKP), hinting at a 'blood and soil romanticism', slanderously described her as a 'new Leni Riefenstahl'.[210]

New opportunities and frustrations

In Austria, Switzerland,[211] the Netherlands, Scandinavia[212] and Italy,[213] the political elites dropped nuclear projects (at least for a time) when they became evidently unpopular. In the Federal Republic of Germany a strong, and for a long time passionate, nuclear 'community' did not give up so easily, but there was no powerful, well-equipped and centrally organized military-scientific-industrial complex of the kind that existed in the nuclear weapons states. Anti-nuclear activists often described the German Atomic Commission as a Moloch of 'state monopoly capitalism'; a study of the records shows, however, that it was a poorly organized and, to some extent, even poorly informed hodgepodge of committees made up of honorary members less and less capable of steering the development of nuclear energy.

Parts of the justice system developed a potential to put a brake on things (though this was seldom appreciated by anti-nuclear activists), when the Federal Administrative Court handed down a judgement in 1972 (the 'Würgassen judgement', after the eponymous nuclear plant) that prioritized safety over economic efficiency. The federal character of the Bundesrepublik obstructed the kind of effective pro-nuclear policy that the atomic community increasingly demanded under the pressure of the ongoing controversy. In 1987 Rudolf Schulten, the inventor of a high-temperature reactor that bears his name, said with a heartfelt groan during a public debate at Bielefeld University that the whole development of German nuclear energy had 'happened against everyone's will'; the uncoordinated interplay of divergent interests had given rise to something that no one had wanted in the first place.

It is true that most of the energy industry had no pressing need for nuclear power plants; when the go-ahead was nevertheless given, an order was placed for the American light water reactors – the cheapest option, and the most tried and tested, which cut across the Bonn government's original plans. The RWE did then build the breeder at Kalkar, but on cost grounds it forwent the full breeder effect and hence the aura of renewable energy. Many opponents of nuclear energy sensed that, despite the harshness of the conflict, they were up against a crumbling front. They played on the underlying lack of interest that the energy industry had in breeder reactors and reprocessing. It should not be forgotten that, if the environmental movement is to be successful in the 'ecology versus economics' exhibition bouts, it has to rely on some convergence (however latent) with economic conditions – as well as on its ability to handle conflict, if only for the sake of media effectiveness.

Japan's nuclear history shows a number of similarities to that of Germany. As Hitoshi Yoshioka, the author of a *Social History of Atomic Energy* (1999), noted, the development of nuclear energy in Japan, as in Germany and France, was for a long time characterized by a 'dual structure': that is, competition between the nuclear science community (keen on developing independent national reactors) and the energy industry (eager to acquire the cheaper American light water reactors). In this too the energy industry prevailed, and the outcome was a hermetically sealed state-industrial complex which until Fukushima offered no opportunities to anti-nuclear activists. And such opportunities are necessary if the protest movement is to move beyond desperate and uncoordinated ad hoc reactions. It may be, though, that impressions are deceptive and that the inner cohesion of the Japanese nuclear complex has been exaggerated.[214]

3 Changing Priorities: The Movement in Motion

'Fax and cyberspace skeletons'? The new communications technology and the environmental movement in motion

In 1968 Peter Menke-Glückert, the inventor of environmental policy in Bonn, proclaimed ten 'eco-commandments for Earth citizens' at the Man and Biosphere conference in Paris. The ninth of these read: 'Information about environmental damage belongs to mankind – not to privileged big business! Not to anyone alone! Avoid information pollution!'

No great movement in history has been as dependent on information as environmentalism is. The anti-nuclear protests started with information, and today the greatest problem for activists is still to ascertain how easy or difficult it would be to opt out of nuclear energy, which is in large part a monopoly of the large electricity producers.[215] The link between modern environmentalism and revolutionary change in information and communications technology is one of the most exciting topics, but also one of the most difficult. Since the impact of the new media and new forms of knowledge is so obscure, many things can be projected into this dynamic. On the question of Facebook, for example, books are currently appearing from opposite points of view: one is subtitled 'How the Facebook Generation Is Saving the Planet', another 'How the Social Network Is Selling Our Lives'.[216] Anyone who constantly surfs in eco-networks on the internet prefers to overlook that the other side uses the same technology. It would seem that the internet increases the inner tension in environmentalism described in this chapter; access to information about the environment has grown to a previously unimaginable extent, but so too has the ability to move within, and get puffed up about, a particular network of 'global thinking'.

In 1971 Barry Commoner presented his 'first law of ecology' – 'everything is connected to everything else' – as applied cybernetics,[217] and the following year Frederic Vester said the same of 'networked thinking'.[218] Cybernetics was a fashion of the age when much could be projected into it; the network became the fetish of the electronic revolution. Not the least of the reasons why *Limits to Growth* caused such a stir in 1972 is that it could support itself on mainframe computer simulations, although the absurdity of growth as a permanent state could easily have been demonstrated without them. It seems to us today that, at a time when the revolutionary development of modern information and communications technology had barely commenced, the significance of technological media for the environment was being spoken of in superlatives. Yet there was little investigation of how this impact looked in detail or changed over time. The whole field has been weighed down with overhasty evaluations as well as mutual allocations of blame.

At a conference on 'Climate Research and the Media', held in Bielefeld in late 1996, the accusations flew back and forth between scientists and media people. One climatologist jibed that the media were 'trained dogs eating out of the hands of doomsayers' – to which someone from the press retorted that scientists hyped up their apocalyptic scenarios as bait for journalists. This provoked a researcher to complain: 'You don't earn any money if you just study in an ivory tower.'[219] There's no doubt about it: the environmental movement does not only deal with interactions between man and nature, but is itself subject to alternating currents within a high-tension triangle made up of science, politics and media. This is a central phenomenon of the eco-age: its dynamic contains great creative potential and should not be prejudged in blanket terms.

We should not forget that advances in information technology, including measurement techniques, crucially enlarge the scope for official enforcement of environmental protection. The strategy of setting emission thresholds, already introduced in the late nineteenth century, remained more or less symbolic so long as emissions could not be measured exactly. In the mid-1970s, however, under the self-effacing state secretary Hartkopf, a fully automatic system for the monitoring of air quality was installed in West Germany.[220] Today the effectiveness of global climate policy depends on, among other things, the extent to which supranational monitors can measure a country's various emissions even if it does not wish them to do so.

The influence of modern media goes right back to the early days of environmental protection. The story began with conservation. Although this is the most tangible side of environmental protection (its erotic zone, as it were), the justification for many protected areas and species can be communicated to most people only by means of colour photos and films. The ordinary person wandering the countryside is not supposed to meet the 'endangered species' face to face – otherwise he or she will endanger it even more! 'It would be difficult to exaggerate the impact and influence upon world opinion of the pictorial accompaniment of the conservation movement', wrote Max Nicholson back in 1970, in his *Environmental Revolution*.[221] It is still creating opportunities today, when wildlife films and photography unimaginable two generations ago are regularly broadcast on television. Placards advertising wildlife organizations show us tigers and gorillas; every soil expert knows that earthworms are far more important for the ecology of our planet, but they are the least photogenic creatures apart from microbes.

The ecologization of conservation actually tends to divert attention away from the immediately fascinating. 'In contrast to the traditional focus on charismatic megafauna,' writes Anna Wöbse, 'the stress has been laid on microflora and microfauna.'[222] After all, modern photographic techniques also developed the art of creating exciting images out of unlikely material that was often not visible to the naked eye, or of using collage to present things that would not otherwise be viewable. This applied especially to new kinds of environmental problem – from radioactivity to climate dangers – which no longer produced a direct shock like the old black (or even grey) smoke pouring from factory chimneys, and it was precisely the confrontation of such risks that gave environmentalism its new quality. It was a challenge to the imagination of people working in the media – and not a few of them took it up. The Wadden Sea National Parks, now a UNESCO world heritage site and the epitome of wilderness for most North Sea tourists, were first made visually attractive by aerial photographs and enlarged detail. The flood of ecological publications can easily make us forget how abstract is all that passes under the name 'environment'. Chris Rootes, the organizer of many transnational symposia on the environmental movement, has the impression that 'it is environmentalists who have made greater, more creative and more effective use of these new technologies than the corporations they oppose'.[223]

This situation influenced the whole character of the environmental movement, which, headed by Greenpeace, often shaped its self-image primarily with the media in mind, not to arouse solidarity with those its operations directly concerned, or to have a directly political impact through lobbying and the proposal of solutions that could get something moving. With an eye to the media David Kraft, the campaigns director of Greenpeace Canada, felt bound to warn against shifting the focus of operations from the sea to land: 'Of 25 Greenpeace operations on land, only one is as spectacular and worth as much as any single operation at sea.'[224] Paul Watson, a rival of Greenpeace who hunts whale-catchers and has studied communications, would not even touch the land: 'Survival in a media culture meant developing the skills to understand and manipulate media to achieve strategic objectives.'[225]

Part of the background to the '68 student revolt was the experience that correctly and rationally presented proposals for reform never get anything moving, whereas large numbers of people can be mobilized by creating a din for the media. Many ecological actions built on this lesson. Earlier – and also later in totalitarian systems – the power of a movement had sometimes consisted in its clandestine character, which was a precondition for conspiratorial activity. Now, on the contrary, 'a movement that doesn't get reported doesn't exist!' – a redefinition of the word 'movement' based on the supposed omnipotence of the media.

There was, and still is, a tendency to exaggerate the importance of the media, precisely in relation to nuclear power. As we pointed out before, it was actually citizens' action groups that first got the controversy started, and nuclear energy continued to be widely rejected during periods when the media considered the issue boring. Later on, media experts claimed that the climate alarm had been played out. But the laws of the media alone do not determine environmental awareness, nor are the issues pure constructs. Media-communicated icons obviously played a huge role, and in typical cases public awareness did not feed off direct observation. Yet, unlike Eastern Christianity, environmentalism did not remain fixed on a particular set of icons.[226] Direct observation and tangible experience could not be permanently eliminated from people's consciousness – and this meant there was movement in the environmental movement.

When the environmental movement set priorities, or when the issues changed after a time, this happened to some extent in accordance with the laws of the media and politics. But the very nature of environmentalism meant that there was always a plurality of themes, and shifts ran counter to the need of environmental groups for an identity of their own. In the long run, the dynamic of the eco-age cannot be reduced to that of the media or the social movements. Behind all the toing and froing, a distinctive dynamic can always be recognized in the chameleon-like changes through which environmentalism passed.

The typical opportunities that the media have offered to environmentalists, helping to redefine the movement in comparison with what went before, have changed over the last forty years. In the 1960s, when television was an exciting new medium and colour film and photography were becoming ever more sophisticated, many activists felt attracted to graphic forms of campaigning and to visually exciting presentations of exotic wildlife. A generation earlier, neither rubber dinghy operations against whalers nor gorillas in the African rainforest would have gripped a wide public as they now did thanks to new pictorial techniques. The Greenpeace rainbow warrior had to be immune from seasickness, while the Robin Wood activist who climbed a chimneystack ladder could not be prone to vertigo. In a pacifist milieu that shunned the old heroism of war, environmental campaigners founded a new heroism and demonstrated that the eco-philosophy of foresight and forethought was by no means an expression of personal anxieties.

Not surprisingly, the preoccupation with the media took its toll: in the competition to achieve maximum effect, it could happen for a while

– though rarely for long – that pure sensation-seeking swept all before it or that Bambi kitsch out-trumped a more carefully considered conservationism.[227] Anyone into hype in a big way often wanted some for himself or herself. Media calculation and money-raising promoted rivalry between various environmental activists and their organizations. Jacques-Yves Cousteau, often regarded as France's most famous environmentalist, whose underwater films on whales caused such a stir when shown on French television in 1968, would have been perfectly suited to working with Greenpeace; but he made his own shows, was unwilling to break with accepted opinion in his country, and undermined the protests in 1987 against French atom bomb tests on the Pacific island of Moruroa.[228] Eventually, the effect of dinghy and smokestack operations wore off – a problem that dawned on many environmental groups remarkably early on and caused them to strike out in new directions.

In the 1980s, leading US environmental organizations began to inundate Congressmen and other potential sympathizers with mail shots, but they soon experienced the law of diminishing returns.[229] The internet, ubiquitous by the late 1990s, seemed cut out for the needs of the movement, where information and networking were crucial in circumventing the established monopolies. 'E-mail and the Internet had transformed the environmental debate into a cyberspace war', we read in a history of the American environmental movement first published in 2007.[230] In the internet world, however, visually spectacular actions were far from possessing the decisive significance they had in television. At the same time, the electronic network took over more than before from the traditional activity of evening meetings and agendas, which many younger activists geared to action and information had never much cared for. 'From structure to network': environmentalism was following a general trend of recent times, which is also observable in economic life.[231] In many respects, networks corresponded to the diversity of environmentalism and the changing priorities better than did traditional movements with their fixed programmes, organizations and set-piece demonstrations.

Still, we need to be careful about constructing a fundamental, irreversible turn! The Facebook world contains the danger of fragmentation and a move away from the valiant perseverance of concerted action. Basic laws of human coexistence are not completely nullified even by revolutions in communications technology; trust is never built through electronic contacts alone. It is also doubtful whether coalitions of players capable of taking action can come about through networks that operate only via the internet. Precisely because of new technology, the explosive growth of communication might have the opposite effect, so that the level of action becomes further removed from it and acquires new radical features through a process of autonomization. The mutual trust necessary for common action still crucially depends on face-to-face contact, and action initiatives and the bringing to bear of political influence still operate mainly in regional settings. There is a tension between the levels of communication and action that helps to keep the environmental movement in motion. The deliberately paradoxical slogan 'Think globally, act locally' should not be understood to imply an unproblematic harmony. Marshall McLuhan predicted that the electronic revolution would bring a 'global village' into being, but real life continues to be acted out in small worlds. The central function of the media for environmentalism can be a weakness as well as a strength.

Hostile essay-writing – Michael Crichton's bestseller *State of Fear* (2004) is a prime example – habitually mocks how environmentalists tend to wallow in angst. One of the most intriguing, but also most difficult, questions is the extent to which the fear articulated by the media over the threat to our environment is actually experienced by real people. Are people in Northern countries really afraid of *global* warming, or is it just 'environmentally correct' to show that one is worried? Peter N. Stearns, in his *American Cool* (1994), showed how the modern media present Americans with a world of contrasts: emotions run riot in the media, but in real life – far more than during the ostensibly so repressive Victorian age – the norm is to stay 'cool' under all circumstances. The Viennese meteorologist Reinhard Böhm, who detects an undercurrent of pleasure in displays of fear over future catastrophes, has the impression that this 'has become something like a parlour game, which most people do not take at all seriously'. No wonder, then, that all the commitments to the Kyoto climate targets have had such meagre practical results.[232] The world of media communication is different from the one of actual feeling and behaviour.

In 1998 a large-scale investigation of the international links of environmental NGOs came to the following conclusion: 'Many of these relationships are limited to fragile fax-and-cyberspace skeletons, and the strong ones are often based more on key cross-cultural individuals than on dense institutional bonds. . . . The broadest-based protest movements remain those based on local, previously existing capillary social networks, many of which lack telephones, not to mention computers.'[233] Technological networks by no means automatically generate social networks, nor, a fortiori, coalitions of players. It is not necessarily logical to infer from the inflation of information that we are living in an 'information society'; the conclusion might at least as well be that information is being devalued. The 'information society' construct, which cancels the previous basic laws of existence, ignores this logic and forgets human nature. And electronic scrap, much more complex than earlier kinds of scrap, defies recycling technologies that have existed until now.

From the nuclear controversy to the 'death of the forest':
a confusing turn

The role of the media was particularly conspicuous in the post-1980 leitmotif that marked out German environmental discourse even more strongly than nuclear energy had done in the previous period: namely, the 'death of the forest'. The damaging effects of acid rain on inland waters were discussed from Scandinavia to North America, and even amid the Reaganite rollback of environmentalism in 1983 – when it prompted official protests in Canada and the prime minister, 'with a certain acid humour, jokingly threatened to declare war on the United States over acid rain'[234] – it became the number one issue for the reactivated EPA following the return of William Ruckelshaus.[235] But the phrase 'death of the forest' was a distinctively German concoction. As a 'keen forest walker' himself, the media researcher Rudi Holzberger later said mockingly that only journalists who hardly ever set foot there could have come up with such a clichéd fixed idea.[236]

Der Spiegel set the ball rolling on 16 November 1981, with its cover headline 'The Forest Is Dying – Acid Rain over Germany' superimposed on a forest of chimneys belching out sulphur-yellow smoke and, below them, a cluster of trees already browned at the top. After some hesitation, the chorus of alarm in the German media grew to a climax in 1983. Without anything really horrific to serve as a trigger, *Der Spiegel* then proceeded on 14 February 1983 to speak of an 'ecological Hiroshima': it could scarcely have gone further than that. On 9 January 1984 another headline, 'Acid Rain – A Mortal Danger for Babies', with a picture of a baby wearing a gas mask. Only for babies? 'First the forest dies, then man dies' became the new eco-slogan. In 1984 *Die Zeit* opined: 'Today not even a doubting Thomas could question the scale of the forest's death – at most perhaps a pathological ignoramus.'[237] Precisely such quotes, however, tell us that it was no longer a subject for rational analysis but was on the verge of becoming an article of faith.

How are we to explain this great alarm, which had not been at all widespread in German environmental discourse in the 1970s? Or had it? There is something curious about the thick volume entitled *Rettet den Wald* [Save the Forest], impressively put together in 1979 with an eye for media effect.[238] In retrospect, it is astonishing that 'acid rain' does not appear in the extensive index and that damage caused by sulphur dioxide is mentioned in only a single sentence (p. 345). Instead, the argument follows the traditional line of 'mixed forest versus coniferous monoculture', or the even more traditional one of 'wood-savvy versus deer-savvy foresters' dating back to the forest reforms around the year 1800. Horst Stern, the lead author, was used to such things. On Christmas Eve 1971 he had already caused a furore with a TV broadcast, *Bemerkungen über den Rothirsch*, which argued that the hunting lobby's excessive breeding of red deer was sowing destruction: 'The German forest is mortally ill.' The violent reactions to the film 'laid bare the clash of interests among foresters, hunters and conservationists that had long been kept under wraps'.[239] All through the 1970s, the forest was not an issue that integrated the environmental movement in any way. Where could it have held demonstrations there?

Things changed completely with the new 'death of the forest' alarm. In the first place, it removed hunters and conventional foresters from the firing line and even brought conservationists and environmentalists together.[240] Unlike the spotted owl alarm in the United States, it had an integrative effect. In fact, acid rain had been an issue right from the start of the eco-age. But in 1972, at the Stockholm Conference, the Swedes had tried in vain to fire up delegates from Germany and elsewhere: as soon as they threatened to claim compensation for damages from the Bundesrepublik and other acid rainmakers, the Germans battened down the hatches, and a cabinet decision in Bonn declared the transmission of sulphur dioxide to be a 'non-issue'.[241] However, now that the German forest appeared to be under threat, acid rain became a top priority. The issue did not originate in the environmental movement,[242] and it offered few targets for action groups or demonstrations (apart from Robin Wood chimney-climbing, designed for media effect). The front lines became confused, as the 'dying forest' theme fundamentally changed the landscape of environmentalism in West Germany. The main enemy was now coal, not nuclear energy: a painful shift for Social Democrats, who regarded solidarity with Ruhr miners as a sacred tradition. On the other hand, a link suddenly appeared with the main current of forest romanticism.

Environmentalism becomes a popular movement in Germany

'If the forest is involved, we'll get a popular movement': Hans-Jochen Vogel, the mayor of Munich, saw it coming.[243] In 1985 Carl Amery wrote: 'The death of the forest was the first violent ecological shock to affect the whole nation.'[244] And, later on, two historians concluded: 'Without the debate on the death of the forest, it is doubtful whether the Greens would have entered the Bundestag for the first time in March 1983 with 5.6 per cent of the vote'[245] – a breakthrough that happened even though the dying forest distracted attention from the nuclear issue that had been central to the formation of the Greens. Conservative milieux too, horrified by clashes between baton-wielding police and (mostly Maoist) far-left groups at nuclear construction sites, were beginning to feel an affinity with the environmental movement. And although there was little doing here for citizens' action groups, the new Christian Democrat government under Helmut Kohl saw a golden opportunity to get off to a resounding start in environmental policy, with a higher profile than Helmut Schmidt's previous SPD government had ever managed to achieve. A new Law on Large Combustion Plants, passed in 1983, stipulated that power stations had to provide for flue gas desulphurization – a multibillion-Deutschmark project and by far the largest success to that point for German environmentalism.

It had been known since the nineteenth century that sulphur dioxide was harmful to vegetation, but previously the leading energy providers had always evaded the issue by claiming that such technology was not 'state of the art'. In 1974 the Technical Inspection Agency (TÜV) pointed out that successful trials had already been conducted in Japan – where acid rain was a relatively innocuous but much-discussed issue.[246] In 1980 the Mannheim generating plant, an old rival of the electrical giants, brought a desulphurization facility into service, creating an undeniable 'state of the art' to which the Kohl government could now refer.[247] The dramatic lowering of sulphur emissions helped to make the death of the forest a self-refuting rather than a self-fulfilling prophecy, as well as impelling many people concerned about the environment to go further into issues of forest ecology.[248]

The 'dying forest' remained an article of faith for some time in sections of the eco-scene, but the panic-mongering increasingly became a target of ridicule from the 1990s on. It turned out that – whether because of under-utilization or rising levels of atmospheric CO_2 – the German forests were not dying but growing more strongly than ever;[249] around the end of the millennium, Germany was the European country with the largest area of forest. The whole experience threatened to discredit any future eco-alarm, and environmental discourse began to remind people of the little boy who kept crying wolf.

What had happened? The alarm had its origins not simply in the media but in an interaction between media and science. With the modern image-conscious world already in full swing, it was striking how little the alarm could actually be presented in graphic terms; instead, warnings about the 'deceptiveness' of photos or constructed idylls became standard in alarmist journalism – a perfect illustration of the tense relationship between environmentalism and sense perception.[250] Reporters could not fabricate this dying forest. Journalists appealed to scientific authorities – first and foremost Bernhard Ulrich, a pioneer of the hitherto neglected discipline of forest soil studies at Göttingen University, who in 1980 had thought he could detect that, contrary to previous assumptions, the forests were in a 'phase of destabilization' due to airborne 'acid deposition'.[251] The alarms also repeatedly emphasized what was new in the damage to the forest, although the novelty was far from certain in every case. It should be noted that in all this the forest floor was still largely terra incognita!

Still, the concerns of the time do not appear unjustified today. Ever-increasing soil acidity really does threaten the forest; it has so far been offset by liming, but it is doubtful whether this can be kept up indefinitely. Although it is realized that many questions remain open, the intensive debates and precautionary measures of that earlier period were thoroughly in accordance with the precautionary principle of the eco-age.[252] Ulrich and his supporters were convinced that alarms had to ring out if politicians were finally to get moving and do something to reduce the level of emissions. Hence 'damage to the forest' was blown up into 'death of the forest', a chronic danger into acute disaster, a hypothetical risk into a clearly proven fiasco. The procedure perfectly illustrates the problems of communication among science, public opinion and politics in new kinds of (only partly identifiable) environmental risks. The immediate practical result – the introduction of desulphurization installations – still deserves our respect today. Later too, the Green-minded German public did not blame those who raised the alarm for their exaggeration; many had evidently made the precautionary principle their own and understood that one must react even to risks that are partly hypothetical.

From German to tropical forests

The 'gentle rebels' of Robin Wood split from Greenpeace in 1982 on the grounds that the 'rainbow warriors' were neglecting the forest for whales and the ocean waves, although Greenpeace Deutschland had made its land debut in June 1981 with the climbing of a chimney at the Boehringer chemical plant in Hamburg. But in spring 1987 Robin Wood began to concentrate on a campaign to protect the tropical rainforest. The transition from 'death of the forest' to threatened rainforest merits closer examination. Obviously 'forest' was the connecting link, yet the whole scene change was important for the period. It was later forgotten that it began at least as much with top-down initiatives as challenges from below – that is, with timber industry circles which in 1985 founded the International Tropical Timber Organization, to promote not only the industry itself but also better forestry in the tropics. The UN Food and Agriculture Organization (FAO) declared 1985 the 'International Year of Forests' and commissioned a special report: *Tropical Forests: A Call for Action*.[253] The focus of campaigning was no longer the 'death of the forest' but the climate alarm that first sounded in 1986, with carbon dioxide rather than sulphur dioxide as the target. Previously little noticed, especially as it promotes forest growth, it is released by the burning and decay of forest. 'We protect the climate by protecting the tropical forest': the link, re-emphasized two decades later, has persisted up to the present day. 'We protect our climate together with his habitat': posters with this message, from which a gorilla stares out at the public, add flesh and blood to the issue.

In the early period, fear of rising sea levels was paramount; on 11 August 1986 *Der Spiegel* published its famous 'Climate Catastrophe' cover, with half of Cologne cathedral under water. 'So that Northern Germany does not sink beneath the waves' was one of Robin Wood's motivations for the tropical forest campaign.[254] But dreams of earthly paradise were also involved: many eco-Romantics worked up more enthusiasm for the tropical forests than for those in Germany. In reality, of course, primal forest is often monotonous, but the mediatic rainforest was an ideal projection area for the imagination. The species-rich savannah, more threatened than rainforest by agribusiness, did not embody dreams of paradise.

Unlike the 'death of the forest', the tropical forest alarm was not peculiar to Germany. It is true that, notwithstanding its name, 'Robin Wood' was originally founded in Germany, but the tropical forests campaign immediately gave it links abroad, from Britain to Australia.[255] Radical Earth First! activists took the lead in the fight to protect the tropical wilderness,

172 Networked Thinking and Practical Priorities

and rainforest clearances in Amazonia were already being branded an 'ecological Hiroshima' at the Stockholm Conference in 1972. When people dreamed of 'virgin forest', they now thought first of South America rather than Africa.

Claude Lévi-Strauss (1908–2009) – whose *Tristes Tropiques* (1955), filled with sadness over doomed indigenous cultures, made him world famous – motivated the protection of tropical rainforests not only as human habitats but also, still without the CO_2 argument, as a way of saving the earth's atmosphere:

> The whole of mankind is in danger, for we should not forget that the tropical virgin forests will not grow again once they have been destroyed. . . . They will never come back. As far as I know, a considerable part of the oxygen in the earth's atmosphere derives from the primal forests of Amazonia. Were they to be cleared, the oxygen supply of the whole of mankind would be in danger.[256]

Anti-colonialism or crypto-colonialism?

The issue of wilderness protection is much older than the eco-age. In late 1981, just when the 'dying forest' alarm was ringing out in Germany, the WWF and IUCN (both of which predate the eco-age) launched a global media-oriented campaign to save the tropical rainforests.[257] Later, Greenpeace too mobilized people on the question. The whole campaign was marked by a curious mixture of anti-colonial and crypto-colonial themes; it developed in the spirit of Lévi-Strauss, but also of Grzimek, continuing the national park aspirations of the fifties and sixties that had started with the colonial big game reserves. Rainforest protectors called for a boycott of tropical woods, but, given the past, third world politicians had no difficulty branding this as colonialist interference. Biodiversity and climate protection were issues totally unsuited to making indigenous people aware that forest conservation was in their own interests. Global ecological vision has not infrequently been an obstacle to communication across cultures.[258] We shall come across this dilemma again later, in connection with the 'Debt for Nature' trading that was invented around that time.

The 'noble savage' was resurrected in the eco-scene, although Lévi-Strauss himself had shown that so-called savages also had complex cultural systems; in taking up the tropical forests, left-wing, anti-colonial environmental activists wanted to protect the habitat of humans as well as gorillas. But their culture was disintegrating all around. As in the age of missionaries and wide-eyed Rousseauians, the friends of indigenous peoples regularly discovered that they could easily be corrupted to exploit nature as soon as they came into contact with the money economy, and that the 'native rights' associated with reservations sometimes opened the gates for unrestricted logging.[259]

On the other hand, the murder of Brazilian rubber-tapper Chico Mendes on 22 December 1988 made him a hero and martyr for those fighting to protect the Amazonian rainforest. Acting in the interests of his fellow-*seringueiros*, as chair of the regional agricultural labourers' union, he had opposed the ranchers' drive to expand their grazing land through forest clearances. Chico Mendes became a legend around the world, but what mattered to him – how could it have been otherwise? – was not nature as such but the use to which it was put. Years after his death, his *seringueiros* obtained a large reservation – yet many of them too found livestock farming more profitable in the long run.[260] Recently, indeed, the Amazon basin has achieved a new kind of fame in the international eco-scene: not as wilderness but as *terra preta*, a cultivated landscape where, thousands of years ago, indigenous peoples invented a sophisticated method of converting waste into fertile humus. Anyone who regards the soil as the central environmental problem now looks for the world to be saved in the Amazonian *terra preta* rather than the rainforest.[261]

In the long run, nature can be protected only through sustainable forms of use – not through efforts to ban all modern economic uses. In a way, it is logical that ecological discourse since the 1990s has been dominated by this goal of sustainability; the old magic word 'wilderness' proved to be more and more of a will-o'-the-wisp.[262] It remains an open question what sustainable economic activity should look like in the tropical forests; there anyway seems to be no general answer. Forms of agroforestry – regionally diverse combinations of agriculture and silviculture – are often considered to be the best solution.[263] One is repeatedly struck by the extent to which stories of successful sustainable development, above all in the third world, have a markedly local character.[264] There is sometimes a danger that 'thinking globally' will blur the success of promising ways of 'acting locally'.

Chameleon environmentalism: the ability to change colour

Not surprisingly, 'networked thinking' is not present at every moment in every brain. But the forty-plus years of the international eco-age have involved endless networking, as rigid stereotypes have repeatedly entered a state of flux. Above all, this gives a history of the eco-age its meaning, beyond the inevitable fragmentation of a miscellany of phenomena. Only in their totality do all the initiatives and policies add up to an environmental movement in the genuine sense of the term, different from all other major movements in history by virtue of its fluid multiplicity and constant re-networking. In many individual episodes, the activism, with its particular groups and group interests, is reducible to certain fixed ideas and identities. Yet in the whole, over time, the essence of the matter keeps breaking through, amid a sea of rhetorical figures.

In the broad historical sweep, we need to bear in mind this chameleon-like ability to change colour. There was the switch in West Germany in the early 1980s from the focus on nuclear hazards to the 'dying forest' alarm: what a scene change! What a blurring of fronts and shift in the support base! Then the dying forest gave way to the tropical rainforest campaign – a perspective shift from local German conditions to faraway exoticism, associated with an internationalization of the eco-scene – and on to climate risks and the threat that large-scale cattle-breeding poses to the tropical forest as well as the earth's climate. Unexpectedly, the old vegetarianism acquired a new global-ecological significance, while at the same time a new bridge was created between the Old and the New World. Looking at cows in Swiss Alpine meadows, one would never have dreamed that the earth's ecosystem was endangered by cattle! In 1992 Jeremy Rifkin published in the United States his assault on the worldwide boom in beef production,[265] yet it was easier for people to react to it in Continental Europe, where steak is less central to gastronomy than in America or Britain. Ironically, it was in 1986, the year of Chernobyl, that the first strident voices began to warn of the dire consequences of global warming – although they diverted attention from the nuclear danger to quite different levels of risk, where nuclear energy could even appear to offer salvation. What striking proof that the growth of environmental awareness is governed by the logic of particular discourses only for a while, not in *la longue durée*!

After nuclear energy, the genetic engineering controversy

The campaign against gene technology is particularly instructive about learning and transfer processes, but also about stereotypes in the collective environmental consciousness as well as characteristic differences between the Old and the New World. Supporters and critics alike tried to learn from the nuclear power dispute, each in their own way, of course.[266] Especially in the early days, many saw some striking analogies: while nuclear technology changed the basic elements of inorganic nature, gene technology based itself on those of organic nature; both promised to deliver chain reactions, physical and economic; and both were associated by supporters and opponents with visions of omnipotence. Since organisms reproduce and genes can jump to other organisms, many critics actually thought that the hypothetical risks were higher than in the case of nuclear technology; genetically modified organisms, they pointed out, have no natural enemies, and so neophytes would be able to multiply without restraint at the expense of existing nature; genetic leaps might even make cancer an endemic disease. Against this, it was argued that the recombined species would not pass through a Darwinian process of natural selection – on the contrary, they would have a hard time of it in the wild and, in most cases, would not survive outside the laboratory. It was questionable whether this was a natural law, however, since genetic engineers worked precisely to ensure that their creatures survived in the wild.

'I started thinking in terms of the atomic bomb and similar things', recalled the molecular biologist Janet Mertz, an originator of the American genetic engineering controversy, which was already peaking in the 1970s when the German eco-scene was still preoccupied with nuclear energy. 'I didn't want to be the person who went ahead and created a monster that killed a million people.' This Frankenstein scenario accompanied the heated phases of the controversy, in both the United States and the Federal Republic of Germany, adding spice to the nightly round of discussions. But – so far, at least – it has distracted attention away from the chief risk of gene technology: that a few corporations will standardize and patent their new recombinations and come to hold a global monopoly in agriculture. One may therefore doubt whether critiques of gene technology that drew on the lessons of nuclear chain reactions really got to the heart of the matter. It was still only the breeding of animals and plants, not human beings, that was economically attractive; researchers, not industrial managers, were the main people interested in experiments with human embryos.

Differences in style between America and Germany were also observable in the genetic engineering controversy. The bulk of US molecular biologists tried to learn from the previous nuclear dispute and to keep the discussion of risks inside their own community. In the very early stages of the public debate, in July 1974, leading American scientists published a letter calling for an initial ban on certain experiments because of the risk of epidemics. This so-called 'moratorium', later held up as a document of historic importance for the responsibility of scientists and the self-limitation of research, became the basis of the American debate on gene technology. In February 1975, the Asilomar conference centre in California hosted an international gathering of 140 scientists to thrash out an agreement on safety measures for future research. Outright opponents of genetic engineering were not invited. This 'historic event', as it was billed in advance, was designed to obviate the external regulation demanded by critics.

At first the calculation seemed to misfire: the controversy set up a ripple effect in the American public and it looked for a time as if Asolimar had merely awakened sleeping dogs. But towards the end of the 1970s, the public controversy died down in the United States; local 'biohazard committees' were converted into 'biosafety committees'. Asilomar had been driven by the philosophy of preventive forethought, but the subsequent period saw a return to the old attitude that the harmfulness of a new technology, not its harmlessness, had to be demonstrated, that the burden of proof lay with the critics. James D. Watson, who had won a Nobel Prize in 1962 for his discovery of the double helix structure of DNA, referred to all who spoke of imprecise dangers as a 'bunch of jackasses'.[267] Although government regulation came in 1980, after years of hesitation, its terms were milder than originally planned and later further diluted. The share prices of the mushrooming gene technology firms rose and rose.[268]

In the following years, the controversy finally got going in Germany too. No established research community set the rules to keep it under control, since the powerful position of synthetic chemistry had left the Germans lagging in gene technology;[269] besides, as in other (not all) European countries, the criticism had a more lasting effect than in the United States. Like the nuclear controversy before it, the new dispute generated a whole world of literature and arguments in which those suitably fired up could talk till the cows came home – only now the gulf between proven effects and hypothetical risks yawned wider than ever. Gene technology had no Hiroshima to weigh it down, although major epidemics and neophyte issues could be taken as a taste of things to come. Anglo-American plans to release anthrax bacilli in the Second World War showed that a biological super-Hiroshima was probably in the realm of the thinkable. And it was known that problems in calculating the military effect, rather than any moral scruples, had stayed the hand of those who had wanted to use biological bombs. Modern gene technology now made it conceivable to programme biological weapons in such a way that they affected only the enemy, not one's own population, if the enemy belonged to a different race.[270]

But this grim topic was still a long way off in the Bundesrepublik. The risks of genetic engineering had something hypothetical about them. So long as most activists were absorbed in the nuclear power issue, there was simply not enough time or energy to go deeply into the even more esoteric problem of gene technology; nor were there enough high-profile targets for demonstrations. The controversy came to a head in the mid-eighties, at the time of the great AIDS phobia, and a few mavericks even suspected that this new plague, which put a damper on the sexual freedom opened up by the contraceptive pill, had originated in the gene technology laboratories. Experts hired by the Bundestag were unable to rebut the idea completely,[271] but it was an indication of the relative objectivity of the argument that this vague suspicion rarely set off a major alarm.

Whereas the Bundestag had convened a public inquiry on 'future nuclear policy' only after the major civil disturbances of 1979–80, it acted much earlier in the case of the new controversy, ordering an inquiry in 1984 into 'the opportunities and risks of gene technology'. This produced a mountain of paper, which lay people found rather disorienting, and a certain hesitancy remained in part of the eco-scene. It could not be theoretically excluded that genetic engineering, if developed with careful ecological oversight, would become a 'green' technology that reduced the inputs of energy and chemicals in agriculture. This time *Der Spiegel* kept out of the fray, after it brought discredit upon itself with a headline that announced: 'Genetics: A Thousand Times Worse than Hitler'.[272] And although the legacy of the nuclear power dispute was still fresh, attitudes became more differentiated in the course of time. The hypothetical character of the genetic risk demanded a new style of politics and kept many from digging in their heels on a particular position.

Agonizing over priorities in chemical policy

Although the chemical industry increasingly bought into gene tech-nology, the fact that this was presented as an alternative to chemicals tended to confuse matters. Since Rachel Carson's *Silent Spring* and Barry Commoner's campaigns, the environmental movement had targeted the chemical industry more than any other. But nowhere was it more difficult to set priorities and to make them publicly known than in this shadowy sector. The first step was to define the groups of materials on which action should be taken: synthetic chemicals in general or particular ones such as DDT or dioxin? All chlorine-based chemicals or only chlorinated hydro-carbons?[273] Or perhaps certain stages of development rather than the materials as such?

Two West German experts who in 1988 looked at options for an eco-logical policy on chemicals – a demand that had been around for a decade or more – began by letting out a deep sigh: 'As hazy and impenetrable as the network of pipes that links production units in a chemical factory, the inner structure of the "chemical industry" presents itself as a highly complex system in which it is scarcely possible to make out the beginning and the end.'[274] Rachel Carson's success was due not least to her concen-tration on a single object in a broad panorama of problems: DDT. But thirty years later it was clear that her priority was unsustainable in the long run. In 1992 the future US vice-president, Al Gore, announced that despite the ban on DDT the American chemical industry was producing thirteen thousand times more pesticide than in Rachel Carson's time.[275] All too often, the use of substitutes simply meant replacing a known with an unknown risk – which in many cases turned out to be even more objectionable.[276]

The asbestos alarm

Early environmental initiatives aimed at the chemical industry typi-cally took up substances such as lead, quicksilver, chlorine or sulphur compounds, long known to be potentially harmful and offering the best chance of a successful claim for damages. In the case of pesticides too, it was logical and plausible to suspect that their impact was not confined to weeds and insects. What was not so well known was the carcinogenic effect of a 'magic mineral' used in modern heat insulation and fire prevention, the reserves of which had given rise to international power struggles, and which the newly founded EPA had targeted back in 1971: asbestos. In the medical world, asbestosis had been regarded as an occupational disease since the 1920s, but the risks had not filtered through to the general public. The decisive change took place only with the eco-age – a decade later in Germany than in the United States. Asbestosis then became 'one of the most widely known of the modern industrial hazards'.[277]

While the US Supreme Court partly reversed the EPA ban of 1971 later in the decade, the use of asbestos continued to boom in West Germany in the 1970s; a general prohibition came into force there only in 1993, and in 2005 throughout the EU. In the United States, under the influence of the media, the campaign against the substance temporarily took on some of the features of collective hysteria. 'The phrase "One fiber can kill" was widely repeated by the media and became engraved on the public's consciousness.'[278] Building contractors, some lacking the necessary competence, pocketed huge sums for ripping asbestos out of school walls and replacing it with other materials, even though it had been causing no harm inside the walls and first became dangerous only when the building work released particles into the air. Later, even environmentalists remembered the anti-asbestos campaign as a warning of what could happen if regulation got out of hand and became a single-minded obsession; eco-revisionists, of course, regarded it as manna from heaven.[279] In 2002, however, the asbestos alarm sounded again when it was revealed that in the mining town of Libby (Montana), where the air was thick with asbestos fibres, nearly a fifth of the adult population suffered from related lung conditions, and there had been more than 200 confirmed deaths from asbestosis. Health damage in mining was one of the oldest environmental scandals, having attracted attention as early as the sixteenth century. It had been a marginal issue at first in the new environmentalism, but now the protests of affected miners gained fresh momentum from the Environmental Justice movement.[280]

Are farmers poisoning us?

In Germany, the chemical industry had been held up for a century as a 'science-based' model which, though never popular with local residents, was trusted to convert not only coking plant residue into glowing colours but virtually all waste into valuable products, and in this way to make the dark corners of industrial society both productive and presentable. There were no outside checks, only self-regulation by the industry, and until the 1970s it was agreed that all discussions would be held among its own pool of experts. The first skirmishes occurred in 1978, when environmental damage from the chemicalization of agriculture – which had also struck conservationists in the broader sense – became a target of public criticism as well as environmental politicians in Bonn. *Der Spiegel* of 30 October 1978 carried the cover headline 'Are Farmers Poisoning Us? Chemicals in Agriculture', with a picture of a sower wearing a gas mask and carrying some toxic red stuff in his basket. However, the initial impetus came not from the news magazine but from state secretary Hartkopf, the driving force behind Bonn's environmental policy, under whose leadership negotiations had been held for years with the chemical industry over the drafting of a new chemicals law. In October 1978 he finally snapped and, in the words of Edda Müller, 'publicly threw down the gauntlet' to the industry.[281] And the next year, though not a man given to grand words, he declared: 'It is time for the ecological turn.'[282] It was a shot across the bows for Chancellor Helmut Schmidt, for whom economic growth took precedence over environmental protection.

From the dioxin alarm to Duales System Deutschland

On 10 June 1976, a disaster in the Italian town of Seveso became an internal cause célèbre for the environmental movement and gave a new name to the threat from the chemical industry: *dioxin*. Two years later, in 1978, the title of a superbly documented polemical work, 'Seveso is everywhere – the lethal risks of chemicals', set the alarm bells ringing;[283] one of its two authors, Fritz Vahrenholt, had been since 1976 the director of the 'chemical industry' section of Germany's Federal Environment Agency (UBA) and an influential policy-maker. *Der Spiegel*, however, ran its 'Seveso is everywhere' cover story only on 30 May 1983, when it was clear that dioxin drums had also been heedlessly dumped on German rubbish tips. From then on, dioxin ran like a red thread through German chemical policy. On 24 September 1984, four environmentalists took up position for twelve hours on the chimneystacks of the waste incineration plant (MVA) in Bielefeld, which not long before had been hailed as the most advanced of its kind in Europe. Even the trial judges showed sympathy for the defendants and halted the proceedings.[284] Elsewhere too, campaigners found a new object of attack in the monstrous MVAs; they were the product of an early phase of environmental policy, which had aimed to ensure not only that rubbish was not simply dumped in out-of-the-way corners, but also that disposal sites should not end up bursting at the seams.

In the 1990s there was another scene change: technical improvements reduced the level of harmful emissions, cooperation developed between critics and the targets of their criticism, and waste separation policies made Germany a model of practical, everyday environmentalism. Primary school teachers took to upending a (not too disgusting) rubbish bin in the classroom and skilfully sorting through the contents. Environmentalism was now supposed to mean doing something yourself, instead of pointing the finger at society. The 'dual system' – a term once used for the division of vocational education between school and on-the-job training – now referred to the compulsory separation of rubbish, and a certain national pride was associated with the founding of a large corporation, Duales System Deutschland (DSD), on 28 September 1990, a week before Reunification. Even the Green environment minister Jürgen Trittin opined that Germany was 'admired all around the world' for this,[285] while Volker Hauff, a leading Social Democrat environmental politician, asserted that the Dual System had become a daunting 'negative example' for other countries. In his view, it had 'created a central mega-institution with clearly monopolistic tendencies', which had no interest in innovations to reduce the generation of waste.[286] DSD certainly did not become a great export success. On the other hand, a new law passed on 7 December 1990 made it compulsory for energy companies to feed electricity generated from renewable sources into the grid and to pay smaller providers a price that covered their costs. Over the next two decades, similar regulations were introduced in sixty-one countries.[287]

The Dual System did not have a happy ending, though. Ten years after the founding of DSD, Gertrude Lübbe-Wolff complained that Germany's waste recycling policy had 'degenerated into utter conceptual confusion',[288] and in many places carefully sorted categories of waste ended up together in the MVA. The problems inherent in all 'end of the pipe' solutions became common property in international environmental discussions: if waste disposal is privatized it is run as a profit-making business, all the more attractive because it is conducted in the name of ecology; the higher the fees that private firms can charge, the less interest they have in waste reduction. Besides, disposal is a murky business, in which mafia-like structures can easily develop in the absence of keen public supervision. Rubbish seems to pass on its foul smell to the companies involved in handling it.

MVAs and sewage treatment plants always had a provisional aspect because of the changing nature of waste; recycling functioned only imperfectly, consumed large amounts of energy, was often unprofitable and created environmental problems of its own.[289] In 1996 Fritz Vahrenholt scoffed that 'messing around with yucky yoghurt cartons on sorting belts' was a distraction from the real problems.[290] DSD, then, fitted into a century-old history of solving the problem by moving it somewhere else. Back in the days of sewage-irrigated fields and attempts to 'close the nuclear fuel cycle' through reprocessing, it must have been realized that a perfect cycle is an unachievable ideal unless care is taken from the beginning to produce reusable material.[291] 'The real emissions of the chemical industry are its products': this raised the discussion of chemical policy to a new level.[292] Today the latest bad news, which fills sea lovers with sickness, is that the sea floor is being increasingly covered with plastic rubbish.

Confusions and clarifications

But let us avoid the kind of hypercritical attitude that comes all too easily in environmental politics: the idea that as a rule, measures are just provisional arrangements, not definitive solutions. Although many regulations were ineffective as such, fear of others with more bite did mean that a lot was achieved in the industry. The chemical policy discussion had significant effects behind closed doors[293] – which was a problem for observers outside! But, for all the toing and froing, the fate of environmental initiatives up to the present does not generally appear as a tragicomedy without deeper meaning. Beyond all its fixations, the movement has repeatedly displayed mobility; and this has not been a question of disoriented wandering, but has always involved a circling around central themes in which much became clarified. Since the sanitation movement of the late nineteenth century, environmental initiatives have repeatedly – though to some extent from different angles – returned to the issues of air and water. Since Rachel Carson's *Silent Spring*, warnings about pesticides have found new objects again and again; the issue by no means died down after the ban on DDT. Since the 1980s, climate danger has remained a central issue, with a few ups and downs, despite the media law prescribing variety for its own sake; the old topic of emission reductions has a new topicality; in arid regions around the world, warming is expressed above all in water shortages. The 'limits to growth' are again openly posed, albeit from different sides, as *the* problem of problems, even if it is not so much population growth as the growth programmed into the existing economic system which appears to be the true heart of the problem. Since the crash of 2008, people have again dared to think of turning away from growth economics – no longer just for ecological reasons, but also for economic ones.

Thus, the whole spectrum of environmental issues is not completely diffuse; it refers to a limited number of leitmotifs that repeatedly join together in harmony. From the beginning, the problem of an ecologically sustainable energy supply has kept coming to the fore. Denis Hayes, the organizer of Earth Day in 1970 and later *Time Magazine*'s 'Hero of the Planet', developed into an early champion of solar energy. 'Alternative' became the magic word of the eco-scene in the late seventies. Or, as *Robin-Wood Magazin* wrote in 1986, the year of Chernobyl: 'So let us concern ourselves about the "dead dog" of atomic energy only as much as necessary and as little as possible, and let us devote ourselves above all to the task of helping new energy supply structures to break through.'[294] Should we speak of a learning process? But a word of caution: world history is not a schoolroom but an arena full of power games, and for all the gain in knowledge, secret processes of forgetting also play themselves out. Anyway, there would appear to be no definitive solutions to the great environmental problems facing humanity. One can never be sure that history will not start over again from the beginning, whether in relation to nuclear energy, the climate problem or something else.

Chapter Four

Charismatics and Ecocrats

1 Spiritual Quest and Charismatic Moments

The apocalypse craves prophets

Visions of man's coming ecological suicide stand within old traditions of Christian apocalypse; the Fall in the Garden of Eden already contains the end of the world. In the same way, we read in Green histories of the world, from Clive Ponting (1991) to Jared Diamond (2005), that the demise of the Easter Islanders, who cut down their last tree out of blind greed, contains the basic model for what will happen to mankind[1] – although, in fact, and this is a much more fitting punchline for environmental activists, there are clear indications that what happened on Easter Island was not ecological suicide but murder, at the hands of settlers and slavetraders.[2]

The first boom in eco-apocalypses arose on both sides of the Atlantic around the year 1970. Michael Egan, in his biography of Barry Commoner, has a chapter ('The New Jeremiad') in which he traces the development of his hero into an environmental activist; the motto he chooses for it is a quotation from Commoner himself: 'If you can see light at the end of the tunnel, you are looking the wrong way.'[3] At the same time, Egan describes Commoner as 'exceptionally charismatic' – albeit a charismatic prophet of doom, who did not manage to gather a large or durable flock of disciples. In this connection, Egan quotes the sociologist Deborah Lynn Guber, who followed the 'green revolution' in the United States in a series of opinion surveys: 'By downplaying environmental progress and by using exaggerated doomsday warnings to motivate public awareness and concern, the environmental movement has sacrificed its own credibility by giving in to the politics of chicken little.'[4] Another version of the 'crying wolf' effect: the fearful little chicken of an American children's story suddenly hears a thud, thinks the sky has caved in, throws the other animals into a temporary panic, then exposes himself to ridicule. The role of Jeremiah is not without risk. But we should not forget that, if our civilization really does suffer ecological collapse – which cannot be excluded – the eco-doomsayers will one day be seen as prophets.[5]

The apocalypse craves a messiah; lack of one has a crippling effect. The need for bold, hypnotic leader figures can also be deduced from the hopelessly diffuse character of the environmental problematic, in which no one knows where to begin if there is too much discussion and argument. Here we come to a fundamental tension of environmentalism, which has never denied for long its roots in the Enlightenment. Apocalyptic fear, it seems, is more media-staged than really felt.[6] This is also true of the latest apocalypse: the coming climate disaster associated with global warming.

Barry Commoner reminds Egan of Max Weber, the creator of the modern concept of charisma, whose wife Marianne felt during the First World War that he was also referring to himself when he spoke of Jeremiah.[7] 'Charisma' actually means 'gift of grace', but in Max Weber the charismatic also has an aptitude for dark apocalyptic visions capable of wrenching the masses from their daily grind and setting them in motion. He resembles a madman when the spirit comes over him: 'Jeremiah acts like a drunkard, shaking all over'; 'scorching heat takes hold of him'; he 'goes around with a yoke on his neck'.[8] This is very different from the kind of slick charisma with which the media endow youthful US presidential candidates assured of victory: men like Kennedy or Obama. But the eco-apocalypse is tailor-made for charismatic prophets; no wonder that, in the history of the environmental movement, we find quite a few figures who remind us of Weber's original concept.

One thing does not fit, though. In Max Weber, the hour of the charismatic has sounded in ages of general despair. The Israelites' 'dread' of the cruelty and superior strength of the Assyrians put them in the apocalyptic mood in which they listened to the prophets. For ecology, however, the big moment came in 1970 – and again in 1990, in a global political situation where the nightmare vision of nuclear war was fading in the dawn light. This raises doubts as to whether doomsayers were suited to the period, since the sociological phenomenon of charisma also includes disciples who play along with the prophet. In this respect, the history of the eco-age confronts us again and again with charismatics manqué, and nowhere more so than in the German Greens, where Herbert Gruhl, the first of many would-be leaders to fall flat, detected a 'panic fear of leading figures'.[9] The environmental movement was much fonder of discussion than of discipleship, and on the whole it belongs in the tradition of the Enlightenment rather than of chilliastic movements.

Still, it cannot be understood as an overall phenomenon unless its spiritual elements are also taken seriously.[10] Iconic images of charismatic animals and landscapes show more clearly than written texts that the old dream of Paradise survives on a foundation of popular ecologism.[11] But we are talking primarily of a paradise lost. As the philosopher Hans Jonas showed in *The Imperative of Responsibility* – his counterblast to Ernst Bloch's *Principle of Hope*[12] – ecological thought contains a markedly anti-utopian element. This may be soberly realistic, but it may also harbour an eschatology of its own. In his much-quoted lecture 'Politics as a Vocation'

(1917), Max Weber presented ethic of conviction and ethic of responsibility as a contrasting pair. For Hans Jonas and many other theorists of the new ecological responsibility, the two belong together: the ethic of responsibility acquires all the emphasis of the ethic of conviction.

The Protestant ethic and the spirit of environmentalism? Looking for a more precise definition of Green spirituality

What type of spiritual themes define the environmental movement? Someone inwardly distant from religion tends to lump all religiosity together.[13] As Max Weber realized, however, the differences matter. There are rational and ecstatic, solitary and communal, forms of religious experience. Charisma involves a particular kind of religiosity: one that longs for salvation and enlightenment, and is prepared for suffering and inner turmoil to attain it.

In his celebrated Christmas addresses on 'the historical roots of our ecological crisis' (1966), the medievalist Lynn White detected a religious kernel in our modern environmental problematic: the Judaeo-Christian tradition liberated people from the animated totality of nature and opposed to it the nature of domination and exploitation; Eastern religions were wiser and conceived of man as part of nature. 'The beatniks, who are the basic revolutionaries of our time, show a sound instinct in their affinity for Zen Buddhism.'[14] The environmental crisis can be overcome, if at all, not through still more science and technology, but only through a spiritual turn.

The aged global historian Arnold Toynbee wholeheartedly agreed with this.[15] René Dubos, the inspiration behind the Stockholm Conference of 1972, was more doubtful: he did not dispute the religious roots of the crisis, but he had a more positive view of the historical role and present-day potential of Christianity. Considered use of nature is not harmful, he maintained, and gardening can even bring us closer to paradise.[16] At the same time, the geographer Yi-fu Tuan, originally from China, put paid to the myth of an Eastern harmony with nature, pointing out that the pipe-dreams of philosophical recluses were being confused with the very different reality of their world.[17]

The opposite of Lynn White's thesis may even be argued: namely, that awareness rather than destruction of the environment can be traced back to Christianity. The origin of the environmental movement in Protestant countries is even more striking than the historical link between Protestantism and capitalism – since capitalism also had medieval Catholic roots – so that one is tempted to replace Weber's famous 'elective affinity' between 'Protestant ethic and the spirit of capitalism' with a nexus between Protestantism and ecologism. Much of the Protestant sense of sin, assuaged neither by confession nor by indulgences, can be found in the ecological consciousness; and it is easy enough to detect a secularized theology (a deity who strictly punishes sinners against his commandments) in the idea of nature's revenge. That is a pretty rational, calculating type of religiosity, however, without the aura required by the charismatic crying for grace and redemption. In Weber's *Protestant Ethic*, one would look in vain for the concept of charisma. Not surprisingly, environmentalism is not too fond of the idea that it has such roots in religion.

But there is not only the depressive, guilt-ridden kind of environmental consciousness reminiscent of Weber's 'Puritan ethic' and 'worldly asceticism'. Roderick Nash, in his cult book *Wilderness and the American Mind* (1967), depicted enthusiasm for the wilderness as a disinhibiting rejection of the New England Puritan tradition[18] (although the relationship of the old American Protestantism to the New World wilderness, which after all was God's creation, had probably looked more ambiguous than it did to Nash in those Swinging Sixties). The Norwegian mountaineer-cum-philosopher Arne Naess (1912–2009), who hung by ropes above a fjord and refused to give up until a dam project was cancelled, described the Deep Ecology movement (which he founded in 1973, with features of a pantheistic religion of nature) as a philosophy of joy making us fully aware of our totally earthly existence. He recognized the problem that, since human beings are seldom completely altruistic, the selfless love of nature demanded by eco-fundamentalists brought forth either hypocrites or sour enemies of pleasure and humanity. His solution was not to equate one's self with 'the limited ego', but to see that it goes beyond the confines of our body and unites nature inside us with the infinity of extra-human nature.[19] This sense of self overcomes the fear of death and therefore a basic cause of sadness.

Hubert Weinzierl, a charismatic figure of German conservation and environmentalism since the beginning of the eco-age, announced for the new millennium that terms such as 'eco' and 'bio' should 'no longer be associated with morality and asceticism, but rather with *joie de vivre*'. 'Sustainability must therefore become a cult,' he insisted, 'since then even the fun society will be counted in. For is anything more fun than living pleasurably in harmony with nature?'[20] This highlights the change in a characteristic human type of the eco-scene, and hence one of the most important transformative processes in environmentalism per se, after a time in which it often bore the features of a new Puritanism. However, this change was at the same time a return to the historical roots of conservationism. Since its earliest days, environmental awareness has involved not only concern but also rapture over the blossoming of nature in the wild, and this can intensify to the point of ecstasy. Romantic landscape painting, from the Rhine to the Hudson, reaches its peak not in naturalism but in nature transfigured by an other-worldly sheen. This spirituality is clearest of all in the wilderness cult. For wilderness conservation cannot be justified purely on ecological grounds; many gardens have a greater variety of species than many wildernesses. When conservation culminates in the total exclusion of human beings from a cordoned area, it stands unmistakably in the tradition of sacred taboos, even if it makes ecological sense for the breeding grounds of certain birds.

Such spiritual impulses of conservationism were often expressed most frankly in the period *before* the eco-age. Hardly any other figure of American environmentalism has such a prophet-like habitus as John Muir, the early champion of wilderness and national parks. For him, the struggle for the wild forest was 'a part of the eternal conflict between right and wrong'.[21] The commitment to the wilderness – according to David Brower in 1957 – draws its strength from 'the pressure of conscience, of innate knowledge that there are certain things we may not ethically do to the only world we will ever have'.[22] Wilhelm Lienenkämper – a charismatic Westphalian who, as official conservationist in the Sauerland from 1936 to 1938, single-handedly pushed through no fewer than nineteen new regulations,[23] and whose favourite flower meadow still attracts droves of pilgrims forty years after his death – once referred to an experience of illumination in spring 1926, in a 'hidden paradise' beside a mountain stream.[24] Later, in the period of the Red Lists, he warned that conservation literature should not only consist of 'the bony frame of officially prescribed lists' but also ignite 'the fire of love'.[25] In the 1930s, as a keen Nazi,[26] he eventually found a 'valuable helper' in the church and put forward the argument (perfectly acceptable theologically) that God's 'dominion over the earth' mandate in Genesis 1:28 included an injunction to protect the earth.[27] Noah's Ark became an icon of the ecological movement: a symbol of human responsibility for the earth, in which the conservationist took over the role of a patriarch blessed by God.

Flower and animal religion: 'charismatic megafauna'

Just as there are different kinds of love of nature, so there are different kinds of religion of nature. When Theodore Roosevelt went walking with John Muir in 1903 through Yosemite valley, he was amazed that his companion had no feeling for birds and bird songs: 'The hermit-thrushes meant nothing to him, the trees and the flowers and the cliffs everything.'[28] Hegel distinguished within 'natural religion' between the peaceful and selfless 'innocence of the flower religion' and the aggressiveness of 'animal religions', which brings 'a hostile movement' into 'the multiplicity of passive plant forms'.[29] The mental leap suggests that protectors of animals (especially as they have to deal with hunters) are typically far more aggressive than protectors of plants!

The legendary Dian Fossey (1932–85), who had a passionate love for Rwanda's mountain gorillas, worked herself up into blind fanaticism in her struggle against local poachers, chaining and torturing them, and, in one case, is said to have kidnapped one of their children to exchange him for a baby gorilla they had taken away;[30] in the end she was murdered by an unknown hand in December 1985. Her story becomes more and more

The American zoologist Dian Fossey (1932–85) with mountain gorillas in
Rwanda, three years before she was murdered.

absurd as one goes into the details. For there are reliable indications that
gorilla-hunting was not very common among the local people;[31] the main
ones to be killed were Dian Fossey's own favourites – evidently in revenge[32]
against a woman whom the Africans angrily called 'the ape', and who con-
fided without a hint of regret: 'I have no friends; the more that you learn
about the dignity of the gorilla, the more that you want to avoid people.'[33]
Her feelings of love were completely centred on gorillas. Their habitat
interested her little:[34] she embodied a kind of animal protection unenlight-
ened by ecology. Since she identified with gorillas, not considering them
to be just creatures among others, the scientific yield of her eighteen years
of living with great apes was puny.[35] The irony is that her death opened
the way for the really effective protection of gorillas, which has skilfully
involved local people who profit from the growth of tourism.[36]

    In a world ruled by humans, a combination of misanthropy and love
of animals is a disaster for animal protection. There is a striking contrast here between Dian Fossey and Jane Goodall (b. 1934), the lover of
chimpanzees: perhaps the animals reacted upon the women who loved
them? Both originally went to the African interior as 'ape girls' of the
palaeontologist Louis Leakey, who discovered the continent as the 'cradle
of humanity'; they must have known each other well, but they developed
in opposite directions. Jane Goodall consciously avoided any idealization
of chimpanzees, neither making humans out of them nor treating them

Jane Goodall: philanthropic lover of chimpanzees; a contrast to Dian Fossey, misanthropic lover of gorillas.

as morally superior beings; indeed, she shocked animal lovers with evidence that chimpanzees too are capable of cruel and brutal behaviour.[37] Only this analytical distance offered a path to science, as well as to a link between love of animals and human beings, and from love of animals to environmentalism.

Not only animal protectionists but animals themselves can have charisma. Max Weber, whose concept of charisma had something animal-like about it, detects a 'hero's ecstasy' in intoxicated Indian war elephants.[38] 'Charismatic megafauna' – lions, tigers, elephants, rhinoceroses, pandas, polar bears, for some time even the ill-famed wolves – is now a standard term, although ecologically and in terms of social policy it is not unobjectionable, in fact more geared to fundraising and media impact, when wilderness protection is obsessively equated with them. To those who have to endure life among tigers and elephants, it can even seem like a disrespect for human dignity – or a diversion from the many ways in which the environment is treated ruthlessly. 'Panda politics' has become a stock phrase in relation to China; the agreement that WWF signed with Beijing in 1980 to save the giant panda (the WWF logo since 1961) is one of the events that mark the country's turn from Maoism to its opening to the West.

But small fauna also had their charisma: not only birds but humus-forming earthworms – Darwin's favourite and Switzerland's 'animal of the year' in 2011 – and not least the bat, which until then had given people goose pimples because of its vampire associations, and which finally acquired a face thanks to the sophistication of modern photography. In the 1990s, when a European Batnight Project was launched, many priests were delighted to take part in it, since bats like to live in church towers and their protection helped to give the church ecological legitimacy. They do leave a terrible mess behind, though, so their presence is not uncontested in ecclesiastical circles.

Conservationists who took ecology seriously had mixed feelings about the media hype regarding charismatic animals. Henry Makowski notes of the storm of outrage over the death of seals in 1988 (which was probably caused by a virus rather than North Sea pollution): 'Never before in its history has conservationism been able to communicate and impose its demands as effectively as it did for the dying seals'[39] – seals with their sad, reproachful eyes. Wolfgang Haber joked that the obsession of animal conservationists with 'charismatic' creatures ultimately had the effect of changing the landscape into one big zoo![40]

In 1991 Dave Foreman, the founder of Earth First! and spokesperson for 'ecotage' (ecological sabotage), published his *Confessions of an Eco-Warrior* – 'warrior', not simply 'fighter' – in which he identifies especially with the dangerous grizzly bear, *Ursus arctos horribilis*. 'A Grizzling Bear snuffling along Pelican Creek in Yellowstone National Park with her two cubs has just as much right to life as any human has, and is far more important ecologically.' 'John Muir said that if it ever came to war between the races, he would side with the bears. That day has arrived.' Foreman takes his chapter motto from the other great wilderness prophet, Aldo Leopold: 'Relegating grizzlies to Alaska is about like relegating happiness to heaven; one may never get there.' And at the end, fully in the spirit of Deep Ecology, he writes out the slogan: 'Run those rivers, climb those mountains, encounter the Griz. . . . And piss on the developer's grave.' 'Developer' as the worst swearword! And again: 'Pissing on what was politically correct. And thereby doing sacred work.' 'We absolutely need a mythology to guide us in our work.'[41] *Nota bene*: Foreman's concept of the sacred is associated with abhorrence of the Puritanical tradition of hostility to nature.[42] Wild enthusiasm in the wilderness is a quite different kind of religiosity!

'Small is beautiful': the ecological reinvention of Buddhism

Concern for future generations – not only of humans but of all living creatures – has a powerful spiritual grounding in the belief in reincarnation. A Buddhism centred on peaceful ties with all living things, and associated with elements of Hinduism and doctrines of Gandhi and Albert Schweitzer, was especially typical of the eco-scene. A leading figure here was Fritz (later E. F. = Ernst Fritz) Schumacher (1911–77), an economist from Bonn, who emigrated to England in 1936, rose to become head of the National Coal Board statistical department, and, initially as a lobbyist for coal, developed a critical attitude to nuclear technology. An interesting personal note is that he was a brother-in-law of Werner Heisenberg, the revered physicist and leading light in West Germany's developing nuclear industry in the 1950s,[43] who, though fond of discussion in general, avoided Schumacher and regarded him as a demagogue inimical to the core of his work.[44] In reality, Schumacher was one of those rather genial prophets who did not announce the coming apocalypse but aimed to offer signs of hope and pragmatic suggestions here and now, without requiring the creation of new people in a new world.

He turned to Buddhism in the early 1950s, long before it became fashionable in the West and the Dalai Lama rose to being 'secret Pope of the Protestants'. The key influences for Schumacher were several periods in Burma and a fellow-emigré who proved a brilliant and highly knowledgeable teacher of Buddhism: Edward (originally Eberhard) Conze (1904–79).[45] First and foremost, Conze advised his pupils to immerse themselves in 'serenity of mind'.[46] It was a Middle Path Buddhism, warmer and more congenial than either Japanese Zen (which, as it turned out, was all too well suited to modern managerial religion) or the tantric sexual mysticism of Himalayan Buddhism, which later enraptured hippies, and not only them. For Schumacher, the Coal Board statistician, his stays in Burma and India became an enlightenment when he saw artisans working there in the old way:[47] utterly impoverished by Western criteria, but cheerful and more developed in their skills than many Western assembly-line or office workers. His impressions there, together with his own experiences of 'organic' gardening, increasingly took shape in a new world-view, with a magical triangle of quality of life, ecological agriculture and alternative technology.

From the early 1960s on, Schumacher gave Middle Path Buddhism a thoroughly practical-technological inflection with his concept of 'intermediate technology'[48] – a phrase to which he gradually gave a more and more definite content; it was originally conceived with third world countries like India in mind, but it also inspired thinking about technological alternatives in the West. Medial, intermediate technology, as he understood it, took over various modern achievements but gave them an artisanal character, developing many-sided capacities in the worker and not displacing large quantities of labour-power; it should be so cheap that even small third world businesses could afford to use it. This was a very personal interpretation of Buddhism; many other Buddhist teachers see wisdom in the equanimity that leaves the world as it is, without vainly striving to change it.

Schumacher's pragmatic Buddhism was also rather different from that of animal-loving Buddhists, for whom the Buddha – outdoing Francis of Assisi and his sermon to the birds – actually turned himself into a cuckoo. And it was even further removed from the later shrill Buddhism of a Petra Kelly, who was entirely focused on the great struggle and knew nothing of a self-contained Middle Path. Until the late 1960s Schumacher made economists laugh with his ideas, but in 1973 his *Small Is Beautiful* suddenly converted him into a guru, who spoke in overflowing halls even in the United States and was so overwhelmed with enquiries from around the world that his health soon began to suffer. Probably the greatest success was the book's title, which he did not even come up with himself:[49] *Small Is Beautiful* was a stroke of genius, short and snappy like a saying from Mao's Little Red Book (which had made a big impression on Schumacher[50]), as if tailor-made as a catchy slogan.

On theological grounds alone, it might have been expected that American religious fundamentalists – who took the Bible's creation story literally and defended it against Darwin – would be like German creationists in having a special receptiveness to ecological messages.[51] Yet the exact opposite was the case.[52] If one thinks historically, not theologically, it is hardly surprising that eco-spirituality seeks the broad rather than the narrow, openness rather than orthodoxy. And it is spirit, not theology, that matters. The American origins of Greenpeace were inspired by the pacifist Quaker tradition, not by doctrinaire creationism;[53] Quakers organized a trip to Bikini atoll as early as 1956 to protest against US bomb tests.[54] Curiously, this peaceful, brotherly free church is usually overlooked by eco-activists in their spiritual quest.

Spiritual roaming: Rudolf Bahro

Fortunately, charisma and spirituality have not up to now founded a new orthodoxy in the eco-scene, at least not a lasting one; an element of movement and mental agility has always endured. A model of roaming spirituality is offered us by Rudolf Bahro (1935–97), who, like an ancient prophet from the desert, came out of the GDR into the greening left scene of the Bundesrepublik. In the late seventies, as a left dissident who had spent time in an East German prison, he was far more famous than all other founders of the Green Party. In the United States at least as much as in Germany, he was considered alongside Petra Kelly as the charismatic figure of the Greens' founding period. Like her, however, he was soon playing only a marginal role in the party's regular political life. In 1985 he resigned from the Greens, having turned two years earlier to the worldly, tantric-inspired salvation movement of the guru Bhagwan Shree Rajneesh.[55]

Bahro's *The Alternative in Eastern Europe* (1977), smuggled to the West and published while he was in prison at Bautzen, came as a thunderbolt in the left-intellectual world. Its conceptualization of 'actually existing socialism' – in contrast to the ideal socialism of the future – meant that for the rest of his life Bahro's political capital rested on the book: all the more curious, then, that his further thinking was not marked by the same intellectual discipline. There too one occasionally finds an apocalyptic note: for example, when he remarks that, if things go on like this for another few decades, 'coming generations will have to produce oxygen for the atmosphere, water for the rivers, and cold for the poles'[56] – one of the flashes of

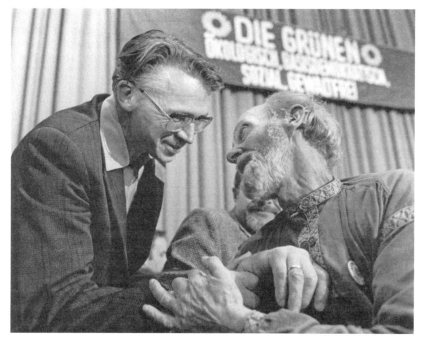

Rudolf Bahro, a founding father of the German Greens, moving from Marxism to Tantrism.

inspiration that remain fixed in the memory. But even sympathetic Greens found his later writings increasingly unreadable. As with so many of his contemporaries on the left, once he threw off the Marxist straitjacket, he lost his intellectual bearings and allowed himself to be carried along by shifting trends.

In 1990, unlike most theorists of the Greens, Bahro became caught up in the new German sense of nationhood. He criticized the Green Party for not using the *völkisch* moment and disgusted many by letting slip: 'There is something in the depths of the *Volk* that calls for a Green Adolf. And the Left is afraid of it, instead of realizing that a Green Adolf would be completely different from the well-known one.'[57] He was probably right in sensing that the Greens could have won far more votes if, instead of slighting the revival of national consciousness, they had uninhibitedly addressed the German love of nature and *Heimat*. But what Treitschke wrote about Friedrich Ludwig Jahn (1778–1852) applies to Bahro's position at the time: 'That cranky saint could not discuss rational matters either except in a clownish manner.'[58] In 1992 Bahro flummoxed his last supporters when he, the ex-prisoner from Bautzen, offered to defend former GDR leader Erich Honecker and discovered promising aspects in the failed Communist dictatorship.[59]

The US environmental activist Charlene Spretnak, who in 1984 published one of the first books on the Greens and was strongly influenced by conversations with Petra Kelly and Rudolf Bahro, had what now seems an absurd impression that the party was essentially a spiritual movement. Bahro himself could speak like a prophet, as when he declared at a Green meeting in Hamburg in December 1984 'The race against the apocalypse can be won only if this becomes a great age of faith, a Pentecostal season in which, as far as possible, the living Spirit pours out over everyone.' That was too much for the ex-pastor Antje Vollmer, who accurately pointed out that Bahro had forgotten one thing: 'You don't make yourself a prophet, but are made into one when people follow you and trust in what you say.'[60]

Indeed! One of the marks of a prophet is his spiritual and human trustworthiness for disciples: something sorely lacking in Bahro, who was self-enamoured to the point of autism. In the GDR, before he became famous, women had often not taken him and his baby-face altogether seriously, and when he left prison for the West he displayed a restless need to make up for lost time – intellectually, spiritually and sexually. Even Petra Kelly, who until then had been intellectually close to him, ran out of patience shortly after the Greens entered the Bundestag (1993), when Bahro, with his horror of any bureaucratization, tried to foil a plan for more efficient running of the party offices.[61] And in late 1983 the minutes of the Green parliamentary group record: 'It was generally held against Rudolf Bahro that he would promote a doomsday mood.'[62]

The Green Bundestag group did not offer a suitable sounding board for an apocalyptic prophet. But even people with religious feelers increasingly regarded him as a loose cannon. As a GDR dissident, he had been a 'great admirer of Luther';[63] then he turned to Meister Eckhart, Spinoza, Buddha, Lao-tse and other thinkers,[64] until he settled on Bhagwan, long known in the media for the tantric sexual practices in which he invited his male and female disciples to take part. But Bahro did not succeed in becoming the Green guru; his charisma was too tied to a particular historical moment. With all his eccentricity, he belonged to a type of the age, more often found in the lower ranks of the eco-scene than at the top: a man who, in his own eyes, was 'searching' for something. In the eyes of a critical observer, however, he latched indiscriminately onto contradictory spiritual trends – from cool Japanese Zen meditation to the sweat lodges of Indian shamans. 'Esotericism' became exhibitionism; 'spirituality' not infrequently degenerated into no more than a trendy slogan.

A Green martyr cult?

Not only organizational structures but also human types and forms of humanity, passion and self-sacrifice matter in Green movements. Robert Michels, for many years a close interlocutor of Max Weber, once pointed out that one of the most important qualities of a charismatic in Weber's sense was a 'preparedness to die'.[65] In trying to pinpoint the various kinds of Green spirituality, it may be instructive to examine any analogies with the Christian martyr cult in the remembrance of environmental activists who have died a violent death or committed suicide, and whose demise has been used to define an obligation for the living. This will shed light on the different forms of religiosity. For the cult of martyrs is not characteristic of religion as such, but only of Christianity (especially Catholicism), post-Maccabi Judaism and Shia Islam. 'Martyr' literally means 'witness'; but *what* the Christian martyr bears witness to is a controversial matter among theologians.[66]

Buddhism, which met with much good will early on in the eco-scene, does not have martyrs – indeed, it condemns careless attitudes to one's own life. As we can see from the Nazi heroization of those who died in the Hitler putsch of 1923, the political (and religious) cult of martyrs is associated with a marked propensity to violence: the fate of one's own martyrs offers legitimacy for doing the same to one's enemies. But even Gandhian non-violent resistance, shared by the environmental movement everywhere down to Greenpeace, may in some situations require a preparedness for martyrdom, as it did in the famous Salt March of 1930, when Gandhi's followers exposed themselves to the clubs of brutal police units. Similarly, the Greenpeace rainbow warriors first fascinated the international public by their willingness 'to die to save the whale', as Monika Griefahn put it,[67] without themselves resorting to violence. (They did plan their operations very carefully, though, so as to stay alive while achieving the greatest possible impact.)

The most famous martyr: Chico Mendes

The murder of Chico Mendes on 22 December 1988 attracted world attention, at a time when the alarm over the destruction of the Amazonian rainforest was reaching its height. As chair of a regional rubber-tapper organization, he was not, strictly speaking, one of the indigenous people for whom the first world eco-scene showed such enthusiasm, but he did belong to a group of workers connected to the rainforest and fighting in their interests to preserve it. He came to prominence in the media for his campaigning activity, although he was not at all keen on the climate-saver image presented there. 'I'm not protecting the forest because I'm worried that in twenty years the world will be affected. I'm worried about it because there are thousands of people living here who depend on the forest and their lives are in danger every day.'[68] He was aware that, in nationalist Brazil, forest conservationists are easily suspected of foreign dependence. But both locally and internationally, he became the object of a remembrance cult after his death. He had known that, although he had trade union backing for his resistance to the cattle barons, he risked being murdered by hired killers.[69] His death has remained in the memory more than other killings of environmental activists. Chico Mendes and his comrades had the Catholic church of their region behind them; and the honouring of martyrs has its place in that church.[70]

The Brazilian Chico Mendes (1944–88) was the first prominent campaigner for rainforest conservation. The picture shows him in December 1988 at the headquarters of his rubber-tappers' union, just a few days before he was killed by two farmers.

Subsequently, under the influence of liberation theology, it happened more and more often – from South America to the Philippines – that Catholic priests gave assistance to movements protesting against the exploitation of local resources by foreign corporations. Erwin Kräutler, a bishop originally from Austria living in Xingu diocese in the heart of Amazonia, more recently became the spokesperson for resistance to the Belo Monte hydropower station planned there, the third largest in the world.[71] Large parts of Latin America are considered so dangerous, however, that even Greenpeace refrains from operations. As Marcie Mersky, the director of Greenpeace Central America, explained: 'Here you'd simply be shot in no time!'[72] Thus, commemorations of that shocking murder have been at least as much warnings as spurs to continue the work of the fallen. Meanwhile, in Colombia, Kimy Pernia Domico, the leader of an indigenous movement against the selling of local water rights to a corporation, was kidnapped on 2 June 2001 and has not been heard of since. An international Water for People and Nature congress, held in July 2001 in Canada (British Columbia), was dedicated to the memory of this activist.[73]

The forgotten martyr: Ken Saro-Wiwa

On 10 November 1995, despite a stream of protests from around the world, the writer and civil rights activist Ken Saro-Wiwa (b. 1941) and eight fellow-campaigners were hanged on the orders of Nigeria's military dictator Sani Abacha. The previous year, already under sentence of death, Saro-Wiwa and the Movement for the Survival of the Ogoni People (MOSOP) – which

The Nigerian civil rights and environmental activist Ken Saro-Wiwa (1941–95)
founded the Movement for the Survival of the Ogoni People. In 1989 he was
executed together with eight others by the military regime of the time. The photo
shows him on 5 January 1993 at an Ogoni Day demonstration.

he founded in 1989 – had received the Alternative Nobel Prize. Even John
Major, UK prime minister at the time, attacked the execution as judicial
murder, Britain being especially affected since the Shell corporation was
involved in the scandal. Two days later, the Commonwealth countries met
in Auckland, New Zealand, and suspended Nigeria's membership with
immediate effect. The prosecutor had accused Saro-Wira of inciting young
people to kill four political opponents, but several witnesses later admitted
to the prosecutor that they had been bribed by the Nigerian government to
give false testimony.[74]

Himself a member of the Ogoni group in Africa's most populous
country, this author of twenty-nine books   who mounted a spirited
and trenchant defence of his positions and personally knew most of the
rulers[75] – had led a movement against the extensive environmental destruction caused by oil leaking from pipelines into densely populated land
around the Niger delta. 'The flares of Shell are flames of hell', began one
of his poems.[76] Although his aim was not to ban oil prospecting but only
to obtain a just share of the proceeds for the Ogoni people, this made him
extremely dangerous for the Nigerian government, which derived half its
budget and nine-tenths of its foreign earnings from oil, with Shell as the
largest private partner in the joint venture. In response to the protests –
some 300,000 people are said to have taken part in one demonstration in
January 1993 – Shell temporarily suspended oil prospecting in the Ogono
areas in 1994. But although in this case environmental protection largely
overlapped with the technical improvement of oil prospecting, the corporation had been covered for decades by the Nigerian power elite and kept
a low profile.[77]

During the Biafra war, Ken Saro-Wiwa had defended the unity of the Nigerian state;[78] its break-up into tribal units was not his objective. In 1987–8 he even temporarily took up a leading position in the Directorate of Mass Mobilisation for Self-Reliance, Social Justice and Economic Recovery (MAMSER), which set out to 'inculcate in Nigerians the virtues of patriotism and positive participation in national affairs'.[79] Evidently he saw the core of many problems facing the third world: a lack of loyalty to the state, which in Nigeria's case was an ethnically heterogeneous structure put together by the British colonial power. But Saro-Wiwa's later life shows that he came to identify politically with his own ethnic group, the Ogoni, so that by 1990 he could publicly call for Nigeria to be reconstituted as a 'federation of 300 ethnic groups'.[80] Under his direction, the MOSOP movement combined protests against the oil plague with demands for regional autonomy and a share in the oil profits: a mix of environmentalism and neo-regionalism typical of many parts of the world. This made MOSOP all the more dangerous for the military rulers of the time, and thousands of people lost their lives in the ensuing reprisals. Ken Saro-Wiwa, who always preached non-violence, accused the regime of genocide.[81] When the environmental movement honours its dead, few would deserve to be remembered more than he. But since the bloody Biafra war (1967–70) the world had grown used to horror stories from countries like Nigeria; many in Africa had lost hope in the rule of law, and for nature lovers the Niger delta – though containing the world's third largest mangrove reserves – was far from playing the same role as Amazonia in dreams of paradise on earth.[82] So the name of Ken Saro-Wiwa, unlike that of Chico Mendes, became only fleetingly known around the world.

Also in 1995 Greenpeace was actively mobilizing against Shell – not over the Nigeria death sentence, though, but over the Brent Spar drilling rig in the North Sea, which eventually became a moral semi-defeat for the rainbow warriors when it turned out that they had been operating with exaggerated figures. Comrades of Ken Saro-Wiwa tried in vain to get Greenpeace to take up the incomparably worse scandal in Nigeria; the whole business was a crude example of how the Green world power prioritized media effect whenever it was in doubt. The organization might have appealed to the basic pedagogic principle: 'You have to start from where people are at.' Its PR consultant reported that it had received roughly 400 protests in connection with Nigeria, but 16,000 on Brent Spar – a disproportion that obviously gave Greenpeace food for thought, even if it was soon forgotten by the public.[83]

The Karen Silkwood mystery

A tragic death is most likely to mobilize people where a constitutional state has to take an environmentally aware public into consideration. The death of 28-year-old Karen Silkwood on 13 November 1974 gave rise to unusual publicity as well as having practical effects. But it has never been proven that it was an assassination by the nuclear lobby rather than a simple traffic accident; speculation continues to this day. Together with the events leading up to it, her death certainly highlighted the health risks of jobs where workers came into contact with highly radioactive substances, and, more generally, the importance of occupational medicine for the new environmentalism. At the same time, it cast the professional ethos of the management in a questionable light, so that sections of the American public felt sure it was a planned murder.

Silkwood, a qualified chemical technician and active trade unionist, worked at a nuclear fuel installation run by the Kerr-McGee corporation near Crescent (Oklahoma). Noticing safety violations in the handling of radioactive substances, she went more deeply into the issue and systematically collected incriminating evidence; she even found traces of highly dangerous plutonium in her body. On her way to a meeting with reporters and trade unionists, at which she was due to make what she knew public, she then suffered her fatal traffic accident. The brown envelope containing all the evidence she had collected was not found later at the scene. The police report spoke of 'over-tiredness', but it did not sound very convincing that she should have nodded off at the wheel in such circumstances.

Karen Silkwood's death caused a huge stir that went beyond the borders of the United States. *Der Spiegel*, which had not covered the occupation at Wyhl a week earlier, ran a report on 24 February 1975 – its first story ever on the seamy side of nuclear technology. Extensive investigations came up with awkward results, and in 1975 Kerr-McGee decided to close down the facility altogether. A feature film, *Silkwood* (1983), was made later, with Meryl Streep in the main role, and there was a strong impetus to get to the bottom of the affair.[84] Yet things never went much beyond the level of cheap sensationalism; one usually looks in vain for 'Karen Silkwood' in the index of academic literature on US environmentalism – which may also have something to do with a certain shyness of real humans in the social sciences.

Death of a rainbow warrior

On 10 July 1985 Fernando Pereira – a Dutch photographer of Portuguese extraction – drowned off the coast of New Zealand, when the Greenpeace ship *Rainbow Warrior* hit two underwater mines laid by the French secret service. This sinking, just as Greenpeace activists were about to stage their largest ever action against French nuclear testing on the island of Mururoa, had a particularly long-lasting impact. (It was a return to the origins of the organization, since it had been a daring operation off Mururoa in 1971, with the soon-famous slogan 'Better Active than Radioactive!', that first shot Greenpeace into the headlines of the world press.) The incoming Labour prime minister of New Zealand, himself opposed to nuclear weapons, lost no time in ordering an investigation of this violation of his country's sovereignty, and the protestations in Paris that the French government had had nothing to do with this act of war in peacetime were exposed as a tissue of lies. The incident acquired the features of a crime thriller.[85]

At first, Greenpeace too was naturally outraged by the killing of its activist, but it was not long before its coffers were overflowing with donations as never before. The publicity effect of the tragedy was even greater than if the Mururoa operation had been successful; only in France did Greenpeace's popularity and membership plummet for a while, leaving this most famous of all environmental organizations with no other option than to close its French section temporarily in 1987. Although an opinion poll showed that 78 per cent of French people thought the secret service killing had been wrong, that was often only a formal expression of 'political correctness'; a majority of the population still supported nuclear weapons testing and 'vigorous measures' against disruption by environmental activists.[86] Thus, the experience was deeply ambiguous for Greenpeace and triggered discussions about whether a confrontational policy geared to spectacular effects was a good idea in the long run. Monika Griefahn, then a member of the Greenpeace directorate, complained that such a collision with ostensible national interests led to acts of defiance that distracted attention from the environmental cause. French people, she argued, felt 'wounded in their national pride', and even in French-speaking Switzerland Greenpeace 'encountered real hatred'; 'it was the worst I have ever experienced in Greenpeace'.[87] After the fatal incident in New Zealand, there was a lively debate inside Greenpeace about whether the damaged ship should be sent across the world to be repaired by volunteers, or whether it should be written off and sunk. Those who thought that the latter would have the greater symbolic value won the argument, but others thought it was the biggest mistake that Greenpeace ever made.[88] The symbolic calculation was not unfounded, however, since pilgrimages were later often organized to the wreck and to Pereira's grave.

Self-immolation in front of Peter's Church

The man who came closest to an ancient Christian martyr was Hartmut Gründler, a 47-year-old teacher from Tübingen, who on 21 November 1977 set fire to himself on the steps of Peter's Church in Hamburg; it was the Day of Prayer and Repentance, and the Congress of the Social-Democratic Party (SPD) was also taking place at the time. The reason that he gave for his action was the misinformation persistently given out by the federal government concerning the risks of nuclear energy. The case merits special attention precisely because Gründler's death remained a non-event in the annals of the German environmental movement. From what we know of his life, he was neither a fanatic nor a psychopath – more like a prototype of the upright idealist prepared to go *jusqu'au bout*. His self-immolation was not a sudden irrational act but had been carefully thought out.

Gründler had been an environmental activist since the word go, who, after a phase in one of the Maoist groups, had become a supporter of Gandhi and split from the militant left on the issue of violence. In 1972 he founded the 'Life Conservation Group for Non-Violent Protection of the Environment' and engaged in extensive leafleting activity in Tübingen. Despite his efforts, the group remained on the margins of the movement against nuclear power plants. But he did make history at one moment in 1975, when he went on hunger strike for three weeks, and the public effect induced the federal research minister, Hans Matthöfer, to accept anti-nuclear groups as a party to talks within the framework of a 'Bürgerdialog Kernenergie'. Before setting fire to himself, Gründler even wrote a letter thanking Matthöfer for his 'chivalrous attitude during our discussions'.[89]

To be sure, Gründler expected that his self-sacrifice – an unprecedented act in the Bundesrepublik – would release shock waves and eventually push the government into reconsidering its policy on nuclear energy. He informed in advance the federal chancellor, the government and the media, putting himself under fateful pressure to go through with his plan, but no one seems to have paid any attention. Such an act did not fit into the political landscape of the time, especially as the public, in that 'German Autumn' of 1977, was obsessed with the Red Army Faction, whose members directed their aggression against others rather than themselves. Moreover, since the German public was already highly sensitive to the risks of nuclear energy, Gründler's gruesome act seemed curiously anachronistic. One has the impression that even many opponents of nuclear power found it rather embarrassing; his name was by no means on everyone's lips in the eco-scene.

A comparison with previous incidents of this kind will help us to gauge the significance of the under-reaction. On 18 August 1976, Pastor Oskar Brüsewitz set fire to himself in front of his church at Zeitz (in East Germany) – an act which sent out a signal well beyond ecclesiastical circles and, together with the arrest of Rudolf Bahro and Wolf Biermann's being stripped of his GDR citizenship, helped to ensure the beginning of a turnaround in the rather favourable attitude of West German intellectuals to the GDR.[90] When the Czech student Jan Palach did the same on 17 January 1969, as a protest against the muzzling of the press in his country, he became a 'new Jan Hus' symbolizing resistance to dictatorship.[91] And when Buddhist monks in South Vietnam excoriated police violence by immolating themselves in May 1963, during processions to mark the Buddha's birthday, this played an essential role in President Diem's loss of US support for his rule.[92]

Against this background, it is understandable that the hapless Gründler had illusions about the likely effect of his self-sacrifice – and also that it had so few repercussions. The age of far-left 'K-groups' risking life and limb drew to an end with the 'German Autumn' of 1977; 'Gorleben must live' became the slogan of the time, as an emphatic commitment to life increasingly defined Green rhetoric. It was precisely in the lonely forest around Gorleben, a remote tip of West Germany rising up into the GDR, that the anti-nuclear movement widened out into a more inclusive environmental movement; the struggle against the nuclear hazard became a struggle for the forest. If this had a spiritual undercurrent, it was rather pantheistic in nature and offered little scope for a sombre martyr-cult. Significantly, the only exception in Europe was the British animal rights movement, which admired Olive Parry's self-immolation in 1972 against vivisection and kept her in its memory;[93] this was not the only respect in which animal rights activism was a rogue element. If we look in the environmental movement for spiritual undercurrents, we find above all a mysticism of life, not death. Nor should we forget how little blood has been shed in it, compared with most other large movements in history, although there was certainly plenty of material for conflict, and in theory much violence could have been legitimated in the name of saving the world. Martyrs were not needed, however, for the legitimation of non-violent resistance.

2 Ten Heroines Embodying Tensions in the Movement

Ecofeminism

Whereas, in the search for a Green martyr-cult, it is rather the lack of one that has a lot to tell us, the worldwide eco-scene has clearly been striving for a new kind of heroism; and heroes are potential martyrs. This whole question has been neglected in the bulk of the literature on environmental movements. Prominent women are particularly good examples: they often embody, more impressively than male combatants, typical tensions of the movement: those between original passion and institutionalization processes that will be the subject of this chapter, as well as those between strategies of conflict and consensus or between cross-border horizons and local sources of activism. The life stories of such women will shed light on the differing internal life of environmental movements in various regions of the world. The selection made here is inevitably at the expense of other high-profile women in the movement, whose number could be extended almost at will. In the majority of cases, the existing literature makes it surprisingly difficult to determine their actual political significance; it depends on the perspective, or makes itself felt at the margins. Not for the first time one has the experience that – contrary to Bourdieu's so-called 'biographical illusion'– the historical meaning of individuals, indeed their very individuality, is called into question by access to their biography.

Cross-connections developed early on between the 'ecological revolution' and the new women's movement. In 1974 Françoise d'Eaubonne coined the term 'ecofeminism', which soon crossed over to the United

States and became much more popular there than in France.[94] The basic idea is that the repression of women is closely bound up with the repression of nature. But feminists disagree about the (easily made) mental leap to a further idea: that women embody nature to a special degree, and that there is a 'female nature' or anyway a distinctively female sense of responsibility for the provision of an environment in which their children and their children's children can have a life worth living. It is in this responsibility for children that Hans Jonas sees 'the archetype of all responsibility', which 'is powerfully implanted in us by nature or at least in the childbearing part of humanity'.[95] But it remains highly contentious: many feminists vehemently reject any notion of a female nature, which they see as providing a biological basis for discrimination.

Often, in environmental initiatives, the female factor becomes stronger if one looks closely and does not focus only on programmatic texts or figures with an international profile. In 1991 Marieluise Beck-Oberdorf and Elke Kiltz pointed to one of the significant small differences that mark local commitment: '[Women] are mobile in a different way – more often on foot, by public transport or on a bicycle, and often still carting around a shopping bag, a pram or both.' For them, cheap and well-organized public transport and bicycle routes are of more vital importance than for many men.[96] One need not speculate about a special 'closeness to nature' to understand women's relationship with environmental issues, and their role is definitely more striking here than it has been in nearly any other large movement in history. It is particularly important to look at the people, not only at the organizational structures.

'The best known Green in the world' and a mass of tensions: Petra Kelly

Scarcely any other figure embodies a cluster of tensions within the environmental movement as stirringly and paradigmatically as Petra Kelly (1947–92) did:[97] tensions between movement and organization, spirituality and realism, charismatic leadership and horror of all hierarchy, global horizon and grassroots base, purposive action and diffuse unease.[98] Having lived and become politicized in the United States from 1959 to 1970, between the ages of twelve and twenty-three, she had a challenging female self-confidence and a natural combination of political interest and spirituality – common character traits in both American and German ecofeminism. Her death was more appropriate to a Shakespearean tragedy – with her lover, the former Bundeswehr general Gert Bastian, in the role of Othello – than in the history of the Bundesrepublik.

In the early years of the German Greens, though from an American vantage point more than a German,[99] Petra Kelly appeared the charismatic leader par excellence: a Joan of Arc[100] of the new eco-age. Yet after Bastian shot first her, then himself, in their Bonn apartment on the night

Petra Kelly (1947–94, here in a photo from 1984) left the SPD in 1979 to become a founding member of the German Greens.

of 1 October 1992, nearly three weeks passed before their bodies were discovered. She had also still been receiving piles of mail from around the world – a harbinger of the internet age, in which someone may have thousands of contacts in various parts but no one who is regularly concerned about him or her.

Petra Kelly's passion for politics stemmed from the women's movement, much as the combination of environmental protection with peace movement activism was constitutive for environmentalism: 'Greenpeace', 'Ökopax'. But the apocalyptic vision of a 'Euroshima', which appalled so many in 1980, had acquired something unreal by the time of the Soviet perestroika of the mid-eighties; she had lost her guiding leitmotif and the power of her charisma survived only from afar, not close up. In Max Weber's work, ideal-typical charisma is rooted in close personal contact among a small circle of people, radiating outward through disciples. Petra Kelly, however, had been isolated in the party for many years and had never really been all that popular with the Greens; when the 'women's council' took power in the party in 1984, she was not one of the six who made up the new all-female executive. She reacted angrily to Antje Vollmer's accusation that she would 'move with breathtaking speed away from rank-and-file decisions and the day-to-day life' of the party.[101] She was a high-pressure woman, always hectic and effervescent – in sharp contrast to the 'laid-back' type common at the grassroots in those days. She saw a kindred spirit in Joseph Beuys, the idol of the alternative arts scene and like her a Green right from the start: she even called him 'the original Green thinker', who 'was humiliated by ten ballots at a candidate selection process in North-Rhine Westphalia and not allowed to stand'.[102] Beuys, for his part, declared Petra Kelly to be a work of art.[103] He too was usable only as a figurehead, not for the daily round of politics.

Petra Kelly increasingly brooked only like-minded people around her, operating on the principle: 'Whoever is not with me is against me.' 'If she doesn't get her way,' wrote Alice Schwarzer, 'she screams, slams doors and shuts herself away in a fit of rage.'[104] In the end, even her lover found her unbearable. Alice Schwarzer, unlike well-meaning Greens who believed in a suicide pact and proposed a joint memorial to the two, caustically pointed out that Petra Kelly's death had been straightforward murder and admitted that, the more she delved into their relationship, the more she understood why the general had finally cracked up and reached in despair for his pistol.[105]

'Right from the start,' Petra Kelly emphasized, 'my involvement with the Greens had a great deal to do with my deeply religious-spiritual orientation. For I consider the genuine Green international movement to be not only a political but a *political-spiritual* movement.'[106] She was aware that 'a number of forces in the Greens' would 'firmly reject such a description'; her statement implies they were not 'authentic'. At the same time, internationality and spirituality were linked to each other in her eyes. More courageous than the majority of Bonn politicians, she established contacts with civil rights activists in the GDR, but when the call went up: 'Deutschland, einig Vaterland!' she, like most of the Green leadership, did not want to know. The crossing of national frontiers had something of a transcendental quality for her; in this she was representative of a widespread exoticism in the eco-scene – that politically irrational mentality which is more committed to the tropical rainforest than to German forests and attacks nothing more aggressively (after nuclear power) than any clinging to borders.[107] 'She was not of this world; she had an incredible spiritual dimension', recalled her former lover Lukas Beckmann after her death.[108]

But 'spiritual' can mean a lot of things. What was her kind of spirituality? Years before her death journalists thought she had 'the air of a martyr',[109] and that fits the basically apocalyptic mood she displayed at a time when her eyes often shone in photos.[110] Parliamentary politics would have meant nothing to her; she could only 'bear witness', as those 'witnesses' called martyrs do. Occasionally she would speak of the 'erotic character of genuine religiosity', mentioning indiscriminately such emotive buzzwords as 'tantric yoga' or 'Tao'.[111] In 1983, as befitted a left Catholic, she showed her support at an Evangelical Academy for the Brazilian archbishop and celebrated liberation theologist Helder Camara,[112] whom the Green press spokesperson Heinz Suhr would have liked to invite over for the entry of the Greens into the Bundestag.[113] To quote Beckmann: 'Petra took on everything – you could almost say she embodied everything. She was a kind of medium.'[114] Again that roving spirituality we came across in

Rudolf Bahro – except that, after an initial sympathy, it soon drove Petra Kelly to distraction.

Her true holy man was eventually the Dalai Lama, whom she first met in Bonn in 1987 and subsequently worshipped without restraint. Disregarding the awkwardness felt by Green non-believers, she now always referred to him as 'His Holiness the Dalai Lama'.[115] Yet she, the living embodiment of restless agitation, was as distant as anyone could be from the serenity and 'middle way' of Buddhism. Rather, in her rigid good-against-evil thinking, she never really got over the provincial Catholicism in which she grew up.

The Dalai Lama, living in exile since 1959, received the Nobel Peace Prize in 1989 and was the object of worldwide attention during these years as he pressed on with his ecological reorientation; 'everything is connected with everything else' was for him the essence of Buddhism. He thus offered an ideal model for the fusion of spirituality and ecologism – except that this was more a synthesis in an exotic fantasy world, set apart from what could be done here and now in the world of German environmental politics. But was Petra Kelly anyway interested in such possibilities? If she had been, her previous experience would have given her excellent prospects; this was later too easily forgotten. From 1972 to 1982 she was an administrator at the EC in Brussels, and in 1971, at the age of twenty-four, she had begun a relationship with the forty-years-older Sicco Mansholt, the leading force at its headquarters. From 1968 on, the EU-funded 'Mansholt Plan' – a massive process of agricultural concentration and modernization that was supposed to see the end of traditional small farmers – had aroused the ire of farmers (apart from the giant beneficiaries) all over Western Europe. Germany, from Schleswig-Holstein in the north to Bavaria in the south, saw the growth of a new kind of 'anti-Mansholt protest action', to which Mansholt himself responded with a smile of superiority.[116]

The Mansholt Plan, then, was the exact opposite of 'Small is beautiful.' The ecological horrors of chemical agriculture, already exposed by Rachel Carson in the United States, were discovered in West Germany precisely in the founding years of the Greens. Brussels farming policy was centrally implicated, and no Green leader was better placed than Petra Kelly – who, in addition to her insider knowledge, had a loathing based on experience for the EU bureaucracy in Brussels[117] – to win over public opinion on this key environmental issue. But there was nothing doing; someone studying the story of her life can almost forget about ecology. The one exception was the issue of 'nuclear energy and cancer'; her sister's death of cancer at the age of ten haunted her all her life, and her statements indicate that it was the starting point for her political involvement. She assumed that she would not be able to have any healthy children of her own, since doctors had exposed her to too many X-rays, and so she had an abortion when she became pregnant.[118] She found her way into the Greens via the movement against the nuclear arms race. Unlike many opponents of nuclear power in the 1970s, she saw a continuum between nuclear bombs and civilian nuclear power, and her hatred of both had its origins in a dread of cancer; a number of her speeches warned of a 'cancerization of humanity'.[119] Always the woman in a hurry, however, she scarcely managed to become competent in any definite spheres of environmental policy.

This points to a general phenomenon in the leadership of the German Greens at the time: there were no genuinely Green issues that generated political dynamism, as the minutes of the Green Bundestag group during its first parliament – from 1983 to 1987 – make abundantly clear. This is a political paradox, since most Green voters were driven by a wish to do something for nature and the environment during that period of the 'dying forest' alarm. The Greens owed their entry into the Bundestag precisely to that wish. Moreover, a basic feeling that much more should be done to protect the environment was widespread also in politically conservative circles, so that the Greens would probably have made even deeper inroads if they had reached out to such milieux instead of alienating them with chaotic affectations, debates on the decriminalization of paedophilia, and contempt for the motherhood of women. At the party congress in Hanover in 1983, Bahro called on the Greens to exploit their electoral potential among people with conservative values. But at the time even Joschka Fischer, rising star of the 'Realos', ridiculed the idea.[120]

Writing in *tageszeitung* in 1985, Michael Vesper, the party whip – who already spent nights in front of a computer when the Greens were still discussing the reliability of the new electronics, and who tried to bring the necessary minimum of rules and professionalism into their group – called on Green Party substitute MPs to become full-blooded parliamentarians at last: 'They must act and keep acting in plenary sessions; they must intrigue, integrate, bow and scrape, show anger and dismay, passion and human concern.'[121] Well, Petra Kelly could display passion and concern more credibly than almost any other Green MP, and she was capable of pulling out the demagogic stops; she demanded 'gentleness' from politicians,[122] yet she certainly contributed to those human 'frictional losses' that came with the Greens' political style in Bonn. In the year before her death, she fairly exploded with rage and despair: the Greens had 'failed first and foremost as human beings'; their eight years in the Bundestag had seen them 'self-destruct' through 'fruitless in-fighting between various mullahs', which had 'crippled political activity and created an unbearable climate of envy and mistrust'.[123] This was an allusion to the vitriolic factionalism between 'Fundis' and 'Realos' that dragged on throughout the eighties. Petra Kelly had been in the USA in 1968 and avoided the experience of Marxism and 'K-groups', but she was not a *Realpolitikerin* either; she kept out of the simmering feud, while opening some new fronts of her own.

Was the human climate in the Greens really colder than in other parties? The main reason for the show of irritability was probably that, at the beginning, typical Greens had looked for an intimate, informal space in politics, rather as in a shared-living commune. Like so many others, Petra Kelly wanted there to be no separation between politics and private life; at the Bundestag, she and her general used to go around together as a pair of lovers – something no one had ever done before. She openly paraded crises in her personal life, to the point of embarrassment; 'bureaucrats and technocrats' were her enemy image.[124] And yet, the experiences in Bonn during those years made many Greens rediscover not only the practical utility but even the human value and defusing effect of certain rules and routines. This was not a peculiarly German phenomenon. All around the world, despite the ideal of 'grassroots democracy', the eco-scene produced virtuous bureaucrats who performed their regulatory duties with commitment and conviction.

Victory over the fast breeder: Dominique Voynet

At this point we should jump from Germany to France and from Petra Kelly to Dominique Voynet (b. 1958), the highest-profile woman the French Greens have produced so far. Michael Bess calls her 'a sort of Gallic Petra Kelly';[125] but in more than one respect the contrast between the two women is ideal-typical. The life of Dominique Voynet has not been at all chaotic: medical studies completed at the age of twenty-three; mother of two daughters; a Euro MP from 1989 to 1991, but also a presence at regional and local level; a politician shuttling between Provence and Paris, not given to globetrotting like Petra Kelly. In 1984 she and Antoine Waechter were among the founders of the French Greens; in 1991 she gave up her seat in the EU Parliament to work as their main spokesperson. In 1997 she became the first Green member of government, under the Socialist prime minister Lionel Jospin, then took over as party chair

Dominique Voynet (b. 1958) was France's first Green member of government, serving as minister for the environment and regional planning from 1997 to 2001. Since 2008 she has been the mayor of Montreuil.

in 2001, and since 2008 has been mayor of Montreuil, a medium-sized town in northern France. (It is true that Brice Lalonde, an early star of the French Greens, had been appointed environment minister in 1988. However, he did not object to the nuclear weapons testing on Mururoa and soon moved away from the party,[126] eventually founding one of his own (*Génération écologie*);[127] he was supposed to possess charisma, but it was not of a kind that most of the Greens played along with.[128])

Dominique Voynet was scarcely interested in projecting herself as a charismatic leader. Quite unlike Petra Kelly, she had an integrative rather than divisive effect, especially in comparison with the male leaders who had previously split the Green milieu and condemned it to political impotence:[129] the 'Parisian dandy'[130] Lalonde and the Alsatian regionalist and eco-fundamentalist Antoine Waechter, who thought a Green would be selling his soul by entering a ministry. She underlined the Greens' capacity for alliance-building and the enlargement of its programme beyond environmental objectives, without a loss of Green identity. Her leading role developed more out of her ministerial office than from the actual movement, where she had previously been just one name among others.[131] As a minister, she showed no ambition to stand out in her external habitus from non-Green colleagues, but set great store by the professional exercise of her duties. Indeed, she displayed no little skill in adapting the administrative centralism that had previously caused so many headaches to the French environmental movement. During her term of office, she managed to achieve a 30 per cent rise in her ministerial budget and an 80 per cent increase in its support for conservation.[132]

Again in contrast to Petra Kelly, Dominique Voynet's name is associated with major policy successes, both symbolic and real. Her first act as minister was to decommission the Super-Phénix fast breeder reactor at Creys-Malville, the scene of twenty years of sometimes bloody struggles.[133] At that time, it was easy enough to justify the decision: the breeder was virtually isolated from the rest of the world, and instead of operating at a profit it increased the deficit of a nuclear industry groaning under the burden of overcapacity. The nuclear power plants in service had already given rise to such a plutonium surplus that – quite apart from the safety risks – it was economically absurd to breed still more. Dominique Voynet also ordered the cancellation of the Rhine–Rhone canal, another bête noire of the environmental movement,[134] which like the Main–Danube canal was questionable on both ecological and economic grounds. At the Kyoto climate summit in late 1997, she cut a good figure when she led the European opposition to American delaying tactics.[135] As Michael Bess put it, she would have had no success if certain leitmotifs of the environmental movements had not meanwhile become part of mainstream thinking in France. Nevertheless, her period as minister marked the historical moment when 'Green visions' became 'an integral part of French modernity'.[136]

On 18 May 2007, the French environment minister announced a 'Grenelle Environnement' panel involving representatives of various political forces, which was supposed to produce by consensus a raft of long-term policy guidelines, and on 24 October 2007 this *table ronde*, chaired by Nicolas Sarkozy and attended by two Nobel prizewinning ecological figures, Al Gore and Wangari Maathai, actually began work on a wide-ranging strategy paper. Conceived as a grand historical initiative, this led partisans of deregulation to conjure up prospects of a 'Green dictatorship' and an unholy alliance between the ministry and 'militant professional tom-tom ecologists'.[137] The 'Grenelle' in the title referred to the compromise agreement between the Gaullist government and the trade union leadership concluded on 25 May 1968 at the social ministry on rue de Grenelle in Paris, under the pressure of student barricades and the strike movement.[138] Since then it had come to stand for any historic compromise. But in 1968 things did not come to an end with 'Grenelle', and the Grenelle Environnement too – as the economic crisis would soon show – was not the end of the story.

If we now look across the Atlantic, we find only one incontrovertible heroine of environmentalism: Rachel Carson, who had not yet become the spokesperson for a movement when she died in 1964. With her ends the gallery of universally recognized icons in the United States. Celia Hunter and Jane Jacobs embody opposing currents of environmentalism, and although admirers often place them alongside Rachel Carson, others mention them only in passing or ignore them altogether.

Celia Hunter: a bomber pilot fights for the wilderness in Alaska

In the Second World War – the contrast with traditional female roles could hardly be greater – Celia Hunter served as a pilot in the US Air Force and would gladly have flown on bombing missions if she had been allowed. She then went to work in Alaska, where no one gets far without an aeroplane, and on 1 January 1947 she landed in Fairbanks in the middle of a blizzard. She began to fly the first organized tourists around, and in 1952 she and some friends set up a tent camp at Denali, the centre of the future national park, with a fine view over the 4,000-metre mountains of the Alaska Range. Tourism was at the origin of wilderness protection too.

From 1956 on, she was joined by enthusiasts who wanted to create large reserves for indigenous wildlife and probably thought it would be easy in the wastes of Alaska. But the few inhabitants vehemently opposed any restrictions on their freedom to use the land as they saw fit. The Alaska Conservation Society (ACS), founded in 1960 and headed for twelve years by Celia Hunter as its executive secretary, got its support almost entirely from outside Alaska – a dilemma that would persist for a long time to come. The first target of the ACS was the Rampart Dam hydropower project on the Yukon, which would have created an artificial lake 480 kilometres long and supplied electricity for a planned aluminium plant. The protest campaign was very unpopular with local people, since they

Celia Hunter (1919–2001) was the first woman to head a US environmental organization. The photo shows her fetching water in the early years of the visitor complex she founded at Camp Denali, at the centre of what would become the National Park.

hoped to obtain cheaper electricity and were proud of the idea of having 'the world's largest artificial lake'. As Roderick Nash remarks, many saw the dam as a 'federal birthday present', which would end 'the long night of colonialism' and finally make Alaska a fully fledged state of the USA![139] When the State Department eventually abandoned the project in 1967 – the beginning of the eco-age had brought growing public sympathy for anti-dam activists – it left deep resentment in its wake.[140]

The opposition to 'Project Chariot' (a plan to blast a harbour on Alaska's Arctic coast with an atom bomb) stood a better chance of gaining local popularity and linked up with the wider movement against the 'Plowshare Program' for the civilian use of nuclear detonations. One account even sees in this the roots of the whole environmental movement: the missing link with the previous movement against nuclear weapons.[141] It is true that 'Project Chariot' was never officially dropped, but nor was it implemented. After Chernobyl, Celia Hunter claimed in a show of superiority that in her day the Atomic Commission had been well on its way to making a Chernobyl out of Alaska.

Dave Foreman, who had gained a kind of charisma from his self-sacrificing militancy since the 1980s, spoke in 1991 of the faceless epigones in the American environmental movement, complaining that one would look in vain for a John Muir, an Aldo Leopold or a Rachel Carson. 'What have we done with their living heirs, like David Brower or Celia Hunter?', he asked.[142] David Brower we know; but it is possible to spend years studying the American environmental movement without coming across the name of Celia Hunter (1919–2001).[143] She became the president (in 1976) and later executive director of the influential Wilderness Society – the first woman to head a major US environmental organization. Yet her leading role in Alaska, the main arena of her activity, continued to be disputed.

In 1879, twelve years after the US acquired Alaska, John Muir set off in search of the last wilderness and underwent an experience far more spiritual than ecological (that would have required a greater eye for detail).[144] Whereas the Everglades National Park marks the ecological turn for many wilderness conservationists, enthusiasm for the 'pristine paradise' basically meant a relapse into old-style monumentalism.[145] In fact, the bare expanse of Alaska – its uniform coniferous forest and its treeless tundra, with snowy peaks in the distance – is far richer than the Everglades in panoramic views that can be captured by modern cameras and aerial photography. Yet very few Americans have ever experienced their northernmost state *in natura*. Even Denali Park, the most popular in Alaska and Celia Hunter's early domain, had no more than 280,911 visitors in 2002 – not even 3 per cent of the total in the easily accessible Great Smoky Mountains National Park between North Carolina and Tennessee.[146] To wander independently in the Alaskan wilderness without a good knowledge of the land had certain obvious dangers; it was rather different from the original wilderness idyll, exemplified by Henry Thoreau's period of solitude in the vicinity of Concord. In 1996 Jon Krakauer's successful *Into the Wild* followed the fate of the young Chris McCandless, who, with a copy of Thoreau's *Walden* in his rucksack, undertook a 'spiritual pilgrimage'[147] of his own into the Alaskan wilderness and died a miserable death from starvation. In Alaska the wilderness was not yet threatened, but it was certainly still threatening. There one could feel for oneself that the wilderness becomes a treasure only when it is in short supply.

'No environmental issue before the American public in the past 20 years has achieved greater symbolic value than preserving the integrity of the Arctic Refuge', stated the executive director of the Sierra Club in 2004.[148] Back in the late 1970s, President Carter stood up for environmentalists (whom he had snubbed earlier under the pressure of the oil crisis) and offered steady support for wilderness conservation in Alaska.[149] However, wonderful dreams could be more readily projected onto Alaska from afar than from close by. A 'New Frontier' was hailed in the North, to replace the legendary one of old in the West, but it could not be so easily filled with life in all its colour. Even Roderick Nash, whose *Wilderness and the American Mind* (1967) became the standard work of Friends of the Wilderness, deals with Alaska in some detail in later editions, but he is remarkably reserved towards the wilderness conservation movement and makes no secret of his indifference to that cold, inhospitable land. Most of the people who drool over Alaska, he suggests, have never set foot there and would not wish to. Only once does he mention Celia Hunter, altogether in passing. Instead, he shows understanding for the great majority of indigenous people who consider it madness to establish strictly run national parks in their region. He quotes Joe Vogler of the Alaskan Independence Party: 'Anybody who says the ecology [of Alaska] is fragile is an ignoramus or a goddamn liar.'[150]

Not surprisingly, the American eco-scene is divided over whether Celia Hunter was an all-time great or one of those who diverted attention from the really important issues and steered environmentalism into a dead end. At least she and her fellow-campaigners eventually had a spectacular victory on 2 December 1980, when Jimmy Carter placed more than a quarter of Alaska (an area larger than California) under protection; 'the greatest single act of wilderness preservation in world history'.[151] The only question is whether that kind of preservation was worthwhile. The sanctity of the wilderness – usually motivated in terms of threatened species and breeding grounds, attractive landscape and tourist interest – was difficult to justify in this conservation area, the largest in the world, especially as most of the people living there, whether Yankee or indigenous, experienced the protection as a form of harassment.

The superlative of wilderness protection coincided, at the beginning of the eco-age, with another, opposite superlative: the largest oil field in North American history was discovered in 1968 at Prudoe Bay, on the Arctic north coast of Alaska, and the pipeline soon planned there counted as 'the most ambitious construction project in American history'. It was the period of Earth Day; the new ecological awakening was on the look-out for targets. Oil disasters were fresh in people's memory; the Trans-Alaska Pipeline, routed through the Arctic National Wildlife Range, triggered a nationwide controversy on a scale never before seen in the history of American conservationism. But then came the oil crisis of autumn 1973, when it became a top national priority to reduce the dependence on Middle East oil to a minimum. The pipeline was now unstoppable.[152] In the following decades, copper, in increasingly short supply, became one of the world's most coveted metals, and there were major reserves in the very regions of Alaska set aside by wilderness conservationists.[153] Predictably, therefore, the 'struggle for Alaska' did not come to an end with the proclamation of the national parks.[154] The *Exxon Valdez* oil tanker disaster off the coast of Alaska in 1989 agitated American public opinion at least as much as the Chernobyl reactor disaster had done. A sarcastic poem, 'Alaska 1984?', which Jay Hammond had written back in the 1960s, now had a prophetic ring. It began with the verse: 'Remember how lousy things used to be? Before we had oil, fish cluttered the sea.'[155]

At the time, the ACS had wound up for lack of resources (in 1980). Anyway, there was no longer any need for it, because wilderness protection in the far North had been pursued since 1971 by the Alaska Coalition, the 'largest and most powerful citizen conservation organization in American history', which had signed up the country's five leading wilderness conservation NGOs.[156] Since the 1970s, the Friends of the Wilderness had worked with Jay Hammond, accepting him with some reservations as a like-minded figure. This bear-like man, first elected governor of Alaska in 1974, had a whiff of the wilderness about him. With Aldo Leopold's phrase 'Thinking like a mountain' in mind, a colleague of his once enthused: 'Hammond is Alaska. He looks like a goddam Alaska mountain.' In his way Hammond did love the wilderness, and above all he understood that, in the eco-age, it was unwise to quarrel with environmentalists head-on; instead, he recommended using the ecological Alaska myth, which attracted more and more tourists and Americans weary of city life. 'Environment', he taught his people, 'is not an obscene, four-letter word. It has eleven letters, just as does the word "development".'[157] In fact, there was enough space in the wilds of Alaska to reconcile 'environment' with 'development'. But as the career of Sarah Palin shows, the old antagonism came alive again. In the history of environmentalism, there has never yet been a happy ending.

Jane Jacobs: a fighter for historic urban districts against the utopian city of classical modernity

In a completely different setting – a colourful city world teeming with human beings – we find Jane Jacobs (1916–2006), the feisty New Yorker who defended her Greenwich Village skilfully and courageously against the hitherto all-powerful developer Robert Moses (1888–1981). In this legendary David-and-Goliath contest, a chain reaction was started which spread across the Atlantic, centring on the preservation of mixed urban districts and neighbourhoods with historical roots.[158] But does Jane Jacobs belong at all in a history of the environmental movement? Certainly she had nothing to do with ecology in a biological sense. But when she attacked previous city planning as a 'pseudo-science' inimical to life, she was outlining a new school of urbanistic thinking that laid bridges to the life sciences. Cities, like life, were a form of 'organized complexity', which could not be schematically planned on a *tabula rasa*.[159] Alexander Mitscherlich, whose polemical blast *Die Unwirtlichkeit unserer Städte* (1965) was inspired by her work, even calls 'the city in which people have lived for centuries' (Jane Jacobs had to content herself with the more youthful New York) a 'biotope', since 'the most diverse forms of life are brought and maintained in equilibrium there'.[160] Still, while Jane Jacobs may lie outside a theoretical ideal type of ecologism, there is undoubtedly a close historical connection between environmental actions and movements to preserve historical neighbourhoods, whether in the United States, Germany or other countries. Not by accident, the Frankfurt housing struggles of the 1970s were an important catalyst of the Green movement, and environmental activists

In her book *The Death and Life of Great American Cities* (1961), Jane Jacobs (1916–2006) protested against the urban planning of her time.

in the late GDR clashed with the Communist regime precisely over questions of 'urban ecology'. The old alliance of natural conservation and cultural heritage, which many Greens regarded as a dubious peculiarity of Germany, found here a worldwide context.

From 1947 Jane Jacobs lived in Greenwich Village, famous for its literary and avant-garde associations from the Belle Époque to the Roaring Twenties, which had become quite run down and, depending on one's viewpoint, was redolent either of *La Bohème* or simply of a slum. Things were clear for Robert Moses and his city planners, and on 20 February 1961, at their instigation, Mayor Robert F. Wagner declared the Village a slum and ordered the clearance of 80 per cent of it.[161] In the same year, Jane Jacobs published her international bombshell *The Death and Life of Great American Cities* – note the resurrection metaphor in the title! It was a frontal attack on everything that planners had hitherto presented as the ideal of modernity, against which the author cleverly pointed to the growing fear of big city crime:

> But look what we have built with the first several billions: Low-income projects that become worse centres of delinquency, vandalism and general social hopelessness than the slums they were supposed to replace. . . . Cultural centres that are unable to support a good bookshop. Civic centres that are avoided by everyone but bums. . . .

Promenades that go from no place to nowhere and have no prome-
naders. Expressways that eviscerate great cities. This is not the rebuild-
ing of cities. This is the sacking of cities.[162]

She did not write in the style of planners conjuring up a utopian vision
of the future, but spoke of the conviviality of actually existing city life. The
point for her, as for conservationists, was not to plan but to preserve. The
neighbourhood and the streets, teeming with people rather than crossed by
cars at speed, were the two focuses of her urban ideal. She idealized street
life in the old districts of New York (which, to European eyes, actually
looked quite new and chaotic) into a kind of blossoming nature that was
creating order and beauty from within itself:

> Under the seeming disorder of the old city . . . is a marvellous order
> for preserving the safety of the streets and the freedom of the city. It
> is a complex order. . . . This order is all composed of movement and
> change, . . . and we may liken it to the dance. . . . The ballet of the
> good city sidewalk never repeats itself from place to place, and in any
> one place is always replete with improvisations.[163]

Robert Moses arrogantly dismissed his adversary as a 'housewife' who
had no clue about city planning. But Jane Jacobs, the wife of an architect,
was the editor of *Architectural Forum* and knew what she was talking
about; she was in tune with a long-term change in the aesthetic sensibility
of New York intellectuals. Also in 1961 the Pennsylvania Railroad published its plan to pull down Penn Station – a fine classical specimen, built
between 1904 and 1910 – and to replace it with the subterranean edifice
that stands there today. Until then, the largest and most splendid station
building in the metropolis had not appealed to New Yorkers as much as
had been expected.[164] Only when the forest of columns was handed over
to the demolition men did architects and historically aware members of
the community voice broad protests against the plan; the end of classical
modernity and the rediscovery of ancient beauty were beginning to shape
up. At first, the protesters stood pretty much alone. But when the first blow
fell, even the *New York Times*, hitherto on the side of Robert Moses,[165] felt
ashamed at this 'monumental act of vandalism against one of the largest
and finest landmarks of its age', in the place of which 'fake architecture for
our fake society' was rising up. Robert Wagner sensed the mood change
and on 19 April 1965 called a monument conservation commission into
being: the first in the United States.

Penn Station was beyond rescue, but old Greenwich Village was saved
from the excavators and Jane Jacobs became a popular figure there and
elsewhere. As the mother of three children, she also brought the interests
of women into play in the discussion of plans for the future, arguing for a
city of neighbourhoods, animated street life and 'short distances', where
people did not have to go far to do their shopping and children could

play safely in the street. Suddenly Robert Moses, who at nearly eighty had dominated New York city planning for four decades, no longer seemed the incarnation of modernity but struck younger municipal politicians as a 'cantankerous, stubborn old man'.[166] But it is easy to forget that in his way Moses also embodied the urban longing for nature. He wanted to build expressways for New Yorkers – or anyway for the car owners among them – so that they could escape to the green countryside and the sea, and he wanted to burst open the old cramped neighbourhoods and to create green spaces among the new skyscrapers. It was nothing other than the late nineteenth-century ideal of bringing 'light and air' into the city, of moving the noise and smoke of industry as far as possible from where people lived. The higher the buildings, the wider the green spaces that could be fitted in between. 'Robert Moses has made an urban desert bloom', rejoiced the *New York World-Telegram* in 1934, thinking not least of the many playgrounds he had created for children. Even Lewis Mumford wrote at the time that Moses had achieved 'the best piece of large-scale planning since the original development of Central Park'.[167]

The dispute between Jane Jacobs and Robert Moses was not a war between Good and Evil. Indeed, it drew a special piquancy from the fact that Jane Jacobs crossed swords with Lewis Mumford too, the founding father of the American environmental movement. 'Nature', when applied to the city, is a polyvalent ideal. Mumford (b. 1895) was from the same generation as Moses and, sharing his vision of 'light and air', remained blind to the social and vital charms of densely built neighbourhoods from the bleak 'ecotechnical' (craft) age. He had spent far more of his life in one than Jane Jacobs and was always glad to escape into a small town with shady avenues and an old church built from roughly hewn stone. He thought he knew New York better than his adversary did, whereas she saw him as having an inveterate 'small-town outlook'.[168] Marked by the utopian *fin de siècle* housing estates, he was especially fond of the garden city, which Jane Jacobs regarded as a sterile refuge of socially isolated middle-class people. Not without reason, she wrote that the urban utopia of a Le Corbusier – which Moses tried to replicate with his New York demolition plans – was nothing but an application of the garden city principle to densely populated areas.[169]

In 1961, the year when *Death and Life* first appeared, Mumford published his own magnum opus: *The City in History*. It was intended for the same liberal, reform-minded intelligentsia that Jane Jacobs was trying to reach, and we can sense a raging jealousy in his criticism of his rival[170] (who suddenly made him look old), even if they shared a horror of rampant suburbanization and he sometimes complained about the loss of neighbourliness as early as back in the nineteenth century.[171] In his view the 'organic city' was long gone, at least in the United States; it could not survive but only be created anew. Although (or because?) he meanwhile pilloried the fourteen- or eighteen-storey apartment blocks built under Robert Moses as 'grim' and 'inhuman', and abhorred the brutally carved expressways as routes from 'megalopolis' to 'necropolis'[172] – again the theme of the death of the city! – he kept up his polemic against Jane Jacobs for a full year in the *New Yorker*.

The Death and Life was indeed directed against both Lewis Mumford and Robert Moses. As far as Jane Jacobs was concerned, Mumford simply could not grasp that people in the neighbourhoods he called slums led perfectly happy lives.[173] But in the decisive battle with Robert Moses, they both fought against the Lomex project for a highway through Lower Manhattan, the old heart of the city.[174] It was one of the most exciting controversies, not only between environmentalists and developers but also within the environmental movement itself, taking place at a high level and with undertones of both love and hate – and even today it is impossible to decide once and for all who was right. Were people really safe on the streets of Harlem, for example, a built-up area initially spared clearances?[175] Crime rates shot up in New York precisely in the 1960s, and it was evident how the city declined after the end of the Moses era. By no means all of its historic neighbourhoods had the charm of Greenwich Village, and anyway few animated old districts teeming with pedestrians remained in many other American cities.

By an irony of history, the countrywide groundswell of support for 'the Village' helped to make it an attractive place to live for high earners, who could appreciate its lively streets. The 'gentrification' typical of such districts all over the world involved expensive restoration and huge rent increases that squeezed poorer residents out. In 1969 even Jane Jacobs packed up and moved to Toronto. She was certainly right to say in her book: 'Cities are an immense laboratory of trial and error.'[176] Alternative concepts of the city also offered no model that was applicable everywhere and at all times. Thomas Menino, as mayor of Boston, prophesied that the right of citizens to veto new construction in their neighbourhood would ultimately lead to the BANANA principle: 'Build absolutely nothing anywhere near anything.'[177]

Whether through urban redevelopment or the preservation of historic neighbourhoods, municipal policy alone cannot solve the problems of society. Besides, the Mumford–Jacobs controversy highlighted a basic tension stretching into the environmental movement itself, right inside people's minds; the writer Kurt Tucholsky had already expressed it in the early twentieth century, when he sighed that his ideal apartment would look on one side over the Kurfürstendamm (the famous avenue in the heart of Berlin) and on the other side over the Baltic coast.

The Save Greenwich Village movement was typical in many ways of similar citizens' initiatives unfolding elsewhere in the world – a sideshow to which the nascent environmental movement owed some of its popularity and vitality. Municipal reformers of the 1960s – Social Democrats at that – considered that the St Georg district of Hamburg or the Jordaan in Amsterdam, for example, had degenerated into slums rife with squalor, prostitution and, to an increasing extent, drugs. 'Neue Heimat', a building cooperative close to the SPD, planned a huge tower block complex in St Georg, which the press – at first admiringly, then mockingly – referred to as 'Manhattan on the Alster'.

In the sixties, this made many Hamburgers proud that they would be competing with New York, but after 1970 they began to rub their eyes and wonder whether they had gone blind. The long-term change of view, which meant that St Georg was discovered as a human habitat worth preserving for its animated street life and neighbourhood networks, went hand in hand with the fundamental redefinition of 'left' and 'progressive' that the environmental movement introduced. Planners around the world were beginning to realize that to build cities around the car would ultimately destroy them by giving a constant boost to motoring.[178] In 1970, initiatives to preserve a human habitat in the cities were often more popular than ecological environmentalism. Still, even successful action groups do not bring everything to a happy conclusion; cities are perpetually changing. The very protest movements that made districts like Jordaan or St Georg fashionable led eventually to their gentrification. It was with mixed feelings that many long-established residents watched an influx of affluent homosexuals turn their neighbourhood into 'St Gayorg'.[179]

Marina Silva: from rubber-tapper to presidential candidate

The life so far of this woman of Portuguese-African descent (b. 1958) – from illiterate adolescent rubber-tapper to Brazilian environment minister, presidential candidate and Latin America's most celebrated female Green – sounds like a fairy tale. But it belongs very much to the real world, and only time will tell whether it will have a happy ending in conservationist terms.[180] In 1978, at the age of twenty, she got to know Chico Mendes and founded with him the regional organization of the Central Workers Union (Central Única dos Trabalhadores/CUT) in the Amazonian state of Acre. This 'Acre connection' in her political background, with forest conservation as her central issue, posed something of a problem in urbanized coastal areas, where other issues were more to the fore. Three years after the murder of Chico Mendes, she fell ill with lead poisoning – a lingering physical effect of environmental pollution, such as none of the other women discussed here had to suffer! – but after another three years she became the youngest Brazilian in history to be elected to the Senate, and in 2003 ecologists were overjoyed when Lula (the Workers' Party leader and newly elected president) brought her into his government.

In 2008, however, Marina Silva resigned from her post, left the Workers' Party and joined the Greens (Partido Verde). In the same year, she received the UNEP Champion of the Earth Award. As a minister, she had increasingly disappointed environmental activists because of her inability to override the growth-obsessed Lula and because of her silence over the construction of large dams and nuclear power plants (which even bishops

Marina Silva: the most famous Green woman of Brazil – moving from liberation theology to the Pentecostal movement.

publicly opposed).[181] In 2011 she stood as a presidential candidate against Lula's favourite Dilma Rousseff, a woman of humble Bulgarian origins (b. 1947), who had experienced prison and torture as a left-wing urban guerrilla under the military dictatorship (1964–82) before serving under Lula as chair of the Petrobas oil corporation and coordinator of the government growth programme. In this line-up, Marina Silva faced not only agribusiness but also large sections of the left, which spread rumours about the dubious connections of the Green candidate. Yet her defeat at the polls was something of a victory, since she surprised the pundits by obtaining nearly 20 per cent of the vote – a figure one should compare with the 0.27 per cent scored by Barry Commoner when he ran as the Citizens Party candidate for the presidency of the United States. At present the duel between the two women – 'Marina versus Dilma' – rumbles on in the Brazilian public arena; there can be few similar cases in the global eco-scene.

Marina Silva's recent evolution testifies to a quest for moral and spiritual bearings – especially important in countries where corruption is a pervasive threat to conservation. Her reputation for integrity and selfless dedication is one of her strongest political cards. Earlier she wanted to become a nun, supported liberation theology, then joined an Evangelical Pentecostalist movement, the Assembleia de Deus, which made a name for itself with miracle healing and anti-abortion activity – a characteristic phenomenon in today's Brazil.

This chameleon, environmentalism! What went on in this woman and around her is not so apparent from a distance; even the internet leaves one feeling high and dry. The Green scene in the North is dismayed when it learns that Marina Silva has spoken out against abortion and used the issue against her more liberal rival Dilma Rousseff. But in Brazil, where sexual licence is paraded by the jet set, traditional morality can well gain the sympathy of ordinary people, not least women in rural areas. When we read that on one summer Sunday in 2011 barely two thousand people turned up to demonstrate against the dam project at Belo Monte, yet two million Evangelicals marched in a procession through the streets,[182] Marina Silva's spiritual turn appears in a new light: as the expression of a longing for enthusiastic crowds headed by ordinary women, though probably also with one eye firmly fixed on the elections.

In scarcely any other large country on earth has environmentalism clashed so much with the hard core of national self-consciousness. Marina Silva is therefore operating in an explosive field of tensions. Two blueprints of national identity have been around for a long time in Brazil: one involving pride in the world's most tremendous natural heritage; the other an ambition to turn this vast country, with its abundant natural resources, into a Latin American United States. If the latter is to apply to agricultural production as well – and the recent price increases for farm produce have been a massive inducement – it means turning large parts of the rainforest into agricultural steppe like the American Midwest. And since pests threaten monocultures much more in hot regions than in the North, the incentive to introduce genetically modified varieties is greater; gene technology is a major topical issue in Brazil.

Such a future would correspond not only to the interests of agribusiness but also to the left's traditional ideal of progress; and Lula, who withdrew his support from the environmentalists – even if he dubbed his 'development' plans 'sustainable' – managed to get both forces behind him and become one of the most popular presidents in Brazilian history. Against this background, Marina Silva naturally had to look elsewhere for support. When Lula gave the go-ahead for genetically modified seeds, she wept in disappointment.[183] In the middle of 2011 she even pulled out of the Partido Verde, for reasons about which one can only speculate. Are there also Green MPs who favour nuclear power, large dams and the cultivation of biofuels in Amazonia? Again and again: tensions within the environmental movement, which it treats as a taboo subject and thereby delivers on a plate to its opponents, manifest themselves most painfully in authentic women – and for that very reason in a way that challenges the movement to come up with new solutions.

Wangari Maathai: the 'tree mother'

Let us now turn from Western cities to Africa. If we take the life story of Wangari Maathai (1940–2011), the Kenyan 'tree mother', we can forget about such themes as the wilderness or national parks for large sections of it; what mattered in her eyes was the planting of trees for local use, to provide firewood or animal fodder and to protect the soil from erosion and desiccation. For a long time one of her bitterest opponents was William ole

The Kenyan activist Wangari Maathai saw the promotion of women's rights as the best environmental policy. In 2004 she became the first African to win the Nobel Peace Prize, for 'sustainable development, peace and democracy'.

Ntimama, the parliamentary representative of the Massai people, the main beneficiary of zebra, gnu and antelope tourism in the protected Massai Mara wildlife area. But wildlife protection is not exactly popular with farmers in this densely populated country: it operates almost inevitably at their expense, especially where the victims of game damage do not receive benefits from tourism.[184]

Wangari Maathai studied biology in Germany and the USA and in 1971 became the first East African woman to receive a doctorate in the subject. In the same year, she was appointed professor in veterinary anatomy at the University of Nairobi, with a special interest in cattle, a cornerstone of the Kenyan farm economy.[185] In 1982 she lost her post when she applied (without success) to be recognized as a candidate in the parliamentary elections. In 2005, after she won the Nobel Prize, the same university awarded her an honorary doctorate.[186] Despite the continuation of tribal loyalties and ever greater population pressure, Kenya was long considered a model Black African country on account of its successful Christian missions, its broad farming base and its high-quality education (though not necessarily for women). When environmental protection became a popular issue internationally, the government set considerable store by raising its profile abroad.[187] In 1989 President Daniel arap Moi, who was shaping up for a twenty-year period of dictatorial rule that Wangari Maathai later described as a 'dark cloud' over Kenya,[188] burned some poached ivory before the world's cameras to demonstrate his commitment to elephant conservation.[189] At first he even supported the tree-planting movement led by Wangari Maathai.[190]

Many episodes in the life of this woman shed a horrific light on the everyday violence in Africa and the unscrupulousness of its new power elites. But Kenya was not Nigeria – otherwise Wangari Maathai would have found it difficult to stay alive. The fact that conservation was official policy and enjoyed respect among the judiciary meant that environmentalists could not be totally excluded from the sphere of legality. Again and again, however, the environmentalist card was played against them by spokespersons of organizations loyal to the government. This was especially painful in the case of the 'Pathfinder' movement (Maendeleo Ya Wanawake), which claimed to represent a majority of rural women.[191]

Wangari Maathai, with her colourful flowing garments, looked to Westerners like the soul of Africa speaking on behalf of its rural women, while her way of thinking also made her part of the international ecological community. In contrast to Dian Fossey, however, she placed her ecologism wholly at the service of indigenous people. Her radiant personality also made her something of an ideal type. Since field labour and wood-gathering are largely women's work in African and other third world countries, the association of women's initiatives with conservation, or indeed with 'development', has a generally more solid material foundation than elsewhere.[192] Shortages of wood, which women experienced most acutely, were a starting point for the environmental activism of the future Nobel prizewinner.[193] In 1985, on her initiative, hundreds of countrywomen lugged large bundles of wood in front of the pompous conference centre in the heart of Nairobi, where an international women's congress was taking place.[194]

Wangari Maathai opened a tree school, without success, and then on 5 June 1977 (World Environment Day) founded the Green Belt Movement (GBM), acting as a member of the National Women's Council. The UN Conference on Desertification (UNCOD), held in Nairobi that year under the impact of the catastrophic drought in the Sahel,[195] assured the new movement of international support from the beginning; and the Nairobi-based UNEP repeatedly came to Wangari Maathai's rescue, as she gratefully acknowledged.[196] Until the 1980s the GBM remained a 'movement' in the literal sense, with the usual ups and downs; only with the support of the Norwegian Forest Society did it start to become an NGO that could afford to have an office of its own. In fact, Wangari Maathai was more geared to achieving an effect through institutions than to 'outdoor' activism; as she herself said, 'visiting the offices gave [her] a sense of purpose' again.[197] But at a time of police harassment, her 'offices' consisted only of a hopeless muddle of papers in her own home;[198] persecution hindered bureaucratization of her movement. She herself was aware of the danger that arises when a movement is run too much out of an office in the capital and loses touch with the village grassroots.[199] The combative autonomy of her movement from the state may be attributed precisely to its *lack* of institutionalization, and this in turn is explained by Wangari Maathai's matchless leadership.[200] Yet is was not she but the tree-planting farmer women who remained the icons of the GBM.[201]

If we compare her with Vandana Shiva (the subject of the next section), with whom she seems at first sight to have many similarities, Wangari Maathai's struggle to gain a following in the countryside indicates how much less she could fall back on the cultural traditions of her own country. Although a member of the all-powerful ruling party, the Kenyan African National Union (KANU), she lacked for years a political base and often found herself terrifyingly isolated: 'I was becoming an outlaw in my own country', she once complained.[202] On the other hand, she and her GBM received the Alternative Nobel Prize in 1984, and the non-alternative one twenty years later. Without support from abroad, she would more than once have been lost. Pure 'grassroots activism' has a very hard time of it in Africa under today's conditions of a weak civil society and deficient rule of law. The career of this woman shows in exemplary fashion the opportunities opened up by a combination of regional and international impulses. 'I always made sure the press was with us, so they could record what was happening and take the news to Kenyans and the world', she reported of operations in the villages.[203]

Over the years, the Green Belt Movement radiated out to other African countries; the eco-age recognized in principle the usefulness of green belts, and so tree-planting women had an evocative symbolism. The act per se was not a sign of protest, but the government of the day was suspicious of the autonomous women's movement associated with it. Strange as the geographical leap appears at first sight, the situation is reminiscent of the GDR in the 1980s. Both there and in Kenya, a movement for democracy developed under the umbrella of conservation and in competition with environmental organizations loyal to the regime (respectively, the Gesellschaft für Natur- und Umweltschutz and the Pathfinders); environmental protection was an official state objective, and the planting of trees could not be simply criminalized. It was treated as critical only when people moved beyond tree-planting and raised questions about the causes of deforestation and environmental destruction, or even ventured into 'urban ecology' and campaigned against prestige projects they considered harmful to the environment.

This was the case with Wangari Maathai, when she placed herself at the head of a protest movement in 1989 against a megalomaniac skyscraper in Nairobi's city park – a sixty-storey tower which, before it was quietly shelved in 1992, was supposed to become the tallest in Africa, complete with a giant statue of President Moi.[204] The prestige implications meant that Wangari Maathai was continually exposed to harassment and, on several occasions, arrested and maltreated. Prominence and persecution had a curious habit of following each other in the course of her life. Once in 1992, while she was still in custody, foreign intervention actually secured her a place on the same plane as President Moi to the environment summit in Rio, where she met Al Gore![205] In 2002, after a regime change in Kenya, she became deputy minister for the environment, and in 2004 she received both the Nobel Peace Prize and the Petra Kelly Prize of the Heinrich Böll Foundation. But in the same week as the Nobel award, her draft forest legislation was defeated in the Kenyan parliament.[206] When she argued that dead people should be buried in plastic coffins to save on wood, she made herself as unpopular as the Holy Roman Emperor Joseph II had done two centuries earlier, when he vainly tried to impose wood-saving coffins in an excess of Enlightenment zeal.

It is hard to tell how far the case of Wangari Maathai shows that one woman can really get things moving on the environmental front even under African conditions, and how far the international women's and ecological movements have played up her role because they wanted to have that kind of heroic figure. It would certainly be wrong to personify in her Kenya's rural-female tree culture; a report dealing with that in 1997, with acacia trees as the main focus, does not mention her name once.[207] Before she received the Nobel Prize, she was scarcely known even in neighbouring countries, and quite a few commentators in the world press were bemused by the honour shown to her; there was some talk of a 'female quota'.[208]

The tree-planting might make one think that Wangari Maathai concentrated too much on symbolic action. She was a city person, an intellectual from the capital, and her autobiography depicts the struggle to save Kairura forest in Nairobi with special drama and passion.[209] Village forests play more of a background role. On the other hand, if village tree-planting is not in accord with local interests, or if care is not taken to protect young trees from loggers or grazing cattle, it can – and all too often does – remain mere play-acting for the media and the aid agencies. Planting is the easy part; what is really decisive is aftercare for the new seedlings.

Wangari Maatai, who started out with no experience of rural tree cultivation, came to this realization only after a series of disappointments: 'This showed me that we needed to make local people feel invested in the projects' – otherwise, trees were under sentence of death.[210] Jomo Kenyatta, the first head of government after independence, had already planted trees wherever he went; yet since the end of colonial rule Kenya has lost nine-tenths of its forest,[211] while at the same time its population has quadrupled from 8 million to 32 million.[212] The metaphor 'demographic explosion' does not seem exaggerated, and the link between population growth and environmental degradation could scarcely be more evident.

Wangari Maathai was opposed to contraceptive methods,[213] justifying this in terms of her Catholic beliefs;[214] another factor, common among female civil rights activists, was her aversion to any state regulation of childbearing. Yet contraception can serve to advance female self-determination. This contradiction poses a typical dilemma for Catholic development aid, which is most acutely felt by people with intense moral scruples. The significance of Wangari Maathai's activity would seem to lie more at a symbolic than a real level – and in that too she is ideal-typical, since most environmental politics is symbolic all around the world.[215] Over time, so long as it is tenaciously pursued, symbolic politics can acquire real substance;[216] not the least attraction of *la longue durée* is that it allows us to follow this process. Only the future will tell whether it is actually unfolding in Kenya.

Vandana Shiva and Medha Patkar: fighting globally and locally in the Gandhian tradition for the autonomy of Indian villages

Here it is worth considering two Indian personalities together, in both their similarities and their contrasts. Vandana Shiva (b. 1952), the daughter of a forester, grew up in and around the famous forestry institute of Dehradun at the foot of the Himalayas. In 1993 she received the Alternative Nobel Prize and, after several further awards, was named one of *Time*'s five Heroes of the Green Century on the occasion of the 2002 environment summit in Johannesburg. As the author of an array of knowledgeable and powerfully written books, covering a wide range of issues and with a spiritual as well as scientific underpinning, she is much better known in the West than Medha Patkar, whom we have already encountered as the spokesperson of the movement against the Narmada dam. Even a critic of hers, Haripriya Rangan, calls Vandana Shiva 'the best-known Indian (and Third World) ecofeminist in the world today'.[217] In India itself things look different: Ramachandra Guha, the leading environmental historian, who knows Vandana Shiva best – they have both written about the Chipko movement – does not mention her once in a survey of the Indian environmental movement, whereas he speaks of Medha Patkar as 'the most celebrated environmental activist in contemporary India'.[218]

While Vandana Shiva, as a government adviser scarcely ever in physical danger, has become known in Western countries through her research institute, international contacts, publications and fiery speeches at mass rallies, Medha Patkar (b. 1954), the daughter of a union leader, has had an impact above all as a grassroots campaigner, not because of any publications, although she was also a lecturer at the Tata Institute of Social

The Indian ecofeminist Vandana Shiva (b. 1952) at a peace festival in Sydney, November 2010.

Sciences.[219] Her fight against the Narmada dam brought about a change in World Bank strategy, yet she belongs more among grassroots activists than in the world of the established NGOs that have regular access to the World Bank.[220] In India, where a readiness for self-sacrifice is highly regarded in the Gandhian tradition of non-violent resistance, Medha Patkar made a deep impression when she took seriously what she had written in a letter in 1989 to the director of the World Bank: that she would throw herself into the rising waters at a secret spot behind the dam. Nevertheless, she was saved in the nick of time, and the government promised an independent inquiry into the Narmada project.[221] From then on, she was a world-famous figure, even in the eyes of the World Bank.[222] In 1993 she told the London *Guardian* that she and her fellow-campaigners would remain on the spot when the flooding took place; it would not be suicide, she said, but 'we will cling to the land like a baby clings to its mother'.[223] More recently, she sought to link up with militant Maoists fighting for the rights of mountain 'tribal people' – a dangerous alliance if ever there was one! But even the former state secretary Tirunellai N. Seshan, who considers any opponent of artificial irrigation to be an enemy of the state, holds the anti-dam campaigner in high regard: she had fought for the rights of the most downtrodden local people, going far beyond women's issues yet demonstrating the strength of women, acting 'almost obsessedly and with scant regard for her own safety and health'.[224]

The Indian ecologist Medha Patkar (b. 1954) went on hunger strike in 2006 to protest against the Sardar-Sarovar dam; she ended the strike after 20 days, when the Supreme Court ordered the return of forcibly evicted local people.

In the case of the Sardar Sarovar dam, an outsider finds it hard to fathom the way in which the ongoing protest movement of 'oustees' led by Medha Patkar has combined with the dispute between the two riparian states – Gujarat (in whose territory the dam lies, and which has always argued for it to have the largest possible dimensions) and Madhya Pradesh (host to the bulk of the Narmada and most of the flooded villages). In 2006, when the planned height of the dam was raised from 110 to 122 metres, Medha Patkar went on a hunger strike that led to her being arrested and force-fed.[225] She suffered another defeat. But the time when large dams were the 'temples of modern India' was now over. The resistance too seems to have grown weaker, though, as the capacity of rural India to prevail politically over the cities has declined.

Vandana Shiva too fought for peasant India, but her impact was different from that of Medha Patkar. When she addressed Western rallies from a microphone: 'You ask: What is Nature? I am Nature!', it sometimes happened that female ecologists burst into tears.[226] Vandana Shiva seemed to them like the embodiment of India's female soul, the incarnation of a spiritually superior nature. While others were reinventing Buddhism in the spirit of ecology, she announced an ecofeminist reinvention of Hinduism: the source of all life in Prakriti, the female incarnation of nature.[227] It fitted this when she counterposed the traditional wisdom of Indian peasants (especially women) to modern Western science, or the ancient Indian elements of village autonomy to the global economy dominated by multinational corporations.

At the time of the Rio summit in 1992, when anti-globalization had not yet appeared on the scene and 'thinking globally' was still valued as a form of solidarity with the third world, Vandana Shiva declared with the assurance of someone who knew what she was talking about: 'Instead of extending environmental concern and action, the recent emergence of a focus on "global" environmental problems has in fact narrowed the agenda.'[228] Lobbying the UN and World Bank instead of local activity geared to specific needs! One can easily overlook, however, that her own career as an environmental activist is by no means typically Indian; it also has very international features and even some that might be considered 'typically German'. In this respect, she is a living example of the fact that an ecological 'global society' really does exist, at least as a communication network, over and above North–South and East–West oppositions.

She came to the environmental movement via the struggle for the forest: for the preservation of the old village forests and use rights against the foreign timber industry, on the southern slopes of the Himalayas where she had grown up. Her first publications, in 1986 – the year of Chernobyl, when environmental initiatives worldwide received a new impetus – were devoted to the Chipko tree-hugging movement. Before that, she tells us, her consciousness had been raised by the dangers of nuclear technology;[229] she had studied nuclear physics in the United States in the early 1970s and worked on the fast breeder project at the Bhabha Atomic Centre in

Mumbai.[230] Far more than Medha Patkar, she can tellingly deploy an extensive arsenal of arguments; her later writings cover a wide spectrum of issues.

The core, however, is neither the nuclear peril nor the conflict over forest and water, but the social and ecological danger to the traditional peasant economy resulting from the 'Green Revolution' that has been hailed as India's salvation from hunger. For more than twenty years Vandana Shiva has been protesting that government agricultural policy, in association with international finance and multinational corporations, lures and compels farmers to give up their old methods based on long experience, to buy specially cultivated seeds and huge quantities of chemical fertilizer and herbicide that plunge them deep into debt, and to destroy the ecological foundations of their existence through the contamination and overuse of groundwater. Picking up on the Western controversy over gene technology, at a time when it had (for the moment?) proved a blind alley regarding the ecological risks, she shifted the focus to the much more evident social-political scandal and found a wide echo in the country. Her reports on the 'epidemic' of suicides among Indian farmers were particularly shocking, revealing a sense of moral shame at indebtedness that is not often found in today's world.[231] Here and there she also took up Rachel Carson's critique of the agrochemical sector, although the priorities she chose corresponded to Indian conditions. There are good reasons to regard the situation she described as India's number one environmental problem, more disastrous even than the consequences of industrial emissions. It calls for the major involvement of civil society, even more than in the case of forest protection (which has had a competent administration dating from British colonial times). Groundwater depletion, resulting not least from the Green Revolution, is probably a far more intractable problem than the destructive impact of large dams, on which Medha Patkar concentrates all her campaigning activity.

'Whose are the forests and the land? Ours, they are ours': so begins the song of the anti-dam activists.[232] The only problem is: who are we? And whom does 'we' exclude? The singers would say that 'we' are the people who live in villages. Vandana Shiva agrees with Medha Patkar that an alternative to the fatal course of things should be sought in village community traditions of autonomy, sociability and knowledge of how to treat the soil, water and forest. Both women have in mind especially the *adivasi* ('tribes'): those ethnic minorities least in the mainstream of modernization. In this recourse to villagers, there would seem to be an element of social romanticism that is more effective from a distance than close up, more likely to affect Westerners than modern Indians, leading them to project an ideal, Gandhian vision of ancient India onto the interior of a country unfamiliar to them. And environmental action groups find their recruits overwhelmingly among urban middle strata with a modern education.[233]

It is precisely against this new middle-class environmentalism, with its focus on urban living conditions, that the celebrated novelist Arundhati

Roy has directed her fire in the last ten years, becoming a mouthpiece of the *adivasi* and a scourge of the whole modern economic system. Although Medha Patkar, for her part, was appreciative of support from World Bank circles, Arundhati Roy now placed Washington among the powers of evil; even the US Supreme Court was part of the detested establishment. This threatened to isolate ecological protests and to divide environmentalism. Since autumn 2000 she has been publicly attacked by Ramachandra Guha: 'What struck one most forcibly was her atavistic hatred of science and a romantic celebration of adivasi lifestyles.'[234] Nor has the fiery author been lost for words in reply; as we can see on the internet, considerable numbers of Indians have become involved in the ongoing controversy.

In large parts of India, it is questionable whether village communities still have the vitality necessary for the kind of action that these women expect of them.[235] Moreover, a serious India-wide strengthening of village rights to forest and water would threaten a conflict between town and country. Since the 'riparian rights' to which Medha Patkar appealed in her letter to the president of the World Bank[236] would inevitably operate at the expense of those living further from the river, it is hardly surprising that her brand of anti-dam activism is not popular in such places.[237] In the cities, it has become a habit to curse Medha Patkar during one of the frequent power cuts.[238] Dam construction is not an issue that lends itself well to fundamentalist positions. There have been compromises on purely technical grounds: a dam can be built higher or lower; population groups can be won over with a more generous water allocation or displaced persons with a higher level of compensation.

The ideal of the old village community stands directly in the tradition of Gandhi, who was influenced in this by British social romantics of the nineteenth century. In a tacit criticism of Gandhi, however, writing to his daughter from prison in 1932, Nehru already kept his distance from such idealization. The village communities, he wrote, were actually 'rather primitive and backward'. 'Growth and progress consist in cooperation among larger and larger units. The more a person or a group keeps to himself or itself, the more danger there is of him or it becoming self-centred and selfish and narrow-minded.' The ruralization of India was the work of British colonial rule, which ruined its urban trades through the competition of British industrial goods; this proliferation of villages at the expense of once flourishing cities became India's misfortune.[239]

One must read such texts to appreciate the extent to which Vandana Shiva – at first sight a fervent anti-imperialist fighting in the name of Indian cultural nationalism[240] – is opposed to the dominant ideology of modern India. When she actually demonizes 'development', a magic word there as in virtually all 'developing countries', Gandhi would be with her heart and soul. Indeed, it is a paradox of the country's national consciousness that, while Gandhi stands beyond all criticism as the 'father of modern India', its modernization policies since independence have been diametrically opposed to his ideas. Against this background, environmental activists such as Vandana Shiva, Medha Patkar and Sunderlal Bahuguna (the Chipko movement leader inspired by Gandhi) may be said to have activated a subversive potential present from the beginning.

'Yangtze! Yangtze!': Dai Qing

With Dai Qing (b. 1941), already known to us from the campaign against the Three Gorges dam, we find ourselves in quite a different world. Of all the female environmentalists discussed here, she is an exception in that she acts within a still largely totalitarian system, although public discussion is now possible there to a degree that was unthinkable in Mao's time. When we see the courage and abandon with which she attacks prevailing conditions, without having to face immediate arrest, we may sometimes think that the freedom to express opinions has already been achieved. But Dai Qing is a special case. It may be exemplary in many respects, but we should be wary of drawing general conclusions from it about the situation in China.

Much about Dai Qing becomes evident only by comparison with the other figures described in this chapter. She displays hardly a trace of ecofeminism or spirituality; her arguments against dam construction are overwhelmingly calm and rational – passionate but not sentimental. Although the title of her documentary record, *Yangtze! Yangtze!*, sounds like a cry from the heart, she only seldom evokes the romantic setting of the Yangtze gorges that the artificial lake created by the dam threatens to engulf. Even the traumas of resettlement are for her – what a contrast with Medha Patkar! – only one argument among others;[241] yet it was clear from

The Chinese dissident Dai Qing (b. 1941), known for her books and other activity against the Three Gorges dam, visited a symposium in 2009 in the run-up to the Frankfurt Book Fair, despite the withdrawal of her invitation.

the beginning that the number of 'oustees' in the Yangtze valley would be a million or more higher than in the Narmada valley. In an interview with Patrick McCully, the author of a global survey of dam conflicts, Dai Qing estimated that the total number of people displaced throughout China was of the order of 40 million to 60 million[242] – so there was never any chance that all would be given equally fertile land in another of the country's densely populated farming regions. Yet Dai Qing did not point to the suffering of 'oustees' with anything like the same intensity as Medha Patkar. Here the 'riparian' argument cut both ways – since it could also be claimed that the dam would tame the river and protect people living downstream from disastrous floods. In fact, that was the original motivation for the Three Gorges project, and *Yangtze! Yangtze!* itself does not fail to mention the catastrophe of 1954 that cost 30,000 people their lives on the middle and lower stretches of the river.[243]

Dai Qing did not present herself as a 'grassroots activist', nor did she think of mobilizing and leading the peasant opposition to resettlement that most probably existed in the area[244] (but which in a regime like the People's Republic of China would have been criminalized and prevented from reaching a wide public). Instead, she aimed to make critical voices heard within the Chinese elites and to generate an atmosphere of free discussion, at least among professionals. As a scion of the Communist elite herself, she was better placed to do this than the great majority of the population. Her father had been a prominent Communist, whose capture and execution at the hands of the Japanese had enshrined him in the gallery of 'revolutionary martyrs'.[245] Dai Qing had then been adopted by Marshal Ye Jianying, one of Mao Zedong's army leaders, who helped to bring down the 'Gang of Four' in 1973 and opened the way for Deng Xiaoping to assume power.[246] This high-profile background should be borne in mind in what follows.

Like so many future oppositionists, she was an enthusiastic Red Guard at the time of the Cultural Revolution, even expressing in an article the fervent wish to invent a way for young people to give Mao their youth, and therefore a longer life. The noted Sinologist Ian Buruma, who knows her well, commented: 'It was perhaps an unconscious variation of Taoist beliefs – held by the Chairman himself – that frequent sex with very young girls adds years to the life of an old man.'[247] However, when Red Guards tortured her mother until she was half dead – the only person who dared to stand by her received the same treatment as a 'class enemy' – and when her stepfather became mentally ill as a result of torture and ended up in an asylum,[248] she began to undergo a rethink, though not as fast or as radical as one might have expected under the circumstances. It would seem that the Cultural Revolution left behind in her a deep mistrust of any radicalism, which she sees as narcissistically caught up in a destructive rage. 'In the long run', she noted in her prison memoirs, 'stability is more important than anything else', because only then is it possible to achieve 'prosperity, education and civilization'. 'Democracy' was not a magic word in her eyes.[249]

Many phenomena in the student movement of 1989 were reminiscent of the Cultural Revolution, and that is also how Dai Qing experienced them.[250] During the demonstrations in Tiananmen Square in May 1989, which the army bloodily repressed in the end on 4 June, she made a speech warning the students of further provocations: they had already won a great victory, she said, and should now accept a compromise – otherwise they risked turning the political clock back at least twenty years. (Later she explained to Buruma her fear that a radical overthrow would be 'far more frightening than maintaining the present political order'.[251]) But in effect she fell between two stools, since neither the demonstrators nor the government wanted a compromise. The Chinese edition of *Yangtze! Yangtze!* appeared at that very moment and was badly misjudged by the government in the light of the unrest: on 14 July 1989 Dai Qing was arrested and sentenced to ten months' imprisonment.

The Western media subsequently promoted her to the position of most famous Chinese dissident, and her invitation to the Frankfurt Book Fair in 2009 turned into a trial of strength between Frankfurt and Beijing. But she herself was not keen on the title – 'What is a dissident?' she would ask Ian Buruma, adding 'with a mocking smile': 'Do you think I am a dissident?'[252] – especially in view of the fighting that had occurred among exiled 'dissidents'.[253] Rather, she wanted to make an impact inside China itself, representing its traditions of 'order and balance between humankind and nature',[254] and speaking on behalf of critical members of its intellectual elite, who were more competent than the mega-planners but were not allowed to voice their own opinions. Her inside knowledge of the regime was greater than that of virtually any other critic: she had once worked as a surveillance expert for the Ministry of State Security and then, until 1982, for military intelligence.[255] So it is all the more surprising that she took up the issue of the Three Gorges project only in autumn 1988, via the press in Hong Kong. Dai Qing felt deeply ashamed of this silence within the elites, over a project filled with risks for the life of the nation.[256] She had no professional competence in hydraulic matters but had to learn from others. In her Yangtze books she presents herself not as a lone campaigner but as a go-between for a respectable team of experts.

For Dai Qing, the main point on the agenda in China was education. Democratization would be a long process: it could not be rushed in this gigantic and, in many respects, still backward country. She admitted – probably with a smile – to feeling 'quite flattered' that many Chinese and foreign newspapers had called her an 'environmentalist'; but that was not how she and others who had worked on *Yangtze! Yangtze!* thought of themselves. Their aim was simply to edge China a small step forward, through decisions in the government, on the road to the free expression of opinion.[257] It had never occurred to her to proclaim a new ecological world-view; the job of a skilled engineer was to discuss projects carefully on the basis of solid technical competence. She and her colleagues repeatedly accused the project-makers of sloppiness and a lack of professionalism, with regard to the cost–benefit analysis, the anticipated silting of the artificial lake, the expenses associated with resettlement, and many other factors.

The large dam, Dai Qing insisted, was not an economically rational project but a question of political prestige; 'it presents fat bureaucrats who hand out contracts, and officials responsible for resettlement, with the opportunity to make a killing'.[258] This sideswipe at corrupt officials was in the best Chinese tradition: none other than Mao had won popularity from such talk. But Dai Qing and her fellow-campaigners were by no means opposed to all dam construction; they simply believed that several smaller dams on tributaries of the Yangtze would be more advantageous than one large one on the main river – and there were indeed good reasons for this view. It too was in an old Maoist tradition of differentiating the Chinese road to industrialization from the mammoth projects of Soviet Stalinism. Nehru once called large dams the 'temples of modern India', whereas Mao, anyway lacking respect for temples, is said to have told Zhou En-lai when the Sanmenxia dam threatened to engulf the city of Xian: 'If nothing works, then just blow up the dam.' (It would have been a difficult proposition, and in the end the dam was rebuilt.) It was one of Dai Qing's colleagues who recalled these words of the Great Chairman![259] The Three Gorges dam was built in the end, but the educational work of Dai Qing and her campaigners was not without effect. When the National People's Congress decided on the project in 1992, a third of the delegates voted against – an open expression of dissent without precedent in Chinese history.[260]

Whereas Vandana Shiva and Wangari Maathai became heated over the issue of 'overpopulation', it was evident to Dai Qing and the post-Maoist leadership that Mao's promotion of demographic growth was a disaster for China.[261] Chinese environmental activists are basically agreed about this, and there is no reason to doubt that it is a realistic viewpoint – especially as it is unpopular. More difficult is the question of how far the anti-dam campaign went to the heart of China's environmental problems. To be sure, it also raised the issues of river sludge load, soil erosion and forest destruction, as well as the decline of the old art of terrace cultivation resulting from the collapse of the village community. But, leaving aside nuclear energy, the only alternative here and now to hydropower was increased coal production and the building of coal-fired power stations. He Bochuan – whose alarming *China on the Edge* (banned from further distribution after 4 June 1989, along with *Yangtze! Yangtze!*) has often been compared to Rachel Carson's *Silent Spring* – thinks there has been too little investment in hydropower and complains at the priority still given to coal. He agreed with Dai Qing about the unprofessional management of large hydropower projects[262] – a surprising shortcoming in a country like China, with its hydraulic tradition going back thousands of years. 'Everyone knows,' he wrote to her in 1998, 'that China is facing an energy shortage, . . . and that we suffer frequent floods'; the point was not to halt all dam construction but to verify whether a number of smaller dams on the Yangtze tributaries would not be a better solution; the unwillingness of the leadership to consider alternatives was the heart of the country's dilemma.[263] The diagnosis does not apply to China alone.

Ishimure Michiko: a Japanese Rachel Carson

If one asks in Japan for a counterpart to Rachel Carson, the name Ishimure Michiko (b. 1927) crops up – and indeed, on the surface, none other of the women discussed here resembles her so much. *Kugai Jodo* (*Paradise in the Sea of Sorrow*, first published in 1969) was, like *Silent Spring*, a combination of specialist work, polemic and poetic fantasy. The contamination of Minamata Bay with discharge from the Chisso chemical corporation was already known – to those who wanted to know – back in 1956 at the latest. But although, over the years, more than a thousand fish died an agonizing death there from methyl mercury poisoning, this unparalleled environmental disaster was persistently hushed up. Reports began to appear in the press in 1967, but Ishimure Michiko's book first brought the scale of the human suffering to wide public attention, in powerful prose and with lofty symbolic power. Together with Hiyoshi Fumiko, a Japan Socialist Party assemblywoman, she founded a citizens' council to assist victims of the disaster in obtaining their rights.[264] Ever since, women have played a role at the forefront of Japanese environmentalism.[265] But this is apparent only to close observers, since most of the women in question do not have any publications to their name. Ishimure Michiko is the major exception.

Ishimure Michiko (b. 1927) is considered the Japanese Rachel Carson. In her trilogy *Paradise in the Sea of Sorrow* (1969/70) she describes the so-called Minamata disease, caused by the eating of seafood contaminated with mercury. Its symptoms include visual, aural and cognitive disturbances, as well as paralysis and deformed foetuses.

Like *Silent Spring*, *Kugai Jodo* has been compared to *Uncle Tom's Cabin* in its stirring effect.[266] Precisely because the author's basic tone is fairly restrained, her account gets right under our skin when anger and dismay pour forth over what the local fisherfolk suffered. Rachel Carson's *Silent Spring* was a vision of the future; the *Sea of Sorrow* was present-day reality. Ishimure Michiko was writing not about a fictitious place but about the town of her birth and an ocean bay that had once been considered paradise. The dangers of DDT for human beings, as described in *Silent Spring*, were partly hypothetical; the toxicity of mercury was well established. But in its haste to industrialize, Japan had turned a blind eye to many of the lessons of the Western health and safety movement in the late nineteenth century.[267] The Minamata scandal is now recognized as one of the four main cases of mass poisoning that lay behind the growth of Japanese environmentalism and the changes in environmental policy.

Yet there is also a remarkable difference between Ishimure Michiko and Rachel Carson. Despite the success of her book – reviewers called it the country's most important literary work since the Second World War[268] – the Japanese author was terrifyingly isolated as a human being. Of course, Rachel Carson too was exposed to attacks from the chemical industry, but she could rely from the beginning on widespread, indeed overwhelming, solidarity. Ishimure Michiko stood alone. For unlike other Japanese intellectuals, who flock to the big cities at the first opportunity, she continued to live in her native Minamata, where the Chisso corporation, dominating the townscape with its cement plant, continued to exercise an authority that demanded respect,[269] and treated the whole furore as altogether unseemly. Even her relatives saw her as a stain on the family.[270]

So why did she go on living there? In her eyes, love of one's home region, even when it becomes both love and hate,[271] is one of the origins of what it means to be human. Home ties as the emotional basis of environmental awareness: it is a nexus we find again and again all around the world. Germans are very wrong to think of it as a disreputable peculiarity of their own. What most horrifies Ishimure Michiko is that this identification with a *Heimat* has been increasingly lost under the conditions of modern Japan; she sees a connection with the alarming number of suicides. The author admits to her own kind of traditional Japanese consciousness, and informs us that her book is not only a documentary record but also a projection of personal fantasies:

The figures in *Paradise in the Sea of Sorrow* are not only reincarnations of farmers from the village of Yanaka, but also projections of ourselves into the past: that is, embodiments of our ancestors, who believed in certain values and a certain philosophy of life that we have long since forfeited. The figures in this book are rooted in what might be described as the original matrix of our thinking.[272]

The title is an allusion to *jodo*, the 'Pure Land' paradise of Amida Buddhism.[273] One senses some of the anti-capitalist bitterness of 1968 – as least as strong in Japanese universities as in German – but the author does not display any political activism or articulate any political ideology.

For Ishimure Michiko, the Minamata disaster was not a challenge to perfect industrial technology but a metaphor for the fundamentally destructive character of modern civilization. In this she is in tune with the radical anti-modernism and generally apocalyptic mood of Ivan Illich, with whom she entered into contact;[274] but this divides her from the mainstream of the environmental movement. Her work has Buddhist but also archaic-animist features, testifying to her faith in an originally animate nature whose soul is being destroyed by modernity.[275] Such ideas are not out of place in Western ecological literature, either. But in her case they have a seriousness rooted in religion that is not so easy to find among Western nature lovers. Later, she and some like-minded people founded a Buddhist community, where she lived the life of a nun.

Scandals involving toxic emissions arouse special horror, but this is also the area in which new policies can produce visible results without too much difficulty. Leading Japanese corporations have themselves changed gear and demonstrated an environmental awareness when they have been in danger of losing face in public. Thus, the president of Nippon Chisso went so far as to kneel before mercury victims and to beg their forgiveness for the suffering caused by his company – an act that was broadcast on nationwide television. (The German press drew guilty comparisons with the thick-skinned behaviour of Chemie Grünenthal in the Contergan affair.[276]) For Ishimure Michiko, however, his words of apology were 'like air bubbling on the surface of a pond';[277] she saw only an empty gesture, not a fundamental turning away from the arrogant attitude of industrialists towards the population. A number of harmful agents that had attracted special attention were removed, but the general procedures for dealing with toxic waste remained woefully inadequate.[278] Although at times, in response to particularly glaring scandals, Japan has played a leading role internationally on environmental issues, this has not lasted for long. The bitterness remained in Ishimure Michiko; one has hardly any sense of triumph.

What significance does Ishimure Michiko have for the partial turn in the environmental policies of Japanese industry around the year 1970? The first point to make is that the bureaucracy very soon took the initiative: it was a world in which a writer, and a female one at that, simply did not feature. Nor does she receive a mention in surveys of the rise of Japanese environmentalism.[279] She does not seem to have had a direct impact on policy. The decisive turn came when the local chemical workers' union, which had previously sided with the company, came out in support of the victims in 1967;[280] mere protests on the part of the fisherfolk, though increasing all the time, had been powerless to produce results. The Japanese courts did also play a key role, however, by allowing statistical evidence for the causes of poisoning that made it much more likely that victims would receive appropriate compensation. Formerly, the difficulty of proof in individual cases had often left them in a hopeless position.[281]

Ishimure Michiko never showed any desire to emphasize her role in the advance of Japanese environmentalism; none of the other activists considered here was as self-effacing in public. In 2013 the Wikipedia entry for Japan's 'Rachel Carson' is of the skimpiest, and one would search in vain for spectacular appearances abroad. It would seem that, whereas the others looked to international resonance at least as much as national impact, her ambitions did not lie in that direction. Her sense of roots was so strong that she allowed the Minamata dialect to enter her verse, thereby putting off many fellow-Japanese.[282] The fate of her home region is also the main theme in a sequel to *Kugai Jodo* published in 1997: *Tenko* (Lake of Heaven), which follows the destruction of a mountain village after the construction of a large dam. She is further proof of the intensity of reactions to large dam projects. Even activists who do not seek a presence at international level are inserted into global contexts.

3 Institutionalization, Routinization, Revitalization

Research problems

Let us now cut to anonymous processes, which also abound in source problems. In any attempt to describe collective histories, it should not be forgotten that one is operating on an insecure empirical foundation, whether in relation to campaign groups or to the environmental commitment of public authorities. About both there is a lack of good theoretical models, but solid investigatory material is much scantier still. The number of groups around the world that bill themselves as 'the environmental movement' is so huge that no individual can hope to survey them even approximately. Many have no proper archives, and even more – for various reasons – do not allow outsiders to peruse their internal documents. The easiest to get information about are their statutes, the hardest what they actually do, their reasons for doing it and the priorities they set for themselves; here researchers are forced to base themselves on interviews and newspaper articles.[283] This dilemma also applies to information in well-ordered Germany. Even in India and China the number of registered environmental groups runs into the thousands, and no one has the overview or perspective with which to gauge what lies behind such figures. Nevertheless, in the eco-age the term 'environmentalist' has become a seal of approval, which rightly or wrongly attests to a concern with public welfare deserving of financial support.

We do not have broadly based, scientifically rigorous accounts even of the anti-nuclear movement or Greenpeace. Michael Cohen's well-documented 550-page history of the Sierra Club, the most traditional of the American environmental organizations, ends in 1970 – just as things were getting most exciting. There are certainly plenty of official records, perhaps too many for our own times, but most of those pertaining to the eco-age are still under wraps. As to the histories of environmental policies carried out by various authorities, few provide the kind of supporting evidence that historians expect. One is therefore forced to start from general storylines, and then to look for clues as to how far they correspond to reality.

One familiar, and not exactly fruitful, approach plots the transition from charisma to everyday activity, from movement to ossification, from spontaneity to regulation and routinization, from civil initiative to bureaucratization. There is nothing specific to environmentalism here. 'The future belongs to bureaucratization' is one of Max Weber's best-known prophecies in *Economy and Society*, all the more as it has actually come true. At first sight, there is much to be said for narrating the history of the environmental movement in accordance with a Weberian progression from charisma to institutionalization and bureacratization. Conservation has 'moved on from movement to management', explained the landscape ecologist Ulrich Eisel in 2001, not without elegiac undertones.[284] Or, as Niklas Luhmann put it sarcastically: 'As the sediment of extinct social movements, we find on the one hand organized, decision-making structures of responsibility defined in terms of permanent staffing and on the other hand a potential for protest – and in a mediating role as it were, a nostalgia for the civic virtue of public man.'[285]

If we assume with Weber that this is an inevitable process, there is no need to be spiteful about it. For we are dealing with a worldwide phenomenon, not something distinctively German, which may be found even in countries not known for their fanatical sense of order. As we have seen, Wangari Maathai, the 'tree mother', later felt best in her office. In the 1980s the Mexican 'Party of the Institutionalized Revolution' (PRI), in power for decades more as institution than revolution, created an environmental movement and fused it with the party and state in an attempt to bolster the regime;[286] President Carlos Salinas de Gortari took over the term 'ecocide' in 1982 from the rhetoric of environmentalism.[287] And in the Dominican Republic, beginning as early as 1967 but with greater force after his return to power in 1986, Joaquín Balaguer offered the world the amazing spectacle of a regime with the features of an eco-dictatorship.[288]

In many though admittedly not all respects, conservation was attractive early on to state apparatuses. Back in the sixteenth century, forest ordinance was already used as a way of expanding the ruler's control of the countryside in Central and Western Europe, especially in the German-speaking lands; today it has spread to the whole world. In 1972, at the beginning of the eco-age, the government of Guinea draconically intensified colonial traditions by making slash-and-burn techniques punishable by death;[289] a form of economy known all over the world since ancient times thus became branded as arson.[290] Environmentalism, originally a stamping ground for 'social movement' researchers, has increasingly become the domain of institutional theory and political science. Whereas in the 1970s and 1980s 'new social movements' (NSMs) were the stock in trade of those seeking to make environmental campaigns an academic subject, the focus has shifted to NGOs since the Rio Earth Summit of 1992.[291] In an eighties perspective, NSMs and NGOs were still muddled together,[292] but the latter have long since shown themselves to be an establishment raised above grassroots movements, complete with their articles of association and white-collar staff.

Grassroots movements, NGOs, BINGOs and GONGOs: not only in China

When we look at particular cases, the transitions are still fluid and there are constant shifts; grassroots movements can become NGOs. In Germany, a Bundesverband Bürgerinitiativen Umweltschutz (BBU) was founded in 1972, combining two terms, *Verband* (association) and *Bürgerinitiative* (civil initiative), that already sounded old-fashioned; it has remained for years the largest in terms of membership. But its affiliates have retained their autonomy, so that the BBU has been constantly threatened by fissiparous tendencies. Unlike the BUND, it has not been able to exert an influence on official policy, but has operated mainly through the political connections of board members such as Jo Leinen and Manfred Wüstenhagen.[293]

Other neologisms that have appeared meanwhile are the BINGO (big international non-governmental organization) and the GONGO (government-organized non-governmental organization – an antilogy on the borderline between seriousness and sarcasm).[294] In Nepal in 1984, the king personally founded a conservationist NGO, while a publicity slogan for Royal Nepal Airlines announced that alongside Buddhism and Hinduism the country now had a third religion: tourism. Many leading German environmental associations are now in receipt of state funding, and cooperate with government officials to a degree that brings them close to GONGO status. German corporatist traditions make themselves felt here, in sharp contrast to the United States.

A textbook example of a country where GONGOs are dominant is post-Maoist China. In principle, the elites and large sections of the population are aware that environmental damage is seriously jeopardizing the spectacular economic boom.[295] In typical cases, the central government tries to impose conservation on provincial authorities intricately entangled with commercial enterprises; GONGOs serve as major instruments for this purpose.[296] It would therefore be wrong to think of them as fanciful structures designed to dupe the public with a non-existent environmental awareness. One especially popular aspect is so-called 'panda politics': the preservation of charismatic wildlife and famous landscapes, which, unlike the construction of large dams, provides an opportunity for national consensus. In the 1980s Tang Xiyang – whose wife was clubbed to death by Red Guards during the Cultural Revolution, and who later married the

American environmental activist Marcia Bliss Marks – became the editor of *Nature*, the magazine of the Beijing Museum of Natural History, and as such the spokesperson for China's revitalized conservation movement. The fact that this was in principle a politically correct activity did not hold him back from recognizing that China's greatest environmental problem was its lack of democracy.[297] The country's best-known environmental NGO, which was founded in 1994 (the take-off year for Chinese environmental organizations), is dedicated to conservation and calls itself 'Friends of Nature'. Under the 'strong, charismatic leadership' of the renowned historian and government adviser Liang Congjie, it enjoys considerable freedom of action.

Up to now it has been difficult for outsiders to fathom the extent to which most other Chinese NGOs and GONGOs have a free hand and an ability to wage campaigns. Even formally independent NGOs, of which there are now many in China too, are urged to respect the government's wishes, and for most of them the guiding principles are 'Be of help, but don't make trouble; get involved, but don't interfere; act, but don't cause offence.' It is clear that charismatic leaders, as well as financial support from large overseas NGOs, are vitally important for many Chinese environmental organizations;[298] they are not merely agencies of the state. The ecological movement has an unmistakable dynamic of its own, not least because environmental problems are such a live issue in Chinese society. Indeed, since the early 1990s, it has provided some amazing stories that do not fit the picture of a totalitarian state – the drama of the Wild Yak Brigade, for example, an unofficial group of activists founded in 1992, which, to much acclaim in the media, campaigned to protect the dwindling stock of Tibetan antelope from poachers and (though sometimes under a cloud even within the eco-scene) became 'a sort of flag for the Chinese environmental community'.[299]

Greenpeace has become increasingly skilled in the art of diplomacy and since the late 1990s, based at first in Hong Kong, it has been remarkably successful in establishing a presence in the People's Republic. Above all in a campaign over water pollution[300] it has supported Beijing against defiant provincial bosses, just as *Rainbow Warrior* – flying in the face of the fashionable distinction between state authorities and civil society – performed police services for Russia against Japanese trawlers when the country was still reeling from the collapse of the Soviet Union.[301] Many of Greenpeace's operations have skilfully appealed to Chinese national consciousness: for example, the campaigns against the patenting of a Chinese variant of soya and against the shipping of Australian electronic waste to China. According to information that it posted on the internet, Greenpeace was the only NGO to be consulted in 2006 by the Chinese National People's Congress for the drafting of a new law on the promotion of renewable energy. This is an indication of the extent to which the erstwhile dinghy warriors have now prioritized competence in particular fields.

The Big Ten in the USA

The United States, with its traditionally strong civil society, represents a countermodel to China, but there too – especially where wilderness protection is concerned – an establishment of environmental organizations has consolidated itself and conducts effective lobbying in Washington, where it is a privileged interlocutor of Congressmen and government officials. As in other countries, this establishment has been remarkably stable for a number of decades; the 'Big Ten' sometimes appear in the literature as a standard term, even if there are not always precisely ten (some authors count up to twelve). The list certainly includes the Sierra Club, the Wilderness Society, the National Audubon Society, Friends of the Earth, the Natural Resources Defense Council (NRDC), the Environmental Defense Fund (EDF), probably also the National Parks and Conservation Association, the National Wildlife Federation and Nature Conservancy, as well as the international organizations Greenpeace and the WWF. Perhaps one should add the American Forestry Association or the American Rivers Conservation Council or Zero Population Growth[302] – things are less clear between the tenth and twelfth places.

The top people in the Big Ten know one another and keep in touch. There are rivalries, but also a division of labour. Michael McCloskey, then chair of the Sierra Club, but eager to be fair towards other frontrunners, observed in 1992 that many of these organizations 'are very good at certain things: the Sierra Club in mobilizing its large cadre of grassroots activists' (his Sierra Club, with the charm of a grassroots movement!); 'the Wilderness Society at research and public relations; Nature Conservancy at habitat surveys; the National Wildlife Federation in reaching middle-class and working-class people with an environmental message; the NRDC in mastering the complexities of federal programmes; the Audubon Society in running sanctuaries; and the Sierra Club Legal Defense Fund in litigating'.[303]

Robert Gottlieb, the historian of the American environmental movement, detected in 1993 – after the end of the rollback of early environmentalism during Reagan's first presidency – 'a revolving door between staff positions in the mainstream groups and government and industry'.[304] This is reminiscent of the surprise that a British visitor expressed at the German Environmental Agency (UBA), not a few of whose staff had come from NGOs: 'Am I in a government authority here or in Greenpeace?' In the United States, things never went as far as a German-style corporatist amalgamation of governmental and non-governmental organization; tensions always remained with the Environmental Protection Agency (EPA). One staff member, who would have dearly liked the cooperation to have been closer, admitted: 'Unfortunately the EPA too often treats the NGOs as antagonists, instead of seeing them as natural allies. There are many good examples of collaboration, but too many examples of people working against each other.'[305] More generally, the Big Ten seem to have first constituted a broad Green alliance in 1981, as a defensive measure against Reagan's onslaught on environmentalists.[306]

'Mainstream' as a swearword

Like so many organizations in this world, the large environmental NGOs look different from the outside and from the inside. The established 'mainstream' became a swearword for activists new to the movement; they accused it of working hand in glove with the government and industry, of being interested only in money and special privileges, and of becoming arrogant, bureaucratic and cut off from its base.[307] The Australian Timothy Doyle, who sides with grassroots campaigners in the third world, writes of top managers in the EDF and other Big Ten organizations that they 'understand the earth itself as a massive corporation which, if run on correct *best-practice* business strategies, will survive the current environmental hiccups'.[308]

This sounds like a typical clash between yesterday's arrivistes and today's new fighters, such as has existed, and continues to exist, in many parts of the (not only first) world. Sunderlal Bahuguna, the spiritual leader of the Chipko movement, once stressed that the forces for change must come from the people – which means 'out of small local initiatives, small groups of volunteers, not out of NGOs, which are government appendages and part of the establishment'.[309] In Germany Jörg Bergstedt, co-founder of an environmental youth movement, has collected a wealth of material on the links between leading conservationist organizations and government and industry. He distinguishes between 'two environmental movements' in the 1990s: the campaigns against nuclear power and genetic engineering, whose aims made them immune to co-opting from above; and the 'large environmental associations', most of which 'had a cosy relationship with politicians and business leaders'.[310] Unlike in the United States, no government in the Bundesrepublik since 1970 has gone for a head-on collision with the whole environmental movement, and so the external pressure has not existed for a broad anti-government alliance. In Bergstedt's view, autonomy from the state and industry is a value in itself and conflict always something good, even if one can draw closer to certain objectives by cooperating with those in power. Those for whom the environment is more important than autonomy behave differently.

Mark Dowie, the critical chronicler of the American environmental movement, characterizes the activity of the Big Ten in terms of 'the three Ls: legislation, litigation and lobbying'.[311] He does concede that without them nothing effective can be done in environmental politics. Yet the basic dividing line in his account is between 'grassroots movements' and 'mainstream environmentalism'. This schematic distinction is a classic example of how momentary snapshots are interpreted as structures. For, over a period of time, the mainstream changes direction and grassroots activists often become part of it. Nor should we forget the metaphorical character of the term 'grassroots': human beings have legs, not roots.

A World Bank director of Venezuelan origin, who describes himself as an NGO man and takes NGOs only partly seriously, drew a differentiated picture of those which seek contact with the World Bank (especially important for many in the third world since the 1980s): 'In general terms, you could classify them into three types: the seriously concerned and truly interested, the bona fide NGOs; the self-interested NGOs (there are plenty of money and business or consultancy opportunities in development); and, finally the groupies, those who just get a kick in life out of hanging around.' 'Many NGOs in the developing countries are frequently totally subordinated to sophisticated NGOs from developed countries, and I find this very sad.'[312]

Bureaucratization: a law of nature?

Evidence of the affinity between environmental associations and state apparatuses, and of bureaucratic structures within those associations, can be found in abundance all around the world. Wolfgang Sachs, who himself later went to the Wuppertal Institute, detected a 'rising global ecocracy' in the post-Rio period.[313] The question, however, is whether there is an inevitable, law-like evolution from spontaneous civil movements – charismatically inspired or not – towards institutionalization and regulation. No doubt there is such a trend over limited periods, but that is not the whole story. This is immediately apparent if, instead of taking the Earth Day mega-happening of 22 April 1970, with its whiff of Woodstock, as the point of departure, we follow the environmental movement back a century to the time 'before the environmental movement'. Then we can see that an affinity with the state and a tendency to institutionalization were there from the beginning, both in the United States (with Gifford Pinchot) and in Prussia-Germany (with Hugo Conwentz). Dave Foreman, the 'eco-warrior' and advocate of non-law-abiding 'ecotage' to save the wilderness, notes with some justice (and an undertone of contempt): 'The early conservation movement in the United States was a child – and no bastard child – of the Establishment. The founders of the Sierra Club, the National Audubon Society, the Wilderness Society and the wildlife conservation groups were, as a rule, pillars of American society.'[314] And demands for the protection of natural resources already amounted to an enlargement of the powers of government – in Washington, not in the individual states.

In Germany, the federal structure of the country showed through more in relation to conservation, but there too a penchant for organization made itself felt from the beginning – not efficiency-oriented, though, and for a long time mainly within the tradition of clubs and societies. In 1910, as the German cultural heritage leagues endlessly chewed over whether to form an umbrella organization, the musician Ernst Rudorff, the spiritual father of German conservation, was at the end of his tether: 'We would again be organizing our league to death.'[315] The (seemingly) unselfish love of nature and *Heimat* threatened to turn into a self-centred clubbiness; the umbrella organization made sense only as a result of political lobbying. Here, at least as much as in the USA, a close affinity developed early on between environmental activists and public authorities. In the first few decades after the Second World War, the big man of Bavarian conservation was Otto Kraus, director from 1949 to 1967 of the Bayerische Landesstelle für Naturschutz. Although acting in an official capacity, he quite often did so in the style of a people's tribune representing the public good against narrowly egoistic considerations. In his case, it is misleading to separate the state and civil society from each other.

The BUND had the greatest presence in postwar German environmental policy, until the rise of the NABU (Naturschutzbund Deutschland) in the 1990s.[316] 'By far [the BUND's] strongest and most influential base' was Bavaria, where it had originally seen the light of day on 26 June 1913,[317] and where it recruited mainly from the conservative CSU. In the mid-1970s, however, the BUND developed in North-Rhine Westphalia in SPD circles, while sharing with its Bavarian sister organization a closeness to government bodies.[318] Peter Menke-Glückert, the architect of environmental policy at the interior ministry in Bonn, claimed in his blunt way that one of state secretary Hartkopf's 'masterly achievements' was to have 'won over and instrumentalized [*sic*!] individual environmental associations for the purposes of the federal government, by means of various devices and dialogues'.[319] Instrumentalization is a two-way business, though. Jochen Flasbarth – the dynamic president of the NABU from 1992 to 2003, who had converted it from a tranquil bird conservation society into a combative environmental organization – took over in August 2009 as the president of the UBA and adopted a radical activist's tone unusual for a head official. For example: let it be stated clearly for once that 'a half of the world's fishing fleets must be simply laid up!'[320]

Still, we should not conclude that everything was hunky-dory between the government and environmentalists. If only to avoid losing face with their supporters, the BUND and NABU alike had to show from time to time that they were capable of a fight.[321] Thus, the North-Rhine Westphalia BUND waged a fierce campaign against an autobahn through the Rothaar mountains – a project massively supported by the *Land* government. The regional BUND chair Michael Harengerd (1992–8) spoke of an 'SPD Mafia', and a banner at a BUND meeting in the early nineties referred to the Social Democrat first minister, Johannes Rau, as an 'environmental criminal'.[322] Hubert Weinzierl, the dynamic new chair of the BUND from 1969, drew inspiration from the dawning 'ecological revolution' and, paying no heed to the high level of public funding, struck a more offensive tone. Yet he also firmly believed 'that conservation has a chance of survival today only if it is properly managed'.[323] In theory, there may be a contradiction between charismatic leadership and rational management. The historical reality is that the two are often combined.

In the United States, the Sierra Club – suddenly in danger of looking old amid the 'ecological revolution' – tried to keep pace with a new militant tone. On Earth Day itself, in April 1970, it published a *Handbook for Environment Activists* under the title *Ecotactics*, which began with the thesis 'A revolution is truly needed' (a revolution 'in our values, outlook and economic organization') and went on incessantly about 'action', revolution and struggle against enemies of the earth, without actually arguing for violation of the law. But when one of the editors approvingly quoted something a girl had said: 'General Motors is killing us' (with exhaust gases), everything became permissible against such an enemy.[324]

What lay behind that regulation, institutionalization and bureaucratization, which did not exactly make the environmental movement more attractive to young people bringing fresh enthusiasm to it? Or is that a stupid question? If we stick to Max Weber, it operates like a natural process: enthusiastic, charismatic conditions are inherently provisional; the inevitable routinization bears the marks of the time, in the modern polities governed by bureaucratic administrations and institutions where finance too is usually an important factor. In this 'natural history' model of social movements, there is also the likelihood that decline will set in as soon as the first impetus is spent and no solid institutionalization is achieved.[325] Even rock groups and their managers, precisely if they are successful, sooner or later turn into apparatuses that obey the laws of the entertainment industry.

In the case of the environmental movement, however, there are further specific reasons for the tendency to institutionalization. Many of its objectives, especially where large areas are concerned, cannot possibly be achieved without state intervention. This has been the basic contradiction since the beginning of the movement: campaigns acquire group cohesion and combative dynamism mainly by setting themselves definite goals, but the holistic concept of 'environment', with its claims beyond particular groups and its requirement for networked thinking, amounts to the exact opposite. If they are consistent, environmental campaigns regularly come to see that they need the state. As lobbyists and as contact and negotiation partners, they must make a serious impact on government bodies and adapt to their codes and fields of competence. And even if, like Greenpeace, they want to enlist the media on their side by means of spectacular actions, strict organization can serve to optimize the balance between risks and chances of success. One can have endless public discussions about priorities, only to be too late in acting and to lose the opportunity to make an impact. It is also advisable to plan operations as professionally as possible, with one eye on upcoming law suits and any counteroffensives that opponents might launch.

Litigation was a major weapon in the United States, where environmental NGOs were soon conducting hundreds of law suits simultaneously.[326]

Lawyers were needed for this, and plenty of exciting assignments existed in the initially confusing but rapidly expanding field of environmental law. In 1967 a Sierra Club employee could gloomily predict to its chair, David Brower, that within a year New York lawyers would be joining in such numbers that it would be on the point of becoming the New York Bar Association.[327] The major financial backing needed for particularly contentious cases could best be obtained from industrial sponsors. And for that too it is important to be a legal person, to appear serious, and to have statutes and proper offices.

EU, UNO, World Bank: transnational lobbying and the development of an NGO establishment

Since groups differ widely in their level of success, only few having access to top government bodies, an establishment inevitably takes shape within the environmental movement as it becomes more developed. The higher the political level, the smaller is the group of NGOs capable of playing an active role. The UN and UNESCO were an early influence on the environmental movement, with 'NGO' becoming a sort of trademark. In Europe, the growing importance of the EU also had an impact on the movement, especially after it began to take the initiative in environmental policy in the 1990s. Although the eco-scene had previously been suspicious of the EU, seeing it as a machine to force industrial growth and to technologize agriculture, the 'Flora, Fauna, Habitat' (FFH) directives that it began to issue in 1992 spread a mood of triumph among conservationists. 'Never before in its history', writes Frank Uekötter, 'had conservationism invested so much in the power of the interventionist state.'[328]

The World Bank in Washington played a prominent role in globally shaping the environmental movement. It participated in the funding of large dams and other major development projects against which activists campaigned, but as an institution it was officially bound to pursue the common good and to take heed of international public opinion. The growing salience of environmental issues therefore had an impact on it, especially from the late 1980s on, when environmental organizations increasingly addressed themselves to it and later received its sponsorship. In the 1990s, one detects a kind of ecological turn in the World Bank; this was given a huge impetus by mounting criticism of the Narmada dam project, which caused it more trouble than any previous controversy. Whereas Vandana Shiva still sees the World Bank today mainly as an adversary, especially because of its loan conditions that promote the commercialization of water,[329] Medha Patkar appealed to it as long ago as 1989 in a letter to its new president, Lewis Preston: one of the most powerful documents of hers in circulation.[330] Evidently she expected to find greater understanding in Washington than in Delhi or even Mumbai – and she was not disappointed. As a grassroots activist without an established

NGO behind her, she understood how to influence people at the top of the World Bank and to induce a climbdown in the end. Philippines activists had a spontaneous horror of the World Bank, feeling that to collaborate with it was tantamount to 'sleeping with the enemy'.[331] Yet in the end they got support from it in their campaign against the Philippine National Oil Corporation's plan to use geothermal energy on Mount Apo.

In Washington people realized the awkwardness of the situation when a few established NGOs managed to gain a monopoly position there as lobbyists. Efforts were then made to include and promote grassroots campaigns from around the world, as Bertrand Schneider, the secretary-general of the Club of Rome, had demanded in 1986.[332] A turn has been shaping up especially since 1989.[333] A report in 2001 on projects promoted by the World Bank in the 1990s under the Global Environment Facility[334] reads like a compendium of environmental initiatives and projects from around the world, most of which receive no mention in the bulk of the extant literature: 26 in China, 16 in India, 14 in Indonesia, 14 in Peru, 13 in the Philippines, 10 in the two Congo republics, 7 each in Senegal and the Seychelles. One suspects how much the scenario of environmental projects around the world is scripted in Washington, even if the initiative comes from the regions in question.

The Arun III dispute: communication worldwide and in Nepal

The ecological turn at the top of the World Bank reached a peak in the mid-nineties with the dispute over the Arun III dam in eastern Nepal.[335] For a long time India's hydraulic engineers were spellbound by the huge energy potential of the Himalayas, beside which the Narmada paled into insignificance, and dizzying profit opportunities opened up even for impoverished Nepal. But territorial divisions within the world's highest mountain range, together with political instability in Nepal and a lack of professional management, had done more than environmentalists to obstruct all major projects.[336] The plan to build a dam in the Arun mountain valley, where fewer people had settled than in the Narmada valley, was attractive from a purely technical point of view, but unlike the Narmada project it got friends of the wilderness up in arms worldwide, since it threatened indigenous ethnic groups hitherto untouched by modernity.[337] Defenders of nature and of local people stood together, and they found a new line-up in Washington. James Wolfensohn, who had just taken over at the World Bank, wanted to shake off its highly capitalist image and to side visibly with the poor;[338] his adviser, Maurice Strong, had previously been the secretary-general of the Stockholm Environment Conference. The new leadership at the World Bank stopped supporting the Arun project, and since Nepal, unlike India, could not fund a large dam independently, the project was eventually mothballed. At an international level, the Arun III controversy had the appearance of an environmental conflict. It raged inside Nepal too, but there the dominant issue by far was who profited from the dam and where the kickbacks had gone.[339] Other large dam projects in Nepal, which were funded by India, caused an uproar because they meant sacrificing the country's valleys to Indian interests and increased the ever-present danger that Nepal would become a mere satellite of its powerful neighbour.[340] This is how globally networked 'ecological communication' casts a veil over local conflicts of interest!

The liberating effect of freedom from value judgements

Still, the question is repeatedly posed: what is to be valued, and how? The literature on environmental issues teems with value judgements, both open and (more often) hidden; they tend to creep in unobtrusively, without being obvious to the author. Not infrequently, the value judgements actually contradict one another. Opposite impulses are discernible in the origins of conservation and environmentalism: the joy in spontaneous natural growth has something anarchic, whereas outrage over the 'free economy' that blights nature with excavators and concrete gives rise to calls for far-reaching state intervention to preserve familiar landscapes.

Those for whom autonomy is the highest value regard any cooperation with government bodies as betrayal. Those for whom only the state is capable of effective action do not think it a good idea that private organizations should be responsible for long-term conservation, and they grade them according to whether and how they are capable of cooperating with government bodies. If you deem state bureaucracies to be essentially sluggish, incompetent and corrupt, you will look to NGOs as the only salvation; if you hold that conservation always needs to be imposed on the broad masses, you will assess nature conservancy societies by their ability to handle conflicts; and if you believe that all successful conservation rests upon the consent of local people, you will judge conservationists by their 'communicative skills'. Someone for whom science is the only basis for a modern environmental policy will be easily disgusted by the emotions found in conservationist movements. Someone who gets involved out of love or passion will consider that drily rational mountains of paperwork, in which hallowed wildlife and landscapes do not exist, add up to an anaemic ecological world of eunuchs. Someone who thinks that true environmentalism is driven by a selfless love of nature for its own sake will feel spite when it turns out that campaigners against a construction project supposedly acting on behalf of an endangered bat species were really interested in keeping their homes undisturbed in an open green space. Someone who judges all environmental groups by whether they observe the 'Think globally, act locally' maxim will treat a mere concern for one's home district as indicative of an egoistic Nimby existence. Someone for whom true environmentalism takes in the whole environment will regard all single-issue movements as narrow-minded.

In short, there is an obvious danger that one-sided, 'over-the-top' evaluative criteria will make it impossible to assess the environmental movement. Max Weber's once overworked postulate of value-free science now raises hackles among many contemporary social scientists, but it could yet revolutionize the study of environmental politics and movements! The first requirement is to give up altogether the completely ahistorical idea that there is just one patent solution to environmental problems, one effective method, one optimum form of organization. Here there are no truths valid for all times and places, irrespective of the particular situation and players. All value judgements are here relative and time-dependent; all are tied to particular conditions and presuppositions.

The basic contradiction of the environmental movement

The once prominent constitutional theorist Ernst Forsthoff (1902–74) declared a precautionary concern for people's livelihoods (*Daseinsvorsorge*) to be one of the noblest tasks of the state, and hence the best philosophical foundation for the demands of the environmental movement on the government. However, in the eyes of many environmental activists, this conservative, who praised the Nazi energy law of 1935 as exemplary, represented an authoritarian tradition of German political thought. It is true that he was too unappreciative of citizens' initiatives (in so far as he was aware of them at all). In 1971 he thought that the environmentalism taking shape in such campaigns would be ineffectual, since its particularist character conflicted with the anti-particularism of environmental protection; only the state, not fragmented among a plurality of interests, was capable of fulfilling this interest akin to *Daseinsvorsorge*.[341]

That was 1971, and periodization is a factor in all judgements concerning the environmental movement. One or two decades later, it would have been hard for Forsthoff to argue that the movement had set nothing in motion. He did not see clearly enough that 'the state' too is not a compact entity, that its bureaucracy tends to spread responsibility, and that its apparatus does not automatically provide for the public good but needs to be constantly pushed into it from outside. The history of environmentalism offers abundant proof of this not exactly new point. As long ago as 1872, the famous legal theorist Rudolf von Jhering – a man who came under attack from Forsthoff – argued in his Vienna lecture 'The Struggle for Law' that, unless individuals fought for their rights, 'abstract law' was a 'mere appearance' that existed only 'on paper'.[342] Jhering had individual rights in mind, but the same applies to environmental laws: this public interest too becomes a reality only through a multiplicity of individual interests; and all too often environmental law remains a dead letter if individuals do not fight for its practical enforcement.

Yet each particular interest, whether of an individual or a group, has its limitations and, if pursued with monomaniac zeal, may well harm the legitimate interests of others. The history of environmentalism affords plenty of examples of this. Forsthoff's critique is therefore not entirely outdated; it is becoming topical precisely in relation to conflicts between different ecological initiatives. Like all organizations, environmental associations develop an egoism of their own: they tend to define success not in terms of greater environmental protection but by the level of donations; and in the rivalry for private donors and government sponsors, their efforts to distinguish themselves from others can overshadow solidarity in a common cause. In 1991 Max Nicholson said it filled him with horror that 'within two years' there might be a dozen or more wildlife funds 'all going for the same source'.[343] The same happens in the fight for publicity, since media attention is not evenly distributed across a broad spectrum of issues and actions. But although there is an urgent need for all groups to band together, this might cut across their organizational interest in self-preservation. The best chance of cooperation probably exists at the level of local voluntary workers.

By 1970, it was clear in the United States that the mushrooming of groups and ad hoc campaigns was not simply a strength but also threatened to fragment the wider ecological complex. America today offers the best example of the dilemma described by Forsthoff. Since the early 1970s it has had the environmental movement with the strongest roots anywhere in civil society, and it can point to a long chain of successes, especially in the banning of certain toxic emissions. Yet it appears as the major obstacle to the reduction of CO_2 emissions, where the common interests of humanity are at stake.

After wretched experiences with development aid in many states around the world, and following a general trend to deregulation since the 1990s, 'NGO' has become a magical word – as if non-governmental status were itself a proof of quality. However, NGOs lack the democratic seal of elections; their legitimacy rests on the fact that democracy needs the impetus provided by campaigning groups and that their members can be assumed to have a certain degree of idealism. Such motivation is not certain in every case, and large, well-equipped NGOs do not escape entirely the law of inertia manifest in state apparatuses (although they offer far lower salaries and much less secure employment). The chances for environmentalism hinge everywhere on a reasonably competent and energetic personnel with at least a minimum of professional ethics and integrity, and on the existence of a critical public opinion to keep tabs on it. Since many countries around the world are deficient in this respect, it would be wrong to conclude from the multiplicity of environmental groups (which fill whole handbooks) that they also produce sizeable results.

With regard to Green activism in state apparatuses, there is also the question of parliament – but here the literature on environmentalism displays the least interest. When the 'new social movements' model was in fashion, the orthodox view was that an ecological party was a contradiction in terms; confident predictions were made, even in their own ranks, that the German Greens would come to a swift end. More than thirty years later they are still the world's best-known ecological party, and there is now a considerable body of literature about them. But this focuses to a striking degree on their early period,[344] when the struggle between 'Fundis' and 'Realos' was at its height, the Green group in the Bundestag was always divided over whether it should act as a party or anti-party in Bonn, and the whole Green scene had the charm of the grotesque.

Again and again the search for order

The 1,100 pages of minutes of Green meetings – public as well as internal – during their first parliamentary period (1983–7), which were published in 2008, have nothing quite like them anywhere in the world; they are unique also in their candour, revealing a series of explosions by frustrated group members and improper remarks by minute-takers. Take, for example, the session on 20 November 1983, which considered whether the Greens should break with custom and form a 'circle of silence' during the Bundestag debate on rearmament. 'Sabine Bard', we read, 'finds the human gesture of silence inappropriate in an inhuman and cynical place like the Bundestag. . . . Upon Joschka Fischer's question, who will do it?, chaos ensues: who, where, how, what, when; in the following vote it turns out that 8 will remain silent, the rest not.' Towards the end there is again 'a little tumult'. 'Somehow the session stops there.'[345] A muddle of parliamentarism and anti-parliamentarism! Moreover, detailed study of Green politics at that time shows how much the party had to rely upon environmental associations, action groups and ecological institutes. Overstretched by the daily parliamentary routine, the Greens alone lacked the resources to develop alternatives to nuclear and coal-fired power stations or to identify new environmental problems.

The records also show an incipient lack of respect for formal rules, while the largely informal character of decision-making processes did nothing to make them more transparent. The allusions and jargon in quite a few documents of the Greens mean that they are harder for a later outsider to understand than Reichstag minutes from the Bismarck period. Somewhere the decisions were taken: if not in daytime meetings, then at night in bars; informality often strengthens in-groups. Young activists coming into the environmental movement often found offputting the web of eco-jargon spun over the decades, especially as it tended to be combined with the jargon of the ageing New Lefts (and things were not much better for them in the various consciousness-raising, esoteric and feminist groups). Even the experienced Reimar Gilsenbach, a secret guru of the eco-scene in the GDR, reported similar feelings after unification when he found himself among conservationists from West Germany.[346] Jargon flourishes not only in institutions but also in informal scenes.

Greenpeace versus Shell: a Pyrrhic victory? Self-examination
in the environmental movement

For all the temptation to be sarcastic, we should never forget that people in
the environmental movement are all too human; the observation that they
too argue over who should take the chair or how money should be spent,
and that they share in the processes of ageing and routinization that affect
all human beings and their social relations, is a banality that can shock only
those who believed in ecological miracles. What is remarkable, however, is
much that does *not* fit this schema. To some extent from the very beginning, but especially since the turn of 1990 in world history that opened a
new phase of environmental politics, many activists had before their eyes
the cautionary example of Socialist and Communist movements which,
having once originated in the revolt of the powerless, toppled blindly into
the worst kind of authoritarian-bureaucratic centralism.

One can marvel at very different things in the environmental movement:
how quickly wild anti-establishment rebels settled into functions where
they made professional use of the instruments of power; but also how
critically, and self-critically, many environmental campaigners followed
this process and tried to avoid excesses. Within the national environmental
bureaucracy, it was for a while the custom that top officials – who normally seldom left their office – spent some time 'at the front' discussing
new conservation requirements in village inns, so that they did not lose all
sense of the problematic nature of purely top-down policies. Only with the
SPD–Green coalition government did this thoroughly sensible practice fall
into disuse.[347]

Greenpeace is a perfect illustration of this dialectic of the environmental
movement. Since the early 1970s it has been by a long way the most famous
environmental organization in the world, and no one has been more effective than the rainbow warriors in establishing a new Green heroism that
can excite even those who cannot stand the sourpuss 'ecological' type. The
daring operations against ocean whalers and nuclear weapons testing did
much to give a new image (and a global horizon) to the 'ecological revolution', worlds apart from the 'small beer' (*Pritzelkram*) derided by Hermann
Löns. But these operations also required planning worthy of a general
staff; the strictly hierarchical structure and self-preoccupation of this
organization flush with donations aroused the growing rancour of other
groups, which stood in Greenpeace's shadow and referred to it ironically
as 'the Empire'.

The Greenpeace strategist Harald Zindler bluntly declared: 'I won't let
anyone be put in a dinghy by some general meeting. . . . Debates like those
all-night quarrels in Bonn between Green Fundis and Realos, which wore
on everyone's nerves, don't exist in Greenpeace.'[348] Or as Matti Wuori,
another general staff member, put it: 'If you want to change something in
the world, you need power to do it. In the end you have to decide whether
you want to go through nice, endless and mostly inconclusive debates or to

accomplish efficient changes (which happen only with a certain hierarchy); there's no getting away from that contradiction.'[349] Of course, discussions do not necessarily have to be inconclusive, but in the eco-scene they do often seem to be never-ending and unstructured. It has sometimes come as a revelation how wonderful strict organization can be.

In its first leading article on Greenpeace (6 September 1982), *Der Spiegel* stuck to the already iconic self-image of the rainbow warriors: two men in a dinghy before a bright-red mushroom cloud. Nine years later, however, on 16 September 1991, the same magazine felt provoked by a Greenpeace satire on paper-devouring 'environmental killers' and fired off a broadside against 'Greenpeace, the money machine', drawing extensively on the build-up of jealousies in the eco-scene. Again dinghy warriors in the cover picture, again an almighty effusion – only this time it was not a mushroom cloud but a tsunami of hundred-Deutschmark notes. 'David has grown into the eco-Goliath', whose incoming donations were almost double the size of world hunger relief, but which had no clear idea what to do with the 60 million marks it had accumulated in fixed-term deposit accounts. This 'McDonald of the environmental scene' was not geared to really important objectives, only to media impact; so, for example, it had only recently discovered the car as an eco-pest, since for a long time it had been unpopular to criticize it.[350] Subsequently, Greenpeace would try to develop an 'eco-car'.

Four years later, Greenpeace's action against the Brent Spar drilling rig in the North Sea was also geared to the media, but this time *Der Spiegel* gave it the old kind of support. Again the heroes in a tiny boat, now before the Brent Spar platform and a Shell logo looking devilishly like a mushroom cloud. The rubber dinghy had long been 'an indispensable element of the classic David and Goliath tale',[351] even after Greenpeace itself became Goliath. The rainbow warriors boarded the platform and came under fire from water cannons, all before the rolling cameras of television crews; the media effect could not have been greater. Motorists boycotted Shell petrol stations all over Europe. Even Helmut Kohl, the German chancellor, supported the campaign, which surpassed all previous environmental actions in popularity.

This unparalleled public success had had an unusually controversial prelude inside Greenpeace, when an abortive operation was launched on 7 April 1991 to prevent a Norwegian test drilling for a pipeline in the Waddenzee.[352] Was its visual appeal too limited, or had eco-piracy on the high seas lost its attractiveness for the media? In the view of many experts who had moved towards the rainbow warriors and called for 'structural reforms', the dinghy type of operation, with its David-versus-Goliath symbolism, was not appropriate to the knowledge society of the twenty-first century; they wanted to dump the old struggles, but seemed to others like mere 'pen pushers'. 'The Brent Spar operation was the revolt of a small group of old troopers who want to rebuild Greenpeace as an activist organization.' Ulrich Jürgens, the leader of the action, did not mince his words: 'You're always lost if you argue academically. It's all the same to me whether there are ten or a thousand tonnes of toxic sludge there. What matters is how a highly developed society deals with its waste.'[353] And the success was beyond all expectations, proving once more that people need simple, vivid images if they are to be aroused. In 2010, the oil disaster in the Gulf of Mexico reminded us that banal perils of technology thought to belong to the past can always become topical again.

Greenpeace forced Shell to retreat – the most spectacular victory ever won by an environmental organization. Whereas a decline in income had forced its Amsterdam headquarters to shed ninety jobs in the preceding years, donations now reached a new record.[354] But then followed an embarrassing epilogue, when it turned out that Greenpeace – not deliberately, it claimed,[355] but because of a measurement error – had for a while been operating with exaggerated totals: there were only 100 tonnes of oil sludge, not 5,000, in the Brent Spar.[356] What had originally appeared to be a stroke of genius now became a Pyrrhic victory, even in the eyes of many friends of Greenpeace. Had not the playing-up of Brent Spar diverted attention from the incomparably greater Shell scandal in the Niger delta, which had not offered targets for dinghy operations? Nevertheless, the symbolic value remained: the protest against ways of using the ocean as a rubbish tip highlighted a scandal that is still growing worse year by year. One Greenpeace activist, who later affirmed the legitimacy of the operation, pointed out that the sinking of this oil rig set a precedent: 'Brent Spar was the pilot project for disposing of some 420 much larger platforms and rigs in the North Sea over the next few years. Discretionary decisions against the deep sea disposal of other platforms would scarcely have been possible if it had been approved in the case of Brent Spar.'[357]

In 1997, Greenpeace published a partly self-critical collection of documents in which there was no shortage of malicious press articles about the organization. Most remarkable was a conversation with Eric Hobsbawm (1917–2012), published in the *Frankfurter Allgemeine Zeitung* of 24 June 1996 under the (not entirely correct) headline: 'Greenpeace, that's the revolution of the rich.'[358] Whereas Shell had at first given public reassurances that it would change, more restrained, self-critical signals now started to come from its adversary, Greenpeace. One idea was that part of its income from donations would be spent on an unprepossessing project for a study of German fiscal reform, to be undertaken by the Economic Research Institute.[359] When Greenpeace launched a campaign in May 1996 against the fishmeal industry, which is especially developed in Denmark, a heated dispute arose with Greenpeace Denmark, which argued that its activists could not break with Danish fishermen if they hoped to gain popular support.[360] The collision course pursued over Brent Spar was not a universal recipe for success; the critics were right about that.

Although it does not look as if the Brent Spar affair was discussed among a wide Green public, it gave rise to some of the most thought-provoking reflections in the history of the German environmental movement. At least since then, the demand for new thinking about the key problems of the earth's ecosystem, beyond any happenings staged for the media, has been a live topic both inside and outside Greenpeace. The subsequent evolution of the climate issue, which in temperate regions has hardly ever (or only superficially) translated into anxiety-producing events, would be difficult to imagine in the absence of such food for thought. In the 1990s the climate alarm seemed for a time to have been exhausted in the media; the famous (or infamous) cover of *Der Spiegel* on 11 August 1986, showing Cologne Cathedral half under water, had proven to be wildly exaggerated, and the magazine itself later joked about climate fears.[361] But the laws of media publicity are not everything. Despite all the ups and downs, the capacity for reflection in the eco-scene promises to be enduring. And within Greenpeace, the sense of crisis also reactivated the tendency to strict organization.[362]

Rebirth of radicalism

As we have seen, the establishment made up of leading environmental organizations has been remarkably stable over the decades, but within it there has been a considerable turnover of activists. Moreover, breaka-way groups and more radical competitors have caused trouble for these NGOs, and they have had to take care that they do not appear too old and decrepit. As early as the end of 1982, when Greenpeace Deutschland had just been constituted, Robin Wood split away on the grounds that the dinghy activists were neglecting the forest, and that – to quote one accuser – 'Greenpeace preferred to market helpless seal pups than to wage long-term campaigns on the spot against the practices of the chemical industry.'[363] From 1977 on, Greenpeace also faced competition on the high seas from the militant apostate Paul Watson, who rammed whalers with the reinforced concrete bow of his *Sea Shepherd* and mocked his former comrades as seat warmers.[364]

In 1969, the Sierra Club deposed the charismatic David Brower – under whom its membership total had shot up from 5,000 to 70,000 – and he went on to found Friends of the Earth.[365] At the time of Earth Day, there-fore, this elite club had every reason to project as activist an image of itself as possible, and its new handbook *Ecotactics* demonstrated this to excess; if the movement stuck to mere lobbying, its membership threatened to melt away. In 1980 Dave Foreman left the Wilderness Society and founded Earth First!; his militant style, with its call for acts of sabotage, matched the counteroffensive then unfolding under Reagan. For a time Foreman appeared to become the charismatic leader of the American wilderness movement; even elite universities gave him standing ovations.

Such challenges played their part in dissuading the Big Ten from too cosy a relationship with government. In 1992 even the president of the Sierra Club recommended 'healthy interaction between the more radical groups and the mainstream groups' and saw the latter's lack of openness to the former as a major defect of the environmental movement. Management alone was not a key to success: 'History shows that organizations typically enjoy greatest success when they manage to combine elements that are often uncomfortable with one another: those who have a passion for the mission and are driven by their own visions and those who can manage finances and personnel well.'[366] A 'theory of history' that one can accept!

In England, where environmentalists – with the exception of the animal rights movement[367] – had long appeared quite respectable and consensus-oriented, a new wave of militancy sprang up mainly through the Reclaim the Streets movement and the campaign against bypasses and motorway projects: where the excavators moved in, objects of attack soon beckoned. Meanwhile in the United States, despite the continuing dominance of the Big Ten or Big Twelve, the Environmental Justice movement and the campaign against the siting of rubbish dumps near poor neighbourhoods brought a new boom in grassroots initiatives.[368] Whereas the EPA, in its first great period, had distinguished itself in the fight against toxic emissions, the anti-toxic movement now welled up again from below. Not even in China were GONGOs and other NGOs close to the regime able to monopolize environmentalism; Franz Alt calculates that, according to official figures, there were 86,000 (sometimes militant) protest movements in 2008 alone, many of them triggered by environmental scandals in which the health risk to the local population was as clear as daylight.[369] By the turn of the millennium, a Chinese observer was recording a sharp increase in environment-related social protests since the end of Maoism. In typical cases a mourning ceremony – where gatherings of people and a collective expression of sorrow are legal – might turn into a protest demonstration.[370]

The commonly voiced expectation – part melancholic, part derisive – that institutionalization will lead to unavoidable rigidity and mummification has so far not been generally confirmed. Surprisingly clear evidence of this comes from quantitative studies of Central and Western Europe,[371] from the 'new radicalism' of Sierra Club presidents since the 1980s,[372] and from a glance at the Far East, whether China or the Philippines. The march of history repeatedly makes fools of social scientists and the models they throw together. The older generation of environmentalists, however, has frequently found it difficult to take young radicals seriously, instead of writing them off as 'unprofessional' dilettantes. So it is a good idea to think back to one's own beginnings.

'The iron law of oligarchy' and the law of small numbers

The premise underlying the rigidity prognosis is expressed most strongly in Robert Michels's 'iron law of oligarchy'. In 1911, when he formulated it, he had German Social Democracy before his eyes as a living example. The 'iron law' then smoothed his path to fascism, since he concluded from it that democratic socialism anyway had nothing to offer in the way of freedom. It was also the ultimate basis for the conviction of Max Weber, Michels's mentor, that historical novelty stems not from mass organizations but from small groups bonded together by strong passions – hence Weber's special interests in religious sects.[373]

Small groups need not involve a powerful elite, especially not at the beginning; Weber's law of small numbers also gives marginal groups a chance. The so-called Olson paradox leads to the same conclusion. As the Austrian cultural ethologist Otto Koenig put it, summarizing years of experience in behavioural research and the environmental movement:

> Man remains a small group creature, whose energies develop most powerfully in a circle with 10-12 members. . . . In an emergency, a large association that consists only of paying members will fare much worse than a small group ever ready to react and defend itself. This is the advantage of an activist entity over the celebrated 'silent majority', which actually is not in agreement and still does not do anything.[374]

Here too lie the ever new opportunities as well as the basic problem facing the environmental movement; it draws its vitality from local groups of activists but would like to represent the interests of humanity as a whole, including those still unborn. One of the most exciting questions for the future is how far internet forums strengthen the advantage of small marginal groups, by bringing together like-minded people who would not otherwise have met, and how far they tend to disperse the capacity for communication, which at some point reaches its limits.

The fullness of time

For Kierkegaard, 'everything in Christianity revolves around the concept of' *kairos* (ancient Greek: 'favourable moment'): the 'fullness of time'.[375] It is also tempting to try it out in relation to the environmental movement. A non-theologian would speak of the 'historical moment'; whereas systems theorists, eager to find structure everywhere, came up in the 1990s with the 'political opportunity structure' (POS) and packed into it all the diversity of real history, hoping to explain why even amply funded movements sometimes never get anywhere but in other situations are a great success.[376]

The *kairos* phenomenon is evidently involved when rigidity develops within the environmental movement and new issues create an opportunity for fresh initiatives. The 'death of the forest' alarm in the early 1980s played real havoc with the German eco-scene. The post-Chernobyl mothers' movement, derided by old anti-nuclear campaigners as 'the becquerel movement', finally put an end to the absurdity of the venomous mothers' (or sisters') conflict in the Greens[377] over whether care for small children entailed a special situation in life – as if 'mother' were a Nazi category. The feminist sociologist Claudia von Werlhof admitted: 'For the first time I explicitly think, feel, write and behave as a mother.'[378] Even for top businesspeople, nothing got under their skin as much as the thought that they might no longer be able to let their children play unattended in the garden.

In the United States, the Three Mile Island accident had already mobilized women,[379] and the subsequent rollback of ecologism under Reagan ultimately brought about a 'rejuvenation' of the movement.[380] It obtained another perfect enemy image in the shape of George W. Bush, such as the German Greens had lacked for a long time. Large dam projects around the world, which it was very difficult to stop, also prevented activists from becoming complacent. But, however useful global eco-networks were, the vitality that regenerated the movement came in many cases out of local initiatives. One is reminded of the mythical travels of Antaeus, who drew strength again and again from his Mother Earth. In the long run, excessive aloofness is as bad for the environmental movement as it was for Antaeus, whom Hercules was able to lift up and strangle.

Small groups, individual persons and events have repeatedly put the movement back into the environmental movement; it is therefore important – not merely a concession to story-telling – to keep focusing on particular instances. This significance of the episodic also has a deeper reason, for it is ultimately the fact that environmental problems are endless and admit of no definitive solutions which constantly requires new approaches and leaves openings for new activists appearing on the scene. One task of the historian might be to sharpen our present-day sense for the *kairos*, the historical moment or situation, even if it is never known in advance how real is the opportunity for something new. History has all too often been used to overdetermine the actual course of things, and the historians considered most successful are those who have suggested most persuasively that everything had to happen as it did. Yet the closer we get to the present, the clearer it becomes that multiple possibilities are contained in events. This realization might have some practical import for the environmental movement, which has been so inclined to fatalism.

Chapter Five

A Friend–Enemy or Win-Win Scenario?

1 From Nuclear Power to the Spotted Owl

Off to battle – but with which weapons?

In the early 1980s, in a lecture to students in Münster on the dangers of nuclear technology, the Bremen physics professor Jens Scheer ended by asking in the matter-of-fact tone that physics professors have: 'What is our conclusion?' And he called: 'Off to battle!' Ever the sober scientist, he surprised the audience with a finale in the tone of Bizet's Toreador Song.

Well, now, in the seventies Scheer had been considered 'Bremen's wildest Communist'– no mean feat, given that Bremen university was then a fortress of the left – who took on both the nuclear lobby and more accommodating critics of nuclear power such as his colleague Dieter von Ehrenstein, but who also argued that the radioactive fallout from Chinese weapons testing was unavoidable. Between 1975 and 1980, his authorization to teach was withdrawn on the grounds that he had supported the violence of certain far-left groups. But he also strengthened the verbal punch of anti-nuclear activists by producing a (for its time – 1975) excellent compendium refuting all the standard arguments of nuclear apologists; it was more user-friendly than most other writings of its kind, when push came to shove in a local discussion and pro-nuclear speakers manoeuvred onto a specialist level in the hope of ridiculing their opponents.[1]

The scenes of fighting outside nuclear construction sites should not make us forget that it was from the beginning a battle of minds, which unleashed a torrent of literature. But it was a real battle, and it lasted longer and mobilized far more people than the militant demonstrations of '68. At first politicians on all sides in Bonn and Washington welcomed the environment as a possible new terrain for consensus politics[2] – a new version of the public good concerning everyone. But then a new conflict scenario took shape over nuclear energy, giving the whole issue of the environment a provocative undertone that had previously been no more than rudimentary.

Do eco-campaigners need enemies?

'Battle' is a polyvalent term: it can refer to anything from a sports match to someone running amok, from an intellectual tussle to physical violence. In politics, economics, science and elsewhere, confrontations are a normal, transitory stage meant to bring everyone together in the end. But there are also contests where the aim is to annihilate the opponent, two examples being the world wars of the twentieth century. For Carl Schmitt, the 'Friend–Enemy distinction' is essential to all political action; it 'cannot be derived from other categories' but is contained axiomatically in the very 'concept of the political', even in the absence of a morally evil or otherwise repugnant enemy.[3] This assertion has apodictic force: it does not come about through political experience or reflection, but corresponds to the hate-filled postwar period and the tough, dashing style that Schmitt liked to display.

At first sight, Schmitt seems to push an aspect of Max Weber's thinking to a radical conclusion. In the electronic edition of Weber's works, the word *Kampf* (struggle, battle, combat, contest) appears no fewer than 785 times, and the leitmotif that 'politics is struggle' runs all the way from his inaugural lecture in Freiburg (1895) to his political addresses during the First World War.[4] His main concern was the distinction between politics and administration, statesmen and bureaucrats. He had little experience of the fact that a real fighting spirit may be required to enforce laws administratively – an everyday phenomenon in environmental law – although, to be sure, he would not have denied respect to combative officials. With the Prussian-German bureaucracy in mind, he had what seems today a far too exaggerated notion of the administrator's capacity to regulate things by means of a purely technological rationality. As he saw it, struggle arose mainly out of the 'polytheism of values'; he regarded it positively as an exertion of strength. 'The enemy' was not part of Weber's conceptualization. Enemies and allies have often changed round in the course of history; a Max Weber did not need enemy images in order to struggle.

The German Greens first started out as a party of struggle, but they had their problems with fixed enemy images. Impulses to fight and to embrace frequently alternated with each other – a tension observable throughout the history of the environmental movement, both in Germany and elsewhere. The desirability of struggle depended mainly on the opponents with which one had to deal, but also on how the essence of environmentalism was interpreted. Was it a question of obeying the imperative demands of nature? If so, any compromise was weakness, or even betrayal. Fernand Braudel wrote (probably with an ironical undertone[5]) about the Nature tirelessly evoked by the Enlightenment: 'The argument swept all before it.'[6] Or are we speaking of a field of action in which positions were at least partly matters of opinion, interest and taste, and solutions too usually had a provisional character? In that case, there was a danger of finding oneself in a blind alley if one dug in too firmly.

The upshot was similar if one assumed that environmental protection was in everyone's interests and that many had only to become aware of this. Then the process of comprehension – which was ultimately one of self-knowledge – would clog up if the battle lines were drawn too rigidly. 'Communication' became a buzzword in the 1970s and has remained that ever since; it depended on the situation whether it smacked more of controversial debate or mutual understanding. The whole issue of the environment seemed an ideal playing ground for communication. The penchant for endless discussion in the early days of the Green Party, which made many activists edgy, testifies to a faith in the limitless power of communication. Ulrich Beck coined the striking formula 'Poverty is hierarchic, smog is democratic.'[7] At best, however, this was a half-truth: much damage to the environment struck very unevenly at different population groups. The whole field contained abundant material for conflict that could not be cleared away just through communication.

The anti-nuclear campaign as the model of a (time-specific) friend–enemy constellation

For the German Greens, the enemy was clear at the very beginning: the nuclear lobby. But when they entered the Bundestag in 1983, that frontline had fallen silent: hardly any new nuclear power plants were commissioned – the ambitious programme launched ten years earlier under the impact of the oil price shock was forgotten – and the 'death of the forest' alarm dominated environmental consciousness. When the SPD went from government to opposition, nuclear scepticism was rife there too (supported by the Ruhr coal lobby); it was no longer a monopoly of the Greens, or a reliable criterion of who was one of theirs.

The movements against the nuclear power project at Wyhl and the reprocessing plant at Gorleben are the struggles that people have most cultivated in their memory; both ended in success – although it is not obvious how much this was due to the protests and how much to economic factors – and both involved an alliance, under the banner of non-violence, between ecological activists and sections of the local farming community.[8] Opponents liked to poke fun at 'anti-nuclear tourists', but here the protests had elements of a grassroots movement. More traumatic for many of those who took part were the violent clashes with the police at the Brokdorf and Grohnde construction sites. One has to look at film and posters from those struggles to get an idea of how close the atmosphere was to one of civil war and of how certain far-left groups deliberately stoked it up. Many supporters of the Greens later looked back with something more like embarrassment.

Sheer hatred was prevalent at first in the Gorleben movement too. The 'Gorleben Diary', a realistic document of the time by the writer and Rowohlt editor Hans Christoph Buch (b. 1944), notes on 12 January

1977 that no one really knew what a reprocessing plant was, 'only that it is something terrible, a thousand times worse than any nuclear power plant – everyone knows that'.[9] The CDU first minister of Lower Saxony, Ernst Albricht, who two years later called a halt to the 'politically unsustainable' Gorleben project, was the evil enemy: 'I think a man like Albricht is capable of any, yes any, vile deed.' 'I could have vomited with rage, or punched that prize crook Albricht in the face.' And on 14 February 1979: 'I suggest mining the construction site, so the excavators are blown sky-high.' And a repeated equation of the enemy with the Nazis, as in the '68 tradition: 'The terminology – final storage, final disposal, etc. – reminds you of the final solution to the Jewish question.'

But in March 1979, when the anti-nuclear activists felt the wind in their sails and even knew they had Washington behind them, Buch pleaded for non-violence and found himself ridiculed as a 'Gandhi freak':

> The danger comes not from the few trouble-makers, who exist in the ranks of the police as well as the demonstrators, but from the pent-up aggression and prejudice on both sides; everyone sees the enemy in the other. Instead of breaking down these enemy images, many of us reinforce them by trying to justify acts of violence like those at Grohnde.

There he had chatted with some frontier police, who told him that they had been 'shown a film about Grohnde to psych them up for the coming clashes'; 'demonstrators at Grohnde were supposed to have fired steel balls at the police'.[10]

In 1977 Buch and the trade union dissident Heinz Brandt had written a manifesto, 'Gorleben Must Live!', which became the classic text of the anti-nuclear movement and was adopted as its watchword. At its heart was no longer combat but a positive programme: 'reforestation instead of reprocessing', renewable energies instead of nuclear energy.[11] For one participant looking back shortly afterwards, 'Gorleben Must Live!' signalled an 'offensive for vital needs', after an attempt by certain far-left groups to take over the movement had been foiled.[12] The general reversal of mood on the left since the 'German Autumn' of 1977, the deadly climax of Red Army Faction terrorism, contributed to the changed atmosphere – which explains why the self-immolation of Hartmut Gründler on the Day of Prayer and Repentance in November 1977 went curiously unnoticed. Environmental activists now wanted signs of life, not of death! The greatest historical hour of the German anti-nuclear movement followed in late March 1979, when an international symposium on Gorleben in Hanover, under the direction of Carl Friedrich von Weizsäcker, coincided with the Three Mile Island incident and the arrival of a huge demonstration in the streets of Hanover. Albrecht announced the suspension of the Gorleben project, and the nuclear 'community' suffered its Cannae-like defeat.

*The German commission on the future of nuclear energy as the
model of a consensus strategy on several fronts*

On 14 December 1978, after bitter mass demonstrations at the Kalkar construction site, the Bundestag adopted a curious compromise: to continue building the SNR-300 fast breeder reactor, but to schedule further deliberation about its entry into service. A special commission of inquiry on 'Future Nuclear Energy Policy', at which MPs would discuss with experts in the field, was set up to ensure that the eventual decision was competent and well-founded. This body, sometimes named after its chair, the young SPD deputy Reinhard Ueberhorst, convened on 29 March 1979, in the international context just evoked.

Instead of plunging into the usual pros and cons of nuclear energy alone – which would have immediately led to polarization and deadlock – the commission decided to run through several possible directions for energy policy, before establishing science-based criteria for the evaluation of various options. Thus, as if by itself, a direction that did not involve nuclear energy also came up for discussion,[13] and the conclusion could not be avoided that it too was perfectly feasible. For the first time, it was officially conceded that – so long as serious energy-saving measures were introduced – a way forward *without* nuclear energy lay in the realm of the possible and deserved to be carefully tested. It turned out that the middle two of the four paths under consideration ran parallel to each other, at least for the decade to come, making it unnecessary to make a firm choice between them *hic et nunc*. Everyone could hope that the potential for energy-saving and a switchover to renewable energies (which could not be even approximately quantified in 1980) would be much easier to determine ten years later. This presupposed, however, that proper use would be made of the interval, and at least until Chernobyl that was mostly not the case.

The communicative search for consensus on new terrain – even if that simply meant a clearer definition of differences on both sides – reached unique heights in this commission of inquiry; it represented a remarkable episode, both in Germany and internationally, in which the environmental movement and policy-making were intertwined with the testing of controversial positions and potential areas of agreement.[14] The achievement is all the more considerable if we remember the scenes akin to civil war that had gone before. Also noteworthy is the clear and concise final report; its list of specific policy recommendations was utterly unlike those of most subsequent commissions, whose (often self-serving) academic advisers produced masses of paper heavy with specialist jargon for which practical politicians could find little use.[15]

This first commission of inquiry, operating in a highly tense situation, also contributed to a relative consensus which sections of the media hailed as a 'historic compromise', and which a 2010 study still describes as a 'mini-revolution' in the political handling of energy issues.[16] It enabled a mainly extra-parliamentary controversy to become part of the political (and above all parliamentary) process, and created a model of rational communication in a situation polarized along militant lines. Whereas nuclear policy had previously been conceived as making a virtue out of necessity, the airing of a range of options now converted it into politics in the full sense of the term, as something that required the taking of decisions.

A guiding thread of this book is that several narratives of environmentalism are possible. The first inquiry is a perfect case in point: there are two different ways in which it can be read. We might call these the Habermas version and the Luhmann version: the former an example of successful communicative action, the latter a comedy of pseudo-communication between two subsystems with their thoroughly different codes. It is worth considering this in greater detail.

First version of history: The Ueberhorst inquiry is the best proof that, among people of intelligence and integrity who conform to Kant's definition of enlightenment as the autonomous use of reason, political communication in the Habermasian sense really can succeed, even in a seemingly hopeless, hate-filled situation: that is to say, rational communication that involves putting oneself in the other's place, leading to a victory of reason and an understanding of the plurality of policy options that goes beyond a doggedly 'positional' mode of thought.

Energy policy in general and nuclear energy policy in particular concerned problem areas with a number of unknowns. Rightly understood, it was a way of handling uncertainty; the point was to grasp this and to draw consequences from it. The consequences lay in the direction of identifying several possible policy paths and a 'discursive', experimental politics not set in stone. The commission presented all this in exemplary fashion; its chair, representative of a new political generation, was carried away by the intellectual excitement of the discussions and therefore, to some extent at least, felt inwardly independent of his own 'scene' or 'community'. Ueberhorst set his sights on replacing the old 'positional' style of politics with a 'discursive' one, in accordance with the Swedish model of broad participation in energy policy discussions;[17] it is not only in their sex life that Swedes have developed less rigid roles than in the past. This strategy involved the projection of various paths into the future – and, lo and behold, when all the implications of nuclear energy were thought through, including the number of breeders that would be necessary around the world, the option appeared so absurd to the majority of the commission that it provoked outright laughter.

'Consensus' and 'options' became magic words. Previously, so-called 'product formulas' – based on extent of damage and likelihood of occurrence – had been used for the definition of risk, with the result that a very high 'residual' risk was scaled down almost to zero. But the commission's turn away from this methodology in its final report[18] was of potentially huge significance; if it had been followed consistently, the only conclusion – apart from the abandonment of nuclear energy altogether – would have been a switch to new and far safer reactor types. The ultimate tragedy of this heroic story, as of so many others like it, is that the success did not last long: the next commission stuck to the fruitless weighing of pros and cons in relation to fast breeder reactors and fell apart over the issue; then came the political landslide that swept away the SPD–Liberal government and inaugurated the new Christian Democrat era.

Second version of history: The investigative commission was simply an academic show for the benefit of politicians and the public, playing 'the part of the chorus in ancient tragedy'.[19] It delivered only what had been asked of it:[20] to formulate several policy options and to grace them with scientific authority. But the discussion, for all its input of expertise, did not develop any creative political strength. Science and politics remained distinct subsystems, each with its separate code and rationale, the first seeking after truth, the second interested essentially in power play. A scientist who seriously devotes himself or herself to the search for truth is not usable in politics; an expert who issues policy guidelines has insinuated political premises into his or her expert's report. Someone usually becomes an 'expert' – and offers lucrative political consultations – by virtue of belonging to a relevant institution, and that very fact means that he or she is not a truly non-partisan appraiser. Expert witnesses should anyway not be taken too seriously, since they bear no responsibility and do not have to answer for the consequences of their testimony. Besides, the party divisions among experts are similar to those in the world of politics; we are not talking of a higher level of rationality.

From this critical viewpoint, the 'success' of the Ueberhorst Commission was based not on the quality of communication, but rather on the policy input and the fact that leading exponents of the nuclear party such as Wolf Häfele were shaken by the violence of the resistance ('If I can get a breeder only through civil war, then I don't want it any more'). In the end, the much-vaunted 'historic compromise' came about because of the battles that preceded it, not as the result of rational communication; for people like Häfele, the construction of breeders was a life-or-death issue for our civilization, and it was irrational to give them up. The commission also owed its success to an 'old boys' network':[21] Häfele and Klaus Meyer-Abich, the most prominent speakers on the two sides, had both been assistants of Carl Friedrich von Weizsäcker and could be confident that neither would use the sessions to expose the other in public. At the time, Weizsäcker was keeping his distance from nuclear energy, on the grounds that there was no reliable defence against the threat of terrorist attack. But he had previously been a demigod for the nuclear 'community', and it now found his change of position deeply unsettling. Last but not least, the success of the Ueberhorst Commission rested on its passing the buck on the fast breeder issue to the next commission, so that what it achieved was more an armistice than a full consensus on energy policy. Nor did its energy-saving recommendation amount to much, since no one – at least in the German public – can be in favour of wasting energy.

Nevertheless, the first version (the 'Habermas variant') is not just wishful thinking. If the social subsystems really had been hermetically sealed off from each other, there would have been no chance of communication on broad issues across specialist boundaries. But that was not the case, as the work of the first commission shows. Moreover, the discussion evenings at Elmshorn, which came out of the commission and went on for decades, indicate that at least some of its members found it intellectually stimulating to probe the finer points of a discipline. (A similar atmosphere evidently did not emerge in the second commission.) And even if it is said that the only positive outcome was an agreement to postpone a decision, this was not without its uses. For, in the course of the 1980s, the fast breeder and reprocessing projects sorted themselves out, as did many other problems of the time. It is also true, however, that the Luhmann variant has an element of truth: politics is not a seminar at which people discuss endlessly, but is essentially a question of power play and the taking and implementing of decisions.

Years before the '68 experience left him embittered, Helmut Schelsky, the one-time pope of German sociology, noted that all who wanted reforms without risking anything 'seemingly utopian' did not even achieve the reforms but merely concealed their own impotence.[22] It was an idea that many '68ers would remember. This is the basic problem: violent revolutions may have only rarely made conditions more humane, but *fear* of revolution on the part of ruling elites has often made them more open to dialogue and compromise.

The costs of the conflict

The anti-nuclear campaign was immensely productive. Probably never before have droves of German intellectuals gone so intensely into detailed questions of technology – questions that brought them face to face with basic ecological issues of modernity. But the price of the conflict was also high. Given the new and hypothetical nature of the risks, it would have been rational for everyone concerned to tread carefully and not to lock themselves too soon into fixed positions. In point of fact, the competence assembled in the energy industry would also have been of great use to campaigners for alternative energies. The compliments that Bernd Stoy, a leading electricity company manager, paid to solar energy certainly indicate that both sides had a lot to say to each other;[23] but such overtures never got anywhere at first. The secret of the success of the anti-nuclear movement was that, at least in relation to breeder reactors and reprocessing, its interests converged with those of the energy industry, for which these new technologies were extremely expensive. However, the secret remained hidden from most campaigners. On both sides, a kind of bunker mentality took shape: anyone who questioned even a little the positions of their own side had to fear being considered a traitor. When it comes to the crunch, struggle leads to orgies of righteousness – to a style of thought and discussion unsuited to many environmental problems where unknown factors are involved.

This applies to courtroom battles as well as streetfighting. Frank Uekötter concludes from his review of nearly a century of clean air policies in Germany and the United States that 'the path of litigation has often proved extremely counterproductive'. 'Litigation regularly led to a hardening of fronts; the proceedings were often marked by an intense but fruitless exchange of experts' reports and counter-reports, and the judge was many times as disoriented as any other lay person amid the storm of conflicting opinions. It goes without saying that such cases were famous for their length and complexity.'[24] And smoke from factory chimneys seems child's play in comparison with the hypothetical risks of nuclear power plants. On the other hand, while law suits may have been counterproductive, *fear* of the courts not infrequently had a salutary effect. There is no lack of examples in the history of the anti-nuclear conflict too.

As far as the technology is concerned, various alternative designs that fell between two stools might have been intrinsically safer than the light water reactor that triumphed worldwide in the late 1960s. Should nuclear energy undergo a renaissance in the future, it might turn out to be a disaster that these blueprints were lost in the mists of time. Even Alvin M. Weinberg – the director of the Oak Ridge nuclear research centre from 1955 to 1973, who was responsible for the early decision in favour of light water reactors – publicly called in 1979, after the Three Mile Island accident, for a 'second nuclear era' built around different, and inherently safer, reactor types.[25] And Sir Alan Cottrell, for many years the chief adviser to the Atomic Energy Commission, considered the light water reactor insufficiently safe and blocked its introduction in Britain as long as his word was law.[26]

The violent clashes at reactor construction sites were especially costly, since they put off many who were in principle critical of nuclear technology. It became clear in the 1980s that Green sympathies were much more widespread in Germany than hardline desperadoes had assumed in the conflicts of the previous decade. In France too, the strategy of 'direct action' up to and including Molotov cocktails – which militants tried out in the late seventies as an answer to state violence – proved to be a fiasco for the environmental movement.[27] Battle scenes may have rekindled memories of revolution, but they did nothing to build political alliances.

The strongest argument of the nuclear industry was the lack of convincing energy alternatives other than fossil fuels – and, of course, large hydropower plants, which had also become a target for environmental activists around the world. In order to win the case for decentralized renewable energy sources, broad alliances were always going to be necessary. The advocates of nuclear power had only to persuade the heads of large energy corporations, but regional mixes of solar, wind, water and bioenergy needed the support of local authorities and consumers. Here any strategy involving division and polarization had a blocking effect.

Along with the anti-nuclear campaign, the movement against a new runway (Startbahn West) at Frankfurt airport repeatedly reached the threshold of violence in the 1980s. The protests themselves, triggered by a horror of aircraft noise and backed up by forest conservation arguments, enjoyed widespread sympathy: every homeowner could see that a nearby runway would make life a misery for them, and felt that a degree of militancy was legitimate. Ironically, however, Startbahn West had been planned in the middle of the forest precisely to minimize the disturbance. Frankfurt squatting activists, including Joschka Fischer, whose main concern was human habitat rather than the forest, showed remarkably little interest in the campaign.[28] The 'blackest day' was 2 November 1987, the sixth anniversary of the related clearance of Hüttendorf village, when two policemen were shot during a night-time clash with demonstrators. 'The anti-Startbahn movement never recovered from that. The favourable attitude of citizens and their identification with the campaign went into rapid decline.'[29]

Problems with the enemy image

'Lord, save us from the enemy!' Priests in gowns wearing prophets' beards carried this placard on a demonstration in West Germany against nuclear power. But who was the enemy; how exactly did they imagine him? For the Marxist '68ers who joined the protest movement and quite soon began to produce literature on the subject,[30] it was clear enough: the enemy was capital, big or monopoly capital. But didn't Communist states also build nuclear power plants? And didn't the state anyway play a key role? Didn't the demonstrators at reactor sites have to grapple with the power of the state, with the police?

The best-known enemy image came from the chief bestseller of the West German anti-nuclear movement: Robert Jungk's *Nuclear State* (1977). Here the 'community' was presented as a criminal Mafia, and the Bonn government was 'advised by Hitler's former economic aides' as it ventured into the plutonium industry.[31] But that could make only a limited impression, since any diligent historian easily found old Nazis among the critics of nuclear power too. Besides, had not Germans fleeing the Nazi regime been instrumental in developing the first atom bombs? Two decades earlier, none other than Jungk himself – in *Brighter than a Thousand Suns* – had underlined the Nazi connections of former opponents of 'Jewish' nuclear physics and painted German nuclear physicists during the Second World War as passive resisters of a kind – which, from what we know today, was not the case.[32]

Jungk should have known better than anyone that it was misleading to depict the atomic community in the 'nuclear state' as a thoroughly evil force, and that the atomic euphoria of the 1950s was not so distant from the later environmental movement in its quest for non-polluting renewable energy sources that minimal transport costs would make easily available. In this perspective, nuclear technology was an object lesson in how solutions that in some respects seem ecologically perfect can turn out to be the exact opposite, as soon as their large-scale adoption brings quite different aspects to light. We have seen this again recently in the case of methane, which for decades had an environmentally friendly image[33] but was then discovered to be twenty times worse than carbon dioxide in its impact on the earth's atmosphere.[34] And was the nuclear community really as demonic as its one-time admirer Robert Jungk made it out to be? Many environmental activists who later turned their attention to the car or chemical lobby found that, in retrospect, the nuclear lobby had been comparatively less hard-nosed. The old guard of atomic physicists, under the leadership of Heisenberg and Weizsäcker, had still had a penchant for philosophy, which left other industrial lobbies completely cold.

In 1982 a young SPD parliamentarian perceived the Greens, with Petra Kelly at their head, as an activist scene oozing aggression. 'Every top Green', he wrote, 'carries around a supply of aggressive dictums for any occasion' and immediately constructs an enemy image for anyone who thinks differently.'[35] Yet Petra Kelly found it difficult to make her enemy image sufficiently specific to have an opponent to concentrate on fighting. The haziness of her political activity was reflected in the images that fuelled her hate and persecution mania. 'Like trapped flies – she thought – we wriggle in the web of a big anonymous spider, which sucks itself full at our expense, becoming bigger and fatter and ever more powerful. Whether this monster is called the state, the civil service or the bureaucracy, the result is the same: we are helpless, incapacitated.'[36] Winfried Kretschmann, however, who two decades later was the first Green to become first minister of a German *Land* (Baden-Württemberg), predicted in 1990, following the party's election disaster in the wake of German unification, that the Greens would become 'a socially modern political force' only when they stopped looking for bad guys 'and producing enemy images to fit them'.[37]

The Eurocracy as enemy image?

Petra Kelly's enemy image expressed a diffuse rage, which was often turned against members of her own party. Much more clearly focused was *Die Öko-Bremser* (1993; *The Eco-Twisters*, 1995), a 'Black Book on the environment in Europe',[38] most of whose contributors occupied a leading position in EuroNatur – a foundation embracing several environmental associations, headed by the BUND and NABU, which sought to influence EU policy, attracted funding from industry, but also directly supported conservation projects, with a special focus on East and Southeast Europe. The Black Book offered an unprecedented Europe-wide survey of environmental scandals – from the diversion of the Acheloos river in Greece to the 'silent death' of the Dehesas (the oak forests in Southern Spain yielding pig feed) – together with concrete advice on the bodies to which protests could be submitted.

The 'eco-footdraggers' in question were not just particular individuals or institutions marked down for attack; they were widely dispersed and partly abstract, reaching as far as one's own weaker self. At least a dozen campaigns would be necessary to include them all. But the main target for this first all-European umbrella organization was the EU bureaucracy in Brussels, whose programme of subsidies 'attracts villains as a dungheap attracts flies'.[39] The aim of the Black Book was to open the eyes of city people who had seen nothing but blossoming nature: 'For instance, one spring there might be brilliant yellow rape growing everywhere. Another year in summer there will be sunflowers in bloom as far as the eye can see. This is no accident, but the result of agricultural policy emanating from Brussels, which has long since forced farmers into a vicious circle of subsidies, guaranteed prices, dependency and intensive cultivation.'[40]

On the whole, the book is much more nuanced than the title suggests, corresponding to EuroNatur's pragmatic strategy, to which any aggressive fanaticism is alien; it is not the expression of a frontal opposition to the EU, and indeed the EU's Court of Auditors[41] supplied evidence for the waste of tax money on environmentally harmful projects by the Brussels bureaucracy.[42] The authors recognized that the EU 'indisputably set standards for environmental rights, as with the introduction of environmental compatibility tests, or with the EU Bird Protection Directive'[43] – the Fauna, Flora, Habitat Directive was not yet an issue. It was the time when people in Brussels were on the point of discovering environmental policy as a new cross-border field of EU activity and consigning to oblivion the origins of the new Europe in the European Atomic Energy Community (Euratom).[44] The aim of the EuroNatur polemic was to keep up the reversal of direction. It saw early on that the 'Eurocracy's mania for standardization'[45] may ruin Brussels' environmental policy and lead to busybody forms of pseudo-activity that are of no benefit to nature in the end. Its shock example of 'eco-bluff' was the expensive 'Biological Institute' on the island of Alonnisos, 75 per cent funded by the EU, which was supposed to protect the threatened monk seal but ended up as little more than a ruin.[46]

From 'lead in petrol' to the 'German consensus model'

Even Bonn politicians sometimes got worked up over environmental issues, though not to the point of violence. In 1972 Hans-Dietrich Genscher, then still the interior minister, announced a 'campaign for the environment' to the Stockholm Conference, and thirty years later state secretary Menke-Glückert recalled with pride: 'The word campaign as well as the strategy originated with me. Together with a journalist, I also went to schools to bring the campaigns closer to children. The motto was: the war on nature must be brought to an end, through a people's revolt and a boycott of environmentally harmful products.'[47] At the time, though, demonstrations before the great reactor construction sites, the term 'people's revolt' was thought of metaphorically.

In the campaign to reduce the lead content of petrol over time, environmentalists in the German interior ministry clashed head-on with the Bundesverband der Deutschen Industrie (BDI) employers' federation. The ministry quickly took the offensive, with a so-called 'Petrol Lead Law' that came into force just three days after it was adopted on 5 August 1971. ADAC, the German automobile club, and the oil industry then sounded the alarm in 1973, arguing that if further scheduled reductions went ahead millions of cars would splutter to a halt. The Daimler-Benz house journal wrote that members of the Bundestag should withhold their approval, since they were in no position to understand the finer technical issues, while the Christian Democrat opposition accused the government of acting too hesitantly. This drew an unusually sharp response from Genscher: 'We are not a banana republic that issues laws and is then unable to enforce them.'[48] Menke-Glückert calls the affair 'industry's first major lost environmental battle'. The reversal was not long in coming, however. An ominous closed session at Schloss Gymnich, organized by the chancellor's office on 3 June 1975, marked Helmut Schmidt's retreat from the environmental élan of the previous years[49] and signalled that his government was prepared to heed the complaints of business and trade union representatives. The timetable to reduce harmful substances in petrol was rolled back under pressure from industry, causing Menke-Glückert to observe: 'Since that time I have believed anything industry says only if it has been checked at least ten times.'[50]

The 'German consensus model', subsequently implemented above all in relation to the car lobby,[51] had the result that the Bundesrepublik lagged far behind the United States in environmental aspects of road transport ranging from catalytic converters to speed limits.[52] Leaded petrol was not completely banned until February 1988, and even then, under an agreement with the oil associations, petrol stations had until 1996 to end altogether the selling of leaded Super. The Germans' love of the car was still fairly recent in comparison with that in America, where Henry Ford began assembly-line production of his T-model way back in 1910; even the majority of environmental activists did not really dare to tackle the issue, mostly leaving it to local action groups that wanted to have peace and quiet and clean air in their home surroundings. This shortfall in fighting spirit made itself felt in a lack of staying power among Bonn politicians. When huge industrial interests were in play, nothing happened without a fight using the resources of the legal and administrative system. These did enforce a cut in harmful emissions, though not a rollback of car travel by public transport. There was a tough, American-style crackdown on certain aspects, but the American way of life – the core of the problem – remained undisturbed.

The Environmental Protection Agency (EPA): from 'gorilla in the closet' to lion's feed

The American antagonistic justice system, in which even the ascertainment of facts pits prosecution and defence against each other, has always been geared to the struggle over law; and the EPA developed the same fighting spirit in the 1970s, the 'environmental decade', under its dynamic founder William Ruckelshaus. As Richard N. L. Andrews put it in what is still the standard history of environmental politics: 'From EPA's earliest days, a key policy decision was to emphasize aggressive standard-setting and enforcement rather than negotiation and assistance.' This corresponded to Ruckelshaus's experience of fighting air and water pollution in Louisiana, which had strengthened his conviction 'that strong federal enforcement was essential to make the most intransigent polluters act'.[53] This 'nation-alization' of hitherto local and regional environmental conflicts was typical of the new era dawning in 1970; it meant that it was possible to achieve greater resonance among the critical public, and greater distance from industrial lobbies bent on the exploitation of local resources.

The impact of Earth Day was still fresh in people's minds, and Ruckelshaus could build on the fact that the media likened his hunt for polluters to the legendary sheriff's pursuit of outlaws. Precisely because he belonged to the Republican Party, he was all the more anxious to impress Democrats by courageously standing up to the big corporations. The core of his strategy was to strengthen the EPA's power and credibility through show trials for the media, thereby establishing a counterforce to that of the big polluters. In this he sought support from a public eager to see better environmental protection, not from within the established apparatuses of power.

The EPA emerged from the confluence of existing public hygiene authorities, but in its first sixty days it took enforcement measures five times more often than its predecessors together had ever done in a comparable period. Even when Ruckelshaus lacked legal means of coercion, he overawed his opponents by mobilizing public opinion. He took on the mighty Union Carbide, for example, which until then had shrugged off warnings from government authorities and continued belching out dense black smoke. Without having the legal basis to do so, he issued it with a ten-day ultimatum and released it to the press – which was enough for the corporation to flinch.[54] Its subsidiaries in Indian Bhopal, however, where the largest chemical disaster in history occurred on 2 December 1984, con-tinued to behave in a way that was not exactly scrupulous.

Previously, relations between industry and government on pollution issues had been mostly trustful and cooperative; now Ruckelshaus adopted a sharp new tone that made the EPA seem heroic to sections of the public – at least for a time.[55] With this backing, many individual states also went onto the offensive against air and water polluters. Faced with the power of the industrial lobbies, they were on the surface quite happy to pass the blame on to the EPA, but many secretly welcomed the new EPA standards. As Ruckelshaus put it: 'The EPA was their "gorilla in the closet": the scapegoat they could blame when they imposed new controls on powerful industries.'[56]

The EPA as 'gorilla in the closet': this became something of a catch-phrase. To be precise, the 'gorilla' consisted of a threat to impose fines of up to $25,000 a day on persistent offenders, and under Ruckelshaus and his combative colleague Murray Stein (who enjoyed making an example of corporations[57]) the EPA was quite capable of delivering on the threat. From 1980, however, in the antagonistic climate of the times, the United States witnessed a counteroffensive under Reagan that far exceeded anything seen (so far) in Europe. Even many environmental activists later thought the EPA had gone too far in the 1970s and made it easy for its opponents to brand the agency as an un-American enemy of 'free enterprise'.[58] The weight of the environmental authority was limited and shrank still more as soon as it lost the support of the president. In 1989, when environmental protection was again in the ascendancy and even the Republican George Bush (Senior) claimed that he wanted to be an 'environmental president',[59] the EPA once more came forward as the 'gorilla in the closet', instructing the city of New York, already on the verge of bankruptcy, to safeguard the quality of the water supply. An adequate filtering installation would have cost 6 billion to 8 billion dollars, so it was decided, in the name of 'watershed protection', to make 2,000 square miles of public forest a protected area.[60] The badly rundown city was later famed for its good drinking water. This became an exemplary combination of economics and ecology: not only here was water protection a patented environmental weapon. On health issues too, the proven risks of 'passive smoking' identified tobacco as an environmental hazard and brought it under the remit of the EPA, which during the Bush presidency (and in a favourable international climate) launched a successful campaign against an aggressive industry that was also a frontrunner in terms of publicity.[61] George W. Bush, on the other hand, abolished 223 EPA offices during his first term; a Republican lobbyist on behalf of the pesticide sector had already attacked the EPA under Clinton as a 'Gestapo'. A cartoon showed the erstwhile 'gorilla' as a midget trembling in the arena before the wide-open jaws of a huge lion, 'Business Interests', while in the emperor's box 'Georgius Caesar' gave the thumbs down: 'Eat him!'[62]

The Holy Trinity of the eco-age

In the Federal Republic of Germany, it was usual from the 1970s on to proclaim three basic principles of environmental law: foresight, 'the 'polluter pays', and cooperation. Rather as *fraternité* had once softened the revolutionary edge of *liberté* and *égalité*, so too did cooperation offset the first two principles of the triad. Gertrude Lübbe-Wolff, the chair of the Council of Experts for Environmental Issues from 2000 to 2002 – who as director of the Bielefeld Water Protection Office had developed an eye for the gap between legal principles and reality – aroused a suspicion that the cooperation principle too often functioned as a 'euphemism': that is, it enabled 'cheap use of the environment to obscure the inability or unwillingness of a rundown power of the state to assert itself against industrial interests'. She saw there was a 'two-pronged strategy' in environmental protection: 'Fine laws for those concerned about the environment, weak enforcement for those not concerned about it.'[63] A cooperative style was, to be sure, more agreeable than an inquisitorial one for the officials involved, since it meant that, instead of having to conduct their own surveys and wait in the rain at the gates of a plant, they were wined and dined by industry bosses and supplied with material. But it did not even have the advantage of making things easier: 'In fact, nothing is costlier than "purely cooperative" enforcement.' Often it is much simpler to confront industry point-blank with fixed standards, which everyone can expect to be enforced, but which allow for speedy approval of a project.[64] That was the EPA style under Ruckelshaus in the 1970s. German industrial lobbies constantly complain about the growing complexity of environmental regulations, but this is largely due to the restrictive clauses pushed through by the same lobbies, and to the allowance for special cases that is an obscure and interminable aspect of the German legal process. Nevertheless, it is true everywhere in the world that the best laws and institutions count for little when tranquil officials sit opposite unscrupulous managers.

The cooperation principle tacitly assumes that one is dealing with an honest businessman, who has the will to do his best for the environment. But that is a risky supposition, especially in the case of a faceless corporation not tied to any particular place, with a frequently changing management and an obsession with double-digit rates of profit. Moreover, the principle rests on the fact that a reduction in emissions is essentially a technical problem, and that the necessary technical knowledge is in the hands of industry, not the state administration. So, it is anyway pointless to insist on certain emission levels if engineers in the industry will not play ball. This line of reasoning was not in itself unrealistic: if emission reductions require not only expensive filtering equipment but a change in production processes, the inventiveness of engineers is a *sine qua non* and official regulations can go no further. New technology has undermined traditional recycling techniques, since electronic devices contain many more components than earlier ones, often no more than 'tweaks' in minute precision parts. One central lesson of the eco-age, which is still far from over, is that mere 'end-of-pipe' technologies and ever costlier recycling processes become a dead end for environmental protection, and that lasting solutions must already be developed at the design stage to avoid harmful discharges and to enable repeated use of products. Such a reversal, which would also make environmental protection much less complicated, is possible only through cooperation with industry. The scarcer that certain raw materials become, the more is their reusability also in the interests of producers.

Thus, the German consensus model, which contrasted so sharply with the climate of the anti-nuclear campaign, was not without advantages in comparison with the tougher style of US environmental policy in the 1970s. American society increasingly divided into friends and enemies of environmental protection, whereas Germany in the 1980s overcame the split in society that had been looming in the militant phase of the anti-nuclear struggle. Two American observers noted in 1993: 'Being anti-ecological in contemporary Germany has become nothing short of blasphemous. It is most certainly politically suicidal.'[65] Conflict and consensus are not counterposed alternatives in history, but are often stages of a single process about which no value judgement can be made independently of the situation and the nature of the problem. The conflict issue is a classic example of how meaningless it is to speak of environmental strategies in sweeping transhistorical terms. Dutch environmentalists counterposed their 'Polder model', with its traditions of consensus, to the ideological fronts still cultivated by German co-thinkers. But there too, the 'round table strategy' led in many situations to a weakening of environmentalism, and antagonisms subsequently erupted. There is no end to history.

From the forests of Oregon to the White House: the great spotted owl controversy

An extreme example of the problems of American-style conflict, and of environmental campaign strategies in general, is the 'spotted owl controversy' that broke out in the forests of the American Northwest, and which Steven L. Yaffee, in 1994, divided into no fewer than five phases since its origin in the postwar decades.[66] In the Old World this long-running conflict is almost unknown even in ecological circles. The owl in question, which likes to nest in old trees, became a conservation symbol in East Germany too, and even one of the few GDR emblems that a unified Germany took over in 1990. Yet from a distance it seems curious how seriously, doggedly and energetically the struggle was waged over a period of years and decades – by an ever broader front of activists and an equally large phalanx of foresters, and eventually by Congressmen who carried it all the way to the White House, only to be sent away with the request to agree on a compromise.

But how can a compromise be reached when opposing value systems are at stake: the protection of nature for its own sake, and the use of nature as a resource for human beings? Like the nuclear energy issue in Germany, the position one took on the spotted owl was for a time, in parts of the United States, decisive in determining who was 'ecological' and 'anti-ecological'. How did it acquire this function? How did the energies of so many environmentalists focus on the spotted owl – a creature about which activists in Europe have not so much as heard?

If we follow Yaffee's five-act drama, it began in 1972 with a master's thesis at Oregon State University, when Eric Forsman tracked down pairs of spotted owls at thirty-seven places in Oregon's old-growth forests and started a one-man campaign to make them protected areas.[67] Of course, a student's thesis is hardly a satisfactory explanation for an environmental movement that spread right across the United States; the key point is the magic term 'old-growth', whose appeal came close to that of 'wilderness'; friends of the forest began bumping into friends of the owl. Andy Stahl, who managed to mobilize the Sierra Club behind the spotted owl, declared in 1988 with amazing candour that the bird was so attractive because it served as a 'surrogate' for the old-growth issue. 'I've often thought that thank goodness the spotted owl evolved in the Northwest, for if it hadn't, we'd have to genetically engineer it.'[68] Until then it had attracted scarcely any attention. Often when Eric Forsman told a forestry official there were a couple of spotted owls in his forest, the official would stare at him blankly: 'What?'[69]

A European observer wonders why American friends of the forest did not campaign against clearcutting – still a widespread practice and the heart of the scandal – but concentrated instead on the spotted owl, allowing their opponents to make a laughing stock of them. However, in the age of ecology, it was necessary to argue in terms of habitat protection in order to have something actionable at law. In both the Old and the New World, bird protection campaigners were typically in the forefront of conservancy – and so, with habitat now defined by ecology as a central concern for animal rights, they joined up in this way with the main current of conservation and environmental protection. John Muir (much to Theodore Roosevelt's surprise) paid no heed to the birds in the forest; he fought for the wilderness, because the might of tall trees and the rugged grandeur of cliffs and waterfalls filled him with a sense of the sublime. In the post-1970 age of ecology, however, spiritually informed aesthetic arguments no longer cut much ice in a court of law. When Congress passed the Endangered Species Act in 1973, it provided no more than a potential that environmentalists had to fill in and activate.[70] But if it could be credibly shown that the spotted owl was an endangered species which could survive only in old-growth forests in Oregon and Washington state, there was a hope that the new combative style of environmental politics could be mobilized for this particular cause.

The problem was that the spotted owl, only ever seen by a few, was not a charismatic creature; it could not compete with lions and gorillas, and aroused no passionate feelings. For years the main conservation NGOs, from the Sierra Club to the Wilderness Society, therefore behaved indecisively towards the spotted owl activists,[71] especially since – as the opposing side repeatedly jibed – it was not altogether certain that the creature was really endangered, that it did not exist elsewhere, that it could breed only in old-growth stands or that these had to be as extensive as the environmentalists claimed.[72] In July 1989 a crowd of angry loggers gathered at Forks in Washington state, the 'world's logging capital', and to the speaker's rhetorical question: 'Do you think Spotted Owls can survive in old growth only?' they answered as in a refrain: 'No! No! No!'[73]

The loggers and the lumber industry had support in large parts of the regional Forest Service (FS), which, if necessary, could keep up with their use of ecological jargon. In its heroic early days under Gifford Pinchot in the early twentieth century, the FS had treated as 'poachers' the lumber companies that ate up public forest without caring two hoots about sustainability. But it had long since made its peace with the industry, and at least giants like Weyerhaeuser,[74] acting out of self-interest, could see that the unregulated plunder of forest resources would lead to ruin. The Friends of the Wilderness had gained their national parks, mainly in mountainous areas where timber use was anyway not economically attractive; so until the 1960s peaceful coexistence had been the rule among the various forest interests. In the late fifties, when David Brower became more aggressive towards foresters and complained that the whole wisdom of the FS had shrunk to skill with chainsaws, the Club's committee winced and thought he had gone mad.[75]

At the latest by the eco-age, however, the consensus between foresters and friends of the wilderness entered into crisis. Loggers were pushing into old stands that had previously been untouched (without belonging to national parks);[76] Friends of the Wilderness was showing a new fighting spirit and felt that the ethos and intellectual level of the FS had pitifully declined since Pinchot's time. Yet in important respects this combativeness cut across the 'ecological revolution' of 1970: it was part of a scene staked out by biological specialists with legal frameworks in mind. The stated objective was to save particular wildlife species, not the ecosystem as a whole. Moreover, it did not involve saving the natural foundations of human existence, but rather the protection of nature *against* humans – on a scale that threatened the livelihood of whole logging communities. Not surprisingly, these proactive musclemen mobilized to fight back, no doubt egged on by their companies, but also on their own initiative. Chuck Leavell, the long-time Rolling Stones keyboarder, tetchily remarked after he had become a forest owner: 'Public opinion now shifted, so that the rights of the Northern spotted owl, for instance, are viewed as being just as important as those of the loggers wanting to remove trees from public lands. Frankly, even more so.'[77]

The 'enviros' operated through expert consultants, lawyers and media reports; the loggers demonstrated in Washington. In this case, the grassroots movement sprang up not among environmental activists but on the opposing side. Ron Arnold and Alan Gottlieb (the latter a notorious firearms freak and publisher of *Gun Week*) – the two most aggressive spokespersons of the gathering 'Wise Use' movement, for which the spotted owl controversy was manna from heaven[78] – played their trump card by constructing a core American 'We' against the enviros, as if the farming crises in the West due to wind erosion and overgrazing had never happened. 'We wise users are the real environmentalists', they wrote. 'We are the real stewards of the land. We're the farmers who have tilled this land and the ranchers who have managed this land and we've done it successfully for generations. We're the miners and the loggers who depend for our livelihood on this land. . . . These critics who call themselves environmentalists, they're actually elitists.'[79]

A joke question did the rounds even among American enviros: 'Are you an environmentalist, or do you work for a living?' Sociologically, the 'struggle for nature' was waged by urban middle-class people, who saw the forest as a place for recreation, against sections of the population who had lived there for centuries and were linked to it in very tangible ways.[80] To the public outside the region, however, loggers seemed like mere backwoodsmen in comparison with environmentalists. The mood darkened all the more as the timber industry fell behind the surging 'new economy' and scapegoated the spotted owl and its fans as distractions from the structural causes of the crisis.[81] Blacklists began to circulate, inviting recipients to wage a telephone campaign of terror against the named environmentalists: 'This is a spotted-owl-loving son of a bitch' gives some idea of the tone.[82] The media showed spotted owls that had been shot and nailed to Forest Service notice boards.[83] Violence was in the air; no other environmental issue fuelled it as much.[84]

All this gave the 'anti-enviros' a perfect opportunity to counterattack, as Ronald Reagan and his successor, George Bush, poured scorn on the 'spotted owl people'.[85] It thus became a question of honour for environmentalists to protect the bird, and the new ecological tide that began to build in the late 1980s provided the momentum. This face-off came at a price, however. Unlike in the days of Theodore Roosevelt, who extolled conservation as a beacon of old American virtues and virility, environmentalists active in this new battleground did not convincingly represent the public welfare and American values, but could be branded by their opponents as an influential group of bird lovers obsessed with a fixed idea. This made them an easy target for hate campaigns. Goddamn it, loggers said, the future of our children is more important than the future of spotted owls! By making the owl their *casus belli*, the enviro camp blocked any possibility of agreement.

With an eye to past experiences, leading East German conservationists today warn that a strategy entirely geared to species preservation makes them appear less persuasive and credible to the public; there can be no ecological or political justification for protecting a particular species at the expense of all other interests, so that the building of a bridge over the Elbe at Dresden is halted because of the threat to a certain kind of bat. 'If reduced to species protection, conservation is in danger of losing its cultural dimension.'[86]

The forest would have offered the best chance for an association of economics with ecology, even in the expanses of North America, but the spotted owl conflict put an end to that. It contained nothing of the Rio spirit of 1992 or the new buzzword 'sustainable development'. In comparison, the German forest scene – where so many battles had been fought in the past – remained surprisingly quiet in the eco-age. The 'death of the forest' alarm shifted the main focus to the damaged state of the forest, presenting only an unclear enemy image and few targets for demonstrators other than smokestack-climbers.

Problems in shifting the focus from nuclear power to gene technology

As we have seen, many German activists in the 1980s attempted to transfer the anti-nuclear-power model to the fight against gene technology. This was a success only in words, however, not at the level of action; gene technology lacked the kind of targets and highly visible objects that nuclear power plants presented. Here and there genetically modified plants were ripped out of experimental fields, but in general the question of violence so hotly debated in the anti-nuclear scene did not arise. In 1984 the Bundestag set up a committee of inquiry into the 'opportunities and risks of gene technology' – its title recalled the 'civil dialogue on nuclear energy' a decade earlier, with its discussions of pros and cons, although the chair, SPD parliamentarian Wolf-Michael Catenhusen, thought this premature, since everyone took a more nuanced position than a simple 'no'. In any event, both the risks and opportunities were much more hypothetical than in the case of nuclear energy; the basic dilemma was that they could be established only by trial and error.[87] Both sides tended to exaggerate the differences between genetically modified variants and those artificially cultivated with 'conventional' methods.

In principle, it was possible for there to be 'Green' directions in gene technology that dramatically reduced the need for pesticides. But precisely in the case of robust variants there was an especially high risk of epidemic multiplication – an unclear scenario for supporters and opponents alike. Many critics tried to underpin their position with emotional indictments of artificial human breeding, but this was no more than shadow-boxing, since industry (at least initially) had no interest in the matter and few if any scientists cherished this old Frankenstein ambition.

Things heated up when the agricultural industry began to introduce genetic modification. The opposition centred not so much on safety issues as on the patentability of new variants and the resulting formation of agribusiness monopolies, so that the anti-GM front stretched all the way from Bavaria to Bengal. The left's mistrust of capitalist profit maximization reached breaking point, but now the critics of gene technology also found allies in the Christian Social Union and among Bavarian farmers. An economic card also strengthened their hand, without any need for demonic enemy images: that is, at least in the EU, there was no actual demand for the introduction of GM organisms; the crucial problem for Central and West European farming had always been overproduction, not a shortage of food. The adage on everyone's lips was that the hardest task for GM developers was the invention of demand. Consequently, reservations about gene technology spread in European agriculture even without mass protest actions. Things were different in many sectors of the pharmaceutical industry: it was hard to object, for example, to the development of better-tolerated insulin by means of genetic modification; insulin extraction from pig carcasses was not exactly an appetizing model of 'natural' production methods.

Recently, the basic pattern of the GM controversy has been repeated in relation to nanotechnology. Whereas environmentalist critiques focus elsewhere on the dangers of gigantomania, the even eerier risks in this case stem from entry into realms below the threshold of all human perception. Again, speculation about the risks and opportunities keeps spiralling upward. Even more than 'gene technology', however, 'nanotechnology' is a PR-motivated collective term for a number of discrete sectors, some of which are not as new as they are made out to be.[88] Blanket judgements and simple 'for' and 'against' campaigns make little sense.

The Zurich model of consensus in transport policy

All around the world there are two huge policy areas which, though not usually considered 'ecological', are even more important than classic ones for the environment: *transport* and *farming*. In both, environmentalism requires creative solutions, not a simple decision between existing alternatives, and sharply polarized positions therefore threaten to act as an obstacle to sustainable environmental protection.

Those who dream of putting everyone on a bike are told by seasoned campaigners for alternative transport systems that such a vision plays into the hands of the car lobby by alienating all actual or would-be owners of a motor vehicle. Since 1985 or thereabouts, Switzerland – with Zurich out in front – has unobtrusively become the international model for supporters of an eco-friendly transport revolution. One of the Zurich players, the engineer Willi Hüsler, reported in 1990 to an environmental congress in Frankfurt ('Fortschritt vom Auto') that this turn came out of a distinctively Swiss conservatism: 'There are conservative elements of preservation, involving protection of what already exists, which on key issues lead time and time again to a national bridge-building consensus across party lines, across the left–right schemas.'

Swiss conservatism, though, did not lead in and of itself to the turnaround in transport policy; it needed a strong impetus from the new environmental awareness. According to Hüsler, this combination suddenly generated 'powerful pressure' in Zurich in the mid-1980s, and it has been 'truly wonderful to watch' how self-assertively public transport has taken the initiative since then. 'Crucially, it has not been anti-business: one would be quite wrong to think that many representatives of public transport have a pronounced enemy image of business. The inner-city retail trade itself has a strong interest in public transport, which brings in its customers.'[89] The geography of this mountainous country was evidently an important factor, since any rational person living in its narrow valleys could not fail to see that unlimited growth of car transport would damage the quality of life. Anger over the flood of transit vehicles through the Alpine valleys was widespread, and so reformers could appeal to patriotism and a social conscience.

Harmony with nature against agricultural depradation? *Battle lines and creative opportunities*

Fernand Braudel had good reason to describe the global decline of the traditional peasantry as the twentieth-century process of greatest world-historical significance. That is certainly true for environmental history. Yet the rural economy was only a marginal topic at the time of Earth Day in 1970 – despite Rachel Carson's attack on DDT, which should have made changes to farming a central issue from the start. In the age of the New Deal and the Dust Bowl, the soil had been more at the centre of attention than it was in the years of the 'ecological revolution'. Although (or because?) Petra Kelly had a love affair with Sicco Mansholt, the structural agrarian revolution pursued under the Mansholt Plan was not an issue for her. There was great uncertainty in the eco-scene as to whether farmers should be seen as potential allies or enemies: no wonder, since the movement originated in the cities, and most activists had no close knowledge of farmers. The more that conservationists made protected areas their priority, the less they concerned themselves with the landscape outside.

In German-speaking countries, the tradition of 'bio-dynamic' agriculture founded by Rudolf Steiner had been in existence since 1924; it largely built upon the legacy of peasant knowledge and therefore, in its early period, was still not so distant from actual practice in the countryside. But then the chemical-technological revolution turned it into a small sect, until a new zeitgeist in the eco-age gave it a fresh impetus that led it to join up with other currents of 'organic' and 'ecological' agriculture.[90] In many villages a hostile schism developed between conventional and organic farmers, with the latter a small (but therefore all the more self-assertive) minority. They vigorously took up old farming traditions, but that did not necessarily remain the case. And the line-up was different in other countries. In the Alpine lands – ecology or no ecology – mountain farmers who could not keep pace technologically with the new rationalization processes were subsidized for the sake of tourism and on social-political grounds.

In recent years, French farmers too have mobilized their country's pride in its culture against cheap American 'junk food' and hormone-boosted fish. José Bové, a shepherd from the Larzac, became famous through-out France and beyond when he and other shepherds demolished a McDonald's branch at Millau, a small town in the south of the Cevennes, on 12 August 1999. They gave advance notice of their action, and the police looked on genially enough, but of course Bové found himself under arrest and was photographed in handcuffs with a beaming smile on his face. From then on he was a hero for many of his compatriots, and he soon became a star for the anti-globalization movement and in some Green circles;[91] the global and regional dimensions were here perfectly joined up. It also created a frontline in the popular imagination: a good old culture of regional farming and cuisine, with a plate of cheese at the centre, against the standardized 'crap food' of US corporations; Bové toned down the original *bouffe de merde* to *malbouffe* – a neologism that spread throughout the French-speaking world.[92] Meanwhile, in Italy, a 'slow food movement' took shape from 1986 on; its founder, Carlo Petrini, called it a *movimento di piacere* (pleasure movement), in an explicit rebuff to the asceticism of the environmentalists. It was a new type of movement, which manifested itself in public not through demonstrations but through culinary excursions and internet blogs. Since the 1990s, Slow Food has spread in Germany too. It is a sign of the times that the Greenpeace chairman Thilo Bode,[93] as well as leading representatives of EuroNatur,[94] branched out after 2000 into campaigns against the food industry.

Britain had had its own tradition of natural agriculture since the 1940s. The Soil Association, created in 1946, led a marginal existence for decades, although its upper-class founder, Eve Balfour, travelled widely and preached her ideas around the world. In the eco-age, it actually became the largest 'organic farming' association in the world.[95] Since the victory of free-traders in the nineteenth century, Britain had imported much of its farm produce from the colonies – one of the preconditions of the country's park landscapes, and the reason why traditional agriculture was less strong here than on the continent. Criticisms of genetic engineering gave a new sharpness to the controversy over agrarian technology, and especially in the 1990s the protest movement against 'gene food' reached wide circles of people. The Monsanto corporation became 'a symbol of outright evil', its name being parodied to read 'Nonsanto' or 'Monsatan'.[96]

The picture is very different in the Netherlands, with its farmland wrested from the sea and its giant greenhouses where – to the disgust of many farmers – the futuristic project of a hi-tech agriculture presents itself in multistorey complexes ('vertical farming').[97] Up to now, this vision has encountered stout resistance in its own land and had an opportunity to be fully implemented only in the Shanghai region. In the years around 1990, Dutch hothouse tomatoes became objects of ridicule among self-respecting organic farmers and their clients: the descriptions ranged from 'the world's most tasteless vegetable' through 'water bombs' to 'the fourth state of density of water';[98] but tomatoes that taste of tomatoes can be grown in hothouses, not only in the open air.

Nor do organic agriculture and a gourmet taste necessarily halt the 'death of the traditional farmer'. For, other things being equal, it is easier to do without pesticides in a glass building hermetically sealed from the outside world than it is under open skies. Absurd though it may seem at first sight, there is a convergence between the cult of the wilderness and vertical farming; the less land is used for agriculture, the more can be left to the wild. But this might prove a rude awakening for many nature lovers, since in all likelihood new areas overgrown with forest or scrub will look very different from the landscapes where they like to roam.

In large parts of the third world, a gulf has opened between large farmers or agribusinesses that profit from the Green Revolution and traditional small farmers who have been driven to the sidelines. In India, as we have seen, Vandana Shiva became a powerfully eloquent champion of the traditional rural economy, with its ecological rationality and closeness to nature. Masanobu Fukuoka (1913–2008), the renowned Japanese campaigner for permaculture in accordance with the Taoist principle of *wu wei* (literally 'non-action'), taught that natural processes should as far as possible be left to themselves and, in his old age, spoke of the 'collapse of Japanese agriculture' as if it was a self-evident fact.[99]

Environmentalism therefore has to deal with very different types of agriculture around the world. Many constellations, whether in France or India, offer ammunition for tough battles – but these can achieve something only if they are waged together with local farmers; head-on struggle against them can never establish a new agriculture. The twentieth-century technological revolution, which threw old peasant traditions overboard, was accomplished only through a long process of translating expert knowledge into rules of farming.[100] But where the old know-how has more or less fallen into oblivion, a struggle for the environment can no longer be staged as a defensive campaign by farmers against the agrochemical complex.

In his extensively researched history of agrarian science,[101] Frank Uekötter argues that Central European environmentalists manoeuvre themselves into a hopelessly polarized struggle between 'ecological and conventional agriculture' and – even worse – throw away opportunities presented to them. In his view, there are several reasons for this. Much that has so far counted as organic or ecological farming is simply a niche model, which presupposes a high level of commitment on the part of farmers (crucially often women) and aims at small circles of consumers willing to pay more for their food. A general transformation could only involve intermediate solutions between organic farming and the existing mainstream – a 'middle way' in the sense of E. F. Schumacher's 'Buddhist economics'. In any event, the growth of demand for 'organic' foods has long been imposing such solutions, though not always along the lines of Schumacher's optimum.

Total ecological consistency is not possible in agriculture, if only because there (and not only there!) the term 'ecological' has several different meanings. Apart from soil conservation and the prevention of erosion, it may refer primarily to the banning of environmentally harmful pesticides and of excessive use of fertilizers, as well as optimum material cycles and biogas production affording energy self-sufficiency; or else to natural methods of animal farming or the production of 'natural' food without additives, keeping distinctive regional features and avoiding standardization. Many also understand organic farming to involve a kind of peasant economy, at least visually not so remote from older forms, which preserves something of the atmospheric rural landscape.

These aims can be combined with one another, but a synthesis does not happen as a matter of course. As Dutch and other projects show, perfect material cycles, energy self-sufficiency and the forgoing of pesticides may lead with utmost consistency to a hi-tech agriculture that strips away the last remnant of a country idyll. Biogas installations are most worthwhile for large enterprises, and they tend to horrify nature lovers by making maize crops even more attractive.[102] 'Natural' agriculture does not automatically, in every case, result in particularly flavoursome produce for which consumers will pay more: Karl Ludwig Schweisfurth, the former head of Europe's largest meat corporation, who reinvented himself in the 1980s as a campaigner for organic livestock breeding and food production, was soon reporting his disappointment that free-range pork hardly tasted any different – although this did not prevent his venture from being a major success.[103]

In the early days, an anti-pleasure stigma attached to many organic foods; only gradually did a new kind of eco-culinary enjoyment develop. The triumphal march of Italian, Indian, Thai and Japanese cuisine in the West opened up exquisite new paths for light vegetarian meals,[104] and the meat-eater's equation of 'vegetarian' with 'boring' became an anachronism. Since much in human beings operates through the stomach rather than the head, there are probably quite a few secrets of history to be uncovered in this little-explored territory. But vegetarian food styles did not necessarily lead to organic farming in the same region. The combination of different goals – ecological agriculture, natural and agreeable foods – is a highly creative process, not just a matter of choosing between ready alternatives. In the end, the future of farmers depends on their preserving soil quality and finding consumers for their produce. If organic agriculture results in better produce at affordable prices, there is no need for environmental activists to open a way out of the niche for it. A friend–enemy scenario makes no sense here.

A triumph for organic farmers: the BSE panic

Since no impulse is stronger than fear for one's health, every hormone or antibiotics scandal in animal factories meant hard cash for organic farmers. The BSE alarm, at its height in the 1990s, raised the demand for organic meat by leaps and bounds.[105] Reports that the number of recorded cases of bovine spongiform encephalopathy, or 'mad cow disease' in popular parlance, had soared in Britain from 10 in 1985–6 to 36,000 in 1992 unleashed a wave of disgust and anger at industrial methods of meat production and plunged animal factories into crisis. In late 2000, when the first cow was diagnosed in Germany with BSE, real hysteria broke out there too. The causes of the epidemic are still not entirely clear, but it seems likely that cattle – which are herbivorous by nature – were fed infected waste products from abattoirs and carcass rendering plants.

In this instance, campaigners for organic farming, animal rights and food safety made common cause, and they had consumers on their side. One country after another banned imports of British beef. In Britain itself, nearly four million cattle were slaughtered and burned, so that their meat could not find its way by devious means onto the market or into animal feed.[106] It was a gruesome spectacle, which caused many to lose their appetite for meat. Since the prevailing view was that BSE had an epidemic character, a few cases in a herd were enough for all the rest to be destroyed. In 1994 the use of animal feed for ruminants was prohibited throughout Europe; that had always been the case in organic farming, 'not only for consumer and animal protection, but also because of the moral argument that farm animals should not be fed with members of their own species'.[107] BSE provided a utilitarian justification for this animal ethic.

This vigour of response would be difficult to understand if the ecological sensitivity of the public had not been raised in the preceding years. For the number of people supposedly infected was below twenty, representing a tiny fraction of those suffering from many other causes that had not triggered a major alarm.[108] Satirists could point to the fact that a close proximity to animals and their pathogens on the old peasant farms must have cost incomparably more human lives, and that the risk today of being killed in a traffic accident was a hundred times higher than that of dying from BSE: 'Herds of cars should be culled rather than herds of cattle.'[109] It was an irony of history that – if the hypothesis mentioned above was accurate – the BSE outbreak was a result of the principle dear to ecology: never throw away waste, but use it again. Even the virtues of recycling fall in between light and dark in the canvas of the eco-age.

One aspect was as little understood by the public as in other major controversies of the eco-age: that is, the crisis was not an evident disaster but a *hypothetical risk*. Journalists on the lookout for a sensation blew this up into an acute danger, but their share of the blame was tiny in comparison with that of experts who suggested that the cause and epidemiology of BSE had been clearly demonstrated. If politicians were forced into taking drastic measures, if millions of cattle were slaughtered and huge sums allocated from the EU budget for research and farm subsidies, it was the responsibility of experts to present a 'current state of research' capable of standing up to powerful scrutiny.

For lay people, the scientific issues were as obscure as in the anti-nuclear campaign, and those who went more deeply into modern methods of intensive animal husbandry soon felt nausea rising in their throat. One was on safe ground so long as one stuck to the banning of feed derived from dead animals. As the biochemist Roland Scholz, a critic of the mainstream BSE theory, reminded an interviewer: 'Just think what may lie hidden in this repulsive mixture of corpses and faeces: heavy metals, insecticide, herbicide, and, and, and. . .'[110] In the view of his fellow-campaigner Sievert Lorenzen, all the evidence was that the source of 'mad cow disease' should be sought in 'growth mania' and an unnatural form of livestock breeding suitable only for producing 'high-performance cripples'.[111] Although organic farmers exploited BSE for their own benefit, this seems justified from today's vantage point. But it remains an open question whether the vast, horrific cattle-burning operation was justifiable scientifically or in terms of the philosophy of risk.

Friend–Enemy thinking is particularly dangerous when it may bring old national animosities back to the surface: no wonder the environmental movement was so cautious with them precisely in the international political conjuncture surrounding the Rio Earth Conference of 1992. Jörg Bergstedt, who decries the links between large environmental organizations and government and industry, and who endorses the old anti-nuclear slogan 'Consensus Is Nonsense', complains that 'enemy images got lost' at Rio '92 because of the magical talk of 'sustainability', the 'requirement for consensus and dialogue', and the whole jargon of 'agendas', 'mediation' and 'efficiency revolution'. The new 'trend of the environmental movement in the 1990s' was, in his view, 'to conduct unclear debates, with the motto "Being involved is everything", instead of promoting definite actions and demands'.[112] Anyone who experienced the inflation of 'sustainability' in many platform discussions and came away doubting the practical usefulness of the term will have to admit that Bergstedt makes a strong point. But sweeping judgements of the environmental movement tend not to last long before their expiry date. A historical approach is important not least because of the futility of cut-and-dried choices between conflict and consensus.

The motor pump: more dangerous than large dams?

In large parts of the third world, the question arises whether resistance to large dams has not distracted attention from far more pressing environmental problems. No doubt it would be pointless to campaign against all kinds of dam, but what precisely does the word 'large' mean here? When is it possible actually to support the building of a dam? There is no international committee of inquiry to examine and discuss the various possible answers. If coal and nuclear power plants are rejected, and if the large-scale cultivation of energy crops would be irresponsible in countries where people go hungry, hydropower surely cannot be excluded in principle. Nor, in arid or semi-arid regions, is it possible to maintain that only those living near a river have a right to its water. The alternative to irrigation with river water is the sinking of boreholes to extract groundwater, but today there is much evidence from various parts of the world that the overexploitation of non-renewable deep water resources is the most insidious ecological time bomb. It may turn out that the motor pump, which makes such extraction possible, is an even more dangerous innovation than the large dam. Only it is an inconspicuous technology, which provides no enemy image for protest movements. The use of Saharan groundwater on a large scale to irrigate Libyan farmland – a senseless project, both economically and ecologically, which Colonel Gaddafi launched in 1991 with help from Occidental Petroleum[113] – led to the collapse of many oasis cultures. Not even the spectacular downfall of Gaddafi in 2011 has brought it to the attention of the world.

'We have met the enemy and he is us'

The problem with enemy images is universal. The Sierra Club *Handbook for Environmental Activists*, published in 1970, contains a contribution by a student at the University of Washington (the Lake Washington site, near Seattle) in the American Northwest. Together with other students, he discovered an 'ecological wonderland' of marshes just behind the university and started a campaign to get this 'Union Bay Life-After-Death Resurrection Park' (or Life Park, for short) recognized as a protected area within the campus. When it turned out that the institution had other plans, the environmental group circulated a leaflet with a warning: if the university went ahead with the destruction of this natural paradise, it would stand 'indicted as one of the great, malevolent, environmental villains of our time, along with Georgia-Pacific, Kennecott Copper, the pesticide industry, the Vatican, and the no-return bottle'.[114]

The enemy image sounds serious enough for a copper corporation or the pesticide industry, but the bracketing of them together with the Vatican (an opponent of contraception) and the disposable bottle was, of course, intended for comic effect. No barricades went up, and the university administration declared itself willing to 'cooperate fully' with the environmentalists. Nothing would have been further from the Sierra Club's mind than a violent confrontation; it was just that in 1970 it had to think of how to shake off its image as a tame pensioners' club. However, even the far more militant Barry Commoner, a leading thinker of the New Left, considered a focus on particular enemy images as an aberration – a sign that one had not grasped the complex nature of environmental issues. At the beginning of his *Closing Circle*, he reviewed a long list of possible allocations of blame and pointedly concluded: 'We have met the enemy and he is us.'[115]

2 Violence and the Green Conscience

An anomaly: the British animal liberation movement

The British animal rights movement, as it radicalized in the eco-age, sounds rather exotic in the context of Western environmentalism – and even more against the background of the moderate British environmental movement and the country's well-known traditions of animal protection.[116] The venerable Royal Society for the Prevention of Cruelty to Animals (RSPCA), whose sponsor was once Queen Victoria herself, had a hunting elite among its members until well into the 1970s.[117] This allowed the prevention of cruelty to animals to go together with a professional ethos that justified hunting in the public mind – since, at least in stories, the quarry was dispatched with an accurate shot.

In the nineteenth century, Britain became the international frontrunner also in bird protection, vegetarianism and anti-vivisectionism; it was a quartet of pioneering roles which, though interconnected only loosely and not without tensions, enabled protectionists to make love of animals into a source of national pride. In 1984 an activist could still proclaim that Britain led the world in animal protection because it was 'the most civilized of nations'.[118] The earliest signs of this British peculiarity may be found among the Quakers,[119] although it is true that they were Dissenters as well as pioneers of non-violence. In the eighteenth and nineteenth centuries, Britain's leading role was evident not only in its imperial expansion but also in its love of dogs; the bulldog became the national symbol,[120] rather like the shepherd dog in the German Reich from Bismarck to Hitler.[121] As for old Frederick II of Prussia, who was buried beside his favourite hounds,[122] canophilia went hand in hand with misanthropy, as in the recent British T-shirt slogan: 'The more people I meet, the more I love my dog.'[123] This relationship with dogs, more passionate than with any other animals apart from horses, is also an obscure and paradoxical, highly ambivalent, issue in the history of environmentalism; for no other animal has been changed so unrecognizably by breeding. Furthermore, the history of the man–dog relationship is closely bound up with the history of hunting; it is thus surrounded by an aura of violence and epitomizes the domination of nature.

Nor is this the only potential for violence. Someone who believes in the equal rights of animals and humans will regard an animal-killer as a murderer who deserves to be treated as such. At first, animal rights activists made themselves the objects of violence, in the tradition of martyrs: it was as a protest against vivisection that Olive Parry in 1972 doused herself with paraffin and set herself alight – and the British Union for the Abolition of Vivisection (BUAV) showed not dismay but admiration for her deed.[124] What a contrast with the indifference of most German environmentalists towards the self-immolation of Hartmut Gründler! Although animal protectionists usually had no links with environmental activists, they clearly displayed a new militancy with the coming of the eco-age. The Animal Liberation Front (ALF) was founded in 1976 and spread to many other countries, and in 1982 the Animal Rights Militia (ARM) outtrumped it in terms of direct action.[125] On 6 May 2002 Volkert van der Graaf, co-founder of the Dutch Animal Liberation Front, shot the populist politician Pim Fortuyn: not primarily because of his attacks on Muslim immigrants (which had attracted Europe-wide attention) but because he had ridiculed animal rights activists. 'Vote for me,' he had once bragged, 'and you'll be able to wear your fur coat.' So far, it remains a unique case of assassination carried out by an ecological activist.

Britain's once-respectable animal rights scene began to change in the 1980s: 'Young vegetarians and Positive Punks have replaced kindly middle-aged ladies in hats', observed *The Times* in 1983.[126] Now hunters became enemies, and inventive ways of sabotaging fox hunts were devised. Activists might divert a pack of hounds with hunting horns or use anise spray to put them off the scent, while like-minded people in Germany sawed down tree perches popular with hunters there.[127] The movement divided between moderates and militants, the latter often falling prey to hunters.[128] Things became even livelier in the 1990s, when radicals took up an RSPCA-initiated campaign against the transportation of live animals and the appalling conditions to which they were subjected. For a time, there was a 'real state of siege' in Southern English ports and airports.[129] Militant animal rights groups became a sensation; many did not limit themselves to violence against objects but resorted to letter and car bombs, particularly targeting medical people and firms involved in animal experiments. As in the past, the greatest anger was directed against cruelty to animals – more than their killing. Some activists went to take lessons from the IRA.[130]

Even Eric Hobsbawm, otherwise not squeamish about revolutionary violence, had no sympathy at all for animal rights terrorism, which he saw as the work of 'crazy psychotics and fanatics'.[131] The most radical were consistent in wanting equal rights even for bacteria and tapeworms.[132] Political feasibility did not matter to them – or rather, on the contrary, they were nervous about any precautions that might draw them into pragmatic routinist politics and drive out their rebelliousness. They were not in the least interested in forming a broad front with established animal rights supporters, or in parliamentary lobbying.[133] In the latter case, they would have had excellent chances. Since the 1970s – again we see the effect of the eco-boom – hardly any other issue had claimed the attention of MPs as much as animal protection; nothing had elicited as many letters from their constituents.[134]

How are we to explain such extremism, in Britain of all places? The answer is still open, even today, although it is clear than certain individuals and small groups played a decisive role. There is also a striking parallel with the militancy of the Reclaim the Streets movement. It may be thought that in the 1980s, under the rule of 'Iron Lady' Margaret Thatcher, a tide of anti-Establishment rancour burst onto the scene, with a toughness and arrogance that had not been seen for a long time; and that the new radicalism should be attributed not only to the British love of animals (whose subversive potential it deployed) but at least as much to a rebellion against traditional British culture: the culture of pragmatism, Sunday roasts, colonial imperialism and fox hunting. In 1977, at an animal rights conference in Cambridge, the honorary vice-president of the RSPCA had already observed that those present were pushing for action at any price, as long as it led away from the 'middle-class concept that is conducting our welfare and business'. 'You are on the streets; you break the windows. You may be called vandals but really you are martyrs.'[135] But that too is not the end of the story.

From around 1990, the McDonald's fast food chain became an enemy image for animal rights groups (as it did for environmentalists in general).[136] In 1989 they bombed one of its restaurants in protest against the destruction of the rainforest,[137] echoing the action of José Bové's farmers' movement in France. On the other hand, the literature does not agree on whether animal rights activists – who received by far the most attention in Britain – can really be considered part of the environmental movement.[138] Their links with other environmental groups were certainly not without tensions.[139] For example, campaigners against industrial emissions drew on toxicological findings, and toxicology operated with animal experiments; it was thus at least as important a source as ecology for modern environmentalism. Those involved with bird and wildlife habitat protection flowed into the mainstream of conservationism and environmentalism, but that was not usually the case with animal rights activists. Someone who considers landscape protection and the struggle against pollution as urgent priorities will tend to regard activists obsessed with one animal and nothing else as egomaniacs working out a personal fad. In 1986 the leadership of Greenpeace International fell out with its British bureau, which insisted everywhere on an anti-fur campaign. For most other sections, it was a typical case of British spleen. As Greenpeace leader David McTaggart snorted in his autobiography: 'It's a very small issue compared to the problems the world is facing.' The offices in Sweden and Denmark, and particularly in the USA and Canada, 'went ballistic' over the British move.[140] Still, was the anti-whaling campaign – the Greenpeace leitmotif so long as it was led by its founder, David McTaggart – any different in principle from the campaign against fur fashions?

The much broader and older mainstream, from which the animal rights radicals split away, consisted of the vegetarians. Originally religious and ethical in inspiration, but also driven by health concerns in the eco-age, they gained unexpected support when ecologists raised (in the late 1990s) the destruction of large expanses of rainforest by cattle barons and, worse still, the danger from methane gas that cattle released into the earth's atmosphere.[141] But the implications of the methane alarm were not all animal-friendly: James Lovelock, who saw the global expansion of pastoralism as 'the greatest threat to Gaia's health' and liked to shock the public

Rainbow warriors in their rubber dinghy: the classic Greenpeace icon with David-versus-Goliath symbolism.

from time to time, suggested infecting the world's cattle herds with a virus and planting a tree for every animal killed in this way.[142]

Conservation and hunting: historical affinity and emotional clash

In conflicts over hunting, the threshold of violence is low – not only among animal rights activists, for whom hunters are nothing but people who kill for fun, but also among hunters themselves, who already have a gun in their hand and might object that they are just following their nature: animals hunt one another, and animal rights exist only in human brains. As a matter of fact, there are no purely ecological reasons why environmentalists should be so full of hate for hunters; an alliance between hunting and ecology is not so difficult and has actually occurred in history.[143] As we have seen, hunters used to be a pillar of the RSPCA. And from the Middle Ages on, masters of the hunt knew what many animal protectionists learned only gradually: the preservation of game stocks requires measures to protect their habitat. Historically speaking, the interest of European landowners in forest conservation often stemmed from their passion for hunting; nearly a thousand years of pro-hunting forest ordinance are eloquent proof of this. Among foresters, the keenest hunters tended to be fonder of mixed woodland than were those geared strictly to the maximization of timber yields by coniferous monocultures.

Around the year 1900, British big game hunters who acquired the nickname 'penitent butchers' were creating the first African wildlife reserve; for Theodore Roosevelt bear hunters were the most splendid of all Americans. Herman Melville found whales as fascinating as the hunting of them.

Hermann Löns, the charismatic of German heath romanticism, thought that an ardent love of nature was closely bound up with a passion for hunting (and for wine, women and song); his *Green Book* of 1901, which went through one edition after another,[144] contains typical hunters' tales that end with the shooting of the prey.[145] 'When I hunt,' he wrote, 'I want to have wilderness; I don't want to hear people or cars; I don't want to hear or see anything of culture. I want to be primeval man in primeval nature.'[146] Game [*das Wild*] are the soul of the wild; the magic of the wilderness has its main historical roots in hunting. Aldo Leopold, the second hero, after John Muir, of the US national parks movement, came out of 'game management'.

Bernhard Grzimek – for whom it was also all about game rather than the forest – crossed swords with big game hunters in his fight for the Serengeti National Park, but they promptly hit back and accused him, not without justification, of falsifying the figures to suggest that hunters were a threat to the elephant population. Even Grzimek's friend until then, Henry Makowski, also a combative conservationist, gave *Der Spiegel* some incriminating material for its issue of 14 September 1960, which the wilderness star[147] accused him of having bought from hunters for 300,000 Deutschmarks. But the two later made their peace with each other in a good long drinking session and resumed cooperative relations.[148] Makowski, as a conservationist, had no problem about cultivating contacts with hunters. This was not just a personal matter: as we said, it is not rational ecological considerations but high-running emotions that have led to animosity between hunters and conservationists. Almost nowhere else in the field of environmental issues have passions been such a factor.

If we look around for a work that sparked this escalation of emotions against hunting, we soon find it in the novel *Bambi* by the Viennese Bohemian Felix Salten, which appeared in 1924 in German and 1928 in English, received frenetic acclaim, and was filmed by Walt Disney in 1939. Salten of all people, who had written the porn classic *Josephine Mutzenbacher* under a pen name and bought his own hunting ground 15 kilometres outside Vienna, produced the biggest (though still subtle) bestseller of trivial animal literature. Imbued with the spirit of Schopenhauer,[149] it turned many readers into mortal enemies of hunters; no animal before this little deer had ever been so successfully humanized. Reading Matt Cartmill's history of the Bambi myth, one doubts whether it was really Rachel Carson's *Silent Spring* or simply Salten's *Bambi* that was at the origin of popular environmental awareness. But, of course, the humanization of animals was the opposite of ecology.

Not without reason do experienced hunters feel that they know nature better than ecologists; often it is only they who are capable of identifying protected species in the landscape.[150] So, it cannot simply be claimed that hunting and ecology are on the same wavelength; there is no question of that. When Aldo Leopold had his eureka moment, under the impact of the Kaibab affair, he realized that it had been a huge mistake to shoot all the predators in the national park, since this had allowed mule deer to multiply on a scale that ruined the forest. He concluded that it was best to leave nature to itself in the wild. In large parts of Europe, however, there were no longer any predators, and so hunters had to take over their role. Even today hunters protest that they are the best conservationists: the nurturing of game and winter feeding are sacred to them; but if they get carried away and nurture too much, it is they who ruin the forest. Intelligent landowners, in their own interests, must ensure the right balance of mixed woodland, which offers food to game animals, while deciduous forest cannot regenerate if the game density is too high. And Sunday hunters, who are not very good lookouts, need a large stock of game to get within range of anything. Wilhelm Bode, then the controversial director of the Saar Forestry Service as well as NABU spokesperson on forest matters, attacked more sharply than anyone the damage done to the forest as a result of breeding too much game for Sunday hunters. But he emphasized just as strongly the need to make hunting an 'ecological craft'.[151]

Hunting disputes are not peculiar to Britain and Germany; they have long existed in France and Italy too. But there the opponents of hunting are hardly strong enough to risk going onto the offensive, since in the Latin countries it has remained a popular sport and a component of rural culture, even where affluent city people come and practise it with a special licence. As far as the free hunting of birds is concerned, the split between Germanic and Latin Europe that took shape in the late nineteenth century continued into the eco-age.

In one respect, however, Italian hunters made it easier than Germans for their opponents. For, though not unaffected by the new eco-rhetoric, they did not usually claim to be conservationists.[152] When Italian environmentalists, emboldened by the success of the 1987 poll against nuclear energy, sponsored referendums in May 1990 against hunting and pesticide use, they suffered defeat in both cases, since the turnout was below the required 50 per cent. Hunting and farming associations had called for a boycott and were thus able to check who had taken part and presumably voted in favour of a ban.[153] As it turned out, these new issues were different from nuclear power; it could not be guaranteed that those who voted against nuclear reactors would also oppose hunting and pesticide use. Early in 1992 'the power of Italy's 1,480,000 hunters was deployed to emasculate a new hunting law which failed both to restrict their access to much national parkland or fully to implement EC directives on protected species'.[154] For Italy's Greens, these setbacks came as a major disappointment after a period when they had been on the rise.

Things were more dramatic in France, which also has one and a half million registered hunters. On the famous night of 4 August 1789 the nobility was stripped of its hunting privileges, and since then the freedom to hunt on one's own property has been a symbol of civil rights. Exactly two centuries later, in 1989, a new party was founded with the unusually down-to-earth name Chasse, Pêche, Nature, et Traditions (CPNT), and it straight away won 5 per cent of the vote (a share the Greens had taken many years to achieve).[155] More than their Italian counterparts, French hunters tried to wrest the magic word 'nature' away from the Greens, with whom they were sharply at odds from the moment they launched themselves onto the scene. The more that French environmentalists and anti-hunting activists gained support from the left and the ever greener EU, the more their opponents pulled out the stops of national conservatism and regionalism against the Paris bureaucracy and 'the Green Europe of idiotic restrictions' (in the words of a CPNT leaflet in 2001).[156] Clearly they were speculating on the potential of a silent majority. So far, however, they have not durably gone beyond the level of a mere splinter group.

Newly politicized hunters did display militancy, but in the form of blind rage. In 1998, travelling to a demonstration in Nantes, one of them declared: 'I'm here to destroy everything'; 'we'll show them what real men are like' – that is, we'll beat up security police. Observers see how deep frustration about the general crisis of rural culture and the wasting of people's lives vented itself in this movement in a number of regions, although a hatred of aristocratic hunting also continued to be expressed in some sections of the rural population, as did a resentment over the dominance of licensed hunters from the cities. In 1989 a counterweight to the CPNT appeared in the shape of the Association nationale pour une chasse écologiquement responsable (ANCER), but it could muster no more than 500 members. The Greens reacted cautiously and denied any assumption that they supported a ban on hunting. Since many Green voters too are attached to the old peasant landscapes, the hostility is not insurmountable. There are signs that the CPNT's anti-ecological position is crumbling, and there is even thought to be a chance of presenting hunters as competent conservationists.[157] In German and other regions, meanwhile, disputes over hunting are taking care of themselves, since golf has tended to displace it as an elite sport. For friends of biodiversity, however, golf courses are a far bleaker prospect than forest areas used for hunting; they also require a lot of space and water. In a tourist country like Thailand, protests against golf courses have developed into an environmental movement.[158]

The threshold of violence: thoughts on Homo oecologicus

Among middle strata in the modern Western world – and environmental movements mostly have their roots in them – the inhibition threshold for violence has been very high since the Second World War, and higher in parts of Europe than in the United States.[159] Physical violence, once more or less ubiquitous (as it still is in many parts of the world and among the poor and underprivileged), has become an exceptional phenomenon in the middle strata of the Western world and is seen as that by contemporary historians. The very word is missing in the indexes of most studies of the environmental movement: violence is so remote that one can almost forget about it. This is all the more striking because, in theory, various kinds of eco-apocalytic scenario can be used to justify massive levels of violence. If the survival of humanity is threatened, any means would be legitimate to ward off the danger. If man is the 'cancer of the earth', if there are far too many million human beings on the planet, then human life could be treated with even less regard than Hitler or Stalin showed. Such arguments make it remarkable that the environmental movement sees things quite differently.

An explanation might reach back to Karl Marx: 'Being determines consciousness'; the great majority of eco-activists by no means found themselves in such desperate straits that violence was the only solution left to them. The typical environmentalist is well educated; and someone who can destroy their opponent with words does not tend to provoke police with projectiles. Or, instead of Marx, one might draw on Max Weber (as Wilhelm Hennis has[160]) and recall that all great movements in history have ultimately been about the human types, the human qualities and lifestyles, that they have generated. Opponents of the environmental movement like to assume that it breeds a very definite human type, but all manner of clichés exist about what that type looks like: an eternal flower child, a green frog-like individual, a pleasure-hating sourpuss, an ecocrat with a mania for rules and regulations . . . . None of these has a proclivity for violence, though. Environmentalists tend to make Gandhi – strength of mind expressed in non-violence – the founding father of the movement, however slender his actual continuity with it may have been. For the warriors of Greenpeace, the link between 'green' and 'peace' was already there in the name; simulated clashes trained them to avoid responding to violence in kind, even if one of them saw a company goon club his girlfriend before his eyes. Of course that could be hard in an emergency. In 1983, in an operation against a Linz AG pesticide plant, some Greenpeace activists were 'soundly beaten up by company employees'. But precisely because they did not strike back, they were hailed as heroes and their action, the first by Greenpeace Austria, had 'an enormous PR effect'.[161]

From a world-historical point of view, the environmental movement is a phenomenon of peacetime and (at least relative) détente, when people look to – may indeed search for – common problems that unite humanity. But although eco-activists, even 'Deep Ecology' fundamentalists, liked to invoke Gandhi and his model of non-violent resistance, there is much evidence that violence 'at the base' was greater than the literature has reported – precisely because those who write books favourable to the activists are not that way inclined.[162] Another counter-argument might be the militancy of the anti-nuclear campaign in Germany, and for a time in France; only fortunate coincidences prevented the shedding of more blood. At least in Germany, however, it is clear that the violence came from outside – from the Maoists streaming into the protest movements. The same seems to have been largely true of the role of militant separatists in the Basque Country, where one also finds environmental activists who made a point of distancing themselves from ETA violence.[163] As we have seen, in so far as there was a martyr-cult at all in the environmental movement, it was quite restrained; things would surely have been different if the general mindset had been more open to violence.

Wilderness and wildness

The two Western environmentalists who created the greatest stir, preaching violence against objects that also endangered human lives, were the Canadian Paul Watson (whose ship *Whales Forever* fought illegal whalers) and Dave Foreman, the founder of Earth First! and a campaigner for nature in the wild. Significantly, both are North Americans committed to wilderness protection, rather than environmental protection in the broader, and above all more human-oriented, sense of the term. Foreman actually said: 'I hate the word environment. You can love a forest. You can love a mountain. You can love a plant. But how can you love an abstract concept like the environment?'[164] There is a certain logic in the fact that cultural barriers to violence are overcome most easily with an enthusiasm for the wild. (An exception, perhaps, is when environmentalists are provoked by the violence of others, but hardline opponents usually have a hard time finding environmental activists to go along with their planned escalation of violence.) Ron Arnold, a spokesperson for tough-as-nails American anti-enviros, sent a copy of his *Ecology Wars* to the 'ocean warrior' Paul Watson, penning a dedication: 'To Captain Paul Watson – who understands what the war is about. Salute from an admiring opponent – Best wishes Ron Arnold.'[165] *Ecology Wars* has the subtitle '*Environmentalism as if People Mattered*' – an ironical allusion and riposte to Schumacher's cult book *Small is Beautiful: A Study of Economics as if People Mattered* (1973). Arnold himself had once been part of the Sierra Club; he knew his way around the eco-scene.

Spellbound by the enemy image: the 'ocean warrior' Paul Watson

Paul Watson (b. 1950), who started out as a Canadian coastguard employee, was one of Greenpeace's early ocean heroes; he also claimed to be one of its founders, although this is disputed by Greenpeace. In 1977, however, he took part in a rainbow warrior 'mutiny' against David McTaggart (a term the Greenpeace leader himself used to refer to it!). At the time, McTaggart wanted to suspend an operation against an Icelandic whaler, on the grounds that Greenpeace's legal position was becoming dicey and that, if it pushed things so far as to offend the national honour, a swing he detected in the public mood in Iceland towards the rainbow warriors would be put at risk.[166] This was a basic diplomatic principle for the

In 1977 the 'Ocean Warrior' Paul Watson (b. 1950) walked out of Greenpeace and founded the Sea Shepherd Conservation Society, to campaign against the 'exploitation' of sea creatures. The photo, taken in January 2006, shows him beside his ship, which was detained by the South African authorities in Cape Town.

astute founder of Greenpeace, who was not only a campaigner but also a businessman and an experienced charmer.

It was just that kind of sensitive appraisal which Watson despised with all his being. He broke with Greenpeace and founded his own Sea Shepherd Conservation Society, winning support from Britain's venerable RSPCA[167] and financial sponsorship from Cleveland Amory, the founder of a Fund for Animals,[168] purchasing a ship (*Sea Shepherd*, later renamed *Whales Forever*) and insulting his former comrades as 'Greenpissers'[169] or worse. Whereas Robin Wood split from Greenpeace because the environmental multinational had become too hierarchical for its Hamburg grassroots activists, Watson outdid McTaggart in his captain's ambition to be 'master next God', without actually being in possession of a shipmaster's certificate. Whereas Robin Wood thought Greenpeace too one-sidedly fixated on the ocean, Watson directed all his passion towards whales, all his hatred towards whalers; other issues were of no interest to him. Love and hate, not ecology and environmental politics, were his driving forces. Film people were thrilled with Watson's militancy, and the Ocean Warrior became the theme of a reality TV show. His popularity may be gauged by the fact that he featured in his own cartoon series (*South Park*) as a down-at-heel ship's captain and a 'media whore'. Sea Shepherd and Greenpeace repeatedly competed with each other on the high seas for media attention. It would seem that Watson helped to mobilize Greenpeace on the issue of whale protection.

Watson had his ship's bow coated with 18 tons of concrete, so that it could simply ram whalers and ram them again until they sank. This by no means entailed complete contempt for the law; in fact, he mainly hit out at ships violating international agreements that restricted whale hunting. Appealing to the UN Earth Charter, he argued that on the high seas – where executive force was lacking to enforce international agreements – bold activists must assist the victory of justice, as knightly heroes did in medieval epics. In his view, the pirates were not he and his people but the whalers they had in their sights. Watson's position lacked neither logic nor persuasiveness in terms of legal theory, and indeed, in the court cases he landed himself with, he was not treated as a pirate and more than once regained both his liberty and his ship. The International Whaling Commission (IWC) even recognized Sea Shepherd early on as an environmental organization, although it later withdrew this status after Watson publicly admitted (in 1986) that he had sunk two Icelandic whaling ships and ravaged a whale-processing factory in Reykjavik. From his base in Vancouver, he declared that the Icelandic whalers had been engaged in criminal activity,[170] and given the worldwide disgust Iceland did not even press charges.[171] There was something rather arbitrary about his legal philosophy, however. For when he was no longer covered by IWC law, he made an appeal to natural law – not as the humanist theorists of early modernity understood it, but in the sense of the 'laws of ecology'.[172]

Watson started out as a daredevil maverick. His wake-up call, he tells us, came when he looked into the eyes of a dying sperm whale that had been harpooned from a Soviet ship; the Russians seized him and took him on board, where he jumped onto the now-dead whale. His memoirs, which are filled with a sense of adventure, quote approvingly Captain Ahab's motto from *Moby-Dick*: 'What I've dared, I've willed; and what I've willed, I'll do!' Yet he presents himself as an anti-Ahab – as obsessed with hunting whalers as Ahab was with hunting whales. To begin with, he constructs a thoroughly repulsive enemy image that is hardly of the same stature as Ahab: the whaler *Sierra*, an ocean outlaw on the Japanese payroll, with a Portuguese flag and a Norwegian captain. Before he rammed the ship several times – it was 15 July 1979 – he radioed to the captain: 'You goddamn whale-killer, you son of a bitch, your career is over.'[173] And later he told a Canadian interviewer: 'The ramming of the whaler was the most satisfying thing I've done in my life . . . .'

He was lucky that none of the crew was injured: 'Aggression against the whalers appeared to be socially acceptable. However, public opinion could turn quickly against us if a whaler were killed or injured.'[174] Still, when the *Tonna* – the sister-ship of the *Sierra* – sank in 1978, and the captain went down with it in the old heroic style, Watson 'celebrated the death of the pirate whaling captain'.[175] One gets the impression that he rejected violence against humans mainly out of consideration for the courts and the media. But when it is a question of charismatic animals, violence against hunters is sometimes tolerated even by people fundamentally opposed to it. The Bambi myth has had its effect.

For many others, however, it was going too far to sink a ship, even if the crew managed to escape with their lives. 'The mainstream environmental movement accused me of setting the cause of whale protection back a decade.'[176] Even if one does not blame Watson for unceremoniously ramming a whaler who kills young calves in open breach of quotas and any notion of sustainability, the Friend–Enemy stereotype becomes shakier when he applies it not only to Greenpeace but to ordinary Japanese dolphin fishermen, as he did in his 'dolphin war' of 1981. A Greenpeace press officer had previously warned that *Sea Shepherd* would achieve nothing from it, since the Japanese were 'tired of American environmentalists telling them what to do with their fish.'[177] Yet whaling and fishing off the coast – not, it is true, on the high seas – were an old Japanese tradition, and in the years of hunger after the Second World War many Japanese would not have survived otherwise.

A spokesperson for Greenpeace Japan implored Watson (as he recalls in his memoirs): 'Captain Watson, I am Japanese and I think I understand the Japanese people better than you do. You should go home and let us solve this problem. The Japanese people will stop killing dolphins only through their own efforts.' And a fisherman complained that there were 'over 300,000 dolphins' out there that ate fish and deprived fishing families of food. He asked: 'If you had to choose between saving the life of a dolphin or saving the life of Iki island fisherman, what choice would you make?' To which Watson replied, proud of his brutal candour: 'I would save the dolphin. That is my duty. I did not come to Iki to rescue fishermen.' He actually seems to have enjoyed upsetting the fishermen, who were behaving in a remarkably peaceful manner.[178] One can understand why Stephen Maxwell, an old acquaintance from Greenpeace days, roared at Watson off the Japanese coast: 'Your violence is going to kill more dolphins than the Japanese, you egocentric bastard.'[179]

Watson refers with undisguised pleasure to arguments against his campaigning style: he has absolutely no wish to be reasonable; he's spoiling for a fight, whatever the cost. Whereas Greenpeace, heeding national sensitivities, deliberately avoids always targeting the same countries, Watson is indifferent to such concerns and singles out the Japanese as the most obdurate whale hunters. The open cynicism with which the IWC, mainly under Japanese pressure, allowed the continuation of whaling for 'scientific' purposes lent many of the *Sea Shepherd* operations a higher legitimacy in the eyes of whale lovers. Even supporters of non-violence had to admit that purely legal methods did not get far against hard-boiled whalers. Watson's opponents sought to brand him as a terrorist – a devastating stigma in Western public opinion – but they were not successful. On 26 April 2000, *Time Magazine* even named him one of the environmental heroes of the twentieth century.

At an animal rights convention in 2002, he is said to have made the – unfortunately not altogether unrealistic – statement: 'There's nothing wrong with being a terrorist, as long as you win. Then you write the history.'[180] All the more remarkable is it that in 2003 he was elected onto the board of the Sierra Club for three years. Although he played the wild-eyed maverick, he had taken care to find allies. Early on he had treated Foreman and Earth First! as bedfellows and made contact with British animal rights militants. He also agreed with Foreman that far too many people lived on planet earth. His trajectory is mirrored in his marital life: he was wedded first to a founder of Greenpeace Quebec and then – after a former Playboy model – to an animal rights activist.

Arne Naess, the Norwegian 'Deep Ecology' philosopher, disapproved of whalers: not on rational ecological grounds – that whales were a threatened species or that, as protectionists claimed, they occupied a special position among mammals – but out of a fundamental respect for the 'richness and diversity of life forms on Earth'.[181] We do not hear, however, that he ever took on Norwegian whalers with a spectacular action such as his abseiling over a threatened fjord. This reticence had its reasons: for such a confrontation would have risked losing the sympathy even of environmentally aware compatriots who honoured him as a mentor. His Deep Ecology did not have doctrinaire features; rather, he stood as a philosopher in the tradition of the critique of knowledge, and one of his 'six norms for an objective discussion' was that the opponent should not be set up as a bogeyman. He pleaded for radical thinking, but not for radical action. As a supporter of Gandhi, he tended to steer clear of the direct confrontation that eventually developed on whaling in Norway. Even at the World Wilderness Congress, held in Norway in 1993, an observer found 'a mysterious kind of agreement among all Norwegians, whatever their political stripe, occupation, age or attitude', which was opposed to the consensus among all other participants. 'Norway', it was felt, 'should be allowed to hunt as many whales as it wants, and it knows best for itself what is the acceptable limit of the catch within its sovereign waters.'[182] The Norwegian prime minister Gro Harlem Brundtland, who, as the supposed inventor of 'sustainable development', was hailed as a 'Green goddess' by the international eco-scene at Rio in 1992,[183] nevertheless admitted that in the year before Rio Norwegian whaling vessels had killed nearly one hundred mink whales in breach of IWC directives.[184] In her memoirs she is silent about the whaling issue.[185]

Even bigger than whales: the problem of law at sea

At the World Conservation Congress in Berne in 1913, Paul Sarasin spoke of uncontrolled whaling as one instance of a general scandal: the unrestrained plunder of the global commons.[186] The old ideal of 'the freedom of the seas', first proclaimed in 1609 by Hugo von Grotius and kept up over the centuries, became an ill-fated principle in the age of ecology. Since then, the struggle against illegal whaling – in a broader policy context – has had two sides. It may be seen as central to one of the greatest environmental problems of the present and future, requiring the enforcement of agreed rules on the exploitation of ocean resources. But if it involves a single-minded obsession with whales – whose existence seems to be of much less significance for the ocean ecosystem than their size might suggest – it may divert attention from much larger issues and spread contentment as a result of symbolic victories. For Greenpeace, however great the media impact, this campaign was part of something much wider, as was the operation in 1995 against Brent Spar. And in seeking a solution to the wider problem, it was hardly possible to do without the cooperation of countries such as Japan and Norway, which – when whales were not involved – were in principle open to conservation issues. In the new round of international negotiations on ocean resources – a milestone in 1982 was the UN Convention on the Law of the Sea – the whaling issue proved too sensitive and was generally avoided.[187] Regulation centred mainly on the problem of expanding national utilization zones without hindering maritime transport. Shipping law remains today the best example of global governance without world government.

Another conflict scenario, usually omitted from histories of conservation, may well be more important in this context than the anti-whaling campaign: that is, the 'Cod War' between Britain and Iceland that flared up more than once as Reykjavik gradually extended its territorial waters by invoking the size of the Icelandic continental shelf and the vital importance of fishing for the country's economy. On 15 October 1975, when it pushed the limit out to 200 miles, it employed an argument in the spirit of the eco-age: the shelf was the cod's spawning ground, and only Icelandic government control of fishing there could prevent the rapid disappearance of cod stocks. This echoed Garrett Hardin's case that only exclusive property rights could halt the 'tragedy' of the plundering of 'the commons'. It was the opposite of Watson's position, which asserted an absolute right to protect whales and derived it from the fact that the oceans belonged to mankind.

Iceland's example soon caught on: 'all the world was going to 200 miles'.[188] Even Max Nicholson, the leading British conservationist, thought that the UK's Cod War was a disgrace.[189] The UN Convention on the Law of the Sea – which was ready for signing in 1982 after ten years of talks, and which, although the USA withheld ratification, was described by Henry Kissinger as the most significant agreement in human history – declared the ocean and its resources to be the common heritage of mankind.[190] But what this actually meant is still an open question. The historical evidence so far indicates that common use of a good can function only within a small, easily surveyable space. To be sure, there are truckloads of literature on the law of the sea. But even in times when most judges complain of overwork, those who specialize in maritime law have too little to do; no witnesses means no plaintiffs, and no plaintiffs means no judge. The Indian Admiral Sharma, who wrote the best recent survey of the subject, begins by noting that the law of the sea has changed more drastically in the past few decades than in the past few centuries – yet most captains were ignorant of this, because of the lack of a usable official handbook.[191]

A tricky alliance with Aegean fishermen for the fish-eating monk seal

EuroNatur's creation of the National Marine Park of the Northern Sporades is as great a contrast as there could be with Paul Watson's way of dealing with fishermen. With support from Prince Sadruddin Aga Khan and Daimler-Benz,[192] the European Nature Heritage Fund established the park in the 1990s, in collaboration with a fishing cooperative on the Greek island of Alonnisos in the Sporades. The basic idea was that members of the cooperative would remain undisturbed in their traditional activities – more, that the national park would serve to keep out extraneous fishermen. For dogmatic believers in selfless conservation, this was a morally question-able deal – but politically it was a dream solution. The Riverkeepers on the Hudson, who pioneered the new environmental movement, had applied the same strategy to protect the river from industrial emissions, when they founded the Hudson River Fishermen's Association.[193] It would seem that environmental initiatives in Greece have played a vital role mainly where they have drawn strength from the cohesion and shared interests of a com-munity – and not least from bitterness at the authoritarian paternalism of big city bureaucrats.[194]

The issue in the Aegean was the protection of seals. Their insatiable appetite for fish meant that they were as unpopular with local people as dolphins were with Japanese fishermen, at a time when fish stocks were anyway rapidly declining in the Aegean. However, the Alonnisos fishermen knew 'that what was responsible for the dramatic decline in fish stocks was not the seals but the *gri-gri* boats that came from outside the Sporades at night and, with the help of headlamps and circular drag nets, emptied the area of fish'.[195] The presence of monk seals there, after they were thought to have died out, was first brought to public attention by the naturalist and documentary filmmaker Thomas Schultze-Westrum (b. 1937), who knew how to awaken media interest. He also believed that the American national parks had gone down a false path, since conservation could be successful only when pursued as cultural heritage protection together with the local population. In 1982, before he began to propagandize for conservation, he made himself popular with the fishermen by helping them to acquire an ice maker to preserve their catch.[196]

The IUCN included the monk seal among the twelve most endangered species on earth.[197] In 1978 the first Monk Seal Conference took place on the island of Rhodes; the protection of monk seals became more attractive, and the Dodecanese began to compete with the Sporades for the establishment of a protected area. Unlike the seals of the North that Brigitte Bardot is so mad about, the monk seal was an exciting object for experts to protect, and so a Monk Seal Community even came into being across the Greek–Turkish dividing line, in the Dardanelles off the coast of Turkey. In all this, EuroNatur does not labour under the illusion that the threat to the monk seal is the main ecological problem in the Aegean; the organization points out that, although the EU may want to make treatment plants obligatory all along the coasts, Thessaloniki alone discharges 'sewage from more than a million people every day into the sea'.[198]

The saving of the monk seals through an alliance with local fishermen is an exemplary tale. For mere top-down species conservation is in danger of producing the opposite of what was intended. In Germany, as in the United States, one hears stories of landowners who secretly advise one another to stamp out a threatened species they discover on their property, since they would lose the right to do what they like with it as soon as conservationists got wind of the rare appearance.[199] There does not seem to be a general formula for the association of economics and ecology in such cases; success stories often have a distinctively local character.

Within a hair's breadth of violence: Earth First! in the fight for giant trees and bears

We have already come across Dave Foreman and Earth First!: in the 1980s they epitomized the militant struggle for nature in the wild. Earth First! came into being in 1980 through a split from the well-established Wilderness Society, right at the beginning of Reagan's 'anti-environmental revolution', when activists could show whether they had the guts and the ability to swim against the political mainstream once in a while. The Friends of the Wilderness had expected that public lands with quasi-virgin forest on them would be placed under protection, but now Washington suddenly became petty-minded and gave in to pressure from the timber lobby. Dave Foreman, until then an environmental lobbyist in Washington, became an angry young man – and in the end he let it show. The ostensible success of the large American environmental organizations now looked like defeat, a descent into bureaucratic anaemia. To quote his confessions:

The crisis we now face calls for *passion*. When I worked as a conservation lobbyist in Washington, D.C., I was told to put my heart in a safety deposit box and replace my brain with a pocket calculator. . . . I would lose credibility, I was told, if I let my emotions show.

But, damn it, I am an animal. A living being of flesh and blood, storm and fury. The oceans of the earth course through my veins, the winds of the sky fill my lungs, the very bedrock of the planet makes my bones. . . . When a chainsaw slices into the heart of a two-thousand-years-old Coast Redwood, it's slicing into my guts. When a bulldozer rips through the Amazon rain forest, it's ripping into my side. When a Japanese whaler fires an exploding harpoon into a great whale, my heart is blown to smithereens. I am the land, the land is me.[200]

This was the attitude to life of Arne Naess's Deep Ecology: an expansion of the self to take in the world, but with practical consequences that the Norwegian philosopher avoided. 'No compromise in defence of Mother Earth!' became the watchword of Earth First!: 'man has to retreat when the survival of Nature is at stake'. In Foreman's view, the American environmental movement had made a cardinal error in dropping its campaign against the 'population bomb'; it no longer had the courage to say with brutal frankness that there were too many people on the planet.

The number one enemy for Earth First! was the lumber industry, although it was much too large for the construction of a definite enemy image. In sharp contrast to Sea Shepherd, Earth First! had no hierarchy and no headquarters, and this avoidance of bureaucratization had the intended result that its opponents found it hard to grasp. Another difference is that, whereas Foreman poses on the cover of his memoirs as a gruff muscleman in short sleeves, he was much more bookish than Watson and indeed one of the best-read American environmentalist leaders. Far less than in the 'ocean warrior' does one have the sense of someone who likes fighting for its own sake; he actually tried to avoid direct encounters with the enemy.

Foreman advocated 'ecotage', or 'ecological sabotage', and the tactic that drew most attention was 'tree spiking': the driving of long nails into

Disappointed at the 'professionalizing' of US environmentalism, Dave Foreman (b. 1947) and friends founded the Earth First! movement in the 1980s. As its chief strategist, he made a name for himself well beyond ecological circles.

giant trees, in a way that would break chainsaws without damaging the tree. This could seriously injure loggers, but Foreman was opposed to violence against persons and stressed that workers were warned in advance of any operation; it does seem that there were no victims of such 'ecotage', whereas one activist did lose his life when loggers caused a tree to fall on him.[201] In 1984 a campaign to save old-growth forest in Orgeon led to a dispute between Earth First! hardliners and Gandhi supporters about how careful they should be to avoid violence.[202] Taking inspiration from Edward Abbey's novel *The Monkey Wrench Gang* (1975), Foreman published in 1985 an imaginative handbook in the style of a do-it-yourself manual: *Ecodefense: A Field Guide to Monkey-Wrenching*.[203] A friend objected that even machines deserved respect. But Foreman answered that when a bulldozer tears up the earth it does so against its true essence, since a bulldozer too has its origins in earth. Or, in his half-jokey, half-serious Buddhist-sounding original: 'The monkeywrencher is a boddisattva performing an act of satyagraha, enabling the bulldozer to find its true dharma nature, its Buddhahood, by returning it to Earth as a lump of rusting metal.'[204] Foreman placed sabotage for nature in the 'proud tradition' of the Boston Tea Party, the founding myth of the United States. The illustrations in the book implied that electricity pylons were also fair game: their toppling was a sport that 'sawing cells' of the German *Autonomen* practised around the same time. The inevitable happened in 1989, when Foreman and four fellow-campaigners – later known as the 'Arizona Five', like the legendary 'Magnificent Seven' – were arrested as 'eco-terrorists', although they were later released.[205]

It is remarkable that, despite Foreman's methods and pronouncements, the environmental mainstream of which he was so contemptuous did not treat him as a deranged outsider; audiences at American elite universities even gave him a standing ovation. The *Encyclopedia of World Environmental History*, which was no friend of violence and contained not a single reference to Watson or Sea Shepherd, ended its article on Earth First! on an emphatic note: 'Driven by an uncompromising ethic', this 'tribe' had become 'the conscience of the environmental movement'.[206]

Many top people in the Sierra Club and the Wilderness Society, afraid that money and attention might make conservationists too tame, developed a weakness for Foreman, especially as his thinking was not as simplistic as his speeches often suggested. Unlike Watson, Earth First! was not just hooked on giant trees and grizzly bears – although Foreman did not deny his fascination with grizzlies – but pursued a wide range of objectives and even made a name for itself through campaigns against beef imports from denuded rainforest areas. James Lovelock, the Gaia theorist, appreciated Foreman's visionary perception of the earth as a totality; and David Quammen, one of the most influential nature journalists in the United States, hailed Foreman's completion of the Copernican revolution that had removed man from his imaginary position at the centre of the universe.[207]

Earth First! wanted to remain a grassroots movement, and some of its activists lived a simple life in communes and rode around on bicycles.[208] One group, in England, took part in the animal rights struggle and tried to link up with the left[209] – unlike its American fellow-campaigners and Foreman himself, who in 1983, accused by an excavator operative of being a 'dirty communist bastard', revealed that he was a signed-up Republican.[210] Earth First! always managed to avert an escalation of violence. Foreman rejected any idea that ecotage was the only meaningful kind of eco-activism[211] and in later years actually turned against it. Nor was he a fanatical hate-merchant: he thought it important that campaigners should be able to laugh at themselves.[212] Those who take exception to the misanthropic features of his thinking should bear such statements in mind, instead of taking his 'Back to the Pleistocene!' slogan too literally.

'Water wars', 'wars in the woods' and the potential for escalation

The attitude of the movement to violence also depends on its opponents and the conditions under which it operates. In a social context where hate is in the air, human rights exist only on paper and the threshold of violence is low for both the state and rebels against it, it is naturally much harder to stick to non-violence than in a stable system based on the rule of law and relative social peace. This is not to suggest that non-violent environmental protest has no chance in the third world: as we know, the greatest preacher of non-violence was an Indian, and a homogeneous 'third world' exists only as a rhetorical figure. Just as a large part of environmental history may be told in terms of water and forest, the two classical common goods – and environmental policy is essentially concerned with common goods – so too may conflicts over water and forest afford insights into antagonistic situations and opportunities for consensus. Precisely because such conflicts are so ancient – even more in the case of water than the forest – and because they have obviously necessitated some arrangement in the end, there is also a long tradition of regulatory forms (often in association with authorities having a cooperative component) which contrasts with ways of handling industrial pollution and the exploitation of ocean resources. With regard to large rivers that flow through several countries (Rhine or Danube, Euphrates or Mekong), agreement on a solution is a matter for political institutions, not a field for the activity of campaigning groups. People in Sudan know that a dam on the Nile would mean war with Egypt, or in China that a diversion of the Tsangpo (the Indian Brahmaputra) would inevitably provoke the sharpest of conflicts with the major power to their south. Nevertheless, the technological possibility of diverting water on a large scale over huge distances, together with the rapidly increasing water consumption of modern agglomerations, might encourage governments to drop their traditional inhibitions. The potential for conflict is easy to imagine.

'Water wars', 'wars in the woods': the alliteration is handy in choosing book titles,[213] but a glance inside them usually makes it clear that 'war' is being used metaphorically. Considering the vital importance of water in many drought-affected regions, the surprising thing is not the frequency of conflicts but how seldom they escalate into violence.[214] As we have seen a number of times, conflicts over large dams and artificial lakes are the characteristic hydraulic dispute of the ecological age, and ancient regulatory bodies or generally accepted norms of what is just have usually been lacking here. Allocation disputes, on the other hand, go back a very long time – not only in arid regions but also in rainy Germany (where they have involved watermillers and farmers needing water for their crops).

In arid regions such struggles were often a matter of sheer survival, and in irrigated areas the distribution of water was fastidiously rooted in the social structures.[215] Conflicts abounded, of course, but people knew how and where these were to be thrashed out. As far as today and tomorrow are concerned, the problem lies not so much in the existing disputes[216] as in the fact that, in many water-poor regions, the overextraction of ever deeper groundwater for channelling to the cities offers no eye-catching targets to protest movements. Nomadic groups used to fight over water points, but when a village's wells dry up it is no longer immediately evident who is to blame. Moreover, the present tendency to blame even a long-noticed decline of the water table on global warming threatens to obscure the real causes.

An extreme case: Israel

Ariel Sharon, a hardliner among Israeli politicians, wrote quite openly in his memoirs that the Six Day War of June 1967 – officially an Israeli preventive war – really began two and a half years earlier, when the government decided to counter the diversion of the River Jordan with a similar major project of its own, the National Water Carrier[217] (preparations for which actually went even further back). No other water allocation problem in recent times has been as politically explosive as the longstanding dispute between Israel and its neighbouring states, Syria and Jordan, and the highly unequal way in which water is distributed between Jews and Palestinians inside Israel. The simple facts make provocative reading. In 1975 Arab farmers – who at the time were farming 10 per cent of the arable land in Israel – received all of 2 per cent of the water available for irrigation. In 1996 per capita water consumption was three times higher in the Jewish than in the Arab population.[218] No Arab managed to rise to a senior position in the Israeli water authority.[219] Thirsty Palestinian children staring with hate-filled eyes across a valley at the swimming pools of Jewish villas is one of the iconic images of Arab propaganda.[220] To distribute water resources in such a way that the Palestinians can control and divide up their own share is impossible for hydro-geographical reasons.[221]

Still, in principle there can be calm and rational discussion about water allocation: the needs are the same for Jews and Arabs and their legitimacy is theoretically not in dispute, whereas there can be no basis for agreement between Zionism and Islamism. In fact, there has been progress on the water issue. More productive of hate was the Green Patrol that the Israeli Nature Reserves Authority established in 1977, under the direction of the legendary war hero Avraham Yoffe, which violently expelled Arabs from designated conservation areas. 'Green Patrol brutality and associated intimidation tactics have become almost a new chapter in local Bedouin folklore.'[222] For those affected, there was no indication that this tough, specially trained force served a higher common interest in the protection of nature. Even the afforestation programmes on the Israeli side have created natural bastions against the Palestinians' olive groves.[223]

The situation is further exacerbated by the fact that, as a leading Israeli conservationist complained, Israel did not participate in the West's ecological turn.[224] It is strikingly similar to its Arab enemies in this respect, as the Islamic countries of the Middle East have so far remained blank spots on the global map of environmental movements. Hardly any other country in the world would have had greater reason than sunny Israel to break the power of oil by turning to solar energy – after all, oil is the strongest weapon of its Arab adversaries. You see solar panels on every roof for the heating of water, but the country lags far behind in the generation of electricity with solar cells:[225] this too is an expression of the weakness of its environmental movement.

It is true that Israel has been a pioneer in the development of water-saving drip irrigation, but this makes a virtue of necessity rather than corresponding to a more general environmental awareness. Although Zionism, as we have seen with the New Deal soil conservationist Walter Lowdermilk, once developed its own kind of ecological consciousness, this precisely had irrigation as its central concern. Israeli forest and agriculture policy-makers gambled on eucalyptus groves and orange plantations, both of which use huge quantities of water. Ari Shavit, a leading journalist, complained in 1997 that Zionism was 'caus[ing] an ecological catastrophe in a considerable part of this small and sensitive land'.[226] In 1971 Israel did introduce draconian regulations against water pollution, but Alon Tal notes: 'The trouble was that this formidable environmental arsenal was never really used.'[227] Negligence on a scale one is more used to seeing in third world countries!

For decades the Israeli and Arab publics have watched fatalistically as the famous River Jordan shrinks to a trickle and the level of the Dead Sea falls by a metre a year. There can be few places on earth where one is so conscious that protection of the environment depends upon cooperation. In this tiny country, where the 'limits to growth' are palpable on all sides, there is also an urgent need for social acceptance of birth control, which Arabs and Orthodox Jews alike condemn as unpatriotic.[228] Israel and the Middle East in general thus offer a cross-check for this book's thesis that environmental awareness flourishes best in an atmosphere of peace. When the supply of water becomes a national security issue, it passes from the realm of conservation to that of the military.[229] This would not seem to be only an Israeli problem. In the United States too, 'environmental security' has been a buzzword since the 1990s.

Non-violent struggle for the forest in the Chipko movement

We have already had occasion to dwell on the Chipko tree-hugging movement, itself the origin of the Indian environmental movement, the strongest in the non-Western world. Its beginnings go back to the disastrous floods of 1970 on the southern fringes of the Himalayas.[230] These were not the first of their kind, but the monsoon had been particularly heavy that year. Here too one discerns a far-distant effect of the 'ecological revolution' in the way in which the region reacted. On 27 March 1973, when 300 ash trees that the forest authorities had auctioned off to a sporting goods firm in Allahabad were due to be felled near the village of Mandal (in Garwhal Province), 'the villagers went to the forest, beating drums. They declared that they would embrace the trees and not allow them to be cut. The labourers withdrew.' The news must have travelled quickly, for when the firm acquired concessions elsewhere the loggers had the same experience.[231] Similar movements in defence of forest rights broke out in other regions of India.[232]

In the West, Chipko was later hailed as an ecofeminist movement, on account of the unusual prominence of women within it.[233] But Ramachandra Guha, the leading Indian environmental historian, has argued that the rebellion stood in a 'long series of peasant movements

Tree-hugging activists: Green symbolic act from India to Germany – from the Chipko movement to Gorleben.

In 1973 the Indian Chipko movement, with mainly female activists, set itself the task of preventing commercial deforestation and the associated destruction of people's livelihood. It became known for its practice of embracing trees: *chipko* derives from the Hindi word for 'embrace'.

against commercial forestry', which began under British colonial rule.[234] To be sure, the Chipko movement was about village rights, not ecology and feminism, yet Guha's historicization cannot be accepted without qualification. In the days of the Raj such protests repeatedly took the form of forest-burning,[235] and so *for the forest* the Chipko movement represented a remarkable turn, at a time when Indian authorities had switched to clearcutting and were seeking to drive down the price of wood in favour of industry.

Vandana Shiva and Western ecofeminists trace semi-mythical origins of the Chipko movement.[236] In 1730 – or in other accounts 1763 – loggers working for the maharajah of Jodhpur axed to death 363 (mostly female) villagers led by Amrita Devi, who had clung to *kherji* trees (*Celtis australis*) marked down for felling, not only in defence of their property rights but also as members of the Bishnoi Hindu sect for which the tree was sacred. The ruler was so shaken by the event that he is supposed to have placed the *kherji* under his protection.[237] The hugging of trees, which Indian women practised in similar situations from 1973 on, was thus a highly symbolic act that enchanted Indians aware of this old spiritual tradition.[238] It would seem that, despite the violent response of the forest authorities, the women of Mandal felt confident of being spared the fate of Amrita Devi and her comrades, and their espousal of Gandhian non-violence in defence of the forest, coming shortly after the 1972 Stockholm Conference, did not fail to have an impact on the Indian public. The tree-hugging movement gained widespread sympathy much more quickly than the later protest against large dams. It was also successful, in that the villagers won back their forest rights. But the movement was a victim of this very success and soon began to break up; eloquent spokespersons were invited onto TV talk shows, while women from the village did no more than sing their songs.[239]

As always in history, the happy ending was not the end of the tale. There has since been a demythologization of the Chipko movement in India: even remote villages have not remained immune from commercial considerations and have gradually developed a taste for the marketing of timber. Moreover, the weakening of the government forest authority has opened the way for unchecked deforestation, even for the rise of a 'timber mafia'.[240] Meanwhile, an amazingly similar development occurred among the Kaiapò in Amazonia, who, once revered in Europe as eco-Indians, obtained a reservation and were soon conducting a brisk trade in expensive mahogany.[241] Over time the environmental boundary between Good and Evil starts to become blurred; even friend and enemy images have their season. Nowhere else outside the West has forest history been as well researched as in India; yet no more than in Germany is it possible to say how much villagers there have engaged in sustainable forestry. Given the state of the sources, this is hardly surprising. The value, or lack of value, of the authorities in protecting the forest cannot be determined in blanket terms or once and for all.

In the dark forests of Southeast Asia: rays of hope around 1990

Villagers defending traditional forest rights had a tough fight on their hands in countries like Malaysia, Thailand, Indonesia and the Philippines, which were very attractive to Japanese timber companies in particular. Again and again we find Chipko-type conflicts, although without the cover of a Gandhian tradition and a vibrant civil society to protect them from arbitrary police actions or club-wielding private guards. 'In the Philippines,' writes Timothy Doyle, 'nonviolence is considered a luxury position which activists feel they cannot attain.'[242] Much is typical of certain basic patterns that can also be found in the earlier history of Central and Western Europe: since clearcutting and onward transportation are usually under government control, timber magnates need to have official connections. No wonder that, all the way from Ireland to Indonesia, a thick haze of sleaze and corruption has traditionally shrouded the upper reaches of the timber industry.

Things are all the more obscure because – assuming that anyone wishes to find out – it is hard to verify what actually happens in the forest depths. If we consider that in previous centuries many conflicts turned violent even in German forests, it is hardly surprising that bloody disputes over forest rights are common in parts of the world where legal certainty and a basic social consensus are so weakly implanted. Indeed, given that alien worlds clash with one another there more often than in the Europe of old, it is remarkable how seldom such conflicts have triggered an escalating spiral of violence. Foreign corporations and forest peoples who are considered savages even in their own country: what is the basis for understanding?

In 1981, Papuans in New Guinea drove Japanese loggers from their tribal territory, and their chief threatened that they would be 'killed and eaten' if they ever returned.[243] If prolonged warfare did not result from such conflicts, the primary reason – as historically in parts of Germany – was that a businessperson with an interest did not usually find it difficult to persuade local people to engage in clearcutting for a monetary reward. The Swiss Bruno Manser learned this from experience in the 1980s, when he supported the Penan forest people on Borneo (the Sarawak part, belonging to Malaysia) and tried to mobilize international support for their struggle against a foreign timber company that threatened to destroy its habitat.[244] As a result, he became 'virtually public enemy number one' in Malaysia.[245] The susceptibility of many forest people to such financial bait is eye-opening, if not altogether surprising. But that is not the whole story. Precisely in Southeast and East Asia, the new elites are increasingly open to forest conservation, if only because of the tourist dimension. To be sure, the resistance of forest villages and peoples is not ecologically motivated in the modern sense of the term. But members of the new elites – not least the judiciary – no longer perceive it as mere obstinacy on the part of jungle savages, rather as a theoretically legitimate posture.

In this regard, the environmental conferences in Stockholm (1972) and Rio de Janeiro (1992) cut two ways.[246] On the one hand, they played a key role in the revaluation of forest biodiversity (previously seen as something backward) into a token of modernity; on the other hand, first world representatives – often dreaming of a tropical paradise – regularly tried to talk third world countries out of sustainable forest use (which in many cases existed only on paper) into the maximum possible conservation but met with defiant rejection of their paternalism. Anyone in Brazil who campaigns for protection of the Amazon rainforest tended to be suspected by local nationalists of being remotely guided by gringo environmentalists. At the Rio summit Muhammed Mahathir, the prime minister of Malaysia, vigorously spurred on the Group of 77 (which emerged as representing the South) to resist a binding commitment on the forests.

The tropical wood boycott campaigns of Western environmental organizations were also denounced as examples of foreign neocolonial tutelage. 'What do you want?', roared Lim Keng Yaik, Malaysia's primary industry minister, to a German visitor; 60 per cent of his country was still covered with forest, twice as much as in the Federal Republic of Germany, and its estimated 8 million hectares of primeval forest were eighty times more than Germany's total protected areas. 'And yet you want to tell us that we are pillaging the rainforest!'[247] Mahathir threatened to replace Malaysia's forests with plantations if its wood became unsellable – which assured him of a 'fixed place in the chamber of horrors of the environmental movement'.[248] He did receive Bruno Manser in Rio in 1992, but only to accuse him – a citizen of the country with the world's highest living standard – of wanting the Penan to 'feed on monkeys' for ever more.[249]

Environmental NGOs condemned the Mahathir-sponsored Kuala Lumpur Declaration, which rejected any international interference, as a 'Chainsaw Charter'.[250] But it should not be concluded that these countries have no interest in forest conservation. From 1987 on, Indonesia, the Philippines and Thailand took a series of drastic measures against the threatened destruction of their forests, ranging from a halt to timber exports to a total ban on logging;[251] in 1990 alone, Thailand carried out 11,684 arrests on suspicion of illegal logging.[252] One is reminded of the 1815–48 period in Germany, when wood theft was perpetrated on a mass scale. Even within Malaysia, whose forest destruction alarmed the international eco-scene with as much reason as in Amazonia,[253] Sarawak strengthened its commitment to forest sustainability in 1988, after Dayak tribal people had blocked roads the previous year and aroused sympathy around the world for their struggle against timber extraction.[254] In April 1989 the World Rainforest Movement met in Penang, also part of the Malaysian Federation;[255] so such a gathering was possible even in the lion's den, so to speak. If we bear in mind the great sensitivity of the issue in the internal politics of these countries, the fundamental opposition to any internationalization of forest policy is understandable. Yet Rio 1992 did not fail to make an impression in Southeast Asia;[256] there was a general raising of awareness, and government bodies accepted environmental NGOs more and more as negotiating partners.[257]

However, government activity in the name of sustainability repeatedly clashed with old village use rights. In 1989 it was reported from mountain villages in Thailand that girls were being sold to brothels since the government banned slash-and-burn practices in the forest.[258] The situation generally did little to promote lasting Friend–Enemy divisions on environmental questions. In 1989 even a German government adviser supported campaigns to boycott tropical woods,[259] yet a few years later a Greenpeace forestry consultant persuaded the organization that cooperative strategies were most likely to produce results and that it should back away from a course of boycott and confrontation.[260] The widespread image of the tropical rainforests as a hopeless tragedy does not sufficiently take into account the fact that the chances of agreement are relatively better than on other major environmental issues (one thinks of the oceans!), so long as one does not make a dogma of the wilderness and construct a fundamental conflict between economics and ecology. Adversarial fronts obscure the creative possibilities contained in ecologically stable, species-rich combinations of 'agroforestry'.

A purely ecological approach to the crisis of the tropical rainforests fails to appreciate that the key to a solution lies outside the forest.[261] Rather like German landowners in the early modern period – who, whether they were princes or farmers, regarded the forest as a 'treasure' or a 'provident bank' – the forest in today's third world often functions as a resource for debt repayments; there is typically a link between high debt levels and overexploitation of the forest. In the case of booming Malaysia, however, which in 1983 was reckoned to account for no less than 58 per cent of the world's tropical wood exports,[262] the breast-beating about the pressure of necessity is sheer theatre.[263]

Sustainability as a synthesis of economics and ecology?

An ecologically sustainable combination of commercial forestry and village use presupposes cooperation between the two players. When the struggle over the forest becomes too fierce, it leads the protagonists to compete with one another in exploiting it more intensely. The problem is made worse by the fact that it is more difficult to harmonize economics and ecology in tropical rainforests with a light soil than it is in Central Europe with its heavy soils and comparatively low species diversity. Although experimental stations have shown that sustainable forestry is theoretically possible in the tropics too, this does not mean much in practice: competent foresters with a strong professional ethos are required, and so far they have been a rare breed. In many parts of the world, 'sustainable forestry' may be an official objective, but it seems to exist only on paper.

Let us not forget, however, that sustainability is an ambiguous term. In the case of tropical rainforest, friends of the wilderness understand it to mean undiminished conservation of the original biodiversity – and with that as the ideal all one sees is destruction. But especially on fertile volcanic soil, secondary forest that has grown back after clearing often has its own vitality and biodiversity. Besides, as we now know, many ostensibly prime-val forests are strictly speaking secondary formations that display traces of earlier slash-and-burn. Despite everything, the forest from which the concept of sustainability derives is more likely than other environments to fill 'sustainable development' with real substance.

From legitimacy to legality: win-win games between justice and environmental protection

If the physical violence threshold was generally very high for environ-mental activists – higher than for radical campaigners in most earlier movements throughout history – this may be attributed partly to the human type commonly found in the eco-scene, partly to the comparative peacefulness of the situation in which the state exercised its monopoly of violence, and partly to consideration for the wider public disapproval of violence. But yet another reason became clear in many places in the world: environmentalists often had good opportunities to enlist the law on their side and to acquit themselves respectably in court. During his time as Hesse's environment minister, the ex-streetfighter Joschka Fischer had 'the remarkable experience that one of the sharpest weapons in his hands was the faithful enforcement of laws enacted by non-Green regional and federal parliaments'.[264] Gianfranco Amendola, a 'popular Green guru' in Italy, who made it his strategy to advance the environmentalist cause through the courts, even said that this weapon should be used with caution, so as not to make the Greens unpopular in a country where the state is badly regarded.[265] This was not such a big worry in the Bundesrepublik. It happened time and time again that a judge would uphold the formal charges against an environmental activist, while allowing in mitigation that he or she had acted not out of base motives but out of a well-founded sense of justice. The good sense that they represented a higher law gave activists an inner strength that should not be underestimated.

In 1932 Carl Schmitt once counterposed a higher legitimacy to the formal legality of the Weimar Republic, dismissing the latter as a 'formalism without substance or reference points'.[266] Many environmentalists, however, saw a long-term chance to get formal legality too on their side and to win court cases; this struggle was more and more successful, and violent activity could only jeopardize it. We have seen how carefully Greenpeace calculated its operations so that it could defend itself by invoking a higher justice,[267] and how the militant apostate Paul Watson, though contemptuous of legal experts in his heart of hearts, repeatedly appealed to international law. 'Each year,' he brags in his memoirs, 'dozens of our people were arrested, and each year they were acquitted at great expense to the state.'[268] From the beginning there were areas of convergence between environmentalism and jurisprudence, and so it may seem surprising (or perhaps not, given the middle-class base of the movement) that it took decades for the term 'environmental justice' to take off. There was certainly endless scope for ambitious young lawyers to argue points of law; the various aspects of environmental protection could be linked up at the level of basic legal principles almost more easily than at the ecological level.

We have seen the leading role played by lawyers from early on in the American environmental movement, and one has the impression that they dominated the larger NGOs there.[269] That meant war, by carefully calculated rules. Since US law – and soon Swiss and Scandinavian too[270] – allowed for representative actions, even admitting them in cases where there was no aggrieved individual party,[271] associations had avenues open to them which became available elsewhere only later, if at all – although they could always give financial and legal support to individual claimants.

In the German anti-nuclear campaign, the media were as if spellbound by the scenes of fighting at reactor construction sites, but there too decisive developments took place at a less conspicuous level, especially in administrative courts. The first major protest – this time without the combativeness of old '68ers, but with support from the conservative World League for the Defence of Life and the prominent natural healer Max-Otto Bruker, as well as a local lawyer[272] – was directed against the Würgassen nuclear power plant under construction on the Upper Weser. They were unable to prevent its commissioning, but on 16 March 1972, three years before the beginning of the militant phase of the anti-nuclear campaign, they did obtain the so-called 'Würgassen judgement' from the Federal Administrative Court. This ruled that the safety provisions of nuclear power plants had to be in line with the current 'state of science' – one step further, therefore, than the current 'state of technology'. Equally significant was the clause: 'The protective purpose of the atomic energy law, though listed second in §1 AtG, takes precedence over the facilitation purpose.'[273]

In the 1960s, the RWE energy giant had relied on the absolute precedence of this 'facilitation purpose' when it snubbed the Reactor Safety Commission and, without asking for approval, set out to build the first German experimental reactor at Kahl (close to the Frankfurt conurbation).[274] The tide turned in the early 1970s, however, and a growing flood of applications from concerned citizens did not fail to impress at least some judges. On 14 March 1977, two years after the occupation of the Wyhl site, the Freiburg Administrative Court refused to accept the industry's calculations of probable risks as a multiple of extreme danger scenarios and a minimal likelihood of occurrence, ruling that, even if a disaster was 'extremely unlikely', the consequences of a reactor pressure tank breakdown would be 'so huge' that precautions had to be taken against it.[275] Specifically, this meant surrounding the reactor dome with a further concrete layer to provide additional 'burst protection' – a measure requiring colossal investment that would have placed a question mark over the competitiveness of nuclear energy. 'The best allies of environmentalism', an insider revealed in 1980, 'were the administrative courts, which had meanwhile taken on the '68 student generation as judges.'[276] But the position of the Freiburg court was not uncontroversial in the judiciary. In 1981 Hans-Jürgen Papier, director of studies at a civil service academy and later a judge in the Constitutional Court, complained of 'the latent potential of administrative law to obstruct major facilities'.[277] Particularly after the late 1980s, the European Court of Justice played a 'pioneering role in environmental policy' and strengthened matching initiatives in the European Parliament.[278]

Outside the Western world, the success of environmental campaigns was based not least on their convincing conception of justice and the sympathy of many judges; often their self-confidence came from knowing that they took seriously legal provisions which had previously remained a dead letter. One Indian activist, sharply criticial of British colonial legislation and its prejudice against traditional village rights, stresses that since the 1970s, judicial activism – invoking the 'basic right to life' defined in Article 21 of the Constitution – has developed a 'dramatically different kind of environmental law'. 'It is important to note that many environmentally significant operations in the mountains, such as the banning of an ecologically destructive mine or dam, have found expression in proceedings before the Supreme Court.'[279] The Bhopal disaster of 2 December 1984, however, overstretched the Indian justice system, and, when 25 years of proceedings finally ended with derisory penalties[280] and shamefully inadequate compensation, many of the victims felt it to be a 'second disaster'.[281] The fault lay not only in a lack of judicial good will, but also in the inadequacy of traditional individualist concepts of guilt and responsibility, as well as the demand for precise causal evidence concerning the risks of highly complex modern technologies – a dilemma by no means confined to India.[282] Later, after the Supreme Court threw out protests against large dams, Arundhati Roy angrily declared: 'Based on the absurd notion that a river flowing in to the sea is a waste of water, the Supreme Court, in an act of unbelievable hubris, has arbitrarily ordered that India's rivers be underlinked, like a mechanical water-supply system.'[283]

At times, the courts have played an impressive role in Japan.[284] According to Helmut Weidner, the 'fundamental turn in Japan's environmental policy that began in 1970' was crucially driven by what became known as the 'Big Four': that is, 'four civil lawsuits in which victims of pollution won high damages from the defendant companies'. Some of the awards were so great that the Chisso corporation, particularly notorious from the Minamata scandal, could 'be saved from bankruptcy only by public financial aid' – this in a country where large corporations traditionally enjoy great respect among the elites. Yet the turn was not due only to the justice system. The legal basis had already been there for some time – in 1967 Japan adopted one of the world's first comprehensive environmental laws – but it had previously existed only on paper. Public pressure and the new international trend were necessary to activate the legal potential, and this process was not lasting but situation-dependent.[285] Nevertheless, the potential survived into the future.

Even in Southeast Asian countries that had a bad reputation for the rule of law, and whose resources were ruthlessly pillaged by Japanese firms until the 1980s, the new rights awareness did not remain ineffectual for ever, especially where it could be mobilized against foreign exploitation. In 1993 the Supreme Court of Malaysia ordered the closure of a Japanese-owned factory, which had been illegally dumping radioactive waste in the countryside;[286] it would be rash to draw optimistic general conclusions from this, however. In 1993 the Supreme Court of Indonesia awarded high damages by local standards to thirty-four farming families displaced by the formation of the Kedungombo artificial lake. But it did not publish the verdict, and in 1994 government pressure forced it to backtrack. 'In the name of development, we [judges] are often asked by the government to suspend or postpone implementation of a Supreme Court judgement.'[287]

To recognize the importance of the courts is not to belittle the environmental movement. This has a presence not only in the streets but also in official departments – and without it most environmental legislation would have no teeth. Often, the legal ground for environmental protection predated the eco-age but was not implemented in practice: it was a basic principle of Roman law, for example, that no one should interfere with another's enjoyment of their property, yet the struggle against industrial pollution took a hundred years or more to produce results. The protection of common goods such as air and water was also an age-old principle

– Roman law stipulated *Aerem corrumpere non licet* ('Polluting the air is not permitted') – yet the common good deserving of protection had to be continually redefined and bodies created to enforce it. Rudolf von Jhering's idea of a necessary 'struggle for law', first formulated in 1872, is more topical in relation to the environment – where the gulf between provision and reality is usually very wide – than to almost any other domain. Moreover, information is decisive for effective environmental protection; so long as the civil service maintains its old habits of secrecy where pollution data are concerned, environmental activists often lack the hard facts to argue effectively.

Robert H. Boyle, a joint initiator with Robert F. Kennedy of the Hudson Riverkeeper movement, compared the Consolidated Edison Company, the worst polluter in the area, to Genghis Khan; and one of his fellow-campaigners proposed floating a raft with dynamite under the Con Ed docking station. But then Boyle pointed out that he had discovered the Rivers and Harbors Act of 1888, which not only prohibited any pollution of American waters but promised a generous reward to anyone reporting a violation; the movement should not speak as if it was breaking the law, but as if it was compelling its enforcement.[288] If the story is not true, *è molto ben trovato*. Out of the Riverkeepers came the Natural Resources Defense Council (NRDC), which to this day is one of the 'big ten' American environmental associations. It is said of it that, for all its zealous publicity and political lobbying, 'its heart was in litigation'.[289]

For a time, France offered a counter-example. Robert Poujade, the first environment minister, made it a high priority to create a legal basis for conservation, and his successor described as a 'quiet revolution' the comprehensive law that was finally perfected in 1976. It bore the marks of an engineer more than a legal expert, consisting of a 'vast accumulation of ten thousand very precise technical prohibitions' but lacking a consistently identifiable legal principle or an overall vision from which particular provisions might be derived. Above all, it did not specify any executive powers to enforce them – no mention of investigators to track down violations, or of rangers to arrest offenders and hand them over to the courts.[290] At the same time, one detects a new problem of the eco-age that would become increasingly important in the future: the danger that the administrative mania for regulation would assume such forms that, with the best will in the world, it would be impossible to observe each and every rule, and that a tacit agreement would develop simply to ignore many of them. The more complicated environmental law becomes, the more attractive it is for lawyers aiming for top salaries to specialize in the circumvention of environmental regulations on behalf of big business. This trend, whereby those who were among the initiators of environmentalism become a force against it, has long been discernible. Even from Vienna, the 'model environmental city', the sigh is heard: 'Often whole offices of lawyers seem to be busy undermining environmental legislation.'[291] Once again we see that there is no happy ending in environmental history.

Two limiting cases: urban guerrillas and 'guerrilla gardening'

One exciting example of the precarious relationship between legitimacy and legality is the squatting movement which, along with the anti-nuclear campaigns, did most to create a climate of militancy in the 1970s in the old Federal Republic of Germany. From a narrowly ecological point of view it had nothing in common with environmentalism, but historically there was a close connection between the two. Not by chance did the first house occupations in Frankfurt take place on 19 September 1970. Autumn 1971 saw the beginning of the 'Frankfurt housing struggle': a militant defence of old parts of the Westend district against speculators who were buying up residential blocks and trying to hound out the occupants.[292] One or two decades later, the phenomenal rise of Joschka Fischer from streetfighter to foreign minister had turned this into a piquant memory. But the housing struggle had a historical importance of its own, bringing back what Iring Fetscher calls an 'aura of violence' years after the large demonstrations against the Shah and the Vietnam War.[293] In retrospect, there is a curious ambiguity in the fact that, although these street battles were a kind of bridge between 1968 and the terrorism of the Red Army Faction, they also represented a link to the environmental movement and contributed to the diffuse radicalism of those years. Anger at the destruction of familiar old districts was certainly widespread. And despite their anti-bourgeois gear, the streetfighters enjoyed considerable sympathy among the general population of Frankfurt; even the police chief, Knut Müller, who had a hardline reputation at the time, later accepted that 'they preserved the Westend district from destruction by skyscrapers'.[294] Since land is a limited good that cannot be produced at random, even liberal economic theory cannot tolerate its wholesale monopolization by financiers who evict local people and drive rents sky high. Opposition to this was at the root of the German land reform movement at the turn of the twentieth century, which once had an influence on politicians such as Adenauer and Erhard.

As we saw in Jane Jacobs's campaign against Robert Moses in New York, the preservation of old districts can also defend a city ecologically. In Frankfurt, however, there was no Jane Jacobs. Its housing struggle began without a theory – indeed, it was contrary to various spinoffs from Marxism, for which such struggles in the sphere of reproduction (rather than production) were signs of 'false consciousness'.[295] As Christian Schmidt, the former editor of *Titanic*, remarked: 'It was a typically spontaneist decision to concentrate on squatting simply because more people could be mobilized for that form of action than could workers for strikes and sabotage.'[296] Only gradually was it seen that it could acquire legitimacy and, in the end, even legality; many German *Autonome* did not want to grasp the opportunity.

A parody of the struggle rhetoric of the environmental movement emerged in the 'guerrilla gardening' that spread out from New York's East Village in 1973 and established itself in many corners of Berlin, the birthplace of 'urban ecology'.[297] Its main feature was the independent sowing and planting of rundown areas for which no authority felt itself responsible; eyesores turned into blossoming landscapes as public space was used for the common good or at least for common enjoyment. In this case, the legitimacy of formally illegal actions has a special charm. With the revolutionary romanticism of '68 still fresh in their minds, activists liked to quote from Mao's *Little Red Book* and used a militant vocabulary and heroic pathos, though more in jest than in earnest.[298] The basic idea, however, was ecologically serious and enlightened: namely, that big cities contain numerous niches for a new kind of biodiversity, far more in fact than do many of today's agrarian landscapes. What began as a jovial parody of urban guerrillas took a bloodier turn on 1 May 2000 in London's Parliament Square, when Reclaim the Streets and Critical Mass (a group of several hundred cyclists) issued a call for 'guerrilla gardening', and a spiral of violence developed partly through an influx from far-left groups and partly as a result of major police operations.[299] From today's vantage point, the event seems like a prelude to the Occupy movement. But it is still an open question whether the new potential for social conflict will lead to a revitalization of the environmental movement.

3 Ecology and Economics: The Challenge of Conceptual Analogy

Mere shadow-boxing? A suggestive pair of concepts and the historical experience

The history of the term 'ecology' has a comic side. It was first used by Ernst Haeckel in 1866, but only sporadically and without any suggestion that it was a science, let alone a superscience; like Amerigo Vespucci, who gave his name to the Americas, he did not suspect the dimensions of the new continent he had discovered and named.[300] Many who have no knowledge of Greek imagine that 'eco' has something to do with nature, but *oikos* actually means 'house', and the word coined by Haeckel had much the same meaning as the analogous 'economics' (in German, *Ökologie* and *Ökonomie*). In Haeckel's time, 'economics' in its original sense was already an anachronism; it meant a lot more than the early modern 'housekeeping'. 'Ecology' got its meaning only as a derivative of 'economics' – the theory of the 'housekeeping of nature'.

Only the assonance with *Ökonomie* accounts for the suggestive power that the term *Ökologie* developed in the course of the twentieth century. It gave rise to the idea that there must be some systematic relationship, whether of affinity or antagonism, between ecology and economics – natural housekeeping as a counterpart of human housekeeping. The former still haunts the ecological literature, but is nature really a housewife? Some praise nature's sparingness, some its generosity, with its treasures. But one must be aware of how thoroughly artificial are both the analogy and assonance in order not to be taken in by the confusion. There is no essential theoretical relationship between the two terms, only a historically changing variety of meanings: overlaps as well as real and fancied antagonisms.

Whether their ideological roots are in Marxism or eco-fundamentalism, many environmental activists are far too little conversant with economics; they do not realize that many of the large-scale projects they oppose on ecological grounds do not even have a sound economic foundation. Campaigners who regard nuclear energy as a monstrous invention of capitalism often used to overlook that nuclear power plants are not very solid business ventures, and that if the energy corporations had had to factor in all the incidental costs from the beginning – full accident liability, final waste disposal, dismantling at the end of service – their cost accounting would have collapsed like a pack of cards. William Kapp's *Social Costs of Private Enterprise* first appeared in 1950 – twenty or thirty years later he would have put 'ecological' too in the title – but it stresses what today seems a decisive point: private firms are permitted to externalize social and environmental costs. By contrast, the 'polluter pays' principle fits into the logic of the private economic system. Economics was always one of the best weapons available to the environmental movement. Today it is more important than ever, since the global economic crisis means that the future of environmental protection depends on whether it can be reconciled with economic recovery.

In fact, it may very well be the case that it can be so reconciled. 'Sustainability' is just as much an economic as an ecological ambition; the longing for a more solid economy and an end to the waste of public funds, which has been expressed on all sides after the bursting of various bubbles and the eruption of debt crises in many countries, coincided at a number of points with an intelligently conceived environmentalism. As far as historians are concerned, the opposition between ecology and economics constructed by eco-fundamentalists is mere shadow-boxing. Anyone who imagines they love 'nature in itself' is really in love with their own image of nature. In the long run, and in a global perspective, there can be no doubt that the environmental movement is rooted in human interests; and one cannot help feeling that economic and ecological energies are closely linked to each other. The modern environmental movement first arose in the most successful Western industrial countries. Outside the West, it was Japan which not only closed the industrial gap the earliest, but also, before most other countries in the world, pursued a reasonably sustainable forest policy and, from 1970 on, took the initiative on environmental issues, partly in a process of convergence with the electronic revolution in which Japan became the world leader. Hong Kong and Singapore followed suit – mainly, of course, in fields where environmental protection and business interests were beginning to come together.[301]

As far back as the early 1970s, Japan offered a spectacular paradigm for the convergence of commerce and environmental protection – with the production of cars that met stringent exhaust criteria. Again we encounter one of the many ironies in the history of environmentalism: when the United States followed up the Clean Air Act of 1970 by threatening rigorous measures to reduce exhaust gases, Japan adopted them itself for fear that it would otherwise be shut out of the American market. Subsequently, corporate lobbies managed to water them down in the United States, whereas Japan stuck to its course. There too the powerful motor industry was up in arms, but, while lobbyists fulminated out of habit against the new restrictions, engineers designed 'cleaner' vehicles to comply with them. The boost to Japanese exports was huge, especially as the new models were more energy-efficient in the wake of the oil price shock of 1973.[302] Looking back, however, one suspects that this mega-coup bred overconfidence in technological solutions to environmental problems.

Subsystems with a will of their own

But let us not allow terminological assonance and a global perspective to seduce us into believing in a pre-established harmony of economics and ecology. It will be useful here to recall Niklas Luhmann's theoretical point that the modern economy is not a consistent system capable of relating to ecology as a totality; it breaks down into a multiplicity of subsystems, each with its limited horizon and distinctive code. We have seen how quickly after 22 April 1970 the panerotic euphoria of Earth Day dissipated in the United States, and how Ruckelshaus, the first head of the EPA, though born and bred a Republican, immediately set the Agency on a collision course with industry. Not the least of the reasons why he did this was to gain support among an ecologically awakened public. Indeed, neither in the United States nor in West Germany did anyone get very far with the cooperation principle alone. 'All empirical studies of the implementation of environmental law confirm what everyone familiar with enforcement practice already knows: that it regularly has to contend with economically motivated counterpressure, and that this is the deepest reason for the sluggishness of law enforcement.'[303] Even Günter Hartkopf, the leading light of environmental policy in Bonn in the 1970s, who came out of the liberal Free Democrats and sought consensus whenever possible, tersely stated in 1983: 'Industrial associations and corporations are natural opponents of the Federal government in environmental policy. Business activity regularly leads to adverse effects for the natural environment.'[304] That was 1983, though; such statements too are time-dependent. But even companies in the environmental technology sector, which made money out of stricter environmental standards, initially opposed them simply because of an ingrained anti-ecological reflex in industry.[305]

Market instruments: ecotaxes, emission bonds and certificates

To pre-empt such conflicts, the United States – and more recently the EU – have been calling since the 1970s for ways of protecting the environment that are in line with market requirements. The three principal methods suggested so far are: (1) *ecotaxes*, an extension of (or sometimes just another name for) fuel taxes, which can be applied to everyone indiscriminately by familiar administrative means; (2) *emission bonds or entitlements*, which major producers can purchase from those who forgo a certain quantity of emissions; and (3) *certificates* of environmentally friendly production, so that purchasers of the goods in question may, if they wish, reward the firm for its environmental awareness. As things stand, international ecotaxes in particular have proved to be rather a political dead end, whereas emissions trading has been an 'amazing success' (Hans-Jochen Luhmann),[306] far greater than was expected a few decades ago.[307] The EU, which at Kyoto only reluctantly adopted this method from the United States, has since been able to distinguish itself vis-à-vis the Americans precisely in this regard.

All three methods have their problems. Theoretically, none could be more transparent than high levels of taxation on fossil and nuclear energy, for without doubt, in industry, transport and domestic consumption, there is still a huge energy-saving potential which cannot be tapped through command and control policies, but only by making energy more expensive. The brilliantly simple slogan 'Tax energy not work', first raised in the 1970s, was theoretically suited to win over the trade unions and to mobilize them against the howls of outrage from the oil and car lobby. But long experience suggested that the fiscal interest of the state prevailed, and that large fuel tax increases were not matched by decreases in income tax. What remained of the idea of ecotaxes was a straightforward tax on consumption – the very kind which hits low earners harder than the rich and has therefore been opposed by social reformers for a century or more. Such a strategy soon reaches its limits. Environmentalists tended to remain quiet about tensions between environmental protection and social policy, with the result that their opponents have often been left to put forward social arguments.

Emission bonds have something demoralizing about them, because they make it possible for financially strong companies to get round environmental safeguards and to continue polluting as before, especially since the price of purchasing these entitlements has not been so high that they carry a major inducement to reduce emissions. For poor countries, there is a big temptation to start off emitting as much as possible, so that they can then sell even more emission rights. Meanwhile, certification has become a lucrative branch of its own; but the crucial point is that certifiers are paid by certified enterprises and therefore have an interest in not falling out with them. Moreover, the effectiveness of the last two methods has so far been extremely hard to identify, and there is much to suggest that the devil is in the detail. Is a large plastic sheet over a rubbish tip sufficient evidence of a cut in emissions for which one can receive payment? How 'sustainable' is such a reduction? To what extent can emissions be measured at all in countries that prefer to conceal them? To what extent is emission trading an invitation to bluff?[308] How can it be established whether tropical wood has originated in sustainable forestry, if there is not even agreement about how sustainability can be possible in tropical forests? Even market instruments cannot do without government supervisory bodies. An anti-state environmentalism that stakes everything on 'deregulation' and the myth of an integral 'civil society' is an ideological tendency that ignores a host of real experiences.

Emission bonds and certificates are among those ostensible solutions which reveal many problems in all their sharpness. Again it is clear that effective environmental protection has no chance without the trio of public campaigns, media involvement and environmentally aware civil servants. One problem is that the methods lack transparency for outsiders, and not only outsiders. But let us not be hypercritical! For someone who believes in a grand definitive solution to the problems of the environment, all existing strategies, taken individually, will appear hopelessly limited. Up to now, however, it does not look as if there is such a grand solution. Environmental protection is a never-ending process made up of steps that are never complete in themselves.

Tourism: the dirty secret of conservation

The new global environmentalism broke through around 1970 and spread more or less in parallel to an explosion of charter flights and long-haul tourism; one suspects a hidden link between the two, although in the eco-scene it is good form to turn up one's nose at mass tourism. In the 1990s, German statisticians noted that Green voters took more holidays in faraway destinations than the rest of the electorate,[309] and, despite the climate alarm, the obvious idea of a high tax on aircraft fuel was taboo even in ecological circles. For more than a century there has been something of a love–hate relationship between conservation and tourism, with the hate not infrequently predominant. Though hugely significant in the development of a modern environmental awareness, tourism itself has a discreditable core that it recognizes only with the greatest reluctance. Wolfgang Haber, revered as the 'father of the Bavarian Forest National Park', wrote to this author on 7 May 2012: 'When I pointed out, in my report on the plan, that the national park would be advantageous to the region's tourism and economic development, conservationists took me to task precisely for that.' Their primary activity was in compiling a list of prohibitions for the future national park, instead of publicizing the opportunities that tourism would offer.

It is no accident that conservation was born in the railway age. In *Über das Verhältnis des modernen Lebens zur Natur* (1880), the founding text of German conservationism, Ernst Rudorff had already complained that the train – and the cable car in mountainous regions – was making nature tourism a mass 'craze' that 'prostituted' nature and destroyed 'its very essence'. Today there is a saying among eco-critics: 'Tourism destroys the object of its quest by finding it.' Vituperation against tourists who descend like locusts on the forest may be found throughout the writings of German conservationists; one of these, Rudolf Korb, admitted in 1925 to his 'life-long passionate hatred of the tourist industry'.[310] The more pragmatic Conwentz saw it as a potential ally, mentioning the Norwegian Tourist Association as 'the most splendid example'.[311] John Muir even wanted to mobilize tourists against the timber lobby,[312] although all he ever signed up were ramblers in the vast spaces of the national parks. This impartiality faded away in the age of mass motoring.

Hermann Hesse's *Steppenwolf* (1927) revelled in the fantasy of pedestrians who, tired of being chased by motorists, started a hunt 'to kill all their big satanic cars that filled the air with their coughing, growling and purring'.[313] A few years earlier, in 1922, Robert Sterling Yard of the US National Parks Association had grumbled with car drivers in mind: 'While we are fighting for the protection of the national park system from its enemies, we may also have to protect it from its friends.'[314] A natural parks movement that was active in individual US states from the 1920s on initially worked hand in hand with the car lobby, but nature lovers soon began to shudder as solid lines of cars rolled into the former solitude, and a new wilderness movement sprang up to fight the building of roads in the parks.[315]

The tragedy of the relationship between car and nature has a comic subplot in the coming together of bicycle and nature after early misunderstandings. Around 1900 the bicycle – still a new and exciting vehicle – offered practice in the new speed frenzy, especially for sportsmen and tearaways. The author of a polemical piece against 'the bicycle plague and automobile shenanigans' described the cyclist as worse than the motorist: 'Staring vacantly, back bent far forward, they speed along dusty roads unconcerned with the exquisite charms of nature, paying no heed to the joyful rambler who strays across their path.'[316]

The bicycle ceased long ago to serve as a speed drug. In 1974 Ivan Illich tried to make it the symbol of the new ecological age, arguing that its energy efficiency made it comparable only to 'the invention of the wheel at the dawn of civilization'. 'Equipped with this tool, man outstrips the efficiency not only of all machines, but all other animals as well.' And the top trump, after the end of the Vietnam War: 'A grisly contest between bicycles and motors is just coming to an end. In Vietnam, a hyperindustrialized army tried to conquer, but could not overcome, a people organized around bicycle speed.'[317] The bicycle is the epitome of Schumacher's 'medium technology', which uses modern advances in a way that is accessible to the masses of the third world and spares the environment. But Illich refused at all costs to be tied to a movement; he consciously marginalized himself with his opposition to all institutions and his ever more radical anti-modernism, especially when he picked a fight with leading American feminists.[318]

Christoph Chorherr, the best-known spokesperson of the Viennese Greens, 'enthusiastically' wears a T-shirt emblazoned with 'Cycling Makes You Happy!'[319] And it is true that the bicycle not only offers the most elegant solution to many urban transport problems, but also demonstrates best of all that careful energy consumption makes people healthier and happier. A solution of ingenious simplicity! The bicycle culture connects Central Europe with the third world. On the other hand, the aeroplane marks the latest phase of tourism, precisely in the eco-age. It is no secret that conservation in the third world – and not only there – lives off tourism. In Africa, big game hunters were followed by tourists hunting for photo opportunities; they were the lobby of Grzimek, who worked with the Marco Polo Reisen tourist company founded in 1954,[320] and it was thanks to them that the national parks extended beyond their colonial origins, often at the expense of the local population.[321] The Dominican Republic under Joaquín Balaguer offered the spectacle of an eco-dictatorship (highly unusual for Latin America) and became a magnet for tourists. In Costa Rica it was mainly tourism which triggered an ecological turn: in the 1980s the country still had the highest rate of deforestation in Latin America, but in the 1990s eco-tourism became its principal source of income. No less than a quarter of its territory was placed under protection as Costa Rica sought to present itself to the world as a model of sustainable development (although reports from outside the protected areas were less encouraging and in 1993 Robin Wood denounced the country's eco-tourism as 'the most hypocritical' in the world). It was not always clear whether the areas in question were protected in reality or only on paper; many had to be enforced amid fierce clashes with the local population.[322] Nevertheless, compared with many other Latin American countries, Costa Rica does not stand badly in terms of its (mostly tourist-driven) environmental policy. Not only does this tiny republic have a greater biodiversity than the whole of North America combined; it also has Central America's highest per capita income and average level of education.[323] In Zimbabwe – to take a contrasting example from Africa – the famous CAMPFIRE programme (Communal Areas Management Programme for Indigenous Resources), which was once the model of cooperative wilderness protection, rapidly lost popular support after 2000 amid growing political instability and a decline in tourism.[324]

But we do not need to look so far afield to spot the link between conservation and tourism. Bavaria, a bastion of political conservatism, but also of nature tourism, led not only the rest of Germany but 'the whole world' with its creation of a special environment ministry in 1970.[325] In France, the first car nation in Europe, it was mainly the Touring Club and the Alpine Club that lobbied hard for national parks in the final years before the First World War, and they were also an important driving force behind the First International Conservation Congress, held in Paris in 1923.[326] The phenomenal success of the World Heritage Convention agreed at the Stockholm Environment Conference in 1972 – which declared not only architectural complexes but areas of natural beauty to be part of the 'heritage of mankind'[327] – rested upon the explosive growth of tourism that began around the same period.

Even the pessimistic and alarmist elements in environmentalism have many of their roots in tourism. Precisely because the tourist arrives with so many idealized images, a periodic sobering-up is part of the experience of travel. Witnessing the spread of algae and jellyfish or the demise of coral reefs, seaside holidaymakers, snorkelers and scuba divers become sensitive to the pollution and warming of the oceans. Travel guides and brochures have for a long time offered the kind of synthesis of nature and culture that ecologists and professional conservationists still find hard to absorb. Sweeping Friend–Enemy constructs make it more difficult to analyse the history of the relationship between environmental protection and tourism, which is as fraught with tension as that between environmental protection and hunting – and that is saying something!

The divisiveness of wood and the bumpy road to a 'broad Green alliance'

Let us move on to a substance that seems to epitomize better than any other the synthesis of economics and ecology: wood. Its growth requires nothing but solar energy, improves the soil water balance and delights nature lovers; its use as construction timber ensures an ideal indoor climate and a sense of natural living; and any leftovers can also be utilized. As early as 1949, a UNESCO official reflected on the possible links between conservation and economics: 'Eagles and elephants cannot be cash crops, but trees can be.'[328]

The global aim of 'sustainable development', set in Rio in 1992, has its origins in German forestry, and a precise definition of the term is most likely to be given in relation to the forest. Here too it has a better chance of practical realization than in other areas of environmental policy, since it does not call for expensive technologies and is especially open to cooperation between the first and the third world. In Callenbach's *Ecotopia*, not only houses but also bathtubs are made of wood. As one 'woodworm' from Austria put it. 'If all parties interested in wood – from foresters through the timber industry to academic researchers – could be brought around a table, wood would be an unbeatable material.'[329] But so far such unbeatability has been out of the question; the 'woodworm' himself indicates that a broad Green alliance – not to speak of an even broader alliance between the timber industry and the environmental movement – remains a pipe-dream.[330] A number of alarms in the eco-age seemed almost tailor-made to join the forestry and timber sector in a common front with environmentalists: in particular, the alarm over the damage caused to forests in the North by acid rain, and the alarm over the destruction of forest by cattle barons in the South. Instead, however, the campaign for a boycott of tropical wood has fanned a new animosity. In the United States, where private forest ownership is the rule and the wilderness ideal runs up against highly organized private interests (united, since 1993, in the American Forest and Paper Association), the fronts collide with each other even more violently than in the Old World.[331] Since the American West still has ancient forests with giant trees, such as have all but disappeared from Europe, the struggle for the 'wilderness' is much more emphatic there than on the other side of the Atlantic in the Old World, where it is recognized that the supposed wilderness is not really one.

In theory everything is so simple, even in the age of climate alarms. Sustainable forestry automatically stabilizes carbon dioxide in the atmosphere, so there is no need for huge investment in regulations, controls and sanctions. The point, however, seems to be precisely that wood solutions are too simple and too conventional. Environmental agencies specialize overwhelmingly in other questions. Unlike climate research, solar hydrogen, offshore wind power and ocean wave energy, projects concerning wood or the forest offer little material for what counts as 'cutting-edge research', and new discoveries are not likely to put anyone in the running for a Nobel prize. Fascinated as they are by world horizons, but also spurred on by international seminar tourism, intellectuals tend to gravitate towards models of global management. From both a historical and an ecological point of view, however, a global forest policy would seem to be the most senseless thing imaginable. Success stories from the developing countries have usually been local in character, involving small group initiatives – whether by women in Kenya's Kitui district[332] or by the Kalibo mangrove community on the Philippines island of Panay[333] – to plant trees that correspond to local interests and ecological conditions.

Nowadays, wood is offered as a renewable fuel with a neutral CO_2 balance, with the idea that it will grow back to the same extent that it is consumed. At wood fairs, one already sees whole machine parks for the production of wood fuel. But this situation too has its downside. The exploding demand for wood chips and pellets – which used to be made only from scrap wood – is putting lumber under increasing pressure and provoking cries of alarm. Wood fuel has become a difficult, sensitive issue for both ecologists and economists in the scene. For lovers of the material, it is a disgrace to burn up as fuel what could be made into lasting tools. Someone with a knowledge of history might object that coppice used for the provision of wood fuel was more biodiverse than many timber forests. But will this remain true for the fuel plantations of the future?[334]

Does the climate alarm offer wood a new opportunity? At the Kyoto climate conference in 1997 and in the years that followed, there was much controversy about whether reforestation could compensate for fuel emissions. The doubts were well founded, since reforestation simply in order to cut down more trees in the future has a close to zero effect on the CO_2 balance in the atmosphere. Besides, the mere planting of trees does not mean much: the important thing is to water the trees, to protect them from livestock grazing and to manage them on a sustainable basis. All of that can only be accomplished over time and is difficult to check up on from a distance. There is reason to suspect that, as in the case of development aid, the payment of reforestation premiums is only an invitation to corruption. Again and again, plans are floated to halt desertification by installing a forest belt, a Green 'Great Wall', on the southern edge of the Sahara – even though experts regard such a mega-project as futile.[335]

Be this as it may, a global climate policy based mainly on controls and restrictions, without effective sanctions to back it up, appears doomed to failure. In the long run, such strategies have a chance of success only if those directly affected by them have an interest in taking them up. History shows that this is generally the only route to sustainable forestry. A larger role for wood in the world economy, combined with sustainable forestry, will create a sector in which the CO_2 balance evens out in the long term, without controls or restrictions. Forest and wood are popular, or at least have a chance of becoming so, but restrictions are never popular. There is therefore an opportunity for the forestry and timber sector to take the offensive by participating directly in climate policy formation.

Anyway, for project developers an expensive mega-scheme such as underground CO_2 sequestration is more attractive than conventional CO_2 binding through afforestation. Social policy-makers with third world hunger in mind describe it as a 'crime against humanity' to produce biofuels on areas that might be used to feed people.[336] But all around the world, the traditional locations of forest are highland and other regions unsuitable for agriculture, and technological developments are anyway pulling agriculture out of the mountains. Wood fuel is therefore not subject to the same social policy objections as maize.

The sun on the horizon?

With today's technological possibilities, wood fuel seems a pretty uninteresting way of using solar energy, although it is man's oldest way of producing warmth, and a large part of humanity still uses it for that purpose. At least theoretically, new paths back to solar energy would solve many of the world's environmental problems at a stroke, without a never-ending stream of decrees, restrictions, taxes, checks, and filter, disposal and recycling technologies. They would put an end to emission problems and worries about the earth's atmosphere, as well as addressing the issue of the finite nature of fossil fuels and their highly uneven distribution around the world. Indeed, solar energy would offer a huge opportunity precisely to the hottest countries, which are today also mostly the poorest.

All this has always been known in principle, and even at today's levels the energy content of solar radiation reaching the earth is roughly 15,000 higher than the planet's total energy consumption. This figure is the source of constant fascination, although it has little or no practical significance. 'There is no energy problem, only a lack of technological imagination': such is the slogan of the keenest solar enthusiasts. Should not advances in the direction of solar energy have been the number one issue right from the beginning for environmental movements? And should not all these movements be assessed according to whether they focus on this goal or allow themselves to be distracted from it?

Anyone who goes into the history of solar technology is astonished to find two things that do not fit together: how far its origins stretch back into the past; yet how marginal it remains despite all the advances, and how little the issue seems to interest large parts of the environmental movement itself. The history consists of reversals as well as forward movement. In 1979, Sweden's Secretariat for Futures Studies sketched out a plan for a 'solar Sweden' by the year 2015, half based on the huge areas of forest;[337] today, as the date draws near, the country is on the point of turning once more to nuclear energy.

Gerhard Mener's voluminous 'History of Solar Energy Use in Germany and the USA' – still by far the deepest and most extensive work on the history of renewable energy – begins in the year 1860.[338] By 1900, when futurist visions were in the air, Friedrich Kohlrausch (president of the Physikalisch-Technische Reichsanstalt) was pleading for a solar colonialism in the sun-drenched deserts of the world, since the shape of things to come made it advisable for 'a nation to assure itself a share of such regions'. He continued: 'Very large areas are not necessary; a few square miles in North Africa would be enough for a country like the German Reich.' Evidently he thought it just a matter of time before heat stored there in solar collectors could be transported to Germany – which is the basic idea behind today's Desertec project!

August Bebel, for whom technological and social progress were virtually the same, enthusiastically embraced this vision in successive editions of his bestseller *Woman and Socialism*[339] – and in this way it entered into the heritage of Social Democracy. But it remained more or less latent there, deep beneath the surface, until the post-Chernobyl period; people might believe in a remote solar future, but there was little to be done in the present to achieve it – or anyway, no fascinating mega-projects around which business interests could crystallize. Most of the time, solar energy had neither open enemies to fight against nor powerful friends who professed more than a Platonic love of solar power.

Moreover, it is all but forgotten that for a time the atomic euphoria of the 1950s swallowed up the solar vision, in the belief that nuclear fission reactors would inevitably lead to a new generation of nuclear fusion reactors.[340] It had been known since 1938 that the sun's energy arose from the fusion of hydrogen nuclei, and so the idea was that nuclear fusion would bring solar power down to earth in concentrated form, making it unnecessary to catch the sun's diffuse rays. In 1954, even the serious journal *Außenpolitik* was taken in by the absurd prediction that 'within two years or so' nuclear fusion would be 'practically ready for use'.[341] Among Indian physicists, there was still an enthusiasm for solar energy in the 1940s – what could have been more logical than for this sun-drenched nation to play its trump card against foggy Britain, which had ruled the world with its coal mines? But Homi Bhabha, who came out in 1952 as a firm supporter of solar energy, switched his allegiance to nuclear power amid the Washington-promoted Atoms for Peace euphoria, becoming chair of the Indian Atomic Energy Commission and (in 1955) of the Geneva atomic conference.

The Austrian nuclear physicist Hans Thirring, a vigorous opponent of the Cold War, warned in 1952 that it would be justifiable to use nuclear energy only when the potential of solar and water energy had been fully studied and exhausted. Now there is a logical and historically grounded criterion that could serve as a guide for today's ethics commissions! But Thirring did not believe that decision-makers were capable of acting responsibly on such advice, as his 'Dixi et salvavi animam meam' remark clearly showed.[342] It was literally a salve for his conscience, taken from the Book of Ezekiel: the godless may be on the road to perdition, but one can save one's soul by warning them of it – even if they will not listen. At that time, in fact, there was no policy-making body with broad support among businesspeople and the public at large which could have stayed the course and fully tested every possible renewable energy before turning to nuclear power. Nevertheless, solar energy did not drop out of the picture entirely. And fusion energy, seemingly within reach at the Geneva conference in 1955, receded more and more into the future – so that in the 1970s it became far more unreal than solar energy.

Whereas in the 1960s nuclear power far outstripped solar energy for use on earth, solar cells knocked reactors out of contention for the purposes of manned space flight. But on 19 July 1969, just before the 'ecological revolution' of 1970, the moon landing brought space travel to a zenith that it would never exceed until now. For, like it or not, what the astronauts imparted to the new ecological enlightenment was the basic fact that the cosmos is an unfriendly environment and that all we have is this one planet of ours. US government finances were in crisis as a result of the Vietnam War, and the billions required for space exploration offered themselves as an easy target for cuts; the mighty R&D space complex had to set about making itself useful on earth.[343] A flood of warnings about the dangers of nuclear power and the threats to the oil supply came along just at the right time. At least in principle, the solar cells developed for space travel had refuted the main objection to which solar energy had been exposed so long as it could rely only on large concave mirrors or 'collectors': namely, that the technology produced energy only when the sun was shining.

Yet the alliance between solar technology and the environmental move-ment was anything but easy. Solar collectors encouraged gigantomania; a 'solar oven', located from 1973 at Odeillo in the French Pyrenees, was designed to melt metal with a towering parabolic reflector, which today stands as a monument to a bygone future.[344] Giant mirrors aroused fears of being blinded or even burned. The excitement of miniaturization did attach to the new solar cells. But the first generation of experts came from the research complex corrupted by the arms race – the height of depravity in the eyes of most environmental activists.[345] Worse still: solar cells had been developed in research centres where money was no object; they came out of Star Wars projects and were astronomically expensive. Although they were certainly tiny, the 'small is beautiful' slogan did not apply to them at all in the early days. The costs of the silicon photovoltaic generators used in space travel amounted to 100,000–200,000 dollars per kilowatt.[346] It is true that computers too had exorbitant price tags around 1970, but miniaturization and mass production then led to more dramatic falls than anyone had been expecting. Was something similar likely to happen with solar cells, whose silicon content gave them an affinity with electronics? Their prices began to come down as output increased, but more slowly than with computers, and it took decades for the trend to become clearly established.

Even with falling prices, three further factors weighing on solar energy meant that it did not really have the trust even of people sympathetic to it: first, its dependence on the weather made it seem unreliable; second, there was still no satisfactory storage technology to offset variations in the generation of current; and third, its production was extremely local-ized, except where it took place in large, hot, desert areas. At first it was unclear how the mass of small producers were to be linked up, and how the whole process of generation and consumption was to be managed; the existing structures of the energy industry were not in the least suited to the task. In 1974 Dixy Lee Ray, angry at the winding up of the US Atomic Energy Commission of which she had been the last head, showered solar enthusiasts with derision: 'Making solar energy use technically feasible is about as difficult as getting 10 million fleas to produce useable energy by hopping in the same direction at the same time.'[347] That was a good joke in 1974, but she did not repeat it twenty years later, in her new assault on everything 'eco'; and she did not say a word about solar energy.[348] The *idée fixe* that systems must be managed centrally had become anachronistic in the electronic age. Much more difficult to get out of one's head, however, is the idea that today's colossal demand for energy can be satisfied only by colossal power plant units.

In the course of the eco-age, solar technology development followed very different curves in the United States and Germany. In the 1970s the Americans were initially a long way ahead – after all, they had the largest space research centres (the origin of solar cells) and much larger sunny regions. California, in particular, which had more than enough sun to go round, promised to become the El Dorado of solar energy, and old hippies and young whizz-kids flocked there in search of new pastures. The Mojave Desert became home to nine collector-based solar power plants, with a thermal capacity of 354 megawatts, then equal to 90 per cent of the world total.[349] Most environmental activists – who in those early days included many scientists – were less afraid of contact with military or industrial research than were the German anti-nuclear campaigners of the 1970s (who often had a Marxist background).

But things were about to change. The American solar boom of the seventies proved to be a passing fashion: it lacked a solid economic base, and its impact could not be sustained. President Carter had a solar water heater installed on the roof of the White House, but Ronald Reagan had it taken down when he moved in.[350] Meanwhile, Germany in the 1980s was in the forefront of countries promoting solar energy;[351] this very fact indicates that progress in solar technology crucially depends on the influence of the environmental movement within national politics. In the United States a key impetus came from the anti-nuclear movement, and its special strength in West Germany worked directly or indirectly to the long-term advantage of solar energy. For a long time, though, it was difficult even for German anti-nuclear campaigners to believe in the power of the sun where it was so parsimonious with its blessings. Early exhibitions on solar technology aroused little trust – and, as in the case of nuclear power, trust was what it was about. Today renewable energies still suffer from a lack of it, partly because of inflated promises in the past and an underestimation of the need to learn from experience.[352]

When North German Social Democrats, or indeed Greens,[353] turned against nuclear technology, their alternative was usually quite simple, even if they did not say it out loud or presented it only as a 'transitional strategy':[354] it was coal. Of that there was enough for the foreseeable future; the Ruhr basin, the SPD's largest traditional stronghold, had been suffering since 1957 from a fall in the demand for coal. In the 1980s, however, environmentalist opponents of nuclear power began to see it as a questionable alternative: first because of the 'death of the forest' alarm, then, from 1986, because of the CO_2 global warming revelations that coincided with the shock of Chernobyl. Stormy times lay ahead, and the trend did not change after German unification. From 1990 until 1992, the CDU-led federal government promoted solar energy with its 'thousand roofs programme', which the SPD–Green coalition government later trumped between 1999 and 2003 with its 'hundred thousand roofs programme'[355] – although even that quantum leap did not bring solar power in from the margins.

More recently, solar technology has had the mega-project it was lacking for so long: the Desertec plan to supply Europe with solar electricity from the Sahara, first mooted as a vision more than a century ago.[356] The reasoning behind it is of classical simplicity: nowhere does the sun shine as constantly as under the cloudless desert skies; nowhere do renewable energies conflict so little with the growing of food. The Club of Rome, formerly a think-tank of the eco-age, and the German Aerospace Centre (DLR) have been jointly raising support in the industry for the adventurous scheme;[357] its costs are estimated to total 400 billion euros – and anyone with a knowledge of history will be aware that such projects almost never come in under budget. Münchener Rück, the world's largest reinsurance company, has also stepped in and put its weight behind Desertec.[358] Never before in the history of solar technology have such big fish pushed their way into preparatory bodies, as they did half a century ago into the atomic energy commissions.

Today as then, however, one must look carefully to see whether their participation has a binding character and involves taking on a share of the risk as well as a sizeable investment. In fact, that is still in doubt. There are two other curious points: most of the desert energy would come from conventional collectors, not from photovoltaic cells; and the planned installations would cover a vast area, even though 'upscaling' in the case of solar energy (unlike in that of fossil or nuclear energy) does not promise to save costs and would increase the dependence on politically unstable regions. The project is technically feasible and has a plausible level of insurance cover, especially as it rests essentially on conventional equipment rather than expensive photovoltaics. The only question is whether the implicit overall system is realistic. One effect is evident: this gigantic enterprise would again make large corporations totally responsible for the provision of solar energy, but there would be a danger that control could slip out of their hands because of the decentralized nature of the installations. In this respect, offshore wind parks are more attractive in so far as they avoid conflicts with local inhabitants and environmentalists. There are also strong arguments that the solar power breakthrough will take place not in the energy industry but in construction, where the impetus will not come from giant projects, and where in general the process can be driven from the top to only a limited extent.

Blind spots in 'ecological communication'

The more one reads and thinks about solar energy, the more one is cured of the conceit that we somehow stand at the end of environmental history. The fact is that, after more than a hundred years of technological developments, the solar share of energy provision is still marginal even in countries with long hours of sunshine; its progress has been 'breathtakingly slow' (as Hermann Scheer put it) and sometimes even displayed a regressive tendency. Could this be an indication that, except in a few niche areas, the physical-technological problems are insuperable? Or are certain forces in the energy industry obstructing further advances? Is a changeover to solar energy technically possible? Or would it be too much of a strain only for our existing political and economic systems? How can we tell whether the 'bottom line' will make it worthwhile in certain regions – hence, whether it will generate considerably more energy than is spent on its production and supply? Can it be ascertained whether solar technology still has a really major development potential, and that qualitative leaps in efficiency are to be expected? Could it be that the optimum path has not yet been found and further alternatives will have to be tested? Will state subsidies encourage or obstruct such advances? Has the storage problem been criminally neglected in the promotion of renewable energies? Does the way forward lie with Desertec-style projects or, on the contrary, with a strategy of small steps and careful learning from experience? Is Desertec a sign that solar energy is not a viable proposition in a country like Germany? Are such mega-projects required for solar energy to make a great leap forward, or does history teach us that great leaps often lead nowhere and that mega-projects inevitably suck resources away from more useful purposes? Should we support tendencies to public energy provision, or is it preferable, precisely with renewable energies in view, that the sector should be a playground for private initiative? Is it worth fighting to municipalize the energy supply, or is there reason to fear that city-owned plants would sooner or later fall into their proverbial 'big sleep'? Are large energy corporations usually more capable of bold innovative strategies? Or would we be better off with medium-sized companies, as the history of the last few decades suggests?

And the decisive question: how are we to cope with all these uncertainties? How should we work out the various options and debate them through to a conclusion? The history of 'ecological communication' has no end, yet at this point in time it is especially clear that it has also been a history of deficits. There is no major public discussion on most of these issues, and in smaller circles the opinions vary widely even within the eco-scene. Evaluation of the pros and cons of nuclear energy has not created a style of communication that can handle the range of options. Friend–Enemy categories are here a barrier to thought.

Since the renewable energy yield varies from region to region, it is probably true that discussions cannot clarify everything: that the experience of trial and error is also indispensable. If a powerful coalition of players resolutely presses for the development of renewable energy sources, much that seemed out of the question becomes possible; the history of nuclear technology is a good illustration of this. We should therefore never forget something that well-meaning discussions tend to suppress: energy policy issues are eminently about power; communication alone cannot resolve them. A rational consensus regarding the future can come about only through conflicts. Many oil corporations tried to create the impression that, since they knew best the limits of resources, they could be safely left to develop renewable energies: BP, for example, claimed that it now stood for 'Beyond Petroleum'.[359] The world public has meanwhile been taught a number of different lessons. The Deepwater Horizon disaster in the Gulf of Mexico, for which BP was responsible, offers a taste of what can be expected when oil giants go for major oil resources lying in underwater sands and shales; these are risky areas, and it has been abundantly demonstrated that the energy industry is far from suitably equipped to exploit them. The oil and energy industry has given rise to the largest concentrations of power in economic history, which are highly effective in shaping flows of information. What is imparted about energy matters is seldom completely innocent; many of the issues at stake have their own history and are charged with particular interests, disputes and terminological conventions.

Another question is particularly absorbing, both historically and for us living today. Is it the case that, while nuclear technology is marked by its origins in the military complex, alternative technologies also bear lasting traces of their genesis? Does photovoltaics still reflect its origins in space exploration, at a time when money was no object? Although many would find it comical to hope, with Franz Alt, that reeds will be the salvation of mankind,[360] might it not be vital that we keep open new paths and new ways of thinking? History is change; the historical approach performs its greatest service to the contemporary world when it keeps our eyes open to the possibility of change.

Quite a few recent experiences testify that it is important for the environmental movement to speak rationally about the blind spots of 'ecological communication' – for the sake of environmental protection as well as for its own sake. 'Environmental protection' is an ambiguous term, and as a rule, both in Germany and elsewhere, the more influential the movement becomes, the more its internal tensions come to a head. It first coalesced in 1970 out of a range of heterogeneous aspirations, each with its very different history; the coming together was often only an external phenomenon, a response to common enemies and a common sense of impotence. Once that bond is no longer there, the danger arises that the movement will break apart into its original components.

This is certainly apparent in Germany, where the political influence of the environmental movement became stronger (thanks to the Greens) than in most other countries around the world. The conflict between globally oriented environmentalists and local or national conservationists was especially intense in the wake of the government's massive promotion of renewable energy sources. Hermann Scheer, the most eloquent champion of solar energy, has recently gone so far as to locate the main enemy not only in the energy industry but also in 'the environmental movement' – or, to be more specific, among landscape conservationists who bitterly oppose all wind parks, hydropower schemes and large-scale solar projects. 'Appeals to nature conservation', he writes, 'have blocked countless renewable energy projects.'[361] Although, in Northern Germany, it is often easier to believe in the power of the wind than of the sun, the Hamburg-based *Der Spiegel* – which for many years had lent support to opponents of nuclear power – created uproar with its cover title on 29 March 2004: 'The windmill madness: from the dream of environmentally friendly energy to heavily subsidized landscape destruction.' The lead story gleefully quoted the founder of a 'Save the Uckermark!' campaign, who, with no sense of history, had claimed that wind parks were 'the worst depredations since the Thirty Years War'. If it is agreed not to speak of conflicts between green objectives, the belligerence of the environmental movement turns against itself. In March 2011 in the aftermath of the Fukushima reactor disaster, when the German government announced its intention of not only reducing CO_2 emissions but also disengaging from nuclear energy, it was the greatest triumph of the German environmental movement – it might become its greatest test of strength.

But a basic contradiction? In the early years of the 'ecological revolution', the 'limits to growth' were a leitmotif of discussions about the environment. But when Middle East oil began to flow freely again, it was rather the limitlessness of growth and the unstoppable rise of emissions that gave cause for concern. Besides, environmental activists were then concentrating on more concrete objectives, where something definite could be done. More recently, with the global supremacy of a capitalism divested of all frontiers, many discussions have revolved around the idea that the growth pressure contained in our economic system – or at least the perception of an end to growth as decline – is the ultimate cause of most environmental problems. If this were true, there would be a basic contradiction between economics and ecology.

But is it true? In the worldwide debate that the Club of Rome's famous study triggered in 1972, economic luminaries such as Jan Tinbergen argued that the (undeniable) limits to growth were not necessarily a basic problem for the economic system.[362] Had not market capitalism always rested upon the scarcity of goods? There was no need for economists in the land of Cockaigne.[363]

The growth obsession did not originate with classical economists, from Smith to Keynes, but rather with Walt W. Rostow and his *Stages of Economic Growth: A Noncommunist Manifesto* (1960). In its theoretical level, this book marked a regression to primitive mechanistic thinking; if the rate of investment rose above 14 per cent, whatever the means, then 'take-off' (a telling aeronautic metaphor!) would lead to self-perpetuating growth. This theory became popular in the realm of development aid, although it never seemed to work there. Rostow did contribute to one self-propelling take-off by acting as an influential presidential adviser (later remembered as 'America's Rasputin') during the Vietnam War.[364] But after that his reputation was busted.

In 1991 Jan Tinbergen and the World Bank adviser Herman Daly were among those who, in a Bank 'ecological working paper' assessing the Brundtland report, emphatically argued that 'sustainable development' should by no means be understood in the industrial countries as continuing growth.[365] Seen in this way, ecology leads economics to its original meaning of 'household theory'. Or is there such a thing as 'green growth', not necessarily associated with increased resource consumption? This tempting idea, beloved of optimistic environmentalists, seems to have been refuted by the facts.[366] Instead, we have been seeing spasmodic attempts to push the limits to growth a little further into the future – whether through 'fracking' (pumping down water and chemicals to extract natural resources from unprecedented depths) or through mining operations at the bottom of the sea. The horrific ecological and political dangers of such leaps into the unknown appear to be confirming the 'limits to growth'. The age of ecology has its recurrent leitmotifs. There is a reason for this, since no prospect exists of finally solving most of the great environmental problems.

Chapter Six

Ecology and the Historic Turn of 1990: From Social Justice to Climate Justice?

Third data cluster: the environment from Chernobyl to Rio, 1986–1992

26 Apr. 1986	Chernobyl reactor disaster; special 'operational group' of the Central Committee of the CPSU meets for first time on 29 April.
23 May 1986	India: Environment (Protection) Act, a delayed reaction to the Bhopal chemical disaster on 2 December 1984.
7 June 1986	Violent clashes between demonstrators and police at the planned reprocessing plant at Wackersdorf; large demonstration at Brokdorf nuclear power plant site.
June 1986	German federal ministry for environment, conservation and reactor safety established; first environment minister: Walter Wallmann.
10 June 1986	First anniversary of sinking of *Rainbow Warrior* by French secret service; Greenpeace activists block French embassies and consulates all around the world and call for a halt to nuclear tests.
1986	USA: Emergency Planning and Community Right-To-Know Act, which – in the context of a campaign going back to the Bhopal disaster in India – forces chemical corporations to publish their emission levels and disaster planning. The EPA is given powers to order a complete audit of environmental effects caused by companies in breach of provisions.
1986	Paul Watson and his *Sea Shepherd* comrades destroy the entire whale-processing plant in Reykjavik and sink half of Iceland's whaling fleet, without facing prosecution.
1986	Zimbabwe: CAMPFIRE (Communal Areas Management Programme for Indigenous

	Resources) established after a long preparatory period.
1986	Conservation International becomes an active wilderness protection NGO alongside the World Wildlife Fund (WWF) and The Nature Conservancy (TNC), reaching China and Southeast Asia by the year 2000.
3 July 1986	The Soviet Politburo is fully informed for the first time about the dangers of Soviet nuclear power plants.
Aug. 1986	Gorbachev cancels the Davydov project for the diversion of Siberian rivers to irrigate Inner Asia, which goes back to 1868.
11 Aug. 1986	*Der Spiegel* cover story on 'The Climate Catastrophe', featuring an image of Cologne cathedral half under water.
2 Sep. 1986	Environment Library founded in the precinct of the Zion church in East Berlin.
Oct. 1986	Peter Wensierski publishes *Von oben nach unten wächst gar nichts: Umweltzerstörung und Protest in der DDR* (the first disturbing report on environmental problems in East Germany).
1986	Alfred W. Crosby, *Ecological Imperialism: The Biological Expansion of Europe, 900–1900*.
1986	The International Whaling Commission (IWC) cuts quotas to zero. Subsequently, the ban on whaling under the cover of 'scientific' purposes is relaxed.
1986	India: start of campaign against construction of the Narmada dam.
1 Nov. 1986	Fire at Sandoz corporation near Basle burns 1,351 tonnes of chemicals; fish die in the Rhine; turning-point in European public perception of chemical risks.
Nov. 1986	BSE pathogen first identified.
1986	On the initiative of Ludwig Bölkow, a solar-powered installation for the production of hydrogen is founded with government support at Neunburg vorm Wald (Upper Palatinate).
1986	Ulrich Beck's *Risk Society* first published in German.
1986	Bertrand Schneider publishes *The Barefoot Revolution*, a report to the Club of Rome (of which he is the general secretary), arguing for the inclusion of NGOs in development aid, partly because of ecological problems associated with it.

1987	The European Community acquires powers in environmental policy and the right to take relevant decisions by majority vote.
1987	Founding of the European Nature Heritage Fund (EuroNatur), at first mainly on the initiative of the BUND, but later involving other environmental associations; its first project is aimed at conservation of the Sava-Auen region.
1987	Under pressure from Greenpeace, the second North Sea Conservation Conference orders an end to the dumping of industrial waste at sea by the end of 1989.
1987	Italy: a referendum favours giving up nuclear energy.
1987	Klaus Töpfer becomes environment minister of the German Federal Republic (until 1994).
1987	The 'Brundtland Report' *Our Common Future*, issued by the World Commission on Environment and Development set up by the UN in 1983, argues for a strategy of 'sustainable development': 'development that meets the needs of the present without compromising the ability of future generations to meet their own needs'. Fundamental for Rio 1992.
1987	USA: the Commission for Racial Justice of the United Churches of Christ publishes a report entitled *Toxic Wastes and Race in the United States*: fundamental for the Environmental Justice movement.
1987	Richard Register, *Ecocity Berkeley: Building Cities for a Healthy Future* (also fundamental for Environmental Justice).
1987	Complete ban on the export of wood from Indonesia and the Philippines.
1987	Japan Tropical Forest Action Network founded in response to international criticism of rainforest destruction, in the run-up to the first conference of the International Tropical Timber Association (ITTO) in Yokohama in March.
25 Jan. 1987	German Greens win 8.3 per cent of the vote in federal elections.
Mar. 1987	In Sarawak (Borneo) Dayak tribes blockade roads in protest at foreign logging firms.
18 Mar. 1987	In his government statement, German chancellor Kohl supports the 'debt for nature swap' concept for third world countries, first floated in 1984 by Thomas Lovejoy of the WWF.

Apr. 1987	Soviet Union: a government commission is set up on the ecological situation in the Aral Sea Basin.
1987	On a 'debt for nature' basis, Costa Rica establishes the Guanacaste National Park as a tropical rainforest mega-park, including for the first time traditional indigenous forms of land use (Costa Rica Debt Conservation Plan). The government of Bolivia and Conservation International (CI) conclude the first 'debt for nature swap' agreement.
1987	A broad anti-nuclear movement emerges in Taiwan after the lifting of martial law on 15 July.
Aug. 1987	Broad participation in the first North American Conference on Christianity and Ecology (NACCE); its prospectus predicts global disaster if the economy continues as before: 'The handwriting is now on the wall.'
Sep. 1987	Signing of the Montreal Protocol on Substances that Deplete the Ozone Layer.
24 Nov. 1987	East Berlin: the Environment Library is occupied by the security police; the vigil subsequently mounted by environmental activists is one of the first acts of public resistance that lead to the turn of 1989.
27 Nov. 1987	The Bundestag appoints a commission on 'Precautions to Protect the Earth's Atmosphere' (until 1991). A second commission on the same issue, established in 1991, gains less attention.
1988	The hottest year on record; intense heatwaves in the USA, with droughts and forest fires. James Hansen (NASA) announces: 'Global warming has begun.' The United Nations Environment Programme (UNEP) and the World Meteorological Organization (WMO) jointly establish the IPCC (Intergovernmental Panel on Climate Change).
1988	An international movement to protect the tropical forests (now also a contribution to climate protection) begins to take shape; first calls for a boycott of tropical woods. World Rainforest Week in October; demonstrations outside Japanese embassies.
1988	José Lutzenberger, later Brazilian state secretary for environmental issues, receives the Alternative Nobel Prize for his role in the fight to preserve the rainforest.

1988	The first International Congress for Ethnobiology takes place in Belem (Brazil), leading to the foundation of the International Society of Ethnobiology. A statement declares: 'Indigenous peoples have been stewards of 99 per cent of the world's resources.'
1988	Soviet Union: *Novyi mir* and *Pamir* organize an expedition to the Aral region, which draws public attention to the ecological disaster there.
1988	Soviet Union: founding of the 'Social-Ecological Union', which establishes relations with the international ecological community, distributes information and coordinates activities.
1988	Latvia: public pressure leads to creation of a State Conservation Committee, one of the first steps towards independence for the Baltic states.
1988	Protest movement in Hungary against a planned dam on the Danube near Nagymaros.
1988	Thailand: after persistent protests, the government abandons the plan to build a dam on the largest tributary of the River Kwai.
1988	South Korea: a number of anti-pollution groups merge in the Korean Anti-Pollution Movement Association (KARMA). Sharp protests follow against nuclear waste deposits.
1988	Vandana Shiva, *Staying Alive: Women, Ecology and Survival in India*.
1988	Seal deaths in the North Sea, though probably due to a virus rather than pollution, cause a major outcry and attract unprecedented public support for conservation in the Watten Sea.
1988	Founding of the European Association for Renewable Energies by the SPD politician Hermann Scheer.
Mar. 1988	The World Bank establishes a special department to integrate environmental protection into its activities.
Mar. 1988	Australia: several Green groups unite to form the Rainbow Alliance, under the slogan 'Remaking Australia: People in Control of Politics, the Economy and the Environment'.
27 Apr. 1988	Valerii A. Legasov, deputy director of the Soviet Kurchatov Atomic Energy Institute, who had been made responsible for cleaning-up operations after Chernobyl, hangs himself.
May 1988	Brice Lalonde, the best-known Green politician

	in France at the time, joins the government: first as state secretary, then as minister for environmental issues. In 1990 he founds the Génération écologie party.
May 1988	Estonia's Green movement founded as 'a radical democratic citizens' initiative for the prevention of ecological catastrophe, the development of a nature-friendly way of life, and the liquidation of bureaucratic-technocratic power hostile to the environment'.
1988	Founding of a Green Party in Egypt.
June 1988	At the invitation of the Canadian government, a conference on 'The Changing Atmosphere: Implications for Global Security' takes place in Toronto, against the background of the 'drought of the century' in the USA. It was later seen as the spark for subsequent attempts to agree on a global climate policy. It set the target of 20 per cent cuts in CO_2 emissions by the year 2005.
June 1988	East Berlin: founding of 'Arche Nova' ('Green-Ecological Arche Network'). Its most spectacular action, also in June, is the secret shooting of a documentary film, *Bitteres aus Bitterfeld*, which is smuggled out to West Berlin.
June 1988	Michael Beleites, *Pechblende* (revelations on uranium mining by the East German SDAG Wismut company in Saxony and Thuringia).
1988	The local Berlin-Pankow group of the official East German Gesellschaft für Natur und Umwelt (GNU) founds an urban ecology association, which becomes a rallying point for the opposition.
8 July 1988	The European Parliament approves import restrictions on tropical wood from Malaysia.
Aug. 1988	The Wise Use Movement, the most influential US anti-environmentalist organization, is founded in Reno (Nevada), under the leadership of Ron Arnold and Alan M. Gottlieb, and with support from the Center for the Defense of Free Enterprise (CDFE).
Sep. 1988	In a speech 'which overnight turned the environment from being a minority to a mainstream concern in Britain',[1] Margaret Thatcher warns the Royal Society of the ozone hole discovered in 1985 by the British Antarctic Survey.
Oct. 1988	Krakow hosts the annual meeting of Friends of the Earth International, the only large environ-

	mental organization that has so far extended into Eastern bloc countries.
Nov. 1988	Tree-felling scheduled in the East Berlin district of Prenzlauer Berg causes unrest among the local population. The Potsdam urban ecology group ARGUS, initially part of the official GNU, assumes the character of an autonomous campaign.
Dec. 1988	USA: founding of Ancient Forest Alliance. The spotted owl conservation movement wins broad support.
22 Dec. 1988	Murder of Chico Mendes.
beginning of 1989	Instead of its usual 'Man of the Year', *Time Magazine* features 'Planet of the Year – Endangered Earth', with a cover showing a globe just before sunset.
1989	Founding of Greenpeace Russia.
1989	After disastrous floods, Thailand bans woodcutting throughout the country.
1989	Bruno Manser, who supports the Penan campaign in Sarawak against foreign loggers, alerts the ITTO to the violation of indigenous people's rights. Since 1987 the ITTO has been concerned about the increasing destruction of tropical forest, and it now endorses the idea of certificates as a way of enforcing standards of sustainable forestry.
1989	The Coordinating Body for the Indigenous Organizations of the Amazon Basin (COICA) calls on the 'community of concerned environmentalists' to protect indigenous cultures as well as the tropical forest, accusing it of having 'left us, the Indigenous Peoples, out of your vision of the Amazonian Biosphere'.
1989	The World Bank decides to involve NGOs in decision-making about projects under consideration for its support.
1989	The EPA issues a directive requiring New York to make dramatic improvements in its water quality, whereupon the city, instead of building expensive filter installations, decides to operate a forest conservation project.
Mar. 1989	The *Exxon Valdez* oil tanker runs aground off Alaska.
1989	The Aral Sea divides into two seas – a disaster that attracts the attention of the Western media.

from 1989	More and more information is released about long-term damage in areas around Chernobyl; international aid operations begin. A Green Party is founded in Georgia – the first in the Soviet Union.
1989	The Dalai Lama receives the Nobel Peace Prize.
1989	Dai Qing, *Yangtse! Yangtse!*
1989	A large dam project is abandoned in Georgia because of fears of disastrous flooding.
Apr. 1989	The World Rainforest Movement Meeting is held in Penang (Malaysia).
1989	For the first time, the ITTO argues for the introduction of wood certificates.
1989	Under pressure from the hoteliers' association and conservationists, the regional government of the Balearics places a third of the entire area of the island group under protection. In November 1992 there is a large demonstration against attempts to restrict the scope of this law.
31 May 1989	West Germany: construction work on the Wackersdorf reprocessing plant is called off.
8 June 1989	California: a referendum decides to decommission the Rancho Seco nuclear power plant, which has already had a series of breakdowns; a grassroots group, Sacramentans for Safe Energy, had been waging a campaign against it since 1987.
9 June 1989	The building of a nuclear reprocessing plant is announced at Clairborne (Louisiana), close to mainly black neighbourhoods. Black churches play a leading role in the resistance, which is eventually successful and becomes the first climax of the Environmental Justice movement.
28 Sep. 1989	First mass rally of the newly organized Narmada Bachao Andolan ('Save the Narmada Movement') is held in the Indian town of Harsud (Madhya Pradesh), which is due to be flooded by the artificial lake.
16 Nov. 1989	A week after the opening of the Wall: the West German ARD channel broadcasts a special film: *'The Uninhabitable Republic? Environmental Destruction in the GDR.'*
Dec. 1989	The UN General Assembly calls for a worldwide end to drift-net fishing.
Dec. 1989	UN General Assembly to hold Earth Summit in Rio in 1992, in line with the recommendations of the Brundtland Commission.

1990	Federal Republic of Germany: 'Thousand Roofs Programme' for promotion of solar energy.
1990	Federal Republic of Germany: phasing out of CFCs by 1995, soon after changed to 1993.
1990	The dumping of dilute acid in the North Sea – the target of Greenpeace Deutschland's first campaign in 1980 – is finally banned.
1990	Monika Griefahn, hitherto the chair of Greenpeace Deutschland, becomes environment minister of Lower Saxony.
1990	Ernst Ulrich von Weizsäcker, *Erdpolitik: Ökologische Realpolitik an der Schwelle zum Jahrhundert der Umwelt.*
1990	USA: an amendment to the Clean Air Act of 1970 introduces emission bonds for sulphur dioxide – a decisive breakthrough for emission rights trading.
1990	Paul Watson ('Sea Shepherd') rams two Japanese drift-net ships, without becoming the object of a law suit.
Feb. 1990	Siemens buys Arco Solar, the largest US producer of solar cells.
spring 1990	Japanese NGOs help to set up the first International Narmada Symposium.
Apr. 1990	The European Council resolves to create a European Environmental Agency to develop a Europe-wide system of environmental information.
22 Apr. 1990	US Earth Day centrally features the Save the Ozone campaign; IBM and other Silicon Valley companies are targeted as the world's largest users of CFCs. The Silicon Valley Toxics Coalition (SVTC) is founded.
1990	IPCC report on 'Political Impacts of Climate Change' states: 'Deforestation will cease only when natural forest is economically more valuable than any other land use for people living in and around it.'
1990	The IUCN World Parks Commission sets the goal of making 10 per cent of the earth's surface protected. This was actually exceeded over the next two decades: by 2012 protected areas accounted for a total of 12 per cent.
May 1990	The ITTO publishes a report on Sarawak that recommends limits on woodcutting.
30 May 1990	BSE alarm: France imposes a complete ban on British beef imports.

June 1990	London review conference of parties to the 1987 Montreal Protocol.
12 Sep. 1990	At its final session before German unification, the GDR Council of Ministers approves the most extensive national parks programme in German history.
28 Sep. 1990	Federal Republic of Germany: Der Grüne Punkt – Duales System Deutschland, a 'company for the avoidance of waste and the acquisition of secondary raw materials', emerges in response to the law on rubbish separation and maximum recycling, which had come into force on 12 June.
2 Dec. 1990	German federal elections: the Greens fail to pass the 5 per cent hurdle.
7 Dec. 1990	Federal Republic of Germany: the Electricity Feeding Act, which 10 years later, under the SPD–Green coalition, will be expanded into the Law on the Promotion of Renewable Energy.
1991	Break-up of the Soviet Union.
1991	The 'GDR Conservation League', founded in March 1990, fuses with the German Bird Protection League (DBV) to form Naturschutzbund Deutschland (NABU), which will become the most influential conservancy association under its new (from 1992) president Jochen Flasbarth.
1991	The Wuppertal Institute for Climate, Environment and Energy founded in North Rhine-Westphalia.
1991	An anti-nuclear campaign in the aftermath of Chernobyl gives rise to the alternative Elektrizitätswerke Schönau (EWS) in the Black Forest. It pioneers a growing number of 'rebel power stations', which use a maximum percentage of renewable energy sources while caring for the beauty of the environment.
21 Mar. 1991	For safety and other policy reasons, the German government orders the closure of the SNR-300 fast breeder reactor at Kalkar, which, because of objections by the North Rhine-Westphalia government, had never entered service after its completion in 1985.
from April 1991	Successful Greenpeace campaign against a North Sea pipeline.
1991	The European Parliament calls for a ban on trawling within the EU.

Aug. 1991	President Nazarbaev of Kazakhstan follows up a miners' strike by decreeing that no more nuclear tests will be held on Kazakh soil.
Aug. 1991	Launch of the World Wide Web.
16 Sep. 1991	*Der Spiegel* cover: 'Greenpeace Money Machine – Environmental Corporation Under a Cloud'.
Sep. 1991 to July 1992	On instructions from the World Bank, the Morse Commission reviews the Narmada dam project and reaches a negative judgement.
25–7 Oct. 1991	Washington: First National People of Color Environmental Leadership Summit.
7 Nov. 1991	Salzburg: Alpine countries and EU agree on a convention especially covering environmentally sustainable tourism in the region.
1991	Dave Foreman (Earth First!), *Confessions of an Eco-Warrior*.
1992	England: a militant Earth Liberation Front is founded on the model of the Animal Liberation Front.
1992	Al Gore, *Earth in the Balance: Ecology and Human Spirit*; Clinton becomes US president, with Gore as vice-president.
1992	Founding of the Potsdam Institute for Climate Research.
1992	Friends of the Earth Netherlands publishes *Sustainable Netherlands*, which points the way for the comparable *Zukunftsfähiges Deutschland* study conducted by the Wuppertal Institute for Climate, Environment and Energy.
1992	Fourth UN ozone conference in Copenhagen: the banning of aerosols harmful to the ozone layer is brought forward to 1 January 1996.
1992	USA: the EPA founds an Office of Environmental Equity.
26–31 Jan. 1992	International Conference on Water and Development (ICWD) in Dublin departs from guidelines of previous such conferences and declares that water should 'be regarded as an economic good'.
Feb. 1992	The countries bordering the Aral Sea found an Intergovernmental Coordination Committee for Water Supply (ICCWS).
May 1992	'Flora, Fauna, Habitat' (FFH) directives issued by the European Community.
June 1992	United Nations Conference on Environment and Development (UNCED) meets in Rio.

1992	Wave of redundancies at Greenpeace because of a fall in donations.
11 Sep. 1992	Turkey: founding of the Turkish Foundation for Combating Soil Erosion, for Reforestation and the Protection of Natural Habitats (TEMA), which has since become the country's leading environmental NGO. An environment ministry had already been created in 1991.
1 Oct. 1992	Deaths of Petra Kelly and Gert Bastian.
Dec. 1992	EPA report on 'Respiratory Health Effects of Passive Smoking', which attributes 3,000 lung deaths a year to passive smoking.
Dec. 1992	The UN establishes an Intergovernmental Negotiating Committee for the Elaboration of an International Convention to Combat Desertification (INCD), in which many NGOs also take part.
Dec. 1992	First Israeli–Palestinian International Academic Conference on Water takes place in Zurich.

A new global synergy: surprising data densities and concomitant factors

After a long stretch in which our material has been organized more by leitmotif than chronologically, we should now focus again on timelines for a while. Many events in the field of environmentalism have tended to escape the collective memory in a spiral outside history, and so it will bring some clarity if, in the old style of historians, we fix definite dates for as many facts as possible and order them in a temporal sequence. This may bring a number of surprises. The clustering of data around Earth Day 1970 is not so amazing, even if the degree of it is rather phenomenal. But the existence of a similar nodal point in 1990 is at first unexpected, indeed quite intriguing. This concentration of the data becomes striking only in a global perspective.

Just a few years after Chernobyl, the complaint was often heard in the German eco-scene that the reactor disaster had changed nothing, and a focus only on Germany – or only on America and Japan – would not lead one to think that those years had been a high point of environmentalism. In the old Bundesrepublik, many did initially experience Chernobyl as the biggest watershed since the Second World War and the beginning of a new age of anxiety. But a few years later came the collapse of the GDR and the process of German unification, and the Greens suddenly found that their anti-national slogans had dissipated the anti-nuclear wind in their sails and taken them to their lowest point so far. In the United States, even environmentalist circles did not perceive Chernobyl as a key turning point; it has no entry of its own in the major *Encyclopedia of World Environmental History*, which devotes a special article to the otherwise virtually unknown Chimurenga tree conservation movement.[2] In 1986 America was still deep in the Reagan era, and new worries emerged in his second presidency when he moved away from his hardline anti-enviro position. At the end of the decade the Sierra Club chair still thought that environmentalism was at a nadir, and could see nothing but confusion in the country's environmental politics. Yet over the years, the challenge from a hostile president led to revitalization of the movement, so that fresh militant blood flowed in and the budget of the Sierra Club itself increased tenfold.[3]

Along with the USA and the Bundesrepublik, Japan was a pioneer of the new environmental policy in the 1970s. By 1990, however, it too had other worries: both politicians and the general public were preoccupied with the bursting of the speculative 'bubble economy' that heralded an era of depression and disillusionment. Already Japan had become an 'eco-outlaw' and 'environmental predator', in the language of international ecological communication.[4] Outrage over the destruction of rainforest in Southeast Asia and Chile was directed primarily against Japan, as was anger at the continuation of whaling; it was painful for Japanese environmental activists to watch their country lose face. Japan Tropical Forest Action Network (JATAN) was founded in 1987, partly on the initiative of the international Friends of the Earth.[5] Japanese environmental policy-makers who had previously focused exclusively on their homeland now began to think beyond its frontiers.[6] The Brundtland Commission, whose work relied on sponsorship, received most generous funding from Japan. And at the Earth Summit in Rio in 1992, Japan tried to make a name for itself as the 'leading ecological power'.[7]

Greenpeace, the rising star of the early eco-age, went through a critical period around 1990, especially in the United States: reduced objectives, donations and media impact led to drastic staff cutbacks, and in 1991 its founder David McTaggart stood aside. At the same time, however, the Greenpeace apostate, 'ocean warrior' Paul Watson, made all the greater stir. When Peter Bahouth, the long-time executive director of Greenpeace USA, identified a more general crisis of the environmental movement, relating it to the collapse of Communism and the loss of an enemy image,[8] his diagnosis was patently wrong.

As the above timeline shows, a global perspective tells quite a different story. It also becomes clear that, for all the diversity of the groups and *groupuscules* and all the national and regional specificities, it is still meaningful to watch out for worldwide connections. More doubtful is the extent to which it makes sense – and is not just wishful thinking – to speak of a 'global society'. But anyone who looks back at the world wars and the Cold War will immediately detect the huge change that has come about since the late 1980s. And it was not least ecological communication – previously obstructed by East–West tensions – which gave a content to the new international common ground.

It is true that doubts may still occur. Are we not yoking together events that actually have nothing in common: the West German anti-nuclear movement, the campaign of American wilderness enthusiasts to protect the spotted owl habitat, the blocking of roads to foreign loggers by Dayak tribespeople in Sarawak? Are we not seeing things through the blinkers of our own time when we fall for the suggestiveness of the term 'environment'? In those three cases, very different human groups were certainly fighting for very different reasons. But a look at the series of data is enough to reveal certain cross-connections. The 'Chernobyl effect' boosted anti-nuclear protests as well as movements for democracy as far away as East Asia.[9] And in so far as the reactor disaster contributed to the collapse of the Soviet Union, it became the trigger for whole chain reactions that reshaped the situation facing the environmental movement.

A comparison with the ecological awakening of 1970 is instructive, since this time the spark was much more clearly a major disaster. This raises the question of why the new global surge in environmental awareness did not begin on 3 December 1984,[10] when a highly toxic cloud of methyl isocyanate gas leaked from the Union Carbide (today Dow Chemical) factory at Bhopal, India, killing some five thousand (mostly poor) people within a few days. The number of long-term fatalities is now estimated at 20,000, and the figures for those with impaired health – the gas can cause blindness, nerve and lung disorders, and genetic damage – vary between 150,000 and 500,000. It was the worst catastrophe in industrial history. The chemicals factory in Bhopal produced pesticides – the sector on which Rachel Carson had concentrated in *Silent Spring*. The disaster that hit the Italian town of Seveso on 10 July 1976, leading to the alarm cry 'Seveso Is Everywhere', brought the dangers of chemicals to the centre of public attention,[11] but in comparison with Bhopal it appears almost harmless. No deaths could be attributed unambiguously to the accident. Even in Chernobyl, the number of those who died as a direct result of the accident was far smaller than in Bhopal.

But Chernobyl was eerier and bred far more rumours. Bhopal had brought devastation 'only' to impoverished outlying districts; Chernobyl spread fears of cancer to large parts of Europe. As the radioactive cloud drifted over Scandinavia and Central Europe, upper estimates of the long-term incidence of cancer and misshapen offspring were appallingly high. In the year 2000 even the Russian minister for disaster relief – by then there was one! – attributed roughly 300,000 deaths to the calamity;[12] speculation about the rise in cases of childhood leukemia aroused particular concern. But the number of 'liquidators' alone – people exposed to high radiation levels during cleaning-up operations and later thought to be doomed – rose to 600,000; other estimates put the total number of victims at over one million. Perhaps this was much too high, but who was interested in finding out?[13]

In the case of Bhopal, the weight of blame was rather unclear; there was no straightforward enemy image.[14] Was the risk of disaster part of the very nature of the chemical business, and if so how was it to be recognized and assessed? Or was it a result of sloppy management? Should Indian activists target the multinationals for taking safety less seriously in the third world, or was the enemy closer to home? Did the main responsibility lie at the American corporate headquarters or at the Indian management level? How important was the lack of effective inspection on the part of the Indian government?

This situation made it all too easy for managers and judges to keep passing the buck, so that – as an analysis of the court proceedings shows – the accident itself was followed by a 'second disaster' for the victims: a never-ending ordeal through the justice system.[15] No influential NGO seems to have taken up their cause on the spot; Bhopal was rather a distraction from the main issues of the Indian environmental movements. Chernobyl, on the other hand, shone a bright light on the weaknesses of an already crumbling system. A comparison between the two accidents demonstrates the importance of general historical contexts. Chernobyl activated or reactivated the anti-nuclear movement as far away as Korea and Taiwan, as well as accelerating the disintegration of the Soviet Union; it was easier to construct an enemy image here than in Bhopal and to translate the sense of outrage into an ongoing campaign. The nuclear chain reaction at Chernobyl set off worldwide chain reactions in environmental policy, even in countries where the disaster had not unleashed a wave of anxiety. It could act as a catalyst because a political potential was already present; it is not proof that fear of catastrophe is at the origins of environmentalism. Even in Stockholm, where the major environmental summit took place in 1972, a general breakthrough came only in 1988 and was not directly linked to Chernobyl: 'That year, amid reports of toxic algal blooms and seal deaths and a dawning awareness of climate change to come, the environment became a burning issue as never before.'[16]

Assisted by the collapse of the Eastern bloc, the number of NGOs shot up around 1990; some spoke of a 'global associational revolution' or an 'NGO-ization' of much of the Soviet bankruptcy estate. At the Rio Earth Summit, an elite of NGOs appeared as never before as the vanguard of a blossoming global civil society.[17] Chapter 27 of *Agenda 21*, the Rio action programme, is headed 'Strengthening the Role of Non-Governmental Organizations: Partners for Sustainable Development' and begins with the assertion: 'NGOs play a vital role in the shaping and implementation of participatory democracy. Their credibility lies in the responsible and constructive role they play in society.'[18] The World Bank began to take greater account of environmental aspects in the projects it promoted and to involve NGOs in its decision-making processes.

As 'the environmental movement', protest campaigns that had previously been thought of as a hillbilly phenomenon now became champions of the common good and pioneers of a new modernity. Media, conferences and environmental associations all contributed to transnational networking. When the American *Exxon Valdez* supertanker ran aground off the coast of Alaska in March 1989, spilling some 11 million US gallons of oil, it caused an outcry much greater than the Ixtoc Uno disaster in the Gulf of Mexico had done ten years earlier, when twenty times more oil had been spilled.[19] No death of an environmentalist caused such widespread outrage as the murder of Chico Mendes on 22 December 1988, although he was actually a rubber-tappers' leader and contract killings are an everyday occurrence in Latin America.

In the end, all this was possible not only because of the link word 'environment' but because, at least indirectly, many of the problems were linked with one another by their very nature; the ecological boom of those years cannot be explained in terms of concepts or discourse alone. In the same year as Chernobyl, the first great 'global warming' alarm sounded out and distracted attention from the danger of nuclear technology. It has long been forgotten that, until a few years before, fear of a 'nuclear winter' had still associated the climate alarm with the anti-nuclear movement; the new focus on carbon dioxide broke this association and, at the same time, shifted the ground of struggle away from local toxic emissions and the realm of occupational medicine. The alarm over the destruction of tropical forests, which swept the world not long after Chernobyl, also had no connection with the reactor disaster. It was secondarily linked with the climate alarm but did not arise out of it. No discursive logic led from Chernobyl to Rio; a connection existed by virtue of the historical context. Chernobyl contributed to the collapse of the Soviet power bloc; East–West rivalry in the third world no longer operated as a driving force behind development aid; a new legitimacy was offered by environmentalism and now above all by climate protection.

In the eyes of the media, there was a synergy between the climate alarm and the ozone hole alarm that rang shrilly the following year. As Ernst Ulrich von Weizsäcker (founder in 1991 of the Wuppertal Institute for Climate, Environment and Energy) wrote in his programmatic book *Erdpolitik* (1989), environmental awareness had increased 'almost continually and, it would seem, unstoppably' in the previous two decades around the world, probably 'having crossed a critical threshold' in 1988. 'For the media, the ozone hole, global warming and the tropical forests became one of the lead stories. . . . The world economic summit placed the rainforests on its agenda in 1988. . . . Those who claim today that we are approaching the century of the environment do no more than express what everyone basically knows already.'[20] Gro Harlem Brundtland remarked of her world travels in 1987: 'Environmental interest was increasing. Knowledge was increasing. The ozone layer and climate changes were demonstrating that environmental action was now more than a matter of protecting plants and animals or fighting industrial pollution.'[21] In many countries of the world, the late 1980s and early 1990s appear a formative period on which environmentalism continues to feed today.

In a number of respects, it is instructive to compare the ecological conjuncture in 1990 with the 'revolution' of 1970. In both cases, we are dealing with an interplay between initiatives within civil society and the state apparatus; one-sided approaches that consider only social movements or government bodies fail to capture the reality. In 1970 the global horizon was already in view, but by 1990 globalization – at least of ecological communication, if not necessarily of environmental politics – was much more durable than two decades earlier. Not only had the 'iron curtain' between East and West been removed; a certain kind of North–South confrontation had also more or less resolved itself. It had been evident for a long time that environmental protection was not simply a first world luxury – that environmental problems were at least as burning in the third world as in the old industrial heartlands.

While first world environmental movements already displayed symptoms of old age and 'establishmentization', activism was only now really developing for the first time in large parts of Asia and Eastern Europe. 'Is there an environmental movement in the Soviet Union?' a *Spiegel* interviewer in 1985 asked the novelist Valentin Rasputin, whose peasant-heroine in *Farewell to Matyora* remained in her flooded native village after the building of a dam. 'Yes,' Rasputin replied, 'but unlike your Greens it is spontaneous, not organized.' There were no membership statistics. 'You need very little to belong to this movement: you have to remember and compare what our planet was like twenty or even ten years ago and what has become of it since.'[22] So, it was a Green movement in formation, conscious of a swift and highly topical decline of its own specific environment. In the West, ecological rhetoric combined with 'third world' rhetoric to form a new 'one world' rhetoric. More provocative than before, this associated third world poverty with the global ecological crisis and the type of economy emanating from the first world. From now on, it was mainly environmental issues – above all, the climate danger – which filled the One World with communicative substance.

Meanwhile, the new world without borders acquired a further, very different, substance that threatened to undermine ecological communication, as global financial flows no longer faced a Communist danger to restrain them. Until then the word 'global' had been virtually synonymous with 'good' for quite a few environmental activists, but once the initial One World euphoria had died down globalization began to look more and more unnerving. A latent tension that had existed since the beginning of the environmental movement – and which had been only verbally reconciled with the 'Think globally, act locally' slogan – now developed into a deep rift.

The political and ideological vacuum left by the collapse of Communism had a highly ambivalent aspect. For a time the environmental movement rushed in to fill the void: after the demise of the great political ideologies, it was alone in having something like a vision, a higher meaning, sometimes even spiritual experiences to offer. It was heard from parts of the former Soviet Union that ecology had become the new religion, often with its own esoteric elements.[23] On the other hand, the global power grab of unfettered capitalism took on more and more terrifying features. In India, Ramachandra Guha recorded a 'tremendous backlash against environmentalists' following the turn in world history.[24] Traditionally, whether or not they had more in common, environmental activists had typically been allied with sections of the left, but now they too came to sense the weakness of the left. Especially as unemployment increased, its combativeness on the economic front visibly declined; pragmatic environmentalists bet everything on the convergence of ecology and economics, which – even if it existed in the long term and at a general level – was signally lacking in many particular instances.

All in all, the new era of ecology stretching from 1990 down to the present day has been marked by deep tensions and contradictions. What we see is not a linear 'mainstream' but many ups and downs, especially extreme in Eastern Europe and parts of the former Soviet Union, where a slump often soon followed the eco-boom of 1990. The environmental conjuncture there proved to be context-dependent: when protest movements were no longer needed as a catalyst for democratic change and the creation of new nation-states, they tended to lose much of their impetus. In the second half of 1990, when the Soviet Union stood visibly on the precipice, sections of the press already levelled the charge of 'ecological masochism' against environmentalists; economic fears now ranked far ahead of concern for the environment.[25] Two decades after Chernobyl, Mikhail Gorbachev – by then a more popular figure in Germany than in his own country – expressed the hope to Franz Alt that Germany would become the 'ecological world power'.[26]

In most parts of the world, economic liberalization widened the gap between rich and poor, and partly also between rich and poor countries. Along with environmental problems, this is the greatest challenge for contemporary political thought, yet on no other issue has there been such an ideological vacuum since the decline of socialism. The question of how to deal with social justice has always been the crunch issue for the environmental movement; today we may assume that it will seal its fate.

Chernobyl and the collapse of the Soviet Union

'Death from ecocide' may well be what historians write on the death certificate of the Soviet Union: so begins a book by two renowned American experts that appeared in the year after the demise of the USSR.[27] Chernobyl was the largest single factor in this. It would seem that, at the latest with the reactor disaster of 26 April 1986, the question of how to handle environmental dangers was finally impacting on world history. Twenty years later, Gorbachev had this to say:

> The nuclear meltdown at Chernobyl . . . , even more than my launch of *perestroika*, was perhaps the real cause of the collapse of the Soviet

Union five years later. Indeed, the Chernobyl catastrophe was an historic turning point: there was the era before the disaster, and there is the very different era that has followed. The Chernobyl disaster, more than anything else, opened the possibility of much greater freedom of expression, to the point that the system as we knew it could no longer continue. It made absolutely clear how important it was to continue the policy of glasnost, and I must say that I started to think about time in terms of pre-Chernobyl and post-Chernobyl. . . . Chernobyl opened my eyes like nothing else.[28]

In the period immediately after Chernobyl, one finds no such statements on Gorbachev's part.[29] Moreover, many experts consider his explanation far too simplistic; it might be seen as a *post factum* reconstruction, invoking an external cause to divert attention from his own responsibility for the collapse of the Soviet Union. For the historian Julia Obertreis, it will be necessary to 'free ourselves of [the idea] that ecological problems kept piling up until the point of "ecocide" was reached and the Soviet Union fell apart'; in fact, the 'big question' is still 'the extent to which environmental problems contributed to it', and it has to be proven whether the regime's failings in this respect were 'as some of the literature suggests'.[30] Indeed, what can be demonstrated on the basis of what we know at present? Is it really plausible that a reactor disaster could shake a world power to its foundations?

In the view of German anti-nuclear critics, what Chernobyl highlighted was not so much particular defects of Soviet reactors and crisis management (which were not evident to Western observers at the time) as the extreme hazardousness of nuclear technology in general. Since the first sputnik launch on 4 October 1957, top Soviet technologists had been held in high regard, however abhorrent the system had appeared in other ways. On 10 December 1981, for example, the German CSU politician Matthias Engelsberger reported to the Bundestag on a speech in Moscow by the Soviet environment minister Yurii Israel:[31] 'He knew nothing about reactor disasters. . . . Soviet nuclear power plants were totally and utterly safe.' When the SPD's Wolf-Michael Catenhausen, the future head of the commission on gene technology, interpolated an ironical remark, Engelsberger confirmed: 'Here we see the Russians for the first time as a model, Herr Catenhusen.'[32]

All the more remarkable is it that the top echelons in the Soviet Union, as well as people outside them, saw the nuclear disaster as evidence of a distinctively Russian failing unimaginable on such a scale in the advanced industrial countries of the West. Angela Merkel, who had been working as a physicist in the GDR at the time of Chernobyl, recalled ten years later (when she was Germany's environment minister): 'For me, Chernobyl was mainly one more proof of the sloppiness with which I was familiar from trips to Russia.'[33] The Soviet historian Aleksandr Revalskii went even further, seeing Chernobyl as 'the catastrophe of the Russian mind-set';

Russians behaved with machinery like a cab driver with his horse, constantly resorting to kicks and curses.[34]

The assumption that the operating crew had mishandled the reactor led to the circulation of wild rumours. The official version too, on which the Brundtland Commission relied in 1987, was that the operators had behaved in a grossly negligent manner.[35] This typical shifting of blame onto the weakest – not unknown in reactor accidents in the West either[36] – appears to have lasted until early July 1986, when it became clear to the Politburo that the Soviet-designed RMBK reactor was inherently risky. Evidently a small oversight had been enough to trigger a huge explosion; one credible version suggested that the disaster had actually begun with a safety test![37] It turned out that the reactor had originally been designed to produce plutonium for military purposes, developing in isolation from safety advances in the West – which would fit into Gorbachev's thesis that the preceding decades had been ones of 'stagnation'.

'All countries with developed reactor technology work with a different type of reactor', A. P. Alexandrov, president of the Soviet Academy of Sciences, explained on 3 July 1986 to an apparently surprised Politburo. When Gorbachev irritably followed this up by asking Valerii A. Legasov whether it was true that the RMBK reactor was 'the least researched', he received the laconic answer: 'Yes, that is so.'[38] He would have known: the reactor type had been developed at the Kurchatov Atomic Energy Institute, of which he had been deputy director.[39] And at a public hearing held by the Brundtland Commission in Moscow on 8 December 1986 – another novel departure in the Soviet handling of environmental problems – Legasov (who until Chernobyl had been an unhesitating supporter of Soviet reactor construction[40]) declared: 'The consequences of Chernobyl have made Soviet specialists once again pose a question: Is not the development of nuclear energy on an industrial scale premature? Will it not be fatal to our civilization, to the ecosystem of our planet? On our planet so rich in all sorts of energy sources, this question can be discussed quite calmly.' This statement was incorporated into the final report of the Commission.[41] One of the few to speak out early on, Legasov became increasingly scapegoated and eventually hanged himself in April 1988.[42]

The Ukrainian journalist Alla Yaroshinskaya, a member of the Supreme Soviet in the final period of the USSR, carried out investigations of her own in the Chernobyl area shortly after the disaster. She also managed to rescue and publish secret records of Central Committee meetings (for which she was awarded the Alternative Nobel Prize in 1992), and accused the Soviet leadership of having conducted from the beginning a perfidious policy of systematic misinformation.[43] This was a common charge in the West at the time, but Gorbachev later rejected it: 'In fact, nobody knew the truth, and that is why all our attempts to receive full information about the extent of the catastrophe were in vain.'[44]

The records brought to light by Yaroshinskaya support Gorbachev's defence, at least to some extent. Deliberate disinformation seems to have been practised more at lower levels, with the result that those at the top had an inadequate overview of the situation; the hesitations and downplaying were not so far removed from the way in which Western governments would probably have conducted themselves. To be sure, the 'operational group' set up by the Central Committee to tackle the consequences of the accident tried to present itself as competent and well informed, but the records show between the lines that this was not really the case.

The documents tell us that, without independent media and a critical public, even the pinnacle of a totalitarian dictatorship is incapable of gaining a general, and at the same time penetrating, view of a crisis situation with which the apparatus is not equipped to deal. The Chernobyl fiasco must have taught Gorbachev that 'glasnost' or 'openness' was not only a slogan of democratization but also a requirement for effective rule. In its absence, even the top man in the country was a victim of the bureaucracy. In September 1986, at the special conference in Vienna of the International Atomic Energy Authority, leading Soviet scientists openly stated to the new German environment minister, Walter Wallmann, that Chernobyl had 'finally delegitimized the Soviet system of secrecy and cover-ups', shattering 'the last bastions against the policy of glasnost'.[45] And indeed it was only after Chernobyl that the era of glasnost, as distinct from perestroika (restructuring of the economy and administration), really got under way. When the horrors of the meltdown were uncovered, there was no longer any holding back about the crimes of Stalinism. The media escaped the control of the leadership of the Soviet state.

The Central Committee also revealed something that Gorbachev appears to have recognized too late: that, even with the best will in the world, such crises cannot be totally managed from the top down; there also need to be competent bodies capable of taking decisions on the spot. More than two years after Chernobyl, Gorbachev admitted to the Nineteenth All-Union Conference of the CPSU: 'We had already attempted a lot from above. That brought nothing.'[46] No wonder: for even a totalitarian system can only function to a limited extent through central planning; there too, whether in a planned or a hidden way, decisive things also happen at a lower level.

In 1989 Yurii Lebedinskii thought that the mega-disaster had triggered 'an explosion in social consciousness';[47] there was a new critical tone regarding not only nuclear technology but also river diversions and other previously taboo issues. At a time when incompetence and corruption were being uncovered on all sides, environmentalists were generally seen as trustworthy.[48] Oleg Yanitskii, the early Russian environmental sociologist, remarked from the vantage point of 1995: 'Ecological protest during the years 1987–89 in the USSR was the first legal embodiment of broadly democratic protest and solidarity of citizens as citizens.'[49] At first it looked as if Chernobyl was giving a powerful impetus to Gorbachev's policy of perestroika. Whereas official information policy in the first few months created the suspicion that glasnost was just a new chapter in Soviet hypocrisy, he later succeeded in using the disaster as proof that a new openness was vitally necessary. Yet, in retrospect, it seems rather that the reform policy went out of control as a result of Chernobyl. For the new era it heralded was essentially one of reform from above, its main objective being 'acceleration of the scientific-technological process' or 'a radical breakthrough in all spheres of research and technology'.[50]

Since the first sputnik in 1957, the 'scientific-technological revolution' had been the great hope of reform-minded forces in the Eastern bloc. In this ideal scenario, scientists – no longer the mythical proletariat – would be the heroic protagonists with a natural propensity to intellectual freedom. In the West too, there was a vision of the modern scientific-technological elite as an unstoppable force overcoming the sluggishness and ideological narrow-mindedness of the old system.[51] Science had always been the refuge of conservationism, even if, in their hearts, conservationists had been driven at least as much by spiritual motives.[52]

Most of the time, this conservationism coexisted peacefully with technocratic ambitions. Space travel was the trump card of the new elite, but from the 1950s the nuclear technology growing out of theoretical physics was the epitome of the 'scientific-technological revolution'. At a time when faith in Marxism-Leninism was disappearing, the sputnik religion representing the revolutionary force of cutting-edge technology was also a source of legitimacy for the state-planned economy, which – as many believed even in the West[53] – seemed much more capable than private capitalism of developing and propelling large-scale science-based technological systems. The large number of trained engineers was often seen as an argument that the Eastern bloc countries would emerge victorious in the long run.

Belief in the liberating progress of technology persisted despite all the evidence of inefficiency in Soviet enterprises, but Chernobyl shook the foundations of the myth and left the Soviet system without a vision for the future.[54] The evident inability of the authorities to deal with the consequences of the disaster was the ultimate refutation of the idea that the centrally planned economy and the scientific-technological revolution were 'made for each other'. The root of the problem lay in the system itself, not in corrupt leaders. Even reform-oriented forces in the Soviet Union were unable to cope productively with Chernobyl.

No anti-nuclear movement with an alternative energy policy that might have converted the disaster into a positive signal existed; even today, there are fewer initiatives to develop renewable energies in the countries of the former Soviet Union than there are in China or Japan.[55] The pollution of Lake Baikal by a cellulose complex did mobilize Russian nature lovers in the late 1950s – love of rivers and lakes is an old tradition in Russia, and those who campaigned on their behalf were often regarded as heroes by the Soviet public.[56] Not surprisingly, the Davydov Plan to divert the Onega, Ob and Irtysh rivers from Siberia to Central Asia – which would have flooded many old cultural monuments and changed the landscape incomparably more than any other project around the world – caused widespread outrage.[57] Its origins went as far back as 1868, and it was Gorbachev himself who finally buried it in the same year as Chernobyl.[58] Just one year earlier, Valentin Rasputin had declared: 'Everything now depends on the re-routing of the Siberian rivers. That is the watershed that may play an immense role in the destiny of the nation. If it goes ahead, it will be impossible to stop our industrial managers; we will no longer be able to do a thing.'[59] One sees what a signal its cancellation sent out! At the Party Conference in 1988 Georgii Arbatov, director of the Soviet Academy of Sciences, raged against the madness of the project, arguing that it still existed only because of the lack of a critical public opinion.[60] The reactor disaster, by contrast, had no forces that could be mobilized around it.

The proceedings of the Nineteenth Party Conference are again instructive in this connection. Meeting from 28 June to 1 July 1988, shortly before the disintegration of the USSR became visible, it was one of the rhetorical high points of perestroika, but it is clear that delegates were following the new party line with the same loyalty as in the past. One speaker after another dutifully berated 'the bureaucrats', even though most were themselves part of the ruling apparatus. A great many words were spoken, and a Tolstoyan feeling for truth often clamoured against the duplicity of the past, yet a veil of silence lay over Chernobyl. It was obviously a taboo subject, even for reformers who might have used it to support their cause. Only Anatolii Logunov, the greybeard rector of Moscow's Lomonosov University, complained of how the 'loss of professional honour' had led to 'light-minded projects and ecological disruptions and accidents'. There was 'a whole pleiad of so-called specialists ready to justify and carry out any old job for an official body'. It was 'a serious illness that has spread in our society'.[61] After Chernobyl, what anti-nuclear critics had been saying in the USA since the 1960s became clear in the Soviet Union too: established science was not per se a force for independent critical thinking.

Another way in which Chernobyl thwarted Gorbachev's 'reforms from above' was that it spurred on the 'eco-nationalism' that was beginning to find a voice everywhere in the Soviet Union.[62] Among the Russians, as among the other nationalities, environmental awareness typically went together with a sense of homeland – a combination one finds all around the world, which, involving as it does a comprehensive rather than merely selective environmentalism, should not in principle be judged negatively. As we shall see, however, very different alliances entered into this new nationalism in the Soviet successor states. Given how difficult it must be to process a reactor disaster productively in one's own country, it may seem significant that there was so little of an ecology movement in Belarus[63] – which received 70 per cent of the radioactivity from Chernobyl, and which, after independence, felt its reliance on Russian natural gas as particularly onerous – and that on the other hand Kazakhstan displayed general anger at the systematic misuse of the country for Soviet nuclear weapons testing. In 1989 a protest movement was formed there under the name 'Nevada-Semipalatinsk', the test sites in the USA and the USSR respectively.[64] Over a period of four decades, 456 nuclear explosions took place 150 kilometres from Semipalatinsk, a city of 700,000 people; it was only gradually after the collapse of the Soviet Union that the full scale of the radioactive exposure was revealed, especially since many of the testing sites were not precisely known.[65] Having gained its independence, Kazakhstan voluntarily gave up the nuclear weapons stationed on its territory and, with them, the temptation 'to become the first official nuclear power in the Muslim world', as Artem Ermilow put it. On the other hand, it developed the ambition to become the world's largest uranium producer; it possesses roughly a fifth of global deposits, in second place just behind Australia.[66]

Against the background of Chernobyl, Gorbachev was able to use widespread horror over the radioactive discharge against Reagan's revival of the nuclear arms race – to be sure, in a way that downplayed the effects of the reactor accident. On 14 May 1986 he stated in a TV interview: 'The Chernobyl disaster has again highlighted the chasm that will open for mankind in the event of a nuclear war. Arsenal stockpiles conceal thousands upon thousands of catastrophes much worse than Chernobyl.'[67] Such warnings had been part of Soviet rhetoric since the days of Khrushchev; now Kazakhstan could make use of them against Moscow.

On the border between Kazakhstan and Uzbekistan lies the Aral Sea. In a 600-page survey of world regions facing ecological risks, commissioned by the United Nations in 1995, Nikita F. Glazovskii, director of the Geography Institute of the Russian Academy of Sciences, wrote that the Aral Sea was the 'clearest example of a "crisis region"'.[68] This was a remote effect of Khrushchev's policy of imposing cotton-growing in Central Asia by means of artificial irrigation – a high-risk gamble, like the shrill campaign to promote maize, whose vicissitudes played a role in deciding his political fate. At first, following several years of abundant rainfall, the Soviet Communist leader could show off a sea of white cotton tufts in former desert. But when the drought came, Khrushchev's reputation nose-dived – worse, the enthusiasm for virgin land cultivation, one of the strongest moral sources of strength of Soviet Communism, gave way to a painful hangover.[69] As in the American Dust Bowl half a century earlier, the plough turned from the pride of the agrarian pioneer into the instrument of soil degradation.[70]

Cotton-growing could continue only by means of large-scale irrigation, and the building of the Karakum Canal to ensure this was *the* 'giant prestige project' of the Turkmen Soviet Republic from 1954 on.[71] It drew its water from the Amu Darya, however, with the result that parts of the Aral Sea (into which it had previously flowed) turned into salt steppe; sand storms desertified agricultural land and made the lives of many inhabitants a hell on earth. With the coming of perestroika, the Soviet public became aware of the environmental disaster in the region, and in the year after Chernobyl a special government commission was established under Yurii Israel to investigate the situation. This did not achieve much. But the next year, in the spirit of glasnost, the journals *Novyi mir* and *Pamir* organized Expedition Aral-88, which caused a stir by publishing accounts from people directly affected by the events.[72] Three years later, when the Central Asian republics became independent, Moscow no longer had to concern itself with the consequences and doubtless saw this as a positive aspect of the disintegration of the former world power.

Nevertheless, it is an irony of history that many of those who planned the irrigation projects were aware that the Aral Sea had been considerably smaller in earlier times, and that the rivers feeding it had flowed hither and thither or been diverted on various occasions.[73] 'Did there have to be an Aral Sea?', they asked. Was not the cotton grown with its waters more useful? Unlike Lake Baikal, this unsightly body of water was never an idol for Russian national romanticism. The disaster is thus a warning that, even when 'learning from environmental history', one has to look closely at the evidence and the changing times. Salty sand storms that may have caused little or no trouble when the region was empty of settlers became catastrophic as soon as intensive development began.[74]

The concentration of the world public on the Aral Sea itself diverted attention from the disaster all around it. This was made considerably worse by the horrific levels of pesticide used in the cotton fields, which exceeded the worst visions of Rachel Carson. Dust storms then spread this to the food of the local population, whose mortality rate increased fivefold within a decade. The worst affected region was Karalpakistan, in the Soviet republic of Uzbekistan, where the Amu Darya emptied into the Aral Sea.[75] As in so many other places on earth, from the American West to Australia, the irreversible increase in soil salinity pushed farming and irrigation ever outward: 'In its quest for cotton, the USSR created the single greatest irrigation disaster of the twentieth century' – with its eyes open, moreover.[76] Theoretically, Soviet central planning could have maintained a general oversight of such projects and their side effects, and anyone observing the power apparatus from the outside might easily have believed that this was so. But that was pure theory: what it overlooked was the rampant diffusion of responsibilities within an uncontrolled bureaucracy.

Yet another irony is that the Davydov project, finally scrapped by Gorbachev, would have saved the Aral Sea and perhaps protected the surrounding region from salty sand storms. This was not the least of the reasons why Reimar Gilsenbach, later a semi-official ecologist in the GDR (though watched suspiciously by the Stasi), expressed enthusiasm for the project: indeed, he described it as 'the greatest plan ever thought up for the reshaping of nature'.[77] When Gorbachev visited Central Asia in 1988, he even agreed to reconsider his decision when people living around the Aral Sea sent delegations to plead with him for a resumption of the project.[78] And after the great turn of 1990–1, Uzbek 'Greens' were still demanding that the Ob and Irtysh be diverted to save the lake.[79] For the rulers of the new post-Soviet Russia, however, it was no longer their problem.

Together with Belarus, Ukraine was the worst hit by the Chernobyl disaster: the reactor lay on its territory, a hundred kilometres as the crow flies north of Kiev, at the entrance to an elongated artificial lake on the Dniepr that reaches almost as far as the capital. It is true that the wind blew the radioactive cloud mostly towards Belarus, and then northwest towards Sweden, where the first alarming measurements attracted international concern. But radioactive water contamination affected Ukraine. Mass panic broke out in Kiev even before people in Moscow had realized the scale of the catastrophe.[80]

Chernobyl was the stimulus for a revival of Ukrainian national feeling and for anger with the central authorities in Moscow. But after the break-up of the Soviet Union, when energy independence from Russia became the number one priority, Chernobyl – now spelled Chornobyl – was useful only for obtaining Western subsidies. The 26th of April did not become a day of commemoration in the new Ukraine, and to the disgust of Western observers the Chernobyl reactors not destroyed by fire continued to function. After the 'Orange Revolution' of 2004, which gave increased scope to civil activism, surveys showed that Chernobyl still had an effect on opinion formation, with two-thirds of the population opposed to nuclear power.[81] Yet government policy maintained it as an important energy source.

Officially, the great famine or Holodomor of the early thirties plays a much more important role in the national memory, being seen as a case of deliberate genocide on the part of the Soviet leadership. The very word evokes the Holocaust by assonance, and Ukrainian nationalists have sought to make denial of its intentional nature a crime on a par with Holocaust denial. However, it is doubtful whether Soviet agrarian policy in those years was directed especially against Ukraine; Stalin, the Georgian, wanted to use starvation to break peasant resistance to collectivization, whether it came from Ukrainians or Russians.[82]

Beyond issues to do with the reactor type and Soviet crisis management, what are the general lessons of Chernobyl? Whereas, seven years earlier, it was disputed whether the Three Mile Island accident really had gone beyond a 'maximum credible accident' (MCA) – there were no horror stories of people dying from the immediate effects of radiation – it seemed this time that the hypothetical had actually happened, at a time when nuclear energy was not much of a public issue and even opponents no longer thought of such a disaster as a real possibility. Chernobyl was hard evidence that the need for safety precautions applied not only to known dangers but also to the hypothetical risks of new technologies.

Of course, such thinking was not so easy to implement in practice. Aaron Wildavsky (1930–93), the son of Jewish immigrants from Ukraine and (at the time of Chernobyl) president of the American Political Science Association, used all his ingenuity to argue that society would be crippled if every last consequence of the precautionary principle were to be enforced.[83] Not without venom, he pointed out that even supporters of the arms race operated with a precautionary principle and a 'worst case scenario'.[84] And when he himself was dying of lung cancer – perhaps for that very reason – he did not want to know about the agonizing debates among politicians and the public over the potential causes of cancer.[85] As one of the most influential risk theorists in American political science, he helped to ensure that the precautionary principle has still not fully triumphed in US environmental policy – as is most apparent on climate issues. In most studies of the American environmental movement, one would scour the index in vain for the term 'precautionary principle'; it does not fit the pro-active style of the EPA, which works best in relation to clearly perceived dangers.

In fact, the imagination knows no limits in the construction of hypothetical risks; it would be neither possible nor rational to safeguard against every single one. It is necessary to distinguish among different levels of risk, and to take precautions mainly against those that can be shown to exist on the basis of solid historical material. Even before Chernobyl, however, there was plenty of evidence of the high risks associated with nuclear technology, and the list of near-disasters was ominously long. But since many had been hushed up for most of the time – for example, the consequences of the Windscale incident in Britain or of the Kyshtym disaster in the southern Urals, both in 1957[86] – most of the public was not aware of the full scale of the problem. Often the passing of time had caused the memory to fade.

Today, as the memory even of Chernobyl begins to fade, awareness of the risks associated with nuclear technology has reverted to the level before 26 April 1986. Already in 1997 the prominent environmentalist Alexei Yablokov – initially a member of the Security Council of the Russian Federation under Boris Yeltsin, then pushed into the political wilderness – expressed his frustration that the Russian environmental movement was back where it had been ten years earlier: it was necessary to begin again the task of convincing Russians that 'the environment matters'.[87] The same seems to be true in the successor states of Central Asia.[88] Things are different in some of the others, but there too Chernobyl and its consequences are threatened with oblivion.

The impact of Chernobyl in Germany: the GDR's stranded ecology movement and the Green fiasco after unification

Chernobyl, together with glasnost and perestroika, marked a key turning point in the GDR too,[89] although the East German leadership tried to keep the Soviet new course out of their country. With the USSR no longer the great model, it became less risky to speak of the risks of Soviet nuclear reactors; and those in the GDR came from the Soviet Union, even if they were not of the same type as in Chernobyl. In public, the leaders of the ruling Socialist Unity Party downplayed the effects of the disaster, but internally they were very concerned about the safety defects, especially as it was known that repeated improvements had been necessary before units at the North power plant near Lubmin came into service, and that there had already been a number of significant incidents there.[90] After Chernobyl, the government ordered a series of additional safeguards for the Stendal plant, which had been delayed repeatedly since work began on it in the early 1970s, and which in fact would never come into operation. As elsewhere in the Eastern bloc, however, it was decided to avoid the extra expense of a dome-shaped concrete containment – long standard in the West and the reason why radioactivity from the Three Mile Island incident had not contaminated the surrounding area.[91]

Erich Honecker told Western interlocutors at the time that, if the GDR had had black coal reserves, it would have given up nuclear energy.[92] This was not the position of the minister responsible for economic policy, Günter Mittag, but insiders let it be known that Honecker was not one of those for whom nuclear energy embodied progress in the 'scientific-technological revolution'. Not by accident did he come to power in 1971 as a critic of the technomania of the late Ulbricht era. Under his rule there was a hidden resentment that, for all the lip service to the scientific-technological revolution, GDR industry was becoming more and more stagnant.[93] Let us be clear: it remained politically correct in the GDR, even after Chernobyl, to advocate nuclear power, and some courage was required to refer in public to the risks it involved. Yet a spell was clearly broken in 1986 – and not only with regard to nuclear dangers. The crippling fear of the apparatus of totalitarian control began to subside, so that the regime increasingly became a figure of fun as people sensed that it no longer had the Red Army behind it. Ecological campaigns that clashed with the prevailing political line appeared without exception in the post-1986 period, as did those which had nothing to do with nuclear energy: for example, the movement that gathered in village churches in Thuringia, under the leadership of local pastors, to protest against the huge pig-fattening plant at Neustadt an der Orla and its destruction of the traditional countryside.[94]

The West German environmental movement kept GDR citizens informed via television and numerous other channels;[95] the initiatives in the GDR cannot be understood without that background. It assured people that their criticism of the regime's reckless industrial policy did not mean they were reactionaries, but on the contrary that they were in the forefront of modernity. There is even much to indicate that, unlike in other Eastern bloc countries, the attractiveness of a nearby Western model rather hindered the development of a locally attuned environmental movement. For the truth is that, for many environmentally aware East Germans, the number one issue (present everywhere in the air they breathed) was not nuclear power but the country's dependence on brown coal of an ever worsening quality, which produced increasing amounts of waste and emissions. The 'Schwarze Pumpe' [Black Pump!] complex, built in Hoyerswerda from 1956 on, was by far the largest brown coal refining facility in the world, which for a time absorbed more than half of the total investments in the GDR;[96] lignite was also the foundation of the notorious 'chemical triangle' that took in Bitterfeld, Halle and Merseburg. 'Brown coal is socialism', declared Erich Rammler, the leading technologist at the Freiberg Mining Academy, in the simple style of those red banners that abounded in the GDR. But on his deathbed he sighed: 'This socialism business is harder than I thought.'[97] And the problems of brown coal were not much easier to solve; they increasingly shaped the destiny of the GDR, both economic and ecological.

In the early seventies, in the run-up to the Stockholm Environment Conference, the GDR leadership still believed it could make a name for itself in environmental policy and thereby win the recognition it had long sought in the West.[98] It created an environment ministry as early as November 1971, sixteen years before the Bundesrepublik, and at least on paper its environmental laws were certainly impressive.[99] Left-wing eco-activists in the West were convinced that the private-profit motive was the ultimate reason for the damage to the environment; this was music to the ears of the GDR leadership, and for a long time its assurances that East Germany's ecological problems were a 'legacy of imperialism' – or that the horrors of the 'chemical triangle' went back to Walter Rathenau rather than Walter Ulbricht – sounded more or less credible. In the early 1970s, which are generally regarded as the best period of the GDR, the Honecker leadership appears to have seen environmental protection as a special opportunity for the planned economy to prove its worth. But that all came to an end in 1974, after the first oil crisis; the officially celebrated 'weeks of socialist land culture' were written out of the annual timetable, and in 1976 it was decided to abolish the environment council within the Academy of Sciences.[100] We should not forget that, had it not been for the broad movement in society (and the Federal Environmental Agency inspired by it), the eco-age would have ended in West Germany too with the top-level meeting at Schloss Gymnich called by Chancellor Helmut Schmidt on 3 June 1975.

So long as the GDR had high-quality brown coal as well as cheap oil from the Soviet Union, it had no pressing need for nuclear energy; a word from Ulbricht in the early 1960s was enough to cancel the development of its own reactor types, much to the annoyance of East German technologists.[101] But after 1980 at the latest, the days of brown coal and cheap oil were over. With the GDR completely reliant on Soviet reactors, the party leadership approved the 'state nuclear energy plan' (1983), but it remained unclear how the country, already threatened with bankruptcy, was to fund this programme, the most ambitious in its history.[102] For the time being, it depended on brown coal deposits, which had been mined to such an extent that they were ironically called 'potting compost'. Expensive filtering systems were by now unthinkable.

The gaping wounds in the countryside caused by brown coal extraction were particularly exasperating. Still, as we know today, the 'moon landscapes' were not lost forever to man and nature. Attempts to exploit the slagheaps for agricultural purposes went back to the early period of the GDR, and in 1951 laws were even passed to promote 'topsoil management' (the saving of humus layers during the extraction of brown coal).[103]

Nowhere was so much experience of landscape creation accumulated as in the recultivation of lignite coal fields; the GDR was even ahead of the United States at the time. Moreover, in both East and West, 'renaturation' appeared alongside recultivation in the development of recreation areas – a change which, in the GDR, roughly occurred with the transition from Ulbricht to Honecker and was in keeping with the spirit of the eco-age.

The problem was that, for cost reasons and especially after 1973, the central plans for the mining sector increasingly neglected recultivation,[104] just as greater care for the 'topsoil' was becoming more and more necessary. In this respect too, lethargy prevailed in the latter days of the GDR: the environment ministry seems to have done next to nothing,[105] and Leipzigers were hard put to halt lignite mining at the gates of their city. In a way, nature shifted for itself: huge pitholes gradually filled up with water, coming to resemble natural lakes and even offering new leisure opportunities.[106] Another surprise was that many bio-ecologists were unhappy at the eventual disappearance of the 'moon landscapes', since unusual ecosystems, complete with orchids, had developed there.[107] But such discoveries, which again highlight the problem of value judgements in relation to nature, point well beyond the history of the GDR.

By 1980 the GDR leadership was in the grip of sheer fatalism. Newly available records show that its indifference to environmental damage was even greater than anyone imagined at the time. The environment ministry was little more than a phantom, such that even experts on the subject cannot understand what it actually did during its twenty-year existence.[108] Letters from environment minister Hans Reichelt to the powerful Central Committee economics secretary Günter Mittag were found unopened after the end of the regime:[109] indeed, in the view of Reimar Gilsenbach, Reichelt was a Potemkin figure representing the 'politics of the environmental lie'.[110] On 16 November 1982, the GDR Council of Ministers ordered that the notorious 'Directive for the Classification of Environmental Data' – which especially covered any areas of crisis – should itself be made a state secret![111] This was as deadly as fear of the Stasi for GDR environmentalism, since effective protest actions are in most cases primarily a question of information. Anyone in the GDR who sounded the alarm on an ecological issue was hard pressed to confront conformist professors with statistical material – and it was not surprising that activists, largely left high and dry by scientists, often sounded amateurish in their submissions.

With East Germany's *Naturschutz* one is in a quite different, friendlier world, in which there are idyllic places and success stories.[112] From Mecklenburg to the Uckermark, people still remember Kurt Kretschmann (1915–2007) – who thought up the long-eared owl symbol, now used throughout Germany – as the soul of conservancy. He started out in 1949 as an unpaid conservationist in Freienwalde, working skilfully with his wife, the local education counsellor, and sometimes even bluffing with collective farm people that he had the power of the state behind him. His story throughout the forty years of the GDR is of a fulfilled life with no major breaks, such as one does not often come across in East German biographies.[113] Much as in the West, the Communist rulers regarded conservation as a matter which, though not very important, had some value in principle, so long as it did not clash with powerful economic interests. In fact, its old association with heritage protection persisted more strongly than in the Bundesrepublik, at least in the cadences of popular speech. *Heimat*, a term with Nazi overtones for West German modernizers obsessed with mobility, was always a positively charged emotive word in the GDR. Even top party people were probably under no illusion that what kept citizens in the country was a love of their home region rather than a love of Communism.

Reimar Gilsenbach, at root a lifelong anarcho-socialist with an attachment to Gypsies, started out in 1952 as editor of the conservationist forum *Natur und Heimat*.[114] To create a revolutionary tradition, he combed the writings of the 1848er Emil Adolf Roßmäßler (1806–67) and assigned a prominent place to his journal *Aus der Heimat* in the prehistory of conservationism.[115] From 1981 on, Gilsenbach organized gatherings of writers, artists and environmental experts in the little village of Brodowin, in a lonely, romantic setting among seven lakes in the Uckermark. Then, from 1986, looking like a cross between a hippy and a prophet, he travelled round the GDR performing ecological songs with his new partner Hannelore Kurth.[116] On 28 May 1988 came the 'Oybin Declaration' of the Zittau environmental group belonging to the Arche network. 'In the last few years,' it claimed, 'a sense of *Heimat* has been growing ever stronger in our country.'

Like Roßmäßler and Gilsenbach, the Zittau group operated with a concept of *Heimat* that gained new substance from the living diversity of nature, but which also had a barb directed at official industrial policy: 'Our *Heimat* is not the front garden with a concentration of chemicals greater than in any maize field; it is the little plot in which the blackcap and the hedgehog also have a place.'[117] In the dachas that spread in the late GDR period, and without which many people would have found life unbearable, one detects not only the longing for a petty-bourgeois idyll but also an unarticulated yearning for a life in nature. East German environmental awareness, as it actually existed, should not be looked for only in books! Kurt Kretschmann, who like the older Darwin was fond of earthworms, opposed the dachaphobia of orthodox conservationists and the *noli me tangere* type of natural 'reserve', arguing instead that gardens ought to be incorporated into the world of natural conservation.[118] Saxon conservationists, on the other hand, welcomed German unification as an opportunity to save the Elbe flood plains from the advance of dachas.[119]

Conservancy, without doubt, had a niche existence in East Germany. Since the GDR was less densely populated than the Bundesrepublik, with an ever widening gap in car ownership and highway construction, many tree-lined avenues remained until unification; conservationists could nestle in out of the way corners and coexist more or less peacefully with a ruthless old-style industrialism. Little idyllic places, even in the area around

Bitterfeld, were lovingly depicted in countryside magazines. The honesty and seriousness of most conservationists were beyond question. Yet at the latest in the 1980s, environmentalism acquired a diversionary function in the overall scenario of East Germany's relations with the environment.

The pro-regime Gesellschaft für Natur und Umwelt (GNU), founded in 1980 within the GDR Culture Federation, was devoted mainly to conservation, retaining until the end some 60,000 members in 1,600 local groups. Such dimensions were beyond the wildest dreams of independent ecological groups. Nor were the GNU groups just a farce: membership was voluntary, and their role in conservation was not insubstantial. In this sense, the growth of the GNU may be seen as part of the environmental movement, even though it was founded from above to keep in line any Green stirrings in the population. On the whole, this appears to have been successful. Especially in the final years of the GDR, 'urban ecology societies' within the GNU clashed with the authorities as they ventured out of conservation niches. As two Arche members later recalled: 'The sorry state of the towns' – though 'not an issue for environmentalists' – 'was perhaps the most visible sign of the economic, cultural and social incompetence of the GDR leadership. . . . It is surely no accident that the demonstrations of autumn 1989 began in Leipzig, probably the GDR's most run-down city.'[120] It was also there that the 'Eco-Lion Environmental Association' was founded in November 1989.[121]

Like Jane Jacobs's campaigning in Greenwich Village, the fight to save heritage districts in the late GDR developed a politically explosive force. The GNU chair Harald Thomasius, a professor at the Tharandt Forestry College, associated conservation with 'cultural roots and patriotism', but also emphasized the 'indivisible unity of peace and environmental protection'.[122] The linkage of peace and environment issues in the latent opposition had its pendant within the GNU. In 1987 Thomasius stated that Chernobyl had 'painfully shown to us that environmental problems do not simply vanish with the appearance of socialism on the actual stage of world history'.[123] A new post-Chernobyl tone in the GNU too!

On the eve of German unification, the history of conservation in the GDR ended with a triumph that overshadowed anything in the previous hundred years, when the final session of the Council of Ministers (on 12 September 1990) decreed the creation of fourteen national parks and biosphere reserves comprising one tenth of its territory: the same order of magnitude that the World Parks Commission set in 1990 as the target for the whole world. As the opening of the Wall on 9 November 1989 initiated the GDR's terminal decline, it was East German conservationism that provided the romantic *coup de théâtre* fitting the historic moment. The federal environment minister, Klaus Töpfer, celebrated the great natural paradises now in prospect as the 'silver cutlery of German unity'; it soon became a catchphrase.

Subsequently, it was no longer so clear whether this 'surprise coup' by a 'quartet' of prominent conservationists – with conspicuous support from

Bonn – was not in fact a Pyrrhic victory that attracted the odium of a top-down directive; many people at the grassroots felt that they were being railroaded into something. West German nature lovers, visiting areas from Brandenburg to Usedom, discovered a solitude and sense of expanse they had never known in the old Federal Republic. But quite a few local residents did not want their home to become a Serengeti for 'Wessis', preferring instead to have industries and the jobs that came with them. In 1992 the Brandenburg agriculture minister even asked farmers to dismantle the barriers around conservation areas – and they did not need to be asked twice.[124] But with or without conservation, the hoped-for industry usually did not arrive, and so nature tourism became the main opportunity for many areas in the north of the ex-GDR. As for the former state hunting areas – which the GDR extended beyond those of Hermann Göring's time[125] – there could hardly be any objection to their being placed under protection.

In contrast to the Greens, leading German conservation associations were among the immediate winners from unification: the Deutscher Bund für Vogelschutz (DBV) – which had been in the wilderness for a time after it lost the financial backing of the Hähnle industrialist family in 1965[126] – appointed a dynamic new president in Jochen Flasbarth, transformed itself into the Naturschutzbund (NABU) and fused with the Naturschutzbund der DDR (a spin-off from the GNU).[127] In 1987 the BUND and other organizations had founded the European Nature Heritage Fund (EuroNatur), which, though oriented to Brussels, was especially involved in East European projects.[128] Conservationists far beyond the GDR now discovered with growing enthusiasm 'Europe's Wild East'; EuroNatur called Poland's Narew region 'Europe's Amazonia'.[129] Wilderness romanticism and American-sized national parks gained a new impetus. Nowhere else in 1990 was a common German spirit as demonstrable as in the field of conservation, albeit mainly at the upper levels.

Anti-nuclear activists, who had had only limited success in the old Bundesrepublik, effortlessly secured total victory in the former GDR: existing nuclear power units were decommissioned and work on the Stendal plant was stopped. The main player in this was actually the West German energy industry, whose overcapacity meant that it was capable of supplying the East with electricity, at a time when a mega-accident there would have revived on a much greater scale the panic that had followed Chernobyl. Old anti-nuclear campaigners were not alone in describing the four imported Soviet reactors at Lubmin as 'Chernobyl North', and in early 1990 *Der Spiegel* wrote that their history resembled a 'horror story': 'Two hours by car from Hamburg, Hanover and Berlin a nuclear explosive device is in operation, which could blow up at any minute and release a radioactive plume that would contaminate the whole of Central Europe.'[130]

Since Chernobyl it had seemed that something similar might happen at Lubmin, all the more since there was a basic respect for Soviet engineers and it was not simply assumed that the disaster had been due to

'Russian sloppiness'. Nor had warning voices been lacking in the GDR itself after 1986; the unease reached up to leadership level. Yet Wolfgang Rüddenklau, one of the initiators of the Environment Library in East Berlin's Zion church, thought in retrospect: 'A radical anti-nuclear movement could not have arisen in the GDR.'[131] One would seek almost in vain among the critics of nuclear energy for the passion and courage visible since the late 1970s in the GDR peace movement. Amid the smoke from brown coal, nuclear energy retained the progressive aura of a clean, new, science-based technology much longer than it did in West Germany. Even many of those unhappy at conditions in the GDR felt the Western agitation over Chernobyl to be typical of a country living in the lap of luxury.

But the opponents of nuclear power did achieve one remarkable coup: Michael Beleites's revelations of June 1988 concerning the serious health and environment hazards resulting from Soviet-run uranium mining in Saxony and Thuringia. The Church Research House at Wittenberg, since 1979 a centre for critical information on the environment in the GDR, produced a duplicated copy of his report, entitled *Pechblende: Der Uranbergbau in der DDR und seine Folgen*.[132] Before Chernobyl, such whistle-blowing about the resource base of Soviet nuclear weapons production would have been punished as the worst 'betrayal of the fatherland'.[133] Even now Beleites was not spared the attentions of the Stasi, but he remained at liberty. Also, with the Soviet regime about to lose its threatening aspect, the GDR leadership may have felt angry at being denied free access to the uranium resources of its own country.[134] Studies after 1989 showed that Beleites really had hit upon a potential risk of Chernobyl proportions. According to Carlo Jordan, in his report to the Bundestag inquiry on 'the history and consequences of the SED [Communist] dictatorship': 'The ecological legacy of the Wismut complex is gigantic. We are talking of one of the worst cases of radiation damage in the world; at Ronneburg, for example, roughly 40 million cubic metres of radioactive overburden [soil and rock covering a deposit of ore] on an area of 210 hectares, more than twenty times the volume of the pyramid of Cheops.'[135]

One of the brave actions that broke the forty-year spell weighing on the GDR was the documentary film *Bitteres aus Bitterfeld*, made in strict secrecy in June 1988 by members of the 'Arche Nova Green-Ecological Network', then smuggled out and broadcast to the GDR via West Berlin television. Bitterfeld, well off the tourist routes, had previously had a positive association in the Western literary scene: on 24 April 1959 the cry 'Put pen to paper, mates!' had rung out from the electrochemical complex there, calling on workers to describe their own world of labour, although this proved something of a dead end, since a realistic account of conditions in the infamous 'chemical triangle' would not have passed the censorship. Instead, after June 1988, the symbolism of Bitterfeld turned into its opposite, as it gained the reputation of the 'dirtiest town in Europe'. Two Arche members nevertheless argue that the 'Bitterfeld operation' exemplified 'an important dilemma for GDR ecological groups': 'Many were not unaware of the conditions in Bitterfeld, but very few really knew the situation there; even local people lived with their heads in the West and directly perceived the reality of their own lives only when *Bitteres aus Bitterfeld* was broadcast into their living rooms.'[136]

This was already in the run-up to unification. Whereas media-savvy Western activists aimed to be as conspicuous as possible, the main point in the GDR was to tread softly and adjust chameleon-like to the surroundings, so as not to arouse the wrath of the Stasi. Instead of openly denouncing pollution – and the 'death of the forest' was far more palpable in the Ore Mountains than in many places in the West – environmentalists contented themselves with veiled allusions, by planting trees that no one could possibly object to (although the Stasi did sometimes strike even then); one is reminded of Wangari Maathai's activity under the Kenyan dictatorship. East German environmental activists typically began with tree-planting operations, which, according to the historian of the GDR opposition, 'to some extent took on the features of a mass movement'.[137]

This initial modesty, quite unlike the ebullient, headline-grabbing spontaneity of the West German eco-scene, is reflected in the fact that the founding of environment libraries was often the first and, for a time, the only activity. In particular, the Zion church library, founded on 2 September 1986, 'soon became one of the communication centres of the opposition in Berlin, and then the GDR'.[138] Its greatest success developed out of its greatest crisis, when the Stasi occupied the building on 24 November 1987 and arrested its members. A library thus turned into a beacon; it elicited widespread solidarity action, and the detainees were set free again.[139] It was one of the events directly leading to the public explosion of discontent in autumn 1989.[140] There is much to suggest that the crippling fear of the state was disappearing by 1988 at the latest.[141]

But the various environmental groups did not unite spontaneously into a broader movement. One detects in the surviving documents quite a lot of sectarian narrowness and rivalry, and the old battle between 'grassroots democracy' and 'party democracy' was fought out between the Environment Library and Arche Nova – a bizarre spectacle from the outside, if one thinks of the minimal scope available for initiatives. The lack of a free public sphere, in which differences might have been ironed out, became depressingly palpable – and besides, a climate of mistrust developed because no one ever knew who was or was not a Stasi informer. Fear of infiltration led many groups to shut themselves off from anything new,[142] while disputes rumbled on over those who had resettled in the West: should they be seen as deserters or as useful contacts with the West German environmental movement? The stifling atmosphere of a republic in creeping paralysis, the little tricks of the ruling SED apparatus, the garbled language of official texts that dodged the issues: all this had an effect on attempts to engage in opposition. A historic opportunity was necessary for an irresistible mass movement to emerge out of these groups.

Attitudes that made a virtue of necessity are particularly interesting for an 'ecology of ecologism' in the GDR. In contrast to the helpless brooding in the West about how to drive growth out of the economy, zero growth was an actual reality in the GDR of the 1980s. Was there not a positive side to this situation, which caused more and more frustration inside the SED? Revulsion against the 'throwaway society' had little purchase in a country with a shortage of goods in the shops, where people did not easily discard anything that could be used again. In this respect the GDR was exemplary: it organized a system for the collection and recycling of industrial and domestic waste, achieving just under 40 per cent reuse rates without any expensive outlay on technology.[143] In comparison with the Bundesrepublik, the GDR offered a lesson in the *unintended* benefits of a large degree of self-sufficiency. This ecology of shortage can be observed in other Eastern bloc countries; it has been closely analysed in Hungary in particular.[144] It functioned best in relation to scrap metal. But the more complex industrial waste became, the less the centrally planned economy was fit for purpose.

The ecologism that took shape, mainly under the umbrella of the church, was one of frugality, of the simple life, of self-limitation to life's real necessities. What in the West easily degenerated into a convulsive hostility to pleasure was here a calm acceptance of prevailing scarcity. Protestants discovered the Catholic tradition of fasting, with the result that common fasts too became 'a kind of movement'.[145] At a time when virutally no one thought that German unification was round the corner, East German ecological groups tried to think of socialism as an opportunity for environmental protection; it would be unfair to blame them for this in retrospect.

Bicycles became a characteristic element in the self-projection of East German ecological groups, one advantage being that cyclists were more difficult to arrest than pedestrians in a demonstration. Their vehicles would not fit into police vans, and just to leave them behind in the street unattended would have offended the *Volkspolizei*'s sense of propriety. 'Getting around without a car' (*Mobil ohne Auto*) became 'the environmental activity for which the church was best known'.[146] Even Gilsenbach, who did not need the church for protection, recalled in 1986 out at Brodowin that Jesus did not teach 'May a Mercedes be your highest goal in life!', but 'Do not collect treasures on earth, where moths and rust eat them away and thieves break in and steal them.'[147]

Had the GDR regime not been so stuck in its old conception of progress, it might have welcomed this ecologism as a salvation in its hour of need. In fact, right up to the final years of the GDR, it was thought in church circles that some parts of the SED leadership really did believe this;[148] a clever innovator like Gorbachev might well have devised an eco-centred strategy that turned the GDR from a poor relative into a model for the economic wonderland to its west. On the other hand, such a leader would have had a hard time instilling enthusiasm for his ideal, when that wonderland was the stuff of dreams for GDR citizens. An ecologism of the simple life, which invokes the authority of Jesus, tends to have sectarian features. A more sophisticated appeal to people's existing consciousness involved protests against West German exports of toxic waste to the GDR, which treated it as a third world refuse tip.[149]

Of the German political parties, the Greens could in many ways have been the biggest winners from unification. Early on, leading figures such as Petra Kelly made contact with East German civil rights activists and, on 12 May 1983 – in an unprecedented action at the time – they demonstrated for disarmament on Alexanderplatz until they were led away by the East Berlin police. The situation fostered an elemental solidarity between dissidents in the West and the East. Toxic waste exports to the GDR were also a scandal in the eyes of the West German Greens.

The Gorleben project – a high-risk nuclear site on the piece of the Federal Republic jutting furthest into the GDR – had already been an affront to the regime in East Berlin, although this was not much commented upon at the time. The 'death of the forest', which along with Chernobyl brought the greatest successes for West German environmental activists, was far more evident in Saxony than in the Rhineland; not for nothing had the nineteenth-century search for forest damage caused by pollution begun in the Eastern regions of Freiberg and Tharandt. And the urban ecology groups, one of the courageous parts of the East German environmental movement, had a close affinity with the struggle of West Germans such as Joschka Fischer to preserve old city districts. So why were the Greens eventually among the big losers of unification – just a few years after Chernobyl, when environmentalism was experiencing a worldwide boom?

The solution to the puzzle sheds new light on the 'ecology of ecologism', where ecology is understood in the cultural sense of the term. The Greens – who precisely in 1989–90 behaved in such an anti-German way – were in reality the most German (= West German) of all the political parties; none other sprang so clearly from the special scene of the 1970s in the Federal Republic. For many old '68ers, 'anti-fascist' was still synonymous with 'good', and so even if they did not wish to live in the GDR they regarded it as the better Germany, whereas many non-conformist GDR citizens had long closed their ears to 'anti-fascist' rhetoric, which was all too often used there to demonize anyone out of favour with the regime. Under a 'left' dictatorship, dissidents no longer regarded 'left' as synonymous with 'good'.

Things were very different for Western Greens. The ample documentation on their first period as a force in the Bundestag (1983–7) has revealed the fateful role that Dirk Schneider (then unusually active on inter-German issues) played in blocking contacts with the GDR opposition.[150] Though only exposed in 1991 as an agent for East German state security, he made no secret of his sympathy for the SED and was thus more of an official than unofficial collaborator with the Stasi. But that was not all that separated dissidents in the West and East from each other. Eastern Greens close to the church had a profile not unlike that of the conservative traditionalists who right at the beginning had driven the Green left out of the party. Instead of 'open borders', they argued for an 'immigration law' to govern movement between the two Germanies. Western Greens, who felt inwardly more at home in Nicaragua than in Saxony-Anhalt, blew their top over this. Only after long negotiations was an agreement reached in January 1993 to merge the Western and Eastern Greens in Bündnis 90/Grüne. It was a marriage not of love but of convenience – without which the Greens would have been in danger of failing to enter the Bundestag.[151]

With hindsight, it is curious how late even the eco-scene in the West took notice of the horrific environmental damage in the GDR. Travellers who saw more than the official 'sights' could have known many things about the situation there, but they did not feel like raising an issue that seemed like a distraction. Only Chernobyl created a context to sound the alarm over Bitterfeld too. One deep reason for the electoral disaster in 1989–90 – the Greens lost heavily and only the Eastern Greens entered the new Bundestag – was evidently that many still drew a rigid dividing line for which anything 'national' was the number one enemy, at a time when wars between European nation-states were a thing of the past. They did not see that far greater dangers now stemmed from the economic aspects of globalization and the failing capacity of nation-states to pursue effective social and environmental policies. Despite the fast-growing popularity of environmentalism in the German population, many Greens – as Antje Vollmer admitted after the fiasco of 1990 – clung to the *idée fixe* that they were living in the Bundespublik as in an 'enemy country'.[152]

This obtuseness gave rise to a fatal unity of sentiment between 'Fundis' and 'Realos', the fundamentalist and realist wings of the party; both experienced the new German national consciousness as a pain in the neck. Even Joschka Fischer, the super-Realo, agreed with Günter Grass that the division into two states should be accepted as a consequence of Auschwitz that the Germans had brought upon themselves. To East Germans this must have sounded like pure mockery – as if the Holocaust was being used to conceal West German egoism under a veneer of superior morality; as if they should be punished over again, after forty years in which they had suffered most from the consequences of Nazi crimes. The Greens' recourse in the election campaign to a corny old spontaneist joke – 'Everyone's talking about Germany, we're taking about the weather' (a satire not only of a railway publicity slogan but also of the old Socialist Students' League) – may have been the last nail in the coffin in 1990; it is amazing how long pollsters predicted that the Greens would end up with 10 per cent of the vote, instead of slumping below 5 per cent.[153] When the Greens quickly recovered in the 1990s from the effects of their blindness, this testified not so much to their political acumen as to the strength and durability of environmental consciousness in the German population.

In the new Eastern *Länder* too, the popularity that environmental activists had acquired over the previous period suffered a reversal after unification. Should we conclude that the GDR's ecology movement had never been 'genuine' but had served only as a (theoretically legal) cover for oppositional activity, to be discarded once it was no longer necessary?

Of course, it happens everywhere that environmental movements typically also involve issues of democratization and citizen-based politics; this is further evidence that these movements cannot be deduced from imaginary ecological imperatives but must always be understood in their historical context. It is not surprising that environmentalism lost much of its original impetus at a time when rapid deindustrialization and rising unemployment became the number one problem for people in East Germany; and this does not prove that earlier concerns for the environment had not been meant seriously. Perhaps it will one day even be thought that the GDR's church-centred environmental groups, with their fasting exercises and so on, were one step ahead of many Western environmentalists, and that the growth compulsion of the 'free economy' is ultimately the world's greatest environmental problem.

Debt for nature swap, ozone diplomacy and sustainable development: from the East–West conflict to North–South justice

As early as the 1950s, it was common for anyone who wanted an escape from the Cold War to look towards the so-called third world. What is today almost forgotten is that 'developing country' was not then a euphemism for 'underdeveloped country'; many believed that humanity was on the move especially in the South, that the future lay there, whereas the Northern powers had grown stiff in their trenches. The 'third world', the world of Albert Schweitzer, still held the promise of redemption contained in the magic of the number three. It also had a solid economic perspective; since the greatest potential for growth was assumed to exist there, loans flowed all too lavishly towards it.

At the latest after the oil price rises of 1973, however, it became clear that the third world was falling ever further behind the leading industrial countries. Calls for justice grew all the louder, and it became a standard rhetorical figure that a fixation on the East–West conflict distracted attention from the real North–South issues facing humanity. But how did this fit into the eco-age? It began with the 'debt trap', with the fact that since the 1970s many third world countries had faced a situation where debt service was swallowing up the whole of their development aid. When the alarm over the destruction of the rainforests then spread around the world in the mid-eighties, a causal nexus immediately suggested itself: that is, the environmental crisis lay behind the debt crisis; excessive debt levels were forcing countries in the South to overexploit their forests. Strictly speaking, that was not everywhere the case. Malaysia, for example, the world's top exporter of tropical wood, was also Southeast Asia's boom country, and in parts of Latin America it was the cattle barons who devoured large swathes of forest. But the link between indebtedness and predatory resource use was evident enough, just as, in eighteenth-century Europe, excessive debts led royal courts to make deep inroads into their forest 'treasures'.

Debt cancellation without anything in return would be an affront to governments that took their obligations seriously and kept up sound financial management. In 1984, Thomas Lovejoy of the World Wildlife Fund (WWF) therefore put forward a brilliantly simple idea that gave a key role to the major conservation NGOs and made them more attractive to donors: the idea of 'debt for nature swaps' (DNS). NGOs would purchase the debts of third world countries and offer to cancel them if the government placed a stretch of wilderness under protection and allowed rangers to patrol it. This naturally presupposed that the NGOs had sufficient funds to do this, but also that the bonds could be bought at well under value – since creditor banks would calculate that they would anyway not recover all their money in the foreseeable future, and that large-scale operations of this kind would boost their public image. Furthermore, donations for the purposes of conservation were tax-deductible in the United States and elsewhere.[154]

The novelty of this, in comparison with Grzimek's Serengeti campaigns, was that it mainly concerned the forest rather than the savannah playgrounds of elephants, and that from 1986 forest conservation was also presented as climate protection: the great world forests as CO_2 reservoirs. From 1987 one DNS agreement followed another; it was no longer a question of forest romanticism but of saving mankind. The creation of new national parks in Africa may have been within the colonial tradition, but it had a new legitimacy in keeping with the spirit of the eco-age; it was no longer just about providing photo-ops for safari tourists. As we can see from NGO publicity brochures, the paradisiacal fascination of primal forest, with its 'charismatic megafauna', fuelled this new approach to wilderness conservation; but now it was associated with environmental and human policies that represented a synthesis of romanticism and rationality.

All in all, the DNS was and remains a success: first of all in Latin America, but also in Africa and Southeast Asia. Governments went into action alongside NGOs, and on 18 March 1987 the German chancellor Helmut Kohl formally endorsed the concept. It became popular in third world countries too, not only cancelling part of the debt but promoting tourism at the same time. And since the late 1980s, when the World Bank made its own gradual ecological turn, a deliberate display of environmental awareness has been revamped in a way that is economically useful and enhances the respective country's image. In the years since then, the size of protected areas around the world has increased dramatically; the goal of 10 per cent of the earth's surface, set by the IUCN's World Parks Commission in 1990, had risen to an actual total of 12 per cent by 2009 – more than the whole of Africa and half as much as all the world's farmland.[155] Having foregrounded solitary fighters in remote outposts – in 1982 *Der Spiegel* could still publish a book entitled *Natur ohne Schutz* [Nature without Protection][156] – conservationism had inconspicuously become a world power.

Such a rise to power is seldom a completely innocent process, and it was not so here either. 'Debt for nature' led to a considerable expansion of protected areas, but it also increased the danger of labelling swindles and an empty 'inflation of national parks'.[157] By no means did it reduce third world debt in a similarly dramatic manner; that was anyway hardly to be expected. It is true that the 'swap' business was skilfully attuned to an actual economic interest, but conservation functioned here as a reward by wealthy countries, not as something that third world countries did in their own interest. This was one key problem with the trade-off.

To be sure, advocates of DNS asserted – not without reason – that what third world countries did in return was in their own true interests, since the South had more to fear than the North from global warming. However, this was perceived as a hypothetical risk mainly of concern in the North, whereas the problems facing third world countries were both more concrete and more acute. As we have seen, Chico Mendes objected to being described as a climate saviour; what mattered to him was the livelihood of his own people.[158] For quite different reasons – preservation of their way of life and of their right to use local resources – Zapatistas with a background in the nineties revolt in the Mexican State of Chiapas rebelled in 2002 against the establishment of the Montes Azules biosphere reserve (one of 'the world's last lungs', in the eco-jargon).[159] Whereas anti-ecological rebellions usually command only grudging attention in the West, the Zapatista campaign contained so much of the picturesque romanticism of the Mexican Revolution that it won popularity in the Western third world scene, especially as the genuiness of the ecological motives behind the protection of the Montes Azules was not beyond all doubt. The local press accused Conservation International of having hired soldiers to expel families from forest areas designated for protection.[160]

Here we come to the most delicate aspect: the fate of local inhabitants of the areas in question, which as a rule were *not* empty of people. Already in parts of the American West designated as national parks, there were indications from the beginning that the scenic beauty of the vegetation was the result of carefully controlled Indian slash-and-burn techniques;[161] and yet the cavalry drove the indigenous tribes out of the parks. Wilderness romanticism was not compatible with Indian romanticism; in the presence of Indians John Muir – who tended to keep quiet about such things – could not feel the 'solemn calm' of the wild.[162]

With the dawning of the eco-age, however, popular perceptions of the Indians underwent a fundamental change. 'New Ecological Indians exploded onto the scene' and became part of pop culture.[163] Their ancient ecological wisdom was not only discovered but often exaggerated. One often-quoted text is Chief Seattle's speech in the film *Home* (1972), which is largely fictitious and 'sexed up with ecological thinking'.[164] At a time when Karl May's adventure novels were on the wane in Germany, the American Indians were gaining a new popularity reflected in the squatting struggles of 'urban Indians'. In 1973–4 the Sierra Club found itself in an extremely awkward situation, when it temporarily – still pursuing the old ideal of 'pure wilderness' – opposed the granting of limited land use rights to the Havasupai tribe in the Grand Canyon National Park. The media turned on the club, which, just as it was experiencing a membership boom, suddenly saw new recruits leaving in droves.[165]

Since then, the wilderness conservation movement has presented a confused and contradictory picture. The 'noble savage' ideal dating from Rousseau's time went through another heyday – although its champions could have learned from Claude Lévi-Strauss, one of the great early thinkers of the new era, that the supposed 'savages' were in fact civilized people, by no means organically sprung from their natural surroundings. Of the Amazonian Mbaya, for example, he wrote that they expressed 'the same abhorrence of nature' in their 'facial painting, as well as in their practice of abortion and infanticide'.[166] Nevertheless, with its evocative stories and pictures – not to speak of the title! – his *Tristes Tropiques* probably did more than any other book to demystify the Indians of the Amazonian rainforest and to mourn the threat to their habitat. With this and with *La Pensée sauvage* (1962), possibly just because of misunderstandings suggested by the title, Lévi-Strauss the social ethnologist became world famous.

For the eco-scene and third world activists in Europe and the United States, it has always been a basic assumption that not only the tropical rainforests but also their indigenous peoples must be protected; that was the starting point in the 1980s for both the World Rainforest Movement and the Rainforest Action Network.[167] Their belief that the Indians were the native 'stewards' of the wilderness was written into the Agenda 21 document at Rio. However, this position was easier to adopt from a distance (where wishful projections could play a role) than it was close up. On the spot, it was often hard to tell who was a native and who an immigrant; who still embodied an indigenous culture and who the unified modern civilization. This was most likely to be possible in remote parts of Amazonia or Borneo, or among the Aborigines in the deserts of Australia. (The Swiss environmental activist Bruno Manser combined this protection of wilderness and indigenous cultures in a particularly stirring way.) But it was becoming more and more difficult in Africa, where shifting cultivation and pastoralism were traditionally widespread, and where cultures that had been around for a long time were ever harder to find.

But did they have to be old-established in order to feature as partners for environmental protection? From the late 1980s on, researchers constantly emphasized and confirmed that conservation had to take place in cooperation with people living in the protected area. The old practice of clearing a patch of tropical forest of human habitation came to be derided as 'fortress conservation'.[168] 'Community-based conservation' was the new watchword.

A fashionable new term does not automatically change the reality, however. In 1989 an adviser to the German chancellor's office still highlighted 'the defective, or mostly non-existent, involvement of the local population' in debt for nature projects, describing it as a scandal in terms of efficiency as well as morality, because local people defend their home area against 'settler penetration far more effectively than expensive and, in most cases, utterly unreliable and corrupt police forces ever do'.[169] Although Dian Fossey, murdered in Rwanda in 1985, has been cast as a tragic heroine, there is broad agreement that her kind of love of gorillas – which drew the hatred of indigenous people – was a fatal mistake.

The novelty in the ecological revolution of 1970 was not the idea of wilderness protection but the quest for a friendlier symbiosis between man and nature. In many parts of the world today, biodiversity is threatened not by the spread of human settlement but, on the contrary, by rural exodus and the overgrowth of old cultural landscapes. Yet the wilderness ideal continues to have the upper hand over conservationism, for reasons both practical and spiritual. Not surprisingly, there is no general formula for cooperation with indigenous people – only (if anything) regionally adapted solutions, and even they do not apply once and for all. The simplest way is always that of the old 'fortress conservation': to fence off a stretch of wilderness, to move out the people living there, to win over some by hiring them as armed rangers, and otherwise to enlist the support of the tourism sector. Things get more complicated and unpredictable if one tries to combine nature conservancy with indigenous ways of making a living; people change what they do, and it is virtually impossible to foresee all that will happen if the inhabitants of a protected area are left to get on with their lives. The DNS, on the other hand, demanded something definite in return for financial benefits. With its Man and the Biosphere Programme (MAB), launched in 1977, UNESCO embraced the model of a living interaction between natural diversity and human nature, but in the end many of the newly created 'biosphere reserves' did not differ essentially from national parks. Despite promising first attempts, like the iconic CAMPFIRE in Zimbabwe,[170] the synthesis of nature and culture, without which such reserves cannot work, continues to be a task for the future.

Be it a paradox or tragic irony, while the Western eco-scene fantasized that rainforest conservation was also preserving the way of life of tropical peoples, it not infrequently led to their elimination. Most such cases are known from Africa. The scale of the 'conservation refugee problem' – tens of thousands, hundreds of thousands, millions? – is disputed and difficult to assess, and in the case of semi-nomads almost impossible to quantify exactly; most conservationists and regional authorities have anyway not wanted to find out. Since the late 1980s, dam 'oustees' have had the support of NGOs capable of reaching the international public. Those excluded from national parks lack such advocates, and it is only recently that they have gained wider attention. The expansion of national parks inevitably leads to more intensive agriculture outside their boundaries, and recently the Green public was horrified to learn of cooperation between WWF and the agrochemicals giant Monsanto,[171] which many environmentalists consider even worse than the nuclear industry.

The anthropologist Colin M. Turnbull, once famous for his loving picture of the Mbuti Pygmies' forest culture (1961), shocked his admirers in 1972 with the dystopian vision that he presented of the Ik in Northern Uganda: *The Mountain People*. Ousted from the Kidapo National Park, where they had been used to the life of wandering hunters, they were forced into a wretched sedentary lifestyle in harsh surroundings. In their case, resettlement uprooted a genuinely 'native' people from their environment. This loss of their customary home and way of life robbed the Ik of any cordiality, or even of a feeling for pleasurable sex; it turned them into what Turnbull called a 'loveless people'.[172]

Turnbull's book on the Ik was less discussed than summarily rejected;[173] people in 1972 liked to think of them as a special case. Today it is no longer in doubt that theirs was a typical story, although, of course, the creation of national parks is only one among many causes of deracination in the third world. In comparison with other policy ideas, debt for nature involved a combination of environmentalism and North–South justice, which – and this is the really important point – had the advantage of simplicity. It would be unjust to deny its great effectiveness. And yet it remained caught up in the problematic of 'top-down' conservation and an unclear role for humans in 'natural landscapes'.

One bright spot was the cooperation with Sherpas, so beloved of trekking enthusiasts. In the 1970s even they were in danger of become conservation refugees, when the Sagarmatha National Park was established in their traditional homeland in the Himalayas. In 1978 two whole villages of Hindu Chetris were resettled without compensation after the creation of the Rara National Park in 1978.[174] But the Sherpas, being followers of Tibetan Buddhism with a large proportion of monks, managed to keep their population stable and preserved traditions of careful forest and field management in their fragile mountain habitat,[175] offering a model of 'community-based conservation'. Indeed, although the way this is seen around the world generally ranges from sceptical to pessimistic, the fate of the Sherpas was held up as a happy contrast to that of the once famous Massai in East Africa. New Zealand environmentalists, as well as the WWF and an NGO (with the character of a GONGO) personally founded by the king of Nepal, cooperated with Sherpa villagers, and Sherpas proved their worth as guardians of the national parks.[176] Once more, though, there was no happy ending, as large numbers of male Sherpas have since emigrated to the United States. Over and over again it turns out that there are no general formulas, only local paradigms limited in time, for the association of environmental protection with the vital interests of indigenous people.

Everything is simpler when a small circle of top people from the first world gets together, with a clearly defined and realistic objective. This was the case at the Montreal conference in September 1987 on the threat to the earth's atmosphere from aerosol sprays; over two and a half decades later, the resulting Montreal Protocol on Substances that Deplete the Ozone Layer still counts as the most successful example of global environmental policy.[177] The problem was straightforward, or at least seemed to be, and this time it was quite literally close at hand. Equally clear was the necessary countermeasure: to replace damaging aerosol combinations of fluid and gas with harmless substances. The costs would not be too high, and in fact the chemical corporations in question would have the chance to make a profit. At the other extreme, the recently discovered threat to the atmosphere from ever-increasing CO_2 emissions involved endless numbers of polluters and the tackling of a huge range of problems. A comparison between the ways in which the world has addressed these two threats is full of lessons.

Although the United States later became the great foot-dragger in climate policy, it started out well ahead of Europe in relation to the ozone layer. This is all the more surprising because the causal link between aerosols, the 'ozone hole' and the increased risk of skin cancer was at first partly hypothetical, and the proposed countermeasures invoked the precautionary principle that was never really enforced in the USA. But the EPA – which, in keeping with its focus on environmental cancer risks, took the lead in ozone policy[178] – turned the potential threat into an acute threat to life: one reason why eco-revisionists later used the ozone panic as a stock argument that only clearly proven dangers should call forth countermeasures.[179] To quote Erik Conway: 'Political action against the ozone-depleting chemicals had evolved more quickly than had scientists.'[180] As in other areas, the setting of priorities is not an innocent process governed by pure reason alone. The key point was probably that skin cancer due to solar radiation was at issue – a horror for anyone who likes to spend their holiday lying in the sun. A hypothetical risk was enough to trigger panic.

The first ozone alarm sounded in the early days of the eco-age, serving to bring the boom in supersonic transport development to an abrupt end; it was one of the initial successes of the new environmental movement.[181] From 1974 another object of attack was the chlorofluorocarbons (CFCs) used in refrigerators, air conditioning systems and aerosol cans: characteristic requisites of the American way of life. In this case, unlike in that of lead and mercury pollution, a new substance was harming human beings not directly but through chemical reactions at great heights, which were beyond the lay person's understanding and could be investigated only by NASA's *Discovery* space shuttle and researchers in the laboratory. In themselves, CFCs seem perfectly innocent: 'They are non-toxic and stable. They do not burn and do not react with other substances or corrode material.'[182] But the idea of skin cancer caused terror: it was far more palpable than later warnings of a 'greenhouse effect', in the face of which Northern countries could even take a secret pleasure. Soon came a global boom in research projects on atmospheric chlorine, just as the CO_2 alarm a decade later led to the creation of new research structures. Even Daniel Cohn-Bendit, the legendary student leader of Paris 1968, who felt bored by the nuclear controversy, now considered the ozone hole to be the ultimate crisis.[183]

American activists found here an effective priority amid the welter of environmental issues.[184] First in line was the aerosol can, which, though not posing the greatest threat of CFC overload, seemed especially fit to be targeted: 'It is crazy, they said, to endanger life on earth just for the privilege of spraying on your deodorant.' In 1978 the United States banned the uses of CFCs as propellants,[185] but that was only a prelude to what followed in the 1980s. Now, in the Reagan era, it was Europeans who took the initiative – although this soon revived the movement in the United States too, where Reagan himself was suffering from skin cancer. If nothing else, the ozone alarm helped to ensure that in his second term as president – when the enemy image of the Soviet Union increasingly faded (itself perhaps a sign of America's triumph) – he also backtracked in the struggle against 'enviros'. As in so many other fields, things really got moving in 1986 – a year after a conference in Vienna had ended with virtually no results.[186] Was this new salience due, as one occasionally reads in the literature, to explosive research findings about the ozone problem, especially the discovery of the 'ozone hole' above the Antarctic that caused a sensation in the media?[187]

At first the vanishing ozone at the South Pole, far away from any CFC emissions, was open to various interpretations; none of the atmospheric models had predicted it.[188] None other than Richard E. Benedick, the energetic US negotiator, later frankly admitted the state of knowledge at that time: 'The science was still speculative, resting on projections from evolving computer models of imperfectly understood stratospheric processes – models that yielded varying, sometimes contradictory, predictions of potential future ozone losses.'[189] The essential point is clear: politicians cannot simply rely on experts in the face of such environmental risks; they must dare to take decisions in a situation of uncertainty. Lee Thomas, then the head of the EPA, said exactly the same: we cannot, amid 'all this scientific uncertainty', keep putting things off and wait for empirical verification. We must act, before the crisis is upon us.[190]

Ironically, James Lovelock of all people – who at NASA had developed ways of measuring stratospheric ozone levels and was the most forceful advocate of a holistic approach to the 'Gaia' ecosystem – was among those who thought differently.[191] The decisive point, in his later view, was not the supposed risk of skin cancer but the intensification of the greenhouse effect.[192] Probably not everyone who lived through the media alarm – the *Spiegel* cover title of 30 November 1987 was 'The Ozone Hole: Deadly Danger from a Can'[193] – understood the hypothetical element in the risk they were supposed to tackle. In any event, politicians reacted unusually promptly, at international level too. After the signing of the Montreal Protocol on Substances that Deplete the Ozone Layer, in September 1987, successive follow-up conferences did not water down but further strengthened the demand for an end to the aerosol danger.

No other policy success did as much to nourish hopes that, even without a world eco-dictatorship, there was a real chance of a global regime covering key aspects of the earth's ecosystem. 'Science', Benedick summed up, 'became the driving force behind the formation of public policy on the ozone issue'[194] – although he conceded that the 'state of science' in this case was an unstable foundation. Does 'ozone diplomacy' prove that we have finally entered the 'knowledge society' as well as 'global society'? More than two decades later, it is not possible to give a definitive answer; there are still several ways of reading the history of the global ozone regime. Important advances were initiated and driven forward by the Egyptian Mustafa Tolba, at heart a biologist but also the dynamic head of UNEP, who as early as the mid-1970s attached the highest priority to protection of the ozone layer.[195]

The decisive players, however, were neither the UN nor the EU but nation-states; it was they that constantly renewed the impetus for talks when these ran out of steam. The initiative passed back and forth among the USA, the UK and the Federal Republic of Germany; the government in Bonn overcame forces in the EU opposed to regulation. But at one key moment Margaret Thatcher, otherwise known to be a foe of 'enviros', prevailed on President Reagan to stop opposing government intervention in industrial matters.[196] 'Within a few months the United Kingdom was transformed from a reluctant follower to a world leader in the drive to protect the ozone layer.'[197] In retrospect, Benedick emphasizes – as a lesson of 'ozone diplomacy' for future climate policy – that individual nations should press ahead with initiatives of their own, not always waiting for others to do something or for a general agreement to be reached.[198]

Dennis L. Meadows, a leading figure within the Club of Rome and co-author of the *Limits to Growth* report (1972), distilled the essence of ozone diplomacy together with his wife Donella: 'A world government is not necessary to deal with global problems, but it is necessary to have global scientific cooperation, a global information system, and an international forum within which specific compromises can be worked out.' And more: 'some national government willing to take the political lead; flexible and responsible corporations'.[199] But evidently also a team spirit among leading scientists (who needed a certain paradigm to prevail[200]) and an interplay between science and the media, as in the alarm over the greenhouse effect; plus (perhaps most important) industrial leaders able to make good money from substitutes in the event of a ban on particular substances. And last but not least: a mood of the times, as revealed with special clarity by historical comparisons. In 1987, at the height of perestroika, the East–West conflict was visibly at an end; the former Soviet opposition to CFC restrictions was subsiding, and the Western powers in Montreal made concessions to the inertia of the Soviet planned economy.[201]

The Montreal conference and its sequels also took up issues of North–South justice. For the time being it was agreed to exempt the third world from restrictions and to set up a special fund to support it in the adoption of substitutes for CFC substances. However, the details of this were another matter: 'No other subject required so many meetings and discussions or generated so much documentation.'[202] In this respect, and also because leading environmental NGOs took part in the decision-making processes,[203] Montreal and its follow-up conferences operated as a trial run for Rio 1992 and 'sustainable development'. After some rhetorical outbursts against 'environmental colonialism', India and even China finally accepted the Montreal protocol – especially since the support that Western powers offered for the changeover to alternative products was a way of gaining access to the latest technology.[204]

Rather as a satyr play followed a serious drama in the theatre of ancient Athens, a farce followed earnest 'ozone diplomacy' in the Germany of the 1990s: an 'ozone law' – not directed against the ozone hole but, on the contrary, designed to avert unpleasant concentrations in the form of summer smog – was so chock-a-block with exemptions and inadequate regulations that it was nicknamed the 'Bonn laughing-gas directive'. Since then it has been remembered as a model of 'token environmental politics' (a more fitting term even than 'eco-bluff').[205]

Montreal and Rio, the twin peaks so far of global environmental policy, were close in time yet differed from each other with a truly ideal-typical sharpness. At Rio a line of action initiated in the late 1970s with Willy Brandt's North–South Commission reached its climax. The content, if not the actual wording, of the 'sustainable development' formula also had its origins there and became world famous in its wake. From the beginning it was clear that the aim of the new North–South diplomacy – as Richard Sandbrook, from the International Institute for Environment and Development (IIED), put it at a Brundtland Commission hearing in Oslo – was 'to push the environment lobby of the North and the environment lobby of the South together'.[206]

That was not difficult at a purely conceptual level. But Willy Brandt was aware that the real underlying problem was far more complicated; that it was necessary 'to avoid the persistent confusion of growth with development'.[207] Ulrich Grober, in his history of the idea of sustainability, remarks that it was an attempt to go back to the original conception of 'evolution' as a natural process, from which technocratic 'development' had led away.[208] In nature there is no growth without limits, at least not in a linear sense.

Yet the English word 'development' could not be simply replaced with 'evolution'. 'Development must be central' was by now the premise of all North–South diplomacy.[209] 'Third world' representatives, who had willingly adopted the term 'developing countries' (despite its derogatory overtones), insisted on their right to 'development aid' – and most members of the Brundtland Commission came from the third world. They generally took it for granted that 'development' meant growth, and industrial growth at that, although it was already discernible that, instead of favouring social justice, it typically widened the gap between rich and poor. The 'sustainable development' formula – though this was later forgotten – originated in the world of conservation: it was contained in the declaration of 5 March

1980 on World Conservation Strategy, issued on the initiative of the IUCN and UNEP.[210] In this context it was clear that sustainable development signified a brake on limitless growth, but elsewhere the enigmatic term could also be understood in the sense of self-sustaining growth.

The North–South Commission ushered in a style of political globetrotting not unrelated to the explosion of long-distance tourism and the exotic longings of the eco-scene. Willy Brandt's biographer tells us that he longed to be away from 'dull provincial Bonn' (but were political horizons wider in Bangkok or Bogota?); 'his face lit up as soon as he fastened his seat belt on a flight to somewhere as far away as possible'.[211] Gro Harlem Brundtland seems to have been the same; the commission that bears her name began with a 'two-year world tour',[212] and travel was a value in itself for her, even if the results were often nebulous.

On one point, in particular, she was determined to 'learn from the mistakes of the Brandt Commission': she wanted to expend as much energy spreading the message of her commission as she devoted to the decision-making processes. The Brandt Commission – according to its critics – 'had not had any clear information strategy', 'even though Willy Brandt had given hundreds of lectures'.[213] It is still an open question whether this kind of environmental politics (which continued with Rio) led to substantial results or remained a rather airy phenomenon. The contrast between Montreal and Rio could not be clearer from the literature: Montreal and its follow-up conferences can boast quite a collection of careful and detailed analyses, headed by the work of Richard E. Benedick, whereas there is amazingly little about the 'road to Rio' and the unprecedentedly large conference that took place there. Anyone wanting to get on top of it would have to wade through a mountain of documents, without finding an easy answer to the question of which were really important.

Unfortunately for future historians, no record was kept of discussions in the Brundtland Commission.[214] This certainly contributed to a climate of free debate, and trips together to hearings in faraway parts of the world appear to have created lively 'ecological communication' that developed a dynamic of its own, beyond the usual ping-pong rallies between national positions. Here too, even before Chernobyl, nuclear energy was the most explosive issue. The Japanese argued most vehemently in favour of it – and Japan, along with the Rockefeller Foundation, was among the main sponsors of the Commission. The leader of this discussion was Volker Hauff, a man with considerable experience of the public debate in Germany, who followed the example of the Ueberhorst Commission by asking each side to list the problems as it saw them. It turned out that there was a broad agreement on definitions, and this provided the basis for the chapter headings in the Commission's report. It is striking that both the Soviet and American representatives – none other than Sokolov (the hero of the Lake Baikal struggle) and Ruckelshaus (the strong man at the EPA) – kept a low profile during the Brundtland discussions. One can only conclude that they did not take the commission seriously; it became a legend (reduced to the magical 'sustainable development'[215]) only after the event. Anyone who thinks that 'environment' is basically an emotive term typical of the first world will be amazed that Shridath Ramphal from Guyana, Bernard Chidzero from Zimbabwe and Emil Salim from Indonesia all stood out with their level of commitment.

The Brundtland memoirs tell us little or nothing about what participants thought of 'sustainable development' and its related problems; one suspects that the message of Rio is a myth that does not stand up to close scrutiny. The most often quoted phrase in the Brundtland Report (1987) – indeed, the only one to have stuck in the memory of ecological circles – is the definition of 'sustainable development': 'development that meets the needs of the present without compromising the ability of future generations to meet their own needs'. Otherwise, the distribution of the text was not exactly sustainable. After a few years it was no longer readily available, and it already contained too much explosive material for the Rio conference in 1992. The famous definition was based on the principle of 'intergenerational justice', the cornerstone of Western ecological thought, but third world politicians were far too taken up with today's problems to have much room left over for future generations. In this regard, the main concern in the report was that they become too numerous; its leitmotif of the necessity of birth control contrasted sharply with the priorities at Rio.

The drawback of any future-oriented politics is that, because the future is so uncertain, it is highly suscepible to ideology. This is why Carl Jacob Burckhardt, who lived through the 'Thousand Year Reich', longed for a time when people would 'agree on implementing the immediately useful'.[216] The Brundtland definition of 'sustainable development' at once raised a number of questions: how can we know the needs of future generations? Obviously we cannot provide for any old subjective needs, so which are the legitimate ones that can and should be catered for? And who decides what they are? The report emphasizes 'the essential needs of the world's poor, to which overwhelming priority should be given'.[217] The concept of basic needs could hardly refer to anything other than elementary vital needs. But what would have to change for politics to concentrate on the needs of the poor? These questions often went unanswered; the report, for all its wordiness, often strays from the point when it comes to the delicate issues.

In forestry, the sustainability principle already had a history of more than two hundred years behind it, spreading out from Germany to other parts of the world. It can tell us a lot about the problems of the concept and its practical implementation – but there is nothing to indicate that the Brundtland Commission had any awareness of this. The commitment to sustainability could have rested on much greater historical depth and insight. But the fact is that 'sustainable development' functioned merely as a compromise formulation, a common denominator 'to push the environment lobby of the North and the environment lobby of the South together'. Even for North–South differences within the EU in the year of Rio, sustainable development proved to be a patently 'conciliatory formula'.[218] Its magnification into something larger – which began only a few years after Rio – surprised even those who launched the term into circulation.

In the history of forestry, 'sustainability' became more and more ambiguous.[219] Originally it referred to the mass of wood in a forest, but soon also to its – impossible to predict – future wood yield, and later to its soil quality, biodiversity and regenerative capacity. Above all else there was the question of who defines sustainability, and which methods are used in a particular case to establish and verify it. Right from the start, 'sustainability' was not an innocent term. In a regionally delimited wood market, sustainable use of the forest kept prices high. Use by subsistence farmers generally went unnoticed – coppice regenerated itself even without foresters – except where the postulate of sustainability served to justify the exclusion of farmers from the forest.

The same process – which Rio endowed with a higher legitimacy – unfolded in the eco-age in forest areas of the third world that had previously served farmers as a source of fuel and fodder. It might happen that 'sustainability' decreed from on high struck at local rural interests in the forest and ended up hastening its destruction.[220] The drawbacks known from German history multiply in the tropics, all the more when the criterion of sustainability is applied not only to forestry but to the whole economy, if not the whole society. If 'sustainable development' really had been a serious and meaningful objective, it would have urgently led to detailed specification and operationalization. That has not happened so far, and it remains an open question whether it will become a productive challenge in the future.

Here and there, however, the challenge was taken up early on. At the time of Rio, noted figures in the realm of environmental protection – with World Bank adviser Herman Daly and Nobel Economics prizewinner Jan Tinbergen to the fore – thought highly in retrospect of the Brundtland Report; for on a number of key points it was clearer and more uncompromising than the formulations that were negotiated in the run-up to Rio or at the conference itself. Whereas the advertising industry could later drool over such things as 'sustainable aviation', the Brundtland Report – for all its concessions to the third world – had argued clearly enough that sustainable development should not at all be thought of in terms of endless growth.[221] Since continued population growth would inevitably set up pressure for further economic growth, the report also spoke plainly in its advocacy of contraception, whereas at Rio, and ten years later at Johannesburg, an unholy alliance of US conservatives, the Catholic church and third world nationalists backed away from the issue.

On the question of fossil fuels, the Brundtland Report warned sternly of the danger to the earth's atmosphere.[222] But in the run-up to Rio, Washington vetoed EU initiatives in this direction,[223] giving a foretaste of what was to come at later climate conferences. As expected, the Brundtland Commission did not achieve unanimity on nuclear energy;[224] but it took up the delicate safety issues and incorporated into its report some frank words from the unfortunate Legasov. The report also addressed the ground-swell of protests against the destruction of tropical rainforests, although, under Brazilian pressure, it did so only in very general terms.[225] At Rio people allowed themselves to be cowed by the veto of the host nation plus Malaysia, despite the fact that Rio had put itself forward as the conference site out of a wish to improve its image after the tropical forest campaign and the murder of Chico Mendes.[226] Most of the grassroots move-ments were excluded in Rio, but the Brundtland Report did repeatedly give expression to voices from below – or at least convey the impression of doing so. Thus, although Brazil forbade any explicit mention of the Amazonian rainforest, a representative of the rubber-tappers – a colleague of Chico Mendes – featured in the report with a forceful plea against destruction of the forest.[227] Of course, it should be borne in mind that, whereas the Brundtland Commission contained no more than general rec-ommendations, the Rio conference was meant to take binding decisions; this narrowed the room for manoeuvre over contentious issues. Nor should we forget that Brazil had some justification in insisting that the leading industrial countries should drastically cut their own emissions, before they tried to oblige Brazil to protect the Amazonian rainforest.

There can be no doubt that, especially from a distance, Rio made a powerful, indeed overwhelming, impression – not only as a media spec-tacle, but also against the background of two decades of national and international environmental politics since Stockholm 1972. To many the mammoth conference seemed like the world-historic act of integration that environmentalism had been lacking. All too often nature conservation and environmental protection had developed separately from each other, but at Rio there was also a concern to preserve existing species: 'biodiversity' was the new buzzword, more scientific and less American-sounding than the old 'wilderness'. Ecology and economics, which had engaged in so much fruitless shadow-boxing, were united in 'sustainable development', just as environment and development became the leitmotifs for both North and South. Under the aegis of the new liberalism, with its promotion of 'civil society', an elite of NGOs stepped onto the stage: the more that bureaucra-cies were seen as inefficient and corrupt, the more a mere position outside the state became – rightly or wrongly – a seal of quality.

With Agenda 21 – the action programme for the twenty-first century, whose Chapter 28 foregrounded local environmental initiatives – the old 'Think globally, act locally' slogan finally found large-scale application. 'Sustainability' was to be understood in not only ecological and economic but also social terms: the old tension between environmental and social policy seemingly vanished into thin air. It felt like complete wish fulfil-ment: what more could anyone have hoped for? The only Eastern bloc country with a place in the Brundtland Commission had been the Soviet Union, whose representative had seldom put in an appearance; now the Soviet bloc had fallen apart, and the new governments of the region were eager to join in. Never before had such a broad spectrum of third world

countries been involved; more than 100 of the 175 nations were represented by their head of government; environmental policy had become
visibly global. Maurice Strong, secretary-general both of Stockholm 1972
and now of the UNCED (United Nations Conference on Environment
and Development – the official title of the Rio event), declared in his final
address on 14 June 1992 that it was 'the largest high-level intergovernmental conference held on our planet. And clearly the most important.'[228] And
at the same time, in an awful exaggeration: 'If Rio fails, it will be the signal
for a war between rich and poor.'[229]

Anyone with a modicum of political experience knows that decisions are
impossible at such a heterogenous mega-event unless they have been carefully prepared and negotiated beforehand in small groups. A glance at the
Rio 'agenda' (the new buzzword) would be enough to arouse the suspicion
that those present did not really want to negotiate, or anyway to make
something happen, but were mainly interested in grandstanding and in
confirming one another's sense of responsibility for global environmental
policy. Eco-theorists liked to celebrate Rio, in comparison with Montreal,
as an advance from 'single-issue politics' to a 'holistic approach'. But
Montreal did produce something tangible, and anyone who thinks that
political action needs clear objectives might doubt whether any definite
interest, any practical impulse, stood behind the ambitious programme of
the Rio spectacle.

Did Rio really deliver on the 'Think globally, act locally' slogan? Or was
the secret watchword: 'Raise national prestige by global pseudo-activity'
– a failure of thinking as well as action? Even the official report admitted
that expectations had been of a 'two-week gold-pen cum massive photo
opportunity'.[230] But in the end observers were surprised at the surfeit of
argument in the Brazilian coastal metropolis, most of it centred on essential positions. The Earth Summit was no mere farce. But what was it then?

The key to the answer would seem to lie in the World Bank, the global
institution meant to provide favourable development loans, which was in at
the start of the preparations for Rio. When Gro Harlem Brundtland – then
the only head of government with a background as environment minister
– took the helm of the UN World Commission on Environment and
Development in 1983, she received advice from Willy Brandt, fresh from
his experiences in the North–South Commission. As she later recalled,
Brandt impressed on her that it was critical to 'build further on the [World]
Bank's role', as he had previously been doing. But – typically for her
memoirs – she does not say a word about what this actually meant.[231]

It is not hard to make a plausible guess, however. In the 1980s, World
Bank development aid became increasingly discredited, not only around
pub tables but also among insiders, in Europe as well as the United
States. In 1985 Brigitte Erler, a former SPD member of the Bundestag,
published her incendiary *Tödliche Hilfe* [Deadly Aid], based on her own
experiences;[232] an assessment made of it by the Goethe Institute (the
German equivalent of the British Council) tried to dismiss her as a clinical

hysteric,[233] but a year later the highly regarded Federal German president, Richard von Weizsäcker, in his preface to the Club of Rome's powerful critique of social-ecological monster projects, alluded to her book when he spoke of the new thesis that 'our aid is killing human beings' and that 'to send food to starvation camps in the Sahel simply prolongs its incapacity to survive, instead of promoting the regional production that can alone save it in the long run'.[234]

Of course, development aid was from the beginning conceived as a means to 'self-help' – what else could it be, given that human agents in the third world are neither little children nor cripples? It is significant, however, that this was repeatedly presented as a new discovery, since the reality looked rather different. It had long been an open secret that most aid seeped away into corrupt bureaucracies, but it was turning out that, even when it reached its intended recipients, it often caused more harm than good in the end. 'Hunger relief' weakened the regional subsistence economy; road-building in 'underdeveloped' regions made it easier to pump out resources to the global heartlands; and large dams – the developer's pet project since the days of the TVA – led to the flooding of densely populated valleys and their fertile soil.

Rio's 'sustainable development' thus came as the ideal solution. In a situation where the end of the Cold War had removed one of the chief reasons for development aid, it acquired a new legitimacy from environmental protection – and this promised a degree of forward planning against the negative spin-offs of development projects. What ultimately stood behind Rio's big words was a simple swap: debt for nature, development aid for environmental protection. 'UNCED, from beginning to end, hinged on the question of money', Bruce Rich, the director of the Environmental Defense Fund in Washington, tells us on the basis of thorough World Bank studies.[235] In principle that was not necessarily a bad thing: it might indicate realism on the foundation of Rio. But the basic dilemma of such swaps – that environmental protection operates in the interests of the North – was all the more apparent as the North pushed harder for it and held out the prospect of larger subsidies. Even if it was acting unselfishly in this – and governments seldom act unselfishly – it did not sound convincing to the South. This was particularly unfortunate because in many spheres environmental protection can be effective only if the country in question embraces the cause as it own; only then is there a chance that sustainability will be sustained in the long term.

Another dilemma regarding debt for nature is that the sustainability of economic development, or indeed even of forestry, is incomparably more difficult to verify from outside than the protection of a national park that is fenced off and patrolled by rangers. It should therefore probably not be regretted that this swap – the core idea of Rio – did not really get off the ground, and that the donor countries did not prove very generous. Many environmentalists did not trust 'sustainable development', and they had their reasons. The swap tainted environmental protection not only with the sleaze surrounding aid apparatuses, but also with the dangers of 'development' itself. High-visibility installations were required to demonstrate what had happened to the money, but those very installations made 'development' harmful to the environment. And, however well-intentioned, development aid had a structural propensity to mega-projects that demonstrated expertise and could serve as a showcase.

Hailed a decade before as the great hope for humanity, development aid was already a source of deep disappointment by the beginning of the eco-age. UNESCO had declared the 1960s the 'development decade', but the balance sheet as the decade drew to a close was thoroughly disappointing.[236] Lynton Caldwell, the 'architect of the National Environmental Policy Act of 1970' (which gave birth to the EPA), was himself marked by this sense of a let-down.[237] And a fortiori Ivan Illich! When would-be aid workers from the USA went to see him in Cuernavaca (Mexico), he gave them a cold shower: 'If you really want to help the poor in Latin America, then buy yourselves a ticket home – and do it today.'[238] In his view, the 'development aid' project was fundamentally deceitful: it promoted a form of modernization that mostly profited elites and widened the gap between rich and poor. Although one might imagine many other kinds of 'development', the type currently in operation corresponded to the idea of progress against which the ecological Enlightenment had been fighting. Max Nicholson, the doyen of British conservation, concluded in his *The New Environmental Age* (1987) that 'two of the greatest sources of global environmental damage' were 'the failure of the New York-based United Nations Development Programme and associated aid agencies, and of the largely American-based international lending bank system'.[239] Susan George, co-director of the Transnational Institute (New York and Amsterdam), actually described 'development' – in her preface to the German edition of Vandana Shiva's *Staying Alive* (1988) – as a 'bloodthirsty Moloch'.[240] And, with roots in quite a different philosophy, the 'eco-warrior' Dave Foreman issued the slogan in 1991: 'Climb those mountains, encounter the Griz. . . . And piss on the developer's grave.'[241]

Other environmental activists had trouble with the concept of 'development'. Many found it hard to speak with third world representatives unless they declared a belief in development aid, and there was often a smooth transition between Western environmentalism and third world scenes. They attracted similar human types, with much the same moral sense, exotic yearnings and dreams of salvation. A commitment to development aid – albeit very different from the projects that currently bore that title – relieved these types of a feeling that they shared the responsibility for third world poverty.

For a time, the criticisms were not without effect. Especially around 1990, aid focused more strongly on 'rural development' and support for small farmers left empty-handed by the 'Green Revolution' – a source of traumatic disillusionment for many aid workers. But then there was a switch to feeding the third world state apparatuses more than ever: aid as political-economic kickbacks. Al Gore's *Earth in the Balance* (1992), which appeared in the same year as Rio, ended with an appeal for a 'global Marshall Plan'[242] – although, whatever the myths, the original postwar Marshall Plan was of little significance for the West German 'economic miracle' and would have been ineffectual without the special conditions obtaining in Germany at the time.[243] A global version of the same would have intensified the structural dilemma of development aid. (The fact that a 'global Marshall Plan' would have given the strongest possible stimulus to globalization did not, however, prevent the anti-globalization movement Attac from later adopting the idea.) In any event, as vice-president, Al Gore was not able to bring about a change in US climate policy.

Not only the campaigning groups barred from Rio but also Gro Harlem Brundtland (who vented her anger at Norwegian demonstrators in Brazil) felt disappointed by the outcome of the Earth Summit and distanced themselves from the self-congratulating tone of many political leaders present there. A moderate advance was discernible in some areas, nothing at all in a lot of others. There was special outrage over the blocking of action for birth control,[244] but contraception could anyway not have been organized at a global level. The greatest media attention centred on President Bush's brusque statement in the run-up to Rio that the 'American way of life' was non-negotiable, although no politician anywhere in the world had ever imagined that he would dismantle it. The German environment minister Klaus Töpfer prophesied that, following the loss of Communism as an enemy image, the United States was about to set up ecologism in its place.[245] As the Republican election defeat soon showed, however, anti-ecologism did not win any votes at that time. Ernst Ulrich von Weizsäcker even stated: 'In Rio thousands upon thousands laid the vanishing North American lifestyle to rest.'[246]

Yet the problem is that, in large parts of the world, 'development' has retained its special American flavour. Although the American way of life is out of reach for most of humanity, third world elites, the main beneficiaries of 'development aid', have largely attained it, and the 'development' model helps to make this seem normal and legitimate. Modern environmental awareness contains a very different potential; 'quality of life' was the watchword of the 'ecological revolution' of 1970. Individual happiness consists essentially in what people do for its own sake, not for its exchange-value, and so 'living standards' expressed in dollar terms (according to which most of humanity is utterly wretched) do not necessarily tell us much about their quality of life.[247] An obsession with market value – this is an abiding truth of Marxism – may well mar our sense of the value of life.

For all their inadequacy, European lifestyles do give an inkling of how a higher quality of life might be achieved with a lower consumption of energy and resources. Life is better in a world where much can be done on foot or by bike than in one where you have to rely on cars and planes to get around. Community makes for greater happiness than competition does; conviviality is a more pleasant way of spending your leisure time than aimless wandering in a giant shopping mall. If you can travel safely everywhere in a city, you have a greater sense of freedom than if you have to be constantly on the lookout for 'no go areas'. A degree of tolerance for bodily odours means you are more in touch with your senses than if you spend all your life in air-conditioned rooms and take several showers a day: a truly disastrous lifestyle model in arid regions of the world. At the Rio summit and later international conferences on the environment, EU representatives repeatedly argued against the Americans. But not the least of Europe's charms is its diversity, and no standardized 'European way of life' was offered as an alternative to the much-envied American model.

Still, Rio was a step in that direction. Historical realism suggests that we should refrain from being hypercritical; even a critique of the usual criticisms of Rio is advisable. One big peace conference cannot smooth out the ever tense relationship between man and nature, and for all the rhetorical flourishes anyone who remembers the days of the Cold War can only welcome the changed scenery at the Rio conference centre. The author of the most extensive historical study of American environmental policy sees its greatest deficiency in the lack of 'a broadly shared vision of the common environmental good'; 'sustainable development', he concluded in 1999, is 'the closest current approximation to such a vision'.[248]

The main problem with Rio is that the international eco-boom had overloaded the conference with public expectations – strangely, because leading environmentalists had thought shortly before that the trip there would be a waste of time. The post-Cold War 'peace dividend' was the buzzword which expressed hopes that the billions wasted on the arms race would now be available for development aid and environmental protection. The 'Earth Summit', Klaus Töpfer wrote fourteen years later, 'was undoubtedly a summit of dawning euphoria and optimism'; and it is true that it adopted 'basic principles of global environmental and development policy' which, 'if they had to be renegotiated today, would probably never be accepted with the same succinctness'.[249] 'Sonny' Ramphal, the adviser to secretary-general Maurice Strong, appealed at the outset: 'Rio must be a turning-point for human society, the beginning of a more resolute stage in the process of retrieving our heritage of life on Earth.'[250] A decade or two on, however, Rio seems more like an end: a final burst of international attention to problems of the environment. It is no accident that it also marked the end of a *first* (not, we now know, the only) phase of climate catastrophism.[251]

The title of the official UNCED report alludes ironically to the exaggerated expectations: 'Did We Really Save the Earth at Rio?' The question already contains the answer: 'Of course not!' And the author remarks of the much-touted, though seldom read, *Agenda 21* that it is 'in reality the softest of "soft law", exhortatory in nature, a cafeteria where self-service is the order of the day'.[252] Above all, Rio was 'an almost unmitigated disaster' in respect of forest conservation.[253] What a paradox: Rio failed most on an issue where sustainability had historically been most likely to have a definite meaning! However, it is scarcely less absurd to pursue global forest conservation than it is global contraception from the heights of the UN skyscraper in New York. One should consider it rather fortunate that such megalomanic projects were blocked; third world countries cannot be blamed for refusing to allow themselves to be talked into them. Nor is there any reason to regret that the mega-deals offering 'aid in return for environmental protection' failed to work out so frequently: such protection requires the region in question to take the initiative in its own interests, and a coupling with aid is and always has been highly questionable. The activist José Lutzenberger (1926–2002), who received the Alternative Nobel Prize in 1988 and became Brazil's environment minister in 1990, warned the industrial countries at the UN, three months before Rio, that they should stop giving funds to developing countries for environmental ends, since they 'may well end up in corrupt hands'; his temerity led Brazil's president, Fernando Collor, to remove him from his post without further ado.[254]

Some of the standard criticisms of Rio testify to an affected naïvety. Of course the summit did not renounce the growth economy; of course it did not rise to the complexity of global environmental problems; of course it was not built around grassroots democracy – how could it have been? – but drew on only a select group of NGOs; of course it did not replace utilitarian attitudes to natural resources with awe in the face of nature. To be sure, very few have read the hundreds of pages of *Agenda 21*, whose convoluted officialese bears the marks of late-night compromises, and which has now been displaced by an assortment of new strategy papers that have since appeared under the Agenda 21 heading.[255] A plethora of local Agenda 21 activities, up to and including the creation of green spaces to compensate for overbuilding, were not really inspired by the Earth Summit, but the horizon of Rio did something to give them a touch of something beyond arrow localism in the public perception.

One's assessment of Rio essentially depends on the value one attaches to this change in perception. And that in turn depends on the extent to which patterns of thought and verbal expressions have lastingly marked everyday behaviour: the pivotal question of discourse history. A definitive answer can probably never be given. Between the extremes of trivialization and glorification – vanity fair or prelude to green globalization – the scope of the Rio conference needs to be more precisely and realistically defined. This becomes possible only with the passing of time; the question of whether global ecologism is reaching its goal or heading down a blind alley will accompany us to the end. Someone at Rio recalled that, when Zhou Enlai was asked what he thought was the world significance of the French Revolution, he answered with an eye on the millennia of Chinese history: 'It's too early to say.'

Intergenerational and environmental justice: an ambiguous relationship

Barry Commoner stressed from the beginning that environmental protection and social justice should not be separated from each other: 'The earth is polluted neither because man is an especially dirty animal nor because there are too many of us. The fault lies with human society – with the ways in which society has elected to win, distribute, and use the wealth that has been extracted by human labour from the planet's resources.'[256] In a sense, justice was always a basic principle of the 'ecological revolution': if it is unjust that a private company can offload the social consequences of its business onto society, the same is true of its ecological consequences. 'Polluter pays' has a simple enough logic. But this maxim does not have sufficient purchase amid the diffuse environmental effects of the modern lifestyle.

Ecology is justice is security: this is how a wide-ranging study by the Wuppertal Institute put it forty years later.[257] But it is more a statement of how things should be than a balance sheet of four decades of the eco-age. The tension between ecology and economics was often demonstrated, sometimes even overemphasized, during that period, but the relationship between ecology and justice is probably the greatest *latent* field of tension permeating the eco-age so far. For Wolfgang Haber,[258] one of the 'uncomfortable truths of ecology' is that 'there can be no ecological justice, if only because all vital resources – from the power of the sun to land mass, food, fresh water, vegetation, soil and minerals – are distributed so unevenly across the planet'. Does ecological justice mean pumping water from rainy to dry regions, as modern technology makes possible over ever longer distances? But do the inhabitants of rainy regions well supplied with water not have a right to preserve their familiar environment? Is not the freedom to use water unstintingly not a fair trade-off for the fact that the sun is so often clouded over?

Social imbalances lie hidden behind many 'environmental problems'; an increased awareness of the environment may help to reveal them, but it may also distract attention from them. At the present time, there is a tendency in many parts of the world to blame global warming for droughts that are actually caused by groundwater depletion. The 'population time bomb' alarm, which was at the origin of the ecology movement in the United States and elsewhere, did not necessarily negate social aspects of environmental problems, but in practice it often took people's minds off them; the best precaution for future generations seemed to be to ensure that they did not become too numerous. Only when the Reagan administration attacked birth control did it again acquire rebellious features.[259] The environmental movement is usually listed among the 'new social movements', but this affinity by no means precludes a sense of foreignness or animosity.

Emanating from the United States, 'environmental justice' is the new watchword that has been activating the movement from below since the

1990s – a period when summit diplomacy at the top gave North–South justice a global horizon as never before. Since those who took up environmental justice focused on industrial pollution in urban areas mainly inhabited by non-whites, it produced a laboratory-pure specimen of 'Think globally, act locally.' It actually involved a diversity of local initiatives, but American eco-journalism soon made out of them a cohesive 'environmental justice movement', or 'EJ' for short, which expressed itself politically at rallies in Washington in 1990. Around the time of the Rio conference, it was no longer possible to dismiss such protests as narrowly localist Nimby initiatives.

In this case too, there are a variety of histories about how the movement originated: most often one finds the story of the revolt of 1992 in Warren County, North Carolina, when 414 protesters – or more than 500, in some reports – were arrested for blocking trucks carrying soil contaminated with PCBs (polychlorinated biphenyls) to a depot in the mainly black neighbourhood of Afton.[260] In 1987, a study invested with the authority of the United Church of Christ came to the hardly surprising conclusion that harmful industrial emissions especially affected lower-class black districts; it was a classic environmental scandal, like the one that Friedrich Engels exposed in *The Condition of the Working Class in England* (1845), at the origins of Marxism. In the USA, where environmental activists would have attracted suspicion by associating themselves with that tradition, racial discrimination was more of a target than social injustice; 'environmental racism' became the standard term for the scandal. Until then, blacks had been almost absent from the American eco-scene, and even now they mostly kept to themselves. Fundraising led to tensions with established white NGOs,[261] but these new allies were also a feel-good factor for environmentalism. The theme of 'environmental ethics' experienced a boom, even among philosophers racing to catch up with grassroots activists. Previously they would have dismissed such an association of ecology and justice as a 'naturalistic fallacy'.

Since the hygiene movement of the late nineteenth century, the main 'solution' to environmental problems was to ensure that at least sensitive layers of the population did not perceive them with their senses. This involved shifting them from lower to upper layers of the atmosphere, from inner-city waterways to rivers and lakes, from the world above the earth to the world below, and – typical everywhere – from affluent 'West End' districts to the proximity of lower-class neighbourhoods, where the smoke wafted from chimneys. Urban 'zoning'[262] involved the division of cities into residential, industrial and mixed areas. This background brings out the longer-term significance of the environmental justice movement, whose driving force was far more social than ecological. It helped to stop mere juggling and to get to the heart of problems – the avoidance of pollution. However, this industrial policy objective could not be achieved through local initiatives alone.

In 1986 Ulrich Beck had already declared in italics: '*Poverty is hier-*

archic, smog is democratic'[263] – a lapidary, inclusive formula that erased class boundaries. The old rhetoric of social reform, with its indictment of the upper classes, became passé in the eco-age; even a concentration on familiar toxic substances began to look hackneyed in a context of carbon dioxide and ozone alarms, as if the old dangers had been dispelled. But the reality was very different, whether in the United States, Eastern Europe or the metropolises of the third world. Black revolts in American cities placed a problem of global import on the agenda, while the EPA helped to ensure that these new protests did not blow over but linked up and acquired a political dynamic. The environmental authorities that had fought with their backs to the wall under Reagan found new support in reform-minded sections of the population and the media. Environmental justice brought together impulses that the EPA could accommodate – indeed, which fitted into its existing operations and brought them out of an impasse.

EPA policies in the 1980s had taken shape around the 'Superfund': the popular name for the long-winded Comprehensive Environmental Response, Compensation and Liability Act (CERCLA) of 1980, and in particular for its financial core, the fund to clean up polluted legacy areas, which operated partly in accordance with the 'polluter pays' principle, but in roughly a third of cases (where the guilty party could no longer be traced) drew upon a special tax on the oil and chemicals industry. The first impetus for this came from the Love Canal affair, which the media built up into a huge scandal. The entrepreneur William Love had begun to build a shipping canal above the Niagara Falls in the 1890s, but he went bankrupt and the Hooker Chemical Company used the existing stretch as a garbage dump; it was revealed in 1978 that some of the materials in the dump had been toxic. Until the 1970s, however, not a lot was said about such things on either side of the Atlantic; when the Love Canal was filled in, the company sold the land for one dollar to a local education authority, and a school had stood there in the 1950s and 1960s in idyllic suburban surroundings.

It therefore came as a shock when the idyll proved to be an illusion. It is still not clear how much the dump affected the health of local people, but the scandal had paradigmatic value and one religious group, the Ecumenical Task Force (ETF), made it a cause célèbre.[264] Identifiable cases of toxic contamination were easier targets than cross-border problems for the EPA and environmental lawyers to take up. Besides, in the Reagan era, concentration on abandoned toxic waste had the advantage of not interfering with current industrial production. The field for action seemed endless. Waste disposal had been even more heedless in the wide open spaces of America than in densely populated European regions; there were certainly thousands of dubious sites waiting to be discovered.

But, of course, they could not all be tackled at once, and in most cases it was difficult to prove health damage. It was therefore very important for the litigant to have a good lawyer – and that cost money. If the law suit was successful the 'Superfund' covered the legal costs. Critics later complained that a third of its assets were spent in this way,[265] but even environmental-ists were not really happy with its policy. Huge bureaucratic resources were involved in identifying priority cases, with the result that a mere 16 out of 799 registered 'Superfund sites' were cleaned up in the course of the 1980s. The cost–benefit ratio seemed rather embarrassing.[266] Nor was it necessar-ily the poorest layers of the population who benefited.

In this situation, the ecology movement gained fresh momentum under the aegis of environmental justice. The First National People of Color Environmental Leadership Summit took place in Washington in October 1991, and the following year, towards the end of the Bush Senior presi-dency, the EPA founded an Office of Environmental Equity.[267] A storm broke in the black eastern district on the banks of the Anacosta – which, though only a few minutes by car from the White House, is hardly ever seen by visitors to the city – against the discharge of toxic waste into the river and the carving of a speedway that would cut residents off from the river-side.[268] Similar protests occurred in the Bay Area of San Francisco,[269] all the more spectacular because environmental initiatives on the Californian coast, though politically progressive in theory, had tended to express the wish of chic neighbourhoods to keep their nice views and their peace and quiet.[270] In Louisiana's notorious 'Cancer Alley', a string of oil refineries and chemical plants on the Mississippi between Baton Rouge and New Orleans, where early-industrial recklessness had poisoned the environ-ment, the realities staring people in the face mobilized them on the issue that had been at the origins of the eco-age. Pat Bryant, the director of the Gulf Coast Tenants Association, argued that since most of the 'Cancer Alley' neighbourhoods consisted of former slaves the contamination there was tantamount to 'genocide'.[271]

The Silicon Valley Toxics Coalition, which campaigned against scrap disposal in the legendary home of the electronic revolution, made the public aware that not only old and dirty industries were contaminating the environment.[272] But there too it was very difficult to pinpoint damage to health – especially important in America, where the rights of the indi-vidual are so deeply rooted in the culture and the legal system.[273] This basic dilemma led to frustration and signs of stagnation in the EJ movement.[274] We should remember that many Chernobyl victims would have had a hard time taking legal action in America as well as Russia, given that they could not afford to hire star lawyers.

The transfer of the 'habitat' concept from the forest to the urban jungle was of pioneering significance for the environmental movement in general.[275] In this regard, typical EJ initiatives were closely related to the Greenwich Village campaign led by Jane Jacobs in the 1960s, as well as to the housing struggles in Frankfurt and Berlin, the urban ecology groups in the late GDR, or the anti-pollution initiatives by the nascent Polish move-ment to preserve the old town of Krakow.[276] In a sense, these decidedly local movements were especially global, sharing an affinity with environ-mental groups in many other countries, even if they had no knowledge of one another;[277] there have been some attempts at global networking, but so far these seem to have remained rather weak.[278] The vitality of these initiatives is local in origin. And since particular lifeworlds are at issue, women have been more involved than in other environmental movements.[279]

The demand for environmental justice has also been taken up by an Israeli movement for equal Palestinian rights in the distribution of water; it is one of the most courageous examples of its kind, which touches a raw nerve of national politics but is also of global significance.[280] If there had been an EJ movement at the time of Bhopal in 1984, the disaster would have become the strongest imaginable wake-up call – for the victims definitely belonged to the poorest sections of the population. In the eco-age too, the striving for justice has a productive potential that can get something moving.

The latest drama: environmental politics between globalization and anti-globalization

If we look back at the first two decades of the eco-age, the years from Stockholm to Rio, from 'limits to growth' to 'sustainable development', and if we then consider the still nameless recent period, we certainly find a number of recurrent leitmotifs and scandals, but the main impression is one of novelty. Previously, environmentalism had very different priorities both between and within individual countries; the 'networked thinking' required by ecologism made their definition especially difficult, and this showed time and time again. In the last two decades, however, one priority has imposed itself with extraordinary persistence worldwide: the climate danger resulting from the greenhouse effect. Indeed, 'the climate' has increasingly taken the place of 'the environment', precisely for politicians and advisers who have wanted to take purposive action on a grand scale.

Ecological theorists used to predict that, as the public became more educated, the trend would inevitably move from a 'top issue' to a 'multiple issue' approach. But then global warming pushed to the fore a top issue that has stubbornly remained there ever since. In 1992 the chair of the Sierra Club remarked that, at the end of the day, what really excites people is still the wildness of nature;[281] yet the climate issue sidelined the protests of conservationists against hydropower plants and wind turbines, biofuel plantations and sprawling solar farms. Media researchers were already saying in the 1990s that an alarm inevitably ran out of steam after a few years, especially if no impending disaster was apparent. But although the scorn of sceptics may often have grabbed the headlines, concern for the effects of climate change has repeatedly reasserted itself in the public mind.

There is another reason why this is so striking. In the past, the kind of environmental issue that had the widest resonance was lead, mercury or sulphur emissions; their noxious character had long been known, and occupational medicine had prepared much of the ground on which environmentalism could build. The same was true of asbestos, whose dangers had been discovered more recently. Things were different with carbon dioxide. But it now became such an enemy image that many activists, worked up over the climate alarm, began calling for 'CO$_2$-free cities' and forgot that it is a basic substance of the organic world which, at a certain atmospheric concentration, is part of the human lifeworld.[282]

The dominance of this new priority is all the stranger if we consider that it was propagated by the industrial countries of the North, which until then had produced the world's highest per capita CO$_2$ emissions but had the least to fear from global warming. So, for two decades we have been living through a twofold ambiguity that is ripe for satire: the First Law of Ecological Correctness is to join the public chorus about the threat from global warming; yet in private, people in cold regions smile over the warmer air that has been spreading a Mediterranean leisure culture of outdoor restaurants and pavement cafés. Warmer times have traditionally been seen as good times in Central and Northern Europe: did the troubadours not have their golden age during the medieval climate optimum? It is hard there to feel afraid of warming, at least so long as it continues in the mild form we have seen up to now. On the one hand, the apocalypse has never taken such a definite shape as it has with global warming; on the other hand, it has never seemed less scary to the peoples of the North.

Are the public warnings hypocritical? There is no reason to doubt the serious intention behind them in many cases. Rather, the history of the climate alarm confirms that the main driving force of the eco-age is not panic fear but intellectually mediated concern. Certainly this involves plenty of feelings too, but although it is often ridiculed as an expression of mass hysteria it essentially belongs in the history of the Enlightenment, more in the head than the belly. Surveys in Germany have shown that, although respondents are worried about the state of the planet, they report hardly anything definite that they fear in their own surroundings.

Did the eco-age bring the knowledge or science society to fruition, as many real or would-be scientists like to imagine? The evidence suggests quite otherwise. Indeed, if we think of the cooperation among today's climate researchers, it is surprising how little of a team spirit there was among environmental scientists in the early decades of the eco-age, and how few sonorous demands were placed on policy-makers. The science of ecology, in the strict sense of the term, offers a basis neither for value judgements nor for action programmes. If everything is interconnected, then every action has unintended consequences, nature is in constant flux even without human interventioin, and we can never even approximately survey the infinite world of micro-organisms. From where do sombre eco-prophets derive their authority when they call in a booming voice for repentance?

Those who mock or oppose climate research equate its meteoric rise with an ecological power grab, yet it is by no means synonymous with ecology. An impression has been created that long-range temperature projections carry reliable statements on ecological implications – *en passant*, so to speak. But in fact there can be no question of that. More puzzling is the extent to which recent developments in ecology have passed the public by.

Chaos theory, the most important new direction in ecosystem research since the 1980s, goes beyond static models, underlines the role of tiny unpredictable impulses in the organic world (the 'butterfly effect'), and downplays the predictive value of models in general.[283] Not only changes in ecosystems and populations but also climate shifts contain a 'chaotic' element that allows for no more than limited forecasting. It is not easy to work out what this entails in practice. All the more remarkable is it, then, from a historical as well as an ecological point of view, that climate research has gained such a position of authority since the 1980s: if not for actual policies, then in the realm of ecological postulates. After all, even lay people with a serious interest in the subject, who could keep on top of the risks of nuclear energy and pesticides, find it impossible to follow the computer calculations central to modern climate research. The 'greenhouse effect' concept only appears to involve a simple, directly intuitable, logic. Today, two respected researchers complain that 'the political ideology of climate determinism' is 'a spectre that repeatedly haunts debate on the climate'.[284]

This brings us to something else that is new. Earlier leitmotifs of environmentalism – nuclear power plants, high dams, industrial emission, river pollution – were usually taken up and crucially propelled by grassroots movements. This is more difficult in the case of climate change. Where is the enemy? 'I would have to demonstrate against it from my own chimney', a German Green politican once remarked. Can there ever be a climate movement? If so, only in a new sense of the word 'movement'. In 2006, on the twentieth anniversary of the creation of the Federal Environment Ministry, Volker Hauff even suggested that the leading environmentalists are now to be found in reinsurance businesses worried at the growing number of claims linked to climate change.[285] Is that a movement? Or will something move only when primary schoolteachers organize 'climate breakfasts' that put a minimal burden on the atmosphere? We must rid ourselves of stereotypes in which a movement means demonstrators with placards. Sometimes a government body moves more than many 'movements' do.

Be this as it may, international networking has made a qualitative advance since the Rio period. It is true that the 'Think globally, act locally' slogan was there from the beginning, and David Brower, who launched it, was one of the first to take it seriously with his Friends of the Earth; yet for a long time most environmental campaigners knew little about likeminded people in other countries, if such aspects interested them at all. The 'blue planet' photos from space were an early icon of environmental awareness, in which a new global lust for power also lurked[286] – think of the subtitle of Max Nicholson's *Environmental Revolution* (1970): *A Guide for the New Masters of the World*! But this potential remained more or less latent and diffuse until the 1990s, being spelled out with the project of a global climate regime. As Laurens Jan Brinkhorst, the EU director-general for the environment, said in 1991 at a colloquium in Mainau: 'global dimensions' would make environmental policy 'more and more' a question of 'power politics' – 'together with development policy in general of our whole planet'.[287]

Even if global climate policy has no practical effect, it strengthens the general legitimacy of rule from the centre, and this in turn exacerbates the tension between the regional roots and global horizons of the environmental movement. When the Bundesrepublik set out to become the leader in renewable energies, open conflicts broke out in many cases between conservationists and environmentalists; their mentalities had always been different, although the various organizations tried to build bridges. The anti-nuclear campaign too, by far the largest grassroots movement in Germany, found itself marginalized by the climate alarm, which the nuclear lobby, glad to be out of the firing line at last (unless it also included coal station interests), enthusiastically encouraged. This was further proof that the metamorphoses of environmentalism cannot be derived from an immanent 'logic' of ecological discourse – especially as the CO_2 alarm by no means silenced the protests against nuclear power.

Peter Menke-Glückert – the initiator of German government environmental policy in late 1969 – was downright exuberant in celebrating the birth of a new era at Rio 1992. It had made 'the ecological turn' a reality and shaped a 'global community' around sustainability; 'the business world too – after lengthy filibustering, protestations and bowing and scraping – had learned its lessons on the environment'. Indeed, a single great entity had come into being out of diffuse policy strands. 'Finally abandoning the path of isolated sectoral policies and save-the-corncrake campaigns, the Rio Conference focused again on the core environmental dilemma: the overuse of natural resources for the survival of what will soon be six billion people on earth.'[288]

Klaus Töpfer, German environment minister at the time of Rio, and later (1998–2006) executive director of UNEP, also believed in hindsight that the summit, 'because of its near-elite position on the margins', had moved environmental policy into the mainstream of world politics. But he considered its results to have been 'generally disappointing' – partly, of course, for the personal reason that UNEP did not develop into an authority with greater decision-making responsibilities, but also because, as he now recognized, 'major agreements, principles and agendas, even if adopted at the highest political level, do not directly bring about changes'. The 'real success story' to come out of Rio was the grassroots projects that implemented 'Local Agenda 21'.[289] Such is the dilemma of summitry: effective environmental policy is still essentially regional, and so too are serious initiatives that go beyond 'symbolic politics' and achieve something concrete.

The post-Rio boom in conference tourism was an invitation to mockery.

For Arundhati Roy, the Second World Water Forum of 2000 at The Hague delivered a shock that made her take up arms against the Indian and international elites: 'Every speech was generously peppered with phrases like "women's empowerment", "people's participation" and "deepening democracy". Yet it turned out that the whole purpose of the Forum was to press for the privatization of the world's water.'[290] In March 2003, the Third World Water Forum met in three Japanese cities: Kyoto, Shiga and Osaka. Whereas its predecessor had had just under 6,000 participants, the total this time was four times larger, with three times the number of meetings. The water expert Asit Bitwa complained that the size of the event and the range of topics ensured in advance that no one would be able to gain an overview, and that it would be impossible to come away with a clear result; there could be no question of learning lessons from such a pointless mega-show. The Fifth World Water Forum, held in Istanbul in 2009, again broke the records by attracting 33,058 people from 192 countries, while 'the 192-page final report basically consisted of the programme embellished with greetings and illustrations'.[291] Meanwhile, matters of real importance took place at the G9 summits, where heads of the richest and most powerful countries got together for private talks. The World Summit on Sustainable Development, held in Johannesburg in 2002 and billed as a super-Rio, drew little public attention around the world and was quickly forgotten; hardly anyone could say what it had contributed. This empty round of conferences generated an atmosphere of irresponsibility where everything was vague and non-binding.

There was a time when, precisely in the eco-scene, 'global' was virtually synonymous with 'good' and an erotic thrill – or an elated feeling of worldly transcendence – came over activists at the sound of phrases like '*sans frontières*'. Bird enthusiasts in particular, the earliest crack troops of conservationism, longed for borders to melt away out of a concern for migratory flocks. Nor should we forget that belief in One World had sounded very different during the Cold War, when it had had an apotropaic function in relation to a third world war.

Increasingly, however, the 'open borders' rhetoric spread to commercial advertising, where the apotropaic effect was directed against the spectre of the limits to growth. When the internet really took off across the world, from the mid-1990s on, many environmental activists realized that there had never been such an opportunity to circumvent the established organizations and mass media. (In a way, the writing of this book would have been impossible without the internet.) The impact of this new information and communications network on the vibrancy of environmental groups is still by no means clear. Of course they were not alone when they took advantage of the new possibilities, even if they forgot about other levels of globalization so long as they surfed only in their own networks. The internet has brought a seemingly limitless growth of information and communication, and has also done a lot to revive the illusion of limitless growth in the business world.

The global regime that developed after Rio, and that proved capable of drastic measures if push came to shove, did not revolve around climate protection and 'sustainable development'; it was a regime designed to impose free trade and deregulation in the wake of the collapse of the Communist bloc. This objective was pursued most rigorously by the World Trade Organization (WTO), founded on 1 April 1994 in Marrakesh. Unlike its postwar predecessor, the General Agreement on Tariffs and Trade (GATT), this is not a mere customs union but a supranational organization which – as its arch-enemy Jean Ziegler notes – can resort to a wide range of sanctions and coercive measures,[292] using them most forcefully against weaker third world countries. As for the International Monetary Fund (IMF), founded at Bretton Woods in 1944 at the same time as the World Bank, its interventions (also mainly vis-à-vis the third world) pay little heed to national sovereignty, while making specific provisions to stabilize currencies by reducing levels of government debt.[293]

This corresponded to the general retreat from Keynesianism that economists began to execute around the time of the 'ecological revolution'.[294] Full employment was no longer to be pursued at the expense of free trade and monetary stability, which, according to the new dogma, were not at all harmful to the environment, certainly less than protective tariffs and a large public sector were. Environmentalists, it was (and still is) argued, should not bow too hastily to pressure from anti-globalization demonstrators and throw overboard all the historical insights of economic liberalism: a heavy industry nurtured behind high tariff barriers was just as environmentally unfriendly as forced economic growth reliant on deficit financing rather than needs in civil society; high levels of debt involved enrichment at the expense of future generations, the very opposite of sustainability; inflation too was a deadly enemy of a 'sustainable', future-oriented economy. The ecological longing for sustainability could actually support itself on the new striving for economic solidity; free trade offered every country the opportunity to produce what it was naturally most suited for.

Theoretically, the new global economic regime might have been compatible with care for the environment. But in reality, when combined with the new communications technology and a huge growth in long-distance aircraft and shipping doped on fuel tax relief, it considerably increased the burden on the earth's atmosphere. It also contributed to the weakening of regional economies, where polluters were easier to get at than in a globalized economy and there was a greater chance of environmental protection.

This does not mean, however, that the nation is finished as an environmental policy arena. In the 1990s, it became fashionable to exaggerate the novelty and scale of globalization and to argue that, in today's world, environmental regulations could be successful only if they applied at an international level, since otherwise national industries would fall behind those of their competitors. Yet it was clear in many cases that an international agreement would not be reached in the foreseeable future. Globalization, once a rhetorical figure dear to environmental activists, turned into a lame excuse used by their opponents. Those in today's Germany who seek to block the change in energy policy do not openly proclaim their goals, but point out that Germans cannot go it alone and have to 'think globally'. As Martin Jänicke has shown, the four industries that 'are the toughest obstacles to environmental protection' – energy, transport, agriculture and construction – are exposed to relatively little, if any, global competition.[295] There is undoubtedly wide scope for countries leading the way in environmental protection, and all historical experience indicates that pioneers are the ones who drive innovations forward. That was once true of industrialization, which was not decided on at a global summit conference.

Biodiversity and the spirit of Rio

The meteoric rise of 'biodiversity', unexpected even for conservationists, began in 1992 with the Rio Conference. The word had been coined in 1985 by the American biologist Walter Rosen and then popularized mainly by the influential Edward O. Wilson[296] – with a success so quick and resounding that it surprised him as much as the fate of 'sustainable development' amazed the inventor of that magic formula.[297] At the same time, Wilson put forward the hypothesis (NB: not the thesis[298]) that 'biophilia' was a natural human instinct: a case of inner nature providing a more solid foundation than ecology for the protection of external nature. Along with 'sustainable development', the Convention on Biological Diversity became the trademark of Rio – a conscious synthesis of nature conservation and environmental protection.

In contrast to the UN Framework Convention on Climate Change (UNFCCC), this declaration of intent to do something to preserve biodiversity gained a consensus at Rio without too much difficulty and sent the concept on its journey round the world. On closer examination, though, it was thoroughly open-ended: it failed to define any priorities or specific measures to be taken, apart from one-sidedly singling out certain 'endangered species'. This vagueness made it easier to reach a consensus. Strictly speaking, bacterial micro-organisms were also part of biodiversity, but who would have done anything for them? Maximum species diversity by no means necessarily coincides with sustainability in the sense of long-term soil fertility: on the contrary, deforested regions with worn-out soil not infrequently have high biodiversity. This reverses the usual ranking of environmental model countries, placing Albania, for example, ahead even of the Federal Republic of Germany. Many industrially backward countries may therefore be more friendly towards biodiversity than to expensive measures to protect the environment. Biodiversity is especially high in gardens, which cannot survive without constant care. Maximum species diversity does not harmonize at all well with the idea of 'letting nature get on with it', since many parts of the world, if left to themselves, would become overgrown with thick forest that choked the species diversity of open countryside.

What can be done practically with 'biodiversity' as the key objective? Edward O. Wilson gave some clear indications. Though his own love of nature is more of a personal passion, he tried to mobilize economic interests in support of species diversity, reviving the eighteenth-century concept of 'hidden natural treasures'. 'Biodiversity', he argued, 'is our most valuable but least appreciated resource' – and by that he also meant valuable in an economic sense. Disease-resistant variants that genetic engineers tried to produce, often with only modest success and under attack from conservationists, could be found already tested by evolution in the tropical forests, if only one looked for them carefully enough. He also made the rather exaggerated claim that 'A revolution in conservation thinking in the past twenty years, a New Environmentalism, has led to this perception of the environmental value of wild species.'[299] Finally, under the aegis of 'biodiversity' plus 'sustainable development', the grand synthesis of economics and ecology!

This left its mark in the Rio biodiversity convention, which envisages regulations to simplify industrial access to 'genetic resources'. 'Biotechnology is seen as a component of the technologies relevant to the protection of biodiversity.' In 1989 the Instituto Nacional de Biodiversidad (INBio) was founded in Costa Rica as a 'private autonomous non-profit institution' to study biodiversity, and 'to ensure sustainable use', in a country fast becoming the environmental model for Latin America. In 1992, the year of Rio, INBio hit the headlines by signing an agreement with the US Merck & Co., Incorporated, to 'supply a limited quantity of plant and animal extracts for pharmaceutical research'.[300] Now that East–West barriers no longer restrict the global activity of multinationals, the objective of 'bioversity' has come under a cloud. Pharmaceutical corporations have set themselves up as its trustees, buying third world genetic resources and attempting to patent and monopolize them.[301] This has led to vociferous protests, especially in India. For many today, 'biodiversity' is a slogan not of ecologists but of pharmaceutical and agribusiness multinationals.

From Rio to Brussels: the Flora, Fauna, Habitat (FFH) Directive

The EU headquarters in Brussels soon discovered the cross-border potential of 'biodiversity' and translated it into the grand FFH directive, agreed by member-states in 1992.[302] According to Karl-Heinz Erdmann and Hans Dieter Knapp from the German conservation agency, this marked a new phase 'of tumultuous development of international conservation activity'[303] – which, as Wolfgang Haber put it, eventually led to a 'quantum leap' comparable to debt for nature in wilderness protection.[304] Conservationists now switched from a basically defensive posture to one more inclined to attack. But whereas they had previously seen the Brussels bureaucracy as their enemy, because of its promotion of factory farming and nuclear power plants,[305] it now came as a pleasant surprise to discover what the EU's famous levers could achieve. Activists worked as valuable experts with EU bodies, and Brussels funding for conservation and environmental protection was so generous that for a time NGOs did not have sufficient personnel to take full advantage of it.[306]

Though Rio-style 'biodiversity' set ill-defined goals, the designation of protected areas under the FFH directive was more or less in the old conservationist tradition of focusing on endangered species popular with the public. How could it have been otherwise, once it had been decided not just to 'let nature get on with it'? 'Wild hamster control' was one area that made Saxony-Anhalt an exception in Germany's implementation of the directive,[307] while for other conservationists 'hamster control' had a comical side, and for much of the media its protection caused something akin to the kerfuffle in America over the spotted owl.[308] Previous bird protection zones were now operated as FFH areas.

The FFH model was suited to conditions on the densely populated European continent, where the American national park concept soon reached its limits. FFH areas did not need to be larger than former conservation areas, but they did have to be linked to one another by corridors along which the endangered species could spread and multiply. In keeping with the spirit of the nascent electronic age, this 'biotope network' was the core of the EU's *Natura 2000* vision – a title reminiscent of Rio's *Agenda 21*. From the bird protection guidelines, the FFH directive took over the 'no deterioration of existing conditions' rule, a minimum requirement being habitat conservation for designated species. This was a pragmatic solution, based on the status quo for traditional types of use, but it restricted the freedom of action of farmers in the area, and not infrequently the FFH provisions went beyond mere preservation of the status quo.

Different opinions are still expressed about the (ambiguously worded) FFH directive, and there is also doubt about the extent to which farmers are entitled to compensation for lost earnings. A Europe-wide collection of case studies on the implementation of *Natura 2000* found a general tendency for 'procedural legitimacy' to assert itself at the expense of 'substantive claims to legitimacy'.[309] That is a discreet academic formulation. In ordinary language: the jargon of cooperative do-gooders is all very well, but you won't get anywhere with stubborn peasants unless you take a hard line and are prepared to throw the law at them; however much the old folk grumble, the younger generation will eventually accept conservation or even think it a good idea; all the objections just mask a thirst for larger subsidies; anyway, since farmers nowadays live off tax revenue, it is only right and proper that agriculture should be subordinate to the common good. This trust in 'procedural legitimacy' is probably not altogether unrealistic, but it assumes that the end result for the countryside is in accord with the public welfare. Otherwise, this top-down style of action may have the opposite effect and lead farmers to snub anything 'eco'; there is plenty of evidence of this, particularly in Germany. One continually hears of farmers who mow down their orchids as soon as there is the slightest danger that an area will be placed under FFH protection.

One wonders whether a changeover to more environmentally sound farming methods is not much more important than the issuing of new FFH directives. Would it not be a far more convincing way to reconcile public welfare with farmers' self-interest, and would not such a combination of biodiversity and sustainable development be far more consistent with the spirit of Rio?[310] Are conservationists perhaps too blinkered by the old idea of a protected reserve to appreciate this? Triumphalism over the opportunities opened up by the FFH often made conservationists forget that farm subsidies still accounted for the lion's share of the EU budget, that the power of the agricultural lobby in Brussels was unbroken, and that an (economically and ecologically senseless) agricultural policy subsidized both high-output production and the surpluses generated by it – an obscene scandal if ever there was one.[311] In 1999 EuroNatur drew the sarcastic conclusion that 'Ecological farming is promoted entirely as an extensification measure that helps to reduce agricultural surpluses.'[312] But soon that incentive was a thing of the past, as subsidized biofuels boomed in the name of climate protection.

Opinions are also divided about whether, under these conditions, the FFH directive really is a miracle weapon, or whether it represents a Pyrrhic victory which, by alienating the farmers, will eventually lead to the demise of conservationism;[313] sometimes one and the same observer shifts backwards and forwards between the two positions. Yet, although the need is greater than almost anywhere else, there has been no major public debate on this all-important European conservation issue. Not only here do we see that wordy public discussions on issues relating to nature – of which there have been plenty in recent decades – often have only a slight practical reference. Where power is at stake, words are kept to a minimum. As Winston Churchill is supposed to have said: 'Politics is what people do not talk about.'

High-altitude atmosphere policies from Kyoto to Copenhagen

In the late 1990s, when the EU was coming to the fore on conservation issues, it also began to make a name for itself internationally in relation to climate protection. It has since been forgotten, however, that on this question, as on the ozone hole in the 1970s, the first alarms came from the United States, mainly as a spin-off from space exploration.[314] Following the Kyoto Conference (1997), the EU took on board the concept of emissions trading (previously held in low regard as a typically American idea), with which the United States already had long experience in connection with sulphur dioxide.[315] In the view of David G. Victor, an American critic of Kyoto, the European emissions trading system is now the most important policy experiment anywhere in the world.[316]

At the latest by the Copenhagen Summit of 2009, climate protection gave the (misleading) impression of a specially European cause, facing a powerful, unholy coalition made up of the United States, China and India. The clash on environmental policy between Europeans and Americans was becoming sharper than ever before, although it has often been exaggerated since then in the ecological literature. After Kyoto the United States became the strongest force opposing a global climate regime – assuming that such a regime is possible and that disputes about it are not mere shadow-boxing. A global policy that does not have Washington on its side is a blind alley, especially if China, the new world power, is also opposed to it.

This raises the question of whether the new climate priority did not dissipate the energies bound up with environmental protection. No other issue in its recent history is so explosive: how did this European priority and commitment come about, and what do their results tell us about possibilities for the future? As the whole of the above account indicates, this change in the dynamic of environmentalism is by no means self-explanatory and still presents future researchers with a great deal of work.

In itself, the 'greenhouse effect' theory was anything but new: it went all the way back to Svante Arrhenius in 1896, although it had then been no more than a hypothesis (the role of CO_2 as a dominant factor in climate events was not established until the 1980s). When the medievalist Lynn White noted in 1966 that our massive use of fossil fuels was threatening to change the earth's atmosphere, he said nothing about why this was so: it was merely a passing remark in a piece on the London smog alarm of 1285.[317] But he was aware that this new turn in human history would not remain without fateful consequences of one kind or another.

Even less clear were the consequences for nature and culture. True, there was no lack of theories about the influence of climate change on earlier historical developments, but they did not enjoy a high reputation in academic circles. Even the impact of the Little Ice Age (from the sixteenth to the eighteenth century) has still not been solidly established; climate variations seem to have been so frequent,[318] and human cultures perforce so capable of adaptation, that it is a difficult task to identify them as determinants of history. Causal constructs occur most easily to authors who, for want of broader historical knowledge, can think of no other explanations.

Der Spiegel occasionally sounded the greenhouse alarm as early as 1979 (No. 9 (1979): 'Tod im Treibhaus' [Death in the Greenhouse]), but in those days there were equally vehement predictions of an impending new ice age.[319] In the *Global 2000 Report to the US President*, published in 1980, the Council on Environmental Quality (the most prominent think-tank of its kind) used a similar methodology to that of the German Commission of Inquiry to draw up four scenarios for the climate, ranging from 'strong global cooling' to 'strong global warming'.[320] All begin with a cooling trend observable since the 1940s, with no clear evidence yet of a change. 'The next ice age is coming for sure' had been a common everyday response to a spell of cold weather. Only in the late 1990s was climate history reconstructed in such a way as to yield the alarming 'hockey stick curve': the near-vertical rise of a previously imperceptible warming.[321] More typical of the Cold War period was fear of a 'nuclear winter' caused by fallout from atomic explosions, and this old scenario came to a head amid the arms race of the early 1980s; it then suddenly fell into oblivion after the end of the Cold War. In the mid-1980s, the 'global warming' thesis became dominant (though not uncontested) in a remarkably brief space of time. For those who had been following the environmental discourse of the time in all its diversity, this came as a surprising turn. Was it the result of impressive new discoveries in climate science? Was the climate itself developing in new ways? Or was the historical context decisive: the synergic effects producing a global surge in environmental awareness from Chernobyl to Rio? Or did more specific factors such as the ozone alarm also play a role?

A definitive answer cannot be given in the present state of research. Technological advances were obviously a factor – most notably, the ever deeper ice cores archived in the Arctic and Antarctic since the 1960s, which made it possible to trace atmospheric CO_2 levels back thousands or even hundreds of thousands of years.[322] It turned out that these levels had indeed risen in the course of recent human history. It is true that similar increases had also taken place in earlier geological eras, but anthropogenic causes were the most plausible explanation for the recent changes. Theoretically, CO_2 emissions produced by human activity could have been absorbed by stronger plant growth and by ocean organisms, but it became ever clearer that that had happened to only a limited extent. Self-regulation of the earth's ecosystem could therefore be relied upon only partly, if at all, to deal with the effects of the explosive growth of human civilization.

But, of course, in modern times too man has not been the only influence on the climate. Nor has global warming been a constant feature of the coal and oil age, so could it not have been offset by various countertendencies? Evidently the CO_2 greenhouse effect operates with a delay and is not the only climate factor to be taken into consideration; this makes it difficult to establish causal connections. 'The truth lies not in history but in models' was one response to the ambiguity of previous climate history, but models as such do not contain truth: they require factual verification. Usually the retreat of Alpine glaciers since the 1980s has been held up as visible evidence, but even that does not constitute decisive proof. The 'global warming' thesis has come to seem more convincing the longer the warming that began in the late 1970s has lasted, even if those who believe in computer-generated truth are reluctant to admit the dependence of mainstream science on sense perception. The climate alarm cannot be explained purely in terms of the history of science.[323]

The Swedish climatologist Bert Bolin – the founder and long-term chair of the Intergovernmental Panel on Climate Change (IPCC), which has become the leading scientific authority in climate policy – emphasized that the rise of the climate change issue was mainly science-driven,[324] but in retrospect he freely admitted that climate predictions were by no means certain in the 1980s and later.[325] In early 1989, commenting on an international conference in Delhi that described global warming as the biggest crisis ever to have faced humanity, he called it 'a desperate cry for political action without adequate scientific analysis'.[326] The IPCC too wanted to get things moving politically. It was not simply a debating club but also a think-tank put together on political criteria,[327] which was supposed to send clear signals to politicians. This was an important point for the future course of things.

Bolin himself points out that the hot, dry summer of 1988, which caused severe crop failures in the US, triggered a change in public opinion and spread the idea that global warming was a serious business.[328] Of course, one hot summer was of no consequence for the validity of climate models, but the fact that climate research has generally seen the greenhouse effect as the dominant factor only since about 1980 is evidence that experts who thought in terms of geological eras were also unswayed by current temperature patterns. For it definitely grew warmer in the 1980s: average temperatures were higher than any recorded since the beginning of extensive measurements. But the records did not go back further than the modern age, so once again climate history did not have any clear-cut lessons to offer, even regarding the consequences of a change in the global climate. At temperate latitudes there was nothing inherently scary about the warming of the 1980s and 1990s. Only an interaction of discrete factors led to the alarming headlines that brought it home to everyone.

Bolin also reveals that the motives behind the climate alarm were not all innocent and science-based. One of the first government leaders to join in was Margaret Thatcher, the Iron Lady, for whom the attacks on CO_2 were a highly welcome weapon against the labour movement's base of support in the coal industry, and who saw the future of Britain in the New Economy. She even claimed that warming was taking place at the rate of one degree a decade: a wild exaggeration![329] Remarkably, Helmut Schmidt warned as early as 1977 of the consequences of rising CO_2 levels and would have liked to place the issue on the agenda of Willy Brandt's North–South Commission.[330] Schmidt usually found ecological arguments tiresome, but in this case he could use them to beat anti-nuclear activists at their own game. The Swedish prime minister Olof Palme, who had Bolin as one of his advisers, also used the greenhouse effect to thwart the Green opposition to his extensive nuclear energy programme,[331] while the climate and ozone alarms offered the powerful NASA a golden opportunity to demonstrate its continuing usefulness to humanity after the tide turned against space travel; Robert Watson, who took over from Bolin as IPCC chair and spoke forcefully about the dangers of global warming, also had a background in the US space agency.[332] The climate alarm raisers used to dismiss their opponents, with some justification, as hirelings of the coal, oil and car lobby, but there were material interests and power considerations on their side too – above all, the huge funds that the alarm released for research. In the Bundesrepublik alone, spending on climate studies soared from 3.6 million Deutschmarks in 1983 to 220 million in 1994 – an increase without precedent in the history of science, outside the field of military R&D.[333]

If we consider how much a scientist's prestige depends nowadays on the availability of funding – which would have had a whiff of corruption for an old-style scholar – we can imagine how tempting it is to adopt the hypothesis that promises the most money. Since the empirical findings are usually ambiguous, there is often some room for manoeuvre. Besides, it is not necessary to falsify research results: such deliberate wrongdoing is probably quite rare in the academic community, where colleagues keep a close eye on one another. Talk of a 'climate swindle', sometimes heard in hostile pamphlets, does not tally with the facts; it cannot be reasonably doubted that warming as a result of higher CO_2 levels in the atmosphere is a plausible interpretation of the findings. But the polarization of public debate between alarmists and sceptics, which saddened Bert Bolin towards the end of his life,[334] threatens to obscure matters. For climate predictions do not admit of complete certainty, and it was probably not very clever of climate researchers to allow the other side to make exclusive use of this uncertainty as an argument. The lack of open public debate helps to ensure that, although lip service to climate protection is a matter of political correctness, many inwardly doubt the gravity of the danger and are unable to summon up much energy; they lack a forum to discuss rationally what the uncertainties are and how they should be addressed.

There continued to be grounds for scepticism about the alarmist calls, and in the United States, where, unlike in the EU, opponents of environmentalism were open and above board, a formal Global Climate Coalition (GCC) took shape in the 1990s. Soon, however, leading oil and automobile corporations began to doubt whether such open lobbying was good for their image, and in 2001–2 they withdrew by the dozen from the GCC.[335] Considering that the largest economic powers of our age – the oil and car industries – were born adversaries of the global warming campaign and promised substantial financial support to the other side, it is remarkable how few alternatives to the greenhouse effect theory were known around that time. The most prominent opponent of the IPCC within the climate research elite was a man who had initially collaborated with it: Richard S. Lindzen, professor of meteorology since 1983 at the Massachusetts Institute of Technology (MIT). In his view, increased water vapour due to global warming reduced solar radiation on earth and played a role in climate regulation. But although this model had an intrinsic plausibility, it remained unclear how significant it was for most of the earth's atmosphere; Lindzen refrained from a general offensive in the media against the IPCC.

Fred Singer, on the other hand, who had made a name for himself in the fifties and sixties for the development of weather satellites, and whose criticisms of IPCC calculations even Bolin had initially found constructive, launched into a sharp campaign against the IPCC.[336] He did not deny the possibility of global warming, but only as a hypothesis; and he thought it would be a huge scandal if the USA and other countries ruined their economy to mitigate a climate 'disaster' that existed 'only on computer printouts and in the feverish imagination of professional environmental zealots'. If they absolutely wanted to do something, they could fertilize the oceans so that a larger number of micro-organisms absorbed more carbon dioxide; that would be incomparably cheaper and more effective than a war on industrial and car emissions.[337] Here we see the emergence of the idea of 'geo-engineering'!

The climate campaigners achieved their greatest success so far in 2006, when Nicholas Stern, the former chief economist of the World Bank, reckoned that climate change would cost humanity ten times more than the taking of appropriate countermeasures. This broke major new ground among a public used to thinking in cost–benefit terms. Of course, both Stern's and Singer's calculations contained many unknowns. The only real argument against the alarm raisers was the chaotic character of climate development, which could not be captured in models. Even today there is no serious counter to the global warming thesis that credibly shows how the earth might deal with hugely increased CO_2 levels in a way that is not harmful to humans; rather, the essence of such positions consists in agnosticism, scepticism or avoidance. Mind you, to admit to ignorance can sometimes be a scientifically respectable position.

In any event, the high-profile breakthroughs in climate research have not yet been matched by remotely comparable policy advances. Climate policy has certainly had legitimacy, but although, as Max Weber taught, lasting dominance requires legitimacy, the history of climate policy shows that legitimacy alone cannot establish dominance. This failure to deliver is not hard to explain historically. The road to the Kyoto Protocol began in 1992 with the Rio Climate Framework Convention, but the same year also marked the end of the first period of climate catastrophism.[338] The founding years of international climate policy – from the Toronto Conference in 1988 to Rio in 1992 – fell in a phase when environmental policy in general was undergoing a boom, whereas attempts at implementation – from Kyoto 1997 to Copenhagen 2009 – occurred at a time when the sharp ups and downs of the economy were occupying the main energies of politicians and the public. The fate of environmental protection can be understood only in the overall context of the age. Furthermore, a drastic lowering of global CO_2 emissions was a task without historical precedent, for which adequate institutions and instruments were lacking. It might seem at first that 'ozone diplomacy' just had to be transferred to the CO_2 problem, but that would be a false impression. In the case of ozone-damaging CFCs, it had been possible simply to impose a ban and to replace them with other substances; the political representatives of leading CFC producers could decide this behind closed doors, even by mutual agreement with the firms in question, for which the replacement substances offered higher profits.

A general ban on CO_2 emissions, however, would have been absurd; there was no way in which it would have been technically feasible. There was the strongest economic resistance to the idea, and the circle of those affected by it was potentially vast.

The aim of the Kyoto Protocol was to oblige industrial countries to reduce their greenhouse gas emissions, so that by 2012 they would be 5.2 per cent below their 1990 level. This immediately raised the question of how this could be achieved, in a period of global liberalization when fewer and fewer state leaderships could simply issue commands relating to the economy. The most effective means would have been an energy tax, but it would have had to be so high that both the business world and private motorists would have been up in arms as never before. The other market instrument therefore carried the day: the issuing of emission bonds. The setting of 1990 as the reference year was meant to lure the former Eastern bloc countries, whose CO_2 emissions had since declined so sharply without any policy changes (on account of the collapse of large parts of industry) that they had a lot of 'hot air' to sell: that is, emissions that their industry no longer belched out. This whole business, with its degradation of the earth's atmosphere into a commodity, had something morally repulsive about it.

In criticizing, we should not forget that 'the' big solution is nowhere in sight, and we have every reason to doubt that there will ever be one. It is all too easy to demonstrate that the success of any climate policy measure is highly uncertain or that in an ideal world there would be far fewer people and they would live much more modestly. But such reasoning has no practical value: indeed, it is more likely to discredit environmentalism. We should also be mistrustful of those who require too much of environmental policy. Especially in countries where no one who cares about their reputation can afford to be openly anti-environmentalist, it is a common ploy to paralyse strategic initiatives by tying them in knots with excessive demands. All environmental policy is a patchwork, and unsavoury practices that actually move things forward a little are preferable to perfect solutions that never become more than words. The only question is whether emission bonds achieve something or not, and whether the monitoring of emissions is possible in countries or enterprises that resort to bluff and obfuscation.[339]

Is there a lack only of effective instruments, or is the real dilemma a lack of *will* on the part of most political leaders? It is hard to be sure. One would also have to be familiar with government archives, and perhaps even those would not provide a clear answer. Global warming first became noticeable only a few decades ago and has not yet acquired dramatic forms – retreating glaciers or shrinking ice caps are mostly far off – and so it has failed to put real pressure on the world's major powers. True, the spectacle of floods and hurricanes is often conjured up, but even Bolin admits that such 'extreme events' cannot be directly associated with global warming.[340] In 1999 Christian Pfister, the Swiss pioneer of climate history, summarized the problem of the public perception of climate change: 'The decisive indicators are not spectacular, and the spectacular events are not decisive!'[341] Yet history shows that disasters are not necessary to get something moving, in the Western world or elsewhere. Beijing is the metropolis most threatened with drought, and, although the Chinese leadership opposes CO_2 curbs now because of the country's dependence on coal, it seems to take the danger of warming seriously. So far at least, the increasingly dry conditions in North China are more attributable to deforestation and groundwater depletion, but they do give a foretaste of what lies ahead as a result of global warming. It would be rash to conclude from the state of climate summitry that the world's rulers would simply dismiss all warnings as a 'swindle'. An opposition front is shaping up only against the demand for immediate measures that restrict the freedom of action of most governments.

The climate disaster, though so much talked about, is not yet a reality; it is even questionable whether a large number of popular publications make it out to be such. As in the 'dying forest' alarm of the early 1980s, the underlying assumption is that only dire warnings will force politicians to do something. The lessons of the past rather tend to contradict this, however, since few historians have seen disasters as the cause of policy innovations. In emergencies, which often have an initially paralysing effect or lead to short-sighted panic, the only response has usually been conventional relief measures; fundamental innovations take time. If we think of the 'ecological revolution' of 1970, we would look in vain for an environmental disaster that triggered the decisive breakthrough; the novel factor was a conscious concern about future risks, and since no one then had a really global long-term vision these were often partly hypothetical. It is not even the case that acute disasters have been the main reason propelling people in new directions and causing them to redouble their efforts; many walls around old cities testify to the extent to which they have guarded against future dangers. If things were otherwise, the power of religions that play on fear of eternal damnation would be impossible to explain.

Why not admit, then, that climate predictions have their uncertainties and that, even if ever greater warming is likely in the long run, it is by no means clear that catastrophe is around the corner? Decisions in a state of uncertainty are anyway routine in politics and business. To accept that some questions remain open is not necessarily a formula for inaction; it may be a barrier to ill-considered activism. If politicians seriously believed in the imminence of disaster, they would be rushing into massive countermeasures which – as in the 1950s or 1960s, when the 'peaceful atom' was supposed to be the great saviour – might turn out to be a greater problem than climate change. Catastrophism also encourages a style of forcing through policies at any price, which is counterproductive in the international arena and tends to provoke defiance on the part of countries incapable of immediate drastic CO_2 reductions. It is striking that, in his old age, Bert Bolin distanced himself from the alarmism of Al Gore's *Inconvenient Truth*;[342] the hardly impressive environmental record of Gore's term as US vice-president suggests that alarmism is by no means the same as effective activism.

Especially in the United States – most Europeans still recoil at the prospect – one comes across wild technocratic fantasies of 'geo-engineering' or 'climate engineering' (CE for short), which draw on vulcanology for such ideas as the spraying of sulphur dioxide in the stratosphere to reduce levels of solar radiation.[343] Of course, this carries certain risks: not only that sulphurous yellow streaks would make clear blue skies a thing of the past, but also that the Asian monsoons on which hundreds of millions depend for their food would disappear.[344] Worst of all, even if such science fiction scenarios never come true, they provide an excuse for American politicians to deprioritize CO_2 reductions here and now. For a decade there has been growing evidence that the new Indian and Chinese coal-fired power stations, which do not have desulphurization facilities, already provide for geo-engineering and thus represent a brake on global warming[345] – even though they have other unpleasant side effects. While historians have learned to be supercautious with predictions, there is some evidence that the way to a globally sustainable environment lies more through increased forest growth, cycling and birth control than through geo-engineering, underground CO_2 sequestration or giant wind farms, not to speak of nuclear power plants.

Even if the Kyoto Protocol was ratified by all participants and actually put into practice, it would achieve only little against the measurable effects of climate change. Moreover, a basic problem of global climate diplomacy, with its rhetoric of CO_2 percentage reductions, is that these cover a wide range of national and regional situations and varying scopes for action on the part of different players, especially as far as win-win strategies with inbuilt advantages are concerned. A country like France, which has an extremely high proportion of nuclear power, finds it quite easy to present itself as a model at climate summits, as do heavily deindustrialized England, the former Eastern bloc countries (whose old smokestack industries have partly collapsed) or the Federal Republic of Germany (which claims to be the leader in environmental technology).

This being so, the EU can demand reductions at international conferences that put other countries in a tight corner. It seems as if many opportunities for agreement have been lost in this way. The 'ecology of ecologism' plays a very large role in climate protection too; solutions with a prospect of 'sustainability' look very different from country to country. International mega-conferences – where, on grounds of size alone, creative decision-making processes are unlikely to feature, and oil-producing countries plus their third world client states are able to block many things – tend to involve a style of politics that leads nowhere. The demand for the broadest possible participation sounds democratically correct, but it actually contributes to the blind alley of global climate politics. The UNEP's *Global Environment Outlook 2000* concluded from experiences in Asia: 'Generally, the smaller the membership of the agreement, the wider the coverage in local mass media. For example, the Ganges Water Sharing Treaty is known even to poor farmers in the remotest parts of Bangladesh and West Bengal.'[346]

Also questionable is the well-meaning rhetoric of 'climate justice' popular at church conferences, where 'ecumenical' has increasingly become synonymous with 'ecological' (which in principle makes some sense nowadays). It is often claimed, in justification of development aid, that the main perpetrators of climate change have to suffer the least from its effects. But if that was really so, the situation would be hopeless. No world power will accept major restrictions on its economic activity out of regard for Bangladesh or the Seychelles. It is evidently counterproductive if – as has repeatedly happened – international climate policy gets caught up in conventional North–South diplomacy, so that climate protection appears as a demand of the North to which the South must make concessions in return for aid. Climate protection has a chance of being effective and sustainable, beyond mere shows of activitiy, if it corresponds to the interests of most of the players and if it is managed by competent and honest people. Wangari Maathai declared: 'Efforts to help developing countries adapt to climate change are doomed to failure unless good governance and ethics are integral elements of financial assistance'[347] – and this serves as the epigraph in a *Global Corruption Report: Climate Change*, commissioned by Greenpeace International and published by Transparency International.

Although the EU is the main promoter of climate protection at international conferences today, a false impression often arises in other parts of the world that Europeans have the main interest in safeguards and that they should be made to pay for them. In reality, the United States and China are more threatened than most EU countries by global warming, and China has recently overtaken the US as the largest producer of CO_2 emissions. Methane, which is now known to be a particularly dangerous greenhouse gas also emitted in rice cultivation,[348] has confused previous lines of argument – so much so that it has not even become part of climate discourse. It would seem that methane can be controlled at a global level far less than CO_2; the only strategies that stand a chance are ones that the countries in question pursue in their own interest.

In water policy[349] and the fight against erosion, desertification and soil destruction too – probably the most important ways of protecting the environment in the long term[350] – the global level tends to be a stratosphere where energies fall flat. The problems and solutions are essentially regional, and in the case of desertification, for example, the well-known pointlessness of global management means that the issue has been given comparatively little prominence in the era of (putative) global politics. Hence the desirability of a new style of transnational environmental diplomacy – one more adapted to regional specificities and conducted in smaller circles capable of taking decisions. Only this can do justice to other problems no less serious than climate change. The disappointments since the early 1990s have made these points clearer than they were amid the euphoria of Rio

1992. Experiences so far in environmental policy highlight the particular advantage of smaller countries – from the Alps to Scandinavia, from Costa Rica to Bhutan.

Recent ecological literature often subsumes water shortages and soil degradation in large parts of the world under the heading of global climate change, but a look back over a few decades is enough to remind us that these problems existed before, and can be explained without, the present climate alarm. The first catastrophic drought in the Sahel, coinciding with the 'ecological revolution' and focusing public attention on desertification for the first time since the Dust Bowl era,[351] occurred at a time (1970) when climate researchers still thought they could detect signs of a new ice age. No doubt it is wrong to think that correct policies could solve the world's major environmental problems in one go. On the other hand, there is a danger that talk of climate change might operate as a diversionary manoeuvre. If big cities lower the groundwater level in arid rural areas, or if economic and demographic growth leads to overuse of water resources, it is a cheap trick to blame this on global warming in order to avert the need for action. International climate conference tourism, though attractive to many environmentalists in marginal countries, can distract attention from the truly pressing environmental problems at home.

'Think globally, act locally': solving the paradox

The global climate policy of emission bonds and certificates is highly susceptible to bluff and corruption;[352] a local policy involving low-energy housing, cycle lanes and optimized public transport has far greater substance and brings other tangible benefits. Not only the essence of many issues but also the source of many initiatives continues to have marked regional features, in a part latent, part open tension with the global trend in environmentalism since the time of Rio.

On the basis of dozens of interviews with politicians in Europe and Japan, David G. Victor had the impression that governments which took the initiative in the Kyoto Protocol were pursuing a policy they would have followed anyway under the pressure of 'public opinion'.[353] National and regional politics are not at all in general decline, contrary to what one would suppose from recent literature on the Europeanization and globalization of environmentalism; here statistics offer a good counterweight to some of the globalization rhetoric.[354] Even many environmental lobbyists in Brussels, faced with today's revival of regionalism, are not sure that they could not be achieving more at home. 'When Rebecca Willis of the Green Alliance, for example, is asked the hypothetical question whether she would rather employ an extra person for lobbying work in Brussels or at the newly created Scottish Parliament, she does not think twice before answering Scotland.'[355] Especially surprising is the result of several studies that would evidently have liked the opposite to be the case: environmental policy-makers in a number of EU countries with a strongly ecological image are not drawing closer to one another.[356] That is a clear indication that environmental politics is driven far more by national and regional forces than by anything in 'global society'.

A fascinating question so far scarcely addressed by researchers is the extent to which the environmental movement has grown together with the anti-globalization movement, not only in response to particular situations but in a stable and productive alliance. The best-known transnational anti-globalization network is Attac, and many are not aware that its name originally had nothing to with 'attack' but was an acronym of the French Association pour la Taxation des Transactions financières et l'Aide aux Citoyens. This title set a new tone in the history of protest movements: a clever understatement perfectly in keeping with the existing economic system, yet designed to limit the snowballing of international financial flows since the 1990s and thus to win back space for political action at the level of the nation-state.

The crises of the new millennium have fully vindicated those who predicted that a complete freeing of the economy would not lead to a self-regulating world order but end in chaos. The demand raised by Attac converged with environmentalist efforts to restrict the explosive growth of world trade on the basis of untaxed fuel – and also with a widespread desire to overcome the uncertainty and opaqueness that had been growing *pari passu* with global competition. However, this was not the only trend. For some time now, the ecological and one-world scene has been marked by a curious half-light reflecting moods of both pro-globalization and anti-globalization.[357]

As is so often the case with protest movements, many spokespersons for Attac find it easier to explain what it is against than what is it for. One particular reason is that the network in France comprises two different milieux with partly opposing attitudes: supporters of old-style national sovereignty and descendants of the New Left. The discrepancy is so strong that many shy away from raising any positive models for discussion, out of a fear that the latent tension will erupt into open conflict.[358] Sections of German society mobilizable for protest action tend to consider the national framework as more taboo than their counterparts in France do. But since the nation-state is the only possible counterweight to the pull of globalization, the formulation of positive conceptions inevitably involves all kinds of contortions, or else an escape into phrasemongering. Ironically, in view of its original impetus to do a lot with little, Attac now calls for a 'global Marshall Plan' with an annual budget of 50 billion euros, although this grandiose idea taken over from Al Gore is globalization jargon of the first water, as if tailor-made to legitimize powerful global economic control centres.

But we should not be too scornful. Attac faces the same difficulty as the modern environmental movement: in an age of powers with global reach, whether economic or ecological, it has become anachronistic to act within a purely regional horizon. To be sure, the present account has repeatedly made it clear that the link between nature conservation and the defence of cultural heritage is anything but a German or British peculiarity, and that, like the giant Antaeus of Greek myth, the environmental movement continually needs to make contact with Mother Earth to preserve its vitality. It is significant that Rio's *Agenda 21* – whether read or unread – was effective mainly in providing a higher legitimacy for local initiatives. But it has also become clear that, right from the beginning, the global horizon contributed to the dynamism and integrative power of the environmental movement, and it would be short-sighted to downplay international conferences and transational networks altogether or to build exclusively on regions, local authorities and village communities. There are stories not only of insubstantial conference tourism but also of narrow-minded town councils that do underhand deals with business interests and evade critical public scrutiny.

Vandana Shiva inveighed passionately against globalization, but acted at international level and appears to have been more famous in parts of the Western eco-scene than in her own country. Sunderlal Bahuguna too, the spokesperson of the Chipko movement, drew strength from contacts with like-minded people around the world. Medha Patkar, the campaigner against the Narmada dam, certainly tried to sink roots in the region threatened by the project and was anxious not to gain the reputation of being financed from abroad, yet support from the World Bank and the world public came to her rescue in certain situations. The same was true for Wangari Maathai, Kenya's 'Tree Mother'. And one cannot win against airport or motorway projects simply by using local arguments; the backing of innovative transport concepts is also required.

'All limitation makes us happy', wrote Schopenhauer in his *Aphorisms*. 'The narrower our range of vision, our sphere of action, and our points of contact, the happier we are; the wider these are, the more often we feel anxious and worried.' In his old age, however, Schopenhauer enjoyed his growing fame, and that maxim of his hardly applies any longer in the modern world. One recalls how Hermann Löns in 1911 accused conservationism of being 'small beer'. And it often appeared to many other nature lovers as hopelessly petty. Against this background we can gauge what the new global horizon meant after 1970, and above all in the period since 1990. The 'small beer' accusation is now outdated.

The 'Think globally, act locally' slogan is usually attributed to David Brower. What exactly did he mean by it in 1970, at the time of the 'ecological revolution'? In 1969, while still chair of the Sierra Club, he placed full-page ads in the *New York Times* for the creation of an Earth National Park: a project that struck most conservationists as meaningless and is understandable only amid the euphoria of the time. After all, the specific nature protected in national parks is essentially local and regional: that is its attraction, the value that makes it worth protecting. Brower's publicity campaign proved his downfall as charismatic leader of the elite wilderness club, whose resources he was accused, not without reason, of squandering.[359]

On the other hand, the subsequent international campaign that Brower's Friends of the Earth waged against civilian nuclear technology gave a definite meaning to 'Think globally, act locally.' The flow of information set in train by this transnational network was at the origin of the West German anti-nuclear movement, which went on to outstrip by far its American forerunner. It is true that, as a rule, campaigns against nuclear power plants gathered enough strength to make a breakthrough only when local people became involved. So long as the 'peaceful atom' remained a vision of the future, it offered a screen for the projection of pipe-dreams; only when a nuclear plant appeared just down the road did people grow terrified of the 'residual risk'. Without transregional links and information, however, local resistance tended to be seen as a backwoods affair – a dramatic case in point was the campaign against uranium prospecting in the 1960s near the Black Forest spa of Menzenschwand.[360]

Similarly, the failure of Japanese anti-nuclear campaigns so far – in the country of Hiroshima! – is due not least to their narrow horizon.[361] To be sure, Japan has also witnessed many local campaigns against nuclear power plants, which are usually located on the coast and pipe their cooling water into the sea, threatening marine life with radioactive contamination. But villagers did not have positive experiences with central campaigns, and for a long time the widespread horror of centralization meant that no large environmental NGOs came into being with offices in Tokyo. In Germany, former rebels from '68 sometimes provided a minimum of strategic thinking, but that was lacking in Japan, where '68ers were typically radical Maoists isolated from society.[362] Much that is sobering in the German or US environmental mainstream can be seen to have its advantages from faraway Japan!

Recently, the initiative for climate protection in the United States has passed from the Federal government to the cities. This trend, observable worldwide, has its logic. For, as Hermann Scheer used to preach, the paths to major change in energy policy are essentially local. The Chicago mayor Richard M. Daley, who had launched the 'Greening Chicago' slogan after a trip to Europe, astonished everyone on 30 March 2003 with a sudden cloak-and-dagger operation to dig up the runway of an airport on an Island in Lake Michigan that was spoiling the green downtown lakefront; the talking on the city council had been going on too long.[363] What a contrast with the fruitless struggle against Startbahn West, the new Frankfurt runway! But, of course, merely local initiatives simply displace environmental problems; Chicago itself, a hundred years earlier, had brazenly channelled its wastewater into the Mississippi and hailed this as a great achievement, not caring two hoots about the fate of St Louis and other cities downriver. Such displacement has been a leitmotif of more than a hundred years of environmental policy. It is good to remind ourselves of this today when, out of rage and disappointment

with globalization, 'local' is well on its way to being promoted as synonymous with 'good'.

'Think globally, act locally': it is usually not possible to do both at once,
without falling victim to schizophrenia. When someone acts locally, they
are advised to remain there in their thoughts too. How to reconcile global
thinking and local action is not something that can be prescribed once
and for all by a theoretical model. Only creative imagination can solve
the problem in practice, in ways that vary with the situation: not all of a
sudden but through a long process. History shows that over time many
things become possible that appear impossible at the moment. But it also
demonstrates that the surprises along the way are not all pleasant.

Conclusion

The Dialectic of Green Enlightenment

A Spanish film was showing not long ago in the cinemas: *Cenizas del Cielo*, ashes from heaven. The hero is Bugallo, a farmer from the north of Spain, who lives in the shadow of a gigantic power station and covers his fruit trees when the wind blows smoke their way. His great hope is the Kyoto climate protocol, which he fondly imagines will soon force the plant to close down. He baptises a new-born calf 'Kyoto' accordingly. He even climbs like a Greenpeace activist up the cooling tower of the plant and allows himself to be hauled back down. At first nothing happens, but eventually the environmentalists come to power and the plant, an aged polluter, is taken out of service. Then, for a short time, the fears propagated by the energy industry come true: the lights go out. People even bring out their candles, until at some point the lights shine brightly again. Federico goes happily into the forest to gather firewood, but some rangers arrest him there for illegal cutting. This breaks his heart, and he dies while the little calf romps about in the meadow.

The film was a spoof of the 'Think globally, act locally' slogan – the message of Kyoto reaches every last farmer – but also an allusion to the oft-quoted words of the Girondin Pierre Vergniaud on first seeing the guillotine: 'The Revolution, like Saturn, is devouring its children.' Looking back over the years since the early 1970s, one is indeed struck by the huge number of people, ideas and energies that the environmental movement has used and worn out. The history of the eco-age is the history not only of a new enlightenment but also of a process of forgetting. Many names that seemed to represent the future for a while are today unknown even within the eco-scene; numerous books that briefly stirred people ended up among the junk a long time ago. Charismatic moments of illumination and spontaneous enthusiasm gave way to an endless flood of environmental directives that even experts on the subject cannot hope to assimilate in their entirety. 'Soft' alternative energies sounded delightful so long as they were the music of the future; now quite a few nature lovers shudder at the sight of wind farms and subsidized cornfields churning out biofuel.

In their 'philosophical fragments', which they entitled *The Dialectic of Enlightenment* (1947), Theodor W. Adorno and Max Horkheimer portrayed how the Enlightenment became entangled in the mechanisms of power, producing its own kind of intolerance and turning its highest ideal, Reason, into an instrument of domination. The *philosophes* appealed dogmatically to nature, but at the same time they repressed its wild, untamed element – not least in female nature. The devastating Lisbon earthquake of 1755 famously threw Voltaire, for example, into disarray: those men of the Enlightenment would have liked to believe in a benevolent, orderly nature that enabled human beings to control it in a spirit of friendship. Adorno and Horkheimer, both scholars who fled the Nazi dictatorship, and who themselves turned out to be dab hands at achieving intellectual hegemony, interpreted National Socialism as the 'revolt of nature' and, for all their disgust, ascribed to it a kind of historical logic: a provocation that has curiously more or less vanished in the ocean of research on the Third Reich.[1]

Today we would be inclined to go further. Reviving eighteenth-century nature worship in its own peculiar way, the environmental movement also touched the sorest point of the old Enlightenment, though doubtless more calmly and humanely than the 'revolt of nature' did in the Nazi movement. For the new ecology, nature in its independent existence is infinitely more differentiated and sophisticated than the physico-theologians of the eighteenth century could have dreamed. But it is also much more vulnerable and therefore presents a twofold challenge to human beings: to spare it and to protect it with all their energy, since the survival of the planet is at stake. And yet the Green enlightenment also has its own dialectic.

Max Weber described modernization as a process of disenchantment, but he did so with an undertone of sadness in which we can detect the idea that it brings forth a longing for re-enchantment.[2] Adorno and Horkheimer showed how the Enlightenment, once it had achieved dominance, generated myths of its own and provided them with the authority of truth. The environmental movement has continued the process of disenchantment, by disenchanting the very idea of progress that was the most powerful of the Enlightenment myths. But at the same time, the conservationist offensive with its flood of seductive images contains a splendid blueprint for the re-enchantment of the world. Whereas the enlightened Prince Paphnutius in E. T. A. Hoffmann's 'Little Zaches' chased away the fairies and filled his little country with dead straight avenues of plane trees, the colourful cult of 'biodiversity' is bringing the fairies back again. However, magic is also an instrument of power.

Michel Foucault coined the term 'biopower' to denote a new dimension of rule in the age of enlightened absolutism; politics now embraced not only forestry and agriculture, the growth processes in forest and field, but also the processes of human reproduction among the ruler's subjects, so that sexual practices that did not serve this end were discredited as unnatural and pathological. At the origin of the new environmental movement, the 'population bomb' alarm ran directly counter to the hue and cry about what some people get up to in bed, but the ambition of the old 'biopower' to regulate reproduction has its counterpart in the modern age of elegant contraceptive techniques.

The global rhetoric that characterized the 'ecological revolution' from early on betrays a dream of power beneath the surface;[3] this has become more apparent since 1990, the year of the second great eco-boom, above all in the project of a global climate regime. Of course, considering the opportunities that global environmentalism offers for the legitimation of rule, it may be thought remarkable how little they have been perceived at the various summit conferences. They even lack a suitable player, in the shape of a world government capable of exploiting this potential. Besides, the counterforces have been too powerful up to now: continued economic growth offers far more than environmental protection to those who hold political power. Unless environmentalism becomes a powerful force itself, it will certainly stand little chance against the centres of power. It would therefore be politically naïve to criticize all power aspirations within the movement in the name of grassroots democracy.

In the light of historical experiences and alternative futures, it is a fact of huge importance that powerful interests may crystallize around environmental protection. For we should not forget that the 'environmental' issues of the years since the early 1970s can be labelled in a very different way and assigned very different imperatives. Realization of the finite character of planetary resources, and of their increasingly visible exhaustion, has so far been a powerful impetus for imperialist rivalry over the division of shares; it is by no means excluded that the problems which environmental discourse now identifies as a common task of mankind will in future be redefined in old ways as areas for aggressive action. Signs of this are already clearly visible. Since the 1990s, the buzzword 'environmental security' has been pointing discussion towards the military. And recently the promotion of renewable energies has been meeting competition from the US-based 'shale gas revolution', which involves drawing up natural gas from great depths beneath the earth's surface. At first, even the Sierra Club approved of this energy turnaround, since the coal revival shaping up in parts of the world is an even greater threat to the climate. But in 2012 its executive director Michael Brune changed the club's position.[4] No wonder – for the 'fracking' (pumping down of toxic chemicals) associated with the shale gas revolution is a threat to groundwater reserves, whose contamination and depletion in many areas is a ticking ecological time bomb.

One more point needs to be made today. The Americanization of the world – which, especially since the Second World War, has irresistibly come to define a concrete utopia and a consumerist model for ever larger parts of humanity – has not brought happiness to most. On ecological grounds, the American standard of living is unattainable for the majority of mankind; the very attempt to reach it widens the gulf between rich and poor and intensifies ecological crises. In terms of their per capita dollar income, most countries in the world are bound to appear hopelessly inferior. The spread of aggressive fundamentalism in the Islamic countries is not unintelligible, when seen as a defiant reaction to the frustrating and provocative situations that face people there.

Environmentalism may offer an alternative, in so far as it emancipates itself from the 'American way of life' and returns to its original aim of improving the quality of life; this would imply a new sense of self-esteem and a revaluation of traditional lifestyles suited to the ecological conditions of particular countries. It is hardly an accident that the Islamic world is by far the largest blank in the landscape of environmental movements:[5] it displays impotent rage against the Americanization that is devaluing its culture, yet offers no better substitute to the mass of the population, no counterforce other than religious fanaticism, which is rather like the 'revolt of nature' that vented its spleen in the Nazi movement during the world economic crisis that drove Germany to despair.

Environmental politicians must have a feeling for power and know how to use its instruments. Full-scale environmental protection has no prospect without skilful deployment of the state apparatus, and the crocodile tears shed by environmental sinners over 'rampant bureaucratism' should not be allowed to act as a diversion. The progress from 'movement to government' is to some extent unavoidable – although, to be sure, this always contains a danger. The more environmentalism associates itself with political and economic power, the more it behoves sympathetic historians and policy researchers to accompany this process with critical insights of their own. History teaches us that the state does not automatically embody the public welfare, and even a formally centralized state apparatus by no means guarantees an integral approach to environmental issues; bureaucracy has more of a tendency to spread around powers and responsibilities. Moreover, 'environmental protection' is an ambiguous project; there is already a history of bluff in the realm of ecology. Care must be taken that the age of ecology does not pass into an age of eco-bluff.

Administrative lawyers often tend – in Germany more than other countries – to forms of overregulation in which the effect is not at all proportional to the investment. The president of Germany's federal administrative court, Everhardt Franßen, knows what he is talking about: 'What we have today are not regulation deficits but enforcement problems, which multiply rather than shrink with the tightening of the legal screws.'[6] Environmental policy insiders tend in their own interests to make the issues as complicated as possible, so that lay persons are unable to keep up with the discussion; on the other hand, anyone concerned about practical results should consider how things can be made simpler, instead of arguing, with the usual self-importance of experts, that politics is inadequate to the complexity of the issues.

Even Henry Makowski, who is not usually shy about mobilizing the power of the state behind conservation, can hardly keep a straight face when he notes that he has counted a record number of sixteen international treaties protecting the Wadden Sea in northern Germany.[7] One often hears insiders complain that landscape protection is faring worse and worse in Germany because of excessive demands made by the authorities. The mass of regulations bother large companies least and small ones most: a depressing side effect that makes a mockery of 'Small is beautiful.' Another far from minor complication is the energetic lobbying that manages to secure numerous exemptions. The toughest directives are often the simplest!

The lasting global success of environmentalism will probably hinge on whether it achieves a limited number of clear and simple regulations that any rational person is able to understand; that was the case with the smoking ban in public places, which the eco-age saw enforced more and more around the world. This is one practical benefit of a look back over past decades: the basic themes appear more clearly amid the jumbled heap of environmental directives. If the human right to clean water, pure air, healthy food and restful sleep is enforced with all its consequences, a large percentage of environmental problems is already covered. Man's relationship with nature can be made harmonious only if it is in harmony with human nature.

Climate policy goes down a blind alley if it is nothing other than climate policy; it will have a truly global basis only when it builds upon vital needs of people alive today. As Hegel rightly pointed out in his lectures on aesthetics: 'Man is essentially here and now.' For all the talk of sustainability and biodiversity, we should not forget that environmentalism has a much more solid foundation in life's necessities than in concern for a distant, ill-defined future; it stands a chance of lasting success only if it appeals primarily to man's instinct for self-preservation, not just to a selfless dimension (or rather: to spiritual dissolution of the self into a greater whole). The one does not exclude the other. As Max Weber showed in *The Protestant Ethic and the Spirit of Capitalism*, the strongest force driving world history stems from a synergy of metaphysical and material motives.

The constant pressure to choose priorities amid the plethora of environmental issues, together with the law of inertia affecting not only the state bureaucracy but also established environmental organizations, carries a danger that environmental policy will become one-sidedly focused on certain paths of action and neglect other, possibly more important, issues. Since nature offers surprises all the time – unintended side effects are the essence of the whole environmental problematic – a fixation on certain priorities can be more disastrous here than in other policy areas. Consequently, eco-revisionism is also part of the Green enlightenment. It would be quite wrong to dismiss as a heretic anyone who professes scepticism about a particular eco-alarm. Many such people may be concealing self-interest behind ecological arguments, but even those who are serious must continually ponder whether they are not sticking to certain points out of personal considerations and should not be more tolerant towards those whose experience leads them to think differently.

Let us remind ourselves that the 'environmentalist' project has always involved an alliance between diverse efforts and that tensions and barriers to understanding have always lain beneath the surface. It may well be the case that this alliance will break up in the future, so that the issues of clean air and water, nature and animal conservation, renewable energies and alternative transport systems again lead separate lives of their own. Trends in this direction are already visible. Climate policy, more than any other issue previously, has dominated certain parts of the eco-scene, but this has itself severely tested the cohesion of the whole movement, especially when climate change has been used as a killer argument against doubts that people might have about certain projects operating under the umbrella of climate protection. The two main targets of attack worldwide – nuclear power plants and large dams – have moved out of the firing line because of the climate alarm; indeed, they are sometimes sold as forms of climate protection. Similarly, the prioritization of bioenergy has downgraded landscape protection. And the heady global rush of conservation since the early 1990s, in the name of 'biodiversity', has further intensified the latent clash of aims.

The ability to cope sensibly with internal tensions and competing objectives has probably never been as decisive as it is today for the future of the environmental movement. To place a doubter of the 'iconic' hockey-stick climate curve[8] on a par with a Holocaust denier is to strain the cohesion of the movement as much as if one were to treat as 'enemy behaviour' any hesitation in unconditionally denouncing all forms of nuclear technology, or to accept as members only those for whom the undisturbed mating of toads is more important than a new express train line. Jeremy Bentham, who loved his cats but also the mice in his study, did not fail to appreciate that there can be clashes between objectives in one's love of nature.[9] But the amatory conflict between cat and mouse is as nothing in comparison with the clash of objectives over the future.

It makes things easier if we realize that the world's major environmental issues admit of no definitive solutions; any on offer are inevitably provisional and time-dependent. Again we see the practical usefulness of history, which, when rid of the ballast of dogmatic 'lessons of history', is a good antidote to unnecessary frictional losses, both political and human. There is no reason to imagine that our present environmental awareness is the highest level of ecological understanding. As we have seen, people in many earlier times were actually more advanced on some issues than we are today: in the eighteenth century in their combination of love of nature and love of man; in 1900 in their combination of nature conservancy with lifestyle reform; and in the 1930s in their focus on soil preservation. Perhaps in the future it will be thought an archaic fallacy to set up conservation and environmental protection as separate spheres, instead of treating them as twin policy aspects in agriculture, energy, transport and construction.

An understanding that things have a dimension rooted in a specific time and place is common to both historical science and ecology, although the two disciplines have so far scarcely woken up to this inner affinity. Another benefit of hindsight is to remind us of all that the environmental alliance, however heterogeneous, has actually achieved since the 'ecological revolution' of 1970. The love of nature inherent in human beings is as multifarious as the erotic instinct, indeed probably more diverse and bizarre ('polymorphically perverse', in Freud's terminology); environmental campaigns driven by monomanic passions are not capable, by their separate operation, of capturing the potential for love of nature and environmental awareness contained in human beings, or of converting it into action whose effects go beyond the ad hoc and the momentary.

In his essay *On the Uses and Disadvantages of History for Life* (1873), Friedrich Nietzsche deals mainly with the danger to life in all its intensity posed by a 'consuming historical fever', by the deafening buzz and dazzling flicker of associations from remote pasts. But the text dates from the high point of historicism, and today we have long been living in a period when most of the sciences are dehistoricized. This also applies to the environmental movement, which has had less historical awareness than any of the other major movements of modern times. Yet history contained so much potential for it: not so much classroom 'lessons of history' as stimulating impulses. Rightly understood, historical awareness means not only looking for the past in the present, but also discovering what is new in the world around us, experiencing more intensely and thinking through the transience of the here and now. We know from history that there are moments when the inertia of existing structures breaks down and much that has seemed impossible is suddenly regarded as possible. The best 'use of history for life' is perhaps the sharpening of one's eye for such historical moments in the present. Who knows, perhaps we shall soon be living at such a moment.

Note: The first German edition of this book, published two weeks before Fukushima, ended with the preceding sentence, which has since been quoted many times. It should therefore remain as it is. Perhaps it will soon acquire a new meaning.

Notes

Preface to the English Edition

1 Joachim Radkau and Lothar Hahn, *Aufstieg und Fall der deutschen Atomwirtschaft*, Munich 2013, pp. 321ff., 390ff.
2 Hayden White, *Metahistory: The Historical Imagination in Nineteenth-Century Europe*, Baltimore 1975.

Introduction: The Green Chameleon

1 Niklas Luhmann, *Ecological Communication*, Cambridge 1989. Cf. Luhmann, *Risk: A Sociological Theory*, New York 2003, esp. ch. 7 'Protest Movements', pp. 125ff. The two books form an interconnected core of Luhmann's thinking: see Michael King and Chris Thornhill, *Niklas Luhmann's Theory of Politics and Law*, New York 2003, pp. 182ff. ('Risk and the Environment'). I am grateful to Klaus Danmann, who is working on a biography of Luhmann, for his invaluable advice.
2 See Jörg Requate and Martin Schulze-Wessel, eds., *Europäische Öffentlichkeit: Transnationale Kommunikation seit dem 18. Jahrhundert*, Frankfurt 2002.
3 Jürgen Habermas, 'The New Obscurity: The Crisis of the Welfare State and the Exhaustion of Utopian Energies', in Habermas, *The New Conservatism: Cultural Criticism and the Historians' Debate*, Cambridge MA 1989, pp. 48–70.
4 India, Department of Environment, Forests and Wildlife, ed., *Environmental NGOs in India: A Directory*, New Delhi 1989.
5 Jost Hermand, *Grüne Utopien in Deutschland: Zur Geschichte des ökologischen Bewusstseins*, Frankfurt 1991.
6 René Dubos, 'Franciscan Conservation versus Benedictine Stewardship', in David Spring and Eileen Spring, eds., *Ecology and Religion in History*, New York 1974, p. 124.
7 Josef Boyer and Helge Heidemeyer, eds., *Die Grünen im Bundestag: Sitzungsprotokolle und Anlagen 1983–1987*, Düsseldorf 2008 (*Quellen zur Geschichte des Parlamentarismus und der politischen Parteien*, 4. Reihe, 14/1), second half-volume, p. 912.
8 Ulrich Linse, *Ökopax und Anarchie: Eine Geschichte der ökologischen Bewegungen in Deutschland*, Munich 1986, p. 7.

9 See, e.g., Christopher C. Horner, *The Politically Incorrect Guide to Global Warming and Environmentalism*, Washington DC 2007.

10 Václav Klaus, *Blue Planet in Green Shackles – What Is Endangered: Climate or Freedom?*, Washington DC 1998.

11 Carl Anthony, 'The Environmental Justice Movement: An Activist's Perspective', in David Naguib Pellow and Robert J. Brulle, eds., *Power, Justice, and the Environment: A Critical Appraisal of the Environmental Justice Movement*, Cambridge MA 2005, p. 92.

12 Dave Foreman refers to this in his *Confessions of an Eco-Warrior*, New York 1991, p. 201.

13 Ron Arnold, *Ecology Wars*, Bellevue WA 1993, p. 21.

14 Quoted in Deborah Lynn Gruber, *The Grassroots of a Green Revolution: Polling America on the Environment*, Cambridge MA 2003, p. 175. Two pages further on, however, the author remarks that 'while environmental concern is widespread, behaviour is not'.

15 Dirk van Laak, 'Planung: Geschichte und Gegenwart des Vorgriffs auf die Zukunft', *Geschichte und Gesellschaft* 34 (2008), pp. 317ff.

16 Donald Worster, *Nature's Economy: A History of Ecological Ideas*, Cambridge 1977, p. 340.

17 United Nations Environment Programme, ed., *Global Environmental Outlook 2000*, London 1999, pp. 67, 56.

18 Hermand, *Grüne Utopien*, p. 134.

19 William T. Markham, *Environmental Organizations in Modern Germany: Hardy Survivors in the 20th Century and Beyond*, New York 2008, pp. 5, 11.

20 Ralf Fücks, ed., *Sind die Grünen noch zu retten?*, Reinbek 1991; Hubert Kleinert, *Aufstieg und Fall der Grünen: Analyse einer alternativen Partei*, Bonn 1992.

21 Markham, *Environmental Organizations*, p. 320.

22 Francis Haskell, *History and Its Images: Art and the Interpretation of the Past*, Yale University Press, 1995, pp. 204ff.

Chapter One Environmentalism before the Environmental Movement

1 John Bowle, *John Evelyn and his World: A Biography*, London 1981, pp. 131 and passim.

2 There is a wealth of material on this in Keith Thomas, *Man and the Natural World: Changing Attitudes in England 1500–1800*, London 1984. One reads with astonishment that in 1691 John Ray (*The Wisdom of God Manifested in the Works of Creation*) regarded as 'vulgar' the view that the whole world was created for man alone: 'wise men nowadays think otherwise' (p. 167).

3 Jakob Lehmann, in *Die Entdeckung der Fränkischen Schweiz durch die Romantiker*, Forchheim 1994, p. 13.

4 Reimar Gilsenbach in an interview with Regine Auster, *naturmagazin* 9–10 (2000), pp. 10f.; Karl Friedel and Reimar Gilsenbach, *Das Roßmäßler-Büchlein*, Berlin 1956.

5 Joachim Radkau, 'Warum wurde die Gefährdung der Natur durch den Menschen nicht rechtzeitig erkannt? Naturkult und Angst vor Holznot um 1800', in Hermann Lübbe and Elisabeth Ströker, eds., *Ökologische Probleme im kulturellen Wandel*, Paderborn 1986, pp. 48ff.

Notes to pp. 12–16

6 Wolf Lepenies, 'Historisierung der Natur und Entmoralisierung der Wissenschaften seit dem 18. Jahrhundert', in Hubert Markl, ed., *Natur und Geschichte*, Vienna 1983, pp. 265f.

7 Roy Pascal, *The German Sturm und Drang*, Manchester 1953, p. 209.

8 Translated by Keith Anderson, in *Schubert: The Complete Lieder*, Naxos edn, 8.503801.

9 See Alfred Schmidt, *The Concept of Nature in Marx*, London 1971, pp. 130ff.

10 Wolfgang Riedel, '*Homo Natura*': *Literarische Anthropologie um 1900*, Berlin 1996, p. 53.

11 Jürgen Mittelstraß, 'Der idealistische Naturbegriff', in Heinz-Dieter Weber, ed., *Vom Wandel des neuzeitlichen Naturbegriffs*, Konstanz 1989, pp. 160ff., esp. p. 170.

12 Immanuel Kant, 'Perpetual Peace: A Philosophical Sketch', in *Political Writings*, enlarged edn, Cambridge 1991, p. 110.

13 Joachim Radkau, 'Holzverknappung und Krisenbewußtsein im 18. Jahrhundert', *Geschichte und Gesellschaft* 9 (1983), pp. 513–43.

14 Arlette Brosselin, Andrée Corvol and Francois Vion-Delphin, 'Les doléances contre l'industrie', in Denis Woronoff, ed., *Forges et forêts: Recherches sur la consommation proto-industrielle de bois*, Paris 1990, pp. 11, 13. 'La peur de manquer semble une fièvre récurrente sous l'Ancien Régime': this is the opening sentence in Andrée Corvol's groundbreaking *L'Homme aux Bois: Histoire des relations de l'homme et de la forêt XVIIe–XXe siècle*, Paris 1987.

15 Konrad Rubner, *Forstgeschichte im Zeitalter der industriellen Revolution*, Berlin 1967, p. 105.

16 Joachim Radkau, *Wood: A History*, Cambridge 2012, pp. 156f.

17 A key text on the 'wood shortage debate' is Bernd-Stefan Grewe, *Der versperrte Wald: Ressourcenmangel in der bayerischen Pfalz (1814–1870)*, Cologne 2004, pp. 26–33. Yet his conclusion (p. 33) is that it cannot be 'put away on the shelf as if it has been settled'.

18 Radkau, *Wood*, p. 165.

19 Andrée Corvol, *L'homme et l'arbre sous l'Ancien Régime*, Paris 1984, p. 178; *L'Homme aux Bois*, p. 305.

20 Joachim Radkau, 'Das Rätsel der städtischen Brennholzversorgung im "hölzernen Zeitalter"', in Dieter Schott, ed., *Energie und Stadt in Europa: Von der vorindustriellen 'Holznot' bis zur Ölkrise der 1970er Jahre*, Stuttgart 1997, p. 69.

21 On the commons in general, see Uwe Meiners and Werner Rösener, eds., *Allmenden und Marken vom Mittelalter bis zur Neuzeit*, Cloppenburg 2004; Jeanette M. Neeson, ed., *Commoners: Common Right, Enclosure and Social Change in England, 1700–1820*, Cambridge 1993.

22 See the discussion volume on the Hardin thesis: John A. Baden and Douglas S. Noonan, eds., *Managing the Commons*, 2nd edn, Bloomington 1998.

23 Elinor Ostrom, *Governing the Commons: The Evolution of Institutions for Collective Action*, Cambridge 1990.

24 Bernd Marquardt, *Umwelt und Recht in Mitteleuropa: Von den großen Rodungen des Hochmittelalters bis ins 21. Jahrhundert*, Zurich 2003, pp. 285ff.

25 Wilhelm Roscher, *Nationalökonomik des Ackerbaues*, 13th edn, Stuttgart 1903, p. 351.

26 Thirsk quoted in J. A. Yelling, *Common Field and Enclosure in England 1450–1850*, London 1977, p. 214.

27 Especially detailed on this is Martin Stuber, *Wälder für Generationen:*

Konzeptionen der Nachhaltigkeit im Kanton Bern (1750–1880), Cologne 2008, pp. 217ff.

28 See Richard Pott and Joachim Hüppe, *Die Hudelandschaften Nordwestdeutschlands*, Münster 1991.

29 Ernst Pitz vividly describes how even a head forester became 'grey and old, dull and querulous' before he knew his area inside out. 'Studie zur Entstehung des Kapitalismus', in Otto Brunner et al., eds., *Festschrift für Hermann Aubin zum 80. Geburtstag*, Wiesbaden 1965, pp. 29, 32.

30 Conversation with the author, 28 September 2010.

31 See Ulrike Gilhaus, *'Schmerzenskinder der Industrie': Umweltverschmutzung, Umweltpolitik und sozialer Protest im Industriezeitalter in Westfalen 1845–1914*, Paderborn 1995, pp. 46ff.

32 Wolf Lepenies, *Das Ende der Naturgeschichte*, Munich 1976, p. 200.

33 Corvol, *L'Homme aux Bois*, p. 314.

34 Radkau, 'Warum wurde die Gefährdung', p. 63.

35 Ludger Lütkehaus, *'O Wollust, o Hölle': Die Onanie – Stationen einer Inquisition*, Frankfurt 1992, pp. 94ff.

36 Radkau, *Wood*, pp. 173f.

37 Ernst Moritz Arndt, *Ein Wort über die Pflegung und Erhaltung der Forsten und der Bauern im Sinne einer höheren, d. h. menschlichen Gesetzgebung*, Schleswig 1820, p. 49.

38 Wilhelm Heinrich Riehl, *Die Naturgeschichte des deutschen Volkes* (orig. 1853), abridged edn by G. Ipsen, Stuttgart 1939, pp. 80, 83, 87.

39 Radkau, *Wood*, pp. 189f.

40 Ingrid Schäfer, *'Ein Gespenst geht um': Politik mit der Holznot in Lippe 1750–1850*, Detmold 1992.

41 George P. Marsh, *Man and Nature, Or, Physical Geography as Modified by Human Action*, reissued Cambridge MA 1974, p. 189.

42 Conrad Totman, *The Green Archipelago: Forestry in Preindustrial Japan*, Berkeley 1989, pp. 233f., 96f.

43 See esp. Luke S. Roberts, *Mercantilism in a Japanese Domain: The Merchant Origins of Economic Nationalism in 18th-Century Tosa*, Cambridge 1998, pp. 74ff.

44 Ostrom, *Governing the Commons*, pp. 88ff.

45 Totman, *Green Archipelago*, p. 80.

46 Sendai Sho-ichiro, 'Vers des espaces figés: La gestion des forêts et les Trois Montagnes, depuis la fin du XIXe siècle', in UNESCO, ed., *Atlas historique de Kyoto*, Paris 2008, pp. 413ff.

47 Ostrom, *Governing the Commons*, pp. 32ff.

48 A striking case in point is Nepal: see Joachim Radkau, *Nature and Power*, Cambridge 2008, pp. 280ff. On the African savannah, James Fairhead and Melissa Leach, *Misreading the African Landscape: Society and Ecology in a Forest–Savanna Mosaic*, Cambridge 1996.

49 Radkau, 'Warum wurde die Gefährdung', p. 63.

50 See Engelbert Schramm, ed., *Ökologie-Lesebuch: Ausgewählte Texte zur Entwicklung ökologischen Denkens vom Beginn der Neuzeit bis zum 'Club of Rome' (1971)*, Frankfurt 1984, pp. 62ff.

51 Arndt, *Ein Wort über die Pflegung und Erhaltung der Forsten*, in Arndt, *Agrarpolitische Schriften*, Goslar 1942, pp. 355f.

52 The most groundbreaking reformer in Germany in the 1840s was the Bavarian

Carl Fraas (1810–75), a disillusioned philhellene who had tried his hand at afforestation projects in Greece; see Schramm, *Ökologie-Lesebuch*, pp. 66ff. and 112f.

53 Michael Williams, *Americans and their Forests: A Historical Geography*, Cambridge 1989, p. 381.

54 Gregory A. Barton, *Empire Forestry and the Origins of Environmentalism*, Cambridge 2002, pp. 29ff.

55 The best-known example is the Chipko movement on the edge of the Himalayas; but see also Daniel J. Klooster, 'Forest Struggles and Forest Policy: Villagers' Environmental Activism in Mexico', in Christof Mauch et al., eds., *Shades of Green: Environmental Activism around the Globe*, Oxford 2006, pp. 191f.

56 Ernst Robert Curtius, *European Literature and the Latin Middle Ages*, London 1979, p. 107.

57 Ibid., pp. 118f.

58 Horst Bredekamp, 'Der Mensch als Mörder der Natur: Das "Iudicium Iovis" von Paulus Niavis und die Leibmetaphorik', in Heimo Reinitzer, ed., *All' Geschöpf ist Zung' und Mund: Beiträge aus dem Grenzbereich von Naturkunde und Theologie*, Hamburg 1984, pp. 261–83.

59 Carl Linnaeus, *Nemesis Divina*, ed. Wolf Lepenies and Lars Gustafsson, Munich 1981.

60 F. Engels, *Dialectics of Nature*, Moscow 1964, p. 182; quoted in Jost Hermand, *Grüne Utopien in Deutschland: Zur Geschichte des ökologischen Bewusstseins*, Frankfurt 1991, p. 77.

61 Franz Wieacker, *Privatrechtsgeschichte der Neuzeit*, Göttingen 1952, p. 152.

62 Jean-Jacques Rousseau, *Confessions* (World Classics edn), Oxford 2000, p. 630.

63 Carolyn Merchant, ed., *Major Problems in American Environmental History: Documents and Essays*, Lexington 1993, p. 352.

64 Robert H. Wiebe, *The Search for Order 1877–1920*, New York 1967, p. 45.

65 Jan Holm, *Die angloamerikanische Ökotopie: Literarische Entwürfe einer grünen Welt*, Frankfurt 1998, p. 74.

66 Edward P. Thompson, *William Morris: Romantic to Revolutionary*, 2nd edn, New York 1976, p. 716.

67 Cornelia Regin, *Selbsthilfe und Gesundheitspolitik: Die Naturheilbewegung im Kaiserreich (1889–1914)*, Stuttgart 1995, p. 453.

68 Ulrich Linse, *Ökopax und Anarchie: Eine Geschichte der ökologischen Bewegungen in Deutschland*, Munich 1986, pp. 60ff.

69 Winfried Mogge and Jürgen Reulecke, eds., *Hoher Meißner 1913: Der Erste Freideutsche Jugendtag in Dokumenten, Deutungen und Bildern*, Cologne 1988, pp. 48, 50.

70 Theodore Roosevelt, *An Autobiography*, London 1913, p. 215.

71 Mogge and Reulecke, *Hoher Meißner*, pp. 183, 188.

72 Ibid., p. 181.

73 Riedel, 'Homo Natura', pp. 143–50.

74 Linse, *Ökopax*, p. 44.

75 See Wilhelm Bölsche, *Das Liebesleben in der Natur: Eine Entwicklungsgeschichte der Liebe*, vol. 2, Jena 1908, pp. 278–92.

76 Rolf Peter Sieferle, *Die Krise der menschlichen Natur: Zur Geschichte eines Konzepts*, Frankfurt 1989, p. 109.

77 Mogge and Reulecke, *Hoher Meißner*, p. 173.

78 Joachim Radkau, *Nature and Power: A Global History of the Environment*, Cambridge 2008, pp. 239ff.

79 Ibid., pp. 246ff.
80 Anthony S. Wohl, *Endangered Lives: Public Health in Victorian Britain*, London 1983, pp. 10ff. ('The Massacre of the Innocents').
81 Joel A. Tarr, *The Search for the Ultimate Sink: Urban Pollution in Historical Perspective*, Akron 1996, p. 11.
82 This is the impression conveyed by Alexander Mrkvicka and Petra Schneider in '"Grüne" Wende? Naturschutz im Jahrhundertwende-Wien', in Karl Brunner and Petra Schneider, eds., *Umwelt Stadt: Geschichte des Natur- und Lebensraumes Wien*, Cologne 2005, p. 337.
83 Wohl, *Endangered Lives*, pp. 142ff., 146ff.
84 John von Simson, *Kanalisation und Städtehygiene im 19. Jahrhundert*, Düsseldorf 1983, p. 24.
85 Engelbert Schramm, *Im Namen des Kreislaufs: Ideengeschichte der Modelle vom ökologischen Kreislauf*, Frankfurt 1995, esp. pp. 211ff. ('Vergötzung des Kreislaufs').
86 J. H. Vogel, ed., *Die Verwertung der städtischen Abfallstoffe: Im Auftrage der Deutschen Landwirtschafts-Gesellschaft, Sonderausschuß für Abfallstoffe*, Berlin 1896 (a 700-page manual that also draws heavily on non-German experiences and projects).
87 Tim Cooper, 'Modernity and the Politics of Waste in Britain', in Sverker Sörlin and Paul Warde, eds., *Nature's End: History and the Environment*, Houndmills 2009, p. 260.
88 Justus von Liebig, *Die Chemie in ihrer Anwendung auf Agricultur und Physiologie*, part I, Brunswick 1862, p. 133. This attack on England is deleted in later editions.
89 Vogel, *Verwertung der städtischen Abfallstoffe*, p. 286.
90 Alwin Seifert, *Ein Leben für die Landschaft*, Düsseldorf 1962, p. 129.
91 Heiner Radzio, ed., *75 Jahre im Dienst für die Ruhr*, Essen 1988, p. 299.
92 Jochen Stemplewski, 'Auf dem Weg ins Neue Emschertal: Die Emscher – vom ungeliebten Fluss zum Sympathieträger der Region', *Heimat Dortmund 2* (2006) (*Das Wasser der Emscher*), pp. 39ff.
93 Volker Rödel, *Ingenieurbaukunst in Frankfurt a. M. 1806–1914*, Frankfurt 1983, pp. 71ff.
94 Frank Uekötter, *Von der Rauchplage zur ökologischen Revolution: Eine Geschichte der Luftverschmutzung in Deutschland und den USA 1880–1970*, Essen 2003, pp. 116ff.
95 Ibid., p. 259.
96 Arthur Schopenhauer, *Aphorismen zur Lebensweisheit* (orig. 1851), Stuttgart 1956, p. 8.
97 Richard J. Evans, *Death in Hamburg: Society and Politics in the Cholera Years, 1830–1910*, Oxford 1987, pp. 292ff.
98 Martin Melosi, *The Sanitary City: Urban Infrastructure in America from Colonial Times to the Present*, Baltimore 2000, p. 111.
99 Thomas Gorsboth and Bernd Wagner, 'Die Unmöglichkeit der Therapie: Am Beispiel der Tuberkulose', *Kursbuch* 94 (*Die Seuche*), Berlin 1988, p. 134.
100 Joachim Radkau, *Das Zeitalter der Nervosität: Deutschland zwischen Bismarck und Hitler*, Munich 1998, p. 88.
101 Ibid., pp. 49ff.
102 Otto Dornblüth, *Die Psychoneurosen: Neurasthenie, Hysterie und Psychasthenie*, Leipzig 1911.

103 Radkau, *Zeitalter der Nervosität*, p. 59.
104 Ibid., p. 310.
105 Ibid., pp. 144f.
106 Ibid., pp. 235f.
107 Wilhelm His, 'Medizin und Überkultur', *Deutsche medizinische Wochenschrift* 34 (1908), pp. 627, 625.
108 Ralph Waldo Emerson, *Nature*, Boston 1849 [Kindle edn], p. 8.
109 Alfred Runte, *National Parks: The American Experience*, 3rd edn, Lincoln 1997, p. 82.
110 Tom Lutz, *American Nervousness 1903: An Anecdotal History*, Ithaca 1991.
111 Ibid., pp. 90f., 63ff.
112 Ibid., pp. 224ff.
113 Jan Hollm, *Die angloamerikanische Ökotopie: literarische Entwürfe einer grünen Welt*, Frankfurt 1998, pp. 147ff. ('Herland').
114 See Marijke Gijswijt-Hofstra and Roy Porter, eds., *Cultures of Neurasthenia: From Beard to the First World War*, Amsterdam and New York 2001.
115 Thomas Dupke, *Hermann Löns:. Mythos und Wirklichkeit*, Hildesheim 1994, p. 136.
116 Merlin Waterson, *The National Trust*, London 1994, p. 25.
117 Wohl, *Endangered Lives*, p. 142.
118 Ibid., pp. 155, 187, 185.
119 Keith Thomas, *Man and the Natural World: Changing Attitudes in England 1500–1800*, London 1984, p. 159.
120 Ulrich Tröhler and Andreas-Holger Maehle, 'Anti-Vivisection in 19th-Century Germany and Switzerland: Motives and Methods', in Nicolaas A. Rupke, ed., *Vivisection in Historical Perspective*, London 1987, p. 149.
121 Friedemann Schmoll, *Erinnerung an die Natur: Die Geschichte des Naturschutzes im deutschen Kaiserreich*, Frankfurt 2004, pp. 115ff.
122 Walther Schoenichen, *Naturschutz, Heimatschutz: Ihre Begründung durch Ernst Rudorff, Hugo Conwentz und ihre Vorläufer*, Stuttgart 1954, pp. 279f.
123 Andreas Knaut, *Zurück zur Natur! Die Wurzeln der Ökologiebewegung*, Greven 1993, p. 41.
124 Samuel P. Hays, *Conservation and the Gospel of Efficiency*, New York 1959, pp. 1f.
125 Schmoll, *Erinnerung an die Natur*, pp. 212–18.
126 On Lüneburg Heath as the product of an 'environmental disaster', see Joska Pintschovius, *Heidschnucken und Donnerbesen. Lüneburger Landschaften*, Vienna 2001, p. 17.
127 Florence Shipek, 'Kumeyaay Plant Husbandry: Fire, Water, and Erosion Management Systems', in Thomas C. Blackbourn and Kat Anderson, eds., *Before the Wilderness: Environmental Management by Native Californians*, Melo Park 1993, p. 388.
128 Thomas Welskopp, *Amerikas große Ernüchterung: Eine Kulturgeschichte der Prohibition*, Paderborn 2010.
129 Emil Kraepelin, *Lebenserinnerungen*, ed. H. Hippius, Berlin 1983, pp. 79ff.
130 Sabine Merta, '"Keep Fit and Slim!" Alternative Ways of Nutrition as Aspects of the German Health Movement, 1880–1930', in Alexander Fenton, ed., *Order and Disorder: The Health Implications of Eating and Drinking in the 19th and 20th Centuries*, Edinburgh 2000, pp. 170–202.
131 Albert Wirz, *Die Moral auf dem Teller, dargestellt am Leben und Werk von*

Max Bircher-Benner und John Harvey Kellogg, Zurich 1993. See also the humorous description in T. C. Boyle's novel *The Road to Welville*, New York 1993.

132 Bernd Tenbergen, *Westfalen im Wandel. Von der Mammutsteppe zur Agrarlandschaft: Veränderungen der Tier- und Pflanzenwelt unter dem Einfluss des Menschen*, Gütersloh 2002, p. 68.

133 Reinhard Johler, 'Vogelmord und Vogelliebe: Zur Ethnographie konträrer Leidenschaften', *Historische Anthropologie* 5 (1997), pp. 20–7.

134 Alfred Barthelmeß, *Vögel – Lebendige Umwelt: Probleme von Vogelschutz und Humanökologie geschichtlich dargestellt und kommentiert*, Munich 1981, pp. 146ff.

135 Knaut, *Zurück zur Natur!*, pp. 360, 366.

136 Ibid., pp. 28ff.

137 Hugo Conwentz, *Die Heimatkunde in der Schule*, Berlin 1906, p. 56.

138 Karl Friedel and Reimar Gilsenbach, *Das Roßmäßler-Büchlein*, Berlin 1856.

139 See Reinhard Piechocki and Norbert Wiersbinski, eds., *Heimat und Naturschutz: Die Vilmer Thesen und ihre Kritiker*, Bonn 2007.

140 Karl Ditt, 'Naturschutz zwischen Zivilisationskritik, Tourismusförderung und Umweltschutz: USA, England und Deutschland 1860–1970', in Matthias Frese and Michael Prinz, eds., *Politische Zäsuren und gesellschaftlicher Wandel im 20. Jh.*, Paderborn 1996, p. 517.

141 Thomas Rohkrämer, *Eine andere Moderne? Zivilisationskritik, Natur und Technik in Deutschland 1880–1933*, Paderborn 1999, p. 138.

142 Anna Wöbse, *Der Schutz natürlicher Schönheit und die Ursprünge des Weltnaturerbes*, MS, Bremen 2010, p. 8.

143 Knaut, *Zurück zur Natur!*, p. 170.

144 Wöbse, *Schutz natürlicher Schönheit*, p. 7.

145 Anna Wöbse, 'Naturschutz global – oder: Hilfe von außen. Internationale Neziehungen des amtlichen Naturschutzes im 20. Jahrhundert', in Hans-Werner Frohn and Friedemann Schmoll, eds., *Natur und Staat: Staatlicher Naturschutz in Deutschland 1906–2006*, Bonn 2006, pp. 629ff. Cf. Douglas R. Weiner, *Models of Nature. Ecology, Conservation and Cultural Revolution in Soviet Russia*, Pittsburgh 2000, p. 230.

146 Merlin Waterson, *The National Trust: The First Hundred Years*, London 1994, pp. 23f.

147 Frank Uekötter, *The Age of Smoke: Environmental Policy in Germany and the United States, 1880–1970*, Pittsburgh 2009, p. 50.

148 Ernst Rudorff, 'Über das Verhältnis des modernen Lebens zur Natur', *Preußische Jahrbücher* XLV/3 (1880), pp. 262ff.

149 Wöbse, *Schutz natürlicher Schönheit*, p. 13.

150 Kirsten Brodde, 'Morgens Fango, abends Tango: Eher Mythos als Medizin, doch die Deutschen kuren wie die Weltmeister', *Die Zeit*, 31 January 1992, p. 78.

151 Jonathan S. Adams and Thomas O. McShane, *The Myth of Wild Africa: Conservation without Illusion*, Berkeley 1992, p. 46.

152 Mark Cioc, *The Game of Conservation: International Treaties to Protect the World's Migratory Animals*, Athens OH 2009, pp. 14ff. ('Africa's Apartheid Parks'); William Beinart and Lotte Hughes, *Environment and Empire*, Oxford 2007, pp. 289ff.

153 Wolfgang Krabbe, 'Die Lebensreformbewegung', in Kai Buchholz et al., eds.,

Die Lebensreform, vol. 1, Darmstadt 2001(accompanying the exhibition on the Mathildenhöhe), p. 25.

154 Schmoll, *Erinnerung an die Natur*, p. 257.

155 'We hate meat, yes we hate meat / And milk and eggs, and chaste is our love. / Corpse-eaters are dull and brutish, / Pig breeding – is that as well.' Erich Mühsam, *Ascona* (orig. 1905), Berlin 1982, pp. 31, 37.

156 The importance of this aspect is apparent from the abundant material in Colin Spencer, *The Heretic's Feast: A History of Vegetarianism*, London 1993; and Tristram Stuart, *The Bloodless Revolution: A Cultural History of Vegetarianism from 1600 to Modern Times*, New York 2006.

157 Wolfgang Krabbe, *Die Lebensreformbewegung im 20. Jahrhundert* (= *Frankfurter Historische Abhandlungen* 45), Stuttgart 2006, p. 27.

158 Quoted from Miriam Zerbel, 'Tierschutz und Antivivisektion', in Diethart Kerbs and Jürgen Reulecke, *Handbuch der deutschen Reformbewegungen 1880–1933*, Wuppertal 1998, p. 44.

159 Linse, *Ökopax*, p. 57.

160 Schmoll, *Erinnerung an die Natur*, p. 159.

161 See the documentary study by Harald Szeemann et al. (translated from Italian), *Monte Verità – Berg der Wahrheit: Lokale Anthropologie als Beitrag zur Wiederentdeckung einer neuzeitlichen sakralen Topographie*, Munich 1980.

162 Joachim Radkau, 'Die Verheißungen der Morgenfrühe: Die Lebensreform in der neuen Moderne', in Buchholz et al., *Lebensreform*, pp. 55–60.

163 John Muir, who had taken refuge there from the city, thundered that the citizens of San Francisco might just as well have turned their cathedrals and churches into water tanks, 'for no holier temple has ever been consecrated to the heart of man'. Daniel M. Berman and John T. O'Connor, *Who Owns the Sun? People, Politics, and the Struggle for a Solar Economy*, White River Junction 1996, p. 78.

164 Ulrich Linse, '"Der Raub des Rheingoldes": Das Wasserkraftwerk Laufenburg', in Linse et al., *Von der Bittschrift zur Platzbesetzung: Konflikte um technische Großprojekte*, Bonn 1988, pp. 11–62.

165 Schmoll, *Erinnerung an die Natur*, p. 13.

166 Barthelmeß, *Vögel*, p. 90.

167 Mary Ann Elston, 'Women and Anti-Vivisection in Victorian England, 1870–1900', in Rupke, *Vivisection*, p. 270.

168 Michael P. Cohen, *The History of the Sierra Club 1892–1970*, San Francisco 1988, p. 25.

169 Reinhard Falter, 'Achtzig Jahre "Wasserkrieg": Das Walchensee-Kraftwerk', in Linse et al., *Von der Bittschrift*, pp. 63–127.

170 Joachim Radkau, *Mensch und Natur in der Geschichte*, Leipzig 2002, pp. 27–66.

171 See Udo E. Simonis, *Globale Umweltpolitik: Ansätze und Perspektiven*, Mannheim 1996, pp. 61ff. The author also recognizes, however, that the soil is the least well suited for a global environmental policy.

172 Donald Worster, *Nature's Economy: A History of Ecological Ideas*, Cambridge 1977, pp. 232, 223.

173 Ibid., pp. 233f. Quotation: Donald Worster, *Dust Bowl: The Southern Plains in the 1930s*, Oxford 1979, p. 200.

174 Tom Dale and Vernon Gill Carter, *Topsoil and Civilization*, Norman OK 1955. The threat to the soil is also the main theme in another early eco-bestseller, which was translated into thirteen languages: *Our Plundered Planet* (1948), by

Fairfield Osborn, president of the New York Zoological Society and later one of the founders of WWF.

175 Richard N. L. Andrews, *Managing the Environment, Managing Ourselves: A History of American Environmental Policy*, New Haven 1999, p. 177.

176 Philip Shabecoff, *A Fierce Green Fire: The American Environmental Movement*, New York 1993, pp. 82f.; Benjamin Kline, *First Along the River: A Brief History of the U.S. Environmental Movement*, Lanham 2007, p. 66.

177 Lewis Mumford, *Technics and Civilization* (orig. 1934), New York 1964, pp. 255f.

178 Shabecoff, *A Fierce Green Fire*, p. 81.

179 Worster, *Dust Bowl*, pp. 212ff.

180 Wilhelm Lienenkämper, *Grüne Welt zu treuen Händen: Naturschutz und Landschaftspflege im Industriezeitalter*, Stuttgart 1963, p. 93.

181 Quoted from William E. Leuchtenburg, *Franklin D. Roosevelt and the New Deal*, New York 1963, p. 173.

182 David E. Lilienthal, *TVA: Democracy on the March*, New York 1944, p. 79.

183 Richard S. Kirkendall, 'The New Deal and Agriculture', in John Braeman et al., eds., *The New Deal*, vol. 1, Columbus OH 1975, p. 95; Carolyn Merchant, *The Columbia Guide to American Environmental History*, New York 2002, p. 177.

184 Kirkendall, p. 106.

185 Wilbur Zelinsky, 'The Imprint of Central Authority', in Michael P. Conzen, ed., *The Making of the American Landscape*, New York 1990, p. 327. The claim on p. 326, 'The landscape legacy of the New Deal is rich and varied in kind and effect', is refuted by the illustration on p. 327 showing a monotonous draughtboard pattern.

186 This was the view of William Vogt, the pioneer of ecological economics, quoted in Reimar Gilsenbach, *Die Erde dürstet: 6000 Jahre Kampf ums Wasser*, Leipzig 1961, p. 240.

187 *Water* (= special issue of *National Geographic* 217/4 (2010)), pp. 130f.

188 Geoff Cunfer, *On the Great Plains: Agriculture and Environment*, College Station TX 2005, pp. 196–200.

189 R. Douglas Hurt, *American Agriculture: A Brief History*, Ames IA 1994, p. 292: 'When the war began, the problems of soil conservation remained far from resolved.' Moreover, although the war economy gave work to ruined farmers, it covered up the problem rather than removed it.

190 Merchant, *Columbia Guide*, p. 176. Curiously, however, Carolyn Merchant dates the beginning of the 'era of environmentalism' to 1940!

191 Berman and O'Connor, *Who Owns the Sun?*, p. 100.

192 David E. Lilienthal, *Change, Hope, and the Bomb*, Princeton 1963.

193 Worster, *Nature's Economy*, pp. 205–20, 237f.; Ludwig Trepl, *Geschichte der Ökologie: Vom 17. Jahrhundert bis zur Gegenwart*, Frankfurt 1987, pp. 144–53.

194 Worster, *Dust Bowl*, pp. 213f.

195 See the detailed and provocative historical survey by Marc Reisner, *Cadillac Desert: The American West and Its Disappearing Water*, new edn, New York 1993.

196 Radkau, *Nature and Power*, p. 65.

197 Thomas R. Dunlap, *Nature and the English Diaspora: Environment and History in the U.S., Canada, Australia, and New Zealand*, Cambridge 1999, pp. 181f.

198 See Charles E. Little, *Green Fields Forever: The Conservation Tillage Revolution in America*, Washington DC 1987, pp. 30ff. The book is dedicated to Faulkner's memory.
199 Worster, *Nature's Economy*, p. 271.
200 What he meant, in context, was that the mountain feared deer, not wolves. Stephen J. Pine, *Fire in America: A Cultural History of Wildland and Rural Fire*, Seattle 1982, p. 520.
201 Susan L. Flader, *Thinking Like a Mountain: Aldo Leopold and the Evolution of an Ecological Attitude Toward Deer, Wolves, and Forests*, Columbia MO 1974, p. 29.
202 Around the same time, bird conservationists on Germany's North Sea coast constantly referred to the 'seagull problem'. Protected as the favourite of tourists, silver gulls increasingly antagonized conservationists because their rapid breeding displaced other bird species. In the end, they were seen as the 'rats of the air'.
203 Worster, *Nature's Economy*, pp. 270ff.
204 Quoted (and retranslated) from Georg Sperber, 'Naturschutz und Forstwirtschaft: Die Geschichte einer schwierigen Beziehung', in Stiftung Naturschutzgeschichte, ed., *Wegmarken: Beiträge zur Geschichte des Naturschutzes*, Essen 2000, pp. 72f.
205 Wilhelm Bode and Elisabeth Emmert, *Jagdwende: Vom Edelhobby zum ökologischen Handwerk*, Munich 1998, pp. 139ff.
206 Stephen J. Pyne, *Fire in America: A Cultural History of Wildland and Rural Fire*, Princeton 1982, p. 279.
207 Robert Gottlieb, *Forcing the Spring: The Transformation of the American Environmental Movement*, Washington DC 1993, p. 319.
208 Christopher Sellers, *Hazards of the Job: From Industrial Disease to Environmental Health Science*, Chapel Hill 1997, p. 225.
209 Ibid., pp. 2, 223; Linda Sellers, *Rachel Carson*, London 1997, pp. 347, 356f., 375 et al.
210 Sellers, *Hazards*, p. 225.
211 Ibid., pp. 235f.
212 Frank Uekötter, *The Age of Smoke: Environmental Policy in Germany and the United States, 1880–1970*, Pittsburgh 2009, p. 82; Tarr, *Search for the Ultimate Sink*, pp. 227ff.
213 Joel Tarr and Carl Zimring, 'The Struggle for Smoke Control in St. Louis: Achievement and Emulation', in Andrew Hurley, ed., *Common Fields: An Environmental History of St. Louis*, St. Louis 1997, pp. 199–220.
214 Tarr, *Search for the Ultimate Sink*, pp. 227ff.
215 Robert Proctor, *The Nazi War on Cancer*, Princeton 1999.
216 Ibid., p. 112.
217 'Already pairing in chromosomes seems crass at times; one prefers not to think of what may come to be through radiation.'
218 Dunlap, *Nature and the English Diaspora*, pp. 173ff., 183ff.; Libby Robbin, 'Ecology: A Science of Empire?', in Robbin and Tom Griffiths, eds., *Ecology and Empire: Environmental History of Settler Societies*, Seattle 1997, pp. 70ff.
219 Robbin, 'Ecology', p. 70.
220 Dunlap, *Nature*, p. 186.
221 See Walter Clay Lowdermilk, *Forestry in Denuded China*, Philadelphia 1930.
222 Recently David R. Montgomery (*Dirt: The Erosion of Civilizations*, Berkeley

2007) used Lowdermilk's reports as his main source for a soil history of large parts of the world.

223 See the colourful, vigorous memoirs published by his widow at the age of ninety-five: Inez Marks Lowdermilk, *All in a Lifetime: An Autobiography*, Berkeley 1983, e.g., p. 173.

224 Walter Clay Lowdermilk, *Palestine: Land of Promise*, New York 1944, p. 200; Alon Tal, *Pollution in a Promised Land: An Environmental History of Israel*, Berkeley 2002, p. 55.

225 Diana K. Davis, 'Resurrecting the Granary of Rome: Environmental History and French Colonial Expansion in North Africa', Athens OH 2007. On North Africa as a warning for Lowdermilk, see Inez Marks Lowdermilk, *All in a Lifetime*, p. 173.

226 See Meron Benvenisti, *Sacred Landscape: The Buried History of the Holy Land since 1948*, Berkeley 2000, in which the son of a Zionist geographer (who had described the 'Holy Land' in the spirit of Lowdermilk) offers a highly revisionist approach. This too, however, suffers from a lack of sources to support its argument that city-dwelling Arab intellectuals most often took no interest in the Palestinian countryside.

227 Philip R. Pryde, *Environmental Management in the Soviet Union*, Cambridge 1991, pp. 198ff.

228 Anton Metternich, *Die Wüste droht: Die gefährdete Nahrungsgrundlage der menschlichen Gesellschaft*, Bremen 1949, pp. 184ff.

229 This was the case especially after the great drought of 1890–2. See Willard Sunderland, *Taming the Wild Field: Colonization and Empire in the Russian Steppe*, Ithaca 2004, pp. 202ff.

230 D. G. Wilenski, *Bodenkunde* (Russian orig. 1954), Berlin 1957, pp. 29ff., 198f.

231 Metternich, *Wüste*, p. 185.

232 See Hans Walter Flemming (in 1940–5, chief executive of the Reichsverband der Deutschen Wasserwirtschaft), *Wüsten, Deiche und Turbinen: Das große Buch von Wasser und Völkerschicksal*, Göttingen 1957, p. 122, on the 'splendid prospects for irrigation in today's Russia' and the promise it offers of 'unimaginable wealth'. Such words, in the mouth of a former expert in Nazi Germany, make Khrushchev's agricultural policy more understandable.

233 Stefan Merl, 'Entstalinisierung, Reformen und Wettlauf der Systeme 1953–1964', in Stefan Plaggenborg, ed., *Handbuch der Geschichte Russlands*, vol. 5, Stuttgart 2002, pp. 212ff., 218.

234 Fr. Christoph (Ministerialrat a. D.), ed., *Die Technik in der Landwirtschaft*, Berlin 1926, pp. 405, 410. Carl J. Burckhardt, then League of Nations commissioner in Danzig, reported a conversation with Hitler in which the Nazi leader, having attributed the increase in Germany's agricultural output mainly to chemical fertilizers, continued: 'But one day the soil will have had enough and conk out like a body stuffed with drugs. What then?' Burckhardt, *Meine Danziger Mission 1937–1939*, Munich 1960, p. 266. That was in August 1939: eco-logic as a justification for military expansion!

235 The best historical study is of the Upper Rhine: Dieter Hassler et al., eds., *Wässerwiesen*, Karlsruhe 1995.

236 Christoph, *Technik in der Landwirtschaft*, p. 102.

237 Thomas Zeller, '"Ganz Deutschland sein Garten": Alwin Seifert und die Landschaft des Nationalsozialismus', in Joachim Radkau and Frank Uekötter, eds., *Naturschutz und Nationalsozialismus*, Frankfurt 2003, p. 305.

238 See Franz W. Seidler, *Fritz Todt: Baumeister des Dritten Reiches*, Frankfurt 1988, pp. 118f.

239 Robert A. Caro, *The Power Broker: Robert Moses and the Fall of New York*, New York 1974.

240 See Alwin Seifert, *Gärtnern, Ackern ohne Gift* (orig. 1948, rev. 1957), new edn of 250,000 copies, Munich 1971. Cf. Seifert, *Compost*, London 1962.

241 Alwin Seifert, 'Die Versteppung Deutschlands', in Seifert, *Im Zeitalter des Lebendigen: Natur – Heimat – Technik*, Planegg 1942, p. 25.

242 Ibid., pp. 36f.

243 Ibid., pp. 46, 39.

244 Ibid., p. 29.

245 Ibid., pp. 43f.; Lilienthal, *TVA*, illustration after p. 144.

246 Zeller, 'Alwin Seifert und die Landschaft des Nationalsozialismus', p. 284.

247 Lienenkämper, *Grüne Welt*, p. 99.

248 Seidler, *Fritz Todt*, p. 282.

249 Ansgar Kaiser, *Zur Geschichte der Ems: Natur und Ausbau*, Rheda-Wiedenbrück 1993, p. 113.

250 Frank Uekötter, *The Green and the Brown: A History of Conservation in Nazi Germany*, Cambridge 2006, pp. 116–24.

251 David Blackbourn, *The Conquest of Nature: Water, Landscape and the Making of Modern Germany*, London 2007, p. 189; cf. Joachim Radkau, 'Wasserbaugeschichte als deutsches Drama', *Gaia* 17/2 (2008), pp. 233–5.

252 Adolf Hitler, *Mein Kampf*, Munich 1937, pp. 146f.

253 Uekötter, *Green and the Brown*, p. 53.

254 See the brief discussion of Klose in Hans-Werner Frohn, 'Naturschutz macht Staat – Staat macht Naturschutz: Von der staatlichen Stelle für Naturdenkmalpflege in Preußen bis zum Bundesamt für Naturschutz 1906 bis 2006 – eine Institutionengeschichte', in Frohn and Friedemann Schmoll, eds., *Natur und Staat*, Münster 2006, p. 213. Klose's wish to broaden conservation to include landscape protections and human dimensions set him 'at the opposite pole from Schoenichen'. Klose 'artfully saved the acquisitions of the Reich [Conservation] Agency and handed them on to the Federal Republic', being a highly influential figure in the years after 1945.

255 Thomas M. Lekan, 'Organische Raumordnung: Landschaftspflege und die Durchführung des Reichsnaturschutzgesetzes im Rheinland und in Westfalen', in Radkau and Uekötter, *Naturschutz und Nationalsozialismus*, p. 162.

256 Hitler, *Mein Kampf*, p. 144.

257 Seifert, *Zeitalter*, p. 54.

258 See Luc Ferry, *The New Ecological Order*, Chicago 1995, pp. 91–107 ('Nazi Ecology'); Anna Bramwell, *Ecology in the 20th Century: A History*, New Haven 1989 (pp. 161–74: 'Was There a Generic Fascist Ecologism?' – a question she answers with a definite no, arguing instead that it was a special German path); Uekötter, *Green and the Brown*; Franz-Josef Brüggemeier, Mark Cioc and Thomas Zeller, eds., *How Green Were the Nazis? Nature, Environment, and Nation in the Third Reich*, Athens OH 2005; Radkau and Uekötter, *Naturschutz und Nationalsozialismus* – and cf. the book reviews by Willi Oberkrome in *Neue Politische Literatur* 49 (2004), pp. 515f.; Florentine Fritzen in *Historische Zeitschrift* 279 (2004), pp. 533f.; Verena Winiwarter in *Österreichische Zeitschrift für Volkskunde* (2004), pp. 404ff.; and Charles E. Closmann in *sehepunkte* 4/11 (2004).

259 Werner Ebert et al., *Natur und Geschichte in der Schorfheide*, Eberswalde 2001, pp. 27ff.

260 Seifert, for example, in relation to Fritz Todt; see Seidler, *Fritz Todt*, pp. 279f.

261 'O German forest, o beech green / And power of mighty oaks / O German forest, you fall down there / From the blows of your slayer.'

262 Radkau, *Nature and Power*, pp. 229f.

263 Uekötter, *Green and the Brown*, pp. 85–99.

264 Ludwig Finckh, *Ludwig Finckh 1876–1964: Gedenkgabe des Arbeitskreises für deutsche Dichtung*, ed. Hinrich Jantzen, Kronberg 1964, p. 26.

265 On the striking case of Heinrich Wiepking-Jürgensmann, see Uekötter, *Green and the Brown*, pp. 78 and 157ff.

266 For a recent expression of this view, see Roger S. Gottlieb (in conversation with Rabbi Arthur Waskow), *A Greener Faith: Religious Environmentalism and Our Planet's Future*, New York 2006, p. 200.

267 Hans Klose, *Fünfzig Jahre staatlicher Naturschutz: Ein Rückblick auf den Weg der deutschen Naturschutzbewegung*, Giessen 1957, pp. 32, 35.

268 See, despite its apologetic tendencies, Daniel Heintz, *Tierschutz im Dritten Reich: 'Im neuen Reich darf es keine Tierquälerei mehr geben'*, Müllheim 2008; and the prize-winning book by Daniel Jütte: *Von Mäusen und Menschen: Die Auswirkungen des nationalsozialistischen 'Reichstierschutzgesetzes' von 1933 auf die medizinische Forschung*, Stuttgart 2001.

269 Michael Wettengel, 'Staat und Naturschutz 1906–1945: Zur Geschichte der Staatlichen Stelle für Naturdenkmalpflege in Preußen und der Reichsstelle für Naturschutz', *Historische Zeitschrift* 257 (1993), pp. 389f.

270 Heinrich Rubner, *Deutsche Forstgeschichte 1933–1945: Forstwirtschaft, Jagd und Umwelt im NS-Staat*, St Katharinen 1985, pp. 54, 72ff., 85f., 104ff.

271 Anna Bramwell (*Blood and Soil: Richard Walther Darré and Hitler's 'Green Party'*, Abbotsbrook 1985) goes too far in presenting the Nazi period as the most successful in pioneering organic farming. For a more balanced view, see Gunter Vogt, *Entstehung und Entwicklung des ökologischen Landbaus*, Bad Dürkheim 2000, pp. 136ff.; and Gesine Gerhard, 'Breeding Pigs and People for the Third Reich: Richard Walther Darré's Agrarian Ideology', in Brüggemeier et al., *How Green*, pp. 129–46.

272 Peter Münch, *Stadthygiene im 19. und 20. Jahrhundert*, Göttingen 1993, pp. 105f., 266f., 280f.

273 Uekötter, *Green and the Brown*, p. 142.

274 Vogt, *Entstehung und Entwicklung*, pp. 141ff.

275 Johannes Zscheisler et al., *Handbuch Mais*, 4th edn, Frankfurt 1990, p. 20.

276 Peter-Michael Steinsiek, *Forst- und Holzforschung im 'Dritten Reich'*, Remagen 2008, pp. 179f.

277 Ibid., p. 209.

278 Rubner, *Deutsche Forstgeschichte 1933–1945*, p. 104.

279 Joska Pinschovius, *Heidschnucken und Donnerbesen: Lüneburger Landschaften*, Vienna 2002, pp. 89ff.; Hermann Cordes et al., eds., *Naturschutzgebiet Lüneburger Heide: Geschichte – Ökologie – Landschaftsschutz*, Bremen 1997, p. 311.

280 'Bones, iron, rags and paper we collect, / and knocked-out teeth as well. / Yes, we thank you, Hermann Goering, / there's nothing we don't collect.'

281 Anton Metternich, *Die Wüste droht: Die gefährdete Nahrungsgrundlage der menschlichen Gesellschaft*, Bremen 1947, p. 87.

282 Anna Wöbse, 'Der Schutz natürlicher Schönheit und die Ursprünge des

Weltnaturerbes', MS, Bremen 2010, p. 25. Cf. her book *Weltnaturschutz: Umweltdiplomatie in Völkerbund und Vereinten Nationen 1920–1950*, Frankfurt and New York 2012.

283 Anna-Katharina Wöbse, 'Der Schutz der Natur im Völkerbund: Anfänge einer Weltumweltpolitik', *Archiv für Sozialgeschichte* 43 (2003), pp. 177–90.

284 Wöbse, *Weltnaturschutz*, p. 64.

285 Shepard Krech III, John R. McNeill and Carolyn Merchant, eds., *Encyclopedia of World Environmental History*, New York 2004, vol. 3, p. 1324.

286 Mark Cioc, *The Game of Conservation: International Treaties to Protect the World's Migratory Animals*, Athens OH 2009, pp. 127ff.

287 Richard Ellis, *Men and Whales*, New York 1991, pp. 401f.

288 Ibid., pp. 431–3.

289 Anna-Katharina Wöbse, 'Die Bomber und die Brandgans: Zur Geschichte des Kampfes um den Knechtsand – eine historische Kernzone des Nationalparks Niedersächsisches Wattenmeer', MS.

290 Ludwig Fischer et al., eds., *Das Wattenmeer: Kulturlandschaft vor und hinter den Deichen*, Stuttgart 2005, pp. 28ff.

291 John McCormick, *Reclaiming Paradise: The Global Environmental Movement*, Bloomington 1989, p. 33.

292 Ibid., p. 31: 'The continental Europeans prevailed, thus denying environmentalists an effective input into UN affairs for nearly thirty years.'

293 Anna-Katharina Wöbse, 'Framing the Heritage of Mankind: National Parks on the International Agenda', MS, Bremen 2008.

294 Martin Holdgate, *The Green Web: A Union for World Conservation*, London 1999, p. 34.

295 McCormick, *Reclaiming Paradise*, p. 37.

296 Holdgate, *Green Web*, p. 55.

297 Max Nicholson, *The New Environmental Age*, Cambridge 1987, pp. 104ff.

298 Holdgate, *Green Web*, pp. 41, 19.

299 Wöbse, 'Framing the Heritage', pp. 10ff.

300 McCormick, *Reclaiming Paradise*, p. 35.

301 Holdgate, *Green Web*, p. 33.

302 Ibid., p. 37.

303 Ibid., p. 40. See also Julian Huxley, *Memories*, Harmondsworth 1972.

304 McCormick, *Reclaiming Paradise*, p. 38.

305 Anna-Katherina Wöbse, 'Naturschutz global', in Frohn and Schmoll, *Natur und Staat*, pp. 710f.

306 Gunnar Myrdal, 'Economics of an Improved Environment', in Myrdal, *Against the Stream: Critical Essays on Economics*, New York 1973, p. 197ff.

307 Bill Jay, 'The Family of Man: A Reappraisal of the "Greatest Exhibition of All Time"', *Insight* 1 (1989).

308 Holdgate, *Green Web*, p. 59; Matthew Connelly, *Fatal Misconception: The Struggle to Control World Population*, Cambridge MA 2008, pp. 128ff.

309 Björn-Ola Linnér, *The Return of Malthus: Environmentalism and Post-War Population-Resource Crisis*, Isle of Harris 2003.

310 Thomas Robertson, '"This Is the American Earth": American Empire, the Cold War, and American Environmentalism', *Diplomatic History* 32/4 (2008), p. 571. For Robertson the origins of American environmentalism are less innocent than in other accounts, more bound up with American imperialism and the Cold War.

311 Julian Huxley, *Memories II*, London 1973, p. 181.
312 Radkau, *Mensch und Natur*, pp. 85ff.
313 Bernhard Grzimek, *Kein Platz für wilde Tiere* (orig. 1955), Munich 1973, p. 13.
314 Huxley, *Memories II*, pp. 180f.; Bernard Asbell, rev. edn, *The Pill: A Biography of the Drug That Changed the World*, New York 1995.
315 Huxley, *Memories*, p. 277.
316 Georg Borgstrom, *The Hungry Planet: The Modern World at the Edge of Famine*, New York 1972, p. ix.
317 Joachim Radkau, 'Der atomare Ursprung der Forschungspolitik des Bundes', in Peter Weingart and Niels C. Taubert, eds., *Das Wissensministerium*, Weilerswist 2006, p. 53.
318 Robert Lorenz, *Protest der Physiker: Die 'Göttinger Erklärung' von 1957*, Bielefeld 2011.
319 Joachim Radkau, *Aufstieg und Krise der deutschen Atomwirtschaft 1945–1975: Verdrängte Alternativen in der Kerntechnik und der Ursprung der nuklearen Kontroverse*, Reinbek 1983, pp. 96ff.; Michael Bess, *The Light-Green Society: Ecology and Technological Modernity in France, 1960–2000*, Chicago 2003, p. 93.
320 Radkau, *Aufstieg und Krise*, pp. 67ff.
321 Ernst Bloch, *The Principle of Hope*, Oxford 1986, vol. 2, p. 664.
322 For an English translation, see Hans Jonas, *The Imperative of Responsibility: In Search of an Ethics for the Technological Age*, Chicago 1984.
323 Bloch, *Principle of Hope*, vol. 1, p. 440.
324 Friedrich Wagner, *Die Wissenschaft und die gefährdete Welt: Eine Wissenschaftssoziologie der Atomphysik* (orig. 1964), 2nd edn, Munich 1969, pp. 281f.
325 Ibid., p. 522.
326 Robert Jungk and Hans Josef Mundt, eds., *Das umstrittene Experiment Der Mensch: 27 Wissenschaftler diskutieren die Elemente einer biologischen Revolution*, Munich 1966, p. 384.
327 Ilona Stölken-Fitschen, *Atombombe und Geistesgeschichte: Eine Studie der fünfziger Jahre aus deutscher Sicht*, Baden-Baden 1995, pp. 215ff.
328 Julian Huxley, 'The Future of Man: Evolutionary Aspects', in G. E. W. Wolstenholme, ed., *Man and His Future*, Boston 1963, pp. 17, 20, 21.
329 See R. Samuel Deese, 'A Dialogue on the Destiny of Species: Julian and Aldous Huxley in the Cold War Era', paper for the Environmental History and Cold War conference, German Historical Institute, Washington DC, March 2007.
330 Jan Holm, *Die angloamerikanische Ökotopie*, Frankfurt 1998, p. 232.
331 Ibid., pp. 178, 184.
332 Huxley, *Memories II*, p. 221.
333 Julian Huxley, in his introduction to the British edition of *Silent Spring*, London 1963, p. 20.
334 Huxley, *Memories II*, p. 98.
335 See Albert Schweitzer, *Out of My Life and Thought: An Autobiography*, Baltimore 2009.
336 *Der Spiegel* 38 (1960), p. 84.
337 Huxley, *Memories*, p. 196.
338 Huxley, *Memories II*, p. 213.
339 Wöbse, *Schutz natürlicher Schönheit*, p. 59.

340 Bernhard Grzimek, *Auf den Mensch gekommen: Erfahrungen mit Leuten*, Munich 1974, pp. 315ff.

341 See, for example, Adams and McShane, *Myth of Wild Africa*, p. 52, which claims that Grzimek's propaganda for conservation of the Serengeti steppe was 'filled with misleading, often falsified data'.

342 Manfred Behr and Hans Otto Meissner, *Keine Angst um wilde Tiere: Fünf Kontinente geben ihnen Heimat*, Munich 1959.

343 Grzimek, *Auf den Mensch gekommen*, pp. 331f.

344 Ibid., pp. 437ff.

345 Adams and McShane, *Myth of Wild Africa*, pp. 50f.

346 Huxley, *Memories II*, p. 251.

347 Huxley, *Memories*, p. 236.

348 Holdgate, *Green Web*, p. 55.

349 Ibid., p. 44.

350 *Encyclopedia of World Environmental History*, vol. 1, p. 433.

351 McCormick, *Reclaiming Paradise*, p. 39.

352 Ibid., pp. 41f.

353 Bernard Stonehouse, *Saving the Animals: The World Wildlife Fund Book of Conservation*, London 1981, pp. 11, 19f.

354 Jörg Bergstedt, *Agenda, Expo, Sponsoring: Recherchen im Naturschutzfilz*, Frankfurt 1998, pp. 70ff.

355 See Alexis Schwarzenbach, *Saving the World's Wildlife: WWF – The First 50 Years*, London 2011, pp. 146f. This book, published for an exhibition at the Swiss National Museum in Zurich, is one of the few thorough and wide-ranging studies of life inside a major international NGO.

356 Worster, *Nature's Economy*, pp. 339f.

357 Radkau, *Aufstieg und Krise*, pp. 89ff.

358 Ibid., p. 436.

359 Bodo Manstein, *Im Würgegriff des Fortschritts*, Frankfurt 1961, p. 122.

360 Linda Lear, *Rachel Carson, Witness for Nature*, New York 1997, pp. 374f.

361 On the following, see my introduction to the new German edition of Carson's work: *Der stumme Frühling*, Munich 2007.

362 Holdgate, *Green Web*, pp. 42, 52, 61.

363 Radkau, *Nature and Power*, pp. 131, 268f.

364 Lear, *Rachel Carson*, pp. 364ff.

365 Ibid., p. 373.

366 Christian Simon, *DDT: Kulturgeschichte einer chemischen Verbindung*, Basle 1999, p. 165.

367 See Deutsches Gartenmuseum Erfurt, ed., *Die ganze Welt im Garten*, Erfurt 2003, pp. 80f.

368 Barbara Ward and René Dubos, *Only One Earth: The Care and Maintenance of a Small Planet*, New York 1983, e.g. pp. xiv, xvi, and 165.

369 Allan Abramson to the author, 9 February 2010.

370 *Encyclopedia for World Environmental History*, vol. 3, pp. 1092f.; Richard White, *The Organic Machine: The Remaking of the Columbia River*, New York 1995, pp. 91f: 'Salmon fishing is, and long has been, political; it is ideo-logical.'

371 Ernst Jünger, *Sämtliche Werke*, 2nd section, vol. 10, Stuttgart 1980, p. 331 (Essay 'Forscher und Liebhaber').

372 Lear, *Rachel Carson*, pp. 411f.

373 Philip J. Hilts, *Protecting America's Health: The FDA, Business, and One Hundred Years of Regulation*, New York 2003, pp. 144–65.

374 Willibald Steinmetz, 'Contergan', in Haus der Geschichte der BRD, ed., *Skandale in Deutschland nach 1945*, Bonn 2007, p. 57.

375 Robert Wizinger, *Chemische Plaudereien*, Bonn 1934, p. 5.

376 Gottlieb, *Forcing the Spring*, pp. 240ff.

377 For an English translation, see Günther Schwab, *Dance with the Devil: A Dramatic Encounter*, London 1963.

378 Lear, *Rachel Carson*, p. 318.

379 Ibid., pp. 464f.

380 Cf. Gottlieb, *Forcing the Spring*, p. 308.

381 Martha Freeman, ed., *Always, Rachel – The Letters of Rachel Carson and Dorothy Freeman 1952–1964: The Story of a Remarkable Friendship*, Boston 1994, pp. 525ff.

Chapter Two   The Great Chain Reaction: The 'Ecological Revolution' in and around 1970

1 Martin Holdgate, *The Green Web: A Union for World Conservation*, London 1999, p. 101.

2 Max Nicholson, *The Environmental Revolution: A Guide for the New Masters of the World*, London 1970, p. 7 (unpaginated).

3 Ibid.

4 Max Nicholson, *The New Environmental Age*, Cambridge 1987, pp. 120ff.

5 This was even the view of Denis Hayes, who organized Earth Day; see Philip Shabecoff, *A Fierce Green Fire: The American Environmental Movement*, New York 1993, p. 119.

6 Frank Uekötter, *The Age of Smoke: Environmental Policy in Germany and the United States, 1880–1970*, Pittsburgh 2009, pp. 179ff.

7 Ibid., p. 182.

8 Ibid., p. 243.

9 Hubert Weinzierl, 'Naturschutz ist Menschenschutz', in Karl Stankiewitz, *Babylon in Bayern: Wie aus einem Agrarland der modernste Staat Europas werden sollte*, Regensburg 2004, p. 134.

10 Arbeitsgemeinschaft Naturschutz westlicher Bodensee, *Umweltschutz am Bodensee: Eine Regionalstudie*, Stuttgart 1971, p. 54.

11 The far-right John Birch Society, for example, fulminated that Earth Day was a disguise for commemoration of Lenin's birthday, also on 22 April – to which Senator Gaylord Nelson, relying on the historical ignorance of his opponents, retorted that it was the birthday (in reality, unknown) of Francis of Assisi. Shabecoff, *Fierce Green Fire*, p. 115.

12 Jeremy Rifkin, *The European Dream: How Europe's Vision of the Future Is Quietly Eclipsing the American Dream*, Cambridge 2004, pp. 313ff. ('A Second Enlightenment').

13 In 1991 John McCormick still insisted that 'Britain has the oldest, strongest, best-organized and most widely supported environmental lobby in the world' (quoted from Chris Rootes, 'Britain – Greens in a Cold Climate', in Rootes and Dick Richardson, eds., *The Green Challenge: The Development of Green Parties in Europe*, London 1995, p. 66.

14 Ernst Ulrich von Weizsäcker and Helmut Schreiber, 'Luftreinhaltung: Der schwierige Konsens', in Lothar Gründling and Beate Weber, eds., *Dicke Luft in Europa: Aufgaben und Probleme der europäischen Umweltpolitik*, Heidelberg 1988, pp. 163ff.

15 Irmela Hijiya-Kirschnereit, in the preface to the German edition: Ishimure Michiko, *Paradies im Meer der Qualen*, Frankfurt 1995, p. 8.

16 Michael Egan, *Barry Commoner and the Science of Survival: The Remaking of American Environmentalism*, Cambridge MA 2007, pp. 93ff.

17 J. Brooks Flippen, 'Richard Nixon, Russell Train, and the Birth of Modern American Environmental Diplomacy', *Diplomatic History* 32/4 (2008), pp. 613f.

18 Eva Sternfeld, *Umweltpolitik und Industrialisierung in der Volksrepublik China (1949–1985)*, Berlin 1984, p. 23; Bernhard Glaeser, *Umweltpolitik in China*, Bochum 1983, p. 15. Bao Maohong, professor of environmental history at Beijing University, has fully confirmed to me this significance of Stockholm 1972.

19 Qu Geping and Li Jinchang, *Population and the Environment in China*, London 1994.

20 James Lovelock, *The Ages of Gaia: A Biography of Our Living Earth*, 2nd edn, Oxford 2000, p. 27.

21 Joachim Radkau, *Nature and Power*, Cambridge 2008, p. 291.

22 Kai F. Hünemörder, *Die Frühgeschichte der globalen Umweltkrise und die Formierung der deutschen Umweltpolitik (1950–1973)*, Wiesbaden 2004, pp. 154ff.

23 Joachim Radkau, 'Scharfe Konturen für das Ozonloch: Zur Öko-Ikonografie der *Spiegel*-Titel', in Gerhard Paul, ed., *Das Jahrhundert der Bilder: 1949 bis heute*, Göttingen 2008, p. 535; Günter Küppers, Peter Lundgreen and Peter Weingart, *Umweltforschung, die gesteuerte Wissenschaft? Eine empirische Studie zum Verhältnis von Wissenschaftsentwicklung und Wissenschaftspolitik*, Frankfurt 1978, pp. 114ff.

24 Edda Müller, *Innenwelt der Umweltpolitik: Sozial-liberale Umweltpolitik – (Ohn)macht durch Organisation?*, 2nd edn, Opladen 1995, pp. 51ff.

25 For examples of these tendencies, see Peter Menke-Glückert, *Friedensstrategien: Wissenschaftliche Techniken beeinflussen die Politik*, Reinbek 1969.

26 Hünemörder, *Frühgeschichte*, pp. 156ff.; interview with Menke-Glückert, 7 March 2001, for allowing me to consult which I am grateful to Kai F. Hünemörder; *Die Zeit*, 'Ein aufmüpfiger Beamter: Umweltexperte Peter Menke-Glückert ist ständig im Clinch mit seinen Ministern in Bonn', 11 July 1980.

27 At least this is the impression conveyed by Peter Merseburger's 900-page biography (*Willy Brandt: 1913 – 1992*, Stuttgart 2002).

28 Joachim Radkau, *Aufstieg und Krise der deutschen Atomwirtschaft 1945–1975: Verdrängte Alternativen in der Kerntechnik und der Ursprung der nukleären Kontroverse*, Reinbek 1983, pp. 374f.

29 Henning von Köller in von Köller, ed., *Umweltpolitik mit Augenmaß: Gedenkschrift für Staatssekretär Dr. Günter Hartkopf*, Berlin 2000, p. 7.

30 Günter Hartkopf and Eberhard Bohne, *Umweltpolitik: Grundlagen, Analysen und Perspektiven*, Opladen 1983, pp. 163f.: 'In no other policy sphere was there such close contact between government bodies – especially the interior ministry – and citizens' groups.' The authors depict the position of environmental politics in the Bonn power play as generally frustrating. The relation-

ship in the United States seems to have been tenser. Allan Abramson wrote (7 February 2010 to the author), after thirty-five years of activity in the EPA: 'Unfortunately, the EPA too often has treated NGOs as antagonists, rather than as natural allies. There are many good examples of working together, but there are too many examples of working against each other.'

31 Uekötter, *Age of Smoke*, pp. 260ff.
32 John Opie, *Nature's Nation: An Environmental History of the United States*, Fort Worth 1998, p. 421; Shabecoff, *Fierce Green Fire*, p. 100.
33 This emerges clearly in his memoirs: *For Earth's Sake: The Life and Times of David Brower*, Salt Lake City 1990.
34 Ibid., p. 438.
35 Donald Fleming, 'Roots of the New Conservation Movement', *Perspectives in American History* 67 (1972), pp. 7–91; here p. 40.
36 See his bestseller *The Closing Circle: Nature, Man, and Technology*, New York 1971, pp. 58ff.
37 Fleming, 'Roots of the New Conservation Movement', pp. 47ff.
38 Shabecoff, *Fierce Green Fire*, p. 113. More generally, see Adam Rome, 'The Genius of the Earth Day', *Environmental History* 15 (2010), pp. 194–205.
39 See the largely interview-based article by Flippen: 'Richard Nixon, Russell Train, and the Birth of Modern American Environmental Diplomacy', *Diplomatic History*.
40 J. Brooks Flippen, *Nixon and the Environment*, Albuquerque 2000; Robert Gottlieb, *Forcing the Spring: The Transformation of the American Environmental Movement*, Washington DC 1993, p. 124.
41 Christoph Spehr, *Die Jagd nach Natur: Zur historischen Entwicklung des gesellschaftlichen Naturverhältnisses in den USA, Deutschland, Großbritannien und Italien am Beispiel von Wildnutzung, Artenschutz und Jagd*, Frankfurt 1994, p. 193.
42 Eric M. Conway, *High-Speed Dreams*, Baltimore 2005, pp. 154f.
43 This term circulated mainly through the work of the American political scientist Ronald Inglehard: *The Silent Revolution: Changing Values and Political Styles among Western Publics*, Princeton 1977.
44 Shepard Krech III, John R. McNeill and Carolyn Merchant, eds., *Encyclopedia of World Environmental History*, New York 2004, vol. 3, p. 1206.
45 Ibid., vol. 1, p. 355.
46 Hünemörder, *Frühgeschichte der globalen Umweltkrise*, p. 119.
47 John McCormick, *Reclaiming Paradise: The Global Environmental Movement*, Bloomington 1989, p. 91: 'If there was any single issue that spawned Stockholm, it was acid pollution.' *Encyclopedia of World Environmental History*, vol. 1, p. 43.
48 See Andrew Jamison et al., *The Making of the New Environmental Consciousness: A Comparative Study of the Environmental Movements in Sweden, Denmark and the Netherlands*, Edinburgh 1990.
49 Claes Bernes and Lars J. Lundgreen, *Use and Misuse of Nature's Resources: An Environmental History of Sweden*, Värnamo 2009, p. 121.
50 Rifkin, *European Dream*, pp. 315ff.; Joachim Radkau, 'Die Kernkraft-Kontroverse im Spiegel der Literatur: Phasen und Dimensionen einer neuen Aufklärung', in Armin Hermann and Rolf Schumacher, eds., *Das Ende des Atomzeitalters? Eine sachlich-kritische Dokumentation*, Munich 1987, pp. 307–34.

51 Jost Hermand, *Grüne Utopien in Deutschland: Zur Geschichte des ökologischen Bewusstseins*, Frankfurt 1991, pp. 134ff.
52 Interview with Kai Hünemörder, 7 March 2001.
53 Willem L. Oltmans, ed., *Die Grenzen des Wachstums: Pro und Contra*, Reinbek 1974, p. 120.
54 Ibid. In the twentieth century, or perhaps ever, there can scarcely have been such a broad spectrum of intellectuals represented in a collective volume: from Margaret Mead to Herbert Marcuse, from Ernest Mandel to Sicco Mansholt, from Jan Tinbergen to Claude Lévi-Strauss.
55 Helmut Weidner, 'Entwicklungslinien und Merkmale der Umweltpolitik', in Manfred Pohl and Hans Jürgen Mayer, eds., *Länderbericht Japan*, Bonn 1998, p. 125.
56 Margaret A. McKean, *Environmental Protest and Citizen Politics in Japan*, Berkeley 1981, pp. 17, 21.
57 See Miranda A. Schreurs, *Environmental Politics in Japan, Germany, and the United States*, Cambridge 2002, p. 40.
58 Radkau, *Aufstieg und Krise*, pp. 438ff.
59 David Okrent, *Nuclear Reactor Safety: On the History of the Regulatory Process*, Madison WI 1981, pp. 294ff. et al.
60 Ibid., p. 330.
61 Karl Wirtz, *Im Umkreis der Physik*, Karlsruhe 1988, p. 111.
62 Radkau, *Aufstieg und Krise*, pp. 372ff.
63 Alvin Weinberg, 'Social Institutions and Nuclear Energy', *Science*, 7 July 1972, pp. 33f.
64 John G. Fuller, *We Almost Lost Detroit*, New York 1975; the statement of the 'anonymous engineer': p. 231.
65 See Edda Müller, speaking from her personal experience: *Innenwelt der Umweltpolitik*, 2nd edn, Opladen 1995, p. 65.
66 Egan, *Commoner*, p. 117.
67 Used as a motto in Cornelis Jan Briejèr, *Silberne Schleier: Gefahren chemischer Bekämpfungsmittel* (from the Dutch), Munich 1970.
68 Radkau, *Nature and Power*, pp. 266f.
69 Lovelock, *Ages of Gaia*, p. 166.
70 Louis C. McCabe, ed., *Air Pollution: Proceedings of the U.S. Technical Conference on Air Pollution*, New York 1952, pp. 453, 482.
71 Uekötter, *Age of Smoke*, p. 242.
72 Daniel Fiorino, *Making Environmental Policy*, Berkeley 1995, p. 128. See the detailed account in Mark Landy et al., *The Environmental Protection Agency. Asking the Wrong Questions: From Nixon to Clinton*, New York 1994, pp. 172–203 ('Forging a Cancer Policy').
73 *Encyclopedia of World Environmental History*, vol. 1, pp. 22f.
74 David Zierler, 'Against Protocol: Ecocide, Détente, and the Question of Chemical Warfare in Vietnam, 1969–1975', paper for the GHI Conference 'Environmental History and the Cold War', Washington 2007.
75 Carl Amery, *Hitler als Vorläufer*, Munich 1998, pp. 136f.
76 Brower, *For Earth's Sake*, p. 295.
77 Gregg Easterbrook, *A Moment on the Earth*, New York 1995, p. 232.
78 Egan, *Commoner*, pp. 109f.
79 Gottlieb, *Forcing the Spring*, pp. 106f.
80 Commoner, *Closing Circle*, p. 10.

81 Harold Sprout, 'The Environmental Crisis in the Context of American Politics', in Leslie L. Roos Jr, ed., *The Politics of Ecosuicide*, New York 1971, p. 49.
82 *Encyclopedia of World Environmental History*, vol. 1, p. 355.
83 Michael McCloskey, 'Twenty Years of Change in the Environmental Movement: An Insider's View', in Riley E. Dunlap and Angela G. Mertig, eds., *American Environmentalism*, Washington DC 1992, p. 78.
84 Lynn White Jr, 'The Historical Roots of Our Ecological Crisis', *Science* 155 (1967), pp. 1203–7.
85 René Dubos (striking a critical distance from Lynn White!), 'Franciscan Conservation versus Benedictine Stewardship', in David Spring and Eileen Spring, *Ecology and Religion in History*, New York 1974, p. 118. The hippy magazine *The Oracle* (San Francisco) published White's lecture, and her thesis became a veritable 'article of faith'.
86 John Bassett McCleary, *The Hippie Dictionary*, Berkeley 2004, p. 163.
87 In Theodore Roszak, *The Making of a Counter-Culture*, New York 1969, the most solid overview of the hippy movement *before* 1970, one would look in vain for the topic of damage to the environment. One should therefore be cautious about the later construction of a continuum between the hippies and the environmental movement.
88 Gottlieb, *Forcing the Spring*, pp. 140ff. *Encyclopedia of World Environmental History*, vol. 2, p. 875: 'Since its founding, the NRDC has become one of the largest and most powerful environmental organizations in America.'
89 Shabecoff, *Fierce Green Fire*, pp. 116, 133f.
90 Siegfried Schmidt-Joos and Barry Graves, *Rock-Lexikon*, 2nd edn, Reinbek 1975, p. 385.
91 Hans Christoph Buch, *Bericht aus dem Inneren der Unruhe*, Reinbek 1984, p. 325.
92 Egan, *Commoner*, p. 104.
93 Samuel P. Hays, *Beauty, Health, and Permanence*, Cambridge 1987, pp. 329ff.
94 Cf. Oltmans, *Grenzen des Wachstums*, p. 126.
95 Andreas Daum, *Wissenschaftspopularisierung im 19. Jahrhundert: Bürgerliche Kultur, naturwissenschaftliche Bildung und die deutsche Öffentlichkeit 1848–1914*, Munich 2002 (esp. regarding the Humboldt Societies, Emil Adolf Roßmäßler and Ernst Haeckel).
96 Erik M. Conway, *High-Speed Dreams: NASA and the Technopolitics of Supersonic Transportation, 1945–1999*, Baltimore 2005. Note the point on p. 303: 'How the *space* agency was reoriented toward the *earth* sciences in general is a subject that needs more investigation.' Indeed! James Lovelock, the author of the Gaia hypothesis, came out of NASA.
97 Surprisingly Hans-Dietrich Genscher included Herbert Marcuse, the philosophical star of '68, among the thinkers who influenced the ecological turn: in von Köller, *Umweltschutz mit Augenmaß*, p. 20.
98 *Kursbuch* 33 (1973), p. 40, quoted from Sternfeld, *Umweltpolitik und Industrialisierung*, p. 91.
99 Silke Mende, *'Nicht rechts, nicht links, sondern vorn': Eine Geschichte der Gründungsgrünen*, Munich 2011, p. 263.
100 Jamison et al., *Making of the New Environmental Consciousness*, p. 66.
101 Alvin M. Weinberg, *The First Nuclear Era: The Life and Times of a Technological Fixer*, New York 1994, pp. 176, 178, 195.

102 See also the essay collection by Garrett Hardin, *Living Within Limits: Ecology, Economics, and Population Taboos*, New York 1993.

103 Famine in India is also a central theme in Georg Borgstrom's *The Hungry Planet: The Modern World at the Edge of Famine*, New York 1972.

104 Paul R. Ehrlich, *The Population Bomb*, Cutchogue NY 1971, p. 1.

105 Ibid., p. xi.

106 Egan, *Commoner*, pp. 118ff.

107 Fleming, 'Roots of the New Conservation Movement', p. 53; Lane Simonian, *Defending the Land of the Jaguar: A History of Conservation in Mexico*, Austin 1995, p. 170.

108 Barbara Ward and René Dubos, *Only One Earth: The Care and Maintenance of a Small Planet*, New York 1983, pp. 207f.

109 Paul R. Ehrlich and Anne H. Ehrlich, *Betrayal of Science and Reason: How Anti-Environmental Rhetoric Threatens Our Future*, Washington DC 1996, p. 212.

110 Paul Ehrlich defended himself against this imputation and went so far as to say that 'the birth of each American child is 50 times the disaster for the world as the birth of a child in India'! Matthew Connelly, *Fatal Misconception: The Struggle to Control World Population*, Cambridge MA 2008, p. x.

111 Ibid., pp. 145f.

112 Gunnar Myrdal, *Against the Stream: Critical Essays on Economics*, New York 1973, p. 211.

113 Ward and Dubos, *Only One Earth*, p. 61.

114 Hermand, *Grüne Utopien*, p. 130.

115 Joachim Raschke, *Die Grünen: Wie sie wurden, wie sie sind*, Cologne 1993, p. 126.

116 Gottlieb, *Forcing the Spring*, pp. 227ff.

117 Ehrlich's *Population Bomb* is treated as proven fact in the *Hippie Dictionary*.

118 J. Donald Hughes, *North American Indian Ecology*, El Paso 1996, p. 97.

119 Klaus Taschwer and Benedikt Föger, *Konrad Lorenz*, Vienna 2003, pp. 244ff.

120 Konrad Lorenz, *Civilized Man's Eight Deadly Sins*, London 1974, pp. 13f.

121 Müller, *Innenwelt der Umweltpolitik*, pp. 55, 51.

122 Michael Bess, *The Light-Green Society: Ecology and Technological Modernity in France, 1960–2000*, Chicago 2003, p. 77.

123 Commoner, *Closing Circle*, p. 293.

124 Christian Pfister, ed., *Das 1950er Syndrom: Der Weg in die Konsumgesellschaft*, Bern 1995; see Radkau, *Nature and Power*, pp. 250ff. and 392f. note 4.

125 Shabecoff, *Fierce Green Fire*, p. 134.

126 Ibid., p. 132.

127 Ibid., p. 94.

128 Wolfgang Kunath, 'Die UN-Umweltschutzbehörde hat den Ruf als "Saftladen" weg', *Frankfurter Rundschau*, 25 October 1997, p. 2. There is a friendlier assessment in J. Donald Hughes, *An Environmental History of the World*, London 2001, pp. 224–30. See also, more generally, Anna Wöbse, 'Naturschutz global – oder: Hilfe von außen. Internationale Beziehungen des amtlichen Naturschutzes im 20. Jahrhundert', in Hans-Werner Frohn and Friedemann Schmoll, eds., *Natur und Staat: Staatlicher Naturschutz in Deutschland 1906–2006*, Bonn 2006, p. 701: 'The international administrative apparatuses fell more easily victim to mass inertia than did those at national level.'

129 Michel Batisse, *The UNESCO Water Adventure*, Paris 2005, pp. 165f.

Chapter Three   Networked Thinking and Practical Priorities: An Endless Interplay

1 James Lovelock, *The Ages of Gaia: A Biography of Our Living Earth*, 2nd edn, Oxford 2000, pp. 231–6.
2 Jared Diamond, *Collapse: How Societies Choose to Fail or Survive*, rev. edn, London 2011, p. 498.
3 Daniel J. Fiorino, *Making Environmental Policy*, Berkeley 1995, p. 151.
4 For example, Hans-Dietrich Genscher and Peter Menke-Glückert in Henning von Köller, ed., *Umweltpolitik mit Augenmaß: Gedenkschrift für Staatssekretär Dr. Günter Hartkopf*, Berlin 2000, pp. 18, 121f.
5 Ernst Ulrich von Weizsäcker, *Erdpolitik*, Darmstadt 1989, p. 14.
6 See, e.g., Andrew Jamison et al., *The Making of the New Environmental Consciousness: A Comparative Study of the Environmental Movements in Sweden, Denmark and the Netherlands*, Edinburgh 1990, p. 75.
7 Frank Uekötter, *Von der Rauchplage zur ökologischen Revolution: Eine Geschichte der Luftverschmutzung in Deutschland und den USA 1880–1970*, Essen 2003, pp. 22f.
8 Axel Meyer, 'Die Entstehung der Arten: Neue Theorien und Methoden', in Ernst Peter Fischer and Klaus Wiegandt, eds., *Evolution: Geschichte und Zukunft des Lebens*, Frankfurt 2003, p. 77.
9 John Cronin and Robert F. Kennedy Jr, *The Riverkeepers*, New York 1997, p. 163.
10 Barry Commoner, *The Closing Circle: Nature, Man, and Technology*, New York 1971, p. 33.
11 Ibid., p. 10.
12 Ibid., pp. 31, 202; he places greater emphasis on this ecological argument than on the noise pollution, which was the main preoccupation of the protest movement at the time.
13 Barry Commoner, *The Poverty of Power: Energy and the Economic Crisis*, London 1976.
14 Michael Egan, *Barry Commoner and the Science of Survival: The Remaking of American Environmentalism*, Cambridge MA 2007, p. 161.
15 Michael Kloepfer, 'Umweltrechtsentwicklungen in Deutschland nach 1945', in Kloepfer, ed., *Schübe des Umweltbewusstseins und der Umweltrechtsentwicklung*, Bonn 1995, pp. 108f.
16 In Jochen Bölsche, ed., *Die deutsche Landschaft stirbt*, Reinbek 1983, p. 289.
17 Benjamin Kline, *First Along the River: A Brief History of the U.S. Environmental Movement*, Lanham 2007, p. 78; Philip Shabecoff, *A Fierce Green Fire: The American Environmental Movement*, New York 1993, p. 106; Robert Gottlieb, *Forcing the Spring: The Transformation of the American Environmental Movement*, Washington DC 1993, p. 125, even regards Nader's consumer protection campaigns as more important than wilderness conservation for the new 'environmentalism'. See Nader's introduction to ecotactics: *The Sierra Club Handbook for Environment Activists*, New York 1970.
18 Robert Jütte, *Geschichte der alternativen Medizin*, Munich 1996, p. 65.
19 Joachim Radkau, *Das Zeitalter der Nervosität: Deutschland zwischen Bismarck und Hitler*, Munich 1998, pp. 208–13.
20 For Germany, see Silke Mende, *'Nicht rechts, nicht links, sondern vorn': Eine Geschichte der Gründungsgrünen*, Munich 2011, p. 74.

21 Anna Wöbse, 'Naturschutz global – oder: Hilfe von außen. Internationale Neziehungen des amtlichen Naturschutzes im 20. Jahrhundert', in Hans-Werner Frohn and Friedemann Schmoll, eds., *Natur und Staat: Staatlicher Naturschutz in Deutschland 1906–2006*, Bonn 2006*t*, p. 707.

22 See Hartmut Blick and Horst Obermann, 'Stiefkind Naturschutz: Misere des Naturschutzes in Deutschland', in von Köller, *Umweltpolitik mit Augenmaß*, pp. 107ff.

23 Such is Edda Müller's position in her *Innenwelt der Umweltpolitik* (orig. 1986), 2nd edn, Opladen 1995, although she suspected (in the preface to this second edition) that environmental policy could be asserted against longer-established departments only in periods when interest in 'the environment' was booming.

24 According to the Hegel scholar Ludwig Siep (letter to the author, 13 May 2010), 'The world spirit does repeatedly redefine itself, but always at a higher level within a process of advance and growing consciousness. Can this be said of the environmental movement?' It is indeed to be feared that the analogy with the Hegelian world spirit stops there!

25 Ramachandra Guha, *How Much Should a Person Consume? Environmentalism in India and the United States*, Berkeley 2006, p. 11.

26 Graham Chapman, Keval Kumar et al., *Environmentalism and the Mass Media: The North–South Divide*, London 1997, p. 274.

27 Alois Glück, 'Vorreiter Bayern', in *Die Umweltmacher. 20 Jahre BMU: Geschichte und Zukunft der Umweltpolitik*, Hamburg 2006, p. 115.

28 Michael Bess, *The Light-Green Society: Ecology and Technological Modernity in France, 1960–2000*, Chicago 2003, p. 84.

29 Barbara Ward and René Dubos, *Only One Earth: The Care and Maintenance of a Small Planet*, New York 1983, p. 28.

30 Timothy Flannery, 'The Fate of Empire in Low- and High-Energy Ecosystems', in Tom Griffiths and Libby Robin, eds., *Ecology and Empire: Environmental History of Settler Societies*, Seattle 1997, p. 58.

31 Christopher Rootes, ed., *Environmental Protest in Western Europe*, Oxford 2003, pp. 77, 236, 250f. et al.

32 Wolfgang Rüdig, *Anti-Nuclear Movements: A World Survey of Opposition to Nuclear Energy*, Harlow 1990.

33 Manuel Jiménez, in Rootes, *Environmental Protest*, pp. 177ff.

34 Ibid., p. 174.

35 Michael Flitner, ed., *Der deutsche Tropenwald: Bilder, Mythen, Politik*, Frankfurt 2000.

36 Bernhard Kegel, *Die Ameise als Tramp: Von biologischen Invasionen*, Zurich 1999, p. 299.

37 Wassilij Kliutschewskij, *Geschichte Russlands*, vol. 1, Stuttgart 1925, pp. 57, 59.

38 Douglas R. Weiner, *A Little Corner of Freedom: Russian Nature Protection from Stalin to Gorbachev*, Berkeley 1999, pp. 414ff.

39 Klaus Vollmer, 'Die bemerkenswerte Abwesenheit von Raubtieren. Naturbilder in Japan', *politische ökologie* 99 (March 2006), p. 39.

40 Mitsuo Fujiwara, 'Silviculture in Japan', in Yoshiya Iwai, ed., *Forestry and the Forest Industry in Japan*, Vancouver 2002, pp. 18ff.

41 Takashi Iguchi, 'Depopulation and *Mura-Okoshi* (Village Revival)', in Iwai, *Forestry*, pp. 259–77.

42 Bess, *Light-Green Society*, p. 126.

43 Conrad Totman, *The Green Archipelago: Forestry in Preindustrial Japan*, Berkeley 1989, p. 2.

44 Gregory Clancey, *Earthquake Nation: The Cultural Politics of Japanese Seismicity, 1868–1930*, Berkeley 2006.

45 See Rootes, *Environmental Protest*, pp. ix, 52.

46 David Elliott, 'Supporting Renewables: Feed In Tariffs and Quota/Trading Systems', in Elliott, ed., *Sustainable Energy: Opportunities and Limitations*, Houndmills 2007, pp. 178f.

47 Fritz Vorholz, 'Wüstenstrom, eine Fata Morgana? Weil die Photovoltaik deutlich billiger geworden ist, gerät das vielversprechende Desertec-Projekt in die Bredouille', *Die Zeit*, 26 April 2012, p. 32.

48 Dieter Rucht and Jochen Roose in Rootes, *Environmental Protest*, pp. 81, 108. On the early history of Bavarian environmentalism, see Ute Hasenöhrl, *Zivilgesellschaft und Protest: Eine Geschichte der Naturschutz- und Umweltbewegung in Bayern 1945–1980*, Göttingen 2011.

49 Martin Jänicke, 'Pionierländer im Umweltschutz', in *Die Umweltmacher*, p. 464.

50 Heiner Monheim, 'Zum Eisenbahnland Nr. 1, der Schweiz', and Walter Moser, 'Die Bahnstrategie der Schweiz und der SBB: Mit Systemdenken zum Erfolg', in Heiner Monheim and Klaus Nagorni, eds., *Die Zukunft der Bahn: Zwischen Bürgernähe und Börsengang*, Karlsruhe 2004, pp. 67–82.

51 Kurt Zurfluh, *Steinerne Pfade: 160 Jahre Urner Wirtschaftsgeschichte*, Altdorf 1990, pp. 307ff.

52 Joachim Radkau, *Technik in Deutschland: Vom 18. Jahrhundert bis heute*, Frankfurt 2008, pp. 383ff.

53 Ernst Ulrich von Weizsäcker and Helmut Schreiber, 'Luftreinhaltung: Der schwierige Konsens', in Lothar Gündling and Beate Weber, eds., *Dicke Luft in Europa: Aufgaben und Probleme der europäischen Umweltpolitik*, Heidelberg 1988, p. 168.

54 Kurt Möser, *Geschichte des Autos*, Frankfurt 2002, pp. 276ff.

55 Derek Wall, 'Mobilising Earth First! in Britain', in Christopher Rootes, ed., *Environmental Movements: Local, National and Global*, London 1999, pp. 84ff., and p. x.

56 Christopher Rootes, 'Acting Globally, Thinking Locally? Prospects for a Global Environmental Movement', in Rootes, *Environmental Movements*, p. 291.

57 Michael Kraack et al., *Umweltintegration in der Europäischen Union: Das umweltpolitische Profil der EU im Politikvergleich*, Baden-Baden 2001, pp. 150f.

58 John M. MacKenzie, *Empires of Nature and the Nature of Empires: Imperialism, Scotland and the Environment*, East Linton 1997, esp. pp. 65–85.

59 James Beattie and W. L. Lindsay, 'Scottish Environmentalism and the "Improvement" of 19th-Century New Zealand', in Tony Ballantyne and Judith A. Bennett, eds., *Landscape/Community: Perspectives from New Zealand*, Dunedin 2005, p. 53.

60 Richard Grove, 'Scotland in South Africa: John Crumbie Brown and the Roots of Settler Environmentalism', in Tom Griffiths and Libby Robbin, eds., *Ecology and Empire: Environmental History of Settler Societies*, Edinburgh 1997, pp. 139ff.

61 Brendan Hill et al., 'Popular Resistance and the Emergence of Radical Environmentalism in Scotland', in Bron R. Taylor, ed., *Ecological Resistance Movements*, New York 1995, p. 245; MacKenzie, *Empires of Nature and the Natures of Empires*, pp. 65ff.

62 Reiner Luyken, 'Nur noch dunkler Tann: Londoner Geschäftsleute entdecken die Forstwirtschaft als gewinnträchtige Branche', *Die Zeit*, 31 October 1986, p. 20.

63 Kevin Dunion, *Troublemakers: The Struggle for Environmental Justice in Scotland*, Edinburgh 2003.

64 Cronin and Kennedy, *Riverkeepers*, p. 229.

65 Ibid., p. 20.

66 Kristine Kern, 'Politische Kultur und Umweltpolitik: Amerikanische Erfahrungen und europäische Perspektiven', in *Europas Kulturen und ihr Umgang mit der Natur*, Insel Mainau 1999 (= *Mainauer Gespräche* 14), p. 43.

67 On the thesis of the agrarian historian Avery Craven (1926) that soil exhaustion was the chief factor in the westward expansion, see Joachim Radkau, *Nature and Power*, Cambridge 2008, p. 178.

68 Kern, 'Politische Kultur', pp. 43, 49.

69 See Carolyn Merchant, ed., *Green Versus Gold: Sources in Californian Environmental History*, Washington DC 1998, pp. 429–62. A previous chapter is entitled 'The Rise of Environmental Science', and the structure of the book suggests that science was the main origin of the environmental movement there.

70 Petra Pinzler, 'Besser wohnen: Wie Portland im US-Bundesstaat Oregon in eine grüne Stadt verwandelt wird', *Die Zeit*, 25 August 2011, p. 24.

71 Kevin R. Marsh, '"Save French Pete": Evolution of Wilderness Protests in Oregon', in Michael Egan and Jeff Crane, eds., *Natural Protest: Essays on the History of American Environmentalism*, New York 2009, pp. 223ff.

72 Steven Lewis Yaffee, *The Wisdom of the Spotted Owl: Policy Lessons for a New Century*, Washington DC 1994.

73 Kern, 'Politische Kultur', p. 45.

74 Merchant, *Green Versus Gold*, p. 423.

75 Mike Davis, *Ecology of Fear: Los Angeles and the Imagination of Disaster*, London 1998.

76 According to Joel K. Bourne Jr ('California's Pipe Dream', in *Water*, special issue of *National Geographic* (April 2010), p. 142), a major earthquake could cut off two-thirds of California from the water supply.

77 Sheldon Novick, *The Careless Atom*, New York 1969; Thomas Raymond Wellock, *Critical Masses: Opposition to Nuclear Power in California, 1958–1978*, Madison WI 1998, pp. 17–67.

78 Mario Neukirch, 'Internationale Nutzung der Windkraft zur Stromproduktion', in Hendrik Ehrhardt and Thomas Kroll, eds., *Energie in der modernen Gesellschaft: Zeithistorische Perspektiven*, Göttingen 2012, p. 158.

79 Frank Uekötter, *The Age of Smoke: Environmental Policy in Germany and the United States, 1880–1970*, Pittsburgh 2009, pp, 211, 215.

80 Daniel M. Berman and John T. O'Connor, *Who Owns the Sun? People, Politics, and the Struggle for a Solar Economy*, White River Junction 1996, pp. 197, 191.

81 *Der Spiegel* 41 (2003), p. 118, in the report on California ('Das bedrohte Atlantis', pp. 112–23).

82 Mike Davis, *City of Quartz: Excavating the Future in Los Angeles* (orig. 1990), London 2006, pp. 156ff., 170 ff.

83 Nicholas Targ, 'The States' Comprehensive Approach to Environmental Justice', in David N. Pellow and Robert J. Brulle, eds., *Power, Justice, and the Environment: A Critical Appraisal of the Environmental Justice Movement*, Cambridge MA 2005, pp. 175ff.

84 See, for example, Christopher C. Horner, *The Politically Incorrect Guide to Global Warming and Environmentalism*, Washington DC 2007: 'Consider that communism and anti-Americanism remain vibrant and complementary political forces in those same areas of the world where environmentalists hold their greatest sway: mainly Europe' (p. 7); or 'Europe is harming itself so much that it has decided it needs to harm the U.S., too. Thus, the EU is considering a greenhouse gas *trade war*' (p. 258).

85 Jeremy Rifkin, *The European Dream: How Europe's Vision of the Future Is Quietly Eclipsing the American Dream*, Cambridge 2004, esp. ch. 15, pp. 315–57.

86 Joachim Radkau, *Max Weber* (German edition), Munich 2005, pp. 375ff.

87 G. Knight, *Concorde: The Inside Story*, London 1976, p. 76.

88 In the Federal Republic of Germany, the precautionary principle (*Vorsorgeprinzip*) was already contained in the Environmental Programme of 1970: Hans-Dietrich Genscher in von Köller, *Umweltpolitik mit Augenmaß*, p. 22.

89 See the impressively detailed tableau in Günter Hartkopf and Eberhard Bohne, *Umweltpolitik: Grundlagen, Analysen und Perspektiven*, Opladen 1983, pp. 91ff. For France: Bess, *Light-Green Society*, p. 250.

90 Bess, *Light-Green Society*, p. 197.

91 See Holger Bonus and Ivo Bayer, 'Symbolische Umweltpolitik aus der Sicht der Neuen Institutionenökonomik', in Bernd Hansjürgens and Gertrude Lübbe-Wolff, eds., *Symbolische Umweltpolitik*, Frankfurt 2000, p. 292.

92 See the contributions for and against, in Elmar Altvater and Achim Brunnengräber, eds., *Ablasshandel gegen Klimawandel? Marktbasierte Instrumente in der globalen Klimapolitik und ihre Alternativen: Reader des wissenschaftlichen Beirats von attac*, Hamburg 2008.

93 Erik M. Conway, *High-Speed Dreams*, Baltimore 2005, p. 154.

94 Bruce Bimber, *The Politics of Expertise in Congress: The Rise and Fall of the Office of Technological Assessment*, Albany NY 1996.

95 Timothy Doyle, *Environmental Movements in Majority and Minority Worlds: A Global Perspective*, New Brunswick NJ 2005, pp. viif., 20, 171f.

96 Ibid., p. 162. The origin of the concept – whose two-hundred-year prehistory in German forestry seems to have been unknown to the Brundtland Commission – has retained a curious mystery; not even the memoirs of Gro Harlem Brundtland (*Madam Prime Minister: A Life in Power and Politics*, New York 2002), whose name is closely associated with 'sustainable development', shed any clear light upon it (see esp. pp. 337, 339).

97 Doyle, *Environmental Movements*, p. 68.

98 See the highly pertinent work by the Cameroonian Axelle Kabou, *Et si l'Afrique refusait le développement?*, Paris 1991.

99 See Philip Hirsch's critique of 'third world environmentalism' in Hirsch, ed., *Seeing Forest for Trees: Environment and Environmentalism in Thailand*, Chiang Mai 1996, pp. 4f.

100 Kim Reimann, 'Going Global: The Use of International Politics and Norms in Local Environmental Protest Movements in Japan', in Pradyumna P. Karan and Unryu Suganuma, eds., *Local Environmental Movements: A Comparative Study of the U.S. and Japan*, Lexington KY 2008, pp. 52f.

101 Philip Hirsch and Carol Warren, eds., *The Politics of Environment in Southeast Asia: Resources and Resistance*, London 1998.

102 Joachim Radkau, 'Scharfe Konturen für das Ozonloch: Zur Öko-Ikonographie der *Spiegel*-Titel', in Gerhard Paul, ed., *Das Jahrhundert der Bilder: 1949 bis heute*, Göttingen 2008, pp. 538f.
103 Von Köller, in the dedication to *Umweltpolitik mit Augenmaß*, p. 9.
104 Carolyn Merchant, *The Columbia Guide to American Environmental History*, New York 2002, pp. 185ff.
105 Jackie Smith, 'Global Politics and Transnational Social Movement Strategies: The Transnational Campaign against International Trade in Toxic Wastes', in Donatella della Porta et al., eds., *Social Movements in a Globalising World*, Basingstoke 1999, pp. 170–88.
106 This is referred to in Michael McCloskey, 'Twenty Years of Change in the Environmental Movement: An Insider's View', in Riley E. Dunlap and Angela G. Mertig, eds., *American Environmentalism*, Washington DC 1992, p. 80.
107 Radkau, *Nature and Power*, pp. 86ff.
108 Joachim Radkau, *Mensch und Natur in der Geschichte*, Leipzig 2002, pp. 78ff.
109 Otto Krätz, *Alexander von Humboldt: Wissenschaftler, Weltbürger, Revolutionär*, Munich 2000, pp. 124f.
110 Radkau, *Nature and Power*, p. 161.
111 See Mario Diani and Francesca Forno on the Italian environmental movement (in Rootes, *Environmental Protest*, p. 163): 'In general, environmental activism was driven mainly by urban ecology.'
112 See the illuminating contributions in Susanne Frank and Matthew Gandy, eds., *Hydropolis: Wasser und die Stadt der Moderne*, Frankfurt 2006.
113 Vandana Shiva, *Water Wars: Privatization, Pollution and Profit*, Cambridge MA 2002, p. 97.
114 David Blanchon, *Atlas mondial de l'eau: De l'eau pour tous?*, Paris 2009, p. 65.
115 Frank Sieren, *Angst vor China: Wie die neue Weltmacht die Krise nutzt*, Berlin 2011, pp. 238f. Chinese and Indian reactions may be found on the internet.
116 Petra Dobner, *Wasserpolitik*, Berlin 2010, p. 100.
117 Maude Barlow and Tony Clarke, *Blue Gold: The Fight to Stop the Corporate Theft of the World's Water*, new edn, New York 2005, pp. 154ff.; Hans Huber Abendroth, *Der 'Wasserkrieg' von Cochabamba*, Vienna 2004 (= *Informationen zur Umweltpolitik* 161).
118 Shiva, *Water Wars*, p. 63.
119 Arundhati Roy, *Power Politics: The Reincarnation of Rumpelstiltskin*, Kottayam 2001, p. 32.
120 Sunderlal Bahuguna et al., *India's Environment: Myth and Reality*, Dehra Dun 2007, part A, p. 11.
121 Vandana Shiva, *Staying Alive: Women, Ecology and Survival in India*, New Delhi 1989, p. 188.
122 Arundhati Roy, *Listening to Grasshoppers: Field Notes on Democracy*, New Delhi 2009, p. 6.
123 Edward Goldsmith and Nicholas Hildyard, *The Social and Environmental Effects of Large Dams*, San Francisco 1984, pp. 277ff.
124 A pathbreaking work in this respect was Marc Reisner, *Cadillac Desert: The American West and its Disappearing Water*, New York 1986.
125 Dave Foreman, *Confessions of an Eco-Warrior*, New York 1991, p. 21.
126 Udo E. Simonis, *Globale Umweltpolitik: Ansätze und Perspektiven*, Mannheim 1996, p. 101.
127 Tirunellai N. Seshan, *The Degeneration of India*, New Delhi 1995, pp. 128, 177.

128 This was also true in Germany as early as the beginning of the twentieth century, when artificial lakes were planned for the supply of drinking water and hydropower potential was still an unknown quantity. See David Blackbourn, *The Conquest of Nature: Water, Landscape, and the Making of Modern Germany*, London 2006, ch. 4.

129 See the impressive account in his memoirs: William Willcox, *Sixty Years in the East*, Edinburgh 1935.

130 J. Donald Hughes, *An Environmental History of the World*, London 2001, pp. 162ff.

131 John R. McNeill, 'Sustainable Survival', in Patricia A. McAnany and Norman Yoffee, eds., *Questioning Collapse: Human Resilience, Ecological Vulnerability, and the Aftermath of Empire*, Cambridge 2010, p. 363.

132 Karlernst Ringer, 'Die Landwirtschaft', in Willy Kraus, ed., *Afghanistan: Natur, Geschichte und Kultur*, 2nd edn, Tübingen 1974, p. 323; Heinz Gstrein, 'Die Sozial- und Wirtschaftsordnung des Islam', in Beate Kukertz, ed., *Das grüne Schwert. Weltmacht Islam: Bedrohung oder Erlösung?*, Munich 1992, p. 112.

133 Christian Vogg, *Die Grünen in Ägypten: Die erste Umweltpartei der arabischen Welt*, Münster 1995, pp. 42, 49, 86, 132.

134 Anna-Katharina Wöbse, *Weltnaturschutz*, Frankfurt 2012, p. 321.

135 Hans Walter Flemming (chief executive of the Reichsverband der Deutschen Wasserwirtschaft 1940–5), *Wüsten, Deiche und Turbinen: Das große Buch von Wasser und Völkerschicksal*, Göttingen 1957, pp. 46f.

136 John R. McNeill, *Something New Under the Sun: An Environmental History of the Twentieth-Century World*, New York 2000, p. 161.

137 Roy, *Power Politics*, p. 36.

138 McNeill, *Something New*, p. 161.

139 Shiva, *Water Wars*, pp. 63ff.; the movement was encouraged by successful resistance to two earlier projects: the Silent Valley and Boghdat dams.

140 Ranjit Dwivedi, *People's Movements in Environmental Politics: A Critical Analysis of the Narmada Bachao Andolan in India*, Working Paper No. 242 of the Institute of Social Studies, The Hague 1997, p. 6.

141 Ira Stubbe-Diarra, 'Die Bedeutung des Wassers in den Religionen Asiens', in Thomas Hoffmann, ed., *Wasser in Asien: Elementare Konflikte*, Osnabrück 1997, p. 88.

142 Chapman et al., *Environmentalism and the Mass Media*, p. 77.

143 John R. Wood, *The Politics of Water Resource Development in India: The Narmada Dams Controversy*, Los Angeles 2007, pp. 118, 236; Diane Raines Ward, *Water Wars: Drought, Flood, Folly, and the Politics of Thirst*, New York 2002, p. 212.

144 Shiva, *Water Wars*, pp. 60f.

145 Wood, *Politics of Water Resource Development in India*, p. 142.

146 Lori Udall, 'The World Bank and Public Accountability: Has Anything Changed?', in Jonathan A. Fox and L. David Brown, eds., *The Struggle for Accountability: The World Bank, NGOs and Grassroots Movements*, Cambridge MA 1998, pp. 394ff.

147 Bruce Rich, *Mortgaging the Earth: The World Bank, Environmental Impoverishment and the Crisis of Development*, Boston 1994, pp. 250ff.

148 Sebastian Mallaby, *The World's Banker: A Story of Failed States, Financial Crises, and the Wealth and Poverty of Nations*, London 2004, pp. 58f.

149 Shiva, *Water Wars*, p. 67.
150 Bruni Weißen, "'... aber am Ende werden wir gewinnen": Der Widerstand gegen den Narmada-Staudamm in Indien', in Hoffmann, *Wasser in Asien*, p. 425.
151 Dai Qing, *Yangtze! Yangtze!*, London 1994.
152 *Der Spiegel* 46 (1997), p. 218; *Neue Westfälische*, 13 October 2007.
153 Dai Qing, *Yangtze!*, pp. 66 ff., 135.
154 Ibid., pp. 163f.; Judith Shapiro, *Mao's War Against Nature: Politics and the Environment in Revolutionary China*, Cambridge 2001, pp. 51ff.
155 See the interview with Dai Qing in *Der Spiegel* 25 (2001), pp. 142f.
156 Sieren, *Angst vor China*, p. 237.
157 *Der Spiegel* 48 (2007), p. 169.
158 See part one ('Large Dams, Community and Nation') of Hirsch and Warren, *Politics of Environment in Southeast Asia*, pp. 29–89, and part six ('Wasser als Waffe: Politische Konflikte um Wasser') of Hoffmann, *Wasser in Asien*, pp. 225–61.
159 Philip Hirsch and Carol Warren in the introduction to Hirsch and Warren, *Politics of Environment in Southeast Asia*, pp. 14f.
160 George J. Aditjondro, 'Large Dam Victims and their Defenders. The Emergence of an Anti-Dam Movement in Indonesia', in Hirsch and Warren, *Politics of Environment in Southeast Asia*, pp. 49f.
161 Rich, *Mortgaging the Earth*, pp. 35–8; McNeill, *Something New*, pp. 279ff.
162 Aditjondro, 'Large Dam Victims', pp. 44f.
163 On the significance of Rasputin, see Vera Meyer, 'Idyll, Ware, Ökosystem: Der Wald in der russischen Literatur', *Osteuropa* 4-5 (2008), p. 105. An impressive film was later made of *Farewell to Matyora*, his main literary work.
164 Weiner, *Little Corner of Freedom*, p. 423.
165 Udall, 'World Bank', p. 396.
166 Klaus Taschwer and Benedikt Föger, *Konrad Lorenz*, Vienna 2003, pp. 256ff.
167 Otto Koenig, *Naturschutz an der Wende*, Vienna 1990, pp. 25f.
168 Ibid., pp. 34f., 38, 28.
169 Ibid., pp. 107ff.
170 Robert Jungk, 'Weltweiter Widerstand: Umrisse einer informellen Internationale', in Lutz Mez, ed., *Der Atomkonflikt: Berichte zur internationalen Atomindustrie, Atompolitik und Anti-Atombewegung*, Berlin 1979, pp. 8ff.
171 Joachim Radkau, 'Eine kurze Geschichte der Antiatomkraftbewegung', *Aus Politik und Zeitgeschichte* 61/46-47 (2011), pp. 7–15.
172 Wolf Häfele, *Hypotheticality and the New Challenges: The Pathfinder Role of Nuclear Energy* (IIASA Research Report 73-14), Laxenburg 1973.
173 Wolfgang Rüdig, *Anti-Nuclear Movements: A World Survey of Opposition to Nuclear Energy*, Harlow 1990; Dieter Rucht, 'The Impact of Anti-Nuclear Power Movements in International Comparison', in Martin Bauer, ed., *Resistance to New Technology: Nuclear Power, Information Technology and Biotechnology*, Cambridge 1995, pp. 277–91; Dieter Rucht and Jochen Roose, 'Germany', in Rootes, *Environmental Protest*, p. 104.
174 Joachim Radkau, *Aufstieg und Krise der deutschen Atomwirtschaft 1945–1975: Verdrängte Alternativen in der Kerntechnik und der Ursprung der nuklearen Kontroverse*, Reinbek 1983, pp. 371f.
175 This is one reason why I divided the history of the nuclear industry between a 'speculative phase' and the era of 'creating fait accompli', not (as was usual in

the specialist literature until then) in accordance with the four German nuclear programmes: see ibid., parts II and III.

176 Ibid., pp. 446 ff.
177 Bess, *Light-Green Society*, p. 89; Gerhard Kiersch and Sabine von Oppeln, *Kernenergiekonflikt in Frankreich und Deutschland*, Berlin 1983, p. 53.
178 Joachim Radkau, 'Die Kernkraft-Kontroverse im Spiegel der Literatur: Phasen und Dimensionen einer neuen Aufklärung', in Armin Hermann and Rolf Schumacher, eds., *Das Ende des Atomzeitalters? Eine sachlich-kritische Dokumentation*, Munich 1987, p. 318.
179 See Christian Deubner and Wolfgang Hertle, 'Frankreich: Vive l'atome?', in Lutz Mez, ed., *Der Atomkonflikt: Atomindustrie, Atompolitik und Anti-Atom-Bewegung im internationalen Vergleich*, Berlin 1979, pp. 130–46; Bess, *Light-Green Society*, pp. 13 ff.
180 On this and what follows, see Kiersch and von Oppeln, *Kernenergiekonflikt*; and Joachim Radkau, 'Die Nukleartechnologie als Spaltstoff zwischen Frankreich und der Bundesrepublik', in Yves Cohen and Klaus Manfrass, eds., *Frankreich und Deutschland: Forschung, Technologie und industrielle Entwicklung im 19. und 20. Jahrhundert*, Munich 1990, pp. 302–18.
181 Bess, *Light-Green Society*, pp. 93f.
182 Ibid., 94f.
183 Radkau, *Aufstieg und Krise*, p. 173.
184 Günter Zint, *Gegen den Atomstaat: 300 Fotodokumente von Günter Zint*, Frankfurt 1979, p. 116.
185 Arthur R. Tamplin and John W. Gofman, *'Population Control' through Nuclear Pollution*, Chicago 1970, pp. 68ff.
186 See the pathbreaking study based on internal documents: David Okrent, *Nuclear Reactor Safety: On the History of the Regulatory Process*, Madison WI 1981, pp. 167ff. and passim!
187 Stephanie Cooke, *In Mortal Hands: A Cautionary History of the Nuclear Age*, New York 2009, pp. 367ff.
188 Fundamental for the turn in American nuclear policy under Carter is the Ford Foundation report: *Nuclear Power: Choice and Issues*, Cambridge MA 1977.
189 The records of the Hanover hearings are probably the most extensive and intellectually stimulating document of the whole German conflict over nuclear power: see Deutsches Atomforum, ed., *Rede – Gegenrede: Symposium der Niedersächsischen Landesregierung zur grundsätzlichen sicherheitstechnischen Realisierung eines integrierten nuklearen Entsorgungszentrums*, Hanover 1979.
190 See Anselm Tiggemann, *Die 'Achillesferse' der Kernenergie in der Bundesrepublik Deutschland: Zur Kernenergiekontroverse und der Geschichte der nuklearen Entsorgung von den Anfängen bis Gorleben, 1955 bis 1985*, Lauf 2004.
191 Joachim Radkau, 'Das überschätzte System: Zur Geschichte der Strategie- und Kreislauf-Konstrukte in der Kerntechnik', *Technikgeschichte* 56 (1988), pp. 207–15.
192 David E. Lilienthal, *Change, Hope, and the Bomb*, Princeton 1963.
193 From a pro-nuclear position: Alvin Weinberg, *The First Nuclear Era*, New York 1994, pp. 178, 197.
194 Tamplin and Gofman, *'Population Control' through Nuclear Pollution*, pp. 144, 27 and passim.
195 Radkau, *Aufstieg und Krise*, pp. 96ff.

196 Ilona Stölken-Fitschen, *Atombombe und Geistesgeschichte: Eine Studie der fünfziger Jahre aus deutscher Sicht*, Baden-Baden 1995, pp. 92ff.
197 Monika Sperr, *Petra Kelly*, Munich 1983, pp. 119ff.
198 Robert Jay Lifton, *Death in Life: The Survivors of Hiroshima*, New York 1967; Elke Tashiro and Jannes K. Tashiro, *Hiroshima: Menschen nach dem Atomkrieg*, Munich 1982.
199 Just a year after the bombings, one sometimes finds an optimistic feeling, expressed through tears, that nature is blossoming again, as if nothing has happened: see Lifton, *Death in Life*, pp. 101ff.
200 Hans-Jürgen Mayer, 'Umweltpolitik auf internationaler Ebene: Anpassungsdruck als "Motor des Fortschritts"', in Mayer and Manfred Pohl, eds., *Länderbericht Japan*, Bonn 1998, p. 182.
201 Nathalie Cavasin, 'Citizen Activism and the Nuclear Industry in Japan: After the Tokai Village Disaster', in Karan and Suganuma, *Local Environmental Movements*, pp. 65–73.
202 Ibid., p. 68.
203 Hsin-Huang Michael Hsiao et al., 'The Making of Anti-Nuclear Movements in East Asia: State–Movements Relationships and Policy Outcomes', in Yok-shiu F. Lee and Alvin Y. So, eds., *Asia's Environmental Movements: Comparative Perspectives*, Armonk NY 1999, pp. 262f.
204 Joachim Radkau, 'Angst und Angstabwehr als Regulative der Technikgeschichte: Gedanken zu einer Heuristik der Furcht', in Max Kerner, ed., *Technik und Angst: Zur Zukunft der industriellen Zivilisation*, 2nd edn, Aachen 1997, pp. 91–119.
205 Friedrich Münzinger, *Atomkraft*, 3rd edn, Berlin 1960, pp. 178, 242, 236.
206 Solange Fernex: '"Elsaß-Lothringen werden sie nicht kriegen!"', in Claus Leggewie and Roland de Miller, eds., *Der Wahlfisch* [sic!]: *Ökologie-Bewegungen in Frankreich*, Berlin 1978, pp. 113ff.; on Waechter see Bess, *Light-Green Society*, pp. 107, 121.
207 Radkau, *Aufstieg und Krise*, pp. 92ff.
208 Ibid., p. 21. On the background, see Joachim Radkau, 'Das RWE zwischen Braunkohle und Atomeuphorie 1945–1968', in Dieter Schweer and Wolf Thieme, eds., *'Der gläserne Riese': RWE – Ein Konzern wird transparent*, Essen 1998, pp. 188ff.
209 Günther Schwab, *Morgen holt dich der Teufel: Neues, Verschwiegenes und Verbotenes von der 'friedlichen' Atomkernspaltung*, Salzburg 1968.
210 See the long interview with Nina Gladitz in *Rote Fahne*, 12 January 1977, and the book about the film: Nina Gladitz, *Lieber aktiv als radioaktiv: Wyhler Bauern erzählen*, Berlin 1976.
211 See Susan Boos, *Strahlende Schweiz: Handbuch zur Atomwirtschaft*, Zurich 1999, esp. pp. 79ff.
212 On Sweden and other countries: Dieter Rucht, 'The Impact of Anti-Nuclear Power Movements in International Comparison', in Bauer, *Resistance to New Technology*, pp. 181ff.
213 Martin Rhodes, 'Italy: Greens in an Overcrowded Political System', in Dick Richardson and Chris Rootes, eds., *The Green Challenge: The Development of Green Parties in Europe*, London 1995, p. 171; Radkau, *Aufstieg und Krise*, p. 24.
214 Morris Low, Shigeru Nakayama and Hitoshi Yoshioka, *Science, Technology and Society in Contemporary Japan*, Cambridge 1999, pp. 66–81.

215 Christian von Hirschhausen, 'Nur eine Handvoll Experten weiß, ob im Stromnetz ohne Kernkraft tatsächlich Ausfälle drohen', *Die Zeit*, 26 May 2011.

216 Daniel Boese, *Wir sind jung und brauchen die Welt: Wie die Generation Facebook den Planeten rettet*, Munich 2011; Sascha Adamek, *Die facebook-Falle: Wie das soziale Netzwerk unser Leben verkauft*, Munich 2011.

217 Commoner, *Closing Circle*, pp. 33ff.

218 See Hermand, *Grüne Utopien*, p. 137.

219 The symposium at the Centre for Interdisciplinary Research – which I attended – was part of the 'climate communication' project led by Peter Weingart: see Peter Weingart, Anita Engels and Petra Pansegrau, *Von der Hypothese zur Katastrophe: Der anthropogene Klimawandel im Diskurs zwischen Wissenschaft, Politik und Massenmedien*, 2nd edn, Opladen 2008.

220 Alois Glück in von Köller, *Umweltpolitik mit Augenmaß*, p. 102.

221 Max Nicholson, *The Environmental Revolution: A Guide for the New Masters of the World*, London 1970, p. 223.

222 Wöbse, 'Naturschutz global', p. 710.

223 Rootes, *Environmental Movements*, p. 300.

224 Bernhard Knappe, *Das Geheimnis von Greenpeace: Die andere Seite der Erfolgsstory*, Vienna 1993, p. 30.

225 Paul Watson, *Ocean Warrior: My Battle to End the Illegal Slaughter on the High Seas*, London 2003, pp. 23f.

226 Radkau, 'Scharfe Konturen', pp. 532–41.

227 Matt Cartmill, *A View to a Death in the Morning: Hunting and Nature through History*, New Haven 1996, pp. 161ff. ('The Bambi Syndrome').

228 Richard Ellis, *Men and Whales*, New York 1991, p. 443; Bess, *Light-Green Society*, pp. 72ff.: Cousteau 'ultimately became something of a pariah among French greens, and his achievements are completely ignored in virtually all the French environmentalist literature'.

229 McCloskey, 'Twenty Years of Change', pp. 82f.

230 Benjamin Kline, *First Along the River: A Brief History of the U.S. Environmental Movement*, Lanham MD 2007, p. 141. There too, however, it is unclear whether the internet brought a new quality to the movement: 'Although the Web has become a dominant site of the debate, the environmental movement has not lost its propensity to take direct action' (p. 142). Christopher Rootes, who has embarked on a Transformation of Environmental Activism (TEA) research project, remarks that in a number of countries, contrary to expectations, the most notable change in mid-nineties environmentalism went in the direction of a new radicalism more or less independent of the established NGOs (*Environmental Protest*, p. ix).

231 Anselm Doering-Manteuffel and Lutz Raphael, *Nach dem Boom: Perspektiven auf die Zeitgeschichte seit 1970*, 2nd edn, Göttingen 2010, pp. 98ff.

232 Reinhard Böhm, *Heiße Luft nach Kopenhagen*, 2nd edn, Vienna 2010, p. 249.

233 Jonathan A. Fox and L. David Brown, in the introduction to Fox and Brown, *Struggle for Accountability*, p. 30.

234 Daniel Yergin, *The Quest: Energy, Security and the Remaking of the Modern World*, New York 2011, p. 471; Naomi Oreskes and Erik M. Conway, *Merchants of Doubt: How a Handful of Scientists Obscured the Truth on Issues from Tobacco Smoke to Global Warming*, New York 2010, pp. 77ff.

235 Mark Landy et al., *The Environmental Protection Agency. Asking the Wrong Questions: From Nixon to Clinton*, New York 1994, pp. 254f.
236 Rudi Holzberger, *Das sogenannte Waldsterben. Zur Karriere eines Klischees: Das Thema Wald im journalistischen Diskurs*, Bergatreute 1995.
237 Ibid., pp. 70f.
238 Horst Stern et al., *Rettet den Wald*, Munich 1979.
239 Jens Ivo Engels, *Naturpolitik in der Bundesrepublik: Ideenwelt und politische Verhaltensstile in Naturschutz und Umweltbewegung 1950–1980*, Paderborn 2006, pp. 254f.
240 Edda Müller refers to this aspect in 'Die Beziehung von Umwelt- und Naturschutz in den 1970er Jahren', in Stiftung Naturschutzgeschichte, ed., *Natur im Sinn: Zeitzeugen im Naturschutz*, Essen 2001, p. 39.
241 Müller, *Innenwelt der Umweltpolitik*, p. 224.
242 Holzberger (*Das sogenannte Waldsterben*, p. 149) argues that 'environmental protectionists' were drawn upon only sporadically in the alarmist reports.
243 Ibid., p. 9.
244 Guntolf Herzberg and Kurt Seifert, *Rudolf Bahro*, Berlin 2002, p. 413.
245 Kenneth Anders and Frank Uekötter, 'Viel Lärm ums stille Sterben: Die Debatte über das Waldsterben in Deutschland', in Frank Uekötter and Jens Hohensee, eds., *Wird Kassandra heiser? Die Geschichte falscher Ökoalarme*, Wiesbaden 2004, p. 122. Anders and Uekötter too do not regard the 'dying forest' warnings as nothing but a 'false alarm'!
246 Miranda A. Schreurs, *Environmental Politics in Japan, Germany and the United States*, Cambridge 2002, pp. 107ff.
247 Radkau, 'Das RWE zwischen Kernenergie und Diversifizierung', in Schweer and Thieme, *'Der gläserne Riese'*, p. 240.
248 Cf. Anders and Uekötter, 'Viel Lärm', p. 121.
249 Heinrich Spiecker et al., eds., *Growth Trends in European Forests*, Berlin 1996; see *Der Spiegel* 46 (1996), pp. 256ff.
250 Holzberger, *Das sogenannte Waldsterben*, p. 99.
251 See Bernhard Ulrich's account of the centuries-long history of the forest: 'Die historische Entwicklung des Beziehungsgefüges Wald – Mensch – Umwelt', in Bernd Herrmann and Angela Budde, eds., *Natur und Geschichte: Naturwissenschaftliche und historische Beiträge zu einer ökologischen Grundbildung*, Hanover 1989, p. 103.
252 Despite the 'false alarm' in the title of the book in which their article appeared, Kenneth Anders and Frank Uekötter finally conclude ('Viel Lärm', p. 137): 'In fact, the debate on the death of the forest offers exemplary confirmation of the vitality of the precautionary principle in West German environmentalism.' Their only point is that its foresight presented itself not as a precaution against future eventualities but as the prevention of imminent catastrophe!
253 Duncan Poore, *Changing Landscapes: The Development of the International Tropical Timber Organization and its Influence on Tropical Forest Management*, London 2003, pp. 39ff.
254 Reiner Scholz, *Betrifft. Robin Wood: sanfte Rebellen gegen Naturzerstörungobin*, Munich 1989, p. 98.
255 Ibid., pp. 99ff.; Wall, 'Mobilising Earth First! in Britain', pp. 83, 86.
256 Willem L. Oltmans, ed., *Die Grenzen des Wachstums: Pro und Contra*, Reinbek 1974, p. 93.

257 Beate von Devivere, *Das letzte Paradies: Die Zerstörung der tropischen Regenwälder und deren Ureinwohner*, Frankfurt 1984, p. 149.

258 Susanna Hecht and Alexander Cockburn, *The Fate of the Forest: Developers, Destroyers and Defenders of the Amazon*, London 1990, p. 237.

259 *Der Spiegel* 6 (2003), p. 150; *GEO*, 4 April 2010.

260 *Der Spiegel* 12 (2001), p. 256.

261 Jochen Schilk, 'Staub zu Erde: Terra Preta erobert die Welt', *oya*, January/February 2012, pp. 38–40; Christiane Grefe, '"Wundererde" im Test: Terra Preta, ein fruchtbarer Humus der Indios, wird als vielseitiger Retter zerstörter Böden gepriesen', *Die Zeit*, 1 December 2011, p. 42.

262 This also applies to historical study of the environment: see J. Baird Callicott and Michael P. Nelson, eds., *The Great New Wilderness Debate*, Athens GA 1998.

263 Herbert Hesmer, *Der kombinierte land- und forstwirtschaftliche Anbau*, 2 vols., Stuttgart 1966/70 (= *Wiss. Schriftenreihe des Bundesministeriums für wirtschaft. Zusammenarbeit* 8 and 17); Olaf Christen, 'Wenn Wald und Feld eine Einheit bilden: Agroforstwirtschaft weltweit häufiger genutzt', *Frankfurter Allgemeine Zeitung*, 17 December 1997.

264 See Christian Küchli, *Wälder der Hoffnung*, Zurich 1997; Asia-Pacific Forestry Commission, ed., *In Search of Excellence: Exemplary Forest Management in Asia and the Pacific*, Bangkok 2005.

265 Jeremy Rifkin, *Beyond Beef: The Rise and Fall of the Cattle Culture*, New York 1992; a German translation appeared in 1994, with an introduction by Ernst Ulrich von Weizsäcker, the director of the Wuppertal-Institut für Klima, Umwelt und Energie.

266 Here and on the following see Joachim Radkau, 'Hiroshima und Asilomar: Die Inszenierung des Diskurses über die Gentechnik vor dem Hintergrund der Kernenergie-Kontroverse', *Geschichte und Gesellschaft* 14 (1988), pp. 329–63; Radkau, 'Learning from Chernobyl for the Fight against Genetics? Stages and Stimuli of German Protest Movements – A Comparative Synopsis', in Bauer, *Resistance to New Technology*, pp. 335–55.

267 Jost Herbig, *Die Gen-Ingenieure: Durch Revolutionierung der Natur zum Neuen Menschen?*, Munich 1978, p. 107; cf. James D. Watson and John Tooze, *The DNA Story: A Documentary History of Gene Cloning*, San Francisco 1981.

268 Sheldon Krimsky, *Genetic Alchemy: The Social History of the Recombinant DNA Controversy*, Cambridge MA 1982, esp. pp. 312ff.

269 This is the thesis in Luitgard Marschall, *Im Schatten der chemischen Synthese: Industrielle Biotechnologie in Deutschland (1900–1970)*, Frankfurt 2000.

270 Steven Rose, 'Gentechnologie und biologische Waffen', in Regine Kollek et al., eds., *Die ungeklärten Gefahrenpotentiale der Gentechnologie*, Munich 1986, pp. 9f.

271 Deutscher Bundestag, *10. Wahlperiode, Protokolle der Enquete-Kommission 'Chancen und Risiken der Gentechnologie'*, 26/245 (4 February 1986).

272 *Der Spiegel*, 27 March 1978, pp. 212f.

273 This position is argued in Hans-Jochen Luhmann, 'Die Entdeckung der Gefahr einer ubiquitären Dioxin-Verbreitung: Ein Beispiel einer latent schleichenden Katastrophe', in Günter Altner, ed., *Jahrbuch Ökologie 1993*, Munich 1992, p. 225.

274 Armin Radünz and Andreas Borgmann, 'Chemiepolitik für Chlorkohlen-wasserstoffe', in Henning Friege and Frank Claus, eds., *Chemie für wen? Chemiepolitik statt Chemieskandale*, Reinbek 1988, p. 149.

275 Al Gore, *Earth in the Balance: Ecology and the Human Spirit*, Boston 1992, p. 141.

276 Engelbert Schramm, 'Denken in Entwicklungslinien und Verzweigungen: Die AlkalichloridElektrolyse und ihre Genese als Fallbeispiel', in M. Held, ed., *Leitbilder der Chemiepolitik: Stoffökologische Perspektiven der Industriegesellschaften*, Frankfurt and New York, pp. 42–54; here p. 54.

277 Paul Weindling, 'Asbestose als Ergebnis institutioneller Entschädigung und Steuerung', in Dietrich Milles, ed., *Gesundheitsrisiken, Industriegesellschaft und soziale Sicherungen in der Geschichte*, Bremerhaven 1993, pp. 352f.; and, more generally, Jean Pütz, ed., *Asbest-Report: Vom Wunderstoff zur Altlast*, Cologne 1989; Deutsches Hygiene-Museum, ed., *Feuerfest. Asbest: Zur Geschichte eines Umweltproblems* (accompanying the exhibition), Dresden 1991.

278 Gene D. Robinson in Shepard Krech III, John R. McNeill and Carolyn Merchant, eds., *Encyclopedia of World Environmental History*, New York 2004, vol. 1, p. 69.

279 Allan Abramson to the author, 7 February 2010. Of the eco-revisionists, Aaron Wildavsky (*But Is It True?*, Cambridge MA 1995, pp. 185ff.) allocates a whole chapter to the asbestos alarm: Darren Schulte, 'Is Asbestos in Schoolrooms Hazardous to Students' Health?' Landy et. al., however (*Environmental Protection Agency*), do not present it as one of the EPA's false priorities; it was not quite altogether unfounded!

280 Steve Schwarze, 'The Silences and Possibilities of Asbestos Activism: Stories from Libby and Beyond', in Ronald Sandler and Phaedra C. Pezzulo, eds., *Environmental Justice and Environmentalism: The Social Justice Challenge to the Environmental Movement*, Cambridge MA 2007, pp. 165–87.

281 Müller, *Innenleben der Umweltpolitik*, p. 135. In a letter to the author (21 October 1993), Joschka Fischer says that – despite having been lured with exquisite wines at a Hoechst guesthouse when he was environment minister in the State of Hessen – he learned from the 'trench warfare over the chemicals law' that the chemical lobby was 'much worse even than the nuclear lobby'.

282 Müller, 'Die Beziehung von Umwelt- und Naturschutz in den 1970er Jahren', p. 39.

283 Egmont R. Koch and Fritz Vahrenholt, *Seveso ist überall: Die tödlichen Risiken der Chemie*, with a preface by Erhard Eppler, Cologne 1978.

284 Joachim Radkau, 'Umweltfragen in der Bielefelder Industriegeschichte', in Florian Böllhoff et al., eds., *Industriearchitektur in Bielefeld*, Bielefeld 1986, p. 87.

285 In *Die Umweltmacher*, p. 52.

286 Volker Hauff, 'Reformfähigkeit durch Lernbereitschaft und Dialog', in Karlheinz Bentele et al., eds., *Die Reformfähigkeit von Industriegesellschaften*, Frankfurt 1995, p. 228.

287 Manfred Kriener, 'Die Kraft aus der Luft: Windenergie galt lange als grüne, typisch deutsche Spinnerei – dabei hat sie eine bewegte internationale Geschichte', *Die Zeit*, 2 February 2012, p. 18.

288 In Hansjürgens and Lübbe-Wolff, *Symbolische Umweltpolitik*, p. 56.

289 Frank Hoffmann and Theo Romland, *Die Recycling-Lüge*, Stuttgart 1993.

290 Fritz Vahrenholt, 'Der Ökochonder als Leitbild', *Der Spiegel* 3 (1996), p. 51.

291 With a critical view of the history of the 'cycle' ideal: Engelbert Schramm, *Im Namen des Kreislaufs: Ideengeschichte der Modelle vom ökologischen Kreislauf*, Frankfurt 1997.

292 Karl Otto Henseling to the author, 5 July 2010.
293 Ibid., based on long years of experience in the UBA.
294 Scholz, *Robin Wood*, p. 34.

Chapter Four   Charismatics and Ecocrats

1 Clive Ponting, *A Green History of the World*, London 1991, pp. 1ff. ('The Lessons of Easter Island'); Jared Diamond, *Collapse: How Societies Choose to Fail or Succeed* (orig. 2005), London 2011, pp. 79ff. ('Twilight at Easter').

2 Terry L. Hunt and Carl P. Lipo, 'Ecological Catastrophe, Collapse, and the Myth of "Ecocide" on Rapa Nui (Easter Island)', in Patricia A. McAnany and Norman Yoffee, eds., *Questioning Collapse: Human Resilience, Ecological Vulnerability, and the Aftermath of Empire*, New York 2010, pp. 21–44.

3 Michael Egan, *Barry Commoner and the Science of Survival: The Remaking of American Environmentalism*, Cambridge MA 2007, p. 79.

4 Ibid., p. 104.

5 This is the key point in Kai F. Hünemörder, 'Kassandra im modernen Gewand: Die umweltapokalyptischen Mahnrufe der frühen 1970er Jahre', in Frank Uekötter and Jens Hohensee, eds., *Wird Kassandra heiser? Die Geschichte falscher Ökoalarme*, Wiesbaden 2004, pp. 78–97.

6 On the general problem of reconstructing the history of feelings, see Peter N. Stearns, *American Cool: Constructing a 20th-Century Emotional Style*, New York 1994.

7 Marianne Weber, *Max Weber: Ein Lebensbild* (orig. 1926), Munich 1989, p. 605.

8 Joachim Radkau, *Max Weber* (German edition), Munich 2005, p. 697.

9 Herbert Gruhl, *Überleben ist alles: Erinnerungen*, Frankfurt 1990, p. 217.

10 'Spiritual' is more apposite than 'religious', because 'religion' contains the 'tie' to authorities, whereas 'spirituality' emphasizes individual illumination as a direct link to revelation.

11 Joachim Radkau, 'Scharfe Konturen für das Ozonloch: Zur Öko-Ikonographie der *Spiegel*-Titel', in Gerhard Paul, ed., *Das Jahrhundert der Bilder: 1949 bis heute*, vol. 1, Göttingen 2008, p. 538.

12 This becomes clear only towards the end: Hans Jonas, *The Imperative of Responsibility: In Search of an Ethic for the Technological Age*, Chicago 1984, pp. 201ff.

13 This is the shortcoming of the overly sardonic but otherwise informative article by J. Baird Callicott, 'That Good Old-Time Wilderness Religion', in Callicott and Michael P. Nelson, eds., *The Great New Wilderness Debate*, Athens GA 1998, pp. 387–94, as it is of other contributions to this 700-page volume.

14 Lynn White, Jr, 'The Historical Roots of Our Ecological Crisis', in David Spring and Eileen Spring, eds., *Ecology and Religion in History*, New York 1974, p. 28.

15 Arnold Toynbee, 'The Religious Background of the Present Environmental Crisis', in Spring and Spring, *Ecology and Religion in History*, pp. 137–49.

16 René Dubos, 'Franciscan Conservation versus Benedictine Stewardship', in Spring and Spring, *Ecology and Religion in History*, pp. 114–36.

17 Yi-fu Tuan, 'Discrepancies between Environmental Attitude and Behavior: Examples from Europe and China', in Spring and Spring, *Ecology and Religion in History*, pp. 91–113.

18 Roderick Frazier Nash, *Wilderness and the American Mind*, 4th edn, New Haven 2001, pp. 35ff.

19 Arne Naess, 'Self-Realization: An Ecological Approach to Being in the World', in John Seed et al., *Thinking Like a Mountain: Towards a Council of All Beings*, Philadelphia 1998, pp. 19–31.

20 Hubert Weinzierl, 'Naturschutz ist Menschenschutz', in Karl Stankiewitz, *Babylon in Bayern*, Regensburg 2004, p. 134.

21 Stephen Fox, *John Muir and his Legacy: The American Conservation Movement*, Boston 1981, p. 107.

22 David Brower, *For Earth's Sake: The Life and Times of David Brower*, Salt Lake City 1990, p. 261.

23 Frank Uekötter, *The Green and the Brown: A History of Conservation in Nazi Germany*, New York 2006, p. 142.

24 Almut Leh, *Zwischen Heimatschutz und Umweltbewegung: Die Professionalisierung des Naturschutzes in Nordrhein-Westfalen 1945–1975*, Frankfurt 2006, pp. 152, 157.

25 Wilhelm Lienenkämper, *Grüne Welt zu treuen Händen: Naturschutz und Landschaftspflege im Industriezeitalter*, Stuttgart 1963, p. 62.

26 Uekötter, *Green and the Brown*, pp. 1f.

27 Lienenkämper, *Grüne Welt*, pp. 17f.

28 Theodore Roosevelt, *An Autobiography* (orig. 1913), Whitefish MT 2004, p. 247.

29 Georg Wilhelm Friedrich Hegel, *Phenomenology of Spirit*, trans. A. V. Miller, Oxford 1977, p. 420 ('Plant and Animal').

30 Farley Mowat, *Woman in the Mists*, New York 1987, p. 336.

31 Mark Dowie, *Conservation Refugees*, Cambridge MA 2009, pp. 66ff.

32 Jonathan S. Adams and Thomas O. McShane, *The Myth of Wild Africa: Conservation Without Illusion*, Berkeley 1992, p. 194.

33 Mowat, *Woman in the Mists*, p. 336.

34 Adams and McShane, *Myth of Wild Africa*, p. 192.

35 Harold Hayes, *The Dark Romance of Dian Fossey*, London 1992, pp. 348f.

36 Adams and McShane, *Myth of Wild Africa*, pp. 185f.

37 Jane Goodall and Phillip Berman, *Reason for Hope: A Spiritual Journey*, New York 2000, pp. 112f.

38 Joachim Radkau, 'Die Heldenekstase der betrunkenen Elefanten: Das Natursubstrat bei Max Weber', *Leviathan* 4 (2006), pp. 556ff.

39 Henry Makowski, *Nationalparke in Deutschland*, Neumünster 1997, p. 36.

40 Wolfgang Haber, 'Naturschutz in der Kulturlandschaft: Ein Widerspruch in sich?', *Laufener Spezialbeiträge* 1 (2008), p. 22.

41 Dave Foreman, *Confessions of an Eco-Warrior*, New York 1991, pp. 3, 105, 116, 174, 175; and cf. 19, 51, 73, 90.

42 Ibid., p. 39.

43 See Joachim Radkau, *Aufstieg und Krise der deutschen Atomwirtschaft 1945–1975: Verdrängte Alternativen in der Kerntechnik und der Ursprung der nukleären Kontroverse*, Reinbek 1983, pp. 34–45.

44 According to information given to me in 1979 by Elisabeth Heisenberg, the widow of Werner Heisenberg and sister of Fritz Schumacher.

45 On this and what follows, see Barbara Wood, *Alias Papa: A Life of Fritz Schumacher*, London 1984.
46 Edward Conze, *Buddhism: A Short History*, Oxford 2000, p. 92.
47 Wood, *Alias Papa*, pp. 320f.
48 E. F. Schumacher, *Small is Beautiful: A Study of Economics as if People Mattered*, London 1973.
49 Wood, *Alias Papa*, p. 352.
50 Ibid., p. 342.
51 Michael Schuering, 'The Devil in Brokdorf: The West German Protestant Churches and the Protest against Nuclear Energy', paper for the World Conference for Environmental History in Copenhagen, August 2009.
52 See Roger S. Gottlieb, *A Greener Faith: Religious Environmentalism and Our Planet's Future*, Oxford 2006, p. 223.
53 Bernhard Knappe, *Das Geheimnis von Greenpeace: Die andere Seite der Erfolgsstory*, Vienna 1993, pp. 16f.
54 Greenpeace leader Thilo Bode refers to this in Greenpeace, ed., *Das Greenpeace Buch: Reflexionen und Aktionen*, Munich 1996, p. 255.
55 *Der Spiegel*, 14 November 1983, p. 64 (Hubert Seipel).
56 Rudolf Bahro, *The Alternative in Eastern Europe* (orig. 1977), London 1979, pp. 262–3.
57 'Gespräch mit Prof. Dr. Rudolf Bahro: Die deutschen Linken und die nationale Frage oder Unsere Ölinteressen am Golf', *Streitschrift zur Erneuerung der Politik*, 3 (November 1990), p. 6.
58 Heinrich von Treitschke, *Deutsche Geschichte im 19. Jahrhundert*, 2 vols., 4th edn, Leipzig 1893, p. 386.
59 Guntolf Herzberg and Kurt Seifert, *Rudolf Bahro: Glaube an das Veränderbare*, Berlin 2005, pp. 523 ff.
60 Ibid., p. 407.
61 *Die Grünen im Bundestag: Sitzungsprotokolle 1983–1987* vol. 1, Düsseldorf 2008, pp. 108 f. (session of 28 April 1983).
62 Ibid., p. 334 (15 November 1983).
63 Charlene Spretnak and Fritjof Capra, *Green Politics*, Santa Fe 1986, p. 11.
64 Ibid., p. 56 (Bahro's own statement).
65 Radkau, *Max Weber* (English edition), Cambridge 2009, p. 538.
66 *Religion in Geschichte und Gegenwart*, vol. 3, 2nd edn, Tübingen 1929, Sp. 836.
67 Knappe, *Das Geheimnis von Greenpeace*, p. 39.
68 Andrew Revkin, *The Burning Season: The Murder of Chico Mendes and the Fight for the Amazon Rain Forest*, Boston 1990, pp. 260f.
69 Chico Mendes, *Fight for the Forest!*, rev. edn, London 1992, pp. 76f.
70 Ibid., pp. 55ff.
71 Gerhard Dilger in *Rheinischer Merkur* 13 (2010).
72 Knappe, *Das Geheimnis von Greenpeace*, p. 31; also Svenja Koch (press spokesperson of Greenpeace Deutschland) to the author, 7 July 2006.
73 Maude Barlow and Tony Clarke, *Blue Gold: The Fight to Stop the Corporate Theft of Water* (orig. 2002), New York 2005, p. 231.
74 Manfred Loimeier, *Ken Saro-Wiwa*, Göttingen 1996, pp. 54, 41ff.
75 See Ken Saro-Wiwa, *A Month and a Day: A Detention Diary*, London 1995.
76 Ibid., p. 79.
77 Ibid., pp. 105ff.
78 Loimeier, *Ken Saro-Wiwa*, p. 21.

79 Saro-Wiwa, *A Month and a Day*, p. 60.
80 Ibid., p. 63.
81 Ibid., pp. 101f.
82 Loimeier, *Ken Saro-Wiwa*, p. 15.
83 Anna-Katharina Wöbse, 'Die Brent-Spar-Kampagne: Plattform für diverse Wahrheiten', in Uekötter and Hohensee, *Wird Kassandra heiser?*, p. 153; Greenpeace, ed., *Brent Spar und die Folgen: Analysen und Dokumente zur Verarbeitung eines gesellschaftlichen Konfliktes*, Göttingen 1997; ibid., documents 86 (*Frankfurter Allgemeine Zeitung*, 6 November 1995: 'Wo bleibt Greenpeace im Ogoni-Land?') and 87 (Dirk Kurbjuweit, 'Die Rollen sind uns näher: Warum "Brent Spar" die Menschen mehr aufrüttelte als das Schicksal von Ken Saro-Wiwa').
84 See Joyce Hannam, *The Death of Karen Silkwood*, Oxford 1991 (Oxford University Press, no less!)
85 Jochen Reiss, *Greenpeace. Der Umweltmulti: Sein Apparat, seine Aktionen*, Munich 1990, pp. 192–202.
86 Michael Bess, *The Light-Green Society: Ecology and Technological Modernity in France, 1960–2000*, Chicago 2003, pp. 33–6.
87 Reiss, *Greenpeace*, p. 202.
88 Knappe, *Das Geheimnis von Greenpeace*, pp. 163f.
89 Werner Abelshauser, *Nach dem Wirtschaftswunder: Der Gewerkschafter, Politiker und Unternehmer Hans Matthöfer*, Bonn 2009, pp. 344f.
90 Friedemann Bedürftig, *Geschichte der DDR*, Cologne 2007, pp. 158ff.
91 See, e.g., François Fejtö, *A History of the People's Democracies*, vol. 2: *Europe since Stalin*, Harmondsworth 1972.
92 Jürgen Horlemann and Peter Gäng, *Vietnam: Genesis eines Konflikts*, Frankfurt 1966, pp. 142f.
93 Mieke Roscher, *Ein Königreich für Tiere*, Marburg 2009, p. 392.
94 Luc Ferry, *The New Ecological Order*, Chicago 1995, p. 116. On the following section, cf. the chapter 'In Praise of Difference, or The Incarnations of Leftism: The Case of Ecofeminism', ibid., pp. 108–26.
95 Hans Jonas, *The Imperative of Responsibility*, Chicago 1984, p. 39.
96 Marieluise Beck-Oberdorf and Elke Kiltz, 'Dogmatismus macht nicht stark: Warum die Grünen das Frauenthema an die Etablierten verlieren', in Ralf Fücks, ed., *Sind die Grünen noch zu retten?*, Reinbek 1991, pp. 94f.
97 The quotation in the heading of this section is taken from Sara Parkin, *Green Parties: An International Guide*, London 1989, p. 260.
98 I would like to thank Saskia Richter (Berlin), the biographer of Petra Kelly, for valuable advice and critical points on the first draft of this section.
99 Monika Sperr, *Petra Karin Kelly: Politikerin aus Betroffenheit*, Munich 1983, p. 13; Spretnak and Capra, *Green Politics*, p. 10.
100 Spretnak and Capra, *Green Politics*, p. 10: 'Many journalists who describe Kelly compare her to Joan of Arc.'
101 *Die Grünen im Bundestag*, vol. 2, p. 546 (open letter to Antje Vollmer, 13 July 1984).
102 Petra K. Kelly, '"Zuallererst sind wir menschlich gescheitert": Offener Brief an die grüne Partei', in Fücks, *Sind die Grünen noch zu retten*, p. 29.
103 Benjamin Henrichs in *Die Zeit*, 5 November 1982 ('Weltliche Nonne'), quoted from Sperr, *Petra Kelly*, p. 181.

104 Alice Schwarzer, *Eine tödliche Liebe: Petra Kelly und Gert Bastian*, Cologne 1993, p. 138.
105 Ibid., p. 170.
106 Petra K. Kelly, 'Religiöse Erfahrung und politisches Engagement', in Gunter Hesse and Hans-Hermann Wiebe, eds., *Die Grünen und die Religion*, Frankfurt 1988, p. 35.
107 Joachim Radkau, 'Die Sehnsucht nach Grenzenlosigkeit: Argumente gegen Grundsatzerklärungen über "offene Grenzen"', in Karl A. Otto, ed., *Westwärts – Heimwärts? Aussiedlerpolitik zwischen 'Deutschtümelei' und 'Verfassungsauftrag'*, Bielefeld 1990, pp. 115–31.
108 Schwarzer, *Eine tödliche Liebe*, p. 81.
109 Spretnak, *Green Politics*, p. 10.
110 Sperr, *Petra Kelly*, p. 139: 'Petra Kelly also saw Spaceship Earth rushing head-long towards disaster.'
111 Schwarzer, *Eine tödliche Liebe*, p. 117.
112 Kelly, 'Religiöse Erfahrung', pp. 31f.
113 *Die Grünen im Bundestag, Sitzungsprotokolle 1983–1987*, vol. 1, p. 48.
114 Schwarzer, *Eine tödliche Liebe*, p. 118.
115 Not in print, however: see Petra K. Kelly and Gert Bastian, eds., *Tibet: Ein vergewaltigtes Land*, Reinbek 1988.
116 Erich Thiesen, *Es begann im Grünen Kreml: Agrarpolitik zwischen Rendsburg und Brüssel*, Neumünster 1997, pp. 222–8; Dietmar Stutzer, *Geschichte des Bauernstandes in Bayern*, Munich 1988, pp. 298–304.
117 Sperr, *Petra Kelly*, pp. 93f.
118 Ibid., pp. 113f.
119 Ibid., p. 180.
120 *Der Spiegel*, 13 June 1983, p. 27.
121 *Die Grünen im Bundestag*, vol. 2, p. 812 (*tageszeitung*, 31 August 1985).
122 Saskia Richter, *Die Aktivistin: Das Leben der Petra Kelly*, Munich 2010, p. 396.
123 Kelly, '"Zuallererst sind wir menschlich gescheitert"', p. 27.
124 *Die Grünen im Bundestag*, vol. 1, p. 107 (open letter from Petra Kelly 'to the parliamentary group, Party organizations and the Green rank-and-file'), April 1983.
125 Bess, *Light-Green Society*, p. 207.
126 Sara Parkin, *Green Parties: An International Guide*, London 1989, p. 102.
127 Alistair Cole and Brian Doherty, 'France: Pas comme les autres – the French Greens at the crossroad', in Dick Richardson and Chris Rootes, eds., *The Green Challenge: The Development of Green Parties in Europe*, London 1995, pp. 56 ff.
128 Sara Parkin (*Green Parties*, p. 99) sees this as a typical dilemma for the French Greens: 'a need for a charismatic leader to attract votes yet difficulty in finding one acceptable to the movement'.
129 Cole and Doherty, 'France: Pas comme les autres', p. 61.
130 Bess, *Light-Green Society*, p. 127.
131 See Cole and Doherty, 'France: Pas comme les autres', pp. 52f.
132 Bess, *Light-Green Society*, p. 207.
133 Ibid., pp. 112f.
134 Ibid., p. 113.
135 Ibid., p. 207.
136 Ibid., pp. 208, 114.

137 Eric Le Boucher (chief editor), in *Le Monde*, 30 September 2007 (quoted from Wikipedia).
138 Ingrid Gilcher-Holtey. *'Die Phantasie an die Macht': Mai 68 in Frankreich*, Frankfurt 1995, pp. 328ff.
139 Roderick Frazier Nash, *Wilderness and the American Mind*, 4th edn, New Haven 2001, pp. 288f.
140 Ibid., p. 290.
141 Dan O'Neill, *The Firecracker Boys: H-Bombs, Inupiat Eskimos, and the Roots of the Environmental Movement*, Philadelphia 1994.
142 Foreman, *Confessions of an Eco-Warrior*, p. 201.
143 Even in David Brower's 550-page anthology of first-hand testimonies (*For Earth's Sake*), which ends with a chapter on Alaska, there is no mention of Celia Hunter. This highlights how difficult it is to be sure about the leading figures in the eco-scene.
144 Nash, *Wilderness*, p. 280.
145 Alfred Runte, *National Parks: The American Experience*, Lincoln NE 1979, p. 256.
146 *Our National Parks*, New York (Life Books) 2009, p. 85.
147 Jon Krakauer, *Into the Wild* (orig. 1996), London 2011, p. 162.
148 Carl Pope and Paul Rauber, *Strategic Ignorance: Why the Bush Administration Is Recklessly Destroying a Century of Environmental Progress*, San Francisco 2004, p. 133.
149 Samuel P. Hays, *Beauty, Health, and Permanence: Environmental Politics in the U.S. 1955–1985*, Cambridge 1987, p. 58.
150 Nash, *Wilderness*, pp. 272–5.
151 Ibid., p. 272.
152 Shepard Krech III, John R. McNeill and Carolyn Merchant, eds., *Encyclopedia of World Environmental History*, New York 2004, vol. 3, p. 218 (Peter Coates); Peter Coates, *The Trans-Alaska Pipeline Controversy*, Fairbanks 1993.
153 Runte, *National Parks*, p. 237.
154 Ibid., p. 255.
155 Jay Hammond, *Tales of Alaska's Bush Rat Governor: The Extraordinary Autobiography of Jay Hammond, Wilderness Guide and Reluctant Politician*, Fairbanks 1994, p. 170.
156 Nash, *Wilderness*, p. 299; Runte, *National Parks*, p. 246.
157 Nash, *Wilderness*, pp. 310f.
158 Anthony Flint, *Wrestling with Moses: How Jane Jacobs Took On New York's Master Builder and Transformed the American City*, New York 2009.
159 Jane Jacobs, *The Death and Life of Great American Cities* (orig. 1961), New York 1992, pp. 433f., 443f.
160 Alexander Mitscherlich, *Die Unwirtlichkeit unserer Städte: Anstiftung zum Unfrieden*, Frankfurt 1965, p. 39; on Jane Jacobs see ibid., p. 37, and Mitscherlich, *Thesen zur Stadt der Zukunft*, Frankfurt 1971, pp. 52f.
161 On this section, see Ric Burns and James Sanders, *New York: An Illustrated History*, New York 1999, pp. 510–20; Edmund T. Delaney and Charles Lockwood, *Greenwich Village: A Photographic Guide*, 4th edn, New York 1984.
162 Jacobs, *Death and Life*, p. 4.
163 Ibid., p. 50.
164 Robert A. M. Stern et al., *New York 1900: Metropolitan Architecture and Urbanism 1890–1915*, New York 1983, pp. 40f.

165 Flint, *Wrestling with Moses*, p. 188.
166 Burns and Sanders, *New York*, p. 517.
167 Ibid., p. 434.
168 Donald L. Miller, *Lewis Mumford*, New York 1989, p. 475.
169 Mitscherlich, *Thesen zur Stadt der Zukunft*, p. 52.
170 Miller, *Lewis Mumford*, pp. 473ff.
171 Lewis Mumford, *The City in History: Its Origins, its Transformations, and its Prospects* (orig. 1961), New York 1989, p. 429.
172 Burns and Sanders, *New York*, pp. 496, 506; Miller, *Lewis Mumford*, p. 360. But in *The City in History*, the normally argumentative Mumford remains silent about Robert Moses!
173 Jacobs, *Death and Life*, pp. 20f. and 207 (on Mumford) and pp. 360 ff. (on Moses).
174 Flint, *Wrestling with Moses*, pp. 156ff., 186.
175 Miller, *Lewis Mumford*, pp. 475f.
176 Jacobs, *Death and Life*, p. 6.
177 Flint, *Wrestling with Moses*, p. 190.
178 Sebastian Haumann, *'Schade, dass Beton nicht brennt'* . . . *Planung, Partizipation und Protest in Philadelphia und Köln 1940–1990*, Wiesbaden 2011.
179 It is instructive to compare two books from different recent periods: Ausstellungswerkstatt St Georg, ed., *St. Georg: Vorstadt und Vorurteil?*, Hamburg 1978; and Michael Joho, ed., *St. Georg lebt! 125 Jahre Bürgerverein St. Georg: Ein Lese-Bilder-Buch*, Hamburg 2005.
180 I am grateful to the Brazilian historian José Augusto Pádua, who drew my attention to the importance of Marina Silva and to the book by Kathryn Hochstettler and Margaret E. Keck, *Greening Brazil: Environmental Activism in State and Society*, London 2007. See also Ziporah Hildebrandt, *Marina Silva: Defending Rainforest Communities in Brazil*, New York 2001, although, typically for environmentalism in the North, she focuses one-sidedly on Silva's commitment to the rainforest. I would also like to thank Andrea Queiroz de Souza and Hubertus Rescher for further information.
181 It is recognized, however, that as environment minister she 'helped to create a set of policies that reduced Amazon deforestation by 80 per cent in eight years'. José Augusto Pádua to the author, 27 December 2010.
182 Marian Blasberg, 'Das Judas-Projekt', *Die Zeit*, 22 September 2011, pp. 17ff.
183 Eva Karnofsky and Barbara Potthast, *Mächtig, mutig und genial: Vierzig außergewöhnliche Frauen aus Lateinamerika*, Berlin 2012, p. 256.
184 Stefan Ehlert, *Wangari Maathai: Mutter der Bäume*, Freiburg 2004, pp. 141, 128.
185 Ibid., p. 43.
186 Wangari Maathai, *Unbowed: A Memoir*, New York 2006, pp. 162f.
187 Ehlert, *Wangari Maathai*, p. 80.
188 Maathai, *Unbowed*, p. 162.
189 Ibid., p. 189.
190 Stephen N. Ndegwa, *The Two Faces of Civic Society: NGOs and Politics in Africa*, West Hartford CT 1996, p. 95.
191 Maathai, *Unbowed*, p. 159; Ndegwa, *Two Faces*, p. 96.
192 Ndegwa, *Two Faces*, pp. 93f.
193 Maathai, *Unbowed*, pp. 124f.

194 Ehlert, *Wangari Maathai*, pp. 61, 59.
195 Joachim Radkau, *Nature and Power*, Cambridge 2008, pp. 33, 287.
196 Ehlert, *Wangari Maathai*, pp. 84ff., 122.
197 Maathai, *Unbowed*, pp. 167f., 165f.
198 Ndegwa, *Two Faces*, p. 86.
199 Ibid., p. 85: 'The cornerstone of the GBM's short- and long-term objectives is empowering local communities to respond to local needs.'
200 Ibid., p. 105.
201 Ibid., p. 86.
202 Maathai, *Unbowed*, p. 197.
203 Ibid., p. 240.
204 Ibid., pp. 184ff.
205 Ibid., p. 227.
206 Ehlert, *Wangari Maathai*, p. 137.
207 Christian Küchli, *Wälder der Hoffnung*, Zurich 1997, pp. 86–99 ('Kenya: Die Frauengruppe unter dem Akazienbaum').
208 Ehlert, *Wangari Maathai*, p. 153.
209 Maathai, *Unbowed*, pp. 260ff.
210 Ibid., p. 133.
211 Ehlert, *Wangari Maathai*, pp. 62, 83.
212 Ibid., p. 19.
213 Ibid., pp. 44f.
214 In her autobiography, however, she distances herself from a narrow Puritanical Catholicism: e.g., Maathai, *Unbowed*, p. 81.
215 Bernd Hansjürgens and Gertrude Lübbe-Wolff, eds., *Symbolische Umweltpolitik*, Frankfurt 2000.
216 Radkau, *Nature and Power*, pp. 294f.
217 Haripriya Rangan, *Of Myths and Movements: Rewriting Chipko into Himalayan History*, London 2000, p. 32.
218 Ramachandra Guha, *How Much Should a Person Consume? Environmentalism in India and the United States*, Berkeley 2006, p. 59. He places Medha Patkar alongside Gaura Devi, 'a remarkable and still unsung heroine of the Chipko Andolan': 'The story of this illiterate woman activist provides us in fact a deeper insight into the constituent elements of an "environmentalism of the poor".'
219 John R. Wood, *The Politics of Water Resource Development in India: The Narmada Dams Controversy*, Los Angeles 2007, p. 134. The author's account of the Narmada conflict, the most objective and well-documented so far, has also been used in what follows.
220 Lori Udall, 'The World Bank and Public Accountability: Has Anything Changed?', in Jonathan A. Fox and L. David Brown, eds., *The Struggle for Accountability: The World Bank, NGOs, and Grassroots Movements*, Cambridge MA 1998, p. 395.
221 Udall, 'World Bank', p. 396; Guha, *How Much*, p. 66.
222 David A. Wirth, 'Partnership Advocacy in World Bank Environmental Reform', in Fox and Brown, *Struggle*, p. 62.
223 Patrick McCully, *Silenced Rivers: The Ecology and Politics of Large Dams*, London 1996, p. 299.
224 Tirunellai N. Seshan, *The Degeneration of India*, Delhi 1995, p. 139.
225 Wood, *Politics of Water Resource Development*, pp. 245f.

226 Susan George, in the foreword to Vandana Shiva, *Staying Alive: Women, Ecology and Development*, New Delhi 1989, pp. ix–xiii.
227 Vandana Shiva, 'Concepts of Nature and Ecological Reality: An Indian Perspective', in Joachim Wilke, ed., *Zum Naturbegriff der Gegenwart*, Stuttgart 1993, vol. 1, pp. 185–92.
228 Vandana Shiva, 'The Greening of the Global Reach', in Wolfgang Sachs, ed., *Global Ecology: A New Arena of Political Conflict*, London 1993, pp. 149–56 (here p. 151).
229 Maria Mies, *Das Dorf und die Welt: Lebensgeschichten – Zeitgeschichten*, Cologne 2008, pp. 243f.
230 Vandana Shiva, *India Divided: Diversity and Democracy Under Attack*, New York 2005, pp. 41f.
231 Ibid., pp. 95ff., 102, etc.
232 McCully, *Silenced Rivers*, p. 301.
233 Rangan, *Of Myths and Movements*, p. 157.
234 Ramachandra Guha, 'The Arun Shurie of the Left', *The Hindu*, 26 November 2000.
235 See Anil Agarwal and Sunita Narain, 'Towards Green Villages', in Sachs, *Global Ecology*, pp. 242–56; here p. 248: 'The biggest problem lies in the alienation . . . amongst village communities towards their commons.'
236 In Sunderlal Bahuguna et al., *India's Environment: Myth and Reality*, Dehradun 2007 (non-consecutive pagination), Text L, p. 7.
237 Graham Chapman et al., 'Environmentalism and the Mass Media: The North–South Divide', London 1997, p. 79. The general tendency of this study, which is partly based on the Indian regional press, is critical, if not subtly defamatory, towards the anti-dam movement. For example (p. 78): 'The campaign against the dam is world-wide, mostly because such schemes have become anathema in the eyes of many thinking and all unthinking [!] environmentalists.'
238 Guha, *How Much*, p. 70.
239 Jawaharlal Nehru, *Glimpses of History*, London 1949, p. 422.
240 See, for example, the speech Vandana Shiva gave in Stuttgart in 1993: 'The North has been living parasitically on the earth and the Third World.' Shiva, 'Concepts of Nature', p. 192.
241 See Dai Qing, *Yangtze! Yangtze!*, London 1994, pp. 248–58. Only in her second Yangtze book does the resettlement problem become central, and there too more emphasis is placed on the preservation of beautiful landscapes and archeological sites: Dai Qing, *The River Dragon Has Come! The Three Gorges Dam and the Fate of China's Yangtze River and its People*, London 1998.
242 McCully, *Silenced Rivers*, p. 67.
243 Dai Qing, *Yangtze! Yangtze!*, p. 266.
244 Nor was it without effect, according to Peter Ho, 'Sprouts of Environmentalism in China? Government-Organized NGOs and Green Organizations in Disguise', in Christof Mauch et al., eds., *Shades of Green: Environmental Activism around the Globe*, Lanham MD 1996, p. 140.
245 Elizabeth C. Economy, *The River Runs Black: The Environmental Challenge to China's Future*, Ithaca 2004, p. 144.
246 Jung Chang and Jon Halliday, *Mao: The Unknown Story*, London 2005, pp. 745ff.

247 Ian Buruma, *Bad Elements: Chinese Rebels from Los Angeles to Beijing*, New York 2003, p. 37.

248 Dai Qing, *River Dragon*, p. xxiii.

249 Dai Qing, *Tiananmen Follies: Prison Memoirs and Other Writings*, Norwalk 2005, p. 90.

250 Dai Qing, *River Dragon*, p. xxvi.

251 Buruma, *Bad Elements*, pp. 35f.

252 Ibid., p. 33.

253 Ibid., pp. 87ff.

254 Judith Shapiro, *Mao's War Against Nature: Politics and the Environment in Revolutionary China*, Cambridge 2001, p. 91.

255 Buruma, *Bad Elements*, pp. 37f.

256 Dai Qing, *Yangtze! Yangtze!*, p. 7.

257 Ibid., p. 8.

258 *Der Spiegel* 23 (2003), p. 117.

259 Quoted from Shang Wie, 'A Lamentation for the Yellow River: The Three Gate Gorge Dam', in Dai Qing, *River Dragon*, p. 155.

260 Economy, *River Runs Black*, p. 144.

261 Shapiro, *Mao's War Against Nature*, p. 28.

262 He Bochuan, *China on the Edge: The Crisis of Ecology and Development*, San Francisco 1991, p. 76.

263 Dai Qing, *River Dragon*, pp. 8f.

264 Margaret A. McKean, *Environmental Protest and Citizen Politics in Japan*, Berkeley 1981, p. 56.

265 These observations of mine during a trip to Japan in January–February 2012 have been fully confirmed by conversations with Helmut Weidner and Miranda A. Schreurs on 7 and 9 March 2012.

266 Irmela Hijiya-Kirschnereit, in the introduction to Ishimure Michiko, *Paradies im Meer der Qualen*, Frankfurt 1995, p. 8.

267 Helmut Weidner, 'Von Japan lernen? Erfolge und Grenzen einer technokratischen Umweltpolitik', in Shigeto Tsuru and Weidner, *Ein Modell für uns: Die Erfolge der japanischen Umweltpolitik*, p. 185: 'Nowhere else have such a large number of illnesses and deaths been so clearly attributable to environmental pollution; nowhere else have the illnesses been so harrowing.'

268 Ibid., p. 9.

269 Ibid., p. 121.

270 Ibid., p. 15.

271 Ibid., p. 363.

272 Ibid., p. 360; Ishimure Michiko, 'Reborn from the Earth Scarred by Modernity: Minamata Disease and the Miracle of the Human Desire to Live', *Japan Focus*, 27 April 2008; www.japanfocus.org/articles/print_article/2732.

273 Michiko, *Paradies*, p. 13. For an English translation, see *Paradise in the Sea of Sorrow: Our Minamata Disease*, University of Michigan 1993.

274 Ryuichiro Usui, 'Die Minamata-Krankheit und die Sprache jenseits des ius talionis: Auf der Suche nach der Sprache der Anima im *Paradies im Meer der Qualen* von Michiko Ishimure', in Heinz-Dieter Assmann et al., eds., *Grenzen des Lebens: Grenzen der Verständigung*, Würzburg 2009, pp. 64f. My thanks to Ryuichiro Usui, who is working on a book about Ishimure Michiko, and to Naoko Morita for a number of valuable points.

275 This is the position of Ryuichiro Usui: see the preceding note.

276 *Der Spiegel*, 8 April 1985, pp. 69ff. (Rolf Lamprecht).
277 Michiko, *Paradies*, p. 352.
278 Alex Kerr, *Dogs and Demons: The Fall of Modern Japan*, London 2001, p. 57.
279 Not even in the detailed account of the Minamata 'mercury disaster' in Bo Gunnarsson, *Japans ökologisches Harakiri, oder: Das tödliche Ende des Wachstums*, Reinbek 1974! Similarly, there is no mention of her in Shigeto Tsuru, 'Zur Geschichte der Umweltpolitik in Japan', in Tsuru and Weidner, *Ein Modell für uns* (pp. 25–9 on the Minamata scandal).
280 Gunnarsson, *Japans ökologisches Harakiri*, p. 19.
281 Helmut Weidner, 'Entwicklungslinien und Merkmale der Umweltpolitik', in Manfred Pohl and Hans Jürgen Mayer, eds., *Länderbericht Japan*, Bonn 1998, p. 127.
282 Ryuichiro Usui to the author, 9 September 2010.
283 Thomas Ellwein, in the foreword to Martin Leonhard, *Umweltverbände: Zur Organisation von Umweltschutzinteressen in der Bundesrepublik Deutschland*, Opladen 1986.
284 At the 'Heimat und Naturschutz' conference organized in July 2001 on the island of Vilm by the German Conservation Office.
285 Niklas Luhmann, *Risk: A Sociological Theory*, New York 1993, p. 129.
286 Elizabeth Dore, 'Capitalism and Ecological Crisis: Legacy of the 1980s', in Helen Collinson, ed., *Green Guerillas: Environmental Conflicts and Initiatives in Latin America and the Caribbean*, London 1996, pp. 16f.
287 Lane Simonian, *Defending the Land of the Jaguar: A History of Conservation in Mexico*, Austin TX 1995, p. 207.
288 At least according to Jared Diamond, *Collapse*, pp. 343–9. Frank Moya Pons, author of the most detailed history of the Dominican Republic, characterizes Balaguer's regime as an 'economic dictatorship' and does not honour it with any mention of an environmental policy: *The Dominican Republic: A National History*, Princeton 1998, pp. 427ff.
289 James Fairhead and Melissa Leach, *Misreading the African Landscape: Society and Ecology in a Forest–Savanna Mosaic*, Cambridge 1996, p. 253.
290 Radkau, *Nature and Power*, pp. 216–21.
291 Jörg Bergstedt, *Agenda, Expo, Sponsoring: Recherchen im Naturschutzfilz*, Frankfurt 1998, p. 252.
292 As in Bertrand Schneider (then secretary-general of the Club of Rome), in *The Barefoot Revolution: A Report to the Club of Rome*, London 1988.
293 Bergstedt, *Agenda, Expo, Sponsoring*, pp. 104ff.; Leonhard, *Umweltverbände*, pp. 190ff.
294 The term GONGO is missing from the *Encyclopedia of World Environmental History*. There is no shortage of analogous ironical constructions. FONGOs (F for 'foreign'); MONGOs (M for 'Mafia'); GRINGOs (government-initiated NGOs); QUANGOs (quasi-NGOs)! See, e.g., Le Monde diplomatique, ed., *Planet in Peril: An Atlas of Current Threats to People and the Environment*, Paris 2006.
295 See the alarming lead story by Li Wen, 'China's Environmental Conditions in 1998', in the *All Out for Cleaner Environment* issue of the official English-language *Beijing Review* (42/28, 12 July 1999).
296 *Der Spiegel* 52 (2009), pp. 46ff.
297 Economy, *River Runs Black*, pp. 138–41.
298 Ho, 'Sprouts of Environmentalism', pp. 135–60, esp. pp. 144f. and

149f.; Bao Maohong, 'Environmental NGOs in Transforming China', MS, Beijing University, 2007. Some of the statistics are astounding. It would seem that there are no fewer than 2,768 environmental NGOs in China, with a total of 69,000 full-time and 155,000 part-time employees (source: *Newsletter of the All-China Environment Federation*, 5 (2006): the blue book of ENGOS in China; ENGOs = Environmental NGOs). These figures are conceivable only if government initiatives overlap with a commitment on the part of the Chinese population. For much valuable advice, I am grateful to Bao Maohong, who invited me to lectures in Beijing and Xian in 2005.

299 Economy, *River Runs Black*, pp. 153–5; see also the lively internet disputes over the Wild Yak Brigade.

300 Frank Sieren, *Angst vor China: Wie die neue Weltmacht unsere Krise nutzt*, Berlin 2011, pp. 250f.

301 Oral communication from Gerhard Wallmeyer (Greenpeace Deutschland), 8 December 2010.

302 See Hays, *Beauty, Health, and Permanence*, pp. 465f.

303 Michael McCloskey, 'Twenty Years of Change in the Environmental Movement: An Insider's View', in Riley E. Dunlap and Angela C. Mertig, eds., *American Environmentalism: The U.S. Environmental Movement 1970–1990*, New York 1992, p. 84.

304 Robert Gottlieb, *Forcing the Spring: The Transformation of the American Environmental Movement*, Washington DC 1993, p. 130. Cf. ibid., p. 118: 'this myriad of laws, regulatory agencies . . . , new administrative bodies, and court decisions had developed into an environmental policy system'. The sigh is audible between the lines.

305 Allan Abramson to the author, 7 February 2010.

306 Timothy Doyle, *Environmental Movements in Majority and Minority Worlds: A Global Perspective*, New Brunswick 2005, p. 28.

307 McCloskey, 'Twenty Years of Change', p. 79.

308 Doyle, *Environmental Movements*, p. 32.

309 Sunderlal Bahuguna, 'People's Programme for Change', in Bahuguna, *India's Environment*, Part A, p. 12. Retranslated.

310 Bergstedt, *Agenda, Expo, Sponsoring*.

311 Mark Dowie, *Losing Ground: American Environmentalism at the Close of the Twentieth Century*, Cambridge 1995, p. 173.

312 Per Kurowski, *Voice and Noise*, www.booksurge.com, 2006, pp. xxx, xxxi. In a conversation I had with him on 20 March 2007, Kurowski was especially critical of the fact that first world environmentalists, including World Bank managers, tried to talk the third world into adopting far too expensive conservation techniques.

313 Sachs, *Global Ecology*, p. xv.

314 Foreman, *Confessions of an Eco-Warrior*, p. 11.

315 Andreas Knaut, *Zurück zur Natur! Die Wurzeln der Ökologiebewegung*, Greven 1993, p. 103.

316 Leonhard, *Umweltverbände*, p. 291.

317 Ernst Hoplitschek, 'Der Bund Naturschutz in Bayern: Traditioneller Naturschutzverband oder Teil der neuen sozialen Bewegungen?', dissertation, FU Berlin 1984, pp. 131f.

318 Joachim Radkau, 'Vom Naturschutzverein über die Bürgerinitiativen zum

anerkannten Umweltverband: Der BUND-NRW vor dem Hintergrund der deutschen Umwelt- und Naturschutzbewegung', in Stiftung Naturschutzgeschichte, ed., *Keine Berufsprotestierer und Schornsteinkletterer: 25 Jahre BUND in Nordrhein-Westfalen*, Essen 2003, pp. 11–22.

319 Peter Menke-Glückert, 'Die Mühen der Ebenen: Umweltziele im Behördenalltag', in Henning von Köller, ed., *Umweltpolitik mit Augenmaß: Gedenkschrift für Staatssekretär Dr. Günter Hartkopf*, Berlin 2000, p. 123.
320 Anna-Katharina Wöbse to the author, 4 June 2010.
321 William T. Markham, *Environmental Organizations in Modern Germany: Hardy Survivors in the 20th Century and Beyond*, New York 2008, p. 315.
322 Radkau, 'Vom Naturschutzverein', pp. 20f., 18.
323 Hoplitschek, 'Der Bund Naturschutz in Bayern', pp. 144, 346.
324 John G. Mitchell and Constance L. Stallings, eds., *Ecotactics: The Sierra Club Handbook for Environment Activists*, New York 1970, p. 88.
325 Riley E. Dunlap and Angela G. Mertig, 'The Evolution of the U.S. Environmental Movement', in Dunlap and Mertig, *American Environmentalism*, pp. 3f.
326 McCloskey, 'Twenty Years of Change', p. 82.
327 Michael P. Cohen, *The History of the Sierra Club 1892–1970*, San Francisco 1988, p. 450.
328 Frank Uekötter, 'Ein Zweiter Frühling? Die Krise der Umweltbewegung und Wege zu ihrer Überwindung', MS.
329 Shiva, *Staying Alive*, pp. 193ff.
330 Medha Patkar, 'Suvarnarekha Project: An Untold Tragedy', printed as an appendix to Bahuguna et al., *India's Environment*.
331 Antoinette G. Royo, 'The Philippines: Against the People's Wishes, the Mt. Apo Story', in Fox and Brown, *Struggle for Accountability*, p. 173.
332 See n. 292.
333 Jane G. Covey, 'Is Critical Cooperation Possible? Influencing the World Bank through Operational Collaboration and Policy Dialogue', in Fox and Brown, *Struggle for Accountability*, pp. 84f.
334 Global Environment Facility, *Operational Report on GEF Projects*, 30 June 2001.
335 In Fox and Brown, *Struggle for Accountability*, the Arun III controversy signals a turn in the World Bank to a more critical, multidimensional attitude towards large hydropower stations, traditionally the pet projects of development agencies. See the introduction (pp. 3f.), the article by Lori Udall ('The World Bank and Public Accountability: Has Anything Changed?', pp. 408–22) and the concluding summary ('Lessons from the Arun III Dam Campaign', pp. 486ff.).
336 However, local projects are possible without governments, the World Bank or the aid agencies. A young Sherpa I met in Nepal in 1999 worked with a few villagers and an engineer to build a mini-hydropower station that now supplies eighty homes with electricity – at a time when the Katmandu valley continues to suffer from power cuts.
337 Ulrich Gruber, *Reiseführer Natur: Nepal, Sikkim und Bhutan*, Munich 1995, p. 102.
338 *Der Spiegel* 51 (2000), p. 96.
339 Communication from the musicologist Gert Wegner, who has lived for thirty years in Nepal as a lecturer.

340 Ingrid Decker, 'David und Goliath: Wasser als politischer Konfliktherd zwischen Nepal und Indien', in Thomas Hoffmann, ed., *Wasser in Asien: Elementare Konflikte*, Osnabrück 1997, esp. pp. 231f.

341 Ernst Forsthoff, *Der Staat der Industriegesellschaft, dargestellt am Beispiel der Bundesrepublik Deutschland*, Munich 1971, p. 120.

342 Rudolf von Jhering, *Der Kampf um's Recht*, repub. Felix Ermacora, Berlin 1992, p. 35.

343 Alexis Schwarzenbach, *Saving the World's Wildlife*, London 2011, p. 18.

344 Frank Uekötter, *Umweltgeschichte im 19. und 20. Jahrhundert*, Munich 2007, p. 78.

345 *Die Grünen im Bundestag*, pp. 353, 355.

346 Gilsenbach in conversation with Regine Auster, in *naturmagazin* 9 and 10 (2000), p. 14.

347 Communication from Heinrich Spanier, 26 May 2010.

348 Reiss, *Greenpeace*, p. 39.

349 Knappe, *Das Geheimnis von Greenpeace*, p. 21.

350 *Der Spiegel* 38 (1991), pp. 87–105.

351 Wöbse, 'Die Brent-Spar-Kampagne'.

352 Christian Krüger and Matthias Müller-Hennig, *Greenpeace auf dem Wahrnehmungsmarkt*, Hamburg 2000, pp. 121ff.: 'Die Kampagne gegen die Europipe 1991–93: die Geschichte eines Flops'.

353 Reiner Luyken, 'Blick fürs Wesentliche', *Die Zeit*, 23 June 1995.

354 *Neue Westfälische*, 23 June 1995: Georg Alexander, 'Weltweiter Mitglieder- und Spendenschwund – Für Greenpeace kommt der Sieg wie gerufen.'

355 Ivar A. Aune and Nikolaus Graf Praschma, *Greenpeace: Umweltschutz ohne Gewähr*, Neudamm 1996, pp. 93ff., calls this claim into question. In any event, Krüger and Müller-Hennig, *Greenpeace auf dem Wahrnehmungsmarkt*, pp. 206ff., shows from the sequence of events that the huge impact had nothing to do with these figures.

356 Wöbse, 'Die Brent-Spar-Kampagne', pp. 139–60.

357 Michael Günther, 'Greenpeace und das Recht', in Greenpeace, *Das Greenpeace Buch*, p. 68. For a contrary position, see Udo E. Simonis, *Globale Umweltpolitik: Ansätze und Perspektiven*, Mannheim 1996, pp. 76f.

358 Greenpeace, *Brent Spar und die Folgen*. On Greenpeace's miscalculations, see ibid., document 49. Hobsbawm: ibid., document 9. Although he considered the Greenpeace operation objectively ill-founded, he conceded in the conclusion: 'And yet the Greens are right.'

359 Ibid., document 11.

360 Aune and Graf Praschma, *Greenpeace*, pp. 66ff.

361 Most lavishly in the cover story of 19 (2007): 'Help . . . the earth is melting! The great climate hysteria.'

362 See *Der Spiegel* 45 (2004), pp. 66 ff.

363 Reiner Scholz, *Betrifft Robin Wood: Sanfte Rebellen gegen Naturzerstörung*, Munich 1989, p. 22.

364 Paul Watson, *Ocean Warrior: My Battle to End the Illegal Slaughter on the High Seas*, London 1994, pp. xiiif. 'My experience with Greenpeace underscored Margaret Mead's belief that established institutions were not to be relied upon to bring change. When Greenpeace was a collective of dedicated individuals it was an effective organization. Unfortunately, the collective became an institution and then a bureaucracy, and now it's part of the problem.'

365 *Encyclopedia of World Environmental History*, vol. 1, p. 171.
366 McCloskey, 'Twenty Years of Change', pp. 85, 84.
367 Hobsbawm's sympathy for radicalism stops here, especially as workers are usually difficult to convert to vegetarianism: 'There are also crazy psychotics and fanatics in such movements – in England's animal rights movement, for example.' Document 9 in Greenpeace, *Brent Spar und die Folgen*.
368 Dunlap and Mertig, *American Environmentalism*, p. 6.
369 Interview with Franz Alt in *Brennpunkt Tibet*, 2 (2010), pp. 19f.
370 Jun Jing, 'Environmental Protests in Rural China', in Elizabeth J. Perry and Mark Selden, eds., *Chinese Society: Change, Conflict and Resistance*, London 2000, pp. 143, 155.
371 Christopher Rootes, in the introduction to Rootes, ed., *Environmental Protest in Western Europe*, Oxford 2003, pp. v and xiv.
372 McCloskey, 'Twenty Years of Change', p. 78.
373 Radkau, *Max Weber*, p. 295.
374 Otto Koenig, *Naturschutz an der Wende*, Vienna 1990, pp. 105, 106.
375 *Lexikon für Theologie und Kirche*, vol. 5, Freiburg 1960, Sp. 1243.
376 See Christopher Rootes (in *Environmental Movements: Local, National and Global*, London 1999, p. 91) on this concept, which is actually a contradiction in terms.
377 Joachim Raschke, *Die Grünen*, Frankfurt 1993, pp. 421ff.
378 Claudia von Werlhof, 'Wir werden das Leben unserer Kinder nicht dem Fortschritt opfern', in Marina Gambaroff et al., eds., *Tschernobyl hat unser Leben verändert: Vom Ausstieg der Frauen*, Reinbek 1986, p. 8.
379 Christina Pernicoli, *Die Frauen von Harrisburg oder 'Wir lassen uns unsere Angst nicht ausreden'*, Reinbek 1980.
380 Riley E. Dunlap, 'Trends in Public Opinion toward Environmental Issues: 1965–1990', in Dunlap and Mertig, *American Environmentalism*, pp. 102ff.

Chapter Five   A Friend–Enemy or Win-Win Scenario?

1 Lilo Weinsheimer, 'Held oder Spinner? Professor Scheer gilt als wilder Kommunist', *Die Zeit*, 27 February 1976, p. 14; letters from D. von Ehrenstein in *Der Spiegel*, 21 January 1977, p. 14, and *Die Zeit*, 19 September 1980, p. 53. Compendium: Autorengruppe des Projektes SAIU, Bremen University, ed., *Zum richtigen Verständnis der Kernindustrie: 66 Erwiderungen*, Berlin 1975.
2 See Edda Müller, *Innenwelt der Umweltpolitik: Sozial-liberale Umweltpolitik – (Ohn)macht durch Organisation?*, 2nd edn, Opladen 1995, pp. 89ff.
3 Carl Schmitt, *The Concept of the Political* (German orig. 1932), Rutgers University 1976, pp. 26f.
4 Joachim Radkau, *Max Weber* (German edition), Munich 2005, pp. 131f.
5 Or not so ironical? Claudia Honegger sees in Braudel a marked tendency to geographical determinism: Honegger, ed., *M. Bloch, F. Braudel, L. Febvre u. a. Schrift und Materie der Geschichte: Vorschläge zur systematischen Aneignung historischer Prozesse*, Frankfurt 1977, p. 23.
6 Fernand Braudel, *The Identity of France*, vol. 1: *History and Environment*, New York 1990, p. 322.
7 Ulrich Beck, *Risk Society: Towards a New Modernity*, London 1992, p. 32.

8 Of the abundant material on Wyhl, see esp. the book by the chair of the BBU: Hans-Helmut Wüstenhagen, *Bürger gegen Kernkraftwerke. Wyhl: Der Anfang?*, Reinbek 1975. The Gorleben conflict yielded by the far the most extensive work on the German anti-nuclear movement: Anselm Tiggemann, *Die 'Achillesferse' der Kernenergie in der Bundesrepublik Deutschland: Zur Kernenergiekontroverse und Geschichte der nuklearen Entsorgung von den Anfängen bis Gorleben 1955 bis 1985*, Lauf 2004.

9 Hans Christoph Buch, *Bericht aus dem Inneren der Unruhe: Gorlebener Tagebuch* (orig. 1979), Reinbek 1984, p. 15.

10 Ibid., pp. 17, 72, 313, 323–5.

11 Text in ibid., pp. 177–9. On the significance of Tiggemann's appeal: *Achillesferse*, pp. 496f.

12 Herbert Meyer, *Zur neueren Entwicklung der Bürgerinitiativbewegung im Bereich der Kernenergie*, Bochum (self-published) 1981, p. 9. Cf. Hans Eckehard Bahr, Dorothee Sölle et al., *Franziskus in Gorleben: Protest für die Schöpfung*, Frankfurt 1981.

13 Klaus M. Meyer-Abich to the author, 19 February 2010.

14 Final report: *Zukünftige Kernenergie-Politik. Kriterien – Möglichkeiten – Empfehlungen: Bericht der Enquete-Kommission des deutschen Bundestages*, Bonn 1980. The following account borrows at many points from the dissertation by Cornelia Altenburg, 'Kernenergie und Politikberatung: Die Vermessung einer Kontroverse', Wiesbaden 2010. See also Joachim Radkau, 'Die Kernkraft-Kontroverse im Spiegel der Literatur', in Armin Hermann and Rolf Schumacher, eds., *Das Ende des Atomzeitalters? Eine sachlich-kritische Dokumentation*, Munich 1987, pp. 321f.

15 Andreas Vierecke, 'Die Technik- und Umwelt-Enqueten des Deutschen Bundestages: Vermessene Zukunft – vertane Zeit', in Günter Altner et al., eds., *Jahrbuch Ökologie 1996*, Munich 1995, pp. 255–68.

16 Altenburg, 'Kernenergie und Politikberatung', pp. 21, 193, 270.

17 Volker Hauff, *Das schwedische Modell zur öffentlichen Diskussion über Energiepolitik*, Bonn 1977.

18 *Zukünftige Kernenergie-Politik*, p. 32.

19 Altenburg, 'Kernenergie und Politikberatung', p. 55.

20 Ibid., pp. 111, 143.

21 Ibid., pp. 88, 112.

22 Helmut Schelsky, *Einsamkeit und Freiheit: Idee und Gestalt der deutschen Universität und ihrer Reformen*, Reinbek 1963, p. 64. In the well-thumbed copy that I bought and devoured as a first-year student in 1963, I find the remark 'good!!!' at this point. It has remained in my memory for almost fifty years.

23 See Bernd Stoy, *Wunschenergie Sonne*, 3rd edn, Heidelberg 1980.

24 Frank Uekötter, *Von der Rauchplage zur ökologischen Revolution*, Essen 2003, p. 513. Cf. the variant English edition: *The Age of Smoke: Environmental Policy in Germany and the United States, 1880–1970*, Pittsburgh 2009, pp. 11f.

25 Alvin M. Weinberg, *The First Nuclear Era: The Life and Times of a Technological Fixer*, New York 1994, pp. 227ff.

26 Alan Cottrell, *How Safe is Nuclear Energy?*, London 1981.

27 Michael Bess, *The Light-Green Society: Ecology and Technological Modernity in France, 1960–2000*, Chicago 2003, p. 101.

28 I am grateful to Sabine Dworog for much information on the campaign against Startbahn West.

29 Hartmut Johnsen, *Der Startbahn-West Konflikt: Ein politisches Lehrstück?*, Frankfurt 1996, p. 49.

30 On some of these texts, see Radkau, 'Die Kernkraft-Kontroverse im Spiegel der Literatur', pp. 313f.

31 Robert Jungk, *The Nuclear State* (orig. 1977), London 1979, p. 129 and pp. 124f., 128.

32 Robert Jungk, *Brighter than a Thousand Suns: The Moral and Political History of the Nuclear Scientists*, London 1958, pp. 38, 91ff.; cf. Joachim Radkau, *Aufstieg und Krise der deutschen Atomwirtschaft 1945–1975: Verdrängte Alternativen in der Kerntechnik und der Ursprung der nukleären Kontroverse*, Reinbek 1983, pp. 34ff.

33 See, for example, Shepard Krech III, John R. McNeill and Carolyn Merchant, eds., *Encyclopedia of World Environmental History*, New York 2004, vol. 2, p. 873.

34 Simon A. Levin, ed., *The Princeton Guide to Ecology*, Princeton 2009, p. 357.

35 Hans Wallow, 'Kreativität als Clownerie', *Die Zeit*, 6 August 1982, reprinted in Monika Sperr, *Petra Karin Kelly: Politikerin aus Betroffenheit*, Munich 1983, p. 174.

36 Ibid., 159.

37 Winfried Kretschmann, 'Wie konservativ müssen die Grünen sein? Warum eine ökologische Partei nicht "links" sein kann', in Ralf Fücks, ed., *Sind die Grünen noch zu retten?*, Reinbek 1991, p. 65.

38 Claus-Peter Hutter et al., *The Eco-Twisters*, London 1995.

39 Ibid., p. 12.

40 Ibid., p. 2; Acheloos: pp. 96ff.; Dehesas: pp. 23f.

41 Ibid., pp. 223ff.

42 See also Volker Angres et al., *Bananen für Brüssel. Europa: Wie unsere Steuern vergeudet werden*, Munich 1999.

43 Ibid., p. 101.

44 Radkau, *Aufstieg und Krise*, pp. 170ff.

45 Hutter et al., *Eco-Twisters*, p. 78.

46 Ibid., pp. 13f. In September 2006 I had it reinforced on the spot that this negative judgement was still accurate.

47 In an interview with Kai Hünemörder, 7 March 2001.

48 Werner Filmer and Heribert Schwan, *Hans-Dietrich Genscher*, Düsseldorf 1988, p. 153.

49 Müller, *Innenwelt der Umweltpolitik*, pp. 97ff.

50 In an interview with Kai Hünemörder, 7 March 2001.

51 Kurt Möser, *Geschichte des Autos*, Frankfurt 2002, p. 279.

52 Dictmar Kleuke, *'Freier Stau für freie Bürger': Die Geschichte der bundesdeutschen Verkehrspolitik*, Darmstadt 1995, pp. 104ff.

53 Richard N. L. Andrews, *Managing the Environment, Managing Ourselves: A History of American Environmental Policy*, 2nd edn, New Haven 2006, p. 230.

54 Marc K. Landy et al., *The Environmental Protection Agency. Asking the Wrong Questions: From Nixon to Clinton*, New York 1994, pp. 35f.

55 Andrews, *Managing the Environment*, p. 230.

56 Ibid., p. 231.

57 Allan Abramson to the author (2 September 2010): 'The overall strategy could be called "hang one publicly" to deter hundreds of others.'

58 Allan Abramson to the author (7 February 2010): 'Yes, the early years of EPA

sometimes did go too far, either issuing complicated rules or trying to over-regulate.' As examples he gave the asbestos panic in schools and the costly, exaggerated renovation to which it gave rise. He regards the Ruckelshaus era in general as the great age of American environmental policy!

59 Ernst U. von Weizsäcker, *Erdpolitik*, Darmstadt 1989, p. 12.
60 Gretchen C. Daily and Katherine Ellison, *The New Economy of Nature: The Quest to Make Conservation Profitable*, Washington DC 2002, pp. 63ff.
61 Naomi Oreskes and Erik M. Conway, *Merchants of Doubt: How a Handful of Scientists Obscured the Truth on Issues from Tobacco Smoke to Global Warming*, New York 2010, pp. 140–60.
62 Carl Pope (executive director of the Sierra Club), *Strategic Ignorance: Why the Bush Administration Is Recklessly Destroying a Century of Environmental Progress*, San Francisco 2004, pp. 50, 181, 180.
63 In the discussion following his lecture 'Modernisierung des umwelt-bezogenen Ordnungsrechts': Alexander Roßnagel and Uwe Neuser, eds., *Reformperspektiven im Umweltrecht: Dokumentation der 'Haydener Hochschul-Gespräche 1995'*, Baden-Baden 1996, p. 120.
64 Gertrude Lübbe-Wolff, 'Das Kooperationsprinzip im Umweltrecht: Rechtsgrundsatz oder Deckmantel des Vollzugsdefizits?', *Natur + Recht* 7 (1989), pp. 295, 302.
65 Andrei S. Markovits and Philip S. Gorski, *The German Left: Red, Green and Beyond*, Cambridge 1993, p. 272.
66 Steven Lewis Yaffee, *The Wisdom of the Spotted Owl: Policy Lessons for a New Century*, Washington DC 1994.
67 Ibid., pp. 14ff.
68 Ibid., pp. 215f.
69 Ibid., p. 24.
70 Ibid., p. 216.
71 Ibid., p. 230: 'it is surprising how long it took before the national environmental groups jumped on the old growth/owl bandwagon. The larger groups were not major players in the controversy until 1987 or so.'
72 Ibid., pp. 170ff.; Samuel P. Hays, *Wars in the Woods: The Rise of Ecological Forestry in America*, Pittsburgh 2007, p. 162.
73 Dave Foreman, *Confessions of an Eco-Warrior*, New York 1991, p. 120.
74 Michael Williams, *Americans and their Forests: A Historical Geography*, Cambridge 1989, pp. 310–15.
75 Michael P. Cohen, *The History of the Sierra Club 1892–1970*, San Francisco 1988, pp. 337f.
76 Yaffee, *Wisdom of the Spotted Owl*, p. 45.
77 Chuck Leavell, *Forever Green: The History and Hope of the American Forest*, Dry Branch GA 2001, p. 159.
78 Also for Dixy Lee Ray, *Environmental Overkill: Whatever Happened to Common Sense?*, New York 1993, pp. 85ff.
79 Alan Gottlieb, in the preface to Ron Arnold, *Ecology Wars: Environmentalism as if People Mattered*, 4th edn, Bellevue WA 1993.
80 Yaffee, *Wisdom of the Spotted Owl*, p. 228.
81 Ibid., p. 161.
82 David Hervard, *The War Against the Greens: The 'Wise-Use' Movement, the New Right, and the Browning of America*, Boulder CO 2004, p. 79.
83 Ibid., p. 54.

84 See Paul R. Ehrlich and Anne H. Ehrlich, *Betrayal of Science and Reason: How Anti-Environmental Rhetoric Threatens Our Future*, Washington DC 1996, p. 19.
85 Yaffee, *Wisdom of the Spotted Owl*, pp. 243, 141.
86 Michael Succow, Lebrecht Jeschke and Hans Dieter Knapp, *Naturschutz in Deutschland*, Berlin 2012, p. 313.
87 Joachim Radkau, 'Hiroshima und Asilomar: Die Inszenierung des Diskurses über die Gentechnik vor dem Hintergrund der Kernenergie-Kontroverse', *Geschichte und Gesellschaft* 14 (1988), p. 357n.
88 Joachim Radkau, 'Das Neue in historischer Perspektive', in Christian Kehrt et al., eds., *Neue Technologien in der Gesellschaft*, Bielefeld 2011, pp. 58ff.
89 Willi Hüsler, 'Konservatismus in der Verkehrspolitik: Das Schweizer Beispiel', in Tom Koenigs and Roland Schaeffer, eds., *Fortschritt vom Auto? Umwelt und Verkehr in den 90er Jahren*, Munich 1991, pp. 255, 264f.
90 Gunter Vogt, *Entstehung und Entwicklung des ökologischen Landbaus im deutschsprachigen Raum*, Bad Dürkheim 2000.
91 Daniel Cohn-Bendit, a long-time star of the Green left, also emphasizes this: 'In France there is complete worship of Bové; . . . he stands for food sovereignty. And that is very, very popular in France' (in Christiane Grefe et al., *Attac*, Berlin 2002, p. 203). An illuminating point for the ecology of ecologism!
92 José Bové and Francois Dufour, 'Le monde n'est pas une marchandise. Des paysans contre la malbouffe: Entretiens avec Gilles Luneau', Paris 2000; on *malbouffe*, pp. 77ff.; cf. the interview with Bové in *Der Spiegel* 26 (2001), p. 132.
93 Thilo Bode, *Abgespeist: Wie wir beim Essen betrogen werden und was wir dagegen tun können*, Frankfurt 2007. In 2002 he founded the consumers' organization 'foodwatch'.
94 Volker Angres, Claus-Peter Hutter and Lutz Ribbe, *Futter fürs Volk: Was die Lebensmittelindustrie uns auftischt*, Munich 2001.
95 Joan Thirsk, *Alternative Agriculture. A History: From the Black Death to the Present Day*, Oxford 1997, pp. 224f.
96 Bernhard Gill, *Streitfall Natur: Weltbilder in Technik- und Umweltkonflikten*, Wiesbaden 2003, p. 199.
97 *Der Spiegel* 43 (2000), pp. 238–41; the microbiologist Martin Häusler (*Die wahren Visionäre unserer Zeit*, Munich 2010) even mentions Jakob von Uexküll, the founder of the Alternative Nobel Prize, as one of its pioneers.
98 Hutter et al., *Eco-Twisters*, p. 11.
99 Masanobu Fukuoka, *The Road Back to Nature: Regaining the Paradise Lost*, New York 1987, pp. 27ff.
100 This is the primary object of Frank Uekötter's thesis: *Die Wahrheit ist auf dem Feld: Eine Wissensgeschichte der deutschen Landwirtschaft*, Göttingen 2010.
101 See the previous note.
102 Hans Schuh, 'Biostrom, nein danke!', *Die Zeit*, 14 July 2011, pp. 35f.
103 Karl Ludwig Schweisfurth, *Wenn's um die Wurst geht. Gedanken über die Würde von Mensch und Tier: Autobiographie*, n.p. 1999, pp. 259f.
104 This is an important point made in Mieke Roscher, 'Ein Königreich für Tiere: Die Geschichte der britischen Tierrechtsbewegung', Marburg 2009, p. 292.
105 See the polemical work by the academic director of the Schweisfurth Foundation: Manuel Schneider, *Mythen der Landwirtschaft. Argumente für eine ökologische Agrarkultur: Fakten gegen Vorurteile, Irrtümer und Unwissen*,

2nd edn, Bad Dürkheim 2001, pp. 43ff. He correctly points out (p. 45) that even eco-firms cannot offer 'a hundred per cent protection against BSE'.

106 Roland Scholz and Sievert Lorenzen, *Phantom BSE-Gefahr: Irrwege von Wissenschaft und Politik im BSE-Skandal*, n.p. (Innsbruck) 2005, p. 62.

107 Schneider, *Mythen der Landwirtschaft*, pp. 43, 44.

108 *Encyclopedia of World Environmental History*, vol. 1, p. 316 (Raymond Pierotti).

109 Roland Scholz (formerly of the Munich University biochemistry and cellular biology institute), 'Eine Ansteckung mit BSE grenzt an ein Wunder', in Scholz and Lorenzen, *Phantom BSE-Gefahr*, p. 152.

110 Ibid., p. 151.

111 Sievert Lorenzen, 'BSE: Wie das Rind dem Wachstumswahn geopfert wird', in Scholz and Lorenzen, *Phantom BSE-Gefahr*, p. 134.

112 Jörg Bergstedt, *Agenda, Expo, Sponsoring: Recherchen im Naturschutzfilz*, Frankfurt 1998, pp. 32, 252, 39, 249ff.

113 John R. McNeill, *Something New Under the Sun: An Environmental History of the Twentieth-Century World*, New York 2000, p. 155; Sandra Postel, *The Last Oasis: Facing Water Scarcity*, New York 1997, pp. 32f., 195.

114 John G. Mitchell and Constance L. Stallings, eds., *Ecotactics: The Sierra Club Handbook for Environment Activists*, New York 1970, p. 109.

115 Barry Commoner, *The Closing Circle: Nature, Man, and Technology*, New York 1971, p. 10.

116 The following points are based mainly on the excellent dissertation by Roscher, 'Ein Königreich für Tiere', one of the most thorough and stimulating works anywhere on a single movement. See also Robert Garner, *Animals, Politics and Morality*, Manchester 1993; Rachel Monaghan, 'Animals Rights and Violent Protest', *Terrorism und Political Violence* 9/4 (Winter 1997), pp. 106–16.

117 Roscher, 'Königreich für Tiere', pp. 294f.

118 Ibid., p. 417.

119 Ibid., p. 102 ff.

120 Keith Thomas, *Man and the Natural World*, London 1983, pp. 108f.

121 See Wolfgang Wippermann, *Die Deutschen und ihre Hunde: Ein Sonderweg der deutschen Mentalitätsgeschichte*, Munich 1999. The critical tendency is all the more valuable in that the author is a well-known dog lover.

122 Ibid., pp. 34, 39.

123 Peter Coates, *Nature: Western Attitudes since Ancient Times*, Cambridge 1998, p. 233, n. 92.

124 Roscher, 'Königreich für Tiere', p. 392.

125 Monaghan, 'Animal Rights and Violent Protest', pp. 109ff.

126 Roscher, 'Königreich für Tiere', p. 302.

127 Ibid., pp. 335, 420ff., 514.

128 Ibid., p. 429.

129 Ibid., p. 337.

130 Ibid., pp. 264f.

131 *Frankfurter Allgemeine Zeitung*, 24 June 1996 = Document 9 in Greenpeace, ed., *Brent Spar und die Folgen: Analysen und Dokumente zur Verarbeitung eines gesellschaftlichen Konfliktes*, Göttingen 1997. Admittedly he adds: 'That is not important so long as such people do not dominate the Green movement.'

132 Roscher, 'Königreich für Tiere', p. 286.

133 Ibid., p. 323: 'The militant groups withdrew almost entirely from attempts to exert parliamentary influence.'
134 Ibid., p. 321.
135 Ibid., p. 290.
136 Ibid., p. 293.
137 Christopher Rootes, ed., *Environmental Protest in Western Europe*, Oxford 2003, p. 38.
138 Ibid., pp. 33, 44ff.
139 *Encyclopedia of World Environmental History* (vol. 1, p. 54, Carol J. Adams) laconically notes: 'The relationship between environmental activism and animal rights is vexed.'
140 David McTaggart, *Shadow Warrior*, London 2002, p. 193.
141 In this connection, the work that attracted most public attention was Jeremy Rifkin, *Beyond Beef: The Rise and Fall of the Cattle Culture*, New York 1992, esp. 194ff, 224f.; on the subject of methane it referred to Fred Pearce, 'Methane: The Hidden Greenhouse Gas', *New Scientist*, 6 May 1990. The methane alarm has since grown considerably more intense.
142 See Robert Lawlor, *Voices of the First Day: Awakening in the Aboriginal Dreamtime*, Rochester VT 1991, p. 151.
143 On the question of whether hunting cultivates a feeling for sustainability – a question without a definitive answer – see Joachim Radkau, *Nature and Power*, Cambridge 2008, pp. 45–54.
144 Much more successful, though, was his *Brown Book* of 1906, which contained stories about nature without marksmen. See Thomas Dupke, *Hermann Löns: Mythos und Wirklichkeit*, Hildesheim 1994, p. 84.
145 'Löns himself never shot a red deer or a wild boar. . . . He did not even have a gun of his own.' Henry Makowski to the author, 28 July 2010.
146 Hermann Löns, *Mein grünes Buch*, 10th edn, Hanover n.d., pp. 65f.
147 *Der Spiegel* 38 (1960), pp. 83ff.
148 Henry Makowski to the author, 8 June 2000.
149 Matt Cartmill, *A View to a Death in the Morning: Hunting and Nature through History*, Cambridge MA 1993, p. 163.
150 Josef H. Reichholf (on the whole a critic of the high-handedness of hunters!), *Naturschutz: Krise und Zukunft*, Berlin 2010, p. 38.
151 Wilhelm Bode and Martin von Hohnhorst, *Waldwende: Vom Försterwald zum Naturwald*, 2nd edn, Munich 1994, esp. pp. 41ff., 127ff.; Wilhelm Bode and Elisabeth Emmert, *Jagdwende: Vom Edelhobby zum ökologischen Handwerk*, 2nd edn, Munich 1998.
152 Communication from Charlotte Tacke (10 December 2001), a student of German–Italian comparative hunting history. This too is no longer undisputed: see Sergio Della Bernardina, 'L'invention du chasseur écologiste: Un exemple italien', *Terrain* 13 (1989), pp. 130–9; I am grateful to Antoine Acker for this reference.
153 Mario Diani and Francesca Forno in Rootes, *Environmental Protest in Western Europe*, pp. 137, 149.
154 Martin Rhodes, 'Italy: Greens in an Overcrowded Political System', in Dick Richardson and Chris Rootes, eds., *The Green Challenge: The Development of Green Parties in Europe*, London 1995, p. 183.
155 Bess, *Light-Green Society*, p. 137.
156 Here and on the French hunting conflict, see Antoine Acker, 'Jagdkrise und

Jägerbewegung in Frankreich seit den 70er Jahren: Die Geschichte einer antiökologischen Massenbewegung?', master's thesis, University of Bielefeld 2007. Acker draws especially on Dominique Darbon, *La crise de la chasse in France: La fin d'un monde*, Paris 1997; and Céline Vivent, *Chasse Pêche Nature et Traditions: Entre écologisme et poujadisme? Socio-anthropologie d'un mouvement des campagnes*, Caën 2005.

157 This is the position of Céline Vivent (see preceding note).
158 Anita Pleumarom, 'Golfplätze verschärfen die Wasserkrise: Das Beispiel Thailand', in Thomas Hoffmann, ed., *Wasser in Asien: Elementare Konflikte*, Osnabrück 1997, pp. 312–16.
159 A pathbreaking collection in its time was Hugh Davis Graham and Ted Robert Gurr, eds., *Violence in America: Historical and Comparative Perspectives* (orig. 1969), rev. edn, Beverly Hills 1979.
160 Wilhelm Hennis, *Max Webers Fragestellung*, Tübingen 1987.
161 Bernhard Knappe, *Das Geheimnis von Greenpeace: Die andere Seite der Erfolgsstory*, Vienna 1993, p. 29.
162 See Rootes, *Environmental Protest in Western Europe*, preface to the paperback edition, p. vii.
163 Inaki Barcena et al., 'The Basque Country', in ibid., pp. 205, 210.
164 *The Sun*, December 2005, p. 6.
165 Watson does not seem to have appreciated this comment, since he gave the signed copy of the book to a junk dealer, from whom I purchased it at a derisory price! This was one of the 'eureka experiences' that opened my eyes on the theme of this chapter.
166 McTaggart, *Shadow Warrior*, pp. 146f.
167 Paul Watson, *Ocean Warrior: My Battle to End the Illegal Slaughter on the High Seas*, London 1994, p. 12.
168 Richard Ellis, *Men and Whales*, New York 1991, pp. 451ff.
169 Watson, *Ocean Warrior*, p. 115.
170 Ellis, *Men and Whales*, p. 474; *Neue Westfälische*, 19 January 2008 ('Chaos auf hoher See').
171 Knappe, *Das Geheimnis von Greenpeace*, p. 175.
172 Paul Watson, 'An Open Letter to Norwegians', in *Sea Shepherd Log* 1 (1993), pp. 5ff.
173 Ibid., p. 16 [retranslated from the German].
174 Ibid., p. 29.
175 Ibid., pp. 16f.
176 Ibid., p. 33.
177 Ibid., p. 90.
178 Ibid., p. 98.
179 Ibid., p. 91.
180 Douglass F. Rohrman, 'Environmental Terrorism', *Frontiers in Ecology and the Environment* 2 (2004), p. 332.
181 David Rothenberg, 'Have a Friend for Lunch: Norwegian Radical Ecology Versus Tradition', in Bron Raymond Taylor, ed., *Ecological Resistance Movements: The Global Emergence of Radical and Popular Environmentalism*, Albany NY 1995, pp. 217f.
182 Ibid., p. 212.
183 Ibid., p. 201.
184 Hutter et al., *Eco-Twisters*, pp. 130f.

185 Gro Harlem Brundtland, *Madam Prime Minister: A Life in Power and Politics*, New York 2002.

186 Anna Wöbse, 'Freiheit für die Meere: Eine kurze Geschichte der Kritik der Freiheit der Meere', in Verein für Internationalismus und Kommunikation, ed., *Wem gehört das Meer?*, Bremen 2009, p. 58.

187 Whaling does not feature in O. P. Sharma, *The International Law of the Sea*, Delhi 2009!

188 Mark Kurlansky, *Cod: A Biography of the Fish that Changed the World*, Munich 1999, pp. 181ff.

189 Max Nicholson, *The New Environmental Age*, Cambridge 1987, pp. 140f.

190 Kai Kaschinski, 'Waterworld: Über die Bedeutung der Meerespolitik für das Nord-Süd-Verhältnis', in Verein für Internationalismus und Kommunikation, *Wem gehört das Meer?*, p. 8.

191 Sharma, *International Law of the Sea*, pp. xv, xvi.

192 Gerald Hau and Claus-Peter Hutter, *Nördliche Sporaden: Natur zwischen Inseln und Meer*, Überlingen 1997 (henceforth = Hau and Hutter I), pp. 121, 139; the following accounts are based on this book and a new edition: Claus-Peter Hutter and Gerald Hau, eds., *Ägäis: Nördliche Sporaden. Natur entdecken und erleben*, Radolfzell n.d. (2002) (= Hau and Hutter II); Hutter et al., *Eco-Twisters*, pp. 13–20; *euronatur* 2 (2007) (*20 Jahre Euronatur*), pp. 24f. ('Fischer schützen Mönchsrobben'); and the author's own research in September 2006 at the office of Yannis Vlaikos, the chair of the Ecological and Cultural Movement & Fishermen Cooperative of Alonnisos.

193 John Cronin and Robert F. Kennedy, Jr, *The Riverkeepers*, New York 1997, pp. 40ff.

194 Maria Kousis concludes on the basis of extensive research: 'As in other southern European countries that emerged from dictatorial regimes in the early 1970s, environmental protest in Greece was strongly marked by the presence of community-based groups.' In Rootes, *Environmental Protest in Western Europe*, 131.

195 Hau and Hutter II, p. 31.

196 Ibid., p. 32.

197 Hau and Hutter I, p. 83.

198 Hutter et al., *Eco-Twisters*, pp. 26f.

199 Daily and Ellison, *New Economy of Nature*, p. 158.

200 Foreman, *Confessions of an Eco-Warrior*, pp. 4f.

201 *Encyclopedia of World Environmental History*, vol. 1, p. 357 (Rik Scarce).

202 Foreman, *Confessions of an Eco-Warrior*, pp. 173f.

203 Ibid., p. 119.

204 Ibid., p. 132.

205 Bron Taylor, 'Religion, Violence and Radical Environmentalism: From Earth First! to the Unabomber to the Earth Liberation Front', *Terrorism and Political Violence* 10/4 (Winter 1998), p. 6; *The Sun*, December 2005, p. 4.

206 *Encyclopedia of World Environmental History*, vol. 1, pp. 357f. (Rik Scarce).

207 See the endorsements on the back cover of Foreman's *Confessions of an Eco-Warrior*.

208 *Encyclopedia of World Environmental History*, vol. 1, pp. 357.

209 Roscher, 'Königreich für Tiere', pp. 287f., 386. In Roscher's account, however, Earth First! plays only a marginal role.

210 *The Sun*, December 2005, p. 6.
211 Foreman, *Confessions of an Eco-Warrior*, p. 172.
212 Ibid., p. 175.
213 Two 'water wars' titles in 2002 alone: Vandana Shiva, *Water Wars: Privatization, Pollution and Profit*, Cambridge MA 2002; Diane Raines Ward, *Water Wars: Drought, Flood, Folly, and the Politics of Thirst*, New York 2002. See also Hays, *Wars in the Woods*.
214 Radkau, *Nature and Power*, p. 88.
215 See Clifford Geertz's classic studies of Indonesia, discussed in Radkau, *Nature and Power*, pp. 99ff.
216 Even the overview in the 460-page collective work edited by Hoffmann, *Wasser in Asien* – currently by far the most extensive on the subject in German – is by no means complete. Especially informative and up-to-date are the geographical charts in David Blanchon and Aurélie Boissière, *Atlas mondial de l'eau: De l'eau pour tous?*, Paris 2009; see also the survey (pp. 66–9) of the decades of international conferences on water allocation issues, in which Stockholm 1972 is considered to have been epoch-making.
217 Christian Chesnot, *La Bataille de l'eau au Proche-Orient*, Paris 1993, p. 67.
218 According to *Le Monde diplomatique*, it was five times higher by 2007: *Atlas der Globalisierung spezial: Klima*, Berlin 2008, p. 24 (Rafael Kempf).
219 Alon Tal, *Pollution in a Promised Land: An Environmental History of Israel*, Berkeley 2002, p. 334. This 550-page work is unique in the sparse literature on Israeli environmental history; its author is the founder of the Arava Institute for Environmental Studies, situated in a desert area, and is considered the leading light of the small Israeli environmental movement. He makes no secret of his links with Zionism, and so his objective account of the discrimination towards Palestinians merits special attention.
220 Ibid., p. 356.
221 Ibid., p. 357.
222 Ibid., pp. 347ff.; on Yoffe pp. 166ff., 174ff.; see also Lewis G. Regenstein, *Replenish the Earth*, London 1991, pp. 212ff.
223 Shaul Ephraim Cohen, *The Politics of Planting: Israeli–Palestinian Competition for Control of Land in the Jerusalem Periphery*, Chicago 1993. The cover text reads: 'On the open landscape of Israel and the West Bank, where pine and cypress forests grow alongside olive groves, tree planting has become symbolic of conflicting claims to the land. Palestinians cultivate olive groves as a vital agricultural resource, while the Israeli government has made restoration of mixed-growth forests a national priority.' In several lectures I have given in Israel, I read this aloud and pointed out that it is a perfect example of how environmentalism can turn a deadly hostility into a productive reality that makes the landscape richer. My audience was sceptical, however, and placed greater weight on the occupation of the land.
224 Tal, *Pollution in a Promised Land*, p. 410; also a communication to the author from Israeli historian Moshe Zimmermann (September 2008).
225 Tal, *Pollution in a Promised Land*, p. 427.
226 Ibid., p. 409.
227 Ibid., p. 230.
228 Ibid., p. 365.
229 Christiane Fröhlich sees this as the fundamental problem of water conservation

in Israel: *Der israelisch–palästinensische Wasserkonflikt: Diskursanalytische Betrachtungen*, Wiesbaden 2010.

230 Ramachandra Guha, *The Unquiet Woods: Ecological Change and Peasant Resistance in the Himalayas*, Oxford 1989, p. 156.

231 Vandana Shiva, *Staying Alive: Ecology, Women and Development*, London 1989, p. 73; Alok Kumar Ghosh, 'State Versus People: The Indian Experience of Environmentalism', in Ranjan Chakrabarti, ed., *Situating Environmental History*, Manohar 2007, pp. 66ff.

232 Ramachandra Guha, *How Much Should a Person Consume? Environmentalism in India and the United States*, Berkeley 2006, pp. 118f.

233 Maria Mies, *Indische Frauen zwischen Unterdrückung und Befreiung*, 2nd edn, Frankfurt 1986, pp. 271f.

234 Guha, *Unquiet Woods*, p. xi.

235 Cf. ibid., p. 116, which suggests that farmers set fire only to forests that served commercial interests and were not useful to villagers. But arson is not easy to rationalize: see the counter-arguments in Ajay Skaria, *Hybrid Histories: Forests, Frontiers and Wildness in Western India*, Delhi 1999, p. 275.

236 See also Guha, *Unquiet Woods*, p. 173.

237 Shiva, *Staying Alive*, p. 67; and, more embellished, Ludmilla Tüting, *Umarmt die Bäume: Die Chipko-Bewegung in Indien*, Berlin 1983, pp. 16ff.

238 This is also recognized in Guha, *Unquiet Woods*, p. 175.

239 Richard Tucker to the author, March 2007.

240 Haripriya Rangan, *Of Myths and Movements: Rewriting Chipko into Himalayan History*, London 2000, pp. 164ff. Of course, this demythologization of the movement is based on the premise that most of the people in the region aspire to 'development' and modernization as desirable goals.

241 Udo Gümpel, 'Sündenfall am Amazonas', *Die Zeit*, 22 May 1992.

242 Timothy Doyle, *Environmental Movements in Majority and Minority Worlds: A Global Perspective*, New Brunswick 2005, p. 18; also p. 64. Cf. Marites Danguilan Vitug, 'The Politics of Logging in the Philippines', in Philip Hirsch and Carol Warren, eds., *The Politics of Environment in Southeast Asia*, London 1998.

243 Jörg Becker, *Papiertechnologie und Dritte Welt*, Eschborn 1986, p. 7.

244 See Bruno Manser, *Voices from the Rainforest: Testimonies of a Threatened People*, Selangor n.d. (1996).

245 According to Norbert Kostede in *Die Zeit*, 24 March 1992, p. 8.

246 On Rio: Philippa England, 'UNCED and the Implementation of Forest Policy in Thailand', in Philip Hirsch, ed., *Seeing Forests for Trees: Environment and Environmentalism in Thailand*, Chiang Mai 1997, pp. 53–71.

247 Norbert Kostede in *Die Zeit*, 24 April 1992, p. 8.

248 Dirk Maxeiner and Michael Miersch, *Öko-Optimismus*, Düsseldorf 1996, pp. 230, 227.

249 Ruedi Suter, *Bruno Manser Die Stimme des Waldes*, Oberhofen am Thunersee 2005, pp. 205f.

250 England, 'UNCED', p. 57.

251 Peter Dauvergne, *Shadows in the Forest: Japan and the Politics of Timber in Southeast Asia*, Cambridge MA 1997, p. 171; Christian Küchli, *Forests of Hope*, London 1997, p. 166.

252 England, 'UNCED', p. 61.

253 Michael Leigh, 'Political Economy of Logging in Sarawak, Malaysia', in

Hirsch and Warren, *Politics of Environment in Southeast Asia*, p. 94: Sarawak 'has experienced the most rapid log clearance in the whole Southeast Asian region, an export volume that rivalled the rate of extraction for the whole Amazon basin'.

254 Al Gedicks, 'International Native Resistance to the New Resource Wars', in Taylor, *Ecological Resistance Movements*, p. 96.

255 Ibid., p. 97.

256 England, 'UNCED', pp. 67, 58.

257 Philip Hirsch and Carol Warren, in the introduction to Hirsch and Warren, *Politics of Environment in Southeast Asia*, p. 8. On the Philippines, see Vitug, 'Politics of Logging', p. 128; and Robin Broad and John Cavanagh, *Plundering Paradise: The Struggle for the Environment in the Philippines*, Berkeley 1993, pp. 132ff. On Indonesia: Bernard Eccleston and David Potter, 'Environmental NGOs and Different Political Contexts in South-East Asia: Malaysia, Indonesia and Vietnam', in Michael J. G. Parnwell and Raymond L. Bryant, eds., *Environmental Change in South-East Asia: People, Politics and Sustainable Development*, London 1996, pp. 63f.

258 *Der Spiegel*, 16 October 1989, p. 233.

259 Dieter Oberndörfer, *Schutz der tropischen Regenwälder durch Entschuldung*, Munich 1989, pp. 19f.

260 Knut Sturm to the author, 25 November 1993, at the talk on the island of Mainau: 'Why Do People Need the Forest?'

261 This is the concluding point in Duncan Poore, *Changing Landscapes: The Development of the International Tropical Timber Organization (ITTO) and its Influence on Tropical Forest Management*, London 2003, p. 255. He sees the 'dangerous segregation' of forestry from the political context as one of the basic errors of Rio 1992.

262 Al Gedicks, 'International Native Resistance to the New Resource Wars', in Taylor, *Ecological Resistance Movements*, p. 94.

263 See Manser, *Stimmen aus dem Regenwald*, Gümligen 1992, p. 274.

264 Weizsäcker, *Erdpolitik*, p. 29.

265 Sara Parkin, *Green Parties: An International Guide*, London 1989, pp. 154f.

266 Carl Schmitt, *Legality and Legitimacy*, n.p. (Duke University Press) 2004, p. 10.

267 Michael Günther, 'Greenpeace und das Recht', in Greenpeace, ed., *Das Greenpeace Buch*, Munich 1996, pp. 65–81, esp. p. 66.

268 Watson, *Ocean Warrior*, p. 121.

269 Landy et al., *Environmental Protection Agency*, p. 25. Similarly Benjamin Kline, *First Along the River: A Brief History of the U.S. Environmental Movement*, Lanham 2007, p. 86 ('lawyer-scientist-based organizations').

270 Jochen Bölsche, ed., *Die deutsche Landschaft stirbt*, Reinbek 1983, p. 64.

271 Richard Forrest et al., 'A Comparative History of U.S. and Japanese Environmental Movements', in Pradyumna P. Karan and Unryu Suganuma, eds., *Local Environmental Movements: A Comparative Study of the U.S. and Japan*, Lexington KY 2008, p. 35, emphasizes this as an advantage of American environmental groups over Japanese.

272 Radkau, *Aufstieg und Krise*, pp. 445f.

273 Hartmut Albers, *Gerichtsentscheidungen zu Kernkraftwerken*, Villingen 1980, p. 83.

274 Radkau, *Aufstieg und Krise*, pp. 404ff.

275 Albers, *Gerichtsentscheidungen*, p. 121.
276 Müller, *Innenwelt der Umweltpolitik*, p. 136.
277 *Neue Westfälische*, 16 October 1981.
278 Michael Kraack et al., *Umweltintegration in der Europäischen Union*, Baden-Baden 2001, pp. 49f.
279 Chhatrapati Singh, 'The Framework of Environmental Laws in India', in Sunderlal Bahuguna et al., *India's Environment: Myth and Reality*, Dehradun 2007 (non-consecutive pagination), ch. 9, pp. 8f. [retranslated]. This is not to say that a concession to local demands automatically benefits environmental protection: for example, the Supreme Court decided, against the government of Himachal Pradesh, that a village is legally entitled to a road link.
280 Two years' imprisonment and 2,000-euro fines for the eight defendants – for a disaster estimated to have caused 25,000 deaths! See Birger Heinzow, 'Das ist Verrat an den Opern', *zeozwei* 3 (2010), p. 10.
281 Jamie Cassels, *The Uncertain Premise of Law: Lessons from Bhopal*, Toronto 1993, p. 250.
282 See the classic by Charles Perrow, *Normal Accidents: Living With High-Risk Technologies*, New York 1984.
283 Arundhati Roy, *Listening to Grasshoppers: Field Notes on Democracy*, New Delhi 2009, p. xvi.
284 See several contributions in Shigeto Tsuru and Helmut Weidner, eds., *Environmental Policy in Japan*, Berlin 1989, esp. Takehisa Awaji, 'Pollution Litigation: Developments in Environmental Jurisdiction', pp. 123–38, and Hiroshi Oda, 'The Role of Criminal Law in Pollution Control', pp. 183–95.
285 Helmut Weidner, 'Entwicklungslinien und Merkmale der Umweltpolitik', in Pohl and Mayer, ed., *Länderbericht Japan*, pp. 127, 125; cf. Miranda A. Schreurs, *Environmental Politics in Japan, Germany, and the United States*, Cambridge 2002, pp. 46f., 73.
286 Hirsch and Warren, *Politics of Environment in Southeast Asia*, p. 9.
287 George J. Aditjondro, 'Large Dam Victims and their Defenders: The Emergence of an Anti-Dam Movement in Indonesia', in ibid., p. 41.
288 Cronin and Kennedy, *Riverkeepers*, pp. 23, 42ff.; John Kerry and Teresa Heinz Kerry, *This Moment on Earth: Today's New Environmentalists and their Vision for the Future*, New York 2007, p. 85.
289 Cronin and Kennedy, *Riverkeepers*, p. 39.
290 Bess, *Light-Green Society*, p. 199.
291 Gerald Novara, 'Ist Wien anders?', in Roland Berger and Friedrich Ehrendörfer, eds., *Ökosystem Wien: Die Naturgeschichte einer Stadt*, Vienna 2011, p. 636. Similar, on the basis of US experiences, is Mark Dowie, *Losing Ground: American Environmentalism at the Close of the 20th Century*, Cambridge MA 1995, pp. 78ff.
292 Jürgen Roth, *Die Zerstörung einer Stadt*, Munich 1975, esp. p. 59.
293 Wolfgang Kraushaar, *Fischer in Frankfurt: Karriere eines Außenseiters*, Hamburg 2001, p. 11.
294 Ibid., p. 75.
295 See Christian Fischer, *Wir sind die Wahnsinnigen: Joschka Fischer und seine Frankfurter Gang*, Munich 1998, p. 47.
296 Ibid., p. 50.
297 Herbert Sukopp, ed., *Stadtökologie: Das Beispiel Berlin*, Berlin 1990.
298 Richard Reynolds, *On Guerilla Gardening*, London 2008.

299 Dieter Rucht, 'Antikapitalistischer und ökologischer Protest als Medienereignis: Zur Resonanz der Proteste am 1. Mai 2000 in London', in Achim Brunnengräber et al., eds., *NGOs als Legitimationsressource: Zivilgesellschaftliche Partizipationsformen im Globalisierungsprozess*, Opladen 2001, pp. 259–83.

300 Anna Bramwell, *Ecology in the 20th Century: A History*, New Haven 1989, pp. 39ff.; Ludwig Trepl, *Geschichte der Ökologie: Vom 17. Jahrhundert bis zur Gegenwart*, Frankfurt 1987, p. 114. Trepl does not honour Haeckel with even a section of a chapter.

301 On-Kwok Lai et al., 'The Contradictions and Synergy of Environmental Movements and Business Interests', in Yok-shiu F. Lee and Alvin Y. So, eds., *Asia's Environmental Movements: Comparative Perspectives*, Armonk NY 1999, pp. 269–86.

302 Tokue Shibata, 'The Influence of Big Industries on Environmental Policies: The Case of Car Exhaust Standards', in Tsuru and Weidner, *Environmental Policy in Japan*, pp. 99–108.

303 Gertrude Lübbe-Wolff, 'Modernisierung des umweltbezogenen Ordnungsrechts', in Alexander Roßnagel and Uwe Neuser, eds., *Reformperspektiven im Umweltrecht*, Baden-Baden 1996, p. 101.

304 Günter Hartkopf and Eberhard Bohne, *Umweltpolitik*, Opladen 1983, p. 159. It is important to note the context: Hartkopf's weightiest argument against a special environmental department was that only a strong ministry could break such resistance.

305 Edda Müller to the author, 22 March 2006.

306 Hans-Jochen Luhmann (Wuppertal Institute), in a manuscript sent to the author on 26 July 2010.

307 Wuppertal Institut für Klima, Umwelt, Energie, ed., *Zukunftsfähiges Deutschland in einer globalisierten Welt, Frankfurt 2008, S. 380: Vorbildlich abwägende Analyse der Vorzüge und Probleme des Emissionshandels im Umweltgutachten 2002 des Rates von Sachverständigen für Umweltfragen*, Stuttgart 2002, pp. 231–40.

308 See the controversial contributions in Elmar Altvater and Achim Brunnengräber, eds., *Ablasshandel gegen Klimawandel? Marktbasierte Instrumente in der globalen Klimapolitik und ihre Alternativen*, Hamburg 2008.

309 Walter Krämer and Götz Trenkler, quoted in *Focus* 23 (1996), p. 55.

310 Andreas Knaut, *Zurück zur Natur! Die Wurzeln der Ökologiebewegung*, Greven 1993, p. 407.

311 Anna-Katharina Wöbse, 'Naturschutz global', in Hans-Werner Frohn and Friedemann Schmoll, eds., *Natur und Staat*, Bonn 2006, p. 631.

312 Cohen, *History of the Sierra Club*, pp. 18f.

313 See Joachim Radkau, *Technik in Deutschland: Vom 18. Jahrhundert bis heute*, rev. edn, Frankfurt 2008, pp. 316f.

314 Ibid., p. 169.

315 Paul S. Suter, *Driven Wild: How the Fight against Automobiles Launched the Modern Wilderness Movement*, Seattle 2002, pp. 36ff, 159ff.

316 Joachim Radkau, 'Wie mit dem Fahrrad der Temporausch erfunden wurde', in LVR (Landschaftsverband Rheinland), ed., *FarRadZeit*, Solingen 2001, p. 20.

317 Ivan Illich, *Energy and Equity*, London 1974, pp. 60, 63.

318 Martina Kaller-Dietrich, *Ivan Illich (1926–2002): Sein Leben, sein Denken*, Weitra 2007.

319 Christoph Chorherr, *Verändert! Über die Lust, Welt zu gestalten*, Vienna 2011, p. 141.

320 Otto Schneider, *Die Ferien-Macher: Eine gründliche und grundsätzliche Betrachtung über das Jahrhundert des Tourismus*, Hamburg 2001, pp. 295f.; Grzimek does not mention this cooperation in his memoirs.

321 William Beinart and Lotte Hughes, *Environment and Empire*, Oxford 2007, pp. 289–309 ('National Parks and the Growth of Tourism'), with examples from Africa through India to New Zealand.

322 Radkau, *Nature and Power*, pp. 292f.; 'the most hypocritical ecotourism': Sterling Evans, *The Green Republic: A Conservation History of Costa Rica*, Austin TX 1999, p. 231.

323 Evans, *Green Republic*, pp. 1f.

324 Beinart and Hughes, *Environment and Empire*, p. 304.

325 See Alois Glück, 'Bayern als Vorreiter in der Umweltpolitik', in *Die Umweltmacher: 20 Jahre BMU*, Hamburg 2006, pp. 110–20.

326 Bess, *Light-Green Society*, pp. 68f.

327 Anna-Katharina Wöbse, *Weltnaturschutz: Umweltdiplomatie in Völkerbund und Vereinten Nationen 1920–1950*, Frankfurt 2012, pp. 320ff. ('Meanwhile the world heritage programme has developed into UNESCO's most successful project').

328 Wöbse, 'Naturschutz global', p. 676.

329 Franz Solar in *Holzwirtschaft Österreichs: Ein Rückblick auf die letzten 60 Jahre, geschildert von 22 Zeitzeugen, die diese Epoche wesentlich geprägt haben*, Vienna 2005 (= Lignovisionen 6), p. 117.

330 The following points draw extensively on Joachim Radkau, *Wood: A History*, Cambridge 2012, pp. 7ff.

331 Hays, *Wars in the Woods*.

332 Küchli, *Forests of Hope*, pp. 86ff.

333 Patrick B. Durst et al., *In Search of Excellence: Exemplary Forest Management in Asia and the Pacific*, Bangkok 2005, pp. 39ff.

334 The only book I found on this subject in June 2011 at LIGNA in Hanover – the largest wood fair in the world – gives considerable reason for doubt: Peter Liebhard, *Energieholz im Kurzumtrieb: Rohstoff der Zukunft*, 2nd edn, Graz 2010.

335 'Eine Grüne Mauer quer durch Afrika', *Welt am Sonntag*, 27 March 2011.

336 According to Jean Ziegler, at the Ecumenical Church Congress in Munich, May 2010.

337 Mans Lönnroth et al., *Solar Versus Nuclear: Choosing Energy Futures*, Oxford 1980.

338 Gerhard Mener, 'Zwischen Labor und Markt: Geschichte der Sonnen-energienutzung in Deutschland und den USA 1860–1986', dissertation, Munich 2000. This regrettably little-known work is also unique in the sources it uses, but it ends in 1986 of all years, just when Chernobyl was giving an unprecedented boost to solar energy in Germany.

339 August Bebel, *Woman and Socialism*, trans. of 33rd German edn, New York 1904, pp. 280f.

340 Radkau, *Aufstieg und Krise*, pp. 67ff.

341 *Außenpolitik* 5 (1954), p. 343 (editorial article by Arthur W. Just).

342 Radkau, *Aufstieg und Krise*, p. 88.

343 John Perlin, *From Space to Earth: The Story of Solar Electricity*, Ann Arbor 1999.

344 Bess, *Light-Green Society*, pp. 6ff.
345 Mener, 'Zwischen Labor und Markt', pp. 433ff.
346 Ibid., p. 375.
347 Quoted in [and retranslated from] Bernd Stoy, *Wunschenergie Sonne*, 3rd edn, Heidelberg 1980, p. 47.
348 Ray, *Environmental Overkill*.
349 *Encyclopedia of World Environmental History*, vol. 3, p. 1138.
350 Daniel M. Bermann and John T. O'Connor, *Who Owns the Sun? People, Politics, and the Struggle for a Solar Economy*, White River Junction VT 1996, pp. xvf.
351 See Joachim Radkau, 'Von der Kohlennot zur solaren Vision: Wege und Irrwege bundesdeutscher Energiepolitik', in Hans-Peter Schwarz, ed., *Die Bundesrepublik Deutschland: Eine Bilanz nach 60 Jahren*, Cologne 2008, pp. 478–84; and Radkau, *Technik in Deutschland*, pp. 410–13.
352 This is the historically substantiated thesis of Gerhard Mener, 'Stabilität und Wandel in der Energieversorgung: Geschichte der Sonnenenergie und der Kraft-Wärme-Kopplung': sent to the author on 29 August 2010.
353 See Christa Nickels, *Die Grünen im Bundestag*, vol. 2, p. 586.
354 Hermann Hatzfeld et al., *Kohle. Konzepte einer umweltfreundlichen Nutzung: Eine Übergangsstrategie für die Ökologiebewegung*, Frankfurt 1981.
355 Radkau, 'Von der Kohlennot zur solaren Vision', p. 478.
356 The latest review at the time of writing: Deutsche Gesellschaft Club of Rome, ed., *Der Desertec-Atlas: Weltatlas zu den erneuerbaren Energien*, e. V., Hamburg 2011.
357 Markus Fasse, 'Solarstrom aus der Wüste hat noch weiten Weg vor sich: Sonnenenergie-Initiative gibt sich drei Jahre Zeit zur Klärung ihres Geschäftsmodells', *Handelsblatt*, 14 July 2009, p. 18.
358 Axel Höpner and Jürgen Flauger, 'Saubere Lösung? DESERTEC: Deutsche Konzerne gründen am Montag eine Initiative, um Strom in der Wüste zu produzieren. Doch die Hürden sind hoch', *Handelsblatt*, 10 July 2009, p. 2.
359 BP has since thought better of it and moved beyond, or rather retreated from, its 'Beyond Petroleum' image. See http://www.cnbc.com/id/100647034.
360 Franz Alt, *Die Sonne schickt uns keine Rechnung: Die Energiewende ist möglich*, Munich 1994, pp. 87ff.
361 Hermann Scheer, *Energieautonomie: Eine neue Politik für erneuerbare Energien*, Munich 2005, pp. 209ff., pp. 201 ff. ('Sand oder Öl im Getriebe? Die verlorene Unschuld der Umweltbewegung').
362 See Willem L. Oltmans, ed., *Die Grenzen des Wachstums: Pro und Contra*, Reinbek 1974.
363 Joachim Radkau, 'Wachstum oder Niedergang: Ein Grundgesetz der Geschichte?', in Irmi Seidl and Angelika Zahrnt, eds., *Postwachstumsgesellschaft: Konzepte für die Zukunft*, Marburg 2010, pp. 37–49.
364 David Milne, *America's Rasputin: Walt Rostow and the Vietnam War*, New York 2008; ibid., p. 7: the term 'America's Rasputin' originated with the diplomat Averell Harriman.
365 Bruce Rich, *Mortgaging the Earth: The World Bank, Environmental Impoverishment, and the Crisis of Development*, Boston 1995, pp. 266f.
366 Tim Jackson's widely noted *Prosperity without Growth: Economics for a Finite Planet* (London 2009) is directed against this idea.

Chapter Six   Ecology and the Historic Turn of 1990: From Social Justice to Climate Justice?

1 John Campbell, *The Iron Lady: Margaret Thatcher, from Grocer's Daughter to Prime Minister*, London 2009, p. 436.
2 See my review of this encyclopedia in *Journal of World History* 16/1 (March 2005), pp. 99–102.
3 Michael McCloskey, 'Twenty Years of Change in the Environmental Movement: An Insider's View', in Riley E. Dunlap and Angela G. Mertig, eds., *American Environmentalism: The U.S. Environmental Movement 1970–1990*, Washington DC 1992, p. 83.
4 Morris Low, Shigeru Nakayama and Hitoshi Yoshioka, *Science, Technology and Society in Contemporary Japan*, Cambridge 1999, p. 97. See ibid., p. 90, however, referring to the turn after 1990: 'Environmentalism emerged from its origins in radical culture to became a mainstream concern.'
5 Anny Wong, 'The Anti-Tropical Timber Campaign in Japan', in Arne Kalland and Gerard Persoon, eds., *Environmental Movements in Asia*, Richmond 1998, pp. 140f.
6 Miranda A. Schreurs, *Environmental Politics in Japan, Germany, and the United States*, Cambridge 2002, pp. 112, 143, 162.
7 Georg Blume and Chikako Yamamoto, 'Die Wirtschaftsmacht Japan will jetzt auch noch die Führungsrolle beim Umweltschutz übernehmen', *Die Zeit*, 14 April 1992, pp. 33f.
8 Bernhard Knappe, *Das Geheimnis von Greenpeace: Die andere Seite der Erfolgsstory*, Vienna 1993, p. 158.
9 Hsin-Huang Michael Hsiao et al., 'The Making of Anti-Nuclear Movements in East Asia: State–Movement Relationships and Policy Outcomes', in Yok-shiu F. Lee and Alvin Y. So, eds., *Asia's Environmental Movements: Comparative Perspectives*, Armonk NY 1999, p. 252.
10 In the USA, however, Bhopal seems to have left a stronger impression than Chernobyl; it led to the development of an environmental movement in West Virginia (where similar chemical plants existed), and in 1986 this achieved the passing of a law that forced chemical corporations to give a public account of their emissions and to submit worst-case scenarios.
11 Egmont R. Koch and Fritz Vahrenholt, *Seveso ist überall: Die tödlichen Risiken der Chemie* (orig. 1978), rev. edn, Cologne 1980; 'Seveso ist überall' is also the cover title of *Der Spiegel*, 30 May 1983.
12 Klaus Gestwa, 'Die Explosion des "Roten Atoms"', *Damals* 4 (2001), pp. 6f.
13 Four years after the event, the excellently informed book by Zhores Medvedev – *The Legacy of Chernobyl*, New York 1990 – still assumed that all casualty estimates were uncertain (pp. 129–30, 165–87), but continued to suggest that the Soviet leadership had played down the consequences.
14 Raphael Beguin, 'Bhopal als Beispiel einer komplexen Krise' (research paper), Munich 2007.
15 Jamie Cassels, *The Uncertain Promise of Law: Lessons from Bhopal*, Toronto 1993, p. 250.
16 Claes Bernes and Lars J. Lundgreen, *Use and Misuse of Nature's Resources: An Environmental History of Sweden*, Värnamo (Swedish Environmental Protection Agency) 2009, p. 277.
17 Jim Igoe, *Conservation and Globalization: A Study of National Parks and*

Indigenous Communities from East Africa to South Dakota, Belmont NC 2004, p. 11; partly critical, partly approving is Le Monde diplomatique, ed., *Atlas der Globalisierung: Die neuen Daten und Fakten zur Lage der Welt*, Berlin 2006, pp. 58f. (Régis Genté), 74f. (Bernard Dréano).

18 'Report of the United Nations Conference on Environment and Development (Rio de Janeiro, 3–14 June 1992)': http://sedac.ciesin.columbia.edu/entri/texts/a21/a21-27-NGOs.html.

19 Joanna Burger, *Oil Spills*, New Brunswick 1997; Burger in Shepard Krech III, John R. McNeill and Carolyn Merchant, eds., *Encyclopedia of World Environmental History*, New York 2004, vol. 3, pp. 966f.

20 Ernst Ulrich von Weizsäcker, *Erdpolitik: Ökologische Realpolitik an der Schwelle zum Jahrhundert der Umwelt*, Darmstadt 1989, p. 12.

21 Gro Harlem Brundtland, *Madam Prime Minister: A Life in Power and Politics*, New York 2002, p. 226.

22 *Der Spiegel*, 8 April 1985, p. 126.

23 The Russian pedagogue Marina Ismenok stressed this point in August 1996, at an international seminar on environmental history at the Summer University in Schloss Neubeuern.

24 Ramachandra Guha, *How Much Should a Person Consume? Environmentalism in India and the United States*, Berkeley 2006, p. 69.

25 Klaus Gestwa, 'Ökologischer Notstand und sozialer Protest: Ein umwelthistorischer Blick auf die Reformunfähigkeit und den Zerfall der Sowjetunion', *Archiv für Sozialgeschichte* 43 (2003), p. 382.

26 'Gorbatschow: "Deutschland wird Öko-Weltmacht"': http://www.sonnenseite.com/index.php?pageID=16&article:oid=a7974&template=article_detail.html.

27 Murray Feshbach and Alfred Friendly, *Ecocide in the USSR: Health and Nature Under Siege*, New York 1992, p. 1.

28 http://www.project-syndicate.org/commentary/turning-point-at-chernobyl.

29 See Medvedev, *Legacy of Chernobyl*, pp. 69–70: 'His rather sombre television address on 14 May 1986 was disappointing. . . . A large part of it consisted of traditional agitprop.' But a small part did not – and that was something new coming from the top of the Soviet Union.

30 Julia Obertreis, 'Der "Angriff" auf die Wüste" in Zentralasien: Zur Umweltgeschichte der Sowjetunion', in *Grünbuch Politische Ökologie im Osten Europas* (= *Osteuropa* 4-5)2008)), pp. 37, 42. However, she also provides quite a lot of material that strengthens the position she originally questions.

31 In reality, there was no environment ministry in the Soviet Union at the time. Israel was head of the State Committee for Hydrometeorology, which also had responsibility for environmental issues. (I am grateful to Julia Obertreis for this information.)

32 Joachim Radkau, 'Tschernobyl in Deutschland?', *Der Spiegel* 20 (1986), p. 35.

33 Angela Merkel, 'Die Tschernobyl-Weintrauben', in Karl-Heinz Karisch and Joachim Wille, eds., *Der Tschernobyl-Schock: Zehn Jahre nach dem Super-GAU*, Frankfurt 1996, p. 120.

34 In Svetlana Alexievich, *Voices from Chernobyl*, London 1999, pp. 175f.

35 Zhores Medvedev, a keen observer of Soviet nuclear technology, drew a very different conclusion: 'A young, tired and inexperienced operator, Leonid Toptunov, who died three weeks later in great pain, moved the control rods of Reactor No. 4 to only slightly below the correct position. This seemingly minor oversight resulted in a giant plume' (*Legacy of Chernobyl*, p. ix).

36 See Joachim Radkau, *Aufstieg und Krise der deutschen Atomwirtschaft 1945–1975: Verdrängte Alternativen in der Kerntechnik und der Ursprung der nukleären Kontroverse*, Reinbek 1983, pp. 552f. (n. 147).

37 Medvedev, *Legacy of Chernobyl*, pp. ix, 37f. One of the most unsettling documents is a manuscript by Legasov, published after his death by suicide: 'I have in my safe a transcript of the operators' telephone conversations on the eve of the accident. Reading the transcript makes one's flesh creep.' It points to abysmal and confusing instruction of the operating crew.

38 Alla Jaroshinskaja, *Verschlußsache Tschernobyl: Die geheimen Dokumente aus dem Kreml*, Berlin 1994, pp. 160ff. (proceedings of the Politburo session of 3 July 1986). Cf. Alla A. Yaroshinskaya, *Crime without Punishment*, London 2011.

39 Stephanie Cooke, *In Mortal Hands: A Cautionary History of the Nuclear Age*, New York 2009, p. 308.

40 Medvedev, *Legacy of Chernobyl*, p. 272.

41 *Our Common Future: Report of the World Commission on Environment and Development*, Oxford 1987, p. 187.

42 Karl-Heinz Karisch, '"Da muss sich Furchtbares ereignet haben": Protokoll der Atomkatastrophe von Tschernobyl', in Karisch and Wille, *Der Tschernobyl-Schock*, pp. 37f.

43 Jaroshinskaja, *Verschlußsache Tschernobyl*; Alla Yaroshinskaya, 'The Big Lie: Secret Documents on Chernobyl', published 21 April 2006, http://www.eurozine.com/pdf/2006-04-21-yaroshinskaya-en.pdf.

44 http://www.project-syndicate.org/commentary/turning-point-at-chernobyl.

45 Walter Wallmann, 'Das erste Jahr: Umweltpolitik nach Tschernobyl', in *Die Umweltmacher. 20 Jahre BMU: Geschichte und Zukunft der Umweltpolitik*, Hamburg 2006, p. 18.

46 *Offene Worte: Sämtliche Beiträge der 19. Gesamtsowjetischen Konferenz der KPdSU in Moskau*, Nördlingen 1988, p. 261.

47 Gestwa, 'Ökologischer Notstand und sozialer Protest', p. 377; cf. Oleg Yanitsky, quoted in Laura A. Henry, *Red to Green: Environmental Activism in Post-Soviet Russia*, Ithaca 2010, p. 39.

48 Gestwa, 'Ökologischer Notstand und sozialer Protest', p. 379.

49 Henry, *Red to Green*, p. 39.

50 *Offene Worte*, p. 31.

51 Joachim Radkau, *Technik in Deutschland: Vom 18. Jahrhundert bis heute*, Frankfurt 2008, pp. 398f.

52 See the abundant material in the great work by Douglas R. Weiner: *A Little Corner of Freedom: Russian Nature Protection from Stalin to Gorbachev*, Berkeley 1999. On p. 130 he writes of the *zapovedniki*, the scientists working in protected areas: 'They were the priests, the interpreters, and ultimately the keepers of these sacred territories, which they thought they had saved from the profane Stalinist mire.'

53 Radkau, *Technik in Deutschland*, pp. 387f.

54 Cf. Klaus Gestwa, 'Herrschaft und Technik in der spät- und poststalinistischen Sowjetunion: Machtverhältnisse auf den "Großbauten des Kommunismus", 1948–1964', *Osteuropa* 3 (2001), pp. 192f.

55 Petra Opitz, 'Strom aus erneuerbaren Energien: Stiefkind osteuropäischer Energiestrategien?', in *Tschernobyl: Vermächtnis und Verpflichtung* (= *Osteuropa* 4 (2006)), pp. 187–98.

56 Weiner, *Little Corner of Freedom*, p. 372 (with reference to Lake Baikal): 'Fighting for nature made one a hero.'

57 See *Der Spiegel*, 3 December 1990, pp. 148ff.

58 Dirk van Laak, *Weiße Elefanten: Anspruch und Scheitern technischer Großprojekte im 20. Jahrhundert*, Stuttgart 1999, pp. 174–8.

59 *Der Spiegel*, 8 April 1985, p. 127.

60 *Offene Worte*, p. 173.

61 Ibid., p. 271.

62 Gestwa, 'Die Explosion des "Roten Atoms"', p. 6.

63 David Marples, 'Diktatur statt Ökologie: Krisenmanagement in Lukasenkas Belarus', in *Tschernobyl: Vermächtnis und Verpflichtung*, pp. 117–29.

64 Wladimir Jakimets, 'Erfolgreicher als die Friedensbewegung im Westen: Bürgerproteste stoppen die Atomtests in Kasachstan', in Valentin Thurn and Bernhard Clasen, eds., *Klassenfeind Natur: Die Umweltkatastrophe in Osteuropa*, Giessen 1992, pp. 71–9. Cf. 'Kazakhs Stop Nuclear Testing (Nevada-Semipalatinsk Antinuclear Campaign), 1989–1991', http://nvdata base.swarthmore.edu/content/kazakhs-stop-nuclear-testing-nevada-semipalat insk-antinuclear-campaign-1989–1991.

65 Richard Stone, 'Plutonium Fields Forever', *Science* 300/5623 (23 May 2003), pp. 1220–4.

66 Artem Ermilow, 'Atomtests, Uranförderung und Ölindustrie: Strahlenbelastung und Strahlenschutz in Kasachstan', in *Grünbuch Politische Ökologie im Osten Europas*, p. 174. Ermilov (from the nuclear physics institute in Almaty) emphasizes that, by concentrating on the fallout from nuclear tests, one tends to overlook that radionuclides released by uranium and oil production represent 'a much greater danger' (ibid., p. 169).

67 Jaroshinskaja, *Verschlußsache Tschernobyl*, p. 227.

68 Nikita F. Glazovsky, 'The Aral Sea Basin', in Jeanne X. Kasperson et al., eds., *Regions at Risk: Comparison of Threatened Environments*, Tokyo 1995, p. 135.

69 Stefan Merl, 'Entstalinisierung, Reformen und Wettlauf der Systeme 1953–1964', in Stefan Plaggenborg, ed., *Handbuch der Geschichte Russlands*, vol. 5, Stuttgart 2002, pp. 215ff.

70 See, for example, Fyodor Morgun, chair of the USSR State Committee for the Environment, speaking on 1 July 1988 to the All-Union Conference (*Offene Worte*, pp. 390f.): 'The main blame for the loss of humus and the soil erosion lies with the strip plough and deep ploughing. . . . The plough is the destroyer, and yet we produce 200,000 new ones a year.'

71 Obertreis, 'Angriff auf die Wüste', p. 45.

72 René Létolle and Monique Mainguet, *Der Aralsee: Eine ökologische Katastrophe*, Berlin 1996, p. 328.

73 Ibid., pp. 93, 387–94.

74 Ibid., p. 337.

75 Julia Obertreis to the author, 4 August 2010. According to Glazovsky, 'Aral Sea Basin' (p. 107), pesticide use in this region rose to 54 kilos per hectare, compared with an average of 3 kilos throughout the Soviet Union.

76 John R. McNeill, *Something New Under the Sun: An Environmental History of the Twentieth-Century World*, New York 2000, p. 162.

77 Reimar Gilsenbach, *Die Erde dürstet: 6000 Jahre Kampf ums Wasser*, Leipzig 1961, pp. 290ff.

78 Létolle and Mainguet, *Der Aralsee*, p. 346.

79 Gundula Bahro, 'Steppenbrand in Kasachstan: Vom Katastrophengebiet zum ökologischen Vorreiter', p. 150.
80 Cooke, *In Mortal Hands*, p. 309.
81 Tobias Münchmeyer (Greenpeace), 'Ukrainian Energy Policy: Between Chornobyl and the Kremlin', in Lutz Mez et al., eds., *International Perspectives on Energy Policy and the Role of Nuclear Power*, Berlin 2008; Irina Stavcuk, 'Ukraine: Doppelter Klimawandel', in *Grünbuch Politische Ökologie im Osten Europas*, pp. 237–50.
82 These points are based on a talk by Kerstin S. Jobst at Bielefeld University: 'Katastrophendiskurse: Der Holodomor und das Reaktorunglück von Chornobyl im ukrainischen kollektiven Gedächtnis', and on the ensuing discussion.
83 'Rejecting the Precautionary Principle' is the title of the conclusion to Aaron Wildavsky, *But Is It True? A Citizen's Guide to Environmental Health and Safety Issues*, Cambridge MA 1995.
84 Ibid., p. 428.
85 Ibid., p. 441.
86 Zhores A. Medvedev, *Nuclear Disaster in the Urals*, London 1979.
87 Gestwa, 'Ökologischer Notstand und sozialer Protest', p. 383.
88 Julia Obertreis to the author, 4 August 2010.
89 On this and the following points, see Ehrhart Neubert, *Geschichte der Opposition in der DDR 1949–1989*, 2nd edn, Bonn 1998; here, pp. 626ff. ('Tschernobyl ist überall'). On the 'rise of an anti-nuclear movement' in the GDR (a term that arouses exaggerated expectations in a Western reader), see Wolfgang Rüddenklau, *Störenfried: DDR-Opposition 1986–1989*, Berlin 1992, pp. 61ff.
90 On the basis of internal records: Mike Reichert, *Kernenergiewirtschaft in der DDR: Entwicklungs-bedingungen, konzeptioneller Anspruch und Realisierungsgrad (1955–1990)*, St Katharinen 1999, pp. 311ff.
91 See the groundbreaking report by Peter Wensierski, *Von oben nach unten wächst gar nichts: Umweltzerstörung und Protest in der DDR*, Frankfurt 1986, p. 71.
92 Reichert, *Kernenergiewirtschaft in der DDR*, p. 423.
93 Radkau, *Technik in Deutschland*, pp. 396f.
94 Jan Schönfelder, *Mit Gott gegen Gülle. Die Umweltgruppe Knau/Dittersdorf 1986 bis 1991: Eine regionale Protestbewegung in der DDR*, Rudolstadt 2000.
95 This happened surprisingly little, however, in areas that could not receive Western television, as I discovered myself during a lecture I gave in Dresden shortly after the fall of the Wall.
96 Radkau, *Technik in Deutschland*, p. 394.
97 Communication from Eberhard Wächtler, who wrote the life story of Rammler.
98 Carlo Jordan, 'Umweltzerstörung und Umweltpolitik in der DDR', in *Machtstrukturen und Entscheidungs-mechanismen im SED-Staat und die Frage der Verantwortung*, Baden-Baden 1995 (= *Materialien der Enquete-Kommission 'Aufarbeitung von Geschichte und Folgen der SED-Diktatur in Deutschland'*, vol. II/3), p. 1785.
99 See the (for its time) excellent work published by the Federal Ministry for Inter-German Relations: *DDR Handbuch*, vol. 2, 3rd edn, Cologne 1985, pp. 1372ff.
100 Jörg Roesler, *Umweltprobleme und Umweltpolitik in der DDR*, Erfurt 2006, pp. 38f.

101 Reichert, *Kernenergiewirtschaft in der DDR*, pp. 227ff.
102 Ibid., pp. 342ff.
103 Christoph Bernhardt: 'Von der "Mondlandschaft" zur sozialistischen "Erholungslandschaft"? Die Niederlausitz als Exerzierfeld der Regional-planung in der DDR-Zeit', in Günter Bayerl and Dirk Maier, eds., *Die Niederlausitz vom 18. Jahrhundert bis heute: Eine gestörte Kulturlandschaft?*, Münster 2002, p. 125.
104 Wilhelm Knabe to the author, 30 September 2010.
105 Bernhardt, 'Von der "Mondlandschaft"', p. 313.
106 Michaela Lorck, 'Braunkohletagebau und Rekultivierung: Probleme und Chancen der Wiedernutzbarmachung im Braunkohlentagebau der DDR', master's thesis, Bielefeld 2006.
107 One senses this regret between the lines of the lavishly illustrated volume by Lothar Eissmann and Armin Rudolph, *Die aufgehenden Seen im Süden Leipzigs: Metamorphose einer Landschaft*, 2nd edn, Leipzig 2006.
108 Horst Paucke, *Chancen für Umweltpolitik und Umweltforschung: Zur Situation in der ehemaligen DDR*, Marburg 1994, p. 40.
109 Hans-Peter Gensichen, 'Umweltverantwortung in einer betonierten Gesellschaft: Anmerkungen zur kirchlichen Umweltarbeit in der DDR 1970 bis 1990', in Franz-Josef Brüggemeier and Jens Ivo Engels, eds., *Natur- und Umweltschutz nach 1945: Konzepte, Konflikte, Kompetenzen*, Frankfurt 2005, p. 289 n. 12.
110 Hannelore Kurth-Gilsenbach, *Trostlied für Mäuse*, Eberswalde 1994, p. 25.
111 Jordan, 'Umweltzerstörung und Umweltpolitik in der DDR', p. 1772. This classification nevertheless became known in the days of the GDR: see Peter Wensierki, *Von oben nach unten wächst gar nichts*, Frankfurt 1986, pp. 22f.
112 It is no accident that a collective history of conservation in the GDR greatly surpasses in scale and documentation anything that yet exists on the East German environmental movement: Institut für Umweltgeschichte und Regionalentwicklung (IUGR), ed., *Naturschutz in den neuen Bundesländern: Ein Rückblick*, 2 half vols., Marburg 1998.
113 See Marion Schulz, *Ein Leben in Harmonie. Kurt und Erna Kretschmann: Für den Schutz und die Bewahrung der Natur*, Neuenhagen 1999.
114 Reimar Gilsenbach, *Wer im Gleichschritt marschiert, geht in die falsche Richtung: Ein biografisches Selbstbildnis*, eds. Hannelore Gilsenbach and Harro Hess, Bad Münstereifel 2004, pp. 202ff.
115 Karl Friedel and Reimar Gilsenbach, *Das Roßmäßler-Büchlein*, Berlin 1956; cf. ibid., pp. 43ff.: 'Making nature into *Heimat*.'
116 Hannelore Kurth, 'Kreuzfahrten für die Umwelt: Durch die Öko-Szene von Rostock bis Suhl', in Susanne Raubold, ed., *Go East! DDR: Der nahe Osten*, Berlin 1990, pp. 111ff.
117 In Carlo Jordan and Hans Michael Kloth, eds., *Arche Nova. Opposition in der DDR: Das 'Grün-ökologische Netzwerk Arche' 1988–90*, Berlin 1995, p. 263.
118 Hermann Behrens and Lebrecht Jeschke, in Schulz, *Leben in Harmonie*, pp. 106, 109.
119 Rainer Pfannkuchen, 'Naturschutz in Dresden', *Dresdner Hefte* 67 (*Von der Natur der Stadt: Lebensraum Dresden*), Dresden 2001, p. 75.
120 Jordan and Kloth, *Arche Nova*, p. 297; cf. Hartmut Zwahr, *Ende einer Selbstzerstörung: Leipzig und die Revolution in der DDR*, Göttingen 1993, pp. 8f., 11, 16.

121 Thomas Mayer, *Helden der friedlichen Revolution: 18 Porträts von Wegbereitern aus Leipzig*, Leipzig 2009, pp. 105ff.

122 Harald Thomasius, 'Die Entwicklung der Gesellschaft für Natur und Umwelt im Kulturbund der DDR zu einem Zentrum sozialistischer Umweltpolitik und landeskulturellen Schöpfertums', *Natur und Umwelt* 2 (1987), p. 7.

123 Ibid., p. 13.

124 Lutz Ribbe (director of EuroNatur), 'Neue Hoffnung: Umweltprojekte in Osteuropa', in Akademie für Natur- und Umweltschutz Baden-Württemberg, ed., *Umwelt in Osteuropa: Von der kommunistischen Ausbeutung in den marktwirtschaftlichen Ausverkauf?*, Stuttgart 1993, p. 55.

125 Reimar Gilsenbach, 'Die größte DDR der Welt: Ein Staat ohne Nationalparke: Des Merkens Würdiges aus meiner grünen Donquichotterie', in IUGR, *Naturschutz in den neuen Bundesländern*, p. 544.

126 See the candid anniversary brochure: *100 Jahre NABU: Ein historischer Abriß 1899–1999*, Bonn 1999, pp. 22ff.

127 Ibid., pp. 31ff.

128 See the anniversary volume *20 Jahre EuroNatur: Gemeinsam für Europas Natur* (= *euronatur* 2 (2007)).

129 Title of *euronatur* 2 (2010).

130 *Der Spiegel*, 29 January 1990, pp. 30ff.

131 Rüddenklau, *Störenfried*, p. 129.

132 Michael Beleites, *Untergrund: Ein Konflikt mit der Stasi in der Uran-Provinz*, 2nd edn, Berlin 1992; Rainer Karlsch, *Uran für Moskau. Die Wismut: Eine populäre Geschichte*, Bonn 2007, pp. 192f.

133 Michael Beleites to the Bundestag inquiry on the 'SED dictatorship', 16 March 1994 (vol. VII/1, p. 199).

134 See the revelations in Karlsch, *Uran für Moskau*, pp. 151f., 178f.

135 Jordan, 'Umweltzerstörung und Umweltpolitik in der DDR', p. 1777.

136 Jordan and Kloth, *Arche Nova*, p. 184.

137 Neubert, *Geschichte der Opposition in der DDR*, pp. 451f.

138 Ibid., p. 629.

139 Ibid., p. 645.

140 Jordan and Kloth, *Arche Nova*, p. 65.

141 See Michael Beleites, 'Die unabhängige Umweltbewegung in der DDR', in Institut für Umweltgeschichte und Regionalentwicklung, ed., *Umweltschutz in der DDR*, vol. 3: *Beruflicher, ehrenamtlicher und freiwilliger Umweltschutz*, Munich 2007, p. 208. Encouraging signals also came from many official institutions; see, e.g., Christian Hänsel, 'Die Umweltproblematik in Lehre und Forschung an der Karl-Marx-Universität Leipzig', in ibid., p. 256.

142 Jordan and Kloth, *Arche Nova*, p. 23.

143 Franz-Josef Bruggemeier, *Tschernobyl, 26. April 1986: Die ökologische Herausforderung*, Munich 1988, p. 269.

144 Zsuzsa Gille, *From the Cult of Waste to the Trash Heap of History: The Politics of Waste in Socialist and Postsocialist Hungary*, Bloomington 2007.

145 In Wensierski, *Von oben nach unten wächst gar nichts*, p. 181.

146 Hans-Peter Gensichen, 'Umweltverantwortung in einer betonierten Gesellschaft: Anmerkungen zur kirchlichen Umweltarbeit in der DDR 1970 bis 1990', in Brüggemeier and Engels, *Natur- und Umweltschutz nach 1945*, pp. 287–306.

147 Kurth-Gilsenbach, *Trostlied für Mäuse*, p. 9.

148 See Sabine Rosenbladt, *Der Osten ist Grün?*, Munich 1988, p. 101.
149 Neubert, *Geschichte der Opposition in der DDR*, p. 746.
150 See, e.g., *Die Grünen im Bundestag*, vol. 1, pp. 320ff. Cf. Jordan and Kloth, *Arche Nova*, p. 54 n. 7.
151 Christoph Hohlfeld, 'Bündnis 90/Grüne: Eine neue Partei?', in Joachim Raschke, ed., *Die Grünen: Wie sie wurden, was sie sind*, Cologne 1993, pp. 841 n. 11, 844 n. 22, 846, 839. Cf., even before unification, Klaus-Dieter Feige, 'Wie Ausländer in der eigenen Partei: Anmerkungen eines Ost-Grünen', in Ralf Fücks, ed., *Sind die Grünen noch zu retten?*, Reinbek 1991, pp. 107–15.
152 Antje Vollmer, 'Das Privileg der ersten, viele Fehler zu machen: Gründe für den Niedergang', in Fücks, *Sind die Grünen noch zu retten?*, p. 15.
153 Hubert Kleinert, *Aufstieg und Fall der Grünen: Analyse einer alternativen Partei*, Bonn 1992, pp. 143, 126.
154 Dieter Oberndörfer, *Schutz der tropischen Regenwälder durch Entschuldung*, Munich 1989 (= Schriftenreihe des Bundeskanzleramtes 5), p. 22.
155 Mark Dowie, *Conservation Refugees: The Hundred-Year Conflict between Global Conservation and Native Peoples*, Cambridge MA 2009, p. xx.
156 Jochen Bölsche, ed., *Natur ohne Schutz: Neue Öko-Strategien gegen die Umweltzerstörung*, Hamburg 1982. The editor even claimed (p. 13) that the West German conservation movement was 'as unsuccessful as any other social current'.
157 Henry Makowski (*Nationalparke in Deutschland. Schatzkammern der Natur: Kampfplätze des Naturschutzes*, Neumünster 1997, p. 13) even argues that the main task of the IUCN was always 'to prevent an inflation of national parks around the world'!
158 Andrew Revkin, *The Burning Season: The Murder of Chico Mendes and the Fight for the Amazon Rain Forest*, Boston 1990, pp. 260f.
159 Luz Kerkeling, *La Lucha Sigue! EZLN: Ursachen und Entwicklungen des zapatistischen Aufstands*, Münster 2003, pp. 221ff.
160 Mac Chapin, 'A Challenge to Conservationists', *World Watch Magazine* (Nov./Dec. 2004), p. 29.
161 Alfred Runte, *Yosemite: The Embattled Wilderness*, Lincoln NE 1990, pp. 58ff. Even Runte is silent about the later fate of the Indians. Evidently no one thought of assigning them to manage the national park.
162 Mark David Spence, *Dispossessing the Wilderness: Indian Removal and the Making of the National Parks*, New York 1999, p. 109.
163 Shepard Krech III, *The Ecological Indian: Myth and History*, New York 1999, p. 20.
164 William Arrowsmith and Michael Korth, *Die Erde ist unsere Mutter: Die großen Reden der Indianerhäuptlinge*, Munich 1995, p. 152; see the attempt on pp. 17–25 to reconstruct the original text of the speech.
165 Will McArthur, '"It Seems Like We Should Be on the Same Side!" Native Americans, Environmentalists, and the Grand Canyon', in Michael Egan and Jeff Crane, eds., *Natural Protest. Essays on the History of American Environmentalism*, New York 2009, p. 311.
166 Claude Lévi-Strauss, *Tristes Tropiques* (orig. 1955), London 2012, p. 188.
167 Bron Taylor, 'Earth First! and Global Narratives of Popular Ecological Resistance', in Taylor, ed., *Ecological Resistance Movements*, Albany NY 1995, pp. 18ff.

168 Dowie, *Conservation Refugees*, pp. 88ff.
169 Oberndörfer, *Schutz der tropischen Regenwälder*, p. 25.
170 Roderick P. Neumann, *Imposing Wilderness: Struggles over Livelihood and Nature Preservation in Africa*, Berkeley 1998, p. 208.
171 Wilfried Huismann, *Schwarzbuch WWF: Dunkle Geschäfte im Zeichen des Panda*, Gütersloh 2012.
172 See Colin M. Turnbull, *The Mountain People*, New York 1972.
173 Werner Petermann, *Die Geschichte der Ethnologie*, Wuppertal 2004, pp. 855f.
174 Jack D. Ives and Bruno Messerli, *The Himalayan Dilemma: Reconciling Development and Conservation*, London 1989, p. 61; Ulrich Gruber, *Reiseführer Natur Nepal, Sikkim und Bhutan*, Munich 1995, pp. 47f.
175 Stanley F. Stevens, *Claiming the High Ground: Sherpas, Subsistence, and Environmental Change in the Highest Himalaya*, Delhi 1996.
176 Igoe, *Conservation and Globalization*, pp. 154ff., with reference to Stanley F. Stevens (see preceding note).
177 See the essential account by an American negotiator: Richard E. Benedick, *Ozone Diplomacy: New Directions in Safeguarding the Planet*, Camdridge MA 1991; and Karen T. Litfin, *Ozone Discourses: Science and Politics in Global Environmental Cooperation*, New York 1994.
178 *Encyclopedia of World Environmental History*, vol. 3, p. 975 (Verena Winiwarter). Ironically, the EPA was studying the health risks associated with high ozone concentrations at the same time; see Marc K. Landy et al., *The Environmental Protection Agency. Asking the Wrong Questions: From Nixon to Clinton*, New York 1994, pp. 49ff.
179 Wildavsky, *But Is It True?*, pp. 304–39 ('CFCs and Ozone Depletion: Are they as Bad as People Think?'); Gregg Easterbrook, *A Moment on the Earth*, New York 1995, pp. 528–50 ('Radiation, Natural').
180 Erik M. Conway, *High-Speed Dreams: NASA and the Technopolitics of Supersonic Transportation, 1945–1999*, Baltimore 2005, p. 228.
181 Barry Commoner, *The Closing Circle: Nature, Man, and Technology*, New York 1971, p. 202; Landy et al., *Environmental Protection Agency*, p. 257; Conway, *High-Speed Dreams*, pp. 157ff.
182 Donella Meadows, Dennis Meadows and Jorgen Randers, *Beyond the Limits: Confronting Global Collapse, Envisioning a Sustainable Future*, White River Junction VT 1992, p. 142.
183 See Daniel Cohn-Bendit and Reinhard Mohr, *1968: Die letzte Revolution, die noch nichts vom Ozonloch wusste*, Berlin 1988.
184 Joachim Radkau, *Nature and Power*, Cambridge 2008, pp. 289f.
185 Meadows et al., *Beyond the Limits*, p. 150.
186 Ibid., p. 154.
187 *Encyclopedia of World Environmental History*, vol. 2, pp. 858f. (Reiner Grundmann).
188 Litfin, *Ozone Discourses*, p. 99
189 Richard Elliott Benedick, *Ozone Diplomacy: New Directions in Safeguarding the Planet*, Cambridge MA 1998, p. x.
190 Litfin, *Ozone Discourses*, p. 103.
191 James Lovelock, *The Ages of Gaia: A Biography of Our Living Earth*, Oxford 1995, pp. 225f.
192 Ibid., p. 226.
193 Joachim Radkau, 'Scharfe Konturen für das Ozonloch: Zur Öko-Ikonografie

der *Spiegel*-Titel', in Gerhard Paul, ed., *Das Jahrhundert der Bilder: 1949 bis heute*, Göttingen 2008, pp. 533ff.

194 Benedick, *Ozone Diplomacy*, p. 204.

195 Even Richard E. Benedick, who otherwise likes to stress the importance of the USA as well as himself, has a whole chapter entitled 'UNEP Starts the Process'. Benedick, *Ozone Diplomacy*, pp. 40ff. Cf. p. 208, where he refers to Tolba's leadership qualities as an example of the individual dimension of such policy breakthroughs.

196 Easterbrook, *Moment on the Earth*, p. 538.

197 Benedick, *Ozone Diplomacy*, p. 114.

198 Ibid., pp. 195ff.

199 Meadows et al., *Beyond the Limits*, p. 159.

200 This is the constructivist main thesis in Litfin, *Ozone Discourses* – a critique of Benedick's account, although he too indicates that there was no direct route from scientific experiment to grand policy.

201 Benedick, *Ozone Diplomacy*, pp. 82f., 101f.

202 Ibid., p. 153.

203 Ibid., p. 206.

204 Ibid., pp. 188 ff. ('North–South Endgame').

205 Rudolf Steinberg, 'Symbolische Umweltpolitik unter besonderer Berücksichtigung der Beschleunigungsgesetzgebung', in Bernd Hansjürgens and Gertrude Lübbe-Wolff, eds., *Symbolische Umweltpolitik*, Frankfurt 2000, pp. 79ff.; Monika Böhm, 'Institutionelle Rahmenbedingungen symbolischer Umweltpolitik', in ibid., pp. 243–8.

206 *Our Common Future*, Oxford 1987, p. 64.

207 Willy Brandt, 'Introduction' to *North–South. A Programme for Survival: Report of the Independent Commission on International Development Issues under the Chairmanship of Willy Brandt*, London 1980, p. 23.

208 Ulrich Grober, *Die Entdeckung der Nachhaltigkeit: Kulturgeschichte eines Begriffs*, Munich 2010, p. 257. On the concept of technical development, which in Germany originally had an evolutionary meaning, see Radkau, *Technik in Deutschland*, pp. 184ff.

209 See Brundtland, *Madam Prime Minister*, p. 193.

210 Grober, *Die Entdeckung der Nachhaltigkeit*, p. 249.

211 Peter Merseburger, *Willy Brandt 1913–1992*, Munich 2004, p. 678.

212 Grober, *Die Entdeckung der Nachhaltigkeit*, p. 260.

213 Brundtland, *Madam Prime Minister*, p. 195.

214 The following remarks are based on oral communications from Volker Hauff (28 September 2010), the German member of the Brundtland Commission.

215 Wolfgang Haber to the author, 4 September 2010.

216 Hugo von Hofmannsthal and Carl J. Burckhardt, *Briefwechsel*, Frankfurt 1956, p. 175.

217 *Our Common Future*, p. 43.

218 Christian Hey, *Umweltpolitik in Europa*, Munich 1994, p. 22.

219 Wiebke Peters, 'Nachhaltigkeit als Grundsatz der Forstwirtschaft, ihre Verankerung in der Gesetzgebung und ihre Bedeutung in der Praxis. Die Verhältnisse in der Bundesrepublik Deutschland im Vergleich mit einigen Industrie- und Entwicklungsländern', diss., Hamburg 1984.

220 Joachim Radkau, *Wood: A History*, Cambridge 2012, pp. 317f.

221 Nicholas Hildyard (co-editor of *The Ecologist*), 'Foxes in Charge of the

Chickens', in Wolfgang Sachs, ed., *Global Ecology: A New Arena of Political Conflict*, London 1993, pp. 22–35. This volume is one of the sources for the following remarks.

222 *Our Common Future*, pp. 172ff.
223 Shridath S. Ramphal, *Our Country, the Planet*, London 1992, pp. 389f.
224 See Brundtland, *Madam Prime Minister*, p. 214.
225 Ibid., p. 201: 'The Brazilian authorities made it clear that they did not want us to discuss only the Amazon. They did not want any interference in domestic affairs. We would simply have to discuss rain forests in general. We had no problem with that.'
226 Bruce Rich, *Mortgaging the Earth: The World Bank, Environmental Impoverishment, and the Crisis of Development*, Boston 1994, p. 243.
227 *Our Common Future*, p. 58.
228 *The Earth Summit: The United Nations Conference on Environment and Development (UNCED)*, London 1993, pp. 4, 521.
229 *Der Spiegel*, 18 May 1992, p. 224.
230 *Earth Summit*, p. 4.
231 Brundtland, *Madam Prime Minister*, p. 193.
232 Brigitte Erler, *Tödliche Hilfe: Bericht von meiner letzten Dienstreise in Sachen Entwicklungshilfe*, Freiburg 1985.
233 *Der Spiegel*, 24 February 1986, p. 44.
234 Richard von Weizsäcker, in Bertrand Schneider (general secretary of the Club of Rome), *Die Revolution der Barfüßigen: Ein Bericht an den Club of Rome* (French orig. 1985), Vienna 1986, p. 9.
235 Rich, *Mortgaging the Earth*, p. 261. Subtler, though tending in the same direction, is Pamela S. Chasek et al., eds., *Global Environmental Politics*, Boulder CO 2010, pp. 35f.
236 Chloé Maurel, *Histoire de l'UNESCO: Les trente premières années, 1945–1974*, Paris 2010, p. 282.
237 Thomas Robertson, '"This Is the American Earth": American Empire, the Cold War, and American Environmentalism', *Diplomatic History* 32 (2008), pp. 581f.
238 Martina Kaller-Dietrich, *Ivan Illich*, Weitra 2007, p. 89.
239 Max Nicholson, *The New Environmental Age*, Cambridge 1987, p. 184.
240 Vandana Shiva, *Das Geschlecht des Lebens: Frauen, Ökologie und Dritte Welt*, Berlin 1989, p. 12.
241 Dave Foreman, *Confessions of an Eco-Warrior*, New York 1991, p. 175.
242 Al Gore, *Earth in the Balance: Ecology and the Human Spirit*, Boston 1992, pp. 296ff.
243 See Werner Abelshauser, *Deutsche Wirtschaftsgeschichte seit 1945*, Munich 2004, pp. 130–54.
244 Brundtland, *Madam Prime Minister*, pp. 338, 341.
245 *Der Spiegel* 25 (1992), p. 150.
246 Ibid., pp. 148ff.
247 I owe much here to my conversations with Veronika Bennholdt-Thomsen, who has had many years of experience working as a social anthropologist in Southern Mexico: see her short book *Geld oder Leben: Was uns wirklich reich macht*, Munich 2010.
248 Richard N. L. Andrews, *Managing the Environment, Managing Ourselves: A History of American Environmental Policy*, New Haven 1999, p. 370.

249 In *Die Umweltmacher*, p. 27.

250 Ramphal, *Our Country, the Planet*, p. 269.

251 Peter Weingart, Anita Engels and Petra Pansegrau, *Von der Hypothese zur Katastrophe: Der anthropogene Klimawandel im Diskurs zwischen Wissenschaft, Politik und Massenmedien*, 2nd edn, Opladen 2008, p. 74.

252 Stanley P. Johnson in *Earth Summit*, p. 6.

253 Ibid., p. 5.

254 Rich, *Mortgaging the Earth*, p. 257. See also Siegfried Pater, *Das grüne Gewissen Brasiliens: José Lutzenberger*, Göttingen 1989, pp. 111ff.

255 When I searched for 'Agenda 21' on Amazon in August 2010, no fewer than 1,918 titles came up; but there was nothing for the original Rio text.

256 Commoner, *Closing Circle*, p. 178.

257 *Zukunftsfähiges Deutschland in einer globalisierten Welt: Eine Studie des Wuppertal Instituts für Klima, Umwelt, Energie*, eds. Brot für die Welt, eed (Evangelischer Entwicklungsdienst) and BUND, Frankfurt 2008, p. 88.

258 Wolfgang Haber to the author, 4 September 2010.

259 Robert Gottlieb, *Forcing the Spring: The Transformation of the American Environmental Movement*, Washington DC 1993, pp. 256ff., 259.

260 Robert Benford, 'The Half-Life of the Environmental Justice Frame: Innovation, Diffusion, and Stagnation', in David Naguib Pellow and Robert J. Brulle, eds., *Power, Justice, and the Environment: A Critical Appraisal of the Environmental Justice Movement*, Cambridge MA 2005, pp. 49f.; Dale Jamieson, 'Justice: The Heat of Environmentalism', in Ronald Sandler and Phaedra C. Pezzullo, eds., *Environmental Justice and Environmentalism*, Cambridge MA 2007, p. 88.

261 Richard A. Walker, *The Country in the City: The Greening of the San Francisco Bay Area*, Seattle 2007, pp. 241, 243.

262 Known in Germany from the late nineteenth century, this spread to the United States in the course of the twentieth: see Charles Lord, *Environmental Justice: Process and Inequality*, a report, specially focusing on Baltimore, to the World Congress for Environmental History, held in Copenhagen in August 2009.

263 Ulrich Beck, *Risk Society*, London 1992, p. 36.

264 Elizabeth D. Blum, 'Parting the Waters: The Ecumenical Task Force at Love Canal and Beyond', in Egan and Crane, *Natural Protest*, pp. 246ff.

265 Wildavsky, *But Is It True?*, p. 153.

266 Gottlieb, *Forcing the Spring*, p. 188; Blum, 'Parting the Waters', p. 260. Similarly, Allan Abramson writes from his experience at the EPA (2 September 2010): 'Love Canal was important, but treating every hazardous waste site as a Love Canal was definitely a mistake. . . . Not enough health or environmental impact, for another.'

267 Bunyan Bryant and Elaine Hockman, 'A Brief Comparison of the Civil Rights Movement and the Environmental Justice Movement', in Pellow and Brulle, *Power, Justice, and the Environment*, p. 33.

268 *Encyclopedia of World Environmental History*, vol. 1, p. 453.

269 Walker, *Country in the City*, pp. 229–48 ('Green Justice: Reclaiming the Inner City'); the emergence of the environmental justice movement in San Francisco Bay is the climax and finale of the account.

270 Mike Davis, *City of Quartz: Excavating the Future in Los Angeles*, London 2006, p. 159.

271 Mark Dowie, *Losing Ground: American Environmentalism at the Close of the Twentieth Century*, Cambridge MA 1995, p. 152.
272 Daniel M. Berman and John T. O'Connor, *Who Owns the Sun? People, Politics, and the Struggle for a Solar Economy*, White River Junction 1996, pp. 189ff. ('Manufacturing Photovoltaics: Another Toxic Time Bomb?'); see also Walker, *Country in the City*, p. 239, on the partnership between the Silicon Valley Toxics Coalition and EJ groups.
273 Cassels, *Uncertain Promise of Law*, p. 259; Bryant and Hockman, 'Brief Comparison', p. 32.
274 Benford, 'Half-Life', pp. 45ff.
275 Walker, *Country in the City*, pp. 244ff., 232: 'Urban Habitat grew out of the first Eco-Cities Conference organized in Berkeley by Richard Register', with reference to Richard Register, *Ecocity Berkeley: Building Cities for a Healthy Future*, Berkeley 1987.
276 Rosenblatt, *Der Osten ist grün?*, pp. 12ff.
277 See the examples from around the world in the 'Environmental Justice' article in *Encyclopedia of World Environmental History*, vol. 1, pp. 451–4 (Brett Williams and Jon Adelson).
278 See J. Timmons Roberts, 'Globalizing Environmental Justice', in Sandler and Pezzullo, *Environmental Justice and Environmentalism*, pp. 285–307.
279 *Encyclopedia of World Environmental History*, vol. 1, p. 454.
280 Bei Alon Tal, *Pollution in a Promised Land: An Environmental History of Israel*, Berkeley 2002, pp. 332–6 ('The Elusive Concept of Environmental Justice'); more recently this movement has been gaining ground, as I learned from conversations with two of its initiators, Carmit Lubanov and Dan Rabinowitz.
281 McCloskey, 'Twenty Years of Change', p. 80.
282 Jens Soentgen and Armin Reller, eds., *CO2: Lebenselixier und Klimakiller*, Munich 2009.
283 See Alan Hastings, 'Biological Chaos and Complex Dynamics', in Simon A. Levin, ed., *The Princeton Guide to Ecology*, Princeton 2009, pp. 172ff.; Marten Scheffer, 'Alternative Stable States and Regime Shifts in Ecosystems', in ibid., pp. 395ff.; Erika Zavaleta and Nicole Heller, 'Responses of Communities and Ecosystems to Global Changes', in ibid., pp. 407ff.; and Carolyn Merchant, *The Columbia Guide to American Environmental History*, New York 2002, pp. 171f. ('The Influence of Chaos Theory').
284 Hans von Storch and Werner Krauß, *Die Klima-Falle: Die gefährliche Nähe von Politik und Klimaforschung*, Munich 2013, p. 169.
285 See the illuminating interview with Nikolaus von Bomhard, the head of the Münchener Rück, in *Der Spiegel* 27 (2010), pp. 76–8.
286 Wolfgang Sachs, 'The Blue Planet: On the Ambiguity of a Modern Icon', ch. 7 of *Planet Dialectics: Explorations in Environment Development*, London 1999, pp. 110 28.
287 Laurens Jan Brinkhorst, 'Möglichkeiten und Grenzen europäischer Umweltpolitik aus der Sicht der EG-Kommission', in *Wenn's dem Nachbarn nicht gefällt: Umweltpolitik als europäische Aufgabe*, Mainau 1992 (= *Mainauer Gespräche* 8), p. 41.
288 Peter Menke-Glückert, 'Die Mühen der Ebenen: Umweltziele im Behördenalltag', in Henning von Köller, ed., *Umweltpolitik mit Augenmaß*, Berlin 2000, pp. 121f.

289 *Die Umweltmacher*, p. 29.
290 Arundhati Roy, *Power Politics: The Reincarnation of Rumpelstiltskin*, Kottayam 2001, p. 14.
291 Petra Dobner, *Wasserpolitik: Zur politischen Theorie, Praxis und Kritik globaler Governance*, Frankfurt 2010, pp. 121, 123.
292 Jean Ziegler, *Les nouveaux maîtres du monde et ceux qui leur résistent*, Paris 2002.
293 Joseph Stiglitz, *Globalization and its Discontents*, London 2002, pp. 40ff.
294 Hauke Janssen, *Milton Friedman und die 'monetaristische Revolution' in Deutschland*, Marburg 2006, p. 14.
295 Martin Jänicke, 'Pionierländer im Umweltschutz', in *Die Umweltmacher*, p. 464.
296 *Encyclopedia of World Environmental History*, vol. 1, pp. 125ff. (Vicki Medland).
297 Timothy J. Farnham, *Saving Nature's Legacy: Origins of the Idea of Biological Diversity*, New Haven 2007, pp. 235ff.: Wilson even found it too 'glitzy' at first. In Farnham's view, the concept itself went back further than the invention of this term: it was an ethical norm, not the product of ecological research.
298 Stephen R. Kellert and Edward O. Wilson, eds., *The Biophilia Hypothesis*, Washington DC 1993.
299 Edward O. Wilson, *The Diversity of Life*, New York 1992, pp. 281–2.
300 Marc Auer and Karl-Heinz Erdmann, 'Schutz und Nutzung der natürlichen Ressourcen: Das Übereinkommen über die biologische Vielfalt', in Erdmann, ed., *Internationaler Naturschutz*, Berlin 1997, pp. 102, 111.
301 Udo E. Simonis, *Globale Umweltpolitik: Ansätze und Perspektiven*, Mannheim 1996, pp. 49ff.
302 The most perceptive article I know on the premises and problems of the FFH directive is Wolfgang Haber, 'Zur Problematik europäischer Naturschutz-Richtlinien', *Jahrbuch des Vereins zum Schutz der Bergwelt*, 72 (2007), pp. 95–110. The follow account is based on this study.
303 Hans Dieter Knapp, 'Internationaler Naturschutz: Phantom oder Notwendigkeit?', in Erdmann, *Internationaler Naturschutz*, p. 19.
304 Haber, 'Zur Problematik europäischer Naturschutz-Richtlinien', p. 107.
305 Surprisingly the EuroNatur bestseller (Volker Angres et al., *Bananen für Brüssel Europa: Wie unsere Steuern vergeudet werden*, Munich 1999) mentions the FFH directive only in passing, but it shows the degree to which taxpayers' interests can be mobilized for conservation and environmental protection – an opportunity masked by the 'ecology versus economics' opposition, as in Christian Hey, *Umweltpolitik in Europa*, Munich 1994, p. 149, or Jochen Roose, *Die Europäisierung von Umweltorganisationen: Die Umweltbewegung auf dem langen Weg nach Brüssel*, Wiesbaden 2003, pp. 140ff., 149.
306 Communication from Anna Wöbse (4 May 2005).
307 Martin Trost, 'Erfahrungen mit dem Management des Feldhamsters *Cricetus cricetus* (L.) in Sachsen-Anhalt', in Sandra Balzer et al., eds., *Management- und Artenschutzkonzepte bei der Umsetzung der FFH-Richtlinie*, Bonn 2008, pp. 131–46.
308 Haber, 'Zur Problematik europäischer Naturschutz-Richtlinien', p. 101.
309 Jozef Keulartz and Gilbert Leistra, eds., *Legitimacy in European Nature Conservation Policy: Case Studies in Multilevel Governance*, Berlin 2008 (=

International Library of Environmental, Agricultural and Food Ethics, vol. 14). I am grateful to Wolfgang Haber for this reference.

310 Wolfgang Haber too ('Zur Problematik europäischer Naturschutz-Richtlinien', pp. 101f., 106f.) sees this as the main opportunity contained in the FFH directive.

311 See the harsh but accurate little work by a once-prominent EU adviser: Hermann Priebe, *Die subventionierte Naturzerstörung: Plädoyer für eine neue Agrarkultur*, Munich 1990.

312 Angres et al., *Bananen für Brüssel*, p. 203.

313 See Haber, 'Zur Problematik europäischer Naturschutz-Richtlinien', p. 100.

314 The Swedish climatologist Bert Bolin, one of the earliest warning voices and the founding chair of the IPCC, points out: 'Undoubtedly, the USA was leading the development of global climate models' (Bert Bolin, *A History of the Science and Politics of Climate Change: The Role of the Intergovernmental Panel on Climate Change*, Cambridge 2007, p. 33). The following remarks are also based primarily on this book, which was published shortly before the author's death from cancer and is, in my view, the best-informed source on international climate policy in the 1980s and later. Its reflective tone is all the more pleasing because it contrasts with the bluster typical of popular literature on both sides of the argument.

315 David G. Victor, *The Collapse of the Kyoto Protocol and the Struggle to Slow Global Warming*, Princeton 2001, pp. ix, xi.

316 Ibid., p. 140.

317 Lynn White, Jr, 'The Historical Roots of Our Ecological Crisis', in David Spring and Eileen Spring, eds., *Ecology and Religion in History*, New York 1974, p. 18.

318 Rüdiger Glaser, *Klimageschichte Mitteleuropas: 1000 Jahre Wetter, Klima, Katastrophen*, Darmstadt 2001, p. 208.

319 Wolfgang Behringer, *A Cultural History of Climate*, Cambridge 2010, p. 186.

320 *Global 2000*, German edn, Frankfurt 1980, pp. 212–27.

321 See the illuminating references in Christopher Booker, *The Real Global Warming Disaster*, London 2009, pp. 82ff. ('Enter Dr Mann and the "Hockey Stick"').

322 Behringer, *Cultural History of Climate*, pp. 8ff.

323 See Jobst Conrad, *Von Arrhenius zum IPCC: Wissenschaftliche Dynamik und disziplinäre Verankerungen der Klimaforschung*, Münster 2008, esp. pp. 110ff.; Ralph Boch, 'Die Global Player des Klimawissens: Die Herausbildung der internationalen Klimaforschung', in Walter Hauser, ed., *Klima: Das Experiment mit dem Planeten Erde* (Deutsches Museum exhibition catalogue), Munich 2002, pp. 123–37; Spencer Weart, *The Discovery of Global Warming*, Cambridge 2003. I am grateful to Jobst Conrad for his critical reading of this chapter.

324 Bolin, *History of the Science and Politics of Climate Change*, p. 77.

325 Ibid., pp. 59, 88f.

326 Ibid., pp. 54f.; cf. p. 49 on the overhasty global warming alarm of NASA researcher James Hansen.

327 See ibid., pp. 49f.

328 Ibid., p. 49.

329 Ibid., pp. 56f.

330 Werner Abelshauser, *Nach dem Wirtschaftswunder: Der Gewerkschafter, Politiker und Unternehmer Hans Matthöfer*, Bonn 2009, pp. 349f.

331 Booker, *Real Global Warming Disaster*, p. 32.
332 Erik M. Conway's splendidly documented study comes to the conclusion that 'NASA's role in the American Earth sciences in the 20th century was revolutionary. . . . It has played a fundamental role in altering our understanding of our world and of life's place in its evolution. . . . While they were mourning the lost Moon, their agency rediscovered our own Earth' (*Atmospheric Science at NASA: A History*, Baltimore 2008, p. 320).
333 Peter Weingart, 'Vom Umweltschutz zur Nachhaltigkeit. Förderung der Umweltforschung im Spannungsfeld zwischen Wissenschaftsentwicklung und Politik', in Weingart and Niels C. Taubert, *Das Wissensministerium: Ein halbes Jahrhundert Forschungs- und Bildungspolitik in Deutschland*, Weilerswist 2006, p. 227.
334 Conrad, *Von Arrhenius zum IPCC*, p. 136.
335 Gerald Fricke, *Von Rio nach Kyoto*, Berlin 2001, p. 137.
336 Bolin, *History of the Science and Politics of Global Change*, p. 73.
337 See Fred Singer, *Hot Talk – Cold Science: Global Warming's Unfinished Debate*, Oakland 1997, pp. ix, 85.
338 Weingart et al., *Von der Hypothese zur Katastrophe*, pp. 65–84. Cf. Hey, *Umweltpolitik in Europa*, pp. 10, 24, 27f.
339 See the illuminating references in Victor, *Collapse*, pp. 57ff.
340 Bolin, *History of the Science and Politics of Global Change*, p. 135.
341 Christian Pfister, *Wetternachhersage: 500 Jahre Klimavariationen und Naturkatastrophen*, Berne 1999, p. 268.
342 Bolin, *History of the Science and Politics of Global Change*, p. 212.
343 The most prominent representative of this idea is the Nobel prizewinner and atmospheric chemist Paul Crutzen; see his contribution in Günter Altner et al., eds., *Die Klima-Manipulateure: Rettet uns Politik oder Geo-Engineering?*, Stuttgart 2010 (= *Jahrbuch Ökologie 2011*), pp. 33–6 ('Erdabkühlung durch Sulfatinjektion in die Stratosphäre'); and Samiha Shafy, 'Giftkur fürs Weltklima', *Der Spiegel* 28 (2006), p. 116.
344 Altner et al., *Die Klima-Manipulateure*.
345 Reinhard Böhm, *Heiße Luft nach Kopenhagen*, Vienna 2010, pp. 263f.
346 UNEP, ed., *Global Environment Outlook 2000*, London 1999, p. 240.
347 Transparency International, ed., *Global Corruption Report: Climate Change*, London and Washington DC 2011, p. 288.
348 See the important short overviews in Simonis, *Globale Umweltpolitik*, pp. 11, 22f., 25.
349 See the splendid study by Dobner, *Wasserpolitik*.
350 See the shocking facts in Simonis, *Globale Umweltpolitik*, pp. 62f. (65 per cent of African and 74 per cent of Central African agricultural land has been degraded).
351 Horst G. Mensching, *Desertifikation: Ein weltweites Problem der ökologischen Verwüstung in den Trockengebieten der Erde*, Darmstadt 1990, pp. 52ff.
352 Transparency International, *Global Corruption Report*.
353 Victor, *Collapse*, p. 134.
354 See Christopher Rootes, ed., *Environmental Protest in Western Europe*, Oxford 2007. Its conclusion (p. xv) is: 'There was no evidence at all of any interchange between British and French campaigners; differences in the ways the issues were framed in each country reflected deep-rooted and nationally peculiar attitudes to the countryside and national political contexts.'

355 Jochen Roose, *Die Europäisierung von Umweltorganisationen: Die Umweltbewegung auf dem langen Weg nach Brüssel*, Wiesbaden 2003, p. 213.

356 Christoph Knill, *Europäische Umweltpolitik*, Opladen 2003, p. 214; Michael Kraack et al., *Umweltintegration in der Europäischen Union*, Baden-Baden 2001, pp. 223f.

357 Daniel Cohn-Bendit confirms that 'the Greens did not even put the question of globalization on the agenda': Christiane Grefe et al., *Attac*, Berlin 2002, p. 206. On the other hand, personal links between Attac and environmental organizations were on the increase.

358 See Cohn-Bendit in Grefe et al., *Attac*, p. 204. Similarly, Bernard Cassen warned that a debate on the institutional future of Europe would 'tear apart' the Attac founding group (ibid., p. 118).

359 Thomas R. Wellock, *Critical Masses: Opposition to Nuclear Power in California, 1958–1978*, Madison WI 1998, pp. 90f. (He describes Brower's campaign as 'foolish'.)

360 Radkau, *Aufstieg und Krise*, pp. 442ff.

361 Schreurs, *Environmental Politics*, p. 71: 'Unlike in Germany, the anti-nuclear movement in Japan, however, remained largely a NIMBY phenomenon.'

362 Oral communications from Helmut Weidner and Miranda A. Schreurs (7 and 9 March 2012); Jun Ui, 'Anti-Pollution Movements and Other Grass-Roots Organizations', in Shigeto Tsuru and Helmut Weidner, eds., *Environmental Policy in Japan*, Berlin 1989, pp. 109–19.

363 Sally A. Kitt Chapel, *Chicago's Urban Nature*, Chicago 2007, pp. 193, 59; Dominic A. Pacyga, *Chicago: A Biography*, Chicago 2009, pp. 398ff.

Conclusion: The Dialectic of Green Enlightenment

1 According to Rolf Wiggershaus (*The Frankfurt School*, Cambridge 1994, pp. 349f.), Horkheimer's previous lecture 'The Revolt of Nature' formed the 'pivot' of *The Dialectic of Enlightenment*.

2 Hartmut Lehmann, 'The Interplay of Disenchantment and Re-Enchantment in Modern European History, or, the Origin and the Meaning of Max Weber's Phrase "Die Entzauberung der Welt"', in Lehmann, *Die Entzauberung der Welt: Studien zu Themen von Max Weber*, Göttingen 2009, pp. 9–20.

3 Frank Uekötter (*Am Ende der Gewissheiten: Die ökologische Frage im 21. Jahrhundert*, Frankfurt 2011, p. 145) even thinks he can show 'that the main force driving the ecologization of the Bundesrepublik was administrations that could use it in their own interests, partly because it enabled them to enlarge their powers and budget'.

4 Vikram Rao, *Shale Gas: The Promise and the Peril*, Research Triangle Park 2012, p. 123.

5 Turkey, the most Westernized country in the Islamic world, is probably an exception in this respect. See the highly impressive and informative *A Tale of Water*, ed. Turgay Türker, Istanbul 2000, an outline synthesis of Islam and environmentalism that was republished for the Istanbul water conference in 2009.

6 Rudolf Steinberg, 'Symbolische Umweltpolitik unter besonderer Berücksichtigung der Beschleunigungsgesetzgebung', in Bernd Hansjürgens and Gertrude Lübbe-Wolff, eds., *Symbolische Umweltpolitik*, Frankfurt 2000, p. 78.

7 Henry Makowski, *Nationalparke in Deutschland. Schatzkammern der Natur: Kampfplätze des Naturschutzes*, Neumünster 1997, p. 35.
8 Jobst Conrad, *Von Arrhenius zum IPCC: Wissenschaftliche Dynamik und diszi-plinäre Verankerungen der Klimaforschung*, Münster 2008, pp. 114f.
9 Mieke Roscher, *Ein Königreich für Tiere: Die Geschichte der britischen Tierrechtsbewegung*, Marburg 2009, p. 87.

Index

impact of 149, 153–4, 352
information on 346
Legasov 343
motherhood after 257–8
nuclear lobby 159
Robin-Wood Magazin 181
Soviet Union 352, 353, 356–65
women's mobilization 157
Chicago 27, 423
Chidzero, Bernard 388
chimpanzees 187–8
Chimurenga tree conservation 351
China, People's Republic of
agriculture 124
carbon dioxide emissions 419
coal 233, 417
Dai 230–4
deforestation 417
democratization 231, 232–3
GONGOs 239–40
groundwater depletion 417
panda politics 188, 239–40
population growth 92
Red Guards 231
Stockholm Conference 92
Tiananmen Square 232
water 138–9
see also Three Gorges dam
China on the Edge (He) 233–4
Chipko movement 85, 140, 227, 242,
309–11, 422, 476n218
Chisso corporation 235, 236, 317
chlorine in atmosphere 383
cholera 26, 35
Chorherr, Christoph 326
Christian Democrats 79, 154, 169, 265, 271
Christianity 194, 199–200, 374–5
see also Catholicism
Church Research House 372–3
church-centred environmental groups
372–6, 377, 419
Churchill, Winston 72–3, 410
Ciba Foundation 69
cigarette smoking 39, 52, 87, 99, 273, 350
citizens' council, Japan 234
citizens' initiatives 148–9, 165, 377
Citizens' League against the Sonic Boom
84–5
The City in History (Mumford) 216–17
Civilian Conservation Corps 48, 51
Civilized Man's Eight Deadly Sins (Lorenz)
87, 110, 147
Clairborne reprocessing plant 346
Clean Air Act, US 86, 131–2, 322, 347
Clean Water Act, US 88
clearcutting 276, 312
Cleghorn, Hugh 127

Clements, Frederic 49
climate change 403, 416–17, 430
alarm raisers 255, 413–14
environment 353
forests 22
genetic engineering 131
see also global warming; greenhouse gas
effect
climate policy 383, 419, 429
climate protection 378, 411, 423
Climate Research and the Media conference
163
Clinton, Bill 145, 273
The Closing Circle (Commoner) 87, 287
Club of Rome
Desertec 333–4
founding of 82
grassroots campaigns 247
Schneider 340
see also Limits to Growth
coal production 83, 233, 333, 413, 417
see also brown coal
coal-fired power stations 125, 157, 169, 418
Cochabamba water war 139
Cod War 86, 301
coffins/wood shortage 224
Cohen, Michael 237
Cohn-Bendit, Daniel 106–7, 383, 487n91
Colbert, Jean-Baptiste 15
Cold War 65, 66
Collapse (Diamond) 114–15
Collor, Fernando 396
colonialism 63, 172–3
*Columbia Guide to American Environmental
History* (Merchant) 136
Commission for Racial Justice 341
Committee for Nuclear Information 74
common goods 46, 306, 317–18
common lands 14–15, 41
Commoner, Barry 97, 98
anti-nuclear protests 160
Center for the Biology of Natural
Systems 79–80
Citizens Party 219
Closing Circle 87, 287
Earth Day 104, 116–17
ecology laws 116–17
Egan on 182, 183
on environmental crisis 110
Harvard lecture 102–3
Lake Erie 81
laws of ecology 163
on *Limits to Growth* 101
mercury 92
on population growth 109
St Louis 74
six chief dangers 135

Index